The Defendant's Rights Today

The Defendant's Rights Today

DAVID FELLMAN

28715

The University of Wisconsin Press

Published 1976

The University of Wisconsin Press
Box 1379, Madison, Wisconsin 53701

The University of Wisconsin Press, Ltd.
70 Great Russell Street, London

Copyright © 1976
The Regents of the University of Wisconsin System
All rights reserved

First printing

Printed in the United States of America

For LC CIP information see the colophon

ISBN 0-299-07200-2

Portions of this book appeared in
The Defendant's Rights © 1958 by David Fellman

To Sara

Contents

Preface / xi
1 **The Importance of Procedure / 3**
   The Tilt of the Law / 3
   The Centrality of Due Process / 6
   The Abuses of Police Power / 9
   Equal Justice for All / 10
   The Federal Problem / 15
   Two Models of the Criminal Process / 21

2 **The Preliminaries / 25**
   Arrests / 25
      The Police / 25
      The Nature of Arrest / 28
      The Warrant of Arrest / 30
      Arrests without Warrants / 30
      Reform of the Law of Arrest / 32
      The Expungement of Arrest Records / 33
      The Limited Powers of the Police / 35
      The Right to Resist Arrest / 36
      Remedies for Illegal Arrests / 39
   The Preliminary Hearing / 42
      Legal Basis / 42
      Purpose / 44
      Value / 45
      Waiver / 46
      The Required Procedure / 47
   Bail / 49
      Historical Origins / 49
      Reasons for Bail / 50
      Present Rules / 52
      Forfeiture / 55
      The Judge's Discretion / 56
      Remedies / 60
      Preventive Detention / 64

viii / Contents

3 The Defendant's Right to Notice / 66
    Notice and the Constitution / 66
    The Accusation / 67
    The Right to a Specific Accusation / 71
    The Void-for-Vagueness Rule / 75
    Notice of What? / 82

4 The Defendant's Right to a Fair Hearing / 84
    The Federal Context / 84
    The Right to a Trial / 86
    Juvenile Delinquency Proceedings / 89
    The Right to be Present at the Trial / 91
    The Necessity of Presenting Evidence in Court / 92
    The Right of Confrontation / 94
    Compulsory Process to Secure Witnesses / 98
    The Ex Post Facto Rule / 99
    The Burden of Proof / 102
    The No-Evidence Rule / 105
    Statutory Presumptions of Guilt / 106
    Jurisdiction / 108
    The Right to a Public Trial / 109
    The Right to a Speedy Trial / 111
    The Right to an Unbiased Judge / 116
    Freedom from Mob Domination / 119
    Pretrial Publicity and a Fair Trial / 121
    Knowing Use of Perjured Testimony by the Prosecution / 124
    The Prosecution and the Boundaries of Propriety / 126
    A Note on Contempt of Court Procedure / 127

5 The Writ of Habeas Corpus / 131
    Significance / 131
    English Origins / 131
    American Origins / 134
    The Uses of the Writ / 135
    Habeas Corpus and Appeal / 140
    An Expanding Writ / 142
    Some Limiting Factors / 146
    The Problem of Military Detention / 152
    Suspension of the Writ / 156
    Addendum on Fourth Amendment Claims / 159

6   **Trial by Jury / 160**
    Constitutional Origins / 160
    The Requirement of Twelve Members / 165
    The Requirement of Unanimity / 168
    The Supervisory Responsibility of the Judge / 172
    Scope of the Right to Jury Trial in Federal Courts / 175
    Waiver / 181
    The Representative Jury / 183
    An Impartial Jury / 187
    Exclusion of Negroes from Jury Service / 193
    The "Blue-Ribbon" Jury / 198
    Right to a Trial in the Locality by a Local Jury / 200
    The Merits of Trial by Jury / 202

7   **The Right to Counsel / 208**
    Growth of the Right / 208
    Scope of the Right to Counsel / 210
    Effective Representation by Counsel / 218
    Competence of Counsel / 225
    Plea Bargaining / 231
    Waiver / 235
    The Question of Compensation / 238
    Representation of Unpopular Defendants / 243
    Remedies / 243
    Right to Counsel in Military Justice / 246
    Right to Counsel in Non-criminal Cases / 249

8   **Searches and Seizures / 254**
    Rights of Privacy / 254
    Historical Origins / 256
    Searches and Seizures by Private Parties / 259
    The Fourth and Fifth Amendments / 261
    The Search Warrant / 262
    Scope of the Guaranty / 269
    Administrative Searches / 272
    Search without Warrant: Arrest / 277
    Search without Warrant: Automobiles / 281
    Electronic Surveillance / 284
    The Exclusionary Rule / 292
    The Question of Remedies / 298
    Waiver / 300
    Conclusion / 302

9 Self-Incrimination / 304
Historical Roots / 304
Scope of the Privilege / 306
How the Privilege Is Pleaded / 311
What Is Incrimination? / 311
Waiver / 317
The Issue of Comment / 319
Self-Incrimination and Federalism / 322
The Problem of Immunity / 324
The Problem of Motive / 331
Other Privileged Communications / 333
The Problem of Confessions / 336

10 Double Jeopardy / 352
Nature of the Right / 352
The Nationalization of the Double Jeopardy Concept / 354
Scope of the Right / 357
When Does Jeopardy Attach? / 363
Offenses against Two Sovereigns / 365
Right of the Government to Appeal / 368
Some Exceptions to the General Rule of Jeopardy / 369
Termination of Proceedings / 370
Closely Related Offenses / 375
Included Offenses / 379
Conclusion / 382

11 Cruel and Unusual Punishments / 383
The Constitutional Rule / 383
Scope of the Guaranty / 384
The Death Penalty / 385
Other Forms of Punishment / 395
The Issue of Severity / 398
Fines and Penalties / 407
Due Process and the States / 408
The Treatment of Prisoners / 409
Reduction of Sentences / 416
Addendum on Capital Punishment / 419

Table of Cases / 421

Index / 439

Preface

In 1958, a New York publisher, then known as Rinehart & Company, published a book of mine under the title *The Defendant's Rights.* Since it takes about a year for a publisher to convert a manuscript into a book, this means that *The Defendant's Rights* was completed in 1957. In fact, the latest Supreme Court cases which were included in that volume were those decided in the 1956–57 Term of Court. Obviously, a great deal has happened to our constitutional law since that time. Above all, Earl Warren was appointed Chief Justice in 1953, and the years during which he presided over the Court were years of extraordinary and boldly innovative activity, especially in precisely the branch of our public law which is concerned with the rights of defendants in criminal cases. In fact, these developments have often been described as the "due process revolution" of the Warren Court. Just how much of the basic law of the land was changed in this area is reflected in the fact that almost every other page in the 1958 book had become out of date. Accordingly, this book can be described as no more than a statement of the content of the rights of defendants in criminal cases as these rights were construed before the Warren Court even began the task of renovation, modernization, improvement, and change of American constitutional law. Some of the purely historical material in the 1958 book has survived in this volume, but otherwise almost every doctrine had to be restated and amplified, and indeed, many new sections had to be added, on such diverse topics as the expungement of arrest records, juvenile delinquency proceedings, plea bargaining, and the death penalty.

I included in the 1958 book a rather lengthy chapter to which I gave the title, "The Quasi-Defendants." I was trying to call attention to the fact that while we extend to even the most vicious criminal the protection of an elaborate and complex bundle of rights, many other people get into difficulties with the government, and are exposed to very serious penalties, without the protection of the rights secured to defendants in criminal cases. I discussed in some detail the problems confronting government employees whose loyalty has been challenged, aliens held for exclusion or deportation, persons being investigated by legislative committees, and applicants for passports, who, among others, are often in a position roughly analogous to that of a defendant in a criminal case, but who do not enjoy the benefits derived from procedures which historic experience suggests are essential if justice is to be done. For example, government employees accused of disloyalty are not protected by double jeopardy doctrine. This means that a civil servant who has been cleared of charges of disloyalty by one hearing board can be put through the same agony again and again. Or, to cite another illustration, a civil servant accused of disloyalty does not enjoy the right of confrontation, which means that he cannot as of right demand to know the identity of his accuser and cross-examine him. Furthermore, the statutory and administrative criteria on the basis of which judgments are made as to disloyalty or unreliability are almost meaninglessly vague, certainly far too vague to satisfy the requirements of specificity and certainty demanded of the criminal law. Thus, in regard to the question of disloyalty or unreliability, civil servants have suffered from such distortions of justice as "guilt by association," even "guilt by coincidence." So, also, persons who are commanded to appear before legislative investigating committees may bring their lawyers with them, but prevailing rules do not permit counsel to do very much beyond advising their clients as to when and how they should plead the privilege against self-incrimination. Those who are being interrogated do not even enjoy the right to insist upon a public hearing, much less the right of confrontation.

In the case of aliens held for deportation, the elemental rule which forbids *ex post facto* laws in the area of criminal justice does not apply. More concretely, this means that an alien may be deported for an act which was not a deportable act when it occurred. Aliens who are excluded from the country have no hearing rights at all, and may be denied admission into the country on the basis of confidential information the nature of which is wholly unknown to them. As for persons whose applications for passports have been denied, the crux of their problem arises from the vagueness of the standards set out in the statutes and administrative regulations, and the inadequacy of the hearing rights available to them.

I was reluctant to drop out all this material, but this new book kept growing and growing, and something had to go. Furthermore, in respect to the law relating to what I called quasi-defendants, there has been little change since I first wrote it up for the 1958 book. Thus, I believe that most of the material in that final chapter is still relevant. It is quite true that in this age of détente we exercise more restraint in dealing with some of these problems, but the underlying body of law has remained relatively stable. Accordingly, I refer those who are interested in the subject to chapter 12 of the 1958 book.

This book is designed for reading by persons interested in our constitutional law, and particularly that branch of our public law concerned with criminal justice. While I have included many references to court decisions and the literature of the law, I have made no attempt at any exhaustive gathering of authorities in the manner of extensive, heavily annotated, multi-volumed legal treatises. I have stressed the positions taken by the United States Supreme Court, because its decisions tend to establish minimum national standards for all the other courts. This is even more true today than it was in 1958. It was quite impossible for me to do full justice to the decisions of the fifty state supreme courts, and while I have not ignored them, I have not attempted any exhaustive marshalling of state authorities. In this respect, I have had to be content with rather broad generalizations about general tendencies.

One more caveat seems to be in order. It is very hazardous to write a book in the American constitutional law field, because this law changes so rapidly. After all, the Supreme Court of the United States meets every year from early October to late June, and decisions which alter the pre-existing law come down with a frequency which is bound to pose serious problems for anyone who seeks to describe the state of the law. Thus, in preparing this manuscript, some chapters were locked up well before the end of the 1974-75 Term of Court, and of course before this book is finally published, many other decisions in the criminal justice field will have been made which have a bearing on the various subjects treated herein. I have tried to include the very latest citations by last-minute additions to the footnotes, and will continue to do so as the exigencies of publication will permit. I am, however, resigned to the fact that in some respects the book which finally appears will be a bit out of date here and there, but I have been aware of this problem, and have made every reasonable effort to confront it, though it is in a very real sense insoluble.

I think I should record once more that the 1958 book was made possible by a generous grant from the Fund for the Republic, supplemented by a grant from the University of Wisconsin. As for the preparation of *The Defendant's Rights Today,* the free time I had to have to get the work done was made possible by my Vilas Professorship, for which I am deeply grateful to the University of Wisconsin.

Obviously, no person or institution mentioned here is responsible for what I have written. The University of Wisconsin is fully committed to academic freedom for its faculty and students. It follows, of course, that the views expressed here are my own, and I am responsible for them, including any errors that may have been made.

The author of such a book as this one is invariably indebted to many people for assistance and encouragement. Above all, I should like to express once more, as I did in 1958, my very deep gratitude to the late Professor Charles Bunn, for many years a distinguished member of the faculty of the Law School of the University of Wisconsin. He was an astute lawyer, a fine legal scholar, and a saintly man; I revere his memory, and recall with gratitude how much he helped me in sorting out the ideas which went into the 1958 book. I also take this opportunity to express my appreciation to Professor Maurice D. Leon, Librarian of the Law School, who was always ready to lend a hand cheerfully and skillfully. In addition, I want to record my indebtedness to two scholarly professors of political science who specialize in constitutional law, and from whom I have profited a great deal both in conversations and from their published writings, Professor Wallace Mendelson of the University of Texas-Austin, and Professor Henry J. Abraham, Henry L., and Grace Doherty Professor of Government and Foreign Affairs at the University of Virginia. I am also delighted to take this opportunity to express my thanks to Thompson Webb, Jr., Director of the University of Wisconsin Press, and Joan M. Krager, its general editor, for their continued interest in what I was doing; their sympathetic encouragement helped me see this project through to its completion.

Finally, I welcome this opportunity to record my appreciation to my secretary, Mrs. Norma Lynch, to whom I am deeply indebted for efficient and faithful service.

D. F.

Madison, Wisconsin
September 29, 1975

The Defendant's Rights Today

1 / The Importance of Procedure

The Tilt of the Law

American public law is deliberately weighted in favor of defendants accused of crime. It gives the accused very many assurances that he will be treated fairly. Indeed, our law is generally described as a defendant's law, in contrast with other legal systems which emphasize the necessities of the prosecution and give priority to the interests of society in the apprehension and conviction of criminals. We, too, are concerned with the suppression of crime, but we are equally concerned with the necessities of justice and respect for man's dignity.[1] As Justice Frankfurter once remarked, "Ours is the accusatorial as opposed to the inquisitorial system. Such has been the characteristic of Anglo-American criminal justice since it freed itself from practices borrowed by the Star Chamber from the Continent. . . ."[2]

The bias of American law in favor of persons charged with crime is not a product of recent decisions of the United States Supreme Court, though to be sure that Court has contributed much in clarifying and strengthening the rights to which defendants are entitled. Basic legal principles in this area of the law are deeply rooted in ancient common law doctrine, such as the rules which provide that an accused person is presumptively innocent, that the burden of proving guilt is on the prosecution, and that guilt must be established beyond a reasonable doubt, which is the most demanding quantum of proof known to the law.[3] As Justice Frankfurter once observed, "[F]rom the time that the law which we have inherited has emerged from dark and barbaric times, the conception of justice which has dominated our criminal law has refused to put an accused at the hazard of punishment if he fails to remove every reasonable doubt of his

---

1. See the remarks of Charles E. Merriam, *Systematic Politics* (Chicago: University of Chicago Press, 1945), p. 59: "It was a great day for the human race . . . when the idea dawned that every man is a human being, an end in himself, with a claim for the development of his own personality, and that human beings had a dignity and a worth, respect for which is the firm basis of human association."
2. Watts v. Indiana, 338 U.S. 49, 54 (1949).
3. See the remarks of Lord Sankey in Woolmington v. D.P.P. [1935] A.C. 462, 481, 25 Cr. App. Rep. 72, 95 (H.L.), and of Lord Chief Justice Reading in R. v. Schama (1914) 79 J.P. 184, 24 Cox C.C. 591, 11 Cr. App. Rep. 45 (C.C.A.). See also Abraham S. Goldstein, "The State and the Accused: Balance of Advantage in Criminal Procedure," *Yale Law Journal,* 69 (June 1960): 1149–99.

innocence in the minds of jurors. It is the duty of the Government to establish his guilt beyond a reasonable doubt.[4]

There are various underlying reasons which explain why our jurisprudence is so tender on the subject of the rights of an accused. For one thing, it must be remembered that every criminal case is a contest between an individual defendant and the government. The prosecutor or moving party in a criminal case is always the government, since we no longer have private justice. A crime is by definition an offense against society, even though the victim was an individual. Society, through its chief agency, the government, undertakes the responsibility of prosecution. In our complex federal system, of course, there is a division of labor, since some crimes are defined by the states and others by the national government, though there is a growing measure of supervision of state criminal justice by the United States Supreme Court, which is the ultimate custodian of the federal Constitution, the supreme law of the land.

In any event, the point to bear in mind is that modern government is very powerful. Government is the chief repository of the enormous power of organized society. It follows that a criminal case is inherently an unequal contest, because the parties are of unequal strength. Indeed, the disparity between them is of such magnitude that without safeguards injustice is almost inevitable in many situations, since inequality begets injustice. In order to reduce the possibilities of injustice the law seeks to redress the balance between these parties in some considerable measure by protecting the weaker party from such practices as compulsory self-incrimination, double jeopardy, and unreasonable searches and seizures, and by guaranteeing him the right to trial by an impartial jury before an unbiased judge, representation by counsel, the privilege of cross-examination, and other procedural safeguards.

There is another compelling reason which explains our traditional tenderness on the subject of a defendant's rights. Our experience teaches us that it is a very serious matter for any government formally to accuse a person of having committed a crime. While we are constantly reminded that an accusation is not the equivalent of proof of guilt, still it exerts a powerful influence upon the public temper. In times of high tension and widespread anxiety, an accusation may in and of itself be a cruel weapon which punishes before it hears. Indeed, in such an atmosphere, charges brought informally, outside the established system of justice—by legislators, for example—may do irreparable harm, wholly apart from any question concerning the substantiality of the charges. The phrase "guilt by accusation" describes this unfortunate situation.

---

4. Leland v. Oregon, 343 U.S. 790, 802 (1952) (dissenting opinion).

A very serious thing has happened to a person when a public prosecutor or a grand jury files with a criminal court a formal charge alleging that a crime has been committed. At the very least it means that someone having public authority believes that a crime was actually perpetrated by the accused. The accused, whether guilty or not, is in immediate trouble. He may be imprisoned pending trial, unless he can secure bail, if indeed he is eligible for bail. He may lose his job, or be suspended from it, pending trial. His reputation is under an immediate cloud. His family relationships may be irretrievably altered. If he happens to be in a profession where good reputation is peculiarly indispensable, he may suffer grievously, though completely innocent. All too many people tend to believe that where there is smoke there must be fire. If the accused holds a delicate fiduciary position, such as cashier of a bank, the mere accusation of such an offense as embezzlement, without more, may ruin him. There are many people in our society who, like Caesar's wife, must be completely above suspicion. A defendant, in short, is in a bad spot, merely by virtue of being one, and needs every possible opportunity to establish his innocence, as soon, as publicly, and decisively as possible.

Another fundamental and enduring reason for our solicitude for assuring defendants a maximum of procedural rights is that we are convinced that without respecting these rights justice will not be done. The prevailing rules have as their central purpose the discovery of truth. As Wigmore has noted, the laws of evidence are not arbitrary. "Their aim is to get at the truth by calm and careful reasoning."[5] Or, as Arthur T. Vanderbilt, Chief Justice of the New Jersey Supreme Court, once observed, "[T]here is no more important right in the law than the right to a fair trial, for without a fair trial all the rights vouchsafed by the substantive law are worthless."[6]

Our procedural law does not rest upon any puerile sentimentality about the criminal. The great judges, legislators, and constitution-makers who fashioned this law were not animated by any particular softness toward lawbreakers. The purpose of the law is not to coddle wrongdoers. It does not purport to multiply loopholes through which evil men may escape the consequences of their offenses against society. The purpose of our public law is to make certain, as nearly as the complexities and perplexities of our world will permit, that the truth will be discovered and that justice will be done. For with us justice is the great end of government. That is why,

---

5. John H. Wigmore, *A Student's Textbook of the Law of Evidence* (Brooklyn: Foundation Press, 1935), p. 5.
6. "The Role of Procedure in the Protection of Freedom," in University of Chicago Law School, *Conference on Freedom and the Law,* Conf. Ser., no. 13, May 7, 1953 (Chicago: University of Chicago Press, 1953), p. 68.

for example, a coerced confession is inadmissible in a criminal trial. The rule which excludes rests upon the hard fact that in addition to the danger of brutalizing the police, such evidence is unreliable. The defendant's right to confront and cross-examine his accuser is based upon like considerations. The guarantee of this right helps the defendant, of course, but in a larger sense it helps our society to do right and avoid injustice. For, as Wigmore has observed, we insist upon the opportunity to cross-examine "because the experience of the last three centuries of judicial trials has demonstrated convincingly that in disputed issues one cannot depend on the mere assertion of anybody, however plausible, without scrutiny into its basis."[7]

The Centrality of Due Process

Due process of law is not, primarily, the right of the accused. It is basically the community's assurance that prosecutors, judges, and juries will behave properly within rules distilled from long centuries of concrete experience. For procedural safeguards are absolutely essential for justice. In fact, in large measure justice is fair procedure. The purpose of any system of criminal justice is to convict the guilty and acquit the innocent. It is the legislature's prerogative to say that a particular act is criminal. However, whether a specific individual committed the act is for a court to decide in a proceeding carried on in accordance with time-tested rules. The importance of these rules can hardly be exaggerated. In a remarkable passage Judge Curtis Bok of the Philadelphia Court of Common Pleas once drew attention to this when he said,

In the whole history of law and order the longest step forward was taken by primitive man when, as if by common consent, the tribe sat down in a circle and allowed only one man to speak at a time. An accused who is shouted down has no rights whatever. Unless people have an instinct for procedure their conception of basic human rights is a waste of effort, and wherever we see a negation of those rights it can be traced to a lack, an inadequacy, or a violation of procedure. Hence procedure effectively comes first: the mechanics of argument and discovery are often set up before the rights they serve take full form in practice. Even the common law had its origin in a group of writs drawn for various uses by Henry II.[8]

Justices of the Supreme Court have often drawn attention to the crucial importance of rules of fair procedure. "It is not without significance," Justice Douglas has written, "that most of the provisions of the Bill of Rights are procedural. It is procedure that spells much of the difference between rule by law and rule by whim or caprice. Steadfast adherence to

7. Wigmore, *Student's Textbook*, p. 238.
8. "If We Are to Act Like Free Men," *Saturday Review of Literature*, February 13, 1954, p. 9.

strict procedural safeguards is our main assurance that there will be equal justice under law."⁹ Justice Jackson put the matter in even stronger terms when he said,

> Only the untaught layman or the charlatan lawyer can answer that procedures matter not. Procedural fairness and regularity are of the indispensable essence of liberty. Severe substantive laws can be endured if they are fairly and impartially applied. Indeed, if put to the choice, one might well prefer to live under Soviet substantive law applied in good faith by our common-law procedures than under our substantive law enforced by Soviet procedural practices. Let it not be overlooked that due process of law is not for the sole benefit of the accused. It is the best insurance for the Government itself against those blunders which leave lasting stains on a system of justice but which are bound to occur on *ex parte* consideration.¹⁰

Even in the formal, legalistic sense, the conception of procedural fairness is the most essential element of due process. Due process has a substantive as well as a procedural aspect. Thus, a regulatory statute which is patently arbitrary and capricious may be held by an American court to be violative of due process of law because it is unreasonable. But our courts are increasingly reluctant to declare that on policy matters the legislature overstepped the boundaries of a fair discretion, because that discretion is necessarily broad, and the legislature as a representative body is uniquely capable of translating the will of the community into law. As Justice Douglas remarked in a widely-noted case, "The day is gone when this Court uses the Due Process Clause of the Fourteenth Amendment to strike down state laws, regulatory of business and industrial conditions, because they may be unwise, improvident, or out of harmony with a particular school of thought."¹¹

---

9. Joint Anti-Fascist Committee v. McGrath, 341 U.S. 123, 179 (1951) (concurring opinion).

10. Shaughnessy v. United States *ex rel.* Mezei, 345 U.S. 206, 224 (1953) (dissenting opinion). Justice Frankfurter has observed that "the history of American freedom is, in no small measure, the history of procedure." Malinski v. New York, 324 U.S. 401, 414 (1945) (concurring opinion). Similarly, Justice Fortas once wrote, "Insistence upon procedural standards, commanded by our Constitution, is *not* a technicality. . . . Constitutionalism is not a technicality. Constitutional rights are not technicalities. . . . Constitutional procedure is the heart, the conscience, the soul of a civilized community. It is the basic principle for which men from the earliest days have fought and died. What is liberty if it is not the right to due process of law, in all of its forms, before the state may consign us to prison or take our life?" "The Fight for Due Process," *Case and Comment,* 73 (November–December 1968): 17.

11. Williamson v. Lee Optical Co., 348 U.S. 483, 488 (1955). Justice Douglas gave fresh emphasis to the famous remark of Chief Justice Waite in Munn v. Illinois, 94 U.S. 113, 134 (1876): "For protection against abuses by legislatures the people must resort to the polls, not to the courts."

But the judges are not equally reluctant to correct the executive and legislative branches of the government where matters of procedural fairness are involved, since they regard themselves as competent to decide such matters in the light of their special professional knowledge and the long tradition of which they are the present custodians. There can be no doubt, Justice Jackson once observed, that whatever may have been the original meaning of due process of law, procedural fairness "is at least what it most uncompromisingly requires. Procedural due process is more elemental and less flexible than substantive due process. It yields less to the times, varies less with conditions, and defers much less to legislative judgment. Insofar as it is technical law, it must be a specialized responsibility within the competence of the judiciary on which they do not bend before political branches of the Government, as they should on matters of policy which comprise substantive law."[12]

This explains why a judge like Justice Brandeis was willing to accord to the legislature a very wide latitude of judgment in connection with substantive policy dealing—for example, with the regulation of the economy —whereas he was extremely conservative in cases involving procedural issues. He could see sufficient point in a minimum wage statute to vote in favor of its constitutionality,[13] but he was apprehensive that a defendant did not have a fair trial if he was not permitted to go along with the jury when it left the courtroom for a firsthand view of the scene of the alleged crime.[14] The legislature is quite competent to decide whether wage regulation is a reasonable limitation on freedom of contract in the public interest, but the right of the accused to be present at all phases of his trial is an established element of fair procedure as to which a judge is especially qualified to have an informed opinion.

The willingness of judges like Justice Brandeis to find constitutional even drastic changes in the law dealing with the regulation of the economy, as contrasted with his reluctance to sustain legislative or judge-made changes in the procedures of justice, should give one pause in using such terms as "liberal" and "conservative" too sweepingly to describe points of view. Theoretically the liberal is in favor of change, whereas the conservative is for the status quo. Actually, there are many things that liberals do not want to change at all, and conservatives are often committed to very substantial changes of the going system. Consider the enthusiasm in some so-called conservative circles for the Bricker Amend-

12. Shaughnessy v. United States *ex rel.* Mezei, 345 U.S. 206, 224 (1953) (dissenting opinion).
13. West Coast Hotel Co. v. Parrish, 300 U.S. 379 (1937) (majority opinion by Chief Justice Hughes).
14. Snyder v. Massachusetts, 291 U.S. 97 (1934) (dissenting opinion by Justice Roberts).

ment, which, if adopted, would have resulted in a drastic alteration of the methods of conducting foreign relations that have been in use since the ratification of the Constitution. In days of high tension and widespread anxiety, liberals as well as conservatives are eager to conserve time-honored guarantees of fair procedure which are under severe pressure from many quarters. In such times we have the paradox that the central emphasis of a position committed philosophically to the desirability of change is to hold fast to existing values and institutions.

Perhaps it would be better to abandon altogether the use of such labels as "liberal" and "conservative," since they serve largely to obscure and confuse.[15] Most normal people are conservative about some things, and non-conservative about others. Few indeed welcome change merely for the sake of change. Liberals who are not in power behave differently than when they are in power. Conservatives who acquire power after a considerable period of liberal reform in government are eager for change. At such a moment in history liberals are anxious to conserve their gains. In the liberal's concern for civil rights today one finds an essentially conservative position.

But devotion to civil rights is not merely a liberal value. Men holding all sorts of views about such policy matters as taxation and the regulation of the economy are equally devoted to the concepts of procedural fairness.

The Abuses of Police Power

Furthermore, our legal system lays great stress upon the protection of the rights of the accused because historical experience in various parts of the world in which we live has alerted us to the dangers which flow from the abuse of police power. We should be fully aware of the fact that the abuse of police power is a primary characteristic of all dictatorial or totalitarian systems of government. Our generation should be very well informed about the price which is exacted by an all-powerful police force which is unrestrained by due process rules and independent judges. Contemporary man has very compelling reasons for understanding the fearful significance of the midnight knock on the door, the use of interrogations that break the will, the ransacking of private dwellings without legal warrant, incarceration in brutal concentration camps, and similar police excesses. Unlimited police power seems to be the hallmark of totalitarian systems. The maintenance of a body of fundamental law which seeks to protect the basic rights of defendants to fair treatment by setting limits to police power is one of the major objectives of American constitutional law.

15. "A fertile source of perversion in constitutional theory is the tyranny of labels." Justice Cardozo in Snyder v. Massachusetts, 291 U.S. 97, 114 (1934).

Still another objective of our public law is to give even guilty persons a feeling that they have been treated fairly. Manifestly, a major purpose of our legal system is to avoid the monstrous injustice involved in convicting the innocent. But it is also important that even the guilty should be afforded a full measure of due process, in order to reduce the anti-social feelings they would otherwise have. As Professor Casper has observed, in a very perceptive book, the criminal justice system "should do more than simply shunt the defendant off to prison or probation. . . . It can and should indicate to him that he is not an outsider but a valuable human being."[16]

Thurman Arnold once expressed this idea in a very striking passage:

> The significance of a criminal trial in all civilized countries goes far beyond the question of public order and the enforcement of law. It embodies the notion that every man, however lowly and however guilty he may be, is entitled to a fair and impartial trial in which he must be presumed to be innocent. What is underneath the idea of a fair trial and what are its basic elements? The first premise is that the judge must be impartial. The second is that the accused has the right to have counsel. The third is that the judgment must be based on the evidence before the tribunal and that the accused is entitled to confront and cross-examine the witnesses who testify against him.
>
> These restrictions are unquestionably handicaps in the enforcement of the law. They prevent the trial from having the efficiency of expert investigation. No doubt many guilty men go free. Nevertheless, there is a tremendous psychological need for the appearance of justice which a fair trial creates in the public mind.
>
> This ideal is as old as Western civilization. Its significance in our culture is tremendous. It involves the humanitarian notion that the underdog is always entitled to a chance. It gives us a sense of security against what we are accustomed to call "mob rule."[17]

Equal Justice for All

The nation agrees upon many things, and it is observable that a very broad consensus exists in connection with the basic elements of fair procedure. There are, to be sure, some differences of opinion about the precise scope of a few procedural guarantees, such as the Fifth Amendment protection against self-incrimination.[18] There are grave differences

---

16. Jonathan D. Casper, *American Criminal Justice: The Defendant's Perspective* (Englewood Cliffs, N.J.: Prentice-Hall, 1972), p. 172. As Justice Douglas observed in Brady v. Maryland, 373 U.S. 83, 87 (1963), "Society wins not only when the guilty are convicted but when criminal trials are fair; our system of the administration of justice suffers when any accused is treated unfairly."

17. "The Criminal Trial as a Symbol of Public Morality," in A. E. D. Howard, ed., *Criminal Justice in Our Time* (Charlottesville: University Press of Virginia, 1965), p. 140.

18. See, for example, the remarks of Judge E. Ray Stevens of the Wisconsin Circuit Court, "Archaic Constitutional Provisions Protecting the Accused," *Journal of Criminal Law*

of opinion on such matters as the construction of the permissible limits of free speech. But on the whole Americans of most shades of political opinion agree, at least in the abstract, upon the basic rules of fair play which prevail in the field of criminal justice. On these matters the national and state constitutions say substantially the same things, in about the same language. State and federal statutes and common law decisions spell out these guarantees according to a familiar pattern. So far as formal legal definition goes, one has about the same procedural rights in whatever state or national court he may happen to be tried. The actual administration of these rights is another matter, of course, since in this regard the picture over the country is uneven. For the translation of legal doctrine into concrete results depends upon the temper of the community, the nature of its prejudices and values, the character of its scapegoats, the state of the economy, the quality of its bench and bar, its educational system, and related nonlegal factors. Here there is much room for debate.

The rights which American constitutional law guarantees to defendants, it is important to note, are available for all defendants, whatever and whoever they may be. We do not have one Bill of Rights for nice people, and another one for bad people. All people accused of crime, no matter how wicked or depraved, enjoy the same rights of fair trial under law. For, as Judge Cuthbert Pound of the New York Court of Appeals observed, "Although the defendant may be the worst of men ... the rights of the best of men are secure only as the rights of the vilest and most abhorrent are protected."[19] Or, as Dean O'Meara of the Notre Dame Law School once put it, "The simple truth is that you have to be for the Bill of Rights or not; you can't be for the Bill of Rights for yourself and your friends; it's all or nothing. A breach in the dyke imperils the whole countryside, not just the area adjacent to the break. There is only one protection against the flood and that is to contain it entirely."[20]

Justice for all is one of the basic purposes of our constitutional system. "Our Government," Justice Rutledge wrote shortly before his death, "is not one of mere convenience or efficiency. It too has a stake, with every citizen, in his being afforded our historic individual protections, including those surrounding criminal trials. About them we dare not become careless or complacent when that fashion has become rampant over the

---

and Criminology, 5 (1914): 16–19, 18: "The state and the defendant are represented by their hired champions, while the accused sits serenely watching the contest, wrapped in his mantle of presumption of innocence with the truth securely locked in his breast, because of the constitutional guaranty that he shall not be compelled to be a witness against himself."

19. Dissenting in People v. Gitlow, 234 N.Y. 132, 158, 136 N.E. 317, 327 (1922).

20. Joseph O'Meara, "Freedom of Inquiry Versus Authority: Some Legal Aspects," *Notre Dame Lawyer,* 31 (December 1955): 3–13, 11.

earth."[21] The fact is that it is possible to pay too high a price for efficiency. There can be no possible doubt that without the restraints which the law insists upon the police could catch and prosecutors could convict far more lawbreakers than they do now. For example, if the police had a completely free hand to break into any building, at any hour of the day or night, to search for stolen goods, undoubtedly more thieves and burglars would be apprehended. But the price we would have to pay would be the utter destruction of privacy, and most people would find that to be prohibitively high. Similarly, if the police were free to torture suspects, unquestionably more confessions would be secured, and the conviction rate would go up. But again, that would invite serious dangers, such as the conviction of innocent people who succumb to pain, and the brutalization of the police. Thus, deterring criminals is not and cannot be the only objective of our penal system. There are other equally important objectives, such as maintaining a decent respect for man's dignity and preserving an atmosphere of freedom.[22] A distinguished legal scholar once expressed his disagreement with the notion that the best criminal justice system is one that produces convictions and sentences in 100 percent of the cases of crime. "The paradoxical fact is that arrest, conviction, and punishment of every criminal would be a catastrophe. Hardly one of us would escape, for we have all at one time or another committed acts that the law regards as serious offenses. Kinsey has tabulated our extensive sexual misdeeds. The Bureau of Internal Revenue is the great archive of our false swearing and cheating. The highway death toll statistics inadequately record our predilection for manslaughter. 100% law enforcement would not leave enough people at large to build and man the prisons in which the rest of us would reside."[23]

This observation is supported by the results of a survey made in behalf of the President's Commission on Law Enforcement and Administration of Justice, published in 1967, which indicated that in a well-selected national sample of 1,700 persons, 91 percent of the respondents admitted to having committed acts for which they might have received jail or prison sentences.[24] Surely, perfect law enforcement would pose some very awkward problems for our society.

21. Kotteakos v. United States, 328 U.S. 750, 773 (1946).
22. Compare the remarks of Circuit Judge Craven in Wheeler v. Goodman, 306 F. Supp. 58, 65 (W.D. N.C. 1969), which held a vagrancy statute unconstitutional: "Crime prevention is not an absolute value. Methods of prevention are constantly weighed against the personal liberties enshrined in the Constitution. Here the outrageous police action under color of the vagrancy statute is far too high a price to pay for crime prevention."
23. Louis B. Schwartz, "On Current Proposals to Legalize Wire Tapping," *University of Pennsylvania Law Review,* 103 (November 1954): 157–67, 157.
24. The President's Commission on Law Enforcement and Administration of Justice, *The Challenge of Crime in a Free Society* (Washington: U.S. Government Printing Office, 1967), p. v.

The assertion that all people, the evil as well as the good, are entitled to the protection of the same rights does not carry with it the implication that rights are absolute. To say, for example, that all persons are entitled to due process does not mean that all persons must be given exactly the same procedures. Due process is a flexible concept. Thus, the requirements of due process for juvenile offenders are not identical with those to which adults are entitled. Due process rights before trial are quite different from those one can claim after conviction. In short, due process demands that public authorities observe the rules of fundamental fairness, in all cases, whoever the defendants may be, but it does not impose an iron-clad rule of uniformity of treatment. The claim to due process is absolute, but its application is not. As Justice Frankfurter once pointed out, due process, "unlike some legal rules, is not a technical conception with a fixed content unrelated to time, place and circumstances. Expressing as it does in its ultimate analysis respect enforced by law for that feeling of just treatment which has been evolved through centuries of Anglo-American constitutional history and civilization, 'due process' cannot be imprisoned within the treacherous limits of any formula. Representing a profound attitude of fairness between man and man, and more particularly between the individual and government, 'due process' is compounded of history, reason, the past course of decisions, and stout confidence in the strength of the democratic faith which we profess. Due process is not a mechanical instrument. It is not a yardstick. It is a process. It is a delicate process of adjustment inescapably involving the exercise of judgment by those whom the Constitution entrusted with the unfolding of the process. . . . The precise nature of the interest that has been adversely affected, the manner in which this was done, the reasons for doing it, the available alternatives to the procedure that was followed, the protection implicit in the office of the functionary whose conduct is challenged, the balance of hurt complained of and good accomplished—these are some of the considerations that must enter into the judicial judgment."[25]

Not only are the basic rights of fair procedure guaranteed to all people, the bad as well as the good, but they are also assured to us in times of crisis as well as in times of tranquility. The plea of extraordinary conditions does not and should not be permitted to support an adjournment of our basic rights. In fact, the Constitution itself was written in an age of crisis, and was designed to serve the nation in days of crisis. Furthermore, in a very real sense the modern world seems to be in a constant state of crisis. In all probability, western civilization has been in a state of crisis, more or less, since the beginning of the Industrial Revolution, and perhaps since the invention of printing. In view of the state of the modern world, if crisis

25. Concurring opinion in Joint Anti-Fascist Refugee Committee v. McGrath, 341 U.S. 123, 162–63 (1951).

were a good and sufficient excuse for an adjournment of our rights, then it would seem to follow that we would have no rights. This much Justice Davis made clear in his opinion in the celebrated case of *Ex parte Milligan*,[26] decided a year after the conclusion of the Civil War:

> The Constitution of the United States is a law for rulers and people, equally in war and in peace, and covers with the shield of its protection all classes of men, at all times, and under all circumstances. No doctrine, involving more pernicious consequences, was ever invented by the wit of man than that any of its provisions can be suspended during any of the great exigencies of government. Such a doctrine leads directly to anarchy or despotism, but the theory of necessity on which it is based is false; for the government, within the Constitution, has all the powers granted to it, which are necessary to preserve its existence. . . .

It is noteworthy, of course, that this ringing declaration was made by the Court *after* the Civil War was over. As a distinguished lawyer once wrote, "The dominant lesson of our history in the relation of the judiciary to repressions is that courts love liberty most when it is under pressure least."[27] It is quite true that when the country is in a state of war excitement the judges, who are human, are apt to be excited themselves, and are not likely to stand in the way of the drive to victory. Even so, the *Milligan* opinion is, at the very least, an eloquent statement of a worthy objective.

Finally, it is worth pointing out that it is neither necessary nor wise to sacrifice our rights in our search for security in an uncertain world, for freedom and security are not necessarily antithetical concepts. One is not the negation of the other. We do not have to make a choice between freedom and security; it is not an either-or problem. It is simply not true that we must sacrifice our freedom in order to achieve security, or that we will lose our security if we insist upon our freedom. In fact, our greatest security will be found in maintaining our freedom. We are not free because we are strong; on the contrary, we are strong because we are free. Our whole way of life rests upon the verity of this proposition.

This view does not ignore the nature of the peril of our times. Prudence requires the government to maintain various security programs, and to deny employment to the disloyal or to those who for other reasons are bad security risks. But an employee-screening program, or any other security program, is not an end in itself, only a means to an end. The end of government is defined for us in majestic language by our Constitution. The end is "to form a more perfect union, establish justice, insure domestic tranquility, provide for the common defence, promote the general welfare, and secure the blessings of liberty to ourselves and our

---

26. 4 Wall. (U.S.) 2, 120–21 (1866).
27. John P. Frank in Edmond Cahn, ed., *Supreme Court and Supreme Law* (Bloomington: Indiana University Press, 1954), p. 114.

Posterity. . . . ." It follows that the use of totalitarian methods to achieve security makes little sense in a society committed to the proposition that the purpose of government is to secure the blessings of liberty. However tempting it may be in days of especially great tension to copy the totalitarian methods of our opponents, we must realize that this only subverts our own cherished design of the good life. As Mr. J. Edgar Hoover once observed, "Free government cannot be defended by dictatorial methods—in so doing the defender will devour the very thing to be defended. The protection of the individual is just as important as the safety of the state."[28] Or as Justice Frankfurter expressed the thought, "In a country with our moral and material strength the maintenance of fair procedures cannot handicap our security. Every adherence to our moral professions reinforces our strength and therefore our security."[29] This is what President Eisenhower had in mind when he declared, on March 3, 1954, that "in opposing Communism, we are defeating ourselves if either by design or through carelessness, we use methods that do not conform to the American sense of justice and fair play."

The Federal Problem

In the American system, both the national and state governments enact and enforce criminal laws. But except for such federal enclaves as the District of Columbia, over which Congress exercises full authority, the power of the national government to define crimes is limited to its delegated and implied powers. For example, federal criminal statutes are tied to such delegated powers as those concerned with taxation, interstate commerce, and the postal system. Nevertheless, the federal criminal code is now a substantial body of statute law, and it is growing larger at an ever accelerating pace. Still, most of the criminal laws of the country are state laws, administered by state agencies. That is to say, the states are mainly responsible for the maintenance of law and order; most crimes are defined by the state legislatures or state courts; most criminal trials are conducted in state courts; and most convicted persons are subject to the authority of state penal officials. Thus, at the end of 1970, offenders in state penal institutions numbered 176,391, whereas there were only 20,038 persons in federal institutions.[30]

28. "Civil Liberties and Law Enforcement: The Role of the FBI," *Iowa Law Review*, 37 (Winter 1951): 175–95, 186.

29. Dissenting in United States v. Nugent, 346 U.S. 1, 13 (1953). See the perceptive remarks of Alpheus T. Mason, *Security through Freedom* (Ithaca: Cornell University Press, 1955), pp. 190–91.

30. U.S. Department of Justice, Law Enforcement Assistance Administration, *Sourcebook of Criminal Justice Statistics, 1973* (Washington: U.S. Government Printing Office, 1973), p. 350.

With rare exceptions, such as the price control statute in World War II,[31] federal criminal statutes are enforceable only in federal courts, and state criminal laws are enforced in state courts. In reviewing federal criminal cases, the Supreme Court not only enforces the provisions of the Constitution dealing with the rights of defendants, but also exercises general powers of supervision over the inferior federal courts,[32] just as a state supreme court has general appellate jurisdiction over its inferior courts in respect to all legal issues, whether constitutional or not. The U.S. Supreme Court does not exercise general supervision over the state courts, for, as Justice Harlan has pointed out, even the growing body of recent precedents does not establish the Court "as a rule-making organ for the promulgation of state rules of criminal procedure. And none of the specific provisions of the Constitution ordains this Court with such authority."[33] Justice Harlan emphasized that so long as the challenged state's rules of evidence are not forbidden by any provision of the U.S. Constitution, there is nothing for the Supreme Court to review. Accordingly, one who has been convicted of a crime in a state trial court, and has taken and lost his appeal in the state's appellate courts, or has allowed his right of appeal to lapse, has gone as far as he can go, unless his appeal involves a substantial federal question of law. The U.S. Supreme Court does not sit to correct mere errors alleged to have occurred in state courts. "Our only power over state judgments," the Court has asserted, "is to correct them to the entent that they incorrectly adjudge federal rights."[34]

It follows, of course, that the scope of Supreme Court review of state courts—and the Supreme Court is the only federal court which has jurisdiction to review any state court judgment—depends upon how federal rights are defined. It is elementary law that the federal Bill of Rights, much of which deals with rights of the accused, does not apply to the states.[35] The opening sentence of the First Amendment begins with the phrase "Congress shall make no law . . .," and this would be curious

---

31. In Testa v. Katt, 330 U.S. 386 (1947), the Court held that state courts having jurisdiction over criminal cases could not refuse to take cases involving violations of the federal price control statute. No federal criminal statute is enforceable in a state court at the present time.

32. See, e.g., McNabb v. United States, 318 U.S. 332, 341 (1943): "The principles governing the admissibility of evidence in federal criminal trials have not been restricted . . . to those derived solely from the Constitution. In the exercise of its supervisory authority over the administration of criminal justice in the federal courts, . . . this Court has, from the very beginning of its history, formulated rules of evidence to be applied in federal criminal prosecutions."

33. Spencer v. Texas, 385 U.S. 554, 564 (1967).

34. Herb v. Pitcairn, 324 U.S. 117, 125–26 (1945).

35. The seminal precedent on this point is Barron v. Baltimore, 7 Pet. (U.S.) 243 (1833), opinion by Chief Justice John Marshall.

language indeed if it had been intended to apply the provisions which followed as limitations on state action. The Constitution was amended in 1791, not to impose fresh federally enforceable limitations on the states, but to secure certain basic rights from possible infringement by the newly established and untried national government. Thus, before the Civil War a defendant in a state criminal case had no way of appealing to the U.S. Supreme Court on any claim involving any of the rights listed in the Bill of Rights.

The adoption of the Fourteenth Amendment in 1868, with its provision that no state shall "deprive any person of life, liberty, or property, without due process of law," opened the door to an eventual expansion of the review power of the Supreme Court over the state courts. To be sure, the Fourteenth Amendment got off to a bad start, as a result of restrictive and highly technical interpretations of the Supreme Court.[36] Thus, it was not until 1925 that the Court first ruled that the "liberty" protected against state violation by Fourteenth Amendment due process included liberty of speech,[37] and it was not until 1940 that the Court decided that the First Amendment guaranty of religious freedom fell within the Fourteenth Amendment's scope.[38]

For a very long time the Supreme Court refused to review state appellate court decisions in criminal cases. As recently as 1915, the Court declined to make an independent inquiry into the facts involved in such an appeal, holding that where a state appellate court is empowered to correct errors, its review of the conviction provides adequate assurance that due process was not denied.[39] This posture of extreme comity with respect to state courts was first abandoned in the leading case of *Moore* v. *Dempsey*,[40] in 1923. As in the 1915 case, this one involved the allegation that the challenged conviction had been secured in a state trial court dominated by overwhelming mob pressures. Speaking for the Court, Justice Holmes ruled that the federal district court which had been petitioned for a writ of habeas corpus was obliged to make an independent review and evaluation of the facts, even though the state's appellate court had ruled in favor of the correctness of the verdict. This important decision broke new ground, and soon led to an expanded federal control over state administration of

36. See, e.g., Slaughter-House Cases, 16 Wall. (U.S.) 36 (1873); Civil Rights Cases, 109 U.S. 3 (1883).
37. Gitlow v. New York, 268 U.S. 652 (1925). The free press guaranty was absorbed into Fourteenth Amendment due process in Near v. Minnesota, 283 U.S. 697 (1931).
38. Cantwell v. Connecticut, 310 U.S. 296 (1940).
39. Frank v. Mangum, 237 U.S. 309 (1915). Justices Holmes and Brandeis dissented, asserting that unless the Supreme Court examines the facts for itself, the right to due process is "a barren one." 237 U.S. 348.
40. 261 U.S. 86 (1923).

18 / The Defendant's Rights Today

criminal justice through review by the Supreme Court on the basis of the due process clause of the Fourteenth Amendment.

Just how far it is permissible to go in construing the meaning of due process has always been the subject of intense debate. The first Justice Harlan, who sat on the bench from 1877 to 1911, took the position that the Fourteenth Amendment should be construed as nationalizing the entire federal Bill of Rights, which meant that in his judgment all the provisions of the Bill of Rights were federally enforceable limitations on the states.[41] This theory of total incorporation has been endorsed by some scholars,[42] and was accepted by such recent Justices as Black and Douglas.[43] But while the Court has at long last come fairly close to total incorporation, that has never been accepted by a majority of the Justices, who have preferred a policy of selective incorporation.

The first important breakthrough occurred in 1932, in the first Scottsboro case,[44] when the Court ruled that a state has denied due process if, in a capital case, it does not provide counsel for a defendant, a right which is secured to defendants in federal courts by virtue of a specific provision in the Sixth Amendment. In effect, then, at least for capital cases the Court read the Sixth Amendment guaranty of the right to counsel into the due process clause of the Fourteenth Amendment, thus bringing it within its protective power in reviewing state criminal cases. In 1963, the Court extended this doctrine to all serious cases, whether or not they involved capital offenses,[45] and in 1972 the Court went even farther to hold, by a unanimous vote, that the right to counsel extends to any case where the possible punishment is imprisonment for any period of time.[46] The Court has refused to impose upon the states the Fifth Amendment guaranty of indictment by grand jury,[47] and there have been no cases holding applicable to the states the Second Amendment guaranty of the right to bear arms, the Third Amendment protection against the quartering of troops in private dwellings, or the Seventh Amendment assurance of trial

---

41. See his dissenting opinions in Hurtado v. California, 110 U.S. 516, 538 (1884); Maxwell v. Dow, 176 U.S. 581, 605 (1900); Twining v. New Jersey, 211 U.S. 78, 114 (1908).

42. See Horace E. Flack, *The Adoption of the Fourteenth Amendment* (Baltimore: Johns Hopkins University Press, 1908); Joseph B. James, *The Framing of the Fourteenth Amendment* (Urbana: University of Illinois Press, 1956). The classic scholarly refutation is a long article by Charles Fairman, "Does the Fourteenth Amendment Incorporate the Bill of Rights? The Original Understanding," *Stanford Law Review,* 2 (December 1949): 5–139.

43. See, e.g., the dissenting opinion of Justice Black, with which Justice Douglas joined, in Adamson v. California, 332 U.S. 46, 68 (1947). Garnering four votes in all, the total incorporation theory achieved its greatest strength in this case.

44. Powell v. Alabama, 287 U.S. 45 (1932).

45. Gideon v. Wainwright, 372 U.S. 335 (1963).

46. Argersinger v. Hamlin, 407 U.S. 25 (1972).

47. Hurtado v. California, 110 U.S. 516 (1884).

by jury in suits at the common law where the amount in controversy exceeds twenty dollars. In addition, there has been no clear holding by the Supreme Court that the Eighth Amendment prohibition of excessive bail applies to the states, although several lower federal courts seem to assume that it does.[48] Otherwise, it may now be said that all other provisions of the Bill of Rights have now been nationalized, including all parts of the First Amendment, which is concerned with the great freedoms of speech, press, religion, assembly, and petition. Similarly, most provisions relating to the rights of persons accused of crime are now applicable to the states as elements of Fourteenth Amendment due process. These now include the Fourth Amendment right to be free from unreasonable searches and seizures, including the derivative right to have illegally seized evidence excluded from the trial;[49] the Fifth Amendment right to be free from compulsory self-incrimination;[50] the Sixth Amendment rights to counsel,[51] to a speedy trial,[52] to a public trial,[53] to confrontation of opposing witnesses,[54] and to compulsory process for obtaining witnesses;[55] and the Eighth Amendment prohibition of cruel and unusual punishments.[56] The process of spelling out federal standards for state criminal proceedings reached some sort of a climax in 1968, when the Court finally ruled that the Sixth Amendment guaranty of trial by jury applies to state criminal trials involving serious or nonpetty offenses,[57] and in 1969, when the federal concept of double jeopardy, which is rooted in the Fifth Amendment, was made binding on the states.[58] While the Court has employed various bits of rhetoric to justify why a right stated in the Bill of Rights should apply to the states through the Fourteenth Amendment—e.g., to vindicate "fundamental principles of liberty and justice," principles "basic in our system of jurisprudence," "fundamental rights essential to a fair trial," or "protection against arbitrary rule"—what they all add up to is the general theme that due process is a guaranty of justice and a fair trial, as these concepts have acquired content in the course of our history.

As a matter of fact, far from being a mere shorthand restatement of the federal Bill of Rights, the due process clause has an independent force

48. See chapter 2 of this book, on bail.
49. Mapp v. Ohio, 367 U.S. 643 (1961).
50. Malloy v. Hogan, 378 U.S. 1 (1964).
51. See cases cited in notes 44, 45, and 46, above.
52. Klopfer v. North Carolina, 386 U.S. 213 (1967).
53. *In re* Oliver, 333 U.S. 257, 273 (1948).
54. Pointer v. Texas, 380 U.S. 400 (1965).
55. Washington v. Texas, 388 U.S. 14 (1967).
56. Robinson v. California, 370 U.S. 660 (1962).
57. Duncan v. Louisiana, 391 U.S. 145 (1968).
58. Benton v. Maryland, 395 U.S. 784 (1969), overruling Palko v. Connecticut, 302 U.S. 319 (1937).

wholly outside its provisions. That is to say, the Court has read into due process principles not mentioned in the Bill of Rights at all. For example, in the famous *Mooney* case,[59] decided in 1935, the Court laid down the rule that a state has denied the defendant due process if the prosecution deceives the trial court and jury by presenting testimony known to be perjured. In fact, later on the Court extended this rule to include the suppression by the prosecution of evidence favorable to the accused.[60] Similarly, in 1960 the Court expanded the due process concept in a very important way by holding that a criminal conviction in a state court which is based on no evidence at all must be set aside as being a wholly arbitrary decision.[61]

It is important to stress that when a state criminal case is appealed to the Supreme Court on the ground that a fundamental federal constitutional right has been denied, the Court is not bound by the factual determinations of the state courts. In a leading case which reversed the second conviction of the Scottsboro boys, this time because of the systematic and arbitrary exclusion of Negroes from jury service, in violation of the Fourteenth Amendment guaranty of the equal protection of the laws, Chief Justice Hughes called special attention to this point when he wrote,

That the question is one of fact does not relieve us of the duty to determine whether in truth a federal right has been denied. When a federal right has been specially set up and claimed in a state court, it is our province to inquire not merely whether it was denied in express terms but also whether it was denied in substance and effect. If this requires an examination of evidence, that examination must be made. Otherwise, review by this Court would fail of its purpose in safeguarding constitutional rights. Thus, whenever a conclusion of law of a state court as to a federal right and findings of fact are so intermingled that the latter control the former, it is incumbent upon us to analyze the facts in order that the appropriate enforcement of the federal right may be assured.[62]

Since the early 1930s, the Supreme Court has vastly expanded its power to review state criminal cases, largely through a progressively generous

59. Mooney v. Holohan, 294 U.S. 103 (1935). For later cases on this point, see Mesarosh v. United States, 352 U.S. 1 (1956); Alcorta v. Texas, 355 U.S. 28 (1957); Miller v. Pate, 386 U.S. 1 (1967).

60. Brady v. Maryland, 373 U.S. 83 (1963); Giles v. Maryland, 386 U.S. 66 (1967).

61. Thompson v. Louisville, 362 U.S. 199 (1960). Many later convictions in sit-in cases were set aside on this ground. See, e.g., Garner v. Louisiana, 368 U.S. 157 (1961); Taylor v. Louisiana, 370 U.S. 154 (1962); Barr v. Columbia, 378 U.S. 146 (1964); Shuttlesworth v. Birmingham, 382 U.S. 87 (1965); Johnson v. Florida, 391 U.S. 596 (1968).

62. Norris v. Alabama, 294 U.S. 587, 589-90 (1935). This point is very well established in the jurisprudence of the Supreme Court. See, e.g., Fiske v. Kansas, 274 U.S. 380, 385 (1927); Chambers v. Florida, 309 U.S. 227, 228-29 (1940); Ashcraft v. Tennessee, 322 U.S. 143, 147-48 (1944); Craig v. Harney, 331 U.S. 367, 373 (1947).

reading of the due process clause of the Fourteenth Amendment. This means that increasingly the Court has been establishing more and more minimum standards in the field of criminal justice which the states are obliged to observe. While this has had the result of imposing many controls upon the states' criminal justice systems, it is still true that the crime problem is largely local, and not federal in character, and that most offenses are dealt with by the state authorities alone. This is well understood by all branches of the federal government. For example, in his major message on crime, sent to Congress on February 9, 1968, President Johnson declared, "The Federal Government must never assume the role of the Nation's policeman. . . . Crime is essentially a local matter. Police operations—if they are to be effective and responsible—must likewise remain basically local. This is the fundamental premise of our constitutional structure and of our heritage of liberty." Similarly, in an address to the American Law Institute on May 16, 1972, Chief Justice Burger said, "Our basic system of justice, of course, lies within state power and it should remain that way, with Federal courts functioning, as the Constitution intended they should, as courts of special and limited jurisdiction. Day-to-day justice, in short, is inherently a state function."[63] This is also the view of Congress. In the Declaration of Purpose which introduces Title I of the Omnibus Crime Control and Safe Streets Act of 1968, dealing with Law Enforcement Assistance, Congress made the formal finding "that crime is essentially a local problem that must be dealt with by State and local governments if it is to be controlled effectively. It is therefore the declared policy of the Congress to assist State and local governments in strengthening and improving law enforcement at every level by national assistance."[64]

Two Models of the Criminal Process

A central problem in operating our criminal justice system arises from the fact that two basic objectives underlying that system often collide with each other, and then some very hard choices must be made. On the one hand, we seek to apprehend, try, and punish lawbreakers. On the other hand, we are strongly concerned with maintaining the legal amenities of a civilized community. As Professor Packer once suggested, the basic choice confronting us is between two models, the crime control model and the due process model.[65] The principal objective of crime control is the quick, efficient, and reliable handling of persons accused of crime. The problem

63. Warren E. Burger, "Has the Time Come?" 55 F.R.D. 119, 123 (1972).
64. 42 U.S.C. §3701 (1970).
65. Herbert L. Packer, "Two Models of the Criminal Process," *University of Pennsylvania Law Review,* 113 (November 1964): 1–68.

is essentially administrative and managerial in charcter, and the process operates on the assembly-line principle. But the main interest of due process is to protect the dignity and autonomy of the individual, and the process is adversary and judicial, an obstacle course. While Professor Packer thought that actually the crime control model predominates in the country, the Supreme Court leans in the direction of the due process model.

In his great dissenting opinion in the first wire-tapping case to reach the Court, Justice Holmes explored this point in language which it would be very difficult to improve upon:

We must consider the two objects of desire, both of which we cannot have, and make up our minds which to choose. It is desirable that criminals should be detected, and to that end that all available evidence should be used. It also is desirable that the Government should not itself foster and pay for other crimes, when they are the means by which the evidence is to be obtained. . . . We have to choose, and for my part I think it a less evil that some criminals should escape than that the Government should play an ignoble part.[66]

In a separate dissenting opinion Justice Brandeis warned of the dangers implicit in governmental lawlessness:

In a government of laws, existence of the government will be imperilled if it fails to observe the law scrupulously. Our Government is the potent, the omnipresent teacher. For good or for ill, it teaches the whole people by its example. Crime is contagious. If the Government becomes a law-breaker, it breeds contempt for law; it invites every man to become a law unto himself; it invites anarchy. To declare that in the administration of the criminal law the end justifies the means—to declare that the Government may commit crimes in order to secure the conviction of a private criminal—would bring terrible retribution. Against that pernicious doctrine this Court should resolutely set its face.[67]

Unfortunately, the crime problem not only will not go away; it is steadily becoming more serious, and the victims of crime are heard from.[68] The demand for more draconian measures is heard in many quarters, but this demand must be evaluated in light of the fact that, in the words of Justice Frankfurter, the Bill of Rights was adopted "in the conviction that too high a price may be paid even for the unhampered enforcement of the criminal law and that, in its attainment, other social objects of a free society should not be sacrificed."[69] The "other social

66. Olmstead v. United States, 277 U.S. 438, 470 (1928).
67. 277 U.S. 485.
68. One approach to the crime problem, the compensation of the victims of crime through public funds, is now being explored in various states. See Herbert Edelberg and Gilbert Reis, *Public Compensation to Victims of Crime* (New York: Praeger, 1974).
69. Feldman v. United States, 322 U.S. 487, 489 (1944).

objects of a free society" to which Justice Frankfurter referred must include such basic values as respect for individual privacy, scrupulous adherence to established rules of law, a fair trial on comprehensible charges, and what Justice Stewart has so aply described as "the imperative of judicial integrity."[70]

The search for a tolerable balance between the crime control model and the due process model will probably never cease. Complaints that we have gone too far in tilting the scales in favor of the criminal, at the expense of vital social interests, seem to keep pace with the efforts of the judges to strengthen the due process protections available to defendants. Thus, a former Police Commissioner of New York City declared, in 1965, "It is my firm conclusion that recent Supreme Court decisions have unduly hampered—and will in the future further hamper—the administration of criminal justice. . . . Police are not alone in their conclusion that we are reaching a critical stage in our never-ending search for the illusive balance between the needs of the community and the rights of the individual."[71] Of course, what this statement fails to recognize is that one of "the needs of the community" is maximum respect for "the rights of the individual."

Complaints that we have moved too far, too rapidly on the due process front are voiced even by members of the Supreme Court. Thus, in a leading case involving the right to the assistance of counsel and the permissible scope of police interrogation, Justice White observed, "I do not suggest for a moment that law enforcement will be destroyed by the rule announced today. The need for peace and order is too insistent for that. But it will be crippled and its task made a great deal more difficult, all in my opinion, for unsound, unstated reasons, which can find no home in any of the provisions of the Constitution."[72] Similarly, early in his career at the center chair, Chief Justice Burger wrote a concurring opinion "only to emphasize the importance of allowing the States to experiment and innovate, especially in the area of criminal justice. . . . The circumstances of this case demonstrate again that neither the Constitution as originally drafted, nor any amendment, nor indeed any need, dictates that we must have absolute uniformity in the criminal law in all the States. Federal authority was never intended to be a 'ramrod' to compel conformity to nonconstitutional standards."[73] Furthermore, the following year Chief

---

70. Elkins v. United States, 364 U.S. 206, 222 (1960).

71. Michael Murphy, speaking to the Judicial Conference of the Third Judicial Circuit on September 9, 1965, 39 F.R.D. 425 (1965).

72. Escobedo v. Illinois, 378 U.S. 478, 499 (1964) (dissenting opinion).

73. California v. Green, 399 U.S. 149, 171–72 (1970). This case held that the admission in evidence of preliminary-hearing testimony given under oath and subject to cross-examination did not violate the defendant's constitutional right of confrontation.

Justice Burger seized upon an opportunity to denounce the exclusionary rule (which bars the use in court of evidence secured unlawfully, even though relevant and otherwise trustworthy) as a rule for which we have been paying a "monstrous price."[74] To cite one more example, a trial judge in California published a book in 1974 in which he sharply criticized the drift of current legal doctrine, especially in the criminal law field, arguing that the Supreme Court has been pursuing legal perfectionism with "disastrous" consequences.[75] He recalled Judge Learned Hand's famous remark that "due process of law does not mean infallible process of law."[76]

Quite obviously, in that branch of the law which is concerned with the rights of defendants in criminal cases, there has been a great deal of change since the early 1930s. This is testimony to the fact that American public law is resilient and sensitive to the requirements of a dynamic society. Both objective conditions and conceptions of justice change, and it is fitting and proper that the law should keep pace with both events and the progress of thought. As for the search for a balance between the crime control model and the due process model, there is no ultimate, final solution. The pushing and hauling in both directions will continue. Perhaps what matters most is that inquiry and adjustment should continue freely as we seek to locate tolerable levels of balance. In this search, the Supreme Court has moved carefully, deciding one case at a time, but always within the mainstream of American legal tradition. It is probably trite to say that not all problems can be solved to everyone's satisfaction, but at the very least a serious effort must be made to grapple with them. This is what has been going on, in recent years, in the field of the defendant's rights.

74. Coolidge v. New Hampshire, 403 U.S. 443, 493 (1971) (dissenting opinion).
75. Macklin Fleming, *The Price of Perfect Justice* (New York: Basic Books, Inc., 1974), p. 5.
76. Schechtman v. Foster, 172 F.2d 339, 341 (2nd Cir. 1949).

2 / The Preliminaries

ARRESTS

The Police

Police practices have an important impact upon the civil rights of the citizen. One of the great purposes of law enforcement is to safeguard the freedom of the people, but this includes "freedom from fear of the police, as well as freedom from fear of criminals."[1] There are thus two sides to the matter. On the one hand, there should be public confidence in the integrity of the agencies of law enforcement, and on the other hand, these agencies must respect the rights of private persons. Professionally disciplined policemen, properly instructed in their duties, and scrupulously observing their responsibilities, contribute much to the protection of the basic rights of the citizen. But official misconduct is a corrosive and disorganizing force in society.

According to a study made by a task force reporting, in 1967, to the President's Commission on Law Enforcement and Administration of Justice, there were in that year about 420,000 people working for some 40,000 separate police agencies at a total cost of over $2½ billion a year.[2] Furthermore, this report noted that "law enforcement has always been a difficult task. It is especially difficult in a society such as ours that has so heterogeneous and mobile a population; that has so prosperous an economy; that has so high a degree of urbanization, with its accompanying congestion and anonymity; and that places so high a value on individual freedom, upon equality under the law, and upon local control over the police power."[3] In addition, as the President's Commission pointed out, "it is hard to overstate the intimacy of the contact between the police and the community. Policemen deal with people when they are both most threatening and most vulnerable, when they are angry, when they are frightened, when they are desperate, when they are drunk, when they are violent, or when they are ashamed. Every police action can affect in some way someone's dignity, or self-respect, or sense of privacy, or

---

1. O. W. Wilson, "The Place of Local Law Enforcement in the Total Picture," in University of Chicago Law School, *Conference on Criminal Law Enforcement*, Conf. Ser. no. 7, March 2, 1951 (Chicago: University of Chicago Press, 1951), p. 51.
2. *Task Force Report: The Police* (Washington: U.S. Government Printing Office, 1967), p. 1.
3. *Ibid.*, p. 13.

constitutional rights. As a matter of routine policemen become privy to, and make judgments about, secrets that most citizens guard jealously from their closest friends: relationships between husbands and wives, the misbehavior of children, personal eccentricities, peccadilloes and lapses of all kinds. Very often policemen must physically restrain or subdue unruly citizens."[4]

As these observations indicate, the police are concerned with much more than the apprehension of criminals; they devote much more time to social welfare activities, such as involvement in family disputes. As they go about their business, policemen exercise great discretion and engage in many different sorts of policy-making. A distinguished legal scholar, Professor Kenneth Culp Davis of the Law School of the University of Chicago, has called attention to this point in an important book:

> The police are among the most important policy-making agencies, despite the widespread assumption that they are not. The Crime Commission makes the basic observation that peace-keeping and service activities consume most of the time of policemen, and law enforcement takes only a minority of their time. Policy has to be made about what private disputes to mediate and how to do it, breaking up sidewalk gatherings, stopping undue noisiness during sleeping hours, legally or illegally tapping wires and using listening devices, helping drunks, deciding what to do with runaway boys who refuse to go home, breaking up fights and matrimonial disputes, deliberately destroying valuable property such as gambling devices even when admissible evidence that it has been used illegally is lacking, engaging in preventive detention in violation of the Constitution, stopping citizens on the street, entering and searching premises, and deciding which crimes not to investigate for lack of manpower. Policy has to be made for the enormous field of police control of juveniles. Policy has to be made on such huge and troublesome subjects as the relations between the police and various minority groups.[5]

As a matter of fact, as another noted legal scholar has pointed out, one of the serious difficulties confronting the police today is that the public tends to identify the police "as the ones to blame and hold responsible for the plight of minority groups and the abuses of minority groups. The policeman is the uniformed symbol of all these social ills. He has come to represent a menace in the way of a better life for the socially deprived."[6] He goes on to say that the police did not produce our slums or ghettoes, and did not create segregation and discrimination. The blame, he

---

4. President's Commission on Law Enforcement and Administration of Justice, *The Challenge of Crime in a Free Society* (Washington: U.S. Government Printing Office, 1967), pp. 91–92.

5. *Discretionary Justice* (Baton Rouge: Louisiana State University Press, 1969), p. 81.

6. Fred E. Inbau, "Democratic Restraints upon the Police," *Journal of Criminal Law, Criminology and Police Science,* 57 (September 1966): 265–70, 265.

declares, lies with the whole community, whom the police serve as they think the community wants to be served.

On the other hand, in its 1968 report, the National Advisory Commission on Civil Disorders described the relationship between the police and our black minority, somewhat differently when it observed,

Almost invariably the incident that ignites disorder arises from police action. Harlem, Watts, Newark, and Detroit—all the major outbursts of recent years—were precipitated by arrests of Negroes by white police for minor offenses.

But the police are not merely the spark. In discharge of their obligation to maintain order and insure public safety in the disruptive conditions of ghetto life, they are inevitably involved in sharper and more frequent conflicts with ghetto residents than with the residents of other areas. Thus, to many Negroes, police have come to symbolize white power, white racism, and white repression. And the fact is that many police do reflect and express these white attitudes. The atmosphere of hostility and cynicism is reinforced by a widespread perception among Negroes of the existence of police brutality and corruption and of a "double standard" of justice and protection—one for Negroes and one for whites.[7]

Just how much police lawlessness there is in our society is really unknown; though the subject is often described, it is impossible to find reliable statistics.[8] It is a fair guess, however, that there is less police lawlessness these days than in earlier times, for increasingly police work in the United States is acquiring the status and dignity of a skilled profession. Furthermore, it is all too easy to underestimate the tremendous complexity of the problems of law enforcement, and the extent to which police violations of the law are purely technical. In the case of arrest, for example, many violations result from the fact that the law is out of date to such an extent that it may be suggested that the law ought to be redrafted to meet contemporary realities, rather than force the police to stay in an archaic groove.

Nevertheless, the fact of official misconduct cannot be denied, and

---

7. *Report of the National Advisory Commission on Civil Disorders* (Washington: U.S. Government Printing Office, March 1, 1968), p. 93.

8. See Report of the President's Committee on Civil Rights, *To Secure These Rights* (Washington: U.S. Government Printing Office, 1947), pp. 25-27; National Commission on Law Observance and Enforcement, *Report on Lawlessness in Law Enforcement* (Washington: U.S. Government Printing Office, 1931); Ernest J. Hopkins, *Our Lawless Police* (New York: Viking Press, 1931); Albert Deutsch, *The Trouble with Cops* (New York: Crown Publishers, Inc., 1955); Theodore L. Becker and Vernon G. Murray, *Government Lawlessness in America* (New York: Oxford University Press, 1971); Paul Chevigny, *Police Power: Police Abuses in New York City* (New York: Random House, 1969); 1961 U.S. Commission on Civil Rights Report, bk. 5, *Justice* (Washington: U.S. Government Printing Office, 1961); M. L. Ernst, "The Policeman and Due Process," *Journal of Public Law*, 2 (Fall 1953): 250-53.

though by no means universal, police lawlessness has always been widespread. This lawlessness takes many forms: failure to protect persons against mob violence, physical attacks upon members of minority groups, third-degree methods to extract confessions, unwarranted arrests, shakedowns of innocent people, illegal detention, mistreatment of prisoners, unreasonable searches and seizures, nonenforcement of the law, theft, and tolerance or support of organized crime activities.[9] Furthermore, as the President's Committee on Civil Rights pointed out in 1947, "most of the victims of such abuses are ignorant, friendless persons, unaware of their rights, and without means of challenging those who have violated those rights."[10]

The Nature of Arrest

Since the first point of contact between the citizen and his government is often the policeman, and since arrest by the policeman is usually the first thing that happens to a person accused of crime, the law of arrest is worth looking into. While this law is in fact extremely complicated,[11] a few general principles and problems relating to it may be noted here. The present law of arrest is of very great antiquity, and it bears the marks of this antiquity. It developed in England in the days before professional, trained police forces and modern jail facilities were available. While arrest and imprisonment are never pleasant experiences, under any circumstances, they were extremely serious when men were held for months, even years, without trial, without bail, which was hard to get, without proper food, and in such hideous places that large numbers died in prison. In short, arrest was likely to be a terrible calamity. Furthermore, before the rise of adequate police forces, most arrests were made by private persons, as, for example, by means of hue and cry. Accordingly, a very strict body of law arose which severely circumscribed the powers of those who sought to make arrests.

Even under modern conditions, however, for most people an arrest by the police is not a minor matter. "Arrest," Justice White recently wrote, "is a public act that may seriously interfere with the defendant's liberty,

---

9. See *Task Force Report, The Police,* chap. 7, "Police Integrity"; John A. Gardner, *Traffic and the Police: Variations in Law Enforcement Policy* (Cambridge: Harvard University Press, 1969); James Q. Wilson, *Varieties of Police Behavior* (Cambridge: Harvard University Press, 1968).

10. *To Secure These Rights,* p. 25. See John Edgar Hoover, "Civil Liberties and Law Enforcement: The Role of the FBI," *Iowa Law Review,* 37 (Winter 1951): 175-95.

11. The leading book on this subject is Wayne R. La Fave, *Arrest* (Boston: Little, Brown & Co., 1965). See also Rollin M. Perkins, "The Law of Arrest," *Iowa Law Review,* 25 (January 1940): 201-89; Lester B. Orfield, *Criminal Procedure from Arrest to Appeal* (New York: New York University Press, 1947), chap. 1; Ernest W. Machen, Jr., *The Law of Arrest* (Chapel Hill: Institute of Government, University of North Carolina, 1950).

whether he is free on bail or not, and that may disrupt his employment, drain his financial resources, curtail his associations, subject him to public obloquy, and create anxiety in him, his family and his friends."[12] It follows, of course, that the observance by public authorities of the law relating to arrests has a high priority in the hierarchy of community values.

An arrest is the taking of a person into custody "for the actual or purported purpose of bringing [him] before a court, or of otherwise securing the administration of justice."[13] The normal purpose of an arrest is to take a person into custody that he may be held to answer for a crime. Arrests can be made by peace officers or private persons, with or without warrants. "A warrant is a written order directing the arrest of a person or persons, issued by a court, body or official, having authority to issue warrants."[14] While arrests by private persons are extremely rare in these days of law enforcement by organized police forces, at the common law a private person may arrest without warrant when a felony or misdemeanor has been committed in his presence, and he knows or has reasonable grounds to believe that a particular individual committed the crime. The reliance upon private plaintiffs to help enforce the laws is not at all uncommon. A well-known example is the triple-damage suit under the antitrust laws. During World War II the Emergency Price Control Act was enforced in part by means of private actions for treble damages.

Generally speaking, the peace officer's power of arrest is much broader, since he is not limited to arrests actually committed in his presence, although a very few states have extended the arrest power of the private person to embrace arrest on reasonable suspicion. Furthermore, if asked to do so by an officer, the citizen has a duty to assist in arresting a felon. This also is an outgrowth of the hue and cry of ancient times. Justice Cardozo once wrote, "Still as in the days of Edward I, the citizenry may be called upon to enforce the justice of the State, not faintly and with lagging steps, but honestly and bravely and with whatever implements and facilities are convenient and at hand."[15] This duty is often spelled out in statutes.[16] Prosecutions for failure or refusal to aid the police, however, are almost unknown.

12. United States v. Marion, 404 U.S. 307, 320 (1971).
13. *Restatement, Torts,* §112 (1934). "An arrest is the initial stage of a criminal prosecution." Terry v. Ohio, 392 U.S. 1, 26 (1968).
14. *Restatement, Torts,* §113.
15. Babington v. Yellow Taxi Corp., 250 N.Y. 14, 17, 164 N.E. 726, 727, 61 A.L.R. 1354 (1928).
16. See, e.g., New York Code of Criminal Procedure, §169: "Every person must aid an officer in the execution of a warrant, if the officer require his aid and be present and acting in its execution."

The Warrant of Arrest

Before a warrant is issued, a sworn complaint must be filed with a magistrate or other duly authorized officer, showing that a crime has been committed, and that there is probable cause to suspect that the arrestee was responsible for the crime. This is in accord with the requirement of state constitutions, and of the Fourth Amendment that "no Warrants shall issue, but upon probable cause, supported by Oath or affirmation." The warrant is designed to interpose a judicial process between the individual and the officer seeking to make an arrest. Speaking of search warrants, Justice Murphy once explained the importance of this procedure as follows: "In their understandable zeal to ferret out crime and in the excitement of the capture of a suspected person, officers are less likely to possess the detachment and neutrality with which the constitutional rights of the suspect must be viewed. To provide the necessary security against unreasonable intrusions upon the private lives of individuals, the framers of the Fourth Amendment required adherence to judicial processes wherever possible."[17] Mere suspicion is not enough to justify the issuance of a warrant of arrest. The facts set out must be such, the Supreme Court has explained, "that a reasonably discreet and prudent man would be led to believe that there was a commission of the offense charged. . . ."[18] Thus, an arrest is unlawful if the warrant was based on an unnamed informer's tip without any factual data tending to corroborate the tip.[19] Local warrants are served locally, but a federal warrant may be executed "at any place within the jurisdiction of the United States."[20]

Arrests Without Warrants

Most arrests, however, are made without warrants. At the common law a police officer may arrest without a warrant whenever he has reasonable ground to believe that a felony has occurred and that the arrestee committed it. If these two grounds exist, he is protected even if it turns out that he made a mistake. By statute, states often provide a third ground for arrest without a warrant in the case of felonies, and that is reasonable belief that the person might escape if not arrested at once. At the common law a police officer may also arrest without warrant if the arrestee is an escaped prisoner. The common law rule dealing with arrest without warrant for misdemeanors is stricter. The Massachusetts court once described the rule as follows: "A peace officer, in the absence of statute, . . . may arrest without a warrant for a misdemeanor which (1)

17. Trupiano v. United States, 334 U.S. 699, 705 (1948).
18. Dumbra v. United States, 268 U.S. 435, 441 (1925).
19. Whiteley v. Warden of Wyoming Penitentiary, 401 U.S. 560 (1971).
20. Rule 4 (c) (2), Rules of Criminal Procedure for the United States District Courts.

involves a breach of the peace, (2) is committed in the presence or view of the officer, . . . and (3) is still continuing at the time of the arrest or only interrupted, so that the offence and the arrest form parts of one transaction. . . ."[21] Thus, the difference is that while as regards felonies an officer may arrest without warrant though the felony was not committed in his presence, he may not arrest for a misdemeanor if not committed in his presence. Furthermore, he may arrest a person for a felony on reasonable suspicion, but for a misdemeanor only if the arrestee is actually guilty. He may arrest for a misdemeanor only when the crime was committed or while in hot pursuit, whereas he may arrest felons at any time. The main reason for these differences is that the social interest in apprehending perpetrators of minor offenses is not sufficiently great or urgent to justify the waiving of the preferable procedure of arrest on the authority of a warrant issued by a magistrate.

The United State Supreme Court has emphasized that the requirement of probable cause has roots deep in our history, and that both before and immediately after the adoption of the Fourth Amendment neither common rumor or report, nor mere suspicion, nor even "strong reason to suspect" was adequate to support an arrest with a warrant.[22] While evidence required to establish guilt is not necessary, on the other hand good faith on the part of the arresting officer is not enough. "Probable cause exists," Justice Douglas has written, "if the facts and circumstances known to the officer warrant a prudent man in believing that the offense has been committed."[23] It is important, he added, to enforce this requirement strictly, pointing out that the constitutional standard protects both the officer and the citizen. Thus, an "arrest is not justified by what the subsequent search discloses. Under our system suspicion is not enough for an officer to lay hands on a citizen. It is better, so the Fourth Amendment teaches, that the guilty sometimes go free than that citizens be subject to easy arrest."[24]

Accordingly, a unanimous Court ruled in 1975 that a person who was arrested under a prosecutor's information is constitutionally entitled to an early judicial determination of the existence of probable cause justifying a

21. Com. v. Gorman, 288 Mass. 294, 297, 192 N.E. 618, 619 (1934).
22. Henry v. United States, 361 U.S. 98 (1959).
23. 361 U.S. 102.
24. 361 U.S. 104. The Supreme Court has in recent years expanded its influence in the area of arrest by a willingness to examine the facts to determine whether there was probable cause. See, e.g., Wong Sun v. United States, 371 U.S. 471 (1963); Ker v. California, 374 U.S. 23 (1963); Beck v. Ohio, 379 U.S. 89, 96 (1964): "When the constitutional validity of an arrest is challenged, it is the function of a court to determine whether the facts available to the officers at the moment of the arrest would 'warrant a man of reasonable caution in the belief' that an offense has been committed" (dissenting opinion of Justice Clark).

pretrial restraint of liberty.[25] Under Florida law, except for capital offenses, prosecutors may charge all other crimes by information, without a preliminary hearing and without obtaining leave of any court, and a person so charged may be detained for a substantial period of time solely on the decision of the prosecutor. Holding that the standard for arrest is probable cause, and that whether there is probable cause must be decided by a neutral and detached magistrate wherever possible, the Court ruled that while it would constitute an intolerable handicap for legitimate law enforcement to require a review by a magistrate of the factual justification prior to any arrest, once the suspect is in custody the reasons which justify dispensing with the magistrate's neutral judgment evaporate, and at this point the need for a neutral judicial determination of probable cause increases significantly. Since pretrial confinement is a serious matter, "the Fourth Amendment requires a judicial determination of probable cause as a prerequisite to extended restraint on liberty following arrest." The Court rejected Florida's argument that the prosecutor's decision to file an information is itself a determination of probable cause. Even so, the Court pointed out that it has never invalidated an arrest supported by probable cause solely because the officers failed to secure a warrant.

In most states today the law of arrest, or a good part of it, is statutory. State statutes often authorize arrest without warrant for *all* offenses committed in the presence of the officer, including misdemeanors which are not breaches of the peace,[26] such as motor vehicle violations. Many statutes also authorize a policeman to arrest a person when notified that another state peace officer has a warrant for his arrest.

Reform of the Law of Arrest

A Committee appointed by the Interstate Commission on Crime prepared a Uniform Arrest Act in 1939 which proposed several drastic changes in the prevailing law of arrest.[27] To date only four states have adopted it. The most important and widely debated provision (§2) would authorize the police to stop and question anyone acting in a suspicious manner in a public place, and detain him for a total period not exceeding two hours. This detention is not an arrest, and is not recorded as one. At

---

25. Gerstein v. Pugh, 420 U.S. 103 (1975).

26. "A breach of the peace is a public offense done by violence or one causing or likely to cause an immediate disturbance of public order." *Restatement, Torts,* §116. See Smith v. Wisconsin, 50 Wis. 2d 460, 184 N.W. 2d 889 (1971), cert. denied, 404 U.S. 1000 (1971), where it was held that arrest for a misdemeanor committed in the officer's presence, without a warrant, is proper even though the offense did not constitute a breach of the peace.

27. See Sam B. Warner, "The Uniform Arrest Act," *Virginia Law Review,* 28 (January 1942): 315–47, for the text of the act and an authoritative analysis of its provisions.

the end of the detention the person so detained must be released or arrested and charged with a crime. At the present time arrest on suspicion in order to investigate is not legal, although it is a common occurrence. The Uniform Act also allows arrest (§6(1)(B)) for a misdemeanor not committed in the presence of the officer if he believes the offender will not be apprehended unless arrested immediately. Finally, the Uniform Act provides (§6(2)(B)) that an arrest is lawful, even if originally it was not, if something turns up after arrest which establishes that a felony has been committed. The reluctance of the states to adopt these reforms testifies to the toughness of the law of arrest. Even though the strict law of arrest is frequently violated by the police, American lawmakers are very loathe to tamper with it.

The Expungement of Arrest Records

The right of an individual to challenge the retention in police files of an arrest record has been the subject of a great deal of litigation in recent years. The traditional, and still prevailing view of most courts has been that an arrestee is not entitled to have his arrest record expunged, even if he was acquitted, or if the charges were dismissed for other reasons, such as the government's decision not to prosecute, on the theory that the retention of arrest records promotes effective law enforcement.[28] The requirements of effective law enforcement are said to outweigh any possible harm to the individual. Indeed, it has been asserted that the retention of the arrest record of an individual in the police files is "a humiliation to which he must submit for the benefit of society."[29] Furthermore, many courts have taken the position that they will not order the expungement of arrest records unless a specific statute authorizes the courts to do so.[30] Thus, the courts have usually ruled that if the arrest was legal, retention of the records of arrest in the police files is valid since that serves as an investigative tool; if the arrestee has been acquitted, then his acquittal neutralizes the impact of the arrest record.[31] In fact, the Supreme Court of Washington recently ruled against the expungement of the arrest records of juveniles, even in cases where the charges have been

---

28. Herschel v. Dyra, 365 F.2d 17 (7th Cir. 1966), cert. denied, 385 U.S. 973 (1966); Sterling v. City of Oakland, 208 Cal. App. 2d 1, 24 Cal. Rptr. 696 (1962); Kolb v. O'Connor, 14 Ill. App. 2d 81, 142 N.E. 2d 818 (1957); Weisberg v. Village, 46 Misc. 2d 846, 260 N.Y.S. 2d 554 (1965). See the Comment in *Notre Dame Lawyer,* 46 (Summer 1971): 825-34.

29. Fernicola v. Keenan, 136 N.J. Eq. 9, 10, 39 A.2d 851 (1944).

30. See, e.g., Spock v. District of Columbia, 283 A.2d 14 (Dist. Col. App. 1971); Mulkey v. Purdy, 234 So.2d 108 (Fla. 1970).

31. The leading authorities are assembled in an annotation on the expungement of arrest records in 46 A.L.R. 3d 900-933 (1972).

dismissed, on the ground that these records constitute important and essential information which ought to be available to the police and other public authorities.[32]

On the other hand, a very persuasive argument can be made that where the arrestee has been exonerated—whether by an acquittal or dismissal of the charges—fundamental fairness precludes retention of an arrest record.[33] In a widely noted decision the influential Court of Appeals for the District of Columbia has pointed out that serious disabilities flow from the mere existence of a record of arrest.[34] The record of arrest is likely to carry with it an element of social stigma and substantial injury to reputation. It affects one's credit standing. One who has an arrest record is apt to be subject to greater police scrutiny. It affects such judicial decisions as those involving the granting of bail, release pending appeal, and sentencing. It has a bearing on the decision of a defendant to testify at his trial. It may have an important bearing on the securing of a license in certain fields of work. It affects applications for employment. In fact, a strong argument can be made for the proposition that the use of arrest records is a racially discriminatory employment criterion.[35] Thus, the Court of Appeals of the District of Columbia ruled that one who was arrested, but against whom no criminal complaint was ever filed, has asserted a cognizable legal injury for which he is entitled to a remedy, and further, that "the judicial remedy of expungement is inherent and is not dependent on express statutory provision, and it exists to vindicate substantial rights provided by statute as well as by organic law. . . ."[36]

Accordingly, various federal and state courts have ruled that a court of equity has the inherent power, even in the absence of specific legislative authorization, to order the expungement of an arrest record.[37] In partic-

32. Monroe v. Tielsch, 84 Wash. 2d 217, 525 P.2d 250 (1974).

33. See Note, "Right of Police to Retain Arrest Records," *North Carolina Law Review,* 49, no. 2 (1971): 509–19.

34. Menard v. Saxbe, 498 F.2d 1017 (D.C. Cir., 1974). For earlier phases of this litigation, see Menard v. Mitchell, 430 F.2d 486 (D.C. Cir. 1970); Menard v. Mitchell, 328 F. Supp. 718 (D.D.C. 1971).

35. See Comment, *Harvard Civil Rights–Civil Liberties Law Review,* 6 (December 1970): 165–78.

36. 498 F.2d 1023. The Court decided this case not on constitutional but on statutory grounds, holding that the statute, 28 U.S.C. §534, does not permit the F.B.I. to maintain in its criminal files as an arrest record an encounter with the police that has been established not to constitute an arrest.

37. See, e.g., Sullivan v. Murphy, 478 F.2d 938, 968 (D.C. Cir. 1973), cert. denied, 414 U.S. 880 (1973), where the Court said, "The principle is well established that a court may order the expungement of records, including arrest records, when that remedy is necessary and appropriate in order to preserve basic legal rights." To the same effect is John Doe v. Commander, Wheaton Police Department, 329 A.2d 35 (Md. Crt. of App. 1974); Kowall v. United States, 53 F.R.D. 211, 213 (W.D. Mich. 1971), where the Court said, "In the last

ular, a few courts have ordered expungement where the arrest was illegal,[38] or where the arrest was for the purpose of intimidation or harassment,[39] or where the arrestee was acquitted or otherwise discharged.[40] Finally, some courts have ruled that a court should order the expungement of an arrest record when harm to the individual's right of privacy or the dangers of unwarranted adverse consequences outweigh the public interest in retaining the records in the police files.[41]

The Limited Powers of the Police

The limited scope of the powers of peace officers is not generally understood. Policemen are not judges. They do not decide whether anyone is guilty of any crime, and they do not make general rules of law. They have no power to compel a man to say anything, although they naturally encourage the human tendency of relieving the mind by confession, and are privileged to do so, provided that they stay within the rules prescribed for interrogation by the Supreme Court. Interrogation is important in the administration of the criminal law. Policemen have no power to detain people merely on suspicion. While they may search the person after arrest for weapons and evidence of the crime, only a few states permit the police to "stop and frisk" without arrest, a procedure which the Supreme Court considers valid.[42] The Uniform Act would legalize frisking of persons detained but not arrested, if the peace officer has reasonable ground to believe that he is in danger if the person possesses a dangerous weapon (§3). The law also requires the arresting officer to bring the arrestee promptly before a magistrate, and it is the duty of the magistrate to discharge the accused unless the police have enough evidence in their possession which, if not contradicted, will prove guilt. Actually many people are released by police without being brought before a magistrate. Furthermore, while it is illegal to resist a lawful arrest, it is legal in most jurisdictions to resist an unlawful arrest, by force if necessary. And the ancient rule that it is murder if one kills a policeman while resisting arrest is no longer the law; now the offense is no more than manslaughther.[43]

---

analysis, the logic of the natural law of remedies does not set arbitrary limits on a federal court's jurisdiction to right wrongs cognizable by the common law within the jurisdiction of the court."

38. United States v. McLeod, 385 F.2d 734 (5th Cir. 1967).
39. Hughes v. Rizzo, 282 F. Supp. 881 (E.D. Pa. 1968).
40. United States v. Kalish, 271 F. Supp. 968 (D.C.P.R. 1967).
41. See, e.g., Eddy v. Moore, 5 Wash. App. 334, 487 P.2d 211, 46 A.L.R. 3d 889 (1971); Davidson v. Dill, 503 P.2d 157 (Colo. 1972).
42. Terry v. Ohio, 392 U.S. 1 (1968); Sibron v. New York, 392 U.S. 40 (1968). This problem is discussed in chapter 8, dealing with searches and seizures.
43. Roy Moreland, "Some Trends in the Law of Arrest," *Minnesota Law Review,* 39 (April 1955): 479-92.

The Right to Resist Arrest

The right to resist an unlawful arrest was established in the English common law in the seventeenth century.[44] It is now recognized in most states, and the U.S. Supreme Court so ruled directly only once, in 1900.[45] In addition, there are recent dicta in which Justices have recognized this right. Thus, Justice Jackson observed in 1948 that "one has an undoubted right to resist an unlawful arrest . . .,"[46] and Chief Justice Warren on one occasion referred to "a Fourth Amendment right to resist" such an arrest.[47] A characteristic statement of this right is the following statement by the Supreme Court of Louisiana: "The right of personal liberty is one of the fundamental rights guaranteed to every citizen, and any unlawful interference with it may be resisted. Every person has a right to resist an unlawful arrest; and, in preventing such illegal restraint of his liberty, he may use such force as may be necessary."[48]

Generally speaking, however, it is not wise to exercise the right of resistance to arrest by police officers. The Association of the Bar of the City of New York and the New York Civil Liberties Union once published a pamphlet, *If You Are Arrested,* in which some very good advice was given: "Even if you think you are not guilty, it is a crime to resist an officer who arrests you lawfully. Respect him. Do not talk back or be disorderly. If it turns out that you have been arrested illegally, you can sue the policeman for false arrest. But remember: if the arrest was a lawful one, the fact that you are innocent does not give you the right to collect damages."

Furthermore, the legal right of the citizen to resist an arrest by one who is known to be a peace officer has been subject to sharp challenge. Section 5 of the Uniform Arrest Act, which has been adopted by California, New Hampshire, Delaware, and Rhode Island, abolishes the right to resist an unlawful arrest. Furthermore, the Model Penal Code, adopted by the prestigious American Law Institute in 1958, abrogates the right to resist an arrest which the person being arrested "knows is being made by a peace officer, although the arrest is unlawful."[49] Accordingly, at least six states have adopted statutes abolishing the common law right to resist an unlawful arrest. Thus a recent Illinois statute provides as follows: "A

---

44. Hopkin Hugget's Case, 84 Eng. Rep. 1082 (K.B. 1666). See also The Queen v. Tooley, 2 Ld. Raym. 1297, 92 Eng. Rep. 349 (K.B. 1710).
45. John Bad Elk v. United States, 177 U.S. 529 (1900).
46. United States v. DiRe, 332 U.S. 581, 594 (1948).
47. Wainwright v. New Orleans, 392 U.S. 598, 603 (1967) (dissenting opinion).
48. City of Monroe v. Ducas, 203 La. 971, 979, 14 So. 2d 781, 784 (1943). See Comment, "The Right to Resist an Unlawful Arrest," *Louisiana Law Review,* 31, no. 1 (1970-71): 120-31.
49. A.L.I., *Model Penal Code,* §3.04 (2) (a) (i) (proposed official draft, 1962).

person is not authorized to use force to resist an arrest which he knows is being made either by a peace officer or by a private person summoned and directed by a peace officer to make the arrest, even if he believes that the arrest is unlawful and the arrest in fact is unlawful."[50] The statute has been upheld by the highest court of Illinois,[51] and the Supreme Court of California sustained the validity of a similar statute the same year.[52] Said the California Court, "In a day when police are armed with lethal and chemical weapons, and possess scientific and detection devices readily available for use, it has become highly unlikely that a suspect, using *reasonable* force, can . . . deter arrest."[53] Similarly, Judge Learned Hand, of the Court of Appeals for the Second Circuit, once remarked, "The idea that you may resist peaceful arrest . . . because you are in debate about whether it is lawful or not, instead of going to the authorities . . . seems to me not a blow for liberty but, on the contrary, a blow for attempted anarchy."[54]

The Appellate Division of the Superior Court of New Jersey concluded, in 1965, without benefit of a statute, that the common law right to resist an illegal arrest by a police officer should not be recognized in that state.[55] Noting that both the Uniform Arrest Act and the Model Penal Code so recommended, the New Jersey court pointed out that, unlike the medieval experience, in modern times all that an arrest means is a few hours of detention in a reasonably clean place. It also noted that every American police officer is armed with a pistol, and has orders not to desist from making an arrest even though there is forceful resistance. Thus successful resistance is possible only by shooting the officer to prevent him from shooting first, and, furthermore, when shooting starts there is always a danger to third persons. In addition, whether an arrest is legal or not is often a matter of close debate, and it is therefore much better for the arrestee to rely upon legal remedies which may be available to him later on. Thus the Court concluded: "The concept of self-help is in decline. It is antisocial in an urbanized society. It is potentially dangerous to all

50. Ill. Laws 1961, p. 1983; Ill. Ann. Stat., 38, §7-7 (Smith-Hurd 1972).

51. Illinois v. Birnbaum, 41 Ill. 2d 426, 243 N.E. 2d 244 (1969), appeal dismissed and cert. denied, 398 U.S. 956 (1970); People v. Gnatz, 8 Ill. App. 3d 369, 290 N.E. 2d 392 (1972).

52. People v. Curtis, 70 Cal. 2d 347, 74 Cal. Rptr. 713, 450 P.2d 33 (1969). The statute is §834(a) of the California Penal Code.

53. 450 P.2d 36.

54. American Law Institute, *Proceedings of the 35th Annual Meeting* (Philadelphia, 1958), p. 254.

55. State v. Koonce, 89 N.J. Super. 169, 214 A.2d 428 (App. Div. 1965). A similar position was adopted in Jordan v. State, 17 Md. App. 201, 300 A.2d 701 (1973); Com. v. Beam, 227 Pa. Super. 293, 324 A.2d 549 (1974).

involved. It is no longer necessary because of the legal remedies available."[56]

Of course, whether the available legal remedies are adequate is a highly debatable question. It has been argued, by a prominent scholar, that the remedies—such as bail, injunction, civil suits for damages, etcetera—are so inadequate that "it is unconscionable to convict a man for resisting an injustice."[57] He has also argued: "To assert that adequate legal remedies now exist to redress false arrests and other police abuses is to misconstrue the rationale of the right. The right does not exist to encourage citizens to resist, but rather to protect those provoked into resistance by unlawful arrests."[58]

It remains to be noted that the Supreme Court has made it clear that no inference of probable cause to search can be drawn from the fact that the accused did not protest his arrest or at once assert his innocence.[59] Of course one has a right to resist an unlawful arrest. "But," said Justice Jackson, "courts will hardly penalize failure to display a spirit of resistance or to hold futile debates on legal issues in the public highway with an officer of the law. A layman may not find it expedient to hazard resistance on his own judgment of the law at a time when he cannot know what information, correct or incorrect, the officers may be acting upon. It is likely to end in fruitless and unseemly controversy in a public street, if not in an additional charge of resisting an officer. If the officers believed they had probable cause for his arrest on a felony charge, it is not to be supposed that they would have been dissuaded by his profession of innocence." He went on to say: "It is the right of one placed under arrest to submit to custody and to reserve his defenses for the neutral tribunals erected by the law for the purpose of judging his case." But probable cause to search the person cannot be inferred from the submissiveness of the arrestee; "the presumption of innocence is not lost or impaired by neglect to argue with a policeman."[60]

The policeman may legally use force if necessary to make an effective arrest, but only as much force as is reasonably necessary under the circumstances. Here too ancient law has been modified, for whereas under the early common law the police could even take life, if necessary to make an effective arrest, this rule is effective today only in connection with major, atrocious felonies.[61] There is increasing opposition to permitting

56. 214 A.2d 436.
57. Paul G. Chevigny, "The Right to Resist an Unlawful Arrest," *Yale Law Journal,* 78 (June 1969): 1128-50, 1138.
58. *Ibid.,* pp. 1133-34.
59. United States v. DiRe, 332 U.S. 581 (1948).
60. 332 U.S. 594-95.
61. Moreland, "Some Trends." This is also the view of the American Law Institute, *Restatement, Torts,* §131 (1934). See also Comment, "Use of Deadly Force in the Arrest Process," *Louisiana Law Review,* 31, no. 1 (1970-71): 131-49.

the taking of life in cases involving minor nonviolent felonies. It has been observed that on the subject of the law of arrest "there is bound to be a continual conflict between the great desire of the public for security and protection from those who commit crime on the one hand and the strong political and social insistence on the personal liberty of the individual and protection from physical and/or mental pressures by those who enforce the criminal law on the other."[62]

Remedies for Illegal Arrests

There can be no doubt of the fact that illegal arrests are not at all uncommon in this country.[63] In fact, there are probably several million illegal arrests every year. A leading authority on the criminal law asserts that "the great majority of arrests by police officers are illegal in their inception, continuance, or termination," though he adds that this is due to "the antiquated law on the books."[64] He would remedy the situation by changing the law to conform more adequately with practice. Certainly this is not a novel suggestion. We once solved the bootlegging problem by repealing the laws which made it a crime to sell liquor and drafting new ones. Most of the people who are arrested illegally are the derelicts of society, the homeless and friendless, vagrants, drunkards, members of powerless minority groups. Most states have vagrancy or suspicious persons statutes which are used to circumvent the traditional limitations on the power to arrest without a warrant.[65] In addition, while the theory is that an arrest is supposed to be for the purpose of bringing the arrestee before a court, the police often make arrests for other purposes, such as harassment, delay, investigation or merely to maintain a reputation for vigorous law enforcement.[66]

Various remedies are available in cases of illegal arrest or imprisonment.[67] One is the imposition of criminal penalties, but this is not effective since the police and prosecutors are understandably relectant to punish themselves or each other. For example, we have had a federal statute since 1921 which makes it a misdemeanor for a federal officer to participate in an unlawful search and seizure,[68] but there seems to be no record of a

62. Moreland, "Some Trends," p. 484.
63. See Rocco Tresolini, R. W. Taylor and E. B. Barnett, "Arrest without Warrant: Extent and Social Implications," *Journal of Criminal Law, Criminology and Police Science,* 46 (July-August 1955): 187-98.
64. Warner, "Uniform Arrest Act," p. 315.
65. See Note, "Use of Vagrancy-type Laws for Arrest and Detention of Suspicious Persons," *Yale Law Journal,* 59 (June 1950): 1351-64.
66. The various purposes served by arrests, other than as steps in the ordinary course of criminal procedure, are fully explored by LaFave, *Arrest, passim.*
67. See Caleb Foote, "Tort Remedies for Police Violations of Individual Rights," *Minnesota Law Review,* 39 (April 1955): 493-516: LaFave, *Arrest,* chaps. 18-20.
68. 18 U.S.C. §2236 (1970).

single prosecution under it. There have been a few criminal prosecutions of state officials in the federal courts under the civil rights acts.[69] But Justice Douglas has expressed the opinion that federal prosecution of local police is an ineffective weapon. He once wrote, "The suggestion that the remedy for lawless conduct by the local police is through federal prosecution under the civil rights laws relegates constitutional rights under the Fourth Amendment to a lowly status. An already overburdened Department of Justice, busily engaged in law enforcement, cannot be expected to devote its energies to supervising local police activities and prosecuting police officers, except in rare and occasional instances. And the hostility which such prosecutions have received here . . . hardly encourages putting the federal prosecutor on the track of state officials who take *unconstitutional* short cuts in enforcing state laws."[70]

The principal federal criminal sanction against police lawlessness is 18 U.S.C. §242, which makes it a federal crime for anyone, acting under color of any law, to wilfully deny a person any federal right or privilege. This statute is derived from Reconstruction legislation, the Civil Rights Act of 1866,[71] and the Enforcement Act of 1870.[72] It was applied for the first time in 1882,[73] a second time in 1911,[74] and the third prosecution, in the famous *Screws* case,[75] came in 1945. Since the Supreme Court insists that specific intent to deny a federal right must be proved, there have been very few successful prosecutions under the statute, and the Department of Justice, which counts heavily on the cooperation of the local police, has shown little enthusiasm for prosecuting them.[76]

Another remedy is the disciplining of police officers by their superiors through administrative methods. This has seemingly never been a very important deterring factor.[77] Another possibility lies in the exclusion of evidence secured illegally, and the exclusionary rule that prevails in the federal courts,[78] now applies to the state courts through Fourteenth Amendment due process.[79] Confessions secured during a period of illegal

---

69. There were fifty convictions in the period 1951–53. See appendix to dissenting opinion of Justice Douglas in Irvine v. California, 347 U.S. 128, 153 (1954).

70. Irvine v. California, 347 U.S. 128, 152 (1954) (dissenting opinion).

71. 14 Stat. 27, ch. 31, §2.

72. 16 Stat. 140, ch. 114, §§16-17.

73. United States v. Buntin, 10 Fed. 730 (C.C.S.D. Ohio, 1882).

74. United States v. Stone, 188 Fed. 836 (D. Md. 1911).

75. Screws v. United States, 325 U.S. 91 (1945).

76. See 1961 U.S. Commission on Civil Rights Report, bk. 5, *Justice,* pp. 45–67.

77. See Note, "The Administration of Complaints by Civilians against the Police," *Harvard Law Review,* 77 (January 1964): 499–519.

78. Weeks v. United States, 232 U.S. 383 (1914).

79. Mapp v. Ohio, 367 U.S. 643 (1961).

detention are inadmissible in federal courts,[80] but most states accept such confessions, and due process has been construed not to forbid the practice.[81] The due process test turns on the issue of voluntariness or coercion, whether physical[82] or psychological.[83] Injunctions are not granted to restrain a threatened illegal arrest, mainly because it is impossible to show threat of an irreparable loss to property. It is impossible to sue the city for whom the policeman works because the courts regard the police function as a governmental function, and hence immune from suit.

It is always possible to sue the policeman for money damages for false arrest. Furthermore, many states allow punitive damages, and even in determining "actual damages" juries are often allowed to consider such factors as disgrace, humiliation, and injury to reputation. Nevertheless, this has never been an effective remedy, partly because of the fact that policemen are not usually affluent enough to pay the judgments. In addition, in most states "public policy" forbids garnishment of a policeman's wages to satisfy a judgment. Furthermore, it has been explained that "most police action operates at lower levels of society and the great majority of persons who are subjected to illegal arrests or searches and who are therefore potential tort plaintiffs come from the lowest economic levels, or minority groups, or are criminals or suspected of criminality."[84] Such persons are not likely to sue for damages, and if they sue, are not likely to succeed. It is also possible to sue for damages in the federal courts under a civil rights act. Such actions have been extremely rare, and have not been very successful. The principal federal statute, 42 U.S.C. §1983, authorizes suits for damages against any person who, under color of law, deprives any person of a federal right. While it is established that a policeman can be sued for false arrest under this statute,[85] he has available to him the defense that he acted in good faith and on probable cause.[86] The prevailing view is that a peace officer who arrests someone with probable cause and in good faith is not liable in damages for false arrest simply because the innocence of the suspect is later proved, or

---

80. McNabb v. United States, 318 U.S. 332 (1943); Mallory v. United States, 354 U.S. 449 (1957).
81. Gallegos v. Nebraska, 342 U.S. 55 (1951); Stroble v. California, 343 U.S. 181 (1952); Brown v. Allen, 344 U.S. 443 (1953).
82. The seminal case was Brown v. Mississippi, 297 U.S. 278 (1936).
83. The rule of "inherent coerciveness" as applied to psychological factors was first developed in Ashcraft v. Tennessee, 322 U.S. 143 (1944).
84. Foote, "Tort Remedies," p. 500.
85. The leading case is Monroe v. Pape, 365 U.S. 167 (1961). See 1961 U.S. Commission on Civil Rights Report, bk. 5, *Justice*, pp. 69-77.
86. Pierson v. Ray, 386 U.S. 547 (1967).

because he acted under a statute he reasonably believed to be valid, even though it was later held unconstitutional.

Perhaps the best remedy for illegal arrest or imprisonment would be to permit a suit in tort against the city itself. There has been a great deal of resistance to such a change in the law, but there is much to be said for a policy which assures reparation in cases of official wrongdoing. Surely the government has the greatest obligation to supply remedies where it is itself guilty of the wrong. In addition, the 1947 report of the President's Committee on Civil Rights emphasized the necessity of increased professionalization of state and local police forces.[87] It is advocated more adequate police training programs, with an orientation towards such civil rights problems as the treatment of persons who are arrested and jailed, and more adequate salaries, as necessary steps for the improvement of the quality of police forces. There are other avenues of betterment through such devices as more sophisticated recruitment, pre-employment training in professional schools, extensive in-service training, and continuous research in problems of police administration.[88]

In the last analysis, police lawlessness is objectionable because it is self-defeating. A distinguished student of American law has written,

From the viewpoint of efficiency, police lawlessness is the worst possible practice. It builds the wall between police and public higher than ever. It stops channels of information and blocks the sources of evidence. Realization that the police are a mere handful, impotent to control by sheer physical force, as is demonstrated when rioting breaks out in a large city, makes it evident that the usurpation by the police of judicial or executive functions comes at a very high price in a democratic community. If the police are educated to understand the rules of law which define their particular job, and if they function impartially within the limits of those laws, they will preserve democratic procedures and win the public support that is essential to police efficiency.[89]

THE PRELIMINARY HEARING

Legal Basis

After one has been accused, either by arrest or summons, of having committed a petty offense, he is tried in some lower court having jurisdiction of the case. But with regard to all other offenses, the normal procedure is that following arrest the acused is taken before a magistrate

---

87. *To Secure These Rights,* p. 155.

88. See Charles B. Saunders, Jr., *Upgrading the American Police: Education and Training for Better Law Enforcement* (Washington: Brookings Institution, 1970).

89. Jerome Hall, "Police and Law in a Democratic Society," *Indiana Law Journal,* 28 (Winter 1953): 133–77, 156.

who holds a preliminary hearing (also known as a preliminary examination or examining trial) for the purpose of deciding whether there is probable cause to hold him for trial. At this point the accused may be discharged or bound over for indictment by a grand jury or by the prosecuting attorney. The preliminary hearing is a modern device, for until very recently there was no preliminary inquiry at the common law into the question of probable guilt. Holdsworth has pointed out, "As a matter of fact the establishment of a system of professional police has, in the nineteenth century, more clearly differentiated the functions of the magistrate and the policeman. The magistrate can act as a judge now that he is no longer required to supplement the deficiencies of the police force."[90]

There is no federal constitutional right to a preliminary examination. So far as federal procedure is concerned the right is based on statute and rules of court. Some state constitutions guarantee a preliminary hearing, while in other states the right is wholly statutory. The Supreme Court has ruled that Fourteenth Amendment due process does not require the states to hold a judicial hearing as a prerequisite to prosecution by information.[91] A unanimous Court ruled in 1975, however, that a person who has been arrested pursuant to a prosecutor's information is constitutionally entitled to a judicial determination of probable cause for a pretrial restraint of liberty.[92] Under Florida law, indictments are required only for the prosecution of capital offenses. Prosecutors may charge all other crimes by information, without a preliminary hearing and without obtaining leave of court. In fact, the Florida courts had ruled that the filing of an information foreclosed the suspect's right to a preliminary hearing, and that habeas corpus could not be used to test the existence of probable cause for detention except in exceptional circumstances. Under a special statute, however, a preliminary hearing could be allowed after thirty days, and arraignment was often delayed a month or more after arrest. Accordingly, under this procedure a person charged by information could be detained for a substantial period of time solely on the decision of the prosecutor. Justice Powell, speaking for the Court, held that pretrial confinement is such a serious matter "that the Fourth Amendment requires a judicial determination of probable cause as a prerequisite to

---

90. William S. Holdsworth, *A History of English Law,* 3d ed. (Boston: Little, Brown & Co., 1923), 1: 297. On the preliminary examination, see Orfield, *Criminal Procedure from Arrest to Appeal,* chap. 2; Hazel B. Kerper, *Introduction to the Criminal Justice System* (St. Paul: West Publishing Co., 1972), pp. 279–84.

91. Beck v. Washington, 369 U.S. 541 (1962); Lem Woon v. Oregon, 229 U.S. 586 (1913).

92. Gerstein v. Pugh, 420 U.S. 103 (1975).

extended restraint on liberty following arrest."[93] The Court rejected Florida's contention that the prosecutor's decision to file an information is in itself a determination of probable cause. Even so, the Court ruled that the judicial determination of probable cause did not have to be accompanied by the full panoply of adversary safeguards available at a trial. The issue of whether there is probable cause to detain an arrested person pending further proceedings can be determined reliably without a formal adversary hearing. This issue, said Justice Powell, can be decided by a magistrate with informal methods of proof on the basis of hearsay and written testimony. Of course, guilt must be proved beyond reasonable doubt, but in the case of probable cause we deal with probabilities. Justice Powell noted that on this matter there is a great deal of variation among the states, and that flexibility and experimentation are desirable. But, he added, "Whatever procedure a State may adopt, it must provide a fair and reliable determination of probable cause as a condition for any significant pretrial restraint on liberty, and this determination must be made by a judicial officer either before or promptly after arrest."[94]

Purpose

The purpose of the preliminary hearing is to establish, by means of a judicial inquiry, whether there is probable cause to hold the defendant for further proceedings, and to fix bail if he is not discharged, this is to say, to discover if a *prima facie* case of guilt is made out. The magistrate does not try the defendant on the issue of guilt or innocence, and the preliminary hearing is not a trial. While it is a public proceeding, it is usually a very informal one, and strict rules of evidence are not followed. The magistrate does not try to obtain evidence or interrogate the accused to get evidence against him. The preliminary hearing is not an examination of the accused; it merely seeks to evaluate whatever evidence the public prosecutor chooses to present. If the magistrate finds that an offense has been committed, and that there is probable cause to believe that the defendant is guilty, the magistrate either admits the accused to bail or commits him to custody. The remedy for an improper commitment is through a habeas corpus action. Thus, as a federal judge once said, "everyone threatened

---

93. 420 U.S. 114.
94. 420 U.S. 124–25. Concurring separately, four Justices maintained that it was unwise to specify the procedural protections that are not constitutionally required for incarcerated suspects awaiting trial. There was no need, Justice Stewart argued, to say that the Constitution extends less procedural protection to an imprisoned human being than is required to test the propriety of garnisheeing a commercial bank account, or temporarily suspending a public school student, or lifting a driver's license.

with the charge of the commission of a crime has two rights. One is, of course, the right to a fair and impartial trial upon which the question of his guilt is determined; the other is the no less valuable right, and practically the more valuable right, that he shall not be even called upon to answer to a criminal charge until some duly constituted tribunal has passed upon the preliminary question of whether he ought to be brought to trial."[95]

Value

The right to a preliminary hearing is valuable because it saves the accused from further prosecution if the magistrate finds that no *prima facie* case exists. As a matter of fact, as all crime surveys show, a tremendous number of cases are terminated at this point, usually for failure of witnesses to appear, or because no probable cause has been made out. "The object or purpose of the preliminary investigation," it has been asserted, "is to prevent hasty, malicious, improvident, and oppressive prosecutions, to protect the person charged from open and public accusations of crime, to avoid both for the defendant and the public the expense of a public trial, and to save the defendant from the humiliation and anxiety involved in public prosecution, and to discover whether or not there are substantial grounds upon which a prosecution may be based."[96]

The preliminary hearing has many advantages for the accused. For one thing, it discourages resort to such police excesses as the third degree, and protects the individual's privilege against self-incrimination.[97] It gives the accused a chance to observe and test the reliability of the witnesses the prosecution puts on the stand, and perpetuates their testimony in a record which can be used for impeachment purposes at the trial. In an interesting

---

95. Dickinson, J., in United States v. Fitzgerald, 29 F.2d 573, 574 (E.D. Pa. 1928).

96. Rosenberry, J., in Thies v. State, 178 Wis. 98, 103, 189 N.W. 539, 541 (1922). Speaking of the defendant's right to a preliminary hearing, the Supreme Court of Kansas once declared, "That is a fundamental and basic right, it is substantial, and certainly if he is deprived of it, he is prejudiced." State v. Howland, 153 Kan. 352, 363, 110 P.2d 801, 808 (1941). See also Blue v. United States, 342 F.2d 894 (D.C. Cir. 1964), cert. denied, 380 U.S. 944 (1965).

97. In McNabb v. United States, 318 U.S. 332, 344 (1943), Justice Frankfurter observed that the rule of law which requires "that the police must with reasonable promptness show legal cause for detaining arrested persons, constitutes an important safeguard—not only in assuring protection for the innocent but also in securing conviction of the guilty by methods that commend themselves to a progressive and self-confident society. For this procedural requirement checks resort to those reprehensible practices known as the 'third degree' which, though universally rejected as indefensible, still find their way into use. It aims to avoid all the evil implications of secret interrogation of persons accused of crime. It reflects not a sentimental but a sturdy view of law enforcement. It outlaws easy but self-defeating ways in which brutality is substituted for brains as an instrument of crime detection."

opinion published in 1970, Justice Brennan, against the background of Alabama's preliminary hearing procedure, explained the various uses of the hearing so far as the accused is concerned, in the following language:

> First, the lawyer's skilled examination and cross-examination of witnesses may expose fatal weaknesses in the State's case that may lead the magistrate to refuse to bind the accused over. Second, in any event, the skilled interrogation of witnesses by an experienced lawyer can fashion a vital impeachment tool for use in cross-examination of the State's witnesses at the trial, or preserve testimony favorable to the accused of a witness who does not appear at the trial. Third, trained counsel can more effectively discover the case the State has against his client and make possible the preparation of a proper defense to meet that case at the trial. Fourth, counsel can also be influential at the preliminary hearing in making effective arguments for the accused on such matters as the necessity for an early psychiatric examination or bail.[98]

While the preliminary examination is primarily for the protection of the accused, however, it is also valuable for the prosecution, since it provides an early test of the reliability of the testimony of prosecuting witnesses, and eliminates flimsy prosecutions based on prejudice or misinformation, thus saving expense and avoiding needless delay. It also reduces the possibility of the intimidation of witnesses by the defendant since they commit themselves at this early stage in the proceedings.[99]

Waiver

Persons in federal custody may waive the right to a preliminary hearing, which is a personal privilege for the benefit of the accused, and most states also permit waiver. Particularly in states where indictments are used to charge felonies, the preliminary hearing is often waived. Waiver may take many forms, including waiver by implication. For example, a plea to the merits, without demanding a hearing, is generally regarded as a waiver. The waiver amounts to an admission that a *prima facie* case exists which warrants holding the accused for trial. Since the preliminary hearing has advantages for the prosecution as well as the accused, some states require the consent of the prosecutor for a waiver. A recent study of practice in three states shows that a large majority of persons entitled to preliminary hearings choose to waive the right.[100]

---

98. Coleman v. Alabama, 399 U.S. 1, 9 (1970).

99. For a balanced evaluation of the advantages of the preliminary hearing both for the accused and the prosecution, see Note, "The Preliminary Hearing—An Interest Analysis," *Iowa Law Review,* 51 (Fall 1965): 164–83.

100. See Frank W. Miller and Robert O. Dawson, "Non-Use of the Preliminary Examination: A Study of Current Practices," *Wisconsin Law Review,* 1964 (March 1964): 252–77.

The Required Procedure

While there are many variations in practice among the states in connection with preliminary hearings, the pattern is, generally speaking, like that of the federal government, which is embodied in Rule 5 of the Federal Rules of Criminal Procedure. This Rule provides that an officer who has made an arrest under a warrant or any person making an arrest without a warrant "shall take the arrested person without unnecessary delay before the nearest available federal magistrate," or any other officer empowered to commit persons charged with federal offenses. The Rule formerly referred to the U.S. commissioner, but with the adoption of the Federal Magistrates Act[101] in 1968, the office of court commissioner was abolished, and all of his powers and duties were transferred to U.S. magistrates, who are appointed for eight- or four-year terms by the district court judges, depending upon whether they serve full time or part time.[102] The Supreme Court has attempted in recent years to strengthen the requirement that an arrested person must be taken to a magistrate "without unnecessary delay" by refusing to permit federal courts to receive as evidence a confession made during a period of police interrogation when the accused was entitled to be brought before the magistrate.[103] And it has made it clear that the inadmissibility of such a confession turns entirely upon the illegal detention, so that the issue of the voluntariness of the confession does not in this instance arise.[104] That is to say, though the confession may have been voluntary, it is still inadmissible if it was secured during a period of illegal detention. Some state statutes are very specific in saying that an arrested person must be taken to a magistrate within twenty-four hours, or some other defined period, while others merely provide that the preliminary hearing must be held "promptly" or within a "reasonable time."[105]

---

101. 28 U.S.C. §§631–39 (1970). Enacted in 1968, this statute became fully effective in all federal district courts on July 1, 1971. See Note, "Masters and Magistrates in the Federal Courts," *Harvard Law Review,* 88 (February 1975): 779–803.

102. As of June 30, 1973, there were 103 full-time magistrates and 567 part-time, as authorized by the Judicial Conference. See *Report of the Administrative Office of the United States Courts* (Washington: Government Printing Office, 1973), VI-I.

103. McNabb v. United States, 318 U.S. 332 (1943); Mallory v. United States, 354 U.S. 449 (1957).

104. Upshaw v. United States, 335 U.S. 410 (1948).

105. See State v. Schabert, 218 Minn. 1, 6, 15 N.W. 2d 585, 587 (1944): "While in this state we have no statute such as the federal statute, or such as most states have, requiring that the arrested accused be immediately taken before a judge or magistrate, . . . we believe that fundamental fairness to the accused requires that he should with reasonable promptness be taken before a magistrate in order to prevent the application of methods approaching what is commonly called the 'third degree.' 'Fundamental fairness' prohibits the secret inquisition in order to obtain evidence."

The federal Rule (5(c)) then provides that the magistrate "shall inform the defendant of the complaint against him, and of any affidavit filed therewith, of his right to retain counsel, of his right to request the assignment of counsel if he is unable to obtain counsel, and of the general circumstances under which he may secure pretrial release. He shall inform the defendant that he is not required to make a statement and that any statement made by him may be used against him. The magistrate shall also inform the defendant of his right to a preliminary examination. He shall allow the defendant reasonable time and opportunity to consult counsel and shall admit the defendant to bail as provided by statute or in these rules."[106]

The Rule further provides that if the defendant waives the preliminary examination, "the magistrate shall forthwith hold him to answer in the district court." If the accused does not waive his right, then he is entitled to a preliminary examination within ten days, if he is in custody, and within twenty days if he is not in custody.[107] Continuances may be granted, with the consent of the defendant, "upon a showing of good cause, taking into account the public interest in the prompt disposition of criminal cases. . . ." Furthermore, "in the absence of such consent by the defendant, time limits may be extended by a judge of the United States upon a showing that extraordinary circumstances exist and that delay is indispensable to the interests of justice."

The Rule (5.1(a)) goes on to provide that "if from the evidence it appears that there is probable cause to believe that an offense has been committed and that the defendant committed it, the federal magistrate shall forthwith hold him to answer in district court. The finding of probable cause may be based on hearsay evidence in whole or in part.[108] "The defendant may cross-examine witnesses against him and may introduce evidence in his own behalf." The Rule goes on to declare (5.1(b)) that "if from the evidence it appears that there is no probable cause to believe that an offense has been committed or that the defendant committed it, the federal magistrate shall dismiss the complaint and discharge the defendant." Finally, the Rule provides that at the conclusion of the proceeding, the magistrate shall transmit "forthwith" to the clerk of the district court

---

106. These rules do not apply to petty offenses which are triable by the U.S. magistrate under 18 U.S.C. §3401 (1970).

107. On the distinction between the situation of persons in custody as compared with that of persons not in custody, see Jaben v. United States, 381 U.S. 214 (1965). On the limited significance of a waiver, see Giordenello v. United States, 357 U.S. 480 (1958).

108. It may be noted that a grand jury indictment may properly be based upon hearsay evidence. Costello v. United States, 350 U.S. 359 (1956).

a record of the proceedings which must be made available to the defendant "on timely application."

Though there are local variations, in a general way state law relating to preliminary hearings conforms with this procedural pattern.

BAIL

Historical Origins

The right of an accused to bail is deeply rooted in English law and practice.[109] The ancient common law extended bail in all cases, and Pollock and Maitland explain why:

> It was not common to keep men in prison. This apparent leniency of our law was not due to any love of an abstract liberty. Imprisonment was costly and troublesome. Besides, any reader of the eyre rolls will be inclined to define a gaol as a place that is made to be broken, so numerous are the entries that tell of escapes. The medieval dungeon was not all that romance would make it; there were many ways out of it. The mainprise of substantial men was about as good a security as a gaol. The sheriff did not want to keep prisoners; his inclination was to discharge himself of all responsibility by handing them over to their friends.[110]

But exceptions were gradually introduced by statute, until by the time of Blackstone (1765) bail was not allowable "wherever the offense is of a very enormous nature; for then the public is entitled to demand nothing less than the highest security that can be given, *viz.*, the body of the accused, in order to insure that justice shall be done upon him if guilty. Such persons . . . have no other sureties but the four walls of the prison."[111] Since there were in Blackstone's day about 160 capital crimes, most bailable offenses were minor.

The principle that bail, when available, must be in reasonable amounts, was nailed down in the Bill of Rights of 1689. Here Parliament charged that the ousted monarch, James II, had endeavored "to subvert and extirpate" the liberties of the kingdom, and complained, among other things, that "excessive bail hath been required of persons committed in

---

109. See Elsa De Haas, *Antiquities of Bail* (New York: Columbia University Press, 1940), for the development of the law of bail down to 1275.

110. Frederick Pollock and Frederic W. Maitland, *The History of English Law*, 2d ed. (Cambridge: Cambridge University Press, 1911), p. 584.

111. 4 Bl. Comm. *298. Sir Edward Coke pointed out that bail could be denied to one accused of a felony "if he be an infamous and a notorious thief, and so openly and commonly esteemed and taken. . . ." *A Treatise of Bail and Mainprize*, William Hawkins, ed. (London: J. Worrall, 1764), p. 285.

criminal cases, to elude the benefit of the laws made for the liberty of the subjects." Accordingly, the statute declared "that excessive bail ought not to be required." This principle is carried over into the Eighth Amendment of the federal Constitution, which decrees that "excessive bail shall not be required." The same doctrine exists in the states pursuant to state law, for the constitutions of all states but one also forbid excessive bail. While the Supreme Court has not yet ruled squarely that the Eighth Amendment prohibition of excessive bail applies to the states through Fourteenth Amendment due process, lower federal courts seem to take that for granted.[112]

Reasons for Bail

"The taking of bail," the New York Code of Criminal Procedure says, "consists in the acceptance, by a competent court or magistrate, of the undertaking of sufficient bail for the appearance of the defendant according to the terms of the undertaking, or that the bail will pay to the people of this state a specified sum."[113] The purpose of bail is to give a defendant his freedom, pending final disposition of his case, while at the same time requiring sufficient security to make certain that he will present himself for trial or punishment, as the case may be, at a specified time.

There are very good reasons why persons accused of crime should be allowed to go free on bail. For one thing, in the words of Chief Justice Vinson, "this traditional right to freedom before conviction permits the unhampered preparation of a defense."[114] Furthermore, as the Chief Justice explained, "unless this right to bail before trial is preserved, the presumption of innocence, secured only after centuries of struggle, would lose its meaning." For if an accused is presumed to be innocent until actually convicted of crime, then like all innocent people he does not belong in jail, though society is entitled to take reasonable precautions to make sure that he will be available for trial. Finally, to hold a man in jail pending trial who is ultimately acquitted amounts to a needless infliction of punishment. Thus Justice Gray wrote in a leading case, "The statutes of

112. See, e.g., Mastrian v. Hedman, 326 F.2d 708 (8th Cir. 1964), cert. denied, 376 U.S. 965 (1964); Pilkinton v. Circuit Court of Howell County, Mo., 324 F.2d 45 (8th Cir. 1963).

113. N.Y. Code of Crim. Proc., §551. In addition, material witnesses may be put under bail to insure their attendance when wanted upon the trial. See Note, "Confining Material Witnesses in Criminal Cases," *Washington and Lee Review,* 20 (Spring 1963): 164–68. Aliens held in custody for deportation may, in the discretion of the Attorney-General, be released on bail pending a final determination. As in the case of judicial discretion, this discretion is reviewable on a showing of clear abuse. Carlson v. Landon, 342 U.S. 542 (1952). Even though a juvenile court proceeding is technically civil in nature, the juvenile is entitled to bail since a deprivation of liberty is involved. Tremble v. Stone, 187 F. Supp. 483 (D.D.C. 1960).

114. Stack v. Boyle, 342 U.S. 1, 4 (1951).

the United States have been framed upon the theory that a person accused of crime shall not, until he has been finally adjudged guilty in the court of last resort, be absolutely compelled to undergo imprisonment or punishment, but may be admitted to bail, not only after arrest and before trial, but after conviction and pending a writ of error."[115]

It is incontestible that releasing an arrestee on bail before trial confers many advantages. He retains his job, and thus is able to support his family and earn money to pay for his lawyer's services. He has a chance to put his affairs in order, should he ultimately be convicted. He has an opportunity to investigate his case and cooperate more meaningfully with his lawyer.[116] The main point involved in admitting persons to bail, Justice Jackson once wrote, "is to enable them to stay out of jail until a trial has found them guilty. Without this conditional privilege, even those wrongly accused are punished by a period of imprisonment while awaiting trial and are handicapped in consulting counsel, searching for evidence and witnesses, and preparing a defense."[117] Similarly, the Senate Judiciary Committee reported in 1965 on a bail reform bill, "There was widespread agreement among witnesses that the accused who is unable to post bond, and consequently is held in pretrial detention, is severely handicapped in preparing his defense. He cannot locate witnesses, cannot consult his lawyer in private, and enters the courtroom—not in the company of an attorney—but from a cell block in the company of a marshall. Furthermore, being in detention, he is often unable to retain his job and support his family, and is made to suffer the public stigma of incarceration even though he may later be found not guilty."[118]

The injustices and hardships which are the products of pretrial detention are illustrated by various empirical studies. For example, the Vera Foundation found that in 1960, 114,653 persons were detained for trial in New York City, and only 30,827 were later convicted and sentenced.[119] Clearly many detentions, in the light of subsequent developments, were unwarranted and therefore unjust. Furthermore, a study of pretrial detention in New York for the year October 1961 to September 1962 indicated that whereas 49 percent of all those accused of crime were imprisoned before trial, only 40 percent were imprisoned after conviction.[120] Similarly, the New York study indicated that in a sample of 385

---

115. Hudson v. Parker, 156 U.S. 277, 285 (1895).
116. See the remarks of Justice Douglas, sitting as a Circuit Justice in United States v. Bandy, 81 Sup. Ct. 197 (1960).
117. Stack v. Boyle, 342 U.S. 1, 7–8 (1951) (dissenting opinion).
118. Sen. Jud. Com., Sen. Rep. no. 750, 89th Cong., 1st sess. (1965), p. 7.
119. Ronald Goldfarb, *Ransom* (New York: Harper & Row, 1965), p. 154.
120. Patricia Wald, "Pretrial Detention and Ultimate Freedom: A Statistical Study," *New York University Law Review,* 39 (June 1964): 631–40, 634.

defendants who were continuously in jail from arraignment to adjudication, 64 percent were sentenced to prison, whereas only 17 percent of the 374 persons who made bail received prison sentences.[121] Making allowance for such factors as prior record, bail amount, type of counsel, family integration and employment stability, it was concluded that unfavorable disposition of the cases was strongly related to pretrial detention. That is to say, "pretrial detention increases a defendant's chance of receiving a prison sentence."[122]

Present Rules

The right to bail in the federal courts is now described by the Bail Reform Act of 1966[123] and Rule 46 of the Federal Rules of Criminal Procedure. The grounds upon which the 1966 statute rests were spelled out in a statement of Congressional findings that was in the bill as reported out by the Senate Judiciary Committee, and later eliminated as unnecessary.[124] Even so, these findings are instructive in pointing up the inadequacies of the conventional bail system. The Senate Committee draft declared that

(1) Present Federal bail practices are repugnant to the spirit of the Constitution and dilute the basic tenets that a person is presumed innocent until proven guilty by a court of law and that justice should be equal and accessible to all;

(2) Persons reasonably expected to appear at future proceedings should not be deprived of their liberty solely because of their financial inability to post bail;

(3) Respect for law and order is diminished when the attainment of pretrial liberty depends solely upon the financial status of an accused;

(4) Bail practices which rely primarily on financial consideration inevitably disadvantage persons and families of limited means;

(5) The high cost[s] of unnecessary detention impose a severe financial burden on the taxpayers and deplete public funds which could be better used for other public purposes;

(6) Family and community ties, a job, residence in the community, and the absence of a substantial criminal record, are factors more likely to assure the appearance of a person than the posting of bail; and

121. Ann Rankin, "The Effect of Pretrial Detention," *New York University Law Review,* 39 (June 1964): 641–55, 642.

122. *Ibid.,* p. 655. Thus, at the Senate hearings on what became the Bail Reform Act of 1966, Senator Tydings said, "Those confined because they cannot meet bail requirements serve longer prison sentences and secure fewer acquittals and dismissals than those who are able to secure bail." Sen. Jud. Com., Sen. Rep. no. 750, 89th Cong., 1st sess. (1965), p. 7.

123. Act of June 22, 1966, 80 Stat. 214, 18 U.S.C. §§3141–43, 3146–52 (1970). The ground was prepared for this statute by a national bail conference called by the Department of Justice in 1964.

124. Sen. Jud. Com., Sen. Rep. no. 750, 89th Cong., 1st sess. (1965), pp. 1–2.

(7) Accused persons should not be unnecessarily detained and subjected to the influence of persons convicted of crimes and the effects of jail life; nor should their families suffer needless public derision and loss of support.

Thus, §2 of the Bail Reform Act of 1966 declares that its purpose "is to revise the practices relating to bail to assure that all persons, regardless of their financial status, shall not needlessly be detained pending their appearance to answer charges, to testify, or pending appeal, when detention serves neither the ends of justice or the public interest." The over-all purposes of the Act are to facilitate release from pretrial detention, and to assure that persons convicted of crimes will receive credit for time spent in custody prior to trial. Ever since the Judiciary Act of 1789, federal statute law has provided for bail "for any crime or offence against the United States," except where the punishment is death.[125] This distinction is retained, as is the basic distinction between the right to bail before conviction and after conviction pending the disposition of an appeal. Before conviction, any person charged with an offense not punishable by death "*shall*, at his appearance before a judicial officer, be ordered released pending a trial on his personal recognizance or upon the execution of an unsecured appearance bond in an amount specified by the judicial officer, unless the officer determines, in the exercise of his discretion, that such a release will not reasonably assure the appearance of the person as required."[126] The judicial officer may also impose conditions, such as placing the person in the custody of a designated person or organization, imposing restrictions on travel, associations or place of abode, requiring a cash payment of up to 10 percent of an appearance bond, which is to be returned on performance of the conditions of release, or any other conditions deemed reasonably necessary. In determining the conditions of release, on the basis of available evidence the judicial officer "shall . . . take into account the nature and circumstances of the offense charged, the weight of the evidence against the accused, the accused's family ties, employment, financial resources, character and mental condition, the length of his residence in the community, his record of convictions, and his record of appearance at court proceedings or of flight to avoid prosecution or failure to appear at court proceedings."[127] If a person for whom conditions of release are imposed is detained after twenty-four hours, he is entitled to have the conditions reviewed by the judicial officer who imposed them, and to a statement of written reasons for his continued detention. Release orders are appealable.[128] Finally, where a person is charged with an offense punishable by death, or has appealed from a

---

125. Act of September 24, 1789, 1 Stat. 73, §33.
126. 18 U.S.C. §3146(a).
127. 18 U.S.C. §3146(b).
128. 18 U.S.C. §3147.

conviction, the judicial officer *may* refuse bail if he finds there is danger to any other person or to the community, or risk of flight, of if the appeal is "frivolous or taken for delay."[129] Rule 46(c) declares that "the burden of establishing that the defendant will not flee or pose a danger to any other person or to the community rests with the defendant." Wilful failure to appear in court as required results in forfeiture of any pledged security, and in the case of felony charges, or while awaiting sentence or pending appeal, the person concerned may be fined up to $5,000 or imprisoned for not more than five years, or both. For misdemeanants and witnesses the penalties are a fine up to $1,000, a year in prison, or both.[130]

In a bill-signing ceremony at the White House, President Johnson hailed the adoption of the Bail Reform Act of 1966 as a giant step forward, pointing out that under the statute the judge will have adequate information to determine that many defendants can be released without any need for money bail, and that release on mere personal recognizance will be encouraged.[131]

A similar pattern of law prevails in the states. Many state constitutions draw a line between bailable and nonbailable offenses, like that of the Bill of Rights of the Indiana Constitution, which reads (Art. I, §17), "Offenses, other than murder or treason, shall be bailable by sufficient sureties. Murder or treason shall not be bailable, when the proof is evident, or the presumption strong."[132] Generally speaking, bail after

---

129. 18 U.S.C. §3148. Commenting on this section, the report of the Senate Judiciary Committee declared, "There is no absolute right to bail in capital cases nor in the cases of convicted persons; on the contrary, the courts have recognized that circumstances such as the gravity of the offense or the record of the defendant might militate against release in such cases. Consequently, courts are empowered to elect to detain them." Sen. Rep. 750, 89 Cong., 1st sess., p. 19. While bail is ordinarily granted to one who has taken an appeal if the appeal is not frivolous or taken for purposes of delay, bail was denied pending appeal in the following cases: Leigh v. United States, 8 L. Ed. 2d 269 (1962) (per Warren, C. J.); Binion v. United States, 352 U.S. 1028 (1957) (a repeat offender with a long record of drug violations); United States v. Wilson, 257 F.2d 796 (2d Cir. 1958) (a convicted person who made repeated threats of injury to witnesses); Carbo v. United States, 82 S. Ct. 662 (1962), review denied, 369 U.S. 868 (1962) (per Douglas, J.). Another distinction is found in 18 U.S.C. §3141 (1970): "Bail may be taken by any court, judge or magistrate authorized to arrest and commit offenders, but only a court of the United States having original jurisdiction in criminal cases, or a justice or judge thereof, may admit to bail or otherwise release a person charged with an offense punishable by death."

130. 18 U.S.C. §3150.

131. *Cong. Rec.*, 89th Cong., 2d sess. (June 28, 1966), 112: 14463.

132. In a case of first impression, the Supreme Court of Connecticut ruled, in State v. Menillo, 159 Conn. 264, 268 A.2d 667 (1970), that a defendant charged with an offense punishable by death is entitled to pretrial bail unless proof of guilt "is evident or the presumption great," and that the mere fact of indictment is not conclusive on this point. In State v. Konigsberg, 33 N.J. 367, 377, 164 A.2d 740, 745 (1960), the court ruled that in a capital case "bail should be denied when the circumstances disclosed indicate a fair likelihood that the defendant is in danger of a jury verdict of first degree murder."

conviction is not a matter of right in state law, although such bail is now increasingly available by reason of statutes, especially in noncapital cases.[133] There is a very good reason for distinguishing between preconviction and postconviction bail. Prior to conviction, it has been noted, the defendant "yet stood upon his plea of not guilty, supported with all the presumptions of innocence with which the law delights to surround him. But when his trial has been had, and his plea proven false, the law will not stultify itself by presuming him other than that it has itself adjudged him to be."[134] Thus, "at each step of the proceeding the grounds upon which the prisoner can be let to bail diminish, as the evidence of his guilt increases; because bail is not based upon the grace or favor of the court, but solely upon the doubt which may exist as to his guilt. After conviction and sentence, his claims to be let to bail are further diminished; but as he may still be innocent—as he may have something to urge against the legality of his sentence—he may apply to be bailed, and if it appear that his conviction was unjust, or there is a serious doubt of his guilt, his application may be granted."[135]

Forfeiture

Forfeiture of bail does not give the accused any immunity from arrest on the indictment. Bail is designed to secure the due attendance of the accused at his trial, and his submission to the judgment of the court. "It is not designed as a satisfaction for the offence."[136] In fact, "when bail is given, the principal is regarded as delivered to the custody of his sureties. Their dominion is a continuance of the original imprisonment. Whenever they choose to do so, they may seize him and deliver him up in their discharge; and if that cannot be done at once, they may imprison him until it can be done. They may exercise their rights in person or by agent. They may pursue him into another State; may arrest him on the Sabbath; and, if necessary, may break and enter his house for that purpose. The seizure is not made by virtue of new process. None is needed. It is likened to the rearrest by the sheriff of an escaping prisoner."[137] The bail has a right to pursue the principal to a different state and bring him back without extradition, which is only exercised by a government at the request of a government.[138]

133. Note, "Bail after Conviction," *Michigan Law Review,* 25 (April 1927): 646–54.
134. *Ex parte* Voll, 41 Cal. 29, 32 (1871).
135. People v. Lohman, 2 Barb. (N.Y.) 450, 454 (1848).
136. *Ex parte* Milburn, 9 Pet. (U.S.) 704, 710 (1835).
137. Justice Swayne in Taylor v. Taintor, 16 Wall. (U.S.) 366, 371 (1872).
138. Fitzpatrick v. Williams, 46 F.2d 40 (5th Cir. 1931). As in England, the bail has the power of summary arrest over the accused. See Jordan v. Com., 135 Va. 560, 115 S.E. 569 (1923) ("Bail are the private jailer of the prisoner . . ."); Miller v. Com., 192 Ky. 709, 234 S.W. 307 (1921). See Note, "Indemnification Contracts in the Law of Bail," *Virginia Law Review,* 35 (May 1949): 496–504.

That the surety has some continuing responsibility to the court which survives the forfeiture of the bail was brought out in the aftermath of the government's successful prosecution of the eleven top Communist leaders in the *Dennis* case.[139] The trustees of the Civil Rights Congress Bail Fund had posted bond in the amount of $260,000. When the mandate of the Supreme Court affirming the conviction arrived, four of the convicted men jumped bail.[140] The trustees of the bail fund were then called in as witnesses in order that the court might get some aid in executing bench warrants it had issued for the arrest of the four men who had absconded. The Court of Appeals held that since the trustees "were, in truth, the jailers of the fugitives, responsible for their appearance," it was proper for the court to bring them in as witnesses in an effort to execute the judgment of conviction, and to punish them summarily for contempt for refusing to bring in their records and answer proper questions.[141] The surety's obligation is not fixed and limited by the cash deposit; the crime is not commuted in some stated sum of money, and its payment does not terminate all surety responsibility.[142]

It remains to be noted that no constitutional right is violated if a bail bond act does not provide for jury trial before a judgment of forfeiture is made.[143]

The Judge's Discretion

There is necessarily a large discretionary element in the decisions of judges or magistrates dealing with bail. Where the accused has been convicted in a federal court, and files an appeal, bail may be allowed if the appeal presents a substantial question. The decision of the judge on the matter of the substantiality of the issue raised by the appeal always commands great deference, but it is reviewable, for, as Justice Douglas once observed, "bail is basic to our system of law. . . . Doubts whether it should be granted or denied should always be resolved in favor of the defen-

---

139. Dennis v. United States, 341 U.S. 494 (1951).

140. Under the Act of August 20, 1954, 68 Stat. 747, as amended by the Act of June 22, 1966, 80 Stat. 216, 18 U.S.C. §3150 (1970), jumping bail is now a serious crime. If the charge was a felony, the penalties are a fine up to $5,000, a prison term up to five years or both. In the case of misdemeanors, the penalties are up to the maximum provided for the misdemeanor, or up to a year in jail, or both. In the case of the nonappearance of material witnesses released on bail the penalties are a fine up to $1,000 or imprisonment up to one year, or both. Bail jumping is a crime under state law. See, e.g., Wis. Stat. §946.49(1)(b), which provides that a felony defendant who jumps bail may be fined up to $5,000, jailed for a period up to five years, or both.

141. Field v. United States, 193 F.2d 86 (2d Cir. 1951).

142. United States v. Field, 193 F.2d 92 (2d Cir. 1951).

143. Resolute Insurance Co. v. Seventh Judicial District Court of Oklahoma County, 336 F. Supp. 497 (W.D. Okla. 1971), judgment affirmed on appeal without opinion, 404 U.S. 997 (1971).

dant."[144] It is established, furthermore, that the Eighth Amendment does not accord a right to bail in all cases, but merely provides that in those cases where it is proper to grant bail, it shall not be excessive.[145] Again, the fixing of the amount of bail is a discretionary act, and the judge's decision will not be set aside by a reviewing court unless there is strong proof of an abuse of discretion, since the trial judge is ordinarily in the best position to evaluate the facts of the situation.[146]

In deciding upon bail, "the judge uses his common sense and experience."[147] He considers the past record of the defendant, the nature and seriousness of the offense, the probability of guilt, the likelihood that the accused will or will not show up for trial, his ability to give bail, and the possibility of undue delay. The judge tries to strike a balance between the need to tie the accused to the jurisdiction and the defendant's right to freedom from unnecessary restraint before final disposition of his case. Furthermore, since in modern times the bond is generally furnished by professional bondsmen, excessive bail merely enriches the bonding companies.[148] It is established, however, that the inability of the defendant to raise the bail does not prove that it is excessive, though it may be a factor to be considered, for otherwise a prisoner without means or friends would be entitled to a discharge on his own recognizance.[149] On the other hand, it has been held that it is an abuse of discretion for the judge to fix a very high bail as a means of inducing the accused to cooperate with the district attorney,[150] or to fail to follow the lead of the Supreme Court in a comparable case,[151] or to require the defendant to furnish a surety company bond by ruling out any individual surety.[152]

---

144. Herzog v. United States, 99 L. Ed. 1299, 1301 (1955). Here it was held that a question of law is substantial if circuit courts are in disagreement about it. See the interesting discussion of this problem by Justice Jackson, sitting as a Circuit Justice, in Williamson v. United States, 95 Ed. 1379 (1950).

145. Carlson v. Landon, 342 U.S. 524, 545 (1952).

146. See Connley v. United States, 41 F.2d 49 (9th Cir. 1930); Bennett v. United States, 36 F.2d 475 (1st Cir. 1929).

147. Charles E. Desmond, "Bail—Ancient and Modern," *Buffalo Law Review*, 1 (Spring 1952): 245-48, 247.

148. Leon R. Yankwich, "Release on Bond by Trial and Appellate Courts," 7 F.R.D. 275 (1947).

149. *In re* Scott, 38 Neb. 502, 56 N.W. 1009 (1893). See also White v. United States, 330 F.2d 811 (8th Cir. 1964), cert. denied, 379 U.S. 855 (1964) (mere financial inability of the defendant to post designated bond does not automatically prove excessiveness, so long as the amount is reasonably calculated to insure that the defendant will stand trial and submit to sentence if convicted).

150. People *ex rel.* Rubinstein v. Warden of City Prison, 279 App. Div. 47, 107 N.Y.S. 2d 948 (1951).

151. Spector v. United States, 193 F.2d 1002 (9th Cir. 1952).

152. United States v. Mule, 40 F.2d 503 (2d Cir. 1930).

The leading modern case on the issue of excessive bail was *Stack v. Boyle*.[153] Twelve alleged Communists were indicted in the southern district of California for conspiring to violate the Smith Act. On arrest, bail was fixed at $50,000 each. The government's request for such high bail was based on the argument that four Communists previously convicted under the Smith Act in the southern district of New York had jumped bail, but no evidence was introduced to show that these four had any connection with the California group. The Supreme Court by unanimous vote held that the bail was excessive, in violation of the Eighth Amendment. Noting that the right of the accused to be released is conditioned upon his giving adequate assurance that he will stand trial and submit to sentence if found guilty, Chief Justice Vinson declared that bail is "excessive" if the figure is higher than an amount reasonably calculated to fulfil this purpose. It was pointed out that the maximum penalties under the Smith Act were incarceration for five years and a $10,000 fine, and also, that the $50,000 bail demanded in this instance was much higher than the bail which is usually imposed for other offenses with like penalties. If higher than usual bail is required, there must be supporting evidence adduced at a hearing to support it. The Chief Justice added, "To infer from the fact of indictment alone a need for bail in an unusually high amount is an arbitrary act. Such conduct would inject into our own system of government the very principles of totalitarianism which Congress was seeking to guard against in passing the statute under which petitioners have been indicted."[154]

There have been occasions when very high bail has been exacted. Jefferson Davis, held on a treason charge after the Civil War, was given his freedom on bail of $100,000, at that time a very large sum of money.[155] "Boss" Tweed, charged with defrauding the City of New York of over $6,000,000, was held, in 1875, in bail of $3,000,000, the court asserting that "the amount is unusually large, but the reason of that is the uncommon magnitude of the defendant's depredations."[156] Bail of $250,000 for a material witness in a case dealing with the murder of an election worker has been upheld on the grounds of the seriousness of the

153. 342 U.S. 1 (1951).

154. Justice Jackson wrote a concurring opinion in an effort to spell out more precisely the standards which ought to govern the granting of bail. He stressed that bail is always a calculated risk, that the judge is not free to make the sky the limit, that each defendant is entitled to be considered as an individual, even when charged with conspiracy, that the grand jury has no business making recommendations on the subject of bail, and that it is not within the traditional spirit of bail procedure to rely upon the fact that public opinion demands that Communists should be kept in jail before trial. 342 U.S. 7-18.

155. Case of Davis, 7 Fed. Cas. 63 (No. 3621a) (C.C.D. Va. 1867-71).

156. People v. Tweed, 5 Hun. 382, appeal dismissed, 63 N.Y. 202 (1875).

The Preliminaries / 59

crime, the man's bad reputation and long criminal record, and the chances of flight.[157] Bail in the amount of $100,000 has been sustained in the case of one who was charged with conspiracy to violate the narcotics law, and who had a criminal record, and was also under indictment for another offense.[158] In another instance a $10,000 bail was approved by the reviewing court in the case of a parole violater charged with two felonies under the narcotics law.[159] In still another case, following conviction for the crime of assault to commit rape, a bond of $10,000, pending appeal, was upheld.[160] Furthermore, it has been ruled that the fact that the defendant is indigent does not establish an absolute right to pretrial release on his own recognizance.[161]

On the other hand, the New York Court of Appeals, in 1947, held that a bail of $250,000 was excessive in the case of a man accused of stealing about $780,000.[162] Several factors were stressed: that the accused had surrendered voluntarily; that there was no showing of any intention to flee; that the prosecutor had suggested a bond of $100,000; and that the accused had business interests and relatives in the city, and had lived there for many years. A bail of $40,000 was cut to $7,500 where a lawyer in good standing, who had no criminal record and had lived in the city for many years, was accused of attempting to bomb a building.[163] A man charged with vagrancy was required to put up a bond of $50,000, but the Illinois Supreme Court cut it to $5,000, noting that the maximum penalty for vagrancy was a jail sentence of ten days to six months or a fine of $20 to $100.[164] The only purpose of fixing bail at this level is to render it impossible for the accused to make it. Similarly a bail of $20,000, pending appeal from a liquor law conviction, was held excessive because prohibitive.[165] In the case of a wealthy man accused of making false statements to

---

157. People *ex rel.* Rao v. Adams, 296 N.Y. 231, 72 N.E. 2d 170 (1947).
158. Meltzer v. United States, 188 F.2d 913 (9th Cir. 1951).
159. Moore v. Aderhold, 108 F.2d 729 (10th Cir. 1939).
160. Hairston v. United States, 343 F.2d 313 (D.C. Cir. 1965). Chief Judge Bazelon dissented, arguing that high monetary bail was not justified because the defendant's character was "bad," or because the evidence was heavily against him. He maintained that release on bail pending an appeal is "heavily favored," and that the possibility of flight was the only valid consideration. See also Pannell v. United States, 320 F.2d 698 (D.C. Cir. 1963) ($5,000 bail on appeal from narcotics conviction upheld).
161. Reeves v. State, 411 P.2d 212 (Alaska, 1966). Here the defendant was accused of first-degree murder, burglary, and robbery. He was not gainfully employed, had no relatives or close friends in the state, and owned no property there. Bail at $10,000 was approved, under these circumstances.
162. People *ex rel.* Lobell v. McDonnell, 296 N.Y. 109, 71 N.E. 2d 423 (1947).
163. State v. Wertheimer, 183 La. 388, 163 So. 545 (1935).
164. People *ex rel.* Sammons v. Snow, 340 Ill. 464, 173 N.E. 8 (1930).
165. Barrett v. United States, 4 F.2d 317 (6th Cir. 1925).

his draft board during World War II, bail of $500,000 was reduced by the reviewing court to $50,000.[166] It was noted that the accused had strong local ties, since he lived with his family in the city and owned real estate there. The penalties to which he would be liable if convicted were not very great, and hence "the urge to flee cannot be unusually great." Ability to flee, it was held, does not prove a purpose to flee. Finally, the court held that a bond may be excessive even though the prisoner can furnish it. Finally, in a recent case a federal district judge ruled that a woman charged with unlawful distribution of heroin was entitled to release on her own recognizance.[167] The court held that a bail of $5,000 was excessive in view of the fact that the defendant was forty-three years old, employed by a U.S. government agency, and had five children and relatives in the area.

Remedies

The customary procedure in the states for raising the issue of excessive bail is to apply for a writ of habeas corpus. This was, until recently, the normal procedure in the federal courts, but in *Stack* v. *Boyle*[168] the Supreme Court ruled that the proper procedure for challenging bail is by motion for reduction of bail, and appeal to the court of appeals from an order denying such motion. While habeas corpus is, to be sure, an appropriate remedy for one held in custody in violation of the Constitution, it was ruled that the district court should withhold relief in a habeas corpus action where an adequate remedy is available in the criminal proceeding, and has not been exhausted. It should be added that the Supreme Court ruled in 1894 that the Eighth Amendment provision on bail does not apply as a limitation on the states by way of Fourteenth Amendment due process,[169] but in recent years many lower federal courts have taken jurisdiction in cases involving state bail questions on the clear assumption that there is a federal remedy through the due process guaranty of the Fourteenth Amendment.[170]

A more promising remedy lies in the direction of reforming the bail system, and in particular in regulating or, better still, eliminating the "bail bond racket."[171] Excluding traffic offenses, it is estimated that from

166. U.S. *ex rel.* Rubenstein v. Mulcahy, 155 F.2d 1002 (2d Cir. 1946).
167. United States v. Figueroa, 347 F. Supp. 112 (D.C. Mass. 1972).
168. 342 U.S. 1 (1951).
169. McKane v. Durston, 153 U.S. 684 (1894).
170. See cases cited in note 112, above.

171. There has been a great deal of interest in this problem, in recent years, which is reflected in the unusually large amount of research and writing on the subject. The most readable book is Goldfarb, *Ransom*. But see also Arthur L. Beeley, *The Bail System in Chicago* (Chicago: University of Chicago Press, 1927); Paul B. Wice, *Freedom for Sale* (Lexington, Mass.: D. C. Heath, 1974); Caleb Foote, ed., *Studies on Bail* (Philadelphia: In-

ten to twelve million people need bail bonds each year. In 1963, about 1,500,000 defendants went to jail because they could not afford the price of a bond, which is usually 10 percent of its face amount. In effect, this means that a huge number of people serve jail terms without trials. The system enriches the professional bondsmen, who operate a $250,000,000 business,[172] and discriminates against the poor and the unpopular, such as civil rights demonstrators and persons accused of subversive activity, and indeed against anyone who cannot afford to pay the premium or those whom the bondsman chooses not to serve. A bail survey in Philadelphia published in late 1964 indicated that in the local federal courts 32 percent of the defendants were unable to make a bail of $500; 50 percent were unable to make bail of $1,000; 67 percent were unable to make bail between $1,500 and $4,000; while 97 percent were unable to make bail of $5,000 or over.[173] A profitable business, the bail system corrupts the police and the courts in many cities through involvement in large-scale racketeering. Many professional bondsmen are ex-criminals, racketeers, or hoodlums who have an absolute discretion to refuse to write a bond, and almost unlimited powers of arrest. Furthermore, the futility of the system is reflected in the fact that there are very few forfeitures when defendants fail to appear for trial as directed.

"If it is true," former Justice Arthur J. Goldberg has written, "that 'the quality of a nation's civilization can be largely measured by the methods it uses in the enforcement of its criminal law,' then the American bail system as it now operates can no longer be tolerated. At best, it is a system of checkbook justice; at worst, a highly commercialized racket."[174] Another

---

stitute of Legal Research, Law School, University of Pennsylvania, 1966); Report of the Attorney General's Committee, *Poverty and the Administration of Federal Criminal Justice* (Washington: U.S. Government Printing Office, 1963), chap. 3; Report of the National Conference on Bail and Criminal Justice, May, 1964, *Bail in the United States: 1964* (Washington: U.S. Government Printing Office, 1964); Martin L. Friedland, *Detention before Trial* (Toronto: University of Toronto Press, 1965); D. J. Freed and P. M. Wald, *Bail in the United States* (Washington: Department of Justice and the Vera Foundation, 1964); Comment, "The Administration of Bail," *Yale Law Journal*, 41 (December 1931): 293–300; Note, "The Bail Reform Act of 1966," *Iowa Law Review*, 53 (August 1967): 170–94.

172. Goldfarb, *Ransom*, p. 96. Goldfarb estimated that agents writing bail bonds made $22,500,000 a year, and the companies about $4,500,000.

173. Note, "Bail: The Need for Reconsideration," *Northwestern University Law Review*, 59 (November–December, 1964): 678–85, 680. A similar bail study in New York for 1965 concluded that 28 percent of the defendants were unable to make bail of $500; 45 percent could not make bail of $1,500, and 86 percent were unable to make any bail over $7,500. Note, "A Study of the Administration of Bail in New York City," *Pennsylvania Law Review*, 106 (March 1958): 693–730, 707. See George F. Longsdorf, "Is Bail a Rich Man's Privilege" 7 F.R.D. 309–12 (1947).

174. Foreword to Goldfarb, *Ransom*, p. ix.

distinguished federal jurist, Judge J. Skelly Wright of the Court of Appeals of the District of Columbia, wrote in 1963, "Certainly the professional bondsman system as used in this District is odious at best. The effect of such a system is that the professional bondsmen hold the keys to the jail in their pockets. They determine for whom they will act as surety—who in their judgment is a good risk. The bad risks, in the bondsmen's judgment, *and the ones who are unable to pay the bondsmen's fees*, remain in jail."[175] As Goldfarb put the matter, "[T]he American bail system is a scandal. It typifies what is worst and most cynical about our system of justice. . . . It is not only unfair; it is illogical; it does not even work well. The bail system is to a degree a socially countenanced ransom of people and of justice for no good reason."[176]

Various alternatives to or remedies of the bail bond system have been proposed or are in operation today. Perhaps the mildest reform takes the form of detailed statutory regulation of professional bondsmen, as in New York.[177] The reform which has attracted the greatest amount of favorable attention was the Manhattan Bail Project, undertaken by the Vera Foundation (organized by Louis Schweitzer, a chemical engineer). This project was based on the rather simple proposition that judges will administer the pretrial release system more justly and intelligently if they had more reliable information to go on. Each prisoner was interviewed by a New York University law student who sought to establish the facts relating to the arrestee, including his community ties, so as to determine whether he could reasonably be trusted to return for trial if released merely on his own recognizance. Vera recommended such release in about 65 percent of all cases, and the courts accepted Vera recommendations in about 70 percent of these cases. During the first three years, over 10,000 persons were interviewed, about 3,500 were released on their own recognizance as a result of Vera recommendations, and of these 98.5 percent appeared in court when they were supposed to. In contrast, about three times as many who were on bail failed to appear. This system of pretrial freedom on the basis of verified information worked so well that in January 1964 New York City took over Vera's work, which was assigned to the Office of Probation.[178] This idea has spread to many other cities all over the country.

---

175. Pannell v. United States, 320 F. 2d 698, 699 (D.C. Cir. 1963) (concurring opinion).
176. Goldfarb, *Ransom,* pp. 4–5.
177. See N.Y. Code of Criminal Procedure, §554-b (McKinney's, 1971). See John J. Murphy, "State Control of the Operation of Professional Bail Bondsmen," *University of Cincinnati Law Review,* 36 (Summer 1967): 375–412.
178. See C. E. Ares, A. Rankin and H. Sturz, "The Manhattan Bail Project: An Interim Report on the Use of Pre-Trial Parole," *New York University Law Review,* 38 (January 1963): 67–95.

Another approach to the problem of reforming the bail bond system is found in the enactment in 1963 by Illinois of a statute[179] which, in effect, has put the professional bail bondsman out of business,[180] and which has been adopted by other states.[181] In the words of Justice Blackmun, "[P]rior to 1964 the professional bail bondsmen system with all its abuses was in full and odorous bloom in Illinois."[182] Under the new dispensation, one who has been arrested and accused of crime can obtain pretrial release (a) on a personal recognizance, or (b) by executing a bail bond and paying only 10 percent of the bail, of which only 10 percent is eventually kept by the state, or (c) by executing a bail bond by putting up cash, stocks, bonds, or real estate. Thus, with the second option, if the bail is set at $1,000, the accused deposits $100 with the court, and gets back $90 when he shows up in court as required. In 1971, the Supreme Court upheld the constitutionality of this statute over equal protection objections, since a compelling governmental interest was found to justify the legislative classifications involved.[183] The new approach to bail in Illinois has proved very successful. By way of contrast, it is of interest to note that in 1962, in Cook County, professional bondsmen wrote bonds totaling $18,513,965, received fees amounting to $1,851,396, and paid forfeiture judgments of only $183,930.[184]

There are other approaches to the bail problem. One is to use the summons as a substitute for arrest and bail, as is done in millions of minor traffic cases every year.[185] Still another is the so-called Tulsa plan, which was put into operation in July 1963, and which provides that in misdemeanor cases the arrestee may be released to his attorney without bond, but if he does not appear when required, the attorney is taken off the list of those eligible to participate in the plan.[186] Finally, the most desirable solution to the bail problem is outright release on recognizance, either on trust, or on an unsupported bond of the defendant, or on the making of a very small cash deposit. Experience shows that most people are trustworthy and have substantial ties to the community in which they reside,

179. 38 Ill. Ann. Stat., §110-7 (Smith-Hurd 1970).
180. See Alfred Kamin, "Bail Administration in Illinois," *Illinois Bar Journal,* 53 (April 1965): 674–86.
181. Wis. Act of July 1, 1970, chap. 298, Wis. Stat. 1973, chap. 969. As in the case of the Illinois statute, the Wisconsin statute provides for a cash payment of 10 percent, of which 90 percent is refundable. See §§969.02–03.
182. Schilb v. Kuebel, 404 U.S. 357, 359 (1971).
183. 404 U.S. 357, 359.
184. See Charles H. Bowman, "The Illinois Ten Per Cent Bail Deposit Provision," *University of Illinois Law Forum,* 1965 (Spring 1965): 35–41, 36.
185. Goldfarb, *Ransom,* pp. 166–72.
186. *Ibid.,* pp. 203–12.

64 / The Defendant's Rights Today

and that if released before trial they will not flee. Accordingly, on March 11, 1963, the Department of Justice instructed all United States attorneys to encourage release on recognizance, and it is worth noting that the default rate has been only about 2.5%, which is lower than the default rate for those who are released on bail bonds. What matters most in determining who is to be released on a mere promise to show up when needed is the assembling and verification of the facts bearing upon the issue of personal reliability.

Preventive Detention

When a judge fixes bail at a figure which he knows is beyond the resources available to the defendant, or denies bail altogether, he is in effect subjecting the accused to a form of preventive detention. This is a subterfuge, since American judges are not supposed to have the authority to lock people up as a mere preventive measure, but of course, denial of bail or fixing bail at a figure which is out of reach, amounts to a preventive detention without calling it that.

In enacting the District of Columbia Court Reform and Criminal Procedure Act of 1970,[187] Congress authorized preventive detention in the District "to eliminate from the bail system," as the reporting House committee stated, "the hypocrisy of locking up defendants, without fixed standards, through the device of requiring a high money bond."[188] In making his decision the judge may consider not only the danger of flight, as before, but also the safety of other persons and the community. Thus, the judge may order a person detained prior to trial if that person is dangerous to the community, if he threatens witnesses or jurors for the purpose of obstructing justice, or if he is a narcotics addict charged with a crime of violence who has been convicted of a crime of violence in the past ten years, or was on bail, parole, or probation for a crime of violence at the time of his arrest. The judge must hold a hearing, and find "clear and convincing" evidence that the accused is in one of these categories, that there is no other way reasonably to assure the safety of the community, and that there is a substantial probability that the defendant committed the offense charged. One may be detained preventively for no more than sixty days, and the decision to detain is appealable.

The constitutionality of preventive detention was debated very vigorously in Congress, with Senator Sam Irvin, Jr. arguing that pretrial detention is equivalent to pretrial punishment.[189] Nevertheless, in the first test

187. D.C. Code Ann. §§23-1321 to 1332 (1973).
188. H. R. Rep. no. 907, 91st Cong., 2d sess. (1970), pp. 82, 87–89.
189. Senator Irvin's main speech on the bill was on July 17, 1970. *Cong. Rec.*, 91st Cong., 2d sess., 116: 24836–88.

the Court of Appeals of the District of Columbia upheld the statute in a case involving a defendant who had a lengthy record of committing crimes of violence and who was intimidating witnesses.[190] The court ruled that there was no violation of the presumption of innocence, since the presumption applies only to the trial at which guilt must be established beyond a reasonable doubt. It also held that the detention hearing and the "clear and convincing" standard of proof were consistent with the requirements of due process. In short, the court felt that the government has such a substantial interest in protecting the community and witnesses and in assuring the integrity of the trial process, that it outweighs the interest of the individual, especially since the detention can not extend beyond sixty days.[191]

190. Blunt v. United States, 322 A.2d 579 (D.C. App. 1974).
191. For an exhaustive and learned analysis of this problem, see H. H. Meyer, "Constitutionality of Pretrial Detention," *Georgetown Law Journal*, 60 (May 1972): 1140-94; (June 1972): 1382-474. A very persuasive argument is advanced by the author that the act of Congress providing for pretrial preventive detention is constitutional.

3 / The Defendant's Right to Notice

Notice and the Constitution

The indispensable, classic minimum requirement of due process is that one who is charged with having committed a crime be given adequate notice of his alleged offense and a fair hearing or trial.[1] Some aspects of notice are usually spelled out in very specific terms in bills of rights. The Sixth Amendment of the national Constitution provides that in all criminal prosecutions the accused has the right "to be informed of the nature and cause of the accusation." State constitutions have similar provisions, usually stated in about the same words.[2] Some are even more explicit. Thus, the constitution of Massachusetts provides that "no subject shall be held to answer for any Crimes or offence, until the same is fully and plainly, substantially and formally, described to him. . . ."[3] In addition, the due process clauses of the Fifth and Fourteenth Amendments have been construed as embracing the principle of fair notice. On such grounds, therefore, the United States Supreme Court can ultimately grant relief in cases heard in both federal and state courts.

The due process concepts of notice and fair hearing, with their emphasis upon the discovery of truth through rational methods, are still in a state of evolution. But they constitute a vast improvement over Anglo-Saxon and early Norman methods of determining questions of guilt and innocence by such ritualistic devices as trial by battle or ordeal, or trial by compurgation (oath-taking). While these were ludicrous from our modern point of view, it must be remembered, as Sir James Stephen pointed out in his great historical work on the English criminal law, that in "early times the really efficient check upon crimes of violence was the fear of private vengeance, which rapidly degenerated into private war, blood feuds, and anarchy. . . . Indeed trial by battle was only private war under regulations."[4] While there were several kinds of ordeals, generally speaking

---

1. See Rodney L. Mott, *Due Process of Law* (Indianapolis: Bobbs-Merrill Co., 1926), chap. 13; Virginia L. Wood, *Due Process of Law, 1932-1949* (Baton Rouge: Louisiana State University Press, 1951), chaps. 3-4.
2. See, e.g., N.Y. Const., Art. I, §6.
3. Mass. Const., Decl. of Rights, Art. XII.
4. James Fitzjames Stephen, *A History of the Criminal Law of England* (London: Macmillan Co., 1883), I: 60-61.

they were much the same. Says Stephen, "They were appeals to God to work a miracle in attestation of the innocence of the accused person. The handling of hot iron, plunging the hand or arm into boiling water unhurt, were the commonest. The ordeal of water was a very singular institution. Sinking was the sign of innocence, floating the sign of guilt. . . . In nearly every case the accused would sink. This would prove his innocence, indeed, but there would be no need to take him out. He would thus die honourably. If by any accident he floated, he would be put to death disgracefully."[5] In contrast, our present methods of administering the criminal law seek to assure defendants their rights to a fair trial, and a trial is a sensible effort to inquire into disputed questions of fact and law by presenting proofs and reasoned argument.

The Accusation

Accusations are made either by grand juries or by public prosecutors. Generally speaking, private individuals may initiate criminal proceedings in the case of minor crimes by filing what is known as a complaint. The older states, and most states east of the Mississippi River, require grand jury action for all major offenses. A grand jury, which has from twelve to twenty-three members,[6] makes no effort to determine the issue of guilt or innocence. It does not hear the defendant's case. All it hears is the prosecution's side, or as much as the prosecutor chooses to present, and its sole function is to decide whether its evidence, if true, would warrant a conviction. Its proceedings are secret, and there are very good reasons for the secrecy. The grand jury sits behind closed doors to discourage the escape of the accused, to prevent the accused from trying to tamper with witnesses, to encourage witnesses to give testimony without fear of retaliation, and to allow grand jurors to investigate and deliberate freely.[7] Above all, the grand jury sits in secret to prevent the disclosure of the fact that one who is ultimately not indicted has been under investigation.

---

5. *Ibid.,* p. 73.
6. See George J. Edwards, Jr., *The Grand Jury* (Philadelphia: George T. Bisel Co., 1906). Some seven states, notably Michigan, use a so-called "one-man grand jury" system, in which a single judge is authorized by statute to subpoena and question suspects and to punish for contempt those who refuse to testify or testify falsely. But except for his power to compel testimony, such a magistrate is not acting as a grand jury, but only as a collector of evidence. See Glenn R. Winters, "The Michigan One-Man Grand Jury," *Journal of the American Judicature Society,* 28 (February 1945): 136-51; Robert G. Scigliano, *The Michigan One-Man Grand Jury* (East Lansing: Governmental Research Bureau, Michigan State University, 1957).
7. See Richard H. Kuh, "The Grand Jury 'Presentment': Foul Blow or Fair Play?" *Columbia Law Review,* 55 (December 1955): 1103-36; Note, "The Grand Jury as an Investigatory Body," *Harvard Law Review,* 74 (January 1961): 590-605.

When a grand jury formulates a charge on its own initiative, the accusation is known as a presentment, and it is called an indictment if the initiative came from the public prosecutor. In many states, particularly those west of the Mississippi, most accusations are filed by the prosecutor (whatever may be his actual title, e.g., state's attorney, district attorney, county attorney), and such an accusation is known as an information. In these states, however, the grand jury is available in the discretion of the prosecutors and judges, although it should be noted that when they have a choice prosecutors strongly prefer the information method. Before a prosecutor may file an information, there must have been a preliminary hearing by a magistrate, who has thus made the initial decision to bring a person to trial. It is, of course, well established that so far as Fourteenth Amendment due process is concerned, states are free to substitute indictment by information for the older form of accusation by grand jury action.[8]

Procedure in the federal courts is controlled by the Fifth Amendment provision that "no person shall be held to answer for a capital, or otherwise infamous crime, unless on a presentment or indictment of a Grand Jury, except in cases arising in the land or naval forces, or in the Militia, when in actual service in time of War or public danger." Rule 7(a) of the Federal Rules of Criminal Procedure provides that an offense punishable by death must be prosecuted by indictment;[9] offenses punishable by imprisonment for over a year or at hard labor shall be prosecuted by indictment, or if waived, by information. Any other offense may be prosecuted either way.[10]

This rule conforms with the position of the Supreme Court, which holds to the view that it is the quality of punishment that determines whether a crime is "infamous," and that changes in public opinion may affect a judgment on this point.[11] In a famous case decided in 1896, the Court ruled that a statute authorizing imprisonment at hard labor for one year, as well as deportation of Chinese aliens found to be in the country illegally, defined an infamous offense for which trial could be had only upon an

---

8. Hurtado v. California, 110 U.S. 516 (1884); Gaines v. Washington, 277 U.S. 81, 86 (1928). The grand jury was abolished in England in 1933, 23 & 24 Geo. V. c. 36, §1. See Nathan T. Elliff, "Notes on the Abolition of the English Grand Jury," *Journal of Criminal Law and Criminology,* 29 (May–June 1938): 3–22.

9. See Smith v. United States, 360 U.S. 1 (1959), which held that one charged with violating the Federal Kidnapping Act can be prosecuted only by way of indictment, even though the death penalty was not the only penalty prescribed by the statute.

10. A federal grand jury has twenty-three members; sixteen constitute a quorum; and it need not be unanimous, an indictment being returnable if at least twelve grand jurors agree to it.

11. *Ex parte* Wilson, 114 U.S. 417, 427 (1885). The common law rule was that the nature of the crime, and not the punishment, was the determining factor.

indictment.¹² Such offenses as banking law violations, counterfeiting, conspiracy to commit a crime against the United States, and fraudulent voting have been held to be infamous. On the other hand, the Court has ruled that an offense punishable by a fine of not over $1,000 or imprisonment for not more than six months, or both, was a misdemeanor which could be tried without an indictment.¹³

Whether or not accusation by indictment is preferable to the information method has long been debated.¹⁴ Some years ago Raymond Moley concluded, on the basis of impressive research data, that prosecution by information had many merits: it is cheaper; it saves time; it is more efficient; and "it properly centers responsibility upon the prosecutor for actions which are apparently largely under his control even when indictments only are used."¹⁵ For it was demonstrated that in the overwhelming majority of instances the grand jury followed the lead of the prosecutor. Moley's data indicated that the information, following a magistrate's preliminary hearing, resulted in fewer cases where persons were acquitted as compared with the indictment cases. On the other hand, one of the main weaknesses of the information method is that, unlike the grand jury, which invokes the subpoena and contempt powers of a judge, the prosecutor has no power to compel testimony.

A task force of scholars and lawyers which reported to the Department of Justice on September 17, 1973, recommended, on the basis of a study of state and local criminal justice systems, the abolition of grand juries.¹⁶ It

12. Wong Wing v. United States, 163 U.S. 228, 237 (1896). See also United States v. Moreland, 258 U.S. 433 (1922), which held that imprisonment at hard labor in the workhouse of the District of Columbia was infamous.

13. Duke v. United States, 301 U.S. 492 (1937). See the excellent annotation in 24 A.L.R. 1002.

14. See R. J. Miller, "Informations or Indictments in Felony Cases," *Minnesota Law Review*, 8 (April 1924): 379-408; Note, "Legislative Interference with the Grand Jury," *Harvard Law Review*, 52 (November 1938): 151-57.

15. "The Initiation of Criminal Prosecutions by Indictment or Information," *Michigan Law Review*, 29 (February 1931): 403-31, 430.

16. National Advisory Commission on Criminal Justice Standards and Goals, *Courts*, a report to the Department of Justice, September 17, 1973. Some of the other basic recommendations of this task force are worth noting here. It was suggested that except for very extraordinary cases, and then subject only to the approval of the reviewing court, a convicted defendant should be allowed only one appeal to a higher court. It was also suggested that except for such serious matters as drunk driving, traffic cases should be handled administratively, allowing pleas by mail and eliminating jury trials. The task force also recommended that juvenile courts should be replaced by family courts capable of dealing with all aspects of family life, such as delinquency, neglect, support, adoption, child custody, divorce, and annulment, with an emphasis on counseling and less concern with punishment. It also recommended the abolition of plea bargaining and a modification of the exclusionary rule. It recommended that judges should be nominated in each state to the governor by a

concluded that grand juries serve only to delay prosecutions, and that they are ineffective because they merely do what the prosecutor wants done. It conceded, however, that under some circumstances, where matters of widespread public concern are involved, it might be desirable to invoke the investigatory function of the grand jury.[17] Similarly, an experienced judge on the U.S. District Court in Chicago, Judge William J. Campbell, recently asserted, "This great institution of the past has long ceased to be the guardian of the people for which purpose it was created at Runnymede. Today it is but a convenient tool for the prosecutor—too often used solely for publicity. Any experienced prosecutor will admit that he can indict anybody at any time for almost anything before any grand jury."[18]

It should be emphasized that a grand jury does not decide upon the guilt or innocence of the accused. It does not necessarily hear all the evidence available to the prosecutor; it must decide whether there is a *prima facie* case against the defendant on the basis of whatever evidence the prosecutor chooses to lay before it. It follows that, as the Supreme Court ruled many years ago, an indictment need not be quashed because it is supported by evidence which would be incompetent if offered at the trial.[19] More recently the Court held that an indictment is not invalid merely because the grand jury heard only hearsay evidence.[20] To hold otherwise, said Justice Black, "would run counter to the whole history of the grand jury institution, in which laymen conduct their inquiries unfettered by technical rules. Neither justice nor the concept of a fair trial requires such a change. In a trial on the merits, defendants are entitled to a strict observance of all the rules designed to bring about a fair verdict. Defendants are not entitled, however, to a rule which would result in interminable delay but add nothing to the assurance of a fair trial."[21]

The power of the prosecuting attorney to file charges or to persuade grand juries to do so lends itself to two abuses. On the one hand, subject to

---

seven-member commission consisting of one judge of the state's highest court, three lawyers, and three laymen representing the general public. It also recommended that trial judges should have four-year terms, and appellate judges six-year terms, and that they should stand for re-election uncontested. Finally, the task force urged more speedy trials, with misdemeanor cases to be heard within 30 days, and felonies within 60 day, after arrest.

17. For other evaluations of the grand jury system see Lewis P. Watts, Jr., "Grand Jury: Sleeping Watchdog or Expensive Antique? *North Carolina Law Review,* 37 (April 1959): 290-315; Judge Irving R. Kaufman, "Grand-Jury—Its Role and Its Powers," 17 F.R.D. 331 (1955).

18. 55 F.R.D. 253 (1972).

19. Holt v. United States, 218 U.S. 245 (1910).

20. Costello v. United States, 350 U.S. 359 (1956).

21. 350 U.S. 364. See also Lawn v. United States, 355 U.S. 339 (1958), holding that the accused has no right to have a preliminary trial on the competency and adequacy of the evidence considered by the grand jury.

the possible defense of former jeopardy in some situations, the prosecutor is able to harass a person with repeated or persistent indictments, trying him on one charge after another. The marathon proceedings against the labor leader Harry Bridges, which began in 1936 and the last phase of which was disposed of by the Supreme Court in 1953,[22] and the government's prosecution of William W. Remington on successive charges,[23] illustrate this point. There is, however, some protection against this sort of abuse. Rule 48(a) of the Federal Rules of Criminal Procedure seeks to limit the prosecutor's discretion by providing that an indictment may be dismissed only "by leave of court." State appellate courts also hold that the prosecutor may not drop an indictment in order to get before a friendlier court or at a more favorable time.[24] On the other hand, the prosecutor may abuse his discretion, to the injury of private rights, through inactivity or refusal to bring actions, and existing restraints, administrative, political, and judicial, have proved inadequate.[25] A proposed remedy would authorize judges to appoint special prosecutors for single cases on the motion of aggrieved private parties where abuse of discretion through inaction has been shown.[26]

The Right to a Specific Accusation

An accused must know in advance of trial the precise nature of the accusation against him. Otherwise he cannot prepare a defense and is vulnerable to surprise. Characteristic of modern law is the present requirement in Rule 7(c)(1) of the Federal Rules of Criminal Procedure that the indictment "shall be a plain, concise and definite written statement of the essential facts constituting the offense charged."[27] A vague and indefinite

22. Bridges v. United States, 346 U.S. 209 (1953). For a complete log of all the proceedings in the long Bridges story, see Milton R. Konvitz, *Civil Rights in Immigration* (Ithaca: Cornell University Press, 1953), pp. 114-20.
23. See Note, "Trial by Persistence," *Stanford Law Review,* 4 (July 1952): 537-45.
24. *Ex parte* Lancaster, 206 Ala. 60, 89 So. 721 (1921); State v. Milano, 138 La. 989, 71 So. 131 (1916); Coleman v. State, 83 Miss. 290, 35 So. 937 (1904).
25. For an excellent study of the prosecutor's discretion, see Frank W. Miller, *Prosecution* (Boston: Little, Brown & Co., 1969). See also John Kaplan, "The Prosecutorial Discretion—A Comment," *Northwestern University Law Review,* 60 (May-June 1965): 174-93; Note, "Prosecutor's Discretion," *University of Pennsylvania Law Review,* 103 (June 1955): 1057-87.
26. See the excellent Comment, "Private Prosecution: A Remedy for District Attorneys' Unwarranted Inaction," *Yale Law Journal,* 65 (December 1955): 209-34.
27. It has been emphasized by Justice Minton that the recently revised Rules "were designed to eliminate technicalities in criminal pleading and are to be construed to secure simplicity in procedure." United States v. Debrow, 346 U.S. 374, 376 (1953). By statute a person charged with any capital offense is entitled to receive a copy of the indictment at least three days before the beginning of the trial. 18 U.S.C. §3432 (1970).

charge will not suffice, since it does not convey fair notice to the accused. While it is true that strict common law rules of criminal pleading have been abandoned—indictments are no longer dismissed because of a missing comma—nevertheless an accused still has a right to know just what the charges against him are. The Supreme Judicial Court of Maine has observed, "The statutes prescribing forms of indictment have removed many of the niceties of technical pleading and the indictment is made little more than a simple statement of the offense couched in ordinary language and with due regard for the rights of the accused. But they cannot change the requirements that the indictment must, as at common law, contain every averment that is necessary to inform the defendant of the particular circumstances of the charge against him."[28]

Another succinct statement of the modern rule was made by Justice Sutherland in 1932:

> The rigor of old common law rules of criminal pleading has yielded, in modern practice, to the general principle that formal defects, not prejudicial, will be disregarded. The true test of the sufficiency of an indictment is not whether it could have been made more definite and certain, but whether it contains the elements of the offense intended to be charged, "and sufficiently apprises the defendant of what he must be prepared to meet, and, in case any other proceedings are taken against him for a similar offense, whether the record shows with accuracy to what extent he may plead a former acquittal or conviction." Cochran v. United States, 157 U.S. 286, 290 . . .; Rosen v. United States, 161 U.S. 29, 34.[29]

These principles are now commonly spelled out in state statutes. For example, the Penal Code of California provides that a statement of the offense "may be made in ordinary and concise language without any technical averments or any allegations of matter not essential to be proved. It may be in the words of the enactment describing the offense or declaring the matter to be a public offense, or in any words sufficient to give the accused notice of the offense of which he is accused."[30]

It was precisely upon this ground of vagueness that Judge Luther W. Youngdahl of the United States District Court for the District of Columbia twice dismissed charges brought against the celebrated Professor Owen Lattimore.[31] Lattimore was indicted on two counts of perjury allegedly committed before the Senate Internal Security Sub-

---

28. State v. Popolos, 103 A.2d 511, 513 (Me. 1954).

29. Hagner v. United States, 285 U.S. 427, 431 (1932). It is also to be noted that "in charging the offense, a detailed recital of the evidence by which it will be established is not required." People v. Quider, 172 Mich. 280, 285, 137 N.W. 546, 548 (1912).

30. Calif. Penal Code Ann. §952 (West 1970).

31. United States v. Lattimore, 112 F. Supp. 507 (1953), sustained by the Court of Appeals on the key counts in 215 F.2d 847 (D.C. Cir. 1954); United States v. Lattimore, 127 F. Supp. 405 (1955), sustained by an equally divided Court of Appeals. After the first dismissal, the government rephrased the charges somewhat. See Sen. Jud. Com., Sen. Rep. no. 2050,

committee in 1952. The first count charged that he had perjured himself when he denied that he was a "follower of the Communist line," and the second stated that Lattimore had perjured himself when he testified that he had never been a "promoter of Communist interests." Judge Youngdahl dismissed the indictment on the ground "that it does not, as a matter of law, inform the accused of the nature and cause of the accusation against him. Neither does it charge an offense with reasonable clarity so that the accused can make his defense, nor furnish the accused with such a description of the charge that he would be able to avail himself of his conviction or acquittal for protection against a further prosecution for the same cause."[32] He ruled that the key phrases were not used or understood by men of ordinary intellect in the same way. "To ask twelve jurors to agree and then decide that the definition of the Communist line found in the indictment is the definition that defendant had in mind and denied believing in, is to ask the jury to aspire to levels of insight to which the ordinary person is incapable, and upon which speculation no criminal indictment should hinge."[33] An indictment which is easily subject to such divergent interpretation does not adequately inform the defendant of the charges so that he may prepare a defense. The charges were dismissed as being "formless and obscure."

In insisting that state and federal courts comply with the principles of due notice and a fair hearing, the United States Supreme Court has wisely refrained from attempting to spell out such requirements in terms of any fixed formula. As Justice Stone once explained, "[T]he Fourteenth Amendment is concerned with the substance and not with the forms of procedure. . . . The due process clause does not guarantee to a citizen of a State any particular form or method of state procedure. Its requirements are satisfied if he has reasonable notice, and reasonable opportunity to be heard and to present his claim or defence, due regard being had to the nature of the proceedings and the character of the rights which may be affected by it."[34]

That a person tried for a crime must have specific notice of the alleged offense was underscored in a decision where an accused was charged in the indictment and tried for the offense of promoting an unlawful assemblage, and the state appellate court affirmed on the theory that the evidence supported a conviction under another section of the statute which defined

---

82d Cong., 2d sess (1952), *Institute of Pacific Relations,* by the Internal Security Subcommittee (Washington, 1952). For Lattimore's story, see his *Ordeal by Slander* (Boston: Little, Brown & Co., 1950).

32. 127 F. Supp. 408.

33. 127 F. Supp. 410. Judge Youngdahl dismissed the first indictment with the observation that the charges were "so nebulous and indefinite that a jury would have to indulge in speculation in order to arrive at a verdict." 112 F. Supp. 516.

34. Missouri *ex rel.* Hurwitz v. North, 271 U.S. 40, 42 (1926).

the offense of using force and violence.[35] The Supreme Court reversed on the ground that the two offenses were separate and distinct from each other. "No principle of procedural due process is more clearly established," said Justice Black for a unanimous Court, "than that notice of the specific charge, and a chance to be heard in a trial of the issues raised by that charge, if desired, are among the constitutional rights of every accused in a criminal proceeding in all courts, state or federal. . . . It is as much a violation of due process to send an accused to prison following conviction of a charge on which he was never tried as it would be to convict him upon a charge that was never made."[36] Similarly, in a later case the Supreme Court reviewed the conviction, in a federal district court, of a man who had been indicted on the charge that, through extortion, he had interfered with the movement of sand from outside Pennsylvania to a plant in Pennsylvania, in violation of the Hobbs Act.[37] At the trial, over protest, the judge permitted testimony on the effect of the defendant's practices insofar as they interfered with steel shipments from the plant to points outside the state. A unanimous Court held that to this extent the defendant was tried on a charge which was never made in the indictment. The variation between pleading and proof, the Court ruled, had the effect of destroying a substantial right, and was not merely harmless error. It is reversible error to convict a person on a charge the grand jury never made. On the other hand, it has been held proper to permit an accused who was indicted for one offense (larceny) to plead guilty to a lesser, closely related and overlapping offense (receiving stolen goods), since the defendant had reasonable notice of the charge.[38] The Court declared that "it would be an exaltation of technical precision to an unwarranted degree" and "a strained interpretation of petitioner's constitutional rights" to say that he had not had sufficient notice of the charge against him.

Proper notice is constitutionally necessary in all sorts of noncriminal proceedings where property or other rights are involved. Whether a particular form of notice is adequate depends upon the circumstances of each situation.[39] In general, the rule is that the best possible form of notice

35. Cole v. Arkansas, 333 U.S. 196 (1948).

36. 333 U.S. 201. The Massachusetts court once held that it was a denial of due process to disbar an attorney on the basis of a charge not contained in the complaint against him. Bar Assoc. of City of Boston v. Sleeper, 251 Mass. 6, 146 N.E. 269 (1925). To the same effect was the Supreme Court's decision in *In re* Ruffalo, 390 U.S. 544 (1968), which also dealt with the disbarment of a lawyer on a charge not made in the original notice of charges.

37. Stirone v. United States, 361 U.S. 212 (1960).

38. Paterno v. Lyons, 334 U.S. 314 (1948).

39. Anderson National Bank v. Luckett, 321 U.S. 233 (1944). In Covey v. Town of Somers, 351 U.S. 141 (1956) the Court held it was a violation of due process for a state to foreclose and sell the property of a mental incompetent for tax purposes upon notice to the incompetent before the appointment of a guardian. See also Armstrong v. Manzo, 380 U.S. 545 (1965), which held that failure to give a divorced father notice of a pending proceeding

must be given. In a carefully formulated opinion Justice Jackson once reached this general conclusion: "An elementary and fundamental requirement of due process in any proceeding which is to be accorded finality is notice reasonably calculated, under all the circumstances, to apprise interested parties of the pendency of the action and afford them an opportunity to present their objections. . . . The notice must be of such nature as reasonably to convey the required information, . . . and it must afford a reasonable time for those interested to make their appearance. . . ."[40] Notice is an essential element of proper procedure in administrative situations,[41] and is required by statute or general law in a host of different circumstances.[42]

The Void-for-Vagueness Rule

Notice to the public of what the criminal law forbids is usually given by statutes. Some states still have a limited number of common law offenses, but for the most part offenses are nowadays spelled out in statutes, and all federal crimes, except treason, which is defined in the Constitution, are statutory. Since it is a basic principle of our legal order that one may do, with impunity, whatever is not forbidden by law, it is well established that the law should convey to the individual a reasonably certain command wherever an act is declared to be punishable. That is to say, the statute should give due notice of just what may not be done.[43] This is known in

---

for adoption of his child violated due process. In Fuentes v. Shevin, 407 U.S. 67 (1972) the Court set aside state statutes authorizing summary seizure of chattels by creditors without giving notice or a hearing to the possessor. "Parties whose rights are to be affected are entitled to be heard; and in order that they may enjoy that right they must first be notified." Baldwin v. Hale, 68 U.S. 223, 233 (1864).

40. Mullane v. Central Hanover Bank & Trust Co., 339 U.S. 306, 314 (1950). Here the Court held that notice by publication in a local newspaper for known persons whose whereabouts were known was lacking in due process, since a more effective form of notice by mail was possible. See also Robinson v. Hanrahan, 409 U.S. 38 (1972).

41. Kenneth Culp Davis, *Administrative Law Text*, 3d ed. (St. Paul: West Publishing Co., 1972), chap. 15.

42. Maurice H. Merrill, *On Notice*, 3 vols. (Kansas City, Mo.: Vernon Law Book Co., 1952).

43. For a characteristic statement of the general rule, see Sherwin v. People, 100 N.Y. 351, 3 N.E. 465, 469 (1885): "The multiplication of offenses by construction of penal statutes is in conflict with the general policy of the law, and a statutory crime can only be created by phraseology which is clear, direct, and unquestionable as to its intention." See also the remarks in Com. v. Slome, 321 Mass. 713, 75 N.E. 2d 517, 519 (1947): "A statute creating a crime must be sufficiently definite in specifying the conduct that is commended or inhibited so that a man of ordinary intelligence may be able to ascertain whether any act or omission of his, as the case may be, will come within the sweep of the statute. It must fix with a reasonable degree of definiteness what it requires or prohibits. It should furnish a definite standard as a guide to determine what it denounces and condemns. . . . One ought not to be compelled to speculate at his peril as to whether a statute permits or prohibits any action which he proposes to take."

constitutional law as the void-for-vagueness rule. It means that a criminal statute violates due process if it does not define with reasonable specificity the nature of the proscribed conduct. In perhaps the most famous case on this subject, the Supreme Court held a World War I statute of Congress unconstitutional which made it a criminal act for anyone wilfully to make "any unjust or unreasonable rate or charge in handling or dealing in or with any necessaries."[44] The Court ruled that the statute did not describe an ascertainable standard of guilt adequate to inform persons accused of violating it of the nature and cause of the accusation. To attempt to enforce this statute, Chief Justice White observed, "would be the exact equivalent of an effort to carry out a statute which in terms merely penalized and punished all acts detrimental to the public interest when unjust and unreasonable in the estimation of the court and jury."[45]

Clearly a statute which sweepingly declared that it is a crime to do anything contrary to the public interest would be constitutionally defective because it does not convey an understandable command. One is not obliged in our society to conduct his life on a plan where he must engage in a continuous guessing contest as to what the public interest is, and what its requirements might be in the opinion of prosecutors, judges and juries. On grounds of essential vagueness a few statutes, state and federal, have been held unenforceable.[46] Justice Douglas observed in one of these cases that "words which are vague and fluid . . . may be as much a trap for the innocent as the ancient laws of Caligula."[47] Thus, in 1948 the Court expressed disapproval of a state law which punished conspiracy "to commit any act injurious to the public health, the public morals or to trade or commerce or for the perversion or obstruction of justice or the due administration of the laws. . . ."[48] For under such a law one could be punished

44. United States v. Cohen Grocery Co., 255 U.S. 81 (1921).
45. 255 U.S. 89.
46. Some of the better known early cases are Connally v. General Construction Co., 269 U.S. 385 (1926); Cline v. Frink Dairy Co., 274 U.S. 445 (1927); International Harvester Co. v. Kentucky, 234 U.S. 216 (1914); Collins v. Kentucky, 234 U.S. 634 (1914). For well-known state decisions on this point, see State v. Diamond, 27 N.M. 477, 202 P. 988 (1921); State v. Klapprott, 127 N.J.L. 395, 22 A.2d 877 (1941).
47. United States v. Cardiff, 344 U.S. 174, 176 (1952).
48. Musser v. Utah, 333 U.S. 95 (1948). See also Winters v. New York, 333 U.S. 507 (1948), which held a New York censorship law invalid on grounds of vagueness. Here Justice Reed observed, at p. 515: "The standards of certainty in statutes for offenses is higher than in those depending primarily upon civil sanction for enforcement. . . . There must be ascertainable standards of guilt. Men of common intelligence cannot be required to guess at the meaning of the enactment." Another important case was Lanzetta v. New Jersey, 306 U.S. 451 (1939), which invalidated a statute purporting to make it a crime to be a "gangster." Said Justice Butler, at p. 453, "No one may be required at peril of life, liberty or property to speculate as to the meaning of penal statutes. All are entitled to be informed as to what the State commands or forbids."

for simply failing to anticipate the general views of a judge and jury on an undefined subject.

But legislation is by no means an exact science, and the law is necessarily full of fairly vague statements. The Court has refused to hold Congress and the state legislatures to impossible standards of certainty. Justice Clark has put the prevailing view in the following words:

> A criminal statute must be sufficiently definite to give notice of the required conduct to one who would avoid its penalities, and to guide the judge in its application and the lawyer in defending one charged with its violation. But few words possess the precision of mathematical symbols, most statutes must deal with untold and unforeseen variations in factual situations, and the practical necessities of discharging the business of government inevitably limit the specificity with which legislators can spell out prohibitions. Consequently, no more than a reasonable degree of certainty can be demanded. Nor is it unfair to require that one who deliberately goes perilously close to an area of proscribed conduct shall take the risk that he may cross the line.[49]

Accordingly, the Court has been extremely reluctant to invalidate statutes on grounds of vagueness. As Justice Frankfurter pointed out, indefiniteness "is itself an indefinite concept."[50]

Thus the Sherman Anti-Trust Act, the key provisions of which are certainly couched in general terms, was sustained by the Court, Justice Holmes observing that "the law is full of instances where a man's fate depends on his estimating rightly, that is, as the jury subsequently estimates it, some matter of degree."[51] As Justice Black once stated, "the Constitution does not require impossible standards," and where statutory language "conveys sufficiently definite warning as to the proscribed conduct when measured by common understanding and practices," then "the Constitution requires no more."[52]

The problem of statutory vagueness is, at bottom, one of balancing competing interests against one another. This is, of course, characteristic of civil liberties questions generally. On the one hand, in the interests of

---

49. Boyce Motor Lines, Inc. v. United States, 342 U.S. 337, 340 (1952). Sometimes the Court holds that a vague statute may be enforceable if indictments filed under it are precise. See the famous cases of Cruikshank v. United States, 92 U.S. 542 (1875); Screws v. United States, 325 U.S. 91 (1945).

50. Winters v. New York, 333 U.S. 507, 524 (1948) (dissenting opinion). For the view that there is no constitutional authority for any court to declare a statute invalid for uncertainty, see J. G. Sutherland, *Statutes and Statutory Construction,* 3d ed. (Chicago: Callaghan & Co., 1943, Vol. II, §4920.

51. Nash v. United States, 229 U.S. 373, 377 (1913). For other examples see Fox v. State of Washington, 236 U.S. 273 (1915); Seven Cases v. United States, 239 U.S. 510 (1916); United States v. Wurzbach, 280 U.S. 396 (1930).

52. United States v. Petrillo, 332 U.S. 1, 7 (1947). For other cases see United States v. Spector, 343 U.S. 169 (1952); United States v. Hood, 343 U.S. 148 (1952).

justice, the individual has a right to know in advance where he stands, so that he may understand just what conduct is forbidden. On the other hand, language is at best a deficient medium for expressing ideas, and legislatures should not be held to impossible standards of specificity. Certainly it is a very rare occurrence for an appellate court to invalidate a statute on this ground.[53] It has become routine in constitutional litigation always to attack statutes as being unduly vague, but counsel rarely win cases with this argument. The courts are inclined to sustain the challenged statute if they are convinced that the standard was carefully phrased, after due consideration, and if no better phrasing occurs to them. The historical and administrative background of the statute is also taken into consideration. For example, a statutory phrase which on its face may seem very vague may actually convey a rather definite meaning because of an established common law principle or administrative usage from which it is derived. Much depends upon the total context.[54]

The recent decision of the Supreme Court in *Parker* v. *Levy*[55] is a case in point. The defendant, a physician in the army, was convicted by a general court-martial of violating three articles of the Uniform Code of Military Justice (UCMJ) which provide for the punishment of anyone who, under Art. 90(2), "wilfully disobeys a lawful command of his superior commissioned officer," or, under Art. 133, is guilty of "conduct unbecoming an officer and gentleman," or, under Art. 134, is guilty of "all disorders and neglects to the prejudice of good order and discipline in the armed forces." The defendant had refused an order to establish a training program for Special Forces aide men, published statements urging Negro enlisted men to refuse to obey orders to go to Vietnam, and referred to Special Forces personnel as "liars and thieves" and as "murderers of women and children." He was dismissed from the service, required to forfeit all pay and allowances, and sentenced to three years at hard labor. After exhausting his military remedies, he petitioned for a writ of habeas corpus in a federal district court, relying mainly on the contention that the Articles of the UCMJ he was convicted of violating were too vague to satisfy the requirements of due process. Dividing 6-3, the Supreme Court held that since the military is a specialized society separate from civilian society, it has by necessity developed its own laws and traditions during its long history. Noting that the present language in the Code which was

---

53. See R. A. Collings, Jr., "Unconstitutional Uncertainty—An Appraisal," *Cornell Law Quarterly,* 40 (Winter 1955): 195-237.

54. See, e.g., Omaechevarria v. Idaho, 246 U.S. 343, 348 (1918): "Men familiar with range conditions and desirous of observing the law will have little difficulty in determining what is prohibited by it."

55. 417 U.S. 733 (1974).

under challenge dated from 1806, Justice Rehnquist maintained that it was well established that "the long standing customs and usages of the services impart accepted meaning to the seemingly imprecise standards of Arts. 133 and 134." He pointed out that the UCMJ cannot be equated with a civilian code, and that its provisions must be construed in the context of many years of experience. Custom, usage, and the interpretations of the Court of Military Appeals have limited the contested sections of the Code to situations where there was direct and serious prejudice to good order and discipline in the armed forces. Thus the accused had fair notice that his conduct was punishable. Three dissenting Justices argued that these Code provisions were unconstitutionally vague and uncertain.

Other recent decisions illustrate the ebb and flow of the void-for-vagueness doctrine. For example, the Court held valid, in 1963, a section of the Robinson-Patman Act which makes it a crime to sell goods at "unreasonably low prices for the purpose of destroying competition or eliminating a competitor."[56] The Court emphasized that the need to find a predatory intent was an important factor in concluding that the defendant could reasonably have understood what conduct was proscribed by the statute.[57] In 1971, dividing 7-2 on the issue, the Court upheld a District of Columbia statute which forbade abortions, unless "done as necessary for the preservation of the mother's life or health," by a licensed physician, rejecting the contention that the statute was overly vague because it did not indicate whether "health" included mental as well as physical health.[58] Properly construed, the Court ruled, the statute permits abortions for both physical and mental health reasons, this being consistent with general usage and modern understanding of the term "health." In 1973, the Court upheld a Florida statute which forbade "the abominable and detestable crime against nature, either with mankind or with beast," on the ground that it had acquired a specific content in the prior decisions of the state's highest court.[59]

On the other hand, the Court ruled unconstitutional, in 1965, a Pennsylvania statute which authorized a jury to assess court costs against a defendant, even if he was acquitted, if the jury concluded that he had been guilty of "some misconduct."[60] Such a statute is so vague that it violates due process, since it includes no standards at all to guide the jury

56. United States v. National Dairy Products Corp., 372 U.S. 29 (1963).
57. Three dissenting Justices argued that United States v. Cohen Grocery Co., 255 U.S. 81 (1921), was controlling.
58. United States v. Vuitch, 402 U.S. 62 (1971).
59. Wainwright v. Stone, 414 U.S. 21 (1973).
60. Giaccio v. Pennsylvania, 382 U.S. 399 (1965).

in making a decision. Similarly, the following year the Court held invalid a conviction for common law criminal libel in Kentucky where the judge had defined criminal libel as "any writing calculated to create a disturbance of the peace, corrupt the public morals, or lead to any act, which, when done, is indictable."[61] Noting that the Court is especially strict where First Amendment rights are involved, Justice Douglas ruled that any law which makes an offense of conduct calculated to create disturbances of the peace leaves the standard of responsibility so wide open as to fall within the vagueness doctrine, Furthermore, in 1972, a unanimous Court set aside a conviction of the manager of a drive-in theater for violating a statute making it a crime to display an obscene motion picture.[62] In affirming the conviction, the Washington Supreme Court had not ruled that the movie in question was obscene, under prevailing standards on the subject, but rather that the conviction should stand because some fifteen private homes and a major thoroughfare were within viewing range of the screen. The Supreme Court ruled that the statute was impermissibly vague as applied to this defendant because it failed to give him fair notice that criminal liability depended upon the place where the film was shown.[63]

In recent years, many criminal statutes dealing with such vaguely defined offenses as vagrancy, loitering, and disorderly conduct, long taken for granted, have been challenged in appellate courts on grounds of vagueness. In a landmark decision handed down in 1967, the Supreme Judicial Court of Massachusetts, in *Alegata v. Com. of Massachusetts*[64] set aside several old statutes as being unconstitutionally vague. One statute provided for punishment of an individual who, "being abroad in the night time and being suspected of unlawful design," fails to "give a satisfactory account of himself" to the police. The Court held that not only does the statute violate the rule which forbids arrest on mere suspicion, but also that it left too much discretion in the hands of the police and the courts, leaving the citizen at the mercy of the whim or caprice of policemen and judges. A second statute, dealing with vagrancy, provided for the punishment of one "who was and is an idle person who not having any visible means of support has lived without lawful employment." It was noted that this obviously vague statute was aimed at picking up derelicts or suspected criminals against whom the authorities do not have sufficient evidence to make a lawful arrest. A third statute made it an offense for one "known to be a thief and a burglar" to act "in a suspicious manner around a store." The court noted that the concept, "once a thief always a thief" was

61. Ashton v. Kentucky, 384 U.S. 195 (1966).
62. Rabe v. Washington, 405 U.S. 313 (1972).
63. See also Wright v. Georgia, 373 U.S. 284 (1963), which set aside a conviction for breach of the peace where the act complained of was not conduct prohibited by the statute.
64. 353 Mass. 287, 231 N.E. 2d 201 (1967).

abhorrent to our law, and that the statute was not only vague and indefinite, but also punished conduct which falls far short of constituting a crime.

Similarly, a unanimous Supreme Court set aside convictions in Florida under a city's vagrancy ordinance; four persons had been charged with "prowling by auto," two with being "vagabonds" and two with "loitering" and being "common thiefs."[65] The Court ruled that the ordinance was unconstitutional for two basic reasons: it was so vague that it failed to give persons of ordinary intelligence fair notice of what conduct is forbidden, and it encouraged arbitrary and erratic arrests and convictions. Other federal and state courts have in recent years held vagrancy statutes unconstitutional on such grounds.[66] In addition, though by a 5-4 vote, the Supreme Court ruled unconstitutional a city ordinance making it an offense for "three or more persons to assemble . . . on any of the sidewalks . . . and there conduct themselves in a manner annoying to persons passing by."[67] The Court majority held that the ordinance was too vague "because it subjects the exercise of the right of assembly to an unascertainable standard, and unconstitutionally broad because it authorizes the punishment of constitutionally protected conduct." The city is free, said Justice Stewart, to forbid antisocial conduct on its streets, but this can be accomplished through the enactment and enforcement of ordinances "with reasonable specificity." The dissenters thought that a person of average comprehension would know what sort of conduct is covered by the ordinance.

On the other hand, statutes and ordinances which forbid "disorderly conduct" have been sustained by the Supreme Court[68] and by many state courts.[69] Said Justice White, "The root of the vagueness doctrine is a

65. Papachristou v. City of Jacksonville, 405 U.S. 156 (1972). A similar decision was made in Palmer v. Euclid, 402 U.S. 544 (1971).

66. Ricks v. District of Columbia, 414 F.2d 1097 (D.C. Cir. 1968); Wheeler v. Goodman, 306 F. Supp. 58 (W.D. N.C. 1969); Fenster v. Leary, 20 N.Y. 2d 309, 282 N.Y.S. 2d 739, 229 N.E. 2d 426 (1967); Seattle v. Drew, 70 Wash. 2d 405, 423 P.2d 522 (1967). On the general subject see William O. Douglas, "Vagrancy and Arrest on Suspicion," *Yale Law Journal,* 70 (November 1960): 1-14; Caleb Foote, "Vagrancy-Type Law and its Administration," *University of Pennsylvania Law Review,* 104 (March 1956): 603-50; Comment, "The Vagrancy Concept Reconsidered: Problems and Abuses of Status Criminality," *New York University Law Review,* 37 (January 1962): 102-36.

67. Coates v. Cincinnati, 402 U.S. 611 (1971).

68. Colten v. Kentucky, 407 U.S. 104 (1972). In Grayned v. City of Rockford, 408 U.S. 104 (1972), the Court upheld an antinoise ordinance, Justice Marshall commenting, "Condemned to the use of words, we can never expect mathematical certainty from our language." 408 U.S. 110.

69. Alegata v. Com. of Massachusetts, 353 Mass. 287, 231 N.E. 2d 201 (1967); State v. Givens, 28 Wis. 2d 109, 135 N.W. 2d 780 (1965); State v. Reynolds, 243 Minn. 196, 66 N.W. 2d 886 (1954).

rough idea of fairness. It is not a principle designed to convert into a constitutional dilemma the practical difficulties in drawing criminal statutes both general enough to take into account a variety of human conduct and sufficiently specific to provide fair warning that certain kinds of conduct are prohibited."[70]

In the last analysis, the void-for-vagueness rule, while rarely used to defeat statutes, is always available for the judges to utilize, as a reserve weapon, in exteme situations.[71] In anything less than an extreme situation they are strongly inclined to give the legislative body the benefit of the doubt, as indeed they should.

Notice of What?

In our system of jurisprudence, people are tried for crimes. What is a crime? The emphasis of all definitions is upon the commission of an act, or an attempt, solicitation, or conspiracy to commit an act. Blackstone defined a crime as "an act committed or omitted, in violation of a public law, either forbidding or commanding it."[72] A leading treatise on criminal law defines a crime as "any wrong which the government deems injurious to the public at large, and punishes through a judicial proceeding in its own name."[73] Statutes often define the term in similar language. Thus the New York Penal Code defines an offense as "conduct for which a sentence to a term of imprisonment or to a fine is provided by any law of this state...."[74] Accordingly, the author of a standard hornbook on criminal law declares, "The general rule of the common law is that a mere intent to commit a crime, unaccompanied by any overt act was insufficient to constitute a crime."[75] The point is that men are punished, under the criminal law, for what they do, and not because of the opinions or beliefs they may entertain, or their character or lack of it, or their associations, or their reputation in the community. Even a man's loyalty, in the absence of some overt act defined by law as criminal, cannot be the basis of a trial in court.[76]

70. Colten v. Kentucky, 407 U.S. 104, 110 (1972).
71. See the remarks of Collings, "Unconstitutional Uncertainty," at p. 214: "One cannot say that the doctrine is dead. Counsel are well justified in continuing to urge it."
72. 4 Bl. Com. *5.
73. Joel P. Bishop, *New Commentaries on the Criminal Law,* 8th ed. (Chicago: T. H. Flood, 1892), I: 14.
74. N.Y. Penal Law Ann. §10.00(1) (McKinney 1975).
75. Justin Miller, *Handbook of Criminal Law* (St. Paul: West Publishing Co., 1934), p. 95.
76. See Lambert v. California, 355 U.S. 225 (1957), which held that wholly passive conduct will not support a criminal conviction; the defendant must do something, or it must be proved that he knew he had a duty to do it. Dividing 5-4, the Court held unconstitutional a city ordinance which required all exfelons to register with the police within five days of arriving in Los Angeles.

Nonjudicial bodies, such as legislative investigating committees, are apparently free to inflict punishment for mere opinion, but courts of law are bound by a strict rule limiting the conception of crime to overt acts. Thinking in an unorthodox manner is not an offense in any American criminal code. It is notice of some specific criminal act that defendants are entitled to receive, before they can be put to trial in a law court. The traditional American view was well stated by President Truman in the message in which he explained the reasons for his veto of the Internal Security Act of 1950, when he said: "There is no more fundamental axiom of American freedom than the familiar statement: in a free country, we punish men for the crimes they commit, but never for the opinions they have. And the reason this is so fundamental to freedom is not, as many suppose, that it protects the few unorthodox from suppression by the majority. To permit freedom of expression is primarily for the benefit of the majority, because it protects criticism, and criticism lead to progress."

4 / The Defendant's Right to a Fair Hearing

The Siamese twin of the due process guaranty of notice is the right to a fair hearing. In the classic language of Daniel Webster, "By the law of the land" is meant "a law, which hears before it condemns; which proceeds upon inquiry, and renders judgment only after trial."[1] Or, as Justice Field once observed, "Undoubtedly where life and liberty are involved, due process requires that there be a regular course of judicial proceedings, which imply that the party to be affected shall have notice and an opportunity to be heard. . . ."[2] The requirement of some sort of hearing, appropriate under the circumstances, is a familiar one in all branches of the law, and is by no means peculiar to the criminal law field.[3]

The Federal Context

It is always important to bear in mind that we have a federal system of government, which divides responsibility between the national and state governments. But while power is divided between them, it should never be forgotten that so far as it goes, the federal Constitution is the supreme law of the land, and therefore prevails over state law in cases of conflict. Many of the ingredients of a fair hearing are spelled out specifically in the federal Bill of Rights, but these rights are guaranteed only against the national government. The main federally enforceable guaranty of a fair hearing in the states is the Due Process Clause of the Fourteenth Amendment. The Supreme Court has consistently refused to rule that the Fourteenth Amendment applies to the states all of the procedural clauses of the federal Bill of Rights. The Court has proceeded according to a principle of selective incorporation, holding that only those procedural rights of the national Constitution which are essential to justice are binding upon the states by

  1. Argument in Dartmouth College v. Woodward, 4 Wheat. (U.S.) 518, 581 (1819).
  2. Hagar v. Reclamation District, 111 U.S. 701, 708 (1884). Justice Black has written: "A person's right to reasonable notice of a charge against him, and an opportunity to be heard in his defense—a right to his day in court—are basic in our system of jurisprudence. . . ." *In re* Oliver, 333 U.S. 257, 273 (1948).
  3. The Supreme Court has often ruled, in a wide variety of situations, that a hearing is an indispensable requirement of due process of law. For recent cases, see Wisconsin v. Constantineau, 400 U.S. 433 (1971) (public infamy); Groppi v. Leslie, 404 U.S. 496 (1972) (legislative contempt); Morrissey v. Brewer, 408 U.S. 471 (1972) (revocation of parole).

way of the Fourteenth Amendment.[4] Thus, in federal courts defendants have a right to indictment by grand jury, because the Sixth Amendment so provides, but a state has not denied due process if it abolishes this ancient procedure, and substitutes for it a bill of information filed by the public prosecutor.[5] On the other hand, the Sixth Amendment guaranty of the right to counsel has been read into the great Civil War Amendment.[6]

The principal federal ingredients of a fair hearing are listed in the Fifth and Sixth Amendments. These include such matters as grand jury indictment, freedom from double jeopardy and self-incrimination, due process of law, a speedy and public trial, an impartial jury drawn from the vicinity, confrontation of witnesses, and assistance of counsel. Other federal procedural rights are defined in statutes, in the rules of court, and in judicial decisions. About the same situation exists in the various states. Each state constitution spells out in standardized language a fairly uniform body of procedural rights, and in every state other rights are found in statutes, rules of court and court decisions. State courts, under our federal system, are the final interpreters of the meaning of state law, and only where a federal right has been denied, such as Fourteenth Amendment due process, is it possible to appeal beyond the state courts to the United States Supreme Court.

While the Supreme Court has greatly expanded the meaning of procedural due process since, roughly, 1923,[7] and a considerable area of state criminal practice now falls within the scope of federal judicial supervision, it cannot be gainsaid that the Court has proceeded with considerable caution. It has been unwilling to sit as an appellate court for the mere correction of errors that occur in the state courts, and it has not attempted to standardize all state procedures. It has repeatedly said that federal procedure is not necessarily the measure of due process, that is to say, that the Fourteenth Amendment does not require the states to observe all the procedures that prevail in the national courts. The Court has wished to inhibit neither variety nor experimentation in the states. Indeed, as Justice Jackson

---

4. See Francis A. Allen, "Due Process and State Criminal Procedures: Another Look," *Northwestern University Law Review,* 48 (March–April 1953): 16–35; Austin W. Scott, Jr., "State Criminal Procedure, The Fourteenth Amendment, and Prejudice," *Northwestern University Law Review,* 49 (July–August 1954): 319–32; John A. Gorfinkel, "The Fourteenth Amendment and State Criminal Proceedings—'Ordered Liberty' or 'Just Deserts,'" *California Law Review,* 41 (Winter 1953–54): 672–91; Jacob W. Landynski, "Due Process and the Concept of Ordered Liberty," *Hofstra Law Review,* 2 (Winter 1974): 1–66.

5. Hurtado v. California, 110 U.S. 516 (1884).

6. Powell v. California, 287 U.S. 45 (1932); Gideon v. Wainwright, 372 U.S. 335 (1963); Argersinger v. Hamlin, 407 U.S. 25 (1972).

7. Moore v. Dempsey, 261 U.S. 86 (1923).

once remarked, "The Federal Constitution does not invalidate state legislation because it fails to embody the highest wisdom or provide the best conceivable remedies."[8] In short, so far as state power is concerned, all the requirements of federal due process of law do not apply.

The Right to a Trial

Wholly apart from these technical distinctions, however, it remains true that in all of our courts, whether national or state, one who is accused of having committed a crime is entitled to have his case decided upon the basis of evidence produced at a trial in a court.[9] The Supreme Court will review the conclusions of fact of a state court where a federal right has been denied as the result of a finding shown by the record to be without evidence to support it, since this is unreasonable and arbitrary.[10]

Furthermore, it is highly improper for Congress or for any state legislature to undertake to declare an individual guilty of a crime, since the Constitution flatly forbids all bills of attainder. The ninth section of Article I declares that Congress shall not pass any bill of attainder, and the following section imposes the same prohibition upon the states.[11] This double-barreled limitation was regarded as so essential that it was put into

---

8. Cohen v. Beneficial Industrial Loan Corp., 337 U.S. 541, 550–51 (1949). Cf. the remarks of Justice Roberts in Buchalter v. New York, 319 U.S. 427, 429–30 (1943): "The due process clause of the Fourteenth Amendment requires that action by a state through any of its agencies must be consistent with the fundamental principles of liberty and justice which lie at the base of our civil and political institutions. . . . But the Amendment does not draw to itself the provisions of state constitutions or state laws. It leaves the states free to enforce their criminal laws under such statutory provisions and common law doctrines as they deem appropriate; and does not permit a party to bring to the test of a decision in this court every ruling made in the course of a trial in a state court."

9. See Specht v. Patterson, 386 U.S. 605 (1967). Of course, a defendant may waive the right to a trial by pleading guilty, but the waiver must be voluntary, and the record must show an intelligent and understanding waiver; a proper waiver will not be presumed from a silent record. Boykin v. Alabama, 395 U.S. 238 (1969). It is interesting to take note of a recent decision of the Supreme Court of California which held that it is an unconstitutional violation of due process to permit a nonlawyer justice of the peace to preside over criminal cases involving potential jail sentences. Gordon v. Justice Court, 12 Cal. 3d 323, 525 P.2d 72 (1974). The Court reasoned that since the Constitution now extends the right to counsel to all cases involving any sort of imprisonment, logic suggests that a judge qualified to comprehend and utilize counsel's legal arguments must also be regarded as a requirement of due process. The likelihood of a fair trial is substantially reduced if a layman lacking the necessary expertise serves as judge.

10. Fiske v. Kansas, 274 U.S. 380 (1927).

11. In English usage a bill of attainder which imposed something less than the death penalty was known as a bill of pains and penalties. It is established that the two bill of attainder clauses of the Constitution also forbid bills of pains and penalties. Cummings v. Missouri, 4 Wall. (U.S.) 277 (1867).

the original Constitution, before a Bill of Rights was incorporated by amendment. The conviction of persons by parliamentary statute, without a court trial, became a familiar weapon in English politics in the fifteenth century, as an instrument of royal power. But during the civil disturbances of the turbulent seventeenth century, the bill of attainder was also utilized by Parliament in its struggle against the monarchy, as in the famous attaint of the Earl of Strafford, chief minister to Charles I. The odious character of bills of attainder was so well known to the framers of the Constitution that they adopted the attainder clauses without debate.

In the *Test Oath Cases*,[12] decided soon after the Civil War, the Supreme Court held that any statute "which inflicts punishment without a judicial trial" was unconstitutional. Accordingly, state and federal statutes requiring persons to sign test oaths to the effect that they had never borne arms or committed other offenses against the United States, as a condition for practicing law, or serving as a teacher or minister, or performing other functions, were held to inflict punishment in violation of the bill of attainder clauses of the Constitution. The Court reasoned that unless the persons involved purged themselves by taking the oaths, they were assumed to be guilty of offenses and thereafter punished by being denied access to certain types of employment and other privileges.

In 1946, in the *Lovett* case,[13] the Supreme Court declared an act of Congress unconstitutional as a bill of attainder which declared three named individuals then working for the government to be ineligible for government employment. Note was taken of the historical fact that the act was based upon a finding of a House committee that these three people had engaged in "subversive activities." Justice Black ruled, for the Court, that "permanent proscription from any opportunity to serve the Government is punishment, and of a most severe type." And he observed: "When our Constitution and Bill of Rights were written, our ancestors had ample reason to know that legislative trials and punishments were too dangerous to liberty to exist in the nation of free men they envisioned."[14]

The rule is otherwise, however, where the legislature fixes general standards for public employment. The Court has ruled that a state law forbidding employment in the public service, or requiring discharge therefrom, of any person who does not execute an oath that he had not within the

---

12. Cummings v. Missouri, 4 Wall. (U.S.) 277 (1867); *Ex parte* Garland, 4 Wall. (U.S.) 333 (1867). See also Murphy and Glover Test Oath Cases, 41 Mo. 340 (1867); Burkett v. McCarty, 10 Bush 758 (Ky. 1866).

13. United States v. Lovett, 328 U.S. 303 (1946). For a trenchant criticism of this decision, see Wylie H. Davis, "United States v. Lovett and the Attainder Bogy in Modern Legislation," *Washington University Law Quarterly,* 1950 (Winter 1950): 13–45.

14. 328 U.S. 316, 318.

preceding five years advocated the unlawful overthrow of government or belonged to an organization so believing, presented no attainder issue.[15] The Court was "unable to conclude that punishment is imposed by a general regulation which merely provides standards of qualification and eligibility for employment." The *Lovett* case, it was pointed out, did not deal with "general and prospectively operative standards of qualification and eligibility for public employment," but rather with named individual employees.

Many states provide in their constitutions and statutes that a conviction for a certain type or class of crimes disqualifies the individual so convicted from holding public office, or voting, or serving on juries, or imposes other disabilities. But the general rule is that a full pardon restores all the rights of citizenship. It has been said that "the pardon obliterates the fact of conviction, and makes it as if it never was."[16] This is somewhat of an exaggeration, however, for while a pardon may restore civil rights, it can't restore the convict's good reputation, for lack of which he may be barred from practicing medicine or law, or suffer other disabilities. It has been observed that "a pardon no longer carries the connotation of innocence. The legal shackles are removed, but the marks of the irons remain."[17]

Generally speaking, the right to a trial prevails also in civil cases involving the uses of property, though there are exceptional situations of great public emergency which have been held to justify summary administrative action without a previous hearing.[18] Even in these instances, however, some sort of judicial hearing may be sought after the event. Similarly, more or less summary and quite informal procedures, including trial without jury, are often used in connection with petty offenses, such as minor traffic violations, violations of local sanitary or building laws, breaches of the peace, and cases of nonsupport. The Supreme Court has explained that at the time of the adoption of the Constitution there were numerous petty offenses which were tried summarily, without a jury, by the justices of peace in

15. Garner v. Board of Public Works of Los Angeles, 341 U.S. 716 (1951).
16. Jones v. Board of Registrars, 56 Miss. 766, 31 Am. Rep. 385 (1879).
17. Note, "The Legal Status of Convicts During and After Incarceration" *Virginia Law Review*, 37 (January 1951): 105–17, 114. See also Note, "Civil Death Statutes—Medieval Fiction in a Modern World," *Harvard Law Review*, 50 (April 1937): 968–77.
18. Some well-known precedents: North American Cold Storage Co. v. Chicago, 211 U.S. 306 (1908) (condemnation of spoiled food in a cold storage plant); Murray's Lessee v. Hoboken Land & Improvement Co., 18 How. (U.S.) 272 (1856) (summary seizure of property of defaulting public officer). See the carefully reasoned argument in Affonso Bros. v. Brock, 29 C.A. 2d 26, 84 P.2d 515 (1938), where the Court of Appeals for the Third District of California sustained the summary destruction of diseased dairy cattle without previous notice or hearing.

England and by police magistrates in the colonies.[19] Such a practice was not in its view fundamentally unfair.

Juvenile Delinquency Proceedings

While the departures from normal trial procedures are permissible in certain situations, nevertheless it remains true that such procedures must be fair. In a well-known decision upholding the procedures of the Children's Court in cases of juvenile delinquency, the New York Court of Appeals pointed out, "There must be a reasonably definite charge. The customary rules of evidence shown by long experience as essential to getting at the truth with reasonable certainty in civil trials must be adhered to. The finding of fact must rest on the preponderance of evidence adduced under those rules. Hearsay, opinion, gossip, bias, prejudice, trends of hostile neighborhood feeling, the hopes and fears of social workers, are all sources of error and have no more place in Children's Courts than in any other court."[20]

This statement by the New York Court of Appeals was made in 1932; while it pointed in the right direction, the Supreme Court has in recent decisions gone far beyond the implications of this statement so far as the rights of juveniles are concerned. The die was cast in 1967, in the landmark case of *In re Gault*,[21] in which the Supreme Court served notice that at least some due process rights constitutionally available to adults must be regarded as applying to juveniles accused of delinquent behavior. In this instance, a fifteen-year-old boy in Arizona was taken into custody, for allegedly making obscene phone calls to a woman, and without notice of charges, a hearing was held on the following day in the judge's chambers at which the complainant was not present, and no one gave sworn testimony. The evidence consisted merely in a statement by the arresting police officer that Gault had admitted making the lewd remarks. Gault had not been advised of his right to remain silent, and was throughout without the assistance of counsel. The Court ruled that he had been denied due process in that there had been no notice of charges to Gault or his parents, counsel was neither offered nor provided, no warning had been given regarding the privilege against self-incrimination, which had not been waived, and the boy had been denied the right of confrontation, since no witnesses were sworn and subjected to cross-examination. Stressing the indispensability of due process of law for the protection of individual freedom, Justice Fortas

---

19. District of Columbia v. Clawans, 300 U.S. 617 (1937). The offense in this case was held to be a petty one, though punishable by a jail sentence of ninety days.
20. People v. Lewis, 260 N.Y. 171, 183 N.E. 353, 355, 86 A.L.R. 1001 (1932).
21. 387 U.S. 1 (1967).

made the striking observation that "under our Constitution, the condition of being a boy does not justify a kangaroo court."[22] At the same time, the Court insisted that it was not undermining the juvenile court system, that juveniles can still be handled separately from adults, and treated as delinquents rather than as criminals. The kindly judge approach is still valid, provided that certain basic rights essential for justice are protected, such as the rights to charges, counsel, confrontation and the privilege against self-incrimination. This decision left open the question as to which other rights juveniles can legitimately claim.

Litigation involving this issue quickly reached the Supreme Court. In the case of *In re Winship*[23] the Court ruled that the burden of proving guilt beyond a reasonable doubt was a requirement of due process, and so essential to justice that it applies to juvenile proceedings just as it applies to ordinary criminal trials of adults. In this instance a New York juvenile court judge had determined the guilt of a twelve-year-old boy accused of stealing money on the basis of a finding that the conclusion he reached was supported by a preponderance of evidence, frankly acknowledging that the proof might not establish guilt beyond a reasonable doubt. The Court declared that the standard of proof beyond a reasonable doubt "is a prime instrument for reducing the risk of convictions resting on factual error. The standard provides concrete substance for the presumption of innocence...."[24] In addition, Justice Brennan argued that use of the reasonable doubt standard will not affect adversely such aspects of juvenile proceedings as confidentiality, flexibility, speed, informality, and individualized postadjudicatory treatment.[25] On the other hand, the following year the Court ruled that the right to jury trial does not accrue in juvenile delinquency proceedings.[26] In the plurality opinion, Justice Blackmun argued that jury trial would invite delay, formality, and the clamor of the adversary

22. 387 U.S. 28. In Kent v. United States, 383 U.S. 541 (1966), the Court held, in a 5-4 decision, that when a juvenile judge elects to waive jurisdiction, so that the defendant can be tried in a regular criminal court, due process requires the judge to hold a hearing on the issue of waiver of jurisdiction.
23. 397 U.S. 358 (1970).
24. 397 U.S. 363.
25. Chief Justice Burger and Justices Stewart and Black dissented. The Chief Justice expressed the hope that this decision "will not spell the end of a generously conceived program of compassionate treatment intended to mitigate the rigors and trauma of exposing youthful offenders to a traditional criminal court...." 397 U.S. 376. In Ivan v. City of New York, 407 U.S. 203 (1972), the Court held that the rule of the Winship case should be given complete retroactive effect on the ground that the issue relates substantially to the truth-finding function of the courts. The Supreme Court of Illinois held that the reasonable doubt standard applied to juvenile proceedings on the basis of the Gault decision alone, three years before Winship was adjudicated. *In re* Urbasek, 38 Ill. 2d 535, 232 N.E. 2d 716 (1967).
26. McKiever v. Pennsylvania, 403 U.S. 528 (1971).

system, all of which the juvenile court idea was intended to avoid. Three dissenting Justices maintained that juveniles accused of crime are entitled to the same procedural protection available to adults. This would in effect constitute an abandonment of the juvenile court idea, and clearly a majority of the Justices do not wish to go that far. Whether juveniles are entitled to other rights when involved in delinquency proceedings will depend upon the outcome of future litigation, and undoubtedly the Court will prefer to decide one issue at a time.

The Right to be Present at the Trial

The accused has a right to be present at every stage of his trial, so that he may advise with his lawyer and face his accusers. Rule 43 of the Federal Rules of Criminal Procedure states that "the defendant shall be present at the arraignment, at every stage of the trial including the impaneling of the jury and the return of the verdict, and at the imposition of sentence. . . ." It follows, as the Court has ruled, that a judge may not communicate with the jury,[27] or impose sentence,[28] in the absence of the defendant. But in 1934 the Supreme Court held, in a 5–4 decision, that a state has not violated due process by permitting the judge and jury, along with counsel on both sides, to view the actual scene of the crime without the presence of the defendant, who had demanded the right to go along.[29] Even though the trial judge had instructed the jury that the view was part of the evidence, the majority of the Court, speaking through Justice Cardozo, took the position that the presence of the defendant was necessary to due process only to the extent that a fair and just hearing would be thwarted by his absence. It was felt that the defendant's absence from the view didn't make much difference.

While the defendant has a right to be present at his trial, he does not have a right to defeat justice by voluntarily absenting himself from the proceedings. Rule 43 is clear on this point: "In prosecutions for offenses not punishable by death, the defendant's voluntary absence after the trial has been commenced in his presence shall not prevent continuing the trial to and including the return of the verdict." This is a restatement of several Court decisions holding that voluntary absence in noncapital cases constitutes a waiver of the right to be present.[30] Furthermore, a defendant cannot defeat justice through unruly and boisterous behavior in the courtroom. The Court ruled in 1970 that "a defendant can lose his right to be

27. Shields v. United States, 273 U.S. 583 (1927).
28. United States v. Behrens, 375 U.S. 162 (1963).
29. Snyder v. Massachusetts, 291 U.S. 97 (1934). Justice Roberts dissented with great vigor.
30. Diaz v. United States, 223 U.S. 442 (1912); Taylor v. United States, 414 U.S. 17 (1973).

present at trial if, after he has been warned by the judge that he will be removed if he continues his disruptive behavior, he nevertheless insists on conducting himself in a manner so disorderly, disruptive, and disrespectful of the court that his trial cannot be carried on with him in the courtroom."[31] Holding that "dignity, order, and decorum" are essential in the proper administration of justice, the Court ruled that the obstreperous defendant may, in the discretion of the trial judge, be bound and gagged, or cited for contempt, or taken out of the courtroom until he promises to conduct himself properly. Of course, removal from the courtroom is not a pleasant thing to do, but, said Justice Black, "it would degrade our country and our judicial system to permit our courts to be bullied, insulted, and humiliated and their orderly progress thwarted and obstructed by defendants brought before them charged with crimes."[32] As Justice Brennan observed in a concurring opinion, "due process does not require the presence of the defendant if his presence means that there will be no orderly process at all."[33]

The Necessity of Presenting Evidence in Court

An indispensable element of a fair hearing is the right to have all the evidence presented in court, under the direction of the judge, who administers the laws of evidence. This is essential, above all, for purposes of cross-examination and objection by counsel for the accused, and for the presentation of rebuttal evidence. It is well established, however, that in exceptional circumstances a judge may make some decisions upon the basis of out-of-court evidence, provided that it does not bear directly on the central issue of guilt or innocence. Just as the Supreme Court has ruled that a federal judge has considerable latitude in devising procedures for framing relief in antitrust cases to implement a judgment,[34] so it has been held that a state trial judge has not violated due process when, following conviction of a defendant, he consults out-of-court sources before deciding upon the sentence.[35] English and American courts have always had a wide discretion in determining sentence, and in consulting sources and various types of evidence to assist in arriving at the sentence.[36]

31. Illinois v. Allen, 397 U.S. 337, 343 (1970).

32. 397 U.S. 346. On the procedure for dealing with an unruly defendant through the contempt power, see Mayberry v. Pennsylvania, 400 U.S. 455 (1971). Justice Douglas wrote feelingly that "these brazen efforts to denounce, insult, and slander the court and to paralyze the trial are at war with the concept of justice under law." 400 U.S. 462.

33. 397 U.S. 350.

34. Besser Manufacturing Co. v. United States, 343 U.S. 444 (1952). Said Justice Jackson, at p. 449, "It is true that the procedure adopted below is an innovation in certain respects, but novelty is not synonymous with error."

35. Williams v. New York, 337 U.S. 241 (1949).

36. Rule 32(c) of the Federal Rules of Criminal Procedure provides for the consideration by federal judges of presentence investigations and reports of probation officers.

The Court has also noted that there are sound, practical reasons for making a distinction between the evidentiary rules governing trial and those governing sentencing. The trial is limited narrowly to strictly relevant evidence, to avoid waste of time and confusion, and to prevent influencing the court by evidence of other misconduct. But a sentencing judge is not limited to the issue of guilt, his task being to decide upon a type of punishment within the statutory limits. It is both relevant and essential for the judge to have in his possession the fullest possible information. Furthermore, the philosophy of modern penology emphasizes individualizing the punishment to fit the offender and not merely the crime. The distinction between first and repeated offenders, the general use of indeterminate sentences, probation and parole systems, all rely heavily upon nonjudicial implementation. The due process clause, said Justice Black, should not be treated "as a uniform command that courts throughout the Nation abandon their age-old practice of seeking information from out-of-court sources to guide their judgment toward a more enlightened and just sentence. . . . The due process clause should not be treated as a device for freezing the evidential procedure of sentencing in the mold of trial procedure. So to treat the due process clause would hinder if not preclude all courts—state and federal—from making progressive efforts to improve the administration of justice."[37]

Similarly, in *Spencer* v. *Texas*,[38] decided by a 5–4 vote in 1967, the Court ruled the Texas habitual-criminal statute, which permitted the trial jury to be fully informed of the defendant's previous convictions, did not violate due process, because the jury was charged by the court not to consider such matters in determining the issue of guilt or innocence on the pending charge. The Court held that a two-part jury trial is not compelled as a matter of constitutional law, and that the jury is expected to follow the judge's limiting instructions. In dissent, Chief Justice Warren argued that in recidivist cases there is no connection between the evidence of prior offenses and the guilt or innocence of the accused in the immediate case.

Furthermore, the Court has ruled that a person legally convicted and sentenced to death has no constitutional right to a judicial trial, after sentence, on the question of insanity.[39] Its theory was that postponement of execution by the governor because of insanity is not like a trial for a crime, but rather bears a close affinity to reprieves of sentence, which spring from the executive power of clemency. On the other hand, it is well established that a defendant is constitutionally entitled to a hearing on the issue of his

37. Williams v. New York, 337 U.S. 250–51 (1949).
38. 385 U.S. 554 (1967).
39. Solesbee v. Balkcom, 339 U.S. 9 (1950). Justice Frankfurter dissented alone in a long and spirited opinion in which he argued that due process forbids a state to execute an insane person, and this being so, then it is not within the benevolent discretion of a state to ignore rudimentary safeguards in establishing the fact of insanity.

competence to stand trial, since it is a violation of due process for a state to convict an accused person while he is legally incompetent.[40]

Apart from special circumstances dealing with questions arising after trial, the defendant has a right to a full hearing on all the evidence touching on questions of guilt or innocence. He has a right to know what evidence is presented, and, subject to reasonable control by the judge, to cross-examine those who testify against him.[41] Thus, any private contact with a juror during a trial is presumptively prejudicial, since evidence must be admitted in pursuance of known rules, under direction of the court, with full knowledge of the parties.[42]

The Right of Confrontation

It must be emphasized that in an American court of law, the accused has a right to confront his accusers and cross-examine them. The Sixth Amendment says explicitly that he has a right "to be confronted with the witnesses against him," and this is no more than a restatement of a very old common law rule dating from around 1600. The government cannot use a witness without submitting him to cross-examination.[43] Indeed, one of the relatively few cases in which the Supreme Court has held an act of Congress unconstitutional involved just this issue.[44] An 1875 statute provided that if a person stealing property from the United States has been convicted, "then the judgment against him shall be conclusive evidence in the prosecution against [the] receiver that the property of the United States therein described has been embezzled, stolen or purloined." The Court ruled that this violated the Sixth Amendment, noting that instead of being confronted with the witnesses to controvert, if possible, a vital fact, the defendant was confronted only with the record of another criminal prosecution with which he had had no connection, in which he never had a right to participate, and the evidence in which was not given in his presence. But the Court took notice of the historic exception to the general rule of confrontation in connection with the admissibility of dying declarations, "an exception which arises from the necessity of the case." Furthermore, by a statute adopted in 1936,[45] Congress made admissible as

---

40. Pate v. Robinson, 383 U.S. 375 (1966). On the requirements of due process with reference to the continuing commitment of mental defectives, see Jackson v. Indiana, 406 U.S. 715 (1972); McNeil v. Director, Patuxent Institution, 407 U.S. 245 (1972). In effect, these cases held that an indeterminate or permanent commitment requires a judicial determination.

41. District of Columbia v. Clawans, 300 U.S. 617 (1937).

42. Remmer v. United States, 347 U.S. 227 (1954).

43. Alford v. United States, 282 U.S. 687 (1931); United States v. Douglas, 155 F.2d 894 (7th Cir. 1946).

44. Kirby v. United States, 174 U.S. 47 (1899).

45. 28 U.S.C. §1732 (1970). See also Rule 26 of the Federal Rules of Criminal Procedure.

evidence in any federal court any writing or record made in the regular course of any business.

It has been held, however, that a defendant has no cause to complain if he himself persuaded a witness to absent himself from the trial.[46]

The government cannot, in a criminal case, decline to disclose the identity of the accusers on the ground that they are informers, or because what they know are state secrets. If the government has evidence which is directly relevant to the defendant's case, the government must make the choice between producing the evidence or dropping its prosecution. One Court of Appeals has even ruled that the government may not refuse to produce this evidence on the ground that it is privileged,[47] since one accused of crime is entitled to use evidence of any sort which may tend to prove his innocence.

This was vividly illustrated in the well-known *Coplon* case,[48] where the Court of Appeals for the Second Circuit ruled that a federal trial judge violated the Sixth Amendment by refusing to disclose to the accused evidence secured by wiretapping on the ground that the disclosure might be dangerous to national security. Said Judge Learned Hand,

[W]e can see no significant distinction between introducing evidence against an accused which he is not allowed to see, and denying him the right to put in evidence on his own behalf. . . . Few weapons in the arsenal of freedom are more useful than the power to compel a government to disclose the evidence on which it seeks to forfeit the liberty of its citizens. All governments, democracies as well as autocracies, believe that those they seek to punish are guilty; the impediment of constitutional barriers are galling to all governments when they prevent the consummation of that just purpose. But those barriers were devised and are precious because they prevent that purpose and its pursuit from passing unchallenged by the accused, and unpurged by the alembic of public scrutiny and public criticism. A society which has come to wince at such exposure of the methods by which it seeks to impose its will upon its members, has already lost the feel of freedom and is on the path towards absolutism.

Judge Hand's position was dramatically affirmed by the Supreme Court, in June 1957, in the much-discussed case of *Jencks* v. *United States*.[49] Jencks, a trade union official, had been convicted of falsely swearing when he filed with the National Labor Relations Board a Taft-Hartley non-Communist affidavit. All of the government's evidence was circumstantial, and the prosecution leaned heavily on the testimony of two informers, Harvey F. Matusow and J. W. Ford, who had been Communist Party members paid by the FBI to make oral and written reports of Communist activities. The Supreme Court ruled that the trial judge had

---

46. Reynolds v. United States, 98 U.S. 145, 158 (1878).
47. United States v. Krulewitch, 145 F.2d 76 (2d Cir. 1944).
48. United States v. Coplon, 185 F.2d 629 (2d Cir. 1950).
49. 353 U.S. 657 (1957).

committed reversible error in refusing to direct the government to produce the reports which these witnesses had made to the FBI for inspection and use in cross-examination. The Court held that the request was a proper one since Matusow and Ford had testified that their reports dealt with events and activities related to their testimony, and the demand was for the production of specific documents, and not merely part of a broad or blind fishing expedition. Justice Brennan pointed out that "every experienced trial judge and trial lawyer knows the value for impeaching purposes of statements of the witness recording the events before time dulls treacherous memory." He also emphasized that the interest of the United States in a criminal case is not to win it, but to see that justice is done. Of course the United States may feel that the protection of vital national interests militates against public disclosure of documents in its possession, but it can invoke its evidentiary privilege only at the price of letting the defendant go free.

Finally, in 1965, in the landmark case of *Pointer* v. *Texas*,[50] a unanimous Supreme Court ruled that the Sixth Amendment right of the accused "to be confronted with the witnesses against him" was applicable to the states by way of Fourteenth Amendment due process. The reasoning of the Court was that the right of confrontation is fundamental to a fair trial because cross-examination is extremely valuable in exposing falsehood and bringing out the truth. Pointer had been arrested in Texas on a charge of robbery, and taken before a state judge for a preliminary hearing. At this hearing the district attorney questioned witnesses, including the complainant, but since Pointer was without counsel, there was no cross-examination. Then the complaining witness moved to California, with no intention of returning. At the trial the state offered the transcript of the testimony the complaining witness gave at the preliminary hearing as evidence, over objections of Pointer's counsel. On these facts, since this testimony was not subject to cross-examination, the defendant was in effect denied the right of confrontation.[51]

While the Court has ruled that the defendant's right of confrontation may be waived, provided that the waiver is made expressly, intelligently, and knowingly,[52] it has since 1965 made a considerable number of rulings on the issue. Thus, it is improper to admit into evidence the confession of an accomplice which is not subject to cross-examination.[53] It is also a

50. 380 U.S. 400 (1965).

51. The rule is otherwise where testimony given at an earlier trial, subject to cross-examination, is read to the jury, the witness now being unavailable through residence in a foreign country. Mancusi v. Stubbs, 408 U.S. 204 (1972). See also Mattox v. United States, 156 U.S. 237 (1895), where testimony given at a former trial was permitted to be read to the jury, after the death of the witness, at a later trial.

52. Brookhart v. Janis, 384 U.S. 1 (1966).

53. Douglas v. Alabama, 380 U.S. 415 (1965). A similar ruling was made in Chambers v. Mississippi, 410 U.S. 284 (1973).

denial of the constitutional right of confrontation for the trial court to refuse to permit defendant's counsel to ask the principal prosecution witness, an informer, to give his correct name and address, since this bears directly on the issue of credibility.[54] In another case, the Court reached a similar conclusion where the trial judge refused to permit any questions concerning the previous crimes of a juvenile who was a crucial witness for the prosecution, since these questions relate to such important matters as motivation, bias, and credibility.[55] The state's interest in seeking to preserve the anonymity of a juvenile offender must yield to the vital constitutional right of confrontation, which is "paramount" to the state's policy. Furthermore, the absence of a witness from the jurisdiction does not justify the use at the trial of preliminary hearing testimony unless the state has made a good faith effort to secure the witness's presence.[56] While the witness was in a federal prison outside the state, it was noted that it is the policy of the U.S. Bureau of Prisons to permit federal prisoners to testify in state criminal proceedings pursuant to writs of habeas corpus *ad testificandum* issued out of a state court.

In the case of *Parker* v. *Gladden*[57] the Court made an interesting application of the confrontation rule. Following conviction for second degree murder, it came to the attention of the defendant that during the eight-day trial, the court bailiff assigned to look after the sequestered jury had expressed the opinion to jurors that the accused was a wicked, guilty man, and had advised them not to fear bringing a verdict of guilt, since any mistake could be corrected by appeal. The Supreme Court ruled that what this amounted to was that the bailiff gave testimony not subject to cross-examination. Since the bailiff holds an official position which carries great weight with the jury, the Court ruled that extreme prejudice was inherent in the situation.

Finally, there have been a number of recent cases in the Supreme Court involving the use of confessions of codefendants not subject to cross-examination,[58] the use at the trial of testimony given at the preliminary hearing,[59] or the admission of out-of-court statements of a coconspirator made

---

54. Smith v. Illinois, 390 U.S. 129 (1968).
55. Davis v. Alaska, 415 U.S. 308 (1974).
56. Barber v. Page, 390 U.S. 719 (1968). The rule of this case was given retroactive application in Berger v. California, 393 U.S. 314 (1969), on the ground that the integrity of the fact-finding process was involved.
57. 385 U.S. 363 (1966).
58. Bruton v. United States, 391 U.S. 123 (1968), overruling Delli Paoli v. United States, 352 U.S. 232 (1957); Frazier v. Cupp, 394 U.S. 731 (1969). Denial of the defendant's constitutional right of confrontation by means of admission in evidence of the confession of a codefendant who did not testify was held to be harmless error where all the other evidence against the accused was overwhelming. Harrington v. California, 393 U.S. 250 (1969).
59. California v. Green, 399 U.S. 149 (1970).

during the concealment phase of the conspiracy.⁶⁰ In effect, the Court ruled that the confrontation clause did not have the effect of codifying common law rules on hearsay, and that the right to question the witness at the trial, or the relative unimportance of the departure from usual hearsay rules, may warrant the conclusion that the defendant had a fair trial.

Compulsory Process to Secure Witnesses

The common law rule that a defendant did not have a right to present his own witnesses was set aside by parliamentary statutes adopted around 1700. The right of a defendant not only to offer witnesses, but to invoke the aid of government to compel their appearance is guaranteed in both state and federal law. The Sixth Amendment states that in all criminal prosecutions the accused shall have the right "to have compulsory process for obtaining witnesses in his favor." In addition, ever since 1790 a federal statute has assured a defendant in capital cases the right "to make any proof that he can produce by lawful witnesses, and shall have the like process of the court to compel his witnesses to appear at his trial, as is usually granted to compel witnesses to appear on behalf of the prosecution."⁶¹ It is established, however, that the government is not obliged to pay the expenses of defense witnesses subpoenaed to appear, unless the defendant is indigent.

The right to have compulsory process for obtaining witnesses is assured in most state constitutions, in statutes, and in common law pronouncements. In addition, in 1967, by unanimous vote, in the case of *Washington v. Texas*,⁶² the Supreme Court ruled that this Sixth Amendment right is so fundamental and essential to a fair trial that it is a requirement of due process binding the states. The Court ruled unconstitutional a Texas statute which provided that persons charged as principals, accomplices, or accessories to the same crime could not testify in behalf of one another. It held that the right to present a defense must include the right to present the defendant's version of the facts to the jury. It follows that a state trial judge denies due process if he admonishes a witness offered by the defense in such unnecessarily strong terms that the witness refuses to testify at all.⁶³

---

60. Dutton v. Evans, 400 U.S. 74 (1970). See also Nelson v. O'Neil, 402 U.S. 622 (1971), holding that where a jointly tried codefendant took the stand after his incriminating out-of-court statement implicating the defendant was admitted into evidence, and denied making the statement and testified favorably to the defendant as to underlying facts, there was no violation of the right of confrontation.

61. 18 U.S.C. §3005 (1970).

62. 388 U.S. 14 (1967).

63. Webb v. Texas, 409 U.S. 95 (1972).

The Ex Post Facto Rule

A basic principle of our public law is that one is always permitted to do, with impunity, whatever is not forbidden by law. This is an indispensable element of a free society, in which freedom is always the rule and restraint is the exception. One cannot even be punished by government for committing antisocial acts, unless such acts are forbidden by the law. Needless to say, however voluminous modern criminal codes may be, they do not cover the whole range of human misconduct. Furthermore, it is a fundamental requirement of our legal order that one cannot be punished for an act which was innocent (i.e., not forbidden) when done. Any attempt to punish someone by virtue of a statute adopted after the act occurred would be set aside by our courts as being *ex post facto*. So important is the *ex post facto* principle that the original Constitution (Article I, Sections 9 and 10) specifically forbade both the national and the state governments to violate it. It declares that neither Congress nor the states shall "pass" an *ex post facto* law. As in the case of the attainder clauses, this prohibition was a product of English experience with retrospective parliamentary legislation, used largely as a weapon of political warfare.

At a very early date the Supreme Court decided, in *Calder* v. *Bull*,[64] that the *ex post facto* clauses apply only to criminal legislation, and not to retroactive civil statutes. The Court relied upon the origin of the practice in English law, the technical meaning developed by certain commentators and judges, and upon the fact that the legal tender and obligation of contract clauses of the Constitution were designed to protect civil interests. If the *ex post facto* prohibition was intended to apply to civil cases, Justice Chase maintained, in what has come to be regarded as the leading opinion, then such guarantees as that which forbids the impairment of the obligation of contract would be superfluous and unnecessary. While impressive arguments have been made to show that the *ex post facto* clauses were intended to prohibit all retroactive civil legislation, the real mischief aimed at historically being retroactive statutes of every variety adopted by legislatures,[65] the doctrine of *Calder* v. *Bull* has always prevailed, and is hardly challengeable today. It is also established that the prohibition applies only to retroactive changes in the criminal law by legislation, and not to changes in law brought about by judicial inter-

---

64. 3 Dall. (U.S.) 386 (1798).
65. See the appendix of Justice William Johnson in 2 Peters (U.S.) 681 (1829); Oliver P. Field, "Ex Post Facto in the Constitution," *Michigan Law Review,* 20 (January 1922): 315–31; B. T. De Witt, "Are Our Legal-Tender Laws Ex Post Facto?" *Political Science Quarterly,* 15 (1900): 96–111; William Winslow Crosskey, *Politics and the Constitution* (Chicago: University of Chicago Press, 1953), vol. I, chap. 11.

pretation.[66] The Court's view has been that the clauses refer only to the making of laws, and not to their construction by the courts. But it also holds that the provision reaches every form in which the legislative power of the state is exerted, whether it be a statute, a constitutional provision, a municipal ordinance, or an administrative rule or regulation.

Actually, the term *ex post facto* law reaches any retrospective change in the criminal law which works a substantial disadvantage to the defendant. A famous and concise definition by Justice Washington went as follows: "An *ex post facto* law is one which in its operation makes that criminal or penal, which was not so at the time the action was performed; or which increases the punishment; or in short, which, in relation to the offence, or its consequences, alters the situation of a party, to his disadvantage."[67]

Since the hallmark of a criminal statute is that it inflicts punishment, it becomes a matter of great importance to determine what constitutes punishment. In one of the Reconstruction cases the Court held that an act of Congress which disqualified certain people for the practice of law because of past conduct imposed punishment in violation of the *ex post facto* clause.[68] But on the whole the Court has limited the concept of punishment to the rather traditional confines of the criminal law. For example, the Court has consistently refused to rule that the deportation of aliens is punishment in this sense, and hence it has held many times that Congress may deport aliens for acts, such as membership in the Communist Party,[69] which were perfectly legal when done, or which were not described as grounds for deportation when they occurred.[70] Furthermore, our courts have refused to rule that discharge from public employment is punishment within the meaning of the *ex post facto* clauses.[71] The cancellation of naturalization certificates[72] and the imposition of penalties for tax delinquencies[73] have also been held not to constitute punishment in this sense.

Any change in the law which increases the penalties for the commission

---

66. Ross v. Oregon, 227 U.S. 150 (1913). For a discussion of the reasons for this decision see Breck P. McAllister, "Ex Post Facto Laws in the Supreme Court of the United States," *California Law Review,* 15 (May 1927): 269–88, 272.

67. United States v. Hall, 2 Wash. C.C. 366, 26 Fed. Cas. 84, 86, No. 15,285 (C.C.D. Pa. 1809).

68. *Ex parte* Garland, 4 Wall. (U.S.) 333 (1867). But the Court held later that the state can change the rules for the practice of medicine on people not previously admitted to practice, Dent v. West Virginia, 129 U.S. 114 (1889).

69. Galvan v. Press, 347 U.S. 522 (1954).

70. Harisiades v. Shaughnessy, 342 U.S. 580 (1952); Mahler v. Eby, 264 U.S. 32 (1924).

71. See the remarks of Circuit Judge Prettyman in Bailey v. Richardson, 182 F.2d 46, 57 (D.C. Cir. 1950), aff'd. by an evenly divided Court, 341 U.S. 918 (1951); Garner v. Board of Public Works of Los Angeles, 341 U.S. 716, 722 (1951).

72. Johannessen v. United States, 225 U.S. 227 (1912).

73. Bankers Trust Co. v. Blodgett, 260 U.S. 647 (1923).

of crime is regarded as *ex post facto*.[74] But the Court has ruled that a retroactive change in the method of execution from hanging to electrocution was not invalid, since the change was to a more humane method.[75] Furthermore, a habitual offender statute imposing a more severe penalty for an additional offense after the first two has been upheld in the case of a person who committed his first two offenses before the statute was enacted, on the theory that although the punishment was for the new crime only, it was well within the legislature's power to consider past conduct in fixing punishments.[76] Similarly, a state legislature may provide that one who has been convicted of a felony shall no longer be eligible to engage in the practice of medicine, and apply it to a physician who had been convicted of a felony before the statute was adopted.[77] The Court held that the legislation was not an additional punishment for past offenses, but rather that it prescribed qualifications reasonably related to the issue of professional competence.

Changes in the mode of conducting the trial or in the rules of evidence, to the defendant's substantial disadvantage, are also *ex post facto*. It is agreed that no one has a vested interest in all existing rules of evidence, which in fact are in a state of almost continuous flux. The crucial issue for any particular defendant is whether the effect of the change was substantial, and this, of course, depends upon an assessment of all the circumstances. Thus in a well-known case the Court ruled that a shift from a jury of twelve to a jury of eight was such a change.[78] The theory was that it is simply easier for the state to persuade eight jurors instead of twelve. But a statute which merely enlarged the class of persons who may be competent to testify in criminal cases has been upheld on the ground that it did not alter the amount or measure of proof necessary for a conviction.[79] Finally,

---

74. Lindsey v. Washington, 301 U.S. 397 (1937); Kring v. Missouri, 107 U.S. 221 (1883); Holden v. Minnesota, 137 U.S. 483 (1890); *In re* Medley, 134 U.S. 160 (1890).

75. Malloy v. South Carolina, 237 U.S. 180 (1915). Some courts have held that any change in the method of punishment, whether more severe or not, falls within the *ex post facto* prohibition. See, e.g., Shepherd v. People, 25 N.Y. 406 (Crt. App. 1862), which disapproved of a retroactive change of the penalty from death to life imprisonment at hard labor. This is not the usual rule. See Com. v. Wyman, 12 Cush. (Mass.) 237 (1853); McGuire v. State, 76 Miss. 504, 25 So. 495 (1899). It is generally taken for granted that rational people desire to live as long as possible.

76. McDonald v. Massachusetts, 180 U.S. 311 (1901); Gryger v. Burke, 334 U.S. 728 (1948).

77. Hawker v. New York, 170 U.S. 189 (1898).

78. Thompson v. Utah, 170 U.S. 343 (1898).

79. Hopt v. Utah, 110 U.S. 574, 589 (1884). For other cases holding retroactive alterations in the mode of trial to be valid as not effecting substantial changes to the disadvantage of the defendant, see Thompson v. Missouri, 171 U.S. 380 (1898) (use of handwriting experts); Beazell v. Ohio, 269 U.S. 167 (1925) (separate trials); Duncan v. Missouri, 152 U.S. 377 (1894) (changes in structure of appellate court); Gibson v. Mississippi, 162 U.S. 565 (1896) (selection of jurors).

a statute is not *ex post facto* if it merely forbids the continuance of an act which was originally legal, the punishment being not for the original act, but for continuing beyond the date of enactment of the statute. Thus, in one of the earliest prosecutions under the Sherman Anti-Trust Act, the Court rejected the defense argument that the agreements in question had been entered into prior to the passage of the statute, pointing out that "the continuation of the agreement, after it has been declared to be illegal, becomes a violation of the act."[80]

The Burden of Proof

Not only is the defendant entitled to examine the evidence against him. In a more fundamental sense, there can be no conviction without incriminating evidence, since it is a basic assumption in American law, state and federal, that all men are presumptively innocent, and that it is therefore the duty and responsibility of the prosecution to assume the burden of proving guilt. One does not have to prove to a court his innocence of crime; the prosecution, on the contrary, must prove his guilt. State criminal codes usually say as much. For example, the Penal Code of California (§1096) declares, "A defendant in a criminal action is presumed to be innocent until the contrary is proved, and in case of a reasonable doubt whether his guilt is satisfactorily shown, he is entitled to an acquittal, but the effect of this presumption is only to place upon the state the burden of proving him guilty beyond a reasonable doubt."[81]

The function of the rule of presumption of innocence, as Wigmore points out, is "that it cautions the jury to put away from their minds all the suspicion that arises from the arrest, the indictment, and the arraignment, and to reach their conclusion solely from the legal evidence adduced."[82] But Wigmore also emphasizes that the presumption is not in

80. United States v. Trans-Missouri Freight Association, 166 U.S. 290, 342 (1897). See also Samuels v. McCurdy, 267 U.S. 188 (1925); Chicago & A. R. Co. v. Tranbarger, 238 U.S. 67 (1915).

81. This principle is deeply rooted in English jurisprudence. In the landmark case of Woolmington v. D.P.P., [1935] A.C. 462, 25 Cr. App. Rep. 72 (H.L.), the House of Lords ruled that a trial judge's instruction to the jury in which he said that since the accused had shot his wife, the law presumed him to be guilty of murder unless he could satisfy the jury that death was due to an accident, was clearly wrong. Said Lord Sankey, "No matter what the charge or where the trial, the principle that the prosecution must prove the guilt of the prisoner is part of the common law of England and no attempt to whittle it down can be entertained." [1935] A.C. 481–82.

82. John H. Wigmore, *Treatise on Evidence,* 3d ed. (Boston: Little, Brown & Co., 1940), 9: 407. See also his illuminating essay on "The Presumption of Innocence in Criminal Cases," in James Bradley Thayer, *A Preliminary Treatise on Evidence at the Common Law* (Boston: Little, Brown & Co., 1898), pp. 551–76. He writes, at p. 559, that the presumption of innocence "has, in our inherited system, a peculiarly important

and of itself evidence. "No presumption can be evidence; it is a rule about the duty of producing evidence."[83]

Justice Frankfurter once drew attention to the significance of the presumption of innocence in a dissenting opinion:

[F]rom the time that the law which we have inherited has emerged from dark and barbaric times, the conception of justice which has dominated our criminal law has refused to put an accused at the hazard of punishment if he fails to remove every reasonable doubt of his innocence in the minds of jurors. It is the duty of the Government to establish his guilt beyond a reasonable doubt. This notion—basic in our law and rightly one of the boasts of a free society—is a requirement and a safeguard of due process of law in the historic, procedural content of 'due 'process.'[84]

Thus, the Justice had no doubt that any statute which made an accused presumptively guilty would, in the light of our traditions, so outrage our sense of justice as to deny him due process.

At long last, in 1970, in the leading case of *In re Winship*,[85] the Court held that the rule which provides that the prosecution must prove guilt beyond a reasonable doubt was a requirement of constitutional due process, so that even a juvenile could not lawfully be convicted of an offense on the basis of a mere preponderance of evidence. It was pointed out that this rule plays a vital role in the American system of criminal procedure.

---

function, that of warning our untrained tribunal, the jury, against being misled by suspicion, conjecture, and mere appearances. In saying that the accused person shall be *proved* guilty, it says that he shall not be presumed guilty; that he shall be convicted only upon legal evidence, not tried upon prejudice; that he shall not be made the victim of the circumstances of suspicion which surround him, the effect of which it is always so difficult to shake off, circumstances which, if there were no emphatic rule of law upon the subject, would be sure to operate heavily against him; the circumstances, *e.g.*, that after an investigation by the grand jury he has been indicted, imprisoned, seated in the prisoner's dock, carried away handcuffed, isolated, watched, made an object of distrust to all that behold him. He shall be convicted, this rule says, not upon any mere presumption, any taking matters for granted on the strength of these circumstances of suspicion; but he shall be *proved* guilty by legal evidence, and by legal evidence which is peculiarly clear and strong—clear beyond a reasonable doubt."

83. *Treatise on Evidence,* 9: 409. See United States v. Nimerick, 118 F.2d 464, 468 (2d Cir. 1941); United States v. Dewinsky, 41 F. Supp. 149, 154 (D.C. N.J. 1941).

84. Dissenting opinion in Leland v. Oregon, 343 U.S. 790, 802 (1952). In this case the majority of the Court upheld an Oregon statute which required an accused who pleads insanity to assume the burden of proving insanity beyond a reasonable doubt. While the Court thought that due process concepts of basic justice were not violated, the rule is otherwise in federal courts, Davis v. United States, 160 U.S. 469 (1895), but this is only a rule of court and not one of constitutional necessity.

85. 397 U.S. 358 (1970). It was noted that the Court had often indicated, in dicta, "that proof of a criminal charge beyond a reasonable doubt is constitutionally required." See the numerous citations in 397 U.S. 362.

"It is a prime instrument," said Justice Brennan, "for reducing the risk of convictions resting on factual error. The standard provides concrete substance for the presumption of innocence. . . ."[86] He added that "a society that values the good name and freedom of every individual should not condemn a man for commission of a crime when there is reasonable doubt about his guilt."[87]

An interesting application of the reasonable doubt rule was made by the Court in *Cool* v. *United States*.[88] Convicted of counterfeiting, Cool had relied primarily on the exculpatory testimony of an accomplice who admitted his own guilt, but testified that Cool knew nothing about the offense. Over objection, the trial judge instructed the jury that it should not "Throw this testimony out," if it was convinced that the accomplice's testimony was true "beyond a reasonable doubt." The Court held that this instruction placed an improper burden on the defense, and in effect allowed the jury to convict despite its failure to find guilt beyond a reasonable doubt. It is permissible for the judge to tell the jury that it should receive accomplice testimony "with care and caution," but the instruction was defective in that it had the effect of substantially reducing the government's burden of proof. Indeed, its effect was to require the defendant to establish his innocence beyond a reasonable doubt.[89] The following year, however, in a 6-3 decision, the Court ruled that where a trial judge instructs the jury properly on the reasonable doubt standard and the presumption of innocence, it was not reversible error for him to tell the jury that the witnesses—all of them called by the prosecution—must be presumed to speak the truth, since he also told the jury that it was free to reject any testimony it found not trustworthy or plausible.[90] The three dissenting Justices thought that the challenged instruction in effect converted the state's burden to proving guilt by a preponderance of evidence, rather than beyond a reasonable doubt.

Finally, the 1975 decision of a unanimous Court in *Mullaney* v. *Wilbur*[91] added another dimension to the reasonable doubt standard. Maine required a defendant charged with murder, which upon conviction carried a mandatory sentence of life imprisonment, to prove that he acted in the

---

86. 397 U.S. 363.

87. 397 U.S. 363-64. The Court regards this rule as so vital to the truth-finding function of the trial that it made it fully retroactive. Ivan v. City of New York, 407 U.S. 203 (1972).

88. 409 U.S. 100 (1972).

89. Three Justices dissented, arguing that "the Court's fine-spun parsing of the trial judge's charge to the jury turns the appellate review of this case into . . . [a] 'quest for error. . . .'" 409 U.S. 105. Justice Rehnquist accused the Court of making "nice semantical distinctions," and of indulging in "scholastic jurisprudence."

90. Cupp v. Naughten, 414 U.S. 141 (1973).

91. 421 U.S. 684 (1975).

heat of passion on sudden provocation. If he could prove that, the charge was reduced from homicide to manslaughter, with the punishment a fine or imprisonment not exceeding twenty years. The Court held that the Maine rule violated the due process requirement that the prosecution must prove beyond a reasonable doubt every fact necessary to constitute the crime charged. In other words, it was incumbent upon the state to prove beyond a reasonable doubt the absence of heat of passion on sudden provocation when the issue was properly presented.

The No-Evidence Rule

In the important case of *Thompson* v. *Louisville*,[92] decided by unanimous vote in 1960, the Supreme Court expanded the meaning of due process in a very significant way. Thompson, a Negro and long-time resident of Louisville, was standing in a cafe, at the window, while waiting for a bus. The cafe manager testified that Thompson frequently patronized his establishment, and that neither he nor any customer objected to the fact that Thompson was shuffling his feet on the dance floor while he was waiting. Two police officers arrested him for loitering, and when he protested his arrest, he was also charged with disorderly conduct. The Louisville Police Court convicted him on both charges, and fined him ten dollars on each charge. Since such small fines were not appealable to or reviewable in any other Kentucky court, and a federal right had been asserted and denied, the case went directly to the U.S. Supreme Court. This Court reversed on the ground that since there was no evidence in the record to support either charge, Thompson's conviction violated due process of law. It was noted that under the Kentucky statute, to prove the offense of loitering the prosecution must establish that the accused was without visible means of support, that he could not give a satisfactory account of himself, and that he was loafing or trespassing without the consent of the person in control of the premises. Actually, Thompson worked regularly, owned some property and had money in his pocket. As for the disorderly conduct charge, there was no evidence that when he protested his arrest Thompson raised his voice, or used offensive language, or resisted arrest, or did anything else to disturb the peace and tranquility of the community. It was noted that merely arguing with a policeman was not disorderly conduct under the substantive law of Kentucky.

In effect, then, the Court ruled that in convicting a person of an offense without any probative evidence at all, a state has acted so arbitrarily and unreasonably as to deny due process of law. This new rule of constitutional law was pronounced just in time to supply a doctrinal basis for the dis-

92. 362 U.S. 199 (1960).

106 / The Defendant's Rights Today

position of appeals in sit-in cases which began to reach the Supreme Court in 1961.[93] In these cases the Court reversed numerous convictions for such offenses as disturbing the peace, obstruction of free passage on the sidewalk, criminal trespass, and wandering or strolling about, on the ground that there was no evidence in the record which supported the convictions.[94]

Statutory Presumptions of Guilt

An allied question arises in connection with statutes which declare that as a matter of law, some particular inference follows from the proof of some particular fact, one fact becoming *prima facie* evidence of another. There are indeed many presumptions in various fields of law, but it is an established rule of due process that the inference must be reasonable. The Supreme Court first announced the rule, in 1910, that there must be "some rational connection between the fact proved and the ultimate fact presumed, and that the inference of one fact from proof of another shall not be so unreasonable as to be a purely arbitrary mandate."[95]

The meaning of this general proposition can be appreciated only in the context of specific cases. Thus, it has been held that a state law which, in effect, declared that if a bank became insolvent, it would be presumed that the officers of the bank were guilty of fraud, created an arbitrary and unreasonable presumption.[96] Another statute was disapproved which provided that whenever a railroad in involved in an accident it shall be presumed that the railroad was negligent.[97] In *Tot* v. *United States*,[98] the Court held unconstitutional a section of the Federal Firearms Act of 1938 which made it unlawful for any person who had been convicted of a crime of violence or was a fugitive from justice to receive any firearm or ammunition transported in interstate or foreign commerce. The law declared that

93. The first of the sit-in cases was Garner v. Louisiana, 368 U.S. 157 (1961), wherein a conviction for disturbing the peace was reversed because there was no evidence in the record to support the ultimate finding of fact.

94. See Taylor v. Louisiana, 370 U.S. 154 (1962) (breach of the peace based on sitting in a white waiting room at a bus depot); Barr v. Columbia, 378 U.S. 146 (1964) (criminal trespass for sitting at a lunch counter); Shuttleworth v. Birmingham, 382 U.S. 87 (1965) (standing on a sidewalk); Brown v. Louisiana, 383 U.S. 131 (1966) (sitting in a library reading room); Johnson v. Florida, 391 U.S. 596 (1968) (wandering or strolling about).

95. Mobile, J. & K.C. R.R. v. Turnipseed, 219 U.S. 35, 43 (1910). See Note, "Statutory Presumptions and Due Process of Law," *Harvard Law Review,* 43 (November 1929): 100–104; Paul Brosman, "The Statutory Presumption," *Tulane Law Review,* 5 (December 1930–February 1931): 17–54, 178–210; E. M. Watson, "Use of Statutory Presumptions in Criminal Cases," *Michigan Law Review,* 38 (January 1940): 366–81.

96. Manley v. Georgia, 279 U.S. 1 (1929).

97. Western & Atlantic R. Co. v. Henderson, 279 U.S. 639 (1929).

98. 319 U.S. 463 (1943).

the possession of a firearm or ammunition by any person shall be presumptive evidence that the firearm or ammunition was shipped in interstate or foreign commerce. This was going too far, even for a Court which was extremely reluctant to invalidate acts of Congress. "It is not too much to say," said Justice Roberts, "that the presumptions created by the law are violent, and inconsistent with any argument drawn from experience."[99] Similarly, in a later case the Court held unconstitutional a federal statute which provided that the presence of a person at the site of an illegal still "shall be deemed sufficient evidence to authorize conviction, unless the defendant explains such presence to the satisfaction of the jury. . . ."[100] The Court thought it unreasonable to infer from mere presence that the accused possessed the still.[101] In 1970, in *Turner* v. *United States,*[102] the Court upheld as reasonable a statute which provided that the unexplained possession of heroin supported an inference of illegal importation, because almost all heroin consumed in the United States is imported illegally. However, a similar presumption in respect to cocaine was held unreasonable because more cocaine is lawfully produced in the United States than is illegally imported.[103]

On the other hand, the Court has expressed approval of a provision of the Anti-Narcotics Act of 1914 which declares that the possession of narcotic drugs without the required stamps shall be *prima facie* evidence of a violation of the law.[104] This was declared to be a reasonable presumption, since the facts are peculiarly within the knowledge of the accused and hidden from discovery by the government. Said Justice Holmes, "In dealing with a poison not commonly used except upon a doctor's prescription easily proved, or for a debauch only possible by a breach of law, it seems reasonable to call on a person possessing it in a form that warrants suspicion to show that he obtained it in a mode permitted by the law."[105] In another instance the Court upheld a statute

---

99. 319 U.S. 468. A California statute which provided that the occupation of land by an alien then ineligible for naturalization created a presumption of conspiracy by the tenant and landowner was held unreasonable in Morrison v. California, 291 U.S. 82 (1934).

100. United States v. Romano, 382 U.S. 136 (1965).

101. United States v. Gainey, 380 U.S. 63 (1965) upheld the same inference, but a different conclusion was reached because it dealt with the charge of "carrying on" the illicit business, whereas in Romano the charge was possession and control.

102. 396 U.S. 398 (1970).

103. In Vlandis v. Kline, 412 U.S. 441 (1973), a divided Court ruled unconstitutional a Connecticut statute which created a permanent, irrebuttable presumption of nonresidency with respect to students whose legal address was outside the state at the time they apply for admission to the State University.

104. Casey v. United States, 276 U.S. 413 (1928).

105. 276 U.S. 418. Three Justices dissented.

that raised a presumption of negligence against a railroad in a grade crossing accident upon proof of failure to give prescribed warning signals.[106] It will be noted that there, as in most cases, the presumption was rebuttable, and not a final irreversible conclusion. More recently, the Court sustained the validity of a statute which provided that the unexplained possession of recently stolen mail supported an inference that the possessor knew that the mail was stolen.[107] The Court thought that there was a "rational connection" between the unexplained possession of recently stolen property and knowledge that the property was stolen.

Many state courts have registered their approval of the rational connection rule, but very few decisions have held that a rational connection does not exist.[108] This is, of course, consistent with still another presumption, that acts of legislatures are presumptively constitutional.

Jurisdiction

It is essential that the court which tries an individual for an offense have jurisdiction over the case. Jurisdiction is actually an exceedingly complex question, and largely a technical concern of lawyers and judges, though it often involves profound issues of public policy. Suffice it to say here that no court can try a case over which it lacks jurisdiction, that is, the legal authority to hear it. The jurisdiction of courts is for the most part territorial. Thus, a New York court will not ordinarily hear a civil case between nonresidents the cause of action of which arose in some other state. No state court will hear a criminal case if the crime in question was committed in some other state. The federal district courts and state trial courts are all limited in their jurisdiction in a territorial sense. In addition, jurisdiction may otherwise be described or limited by statute in the discretion of the legislative body. Thus the conditions under which cases reach the various federal courts are all described by acts of Congress.

There are various ways by which a state court acquires jurisdiction over a defendant. He may be present within the state, or live there (domicile), or he may consent to jurisdiction. Corporations chartered in other states may be required to consent to such jurisdiction as a condition of doing business there; since the state may constitutionally exclude foreign corporations altogether, it may admit them on this condition.

A state court which assumes to act in a case where it lacks jurisdiction acts unreasonably and therefore in violation of due process. This problem often arises when jurisdiction is asserted over nonresidents. It is well established that a state may impose terms upon nonresidents wishing to do

106. Atlantic Coast Line R. Co. v. Ford, 287 U.S. 502 (1933).
107. Barnes v. United States, 412 U.S. 837 (1973).
108. See, e.g., State v. Spiller, 146 Wash. 180, 262 P. 128 (1927); Morrison v. Flowers, 308 Ill. 189, 139 N.E. 10 (1923); Roberts v. People, 78 Colo. 555, 243 P. 544 (1926).

business therein, including a consent to be sued in the courts of the state.[109] By the same token, it has been held that the state's power to regulate the use of its highways is such that it may require nonresidents to agree in advance to local suit in case of accident.[110] And it was recently held that "where business activities reach out beyond one state and create continuing relationships and obligations with citizens of another state, courts need not resort to a fictional 'consent' in order to sustain the jurisdiction of regulatory agencies in the latter state."[111]

One final jurisdictional point remains to be noted. It is an old rule of the Supreme Court, recently reaffirmed,[112] that the power of a state court to try a person for a crime is not impaired by the fact that he had been brought within the court's jurisdiction by a forcible abduction. Due process is satisfied if the defendant had been fairly notified of the charges and given a fair trial.

The Right to a Public Trial

The Sixth Amendment assures the accused, in all criminal prosecutions, a speedy and public trial.[113] The constitutions of forty-one states have similar provisions, and in the remaining states the right to a public trial is secured by statute or court decision.[114] While the origins of our accepted practice of guaranteeing a public trial to an accused are obscure, the right was well established in the common law of England before the settlement of America. The Supreme Court has said, on this point: "The traditional Anglo-American distrust for secret trials has been variously ascribed to the notorious use of this practice by the Spanish Inquisition, to the excesses of the English Court of Star Chamber, and to the French monarchy's abuse of the *lettre de cachet*. All of these institutions obviously symbolized a menace to liberty."[115]

109. H. L. Doherty & Co. v. Goodman, 294 U.S. 623 (1935).
110. Hess v. Pawloski, 274 U.S. 352 (1927).
111. Travelers Health Assoc. v. Virginia, 339 U.S. 643, 647 (1950).
112. Ker v. Illinois, 119 U.S. 436 (1886); Frisbie v. Collins, 342 U.S. 519 (1952). See Note, "Illegal Abductions by State Police: Sanctions for Evasion of Extradition," *Yale Law Journal*, 61 (March 1952): 445-50.
113. The right to a public trial does not apply to grand jury proceedings, which are secret. Levine v. United States, 362 U.S. 610 (1960).
114. Dutton v. State, 123 Md. 373, 91 A. 417 (1914). See N.Y. Rev. Stat. (1829), Part LII, c. III, Tit. I, §1: "The sittings of every court within this state, shall be public, and every citizen may freely attend same." See United States v. Kobli, 172 F.2d 919 (3rd Cir. 1949).
115. *In re* Oliver, 333 U.S. 257, 268 (1948). See Max Radin, "The Right to a Public Trial," *Temple Law Quarterly*, 6 (April 1932): 381-98; Lauren Colby, "Recent Developments in the Right to Public Trial," *Syracuse Law Review*, 6 (Spring 1955): 339-46; Charles W. Quick, "A Public Criminal Trial," *Dickinson Law Review*, 60 (October 1955): 21-35. See also the annotation, "Right to Public Trial in Criminal Cases," 4 L. Ed. 2d 2128.

The Supreme Court regards the principle of the public trial to be so important that it is a requirement of due process of law. Accordingly, it ruled in 1948 that the Michigan one-man grand jury system, which permits the judge, sitting as an inquisitor into wrongdoing, to commit summarily for contempt in a secret proceeding, violated the Fourteenth Amendment.[116] It could find no record of a single criminal trial conducted in secret in any federal, state, or municipal court, and none in England since 1641. It noted that secret trials had been instruments for the suppression of political and religious heresies. The Court called attention to the benefits of publicity: it imposes an effective restraint upon the possible abuse of judicial power; it serves notice to witnesses unknown to the parties; spectators learn about their government and acquire confidence in their judicial remedies.[117] Furthermore, as a New York judge recently noted, "Any person acquainted with the prosecution of crime knows that many a witness who may testify glibly and falsely in the secrecy of a grand jury room will nevertheless refuse or be reluctant to give the same untrue testimony upon the trial in open court. When such testimony is publicly given, the witness well knows there may be persons who can and will come forward to testify as to the true facts."[118] Max Radin has added the observation "that, if trials are speedy and public, powerful officials will be far less likely to use their power against innocent men than if trials are protracted and secret."[119]

A judge, however, has considerable discretion in excluding some people from the courtroom.[120] He may close the doors to avoid overcrowding or in

---

116. *In re* Oliver, 333 U.S. 257 (1948).

117. For a case dealing with the principle of public trials in federal courts, see Tanksley v. United States, 145 F.2d 58 (9th Cir. 1944).

118. People v. Jelke, 284 App. Div. 211, 230, 130 N.Y.S. 2d 662, 680 (1st Dept. 1954). Blackstone made this point long ago. 3 Com. *373. For the argument that a public trial offers "security for testimonial trustworthiness," see Wigmore, *Treatise on Evidence,* 6: 332–46.

119. "The Right to a Public Trial," p. 381. See the remarks of the Court in State v. Schmit, 273 Minn. 78, 86–88, 139 N.W. 2d 800, 806–7 (1966): "In our opinion the constitutional mandate contemplates that an accused be afforded all possible benefits that a trial open to the public is designed to assure. Unrestricted public scrutiny of judicial action is a meaningful assurance to an accused that he will be dealt with justly, protected not only against gross abuses of judicial power but also petty arbitrariness. The presence of an audience does have a wholesome effect on trustworthiness since witnesses are less likely to testify falsely before a public gathering. Further, the possibility that some spectator drawn to the trial may prove to be an undiscovered witness in possession of critical evidence cannot be ignored. It is not unrealistic even in this day to believe that public inclusion affords citizens a form of legal education and hopefully promotes confidence in the fair administration of justice."

120. See Davis v. United States, 247 F. 394 (8th Cir. 1917); Melanson v. O'Brien, 95 F. Supp. 230 (D.C. Mass. 1951); United States *ex rel.* Bruno v. Herold, 408 F.2d 125 (2d Cir. 1969), cert. denied, 397 U.S. 957 (1970).

the interests of public health, or exclude disorderly people, or bar minors in cases where testimony is given that youngsters ought not listen to. While courts differ on the question as to just who may be excluded, no court has ever ruled that an accused may be tried when everyone is denied entrance except the officials of the court. At the very least he is entitled to have his friends and relatives present, as well as his counsel.[121]

It is not always true that a public trial is necessary if the accused is to have a fair trial. At a time of great public tension and popular hostility, the presence of a large audience in the courtroom may very well have an intimidating effect upon the judge, or the jury, or the witnesses, or the lawyers. Of course, the audience may also intimidate the prosecutor. Again, all that can be said is that on the balance the advantages of a public trial will for most people and for society as a whole outweigh the disadvantages. Thus American appellate courts will generally rule that the total exclusion of all spectators violates the defendant's right to a public trial.[122]

The Right to a Speedy Trial

It is a familiar observation that justice delayed is justice defeated. It is equally well known that delays in the American criminal justice system pose serious problems.[123] A number of devices are available to cope with these problems. For one thing, statutes of limitations set limits to delay. For example, the federal limitations statute provides that noncapital offenses must be prosecuted within three years,[124] while in Wisconsin prosecution of a noncapital offense must be commenced within six years.[125] "The purpose of a statute of limitations," Justice Black has noted, "is to limit exposure to criminal prosecution to a certain fixed period of time following the occurrence of those acts the legislature has decided to punish by criminal sanctions. Such a limitation is designed to protect individuals from having to defend themselves against charges when the basic facts may have become obscured by the passage of time and to minimize the danger of official punishment because of acts in the

---

121. The New York Court of Appeals has ruled that since the right to a public trial is personal to the defendant, the newspapers and press associations have no enforceable, legal right of their own to attend trials. United Press Associations v. Valente, 308 N.Y. 71, 123 N.E. 2d 777 (1954) (two judges dissenting). The Cuyahoga County Court of Appeals of Ohio has ruled the other way, holding that newspapers have a right to attend even where the accused has signed a waiver of his right to a public trial. E. W. Scripps Co. v. Fulton, 125 N.E. 2d 896 (Ohio App. 1955).

122. See, e.g., Oliver v. Postel, 30 N.Y. 2d 171, 331 N.Y.S. 2d 407, 282 N.E. 2d 306 (1972); State v. Schmit, 273 Minn. 78, 139 N.W. 2d 800 (1966).

123. See Hans Zeisel, *Delay in Court* (Boston: Little, Brown & Co., 1959).

124. 18 U.S.C. §3281 (1970).

125. Wis. Stat. 1973, §939.74 (1).

far-distant past. Such a time limit may also have the salutary effect of encouraging law enforcement officials promptly to investigate suspected criminal activity."[126]

Above all, the Sixth Amendment assures the accused a "speedy" as well as a public trial. The phrase, "a speedy and public trial" is a familiar one in American law, and is found in almost all state constitutions,[127] and is part of the law of every state. The underlying principle is an ancient one. Thus, Magna Carta stated, "To no one will we sell, to no one deny or delay, right or justice." (c. 29) In fact, the Supreme Court regards this principle as so essential to justice that in the landmark case of *Klopfer* v. *North Carolina*,[128] decided by a unanimous vote of 1967, it was read into the Fourteenth Amendment as an element of due process which is federally enforceable upon the states. As Justice White observed, in a recent opinion, the Sixth Amendment guaranty of a speedy trial is "an important safeguard to prevent undue and oppressive incarceration prior to trial, to minimize anxiety and concern accompanying public accusation and to limit the possibilities that long delay will impair the ability of an accused to defend himself."[129]

At the federal level, the constitutional right to a speedy trial is strengthened by Rule 48 (b) of the Federal Rules of Criminal Procedure, which authorizes the judge to dismiss an indictment, information, or complaint if there has been "unnecessary delay" in presenting the charge or bringing the defendant to trial. In addition, in the Speedy Trial Act of 1974,[130] Congress spelled out very specific time limits to assure accused persons a speedy trial. Generally speaking, an information or indictment charging an individual with the commission of an offense must be filed within thirty days from the date of arrest or of service of summons; arraignment must be held within ten days; and the trial must commence within sixty days thereafter.[131] There are certain grounds for delay beyond these time periods, e.g., the absence or unavailability of the defendant or an essential witness, or considerations which the judge grants in order best to serve the ends of justice, as in the instance of an unusually complex case. Each

---

126. Toussie v. United States, 397 U.S. 112,114–15 (1970). See also the remarks of Justice Jackson in Chase Securities Corp. v. Donaldson, 325 U.S. 304, 314 (1945): "Statutes of limitations . . . are practical and pragmatic devices to spare the courts from litigation of stale claims, and the citizen from being put to his defense after memories have faded, witnesses have died or disappeared, and evidence has been lost."

127. See, e.g., Calif. Const., Art. I, §13; Ariz. Const., Art. II, §24; Ark. Const., Art. II, §10; Conn. Const., Art. I, §9; La. Const., Art. I, §16.

128. 386 U.S. 213 (1967).

129. United States v. Ewell, 383 U.S. 116, 120 (1966).

130. 18 U.S.C. §§3161–74 (1975).

131. 18 U.S.C. §3161.

district court is required to formulate plans to dispose of cases according to the objective of the act, and the Director of the Administrative Office of the United States Courts is authorized to create, in ten representative judicial districts, pretrial service agencies to prepare plans and supervise expeditious pretrial release of accused individuals.

Whether a particular trial is speedy enough depends, of course, upon all the circumstances.[132] Nor is speed an end in itself, since "justice both to the accused and to the public, is the prime consideration."[133]

The case of John David Provoo, a former soldier who was charged with having committed treason while a prisoner of war in the hands of the Japanese, underscored the necessity of a speedy trial as a matter of constitutional right. The conduct alleged to have been treasonable occurred in a period from May 6, 1942, to August 14, 1945, in the Philippine Islands and Japan. Provoo was arrested in August 1945, released in April 1946, and later rearrested and indicted in 1949 in the Southern District of New York. He was tried in 1952–53 and convicted, but in August 1954 the Court of Appeals reversed the conviction, partly because it found that venue was in the Maryland and not in the New York district. He was reindicted by the grand jury in Maryland on October 27, 1954, five years after his arrest. On March 14, 1955, concluding that the delay was caused by a deliberate act of the government in bringing the case to trial in New York because of some supposed advantage, though knowing that venue in New York was doubtful, Judge Thomsen of the U.S. District Court of Maryland dismissed the indictment.[134] The Supreme Court affirmed unanimously on October 17, 1955.[135] The evidence showed that Provoo had been ready for trial since the summer of 1951, that he had requested an immediate trial several times, and had objected to most of the government's requests for continuances. The trial court found that because of the lapse of time, many possible witnesses had either died or been lost track of, and that the long confinement in prison seriously impaired Provoo's ability to defend himself. While the judge thought that prejudice

---

132. Thus the existence of a docket congested with civil cases may be a good cause for delay. State v. Kuhnhausen, 201 Ore. 478, 272 P.2d 225 (1954). See Note, "The Right to a Speedy Criminal Trial," *Columbia Law Review,* 57 (June 1957): 846–67.

133. Frankel v. Woodrough, 7 F.2d 796, 798 (8th Cir. 1925). Thus a defendant is not entitled to a speedy trial for one offense in order to defeat prosecution for others. Beavers v. Haubert, 198 U.S. 77, 87 (1905): "The right to a speedy trial is necessarily relative. . . . It secures rights to a defendant. It does not preclude the rights of public justice."

134. Petition of Provoo, 17 F.R.D. 183 (1955). For other illustrations of dismissals of indictments for lack of prosecution, about four and one-half years after the charges were made, see United States v. McWilliams, 163 F.2d 695 (D.C. Cir. 1947); People v. Winfrey, 20 N.Y. 2d 138, 281 N.Y.S. 2d 823, 228 N.E. 2d 808 (1967).

135. United States v. Provoo, 350 U.S. 857 (1955).

may be assumed from a long delay, which is the position that many state courts take, he ruled that in any event prejudice in fact had been shown.

The Court's decision in the *Klopfer* case[136] drew fresh attention to the speedy trial problem. Klopfer, a professor at Duke, was tried in March 1964 on a charge of criminal trespass after refusing to leave a restaurant when ordered to do so. The jury failed to reach a verdict, and the judge granted a mistrial. Thereupon, the judge granted the prosecutor's motion for a *nolle prosequi,* "with leave," which meant that under North Carolina law the judge could restore the case to the trial docket at any later date on application of the prosecutor. The Supreme Court rejected the state court's holding that a defendant has no right to compel the state to prosecute, and pointed out that while Klopfer was free to go about as he desired, that was not the whole story. With the charge hanging indefinitely over his head, he could be subjected to public scorn, deprived of his employment, and suffer curtailment of his rights to free speech and association and participation in unpopular causes. The Court took the position that the right to a speedy trial was as fundamental as any of the rights secured by the Sixth Amendment.

Furthermore, two years later the Court made it clear that the right of a state prisoner to a speedy trial may not be defeated merely because he is serving a sentence in a federal penitentiary, since if the state makes the effort, a federal prisoner will be produced for trial; at the very least the state must make a diligent, good-faith effort to bring to trial one who is accused of a crime and has repeatedly demanded, over a period of six years, that he be brought to trial on the charge.[137]

Some state and lower federal courts have taken the position that a defendant is in no position to assert that he has been denied the right to a speedy trial unless he had taken the initiative in demanding one,[138] that he cannot sit idly by and do nothing, even if in jail,[139] and then for the first time claim at his trial that there had been a delay within the meaning of the Constitution. This notion, that the absence of a request by the accused for a trial establishes a presumption that he acquiesced in the delay, was specifically rejected by a unanimous decision of the Supreme Court in 1972.[140] In rejecting what is known as the waiver-demand rule, the Court

---

136. Klopfer v. North Carolina, 386 U.S. 213 (1967).

137. Smith v. Hooey, 393 U.S. 374 (1969). A similar decision was made in Dickey v. Florida, 398 U.S. 30 (1970), where the federal prisoner had to wait seven years for his state trial.

138. Pietch v. United States, 110 F.2d 817 (10th Cir. 1940), cert. denied, 310 U.S. 648 (1940); Collins v. United States, 157 F.2d 409 (9th Cir. 1946); United States v. Hill, 310 F.2d 601 (4th Cir. 1962).

139. State v. Keefe, 17 Wyo. 227, 98 P. 122, 22 L.R.A. (N.S.) 896, 17 Ann. Cas. 161 (1908); Pines v. District Court of Woodbury County, 233 Iowa 1284, 10 N.W. 2d 574 (1943).

140. Barker v. Wingo, 407 U.S. 514 (1972).

noted that it was following its traditional position that a proper waiver of a constitutional right must take the form of an intentional abandonment of a known right, the presumption being against waiver, a fact which is not deducible from a silent record. Instead, the Court chose to place the primary burden on the courts and prosecutors to make sure that cases are brought to trial in good time. Since the concept of the right to a speedy trial is inherently imprecise, and depends upon an evaluation of all relevant circumstances, the Court adopted a balancing test according to which cases are to be approached on an *ad hoc* basis, with weight being given to four factors: (1) the length of the delay (delay must be long enough to create a presumption of prejudice); (2) the government reason to justify the delay (e.g. an overcrowded docket as compared with a deliberate attempt to hamper the defense); (3) failure of the defendant to assert his right; and (4) prejudice to the defendant (especially impairment of the defense of the accused). The Court also stressed that apart from possible prejudice at the trial, consideration should be given to the fact that pretrial incarceration can entail serious consequences, such as loss of a job, disruption of family life, enforced idleness, and creation of added difficulties to prepare a defense.[141]

Finally, it should be noted that the Court ruled, in 1971, in *United States* v. *Marion*,[142] that the Sixth Amendment right to a speedy trial does not apply until the defendant becomes an accused. In this case, two defendants were indicted in April 1970 on many counts of consumer fraud in respect to home improvements, for acts which occurred between March 1964 and February 1967. The Supreme Court reversed the district court, which had dismissed the indictment for lack of a speedy prosecution on the theory that a delay of three years was bound to be seriously prejudicial. In short, the Court declined to extend the reach of the speedy-trial provision to the period prior to arrest, since until charges are made, a citizen suffers no restraint on his liberty, and is not the subject of public accusations. Furthermore, in cases of prearrest delay, there are other protective mechanisms, such as statutes of limitations, and it was suggested that due process would require dismissal of an indictment if it were shown that the preindictment delay was purposeful to gain a tactical advantage over the accused so as to cause substantial prejudice to the defendant's right to a fair trial. Three concurring Justices argued that the

---

141. This last point was stressed in Moore v. Arizona, 414 U.S. 25 (1973). In Strunk v. United States, 412 U.S. 434 (1973), the Court ruled that dismissal of the charge is the only possible remedy for a denial of a speedy trial, for unlike the denial of other rights, the harm which is entailed by denying a speedy trial cannot be undone except by dismissal. See Anthony G. Amsterdam, "Speedy Criminal Trial: Rights and Remedies," *Stanford Law Review*, 27 (February 1975): 525–43; John C. Godbold, "Speedy Trial—Major Surgery for a National Ill," *Alabama Law Review*, 24 (Spring 1972): 265–94.

142. 404 U.S. 307 (1971).

Sixth Amendment guaranty should apply to preindictment as well as postindictment delays, but could find no showing of actual prejudice on the particular facts before them.

The Right to an Unbiased Judge

A trial is not fairly conducted if the judge is so strongly biased against the defendant that injustice is invited. This is in accordance with an old maxim of the common law that no man ought to be a judge in his own case. Lord Coke thought this principle was so important that he relied upon it to declare an act of Parliament void in the celebrated *Dr. Bonham's Case*.[143] This is particularly noteworthy because the judge's right to declare acts of legislation invalid on constitutional grounds has never prevailed in England. In this instance Parliament had authorized the College of Physicians to control admission to the practice of medicine, and four members of the College constituted an enforcement board of censors with the power to assess fines, half of which went to the College itself. Thus, as Coke noted, the censors were "judges, ministers, and parties" at the same time, sitting in judgment of cases in the outcome of which they had a pre-existing bias. Coke declared that this parliamentary act was "against common right and reason," because no one should in reason be a judge in his own cause.

While the phrase "unbiased judge" is not in the Constitution, the concept falls within the scope of the due process clauses of the Fifth and Fourteenth Amendments. It is also firmly embedded in our statute law and prevailing principles of professional ethics. Thus, an act of Congress provides, "Any justice or judge of the United States shall disqualify himself in any case in which he has a substantial interest, has been of counsel, is or has been a material witness, or is so related to or connected with any party or his attorney as to render it improper, in his opinion, for him to sit on the trial, appeal, or other proceeding therein."[144] Similarly, Canon 33 of Judicial Ethics of the American Bar Association declares that a judge should, "in pending or prospective litigation before him be particularly careful to avoid such action as may reasonably tend to awaken

---

143. 8 Coke 107a, 113b, 77 Eng. Repr. 638, 646 (1610). For a leading modern English case, see Dimes v. Grand Junction Canal Co., 3 H.L. Cas. 759 (1852). Here the House of Lords ruled that a judge, in this instance no less a dignitary than the Lord Chancellor, was disqualified from sitting in a case where the action was brought against a corporation in which the judge was a substantial shareholder. Said Lord Campbell, at 792, "No one can suppose that Lord Cottenham could be, in the remotest degree, influenced by the interest that he had in this concern; but, my Lords, it is of the last importance that the maxim that no man is to be a judge in his own cause should be held sacred."

144. 28 U.S.C. §455 (1970). The procedure for the filing of affidavits of prejudice by any party to a court proceeding is spelled out in 28 U.S.C. §144 (1970). For a typical state statute on the subject see Wis. Stat. 1973, §§261.06–08, 971.20.

the suspicion that his social or business relations or friendships constitute an element in influencing his judicial conduct."

The most famous American case on this point to reach the Supreme Court was *Tumey* v. *Ohio*,[145] decided in 1927. A village in Ohio had an ordinance which provided that where one was convicted of violating the state prohibition law a portion of the fine went to the judge. As a matter of fact, the judge, at the time of this litigation, was getting a substantial income from this source. In addition, half of the fines went to the village, of which the judge was mayor. The Supreme Court held that it is a violation of due process to put a man on trial before a judge who has such "a direct, personal, substantial, pecuniary interest" in reaching a conclusion against the defendant. Furthermore, said Chief Justice Taft, "the requirement of due process of law in judicial procedure is not satisfied by the argument that men of the highest honor and the greatest self-sacrifice could carry it on without danger of injustice. Every procedure which would offer a possible temptation to the average man as a judge to forget the burden of proof required to convict the defendant, or which might lead him not to hold the balance nice, clear and true between the State and the accused, denies the latter due process of law."[146]

The Court was quick to emphasize, however, that the interest of the judge must be both personal and substantial, for in 1928 it ruled, in *Dugan* v. *Ohio*,[147] that where the mayor-judge, in a town having a commission form of government, is paid a fixed salary out of the local treasury, due process has not been violated because half the fine goes to the town. Here the Court thought that, as one of the town's five commissioners, the mayor's relation to the fund contributed to by fines he assessed as a judge was altogether remote. In 1972, however, the thrust of this case was considerably reduced by the Court's decision in *Ward* v. *Village of Monroeville*.[148] Under Ohio law, mayors sit as judges in cases involving ordinance violations and certain traffic offenses. A major part of the income of the village in 1968, $23,439 out of a total of $52,995, was derived from fines, forfeitures, costs, and fees generated by the mayor's court. Under these circumstances the Court ruled that the *Tumey* case was controlling, the test being not merely whether the judge shares directly in the fines, but whether there is a possible temptation to the average judge. The *Dugan* case was distinguished on the ground that there the mayor-judge had very limited executive responsibilities, since he shared authority with four commissioners and a city manager. Nor was it sufficient that a defendant was entitled to a trial *de novo* on appeal to the next highest

145. 273 U.S. 510 (1927).
146. 273 U.S. 532.
147. 277 U.S. 61 (1928).
148. 409 U.S. 57 (1972).

court, for, as Justice Brennan said, he "is entitled to a neutral and detached judge in the first instance."[149]

Of course, the concept of impartiality is necessarily a relative one. Thus it works no denial of due process to have taxpayers on a tax assessment board[150] or on a jury in a suit in which the city is interested.[151] So far as appeals on this issue from the state courts to the United States Supreme Court are concerned, it is established that he who alleges bias on the part of the judge in a criminal case carries the burden of proof.[152]

There are a few states where judges in very minor cases, usually justices of the peace, receive no compensation except from fees collected from the parties. This practice has rarely been challenged and probably continues because of the insignificance of the amounts involved, but on principle it cannot be justified, and some state courts have expressed their disapproval.[153] In fact, in 1966 a three-judge federal district court in Alabama ruled that a trial of a reckless driving charge before an Alabama justice of the peace who takes his fee out of fines imposed after conviction, but receives nothing upon acquittal, violates due process.[154] Citing *Tumey*, the court declared it was illegal for the judge to have a direct, personal, substantial pecuniary interest in reaching a conclusion against the defendant.

There is, in fact, an unfortunate tendency to underrate the importance of the so-called minor courts. "The Magistrate," the Chief City Magistrate of New York once declared, "is one of the most important officials in the city. He has more opportunities for evil or good in a week than a judge of the Supreme Court has in a year. He can nullify the actions of the police; he can curb disorder or encourage it; he can be a terror to evildoers or an ally.... The Magistrate must be freer from ulterior influences and his integrity should be as unquestioned as that of the Judges in our very highest court."[155]

The defendant's right to an unbiased judge was given additional emphasis by the Supreme Court in the case of *In re Murchison*,[156] decided in 1955. Under Michigan law any judge of a court of record may serve as a one-man grand jury, and compel witnesses to appear in secret and testify

---

149. 409 U.S. 61–62. Justices White and Rehnquist, dissenting, thought that this decision was an unwise extension of the Tumey rule, and pointed out that sixteen other states have similar practices. They thought that the absence of a direct financial stake in the outcome of the case was the controlling fact.

150. Hibben v. Smith, 191 U.S. 310 (1903).

151. Omaha v. Olmstead, 5 Neb. 446 (1877).

152. Buchalter v. New York, 319 U.S. 427 (1943).

153. See, e.g., Wagers v. Sizemore, 222 Ky. 306, 300 S.W. 918 (1927).

154. Hulett v. Julian, 250 F. Supp. 208 (M.D. Ala. 1966).

155. William McAdoo, *Report of the New York State Bar Association*, 43 (1920): 415, 416.

156. 349 U.S. 133 (1955).

about suspected crime. As already noted, the Court held in 1948 that the judge-grand jury may not summarily convict a witness of contempt for conduct in the secret hearing, that due process requires a public trial after reasonable notice, with the right to call witnesses, cross-examine adverse witnesses, and be represented by counsel.[157] In Murchison's case the Court decided that due process has been violated if the judge who was the one-man grand jury presides at the contempt hearing. Said Justice Black, "A fair trial in a fair tribunal is a basic requirement of due process. Fairness of course requires an absence of actual bias in the trial of cases. But our system of law has always endeavored to prevent even the probability of unfairness. To this end no man can be a judge in his own case and no man is permitted to try cases where he has an interest in the outcome." He held that this case came within the rule of the *Tumey* decision, that the measure of bias is possible temptation to the average man as judge. Since the single judge-grand jury was part of the accusatory process, he cannot "in the very nature of things," be wholly disinterested in the results. Furthermore, as a practical matter, Justice Black insisted, it is difficult if not impossible for a judge to free himself from the influence of what happened in the secret session. Three Justices dissented on the ground that actual bias had to be proved.

Finally, the impartiality demanded of the judge requires that he avoid prejudicial conduct which injures the defendant's case. For example, he must not disparage defense counsel by suggesting in the presence of the jury, that he is not telling the truth,[158] or otherwise harass him as, for example, by describing a defense motion, as being "silly" or "foolish."[159] Similarly, it is improper for the judge to describe an attorney's motion as "shyster stuff."[160] It is also improper to tell defense counsel to stop wasting the jury's time.[161] Gross mistreatment of the defendant or witnesses by the judge may also be regarded as a failure in the posture of impartiality which the law expects from him.

Freedom from Mob Domination

The Supreme Court has ruled that a state court has not preserved the defendant's due process rights if it permitted the trial to take place under the domination of a mob. In the leading case on this point, *Moore* v. *Dempsey*,[162] five Negroes, following a race disturbance, had been convicted of murder in an Arkansas court and sentenced to death. In a

157. *In re* Oliver, 333 U.S. 257 (1948).
158. Allen v. United States, 115 F.3 (9th Cir. 1902).
159. McAllister v. State, 206 Ark. 998, 178 S.W. 2d 67 (1944); People v. Neal, 290 Mich. 123, 287 N.W. 403 (1939).
160. Moore v. State, 147 Neb. 390, 23 N.W. 2d 552 (1946).
161. People v. Coli, 2 Ill. 2d 186, 117 N.E. 2d 777 (1954).
162. 261 U.S. 86 (1923).

petition for habeas corpus before a federal district court the following facts were alleged: that the principal witnesses had been tortured; that only white people were admitted to the grand and petit juries; that a threatening mob had surrounded the courthouse; that the defense lawyer didn't dare request a delay in the trial, challenge jurymen, or ask for a change of venue or separate trials; that no witnesses were called in defense; that the whole trial lasted about forty-five minutes, and the jury brought in its verdict of guilty in five minutes. The state supreme court having sustained the regularity of these proceedings, the federal district court dismissed the petition for a writ of habeas corpus without itself examining the facts. Reversing, the Supreme Court held that the facts alleged as true presented a federal due process issue. In a famous sentence Justice Holmes said, "If the case is that the whole proceeding is a mask—that counsel, jury, and judge were swept to the fatal end by an irresistible wave of public passion, and that the State Courts failed to correct the wrong, neither perfection in the machinery for correction nor the possibility that the trial court and counsel saw no other way of avoiding an immediate outbreak of the mob can prevent this Court from securing to the petitioners their constitutional rights."[163]

Nevertheless, the general rule, for reasons both of federal-state comity and expediency, is that federal courts will ordinarily assume the correctness of the decisions in state criminal trials, so long as they were procedurally proper. Federal courts will not intervene, either by review or habeas corpus, unless there was a flagrant and especially bad case of injustice. For, as Justice Pitney once observed, the due process clause "does not mean that the operations of the state government shall be conducted without error or fault in any particular case, nor that the Federal courts may substitute their judgment for that of the state courts, or exercise any general review over their proceedings, but only that the fundamental rights of the prisoner shall not be taken from him arbitrarily or without the right to be heard according to the usual course of law in such cases."[164] Since federal intervention is available only in extreme situations, it follows that a mere allegation of mob domination, without more, will not suffice,[165] and something more than a state of public excitement must be shown.[166]

---

163. 261 U.S. 91.
164. Frank v. Mangum, 237 U.S. 309, 334 (1915). For a later holding, see U.S. *ex rel.* Darcy v. Handy, 351 U.S. 454 (1956).
165. Dunn v. Lyons, 23 F.2d 14 (5th Cir. 1928), cert. denied, 276 U.S. 622 (1928).
166. Bard v. Chilton, 20 F.2d 906 (6th Cir. 1927), cert. denied, 275 U.S. 565 (1927). See Henry Schofield, "Federal Courts and Mob Domination of State Courts," *Illinois Law Review,* 10 (February 1916): 479-506.

Pretrial Publicity and a Fair Trial

In 1911, the highest court of Massachusetts declared,

There can be no justice in a trial by jurors inflamed by passion, warped by prejudice, awed by violence, menaced by the virulence of public opinion or manifestly biased by any influences operating either openly or insidiously to such an extent as to poison the judgment and prevent the freedom of fair action. Justice cannot be assured in a trial where other considerations enter the minds of those who are to decide than the single desire to ascertain and declare the truth according to the law and the evidence. A court of general jurisdiction ought not to be left powerless under the law to do within reason all that the conditions of society and human nature permit to provide an unprejudiced panel for a jury trial.[167]

This search for a fair trial is seriously affected by pretrial publicity in the mass media.[168] As Justice Holmes once remarked, "Any judge who has sat with juries knows that, in spite of forms, they are extremely likely to be impregnated by the environing atmosphere."[169] An important part of this "environing atmosphere" is created by the mass media. It is especially prejudical to the accused if the media publish information that may not be legal evidence at the trial, such as the existence of a confession which the judge later holds to be inadmissible. One purpose of the *voir dire* is to permit defense counsel to challenge potential jurors for cause who admit that their minds are already made up on the basis of what they read in the newspapers or heard on radio and television. The mere fact, however, that the prospective juror indicates that he has some knowledge of the case, or has even formed an opinion on the ultimate issue of guilt, does not suffice to require the judge to accept a challenge for cause. As Chief Justice Marshall pointed out in the *Burr* case,[170] there is a difference between "light impressions" and "strong and deep impressions." In addition, in the language of Chief Justice Waite, in an age "of newspaper enterprise and universal education," all cases of public interest are bound to become fairly common knowledge in the community.[171] It is a general rule of law accepted by American courts that mere exposure to publicity does not support a challenge for cause.[172] In fact, half the states have statutes to

---

167. Crocker v. Justices of the Superior Court, 208 Mass. 162, 178-79, 94 N.E. 369, 376-77 (1911).

168. See the excellent survey of this problem in John E. Stanga, Jr., "Judicial Protection of the Criminal Defendant against Adverse Press Coverage," *William and Mary Law Review*, 13 (Fall 1971): 1-74. See also American Bar Association Project on Standards of Criminal Justice, *Fair Trial and Free Press* (March 1968) (Reardon Report).

169. Frank v. Mangum, 237 U.S. 309, 349 (1915) (dissenting opinion).

170. United States v. Burr, 25 Fed. Cas. 49, 51 (No. 14,692g) (C.C.D. Va. 1807).

171. Reynolds v. United States, 98 U.S. 145, 155 (1878).

172. See citations assembled by Stanga, "Judicial Protection of the Criminal Defendant," n. 10.

this effect. For example, a Wisconsin statute provides as follows: "It shall be no cause of challenge to a juror that he may have obtained information of the matters at issue through newspapers or public journals, if he shall have received no bias or prejudice thereby. . . ."[173]

Since most criminal trials in the United States are had in state courts, it follows that most decisions as to whether pretrial publicity had a prejudicial impact upon the defendant's case are made by state trial and appellate judges. Each case is decided *ad hoc,* on the basis of an evaluation of all the circumstances, within the state's judicial system. In 1961, however, in the leading case of *Irvin* v. *Dowd,*[174] the Supreme Court, for the first time, reversed a state conviction because of excessive pretrial publicity. Justice Frankfurter, in a concurring opinion, explained the Court's decision in the following language: "How can fallible men and women reach a disinterested verdict based exclusively on what they heard in court when, before they entered the jury box, their minds were saturated by press and radio for months preceding by matter designed to establish the guilt of the accused. A conviction so secured obviously constitutes a denial of due process of law in its most rudimentary conception."[175] Speaking for a unanimous Court, Justice Clark said, "With his life at stake, it is not requiring too much that petitioner be tried in an atmosphere undisturbed by so huge a wave of public passion and by a jury other than one in which two-thirds of the members admit, before hearing any testimony, to possessing a belief in his guilt."[176] At the same time Justice Clark pointed out that "it is not required, however, that the jurors be totally ignorant of the facts and issues involved. In these days of swift, widespread and diverse methods of communication, an important case can be expected to arouse the interest of the public in the vicinity, and scarcely any of those best qualified to serve as jurors will not have formed some impression or opinion as to the merits of the case. This is particularly true in criminal cases. To hold that the mere existence of any preconceived notion as to the guilt or innocence of an accused, without more, is sufficient to rebut the presumption of a prospective juror's impartiality would be to establish an impossible standard. It is sufficient if the juror can lay aside his impression or opinion and render a verdict based on the evidence presented in court."[177]

Thus, the due process issue posed by adverse pretrial publicity comes

173. Wis. Stat. 1973, §270.17.
174. 366 U.S. 717 (1961).
175. 366 U.S. 729–30.
176. 366 U.S. 728.
177. 366 U.S. 722–23.

down to a matter of degree, to which should be added the Supreme Court's understandable reluctance to reverse the decisions of the state courts in such matters of judgment. There are various protections available to the accused, including the *voir dire* examination of jurors, the right to challenge jurors either for cause or peremptorily, and motions for continuances and change of venue, and a person convicted in a state court, who had ample opportunity to prove a denial of due process on his appeal, carries the burden of showing essential unfairness when he later seeks a federal remedy.[178]

In 1963, the Supreme Court ruled that a Louisiana court had committed a reversible error in refusing a change of venue in a murder case, where the defendant's confession to the sheriff was filmed and repeatedly shown on the local television station.[179] The Court has also ruled that one tried for a misdemeanor must be given the same opportunity to show that a change of venue was needed because of community prejudice that the state extends to persons charged with felonies.[180] In the celebrated case involving Dr. Sam Sheppard, who was accused of murdering his wife, the Supreme Court granted habeas corpus on the ground that massive, pervasive, and prejudicial publicity deprived the petitioner of a fair trial.[181] On the other hand, a well-known labor leader lost his appeal on a showing that the voluminous adverse publicity occurred nine and a half months before the trial, and that the jurors had been carefully examined on the point, all admitting bias having been excused.[182]

Trial judges have great powers at their disposal to exercise control over the judicial environment. With respect to the press, and the other mass media, the judge may lay down reasonable rules, and back them up with the contempt power. Above all, the judge has ample authority, unrelated to delicate issues regarding freedom of the press, to control the activities of the police and the public prosecutors, who can be ordered not to do or say

---

178. United States *ex rel.* Darcy v. Handy, 351 U.S. 454 (1956). Here the Court refused to overturn a decision of the Supreme Court of Pennsylvania, which was supported by the findings of both a federal district court and a federal court of appeals, to the effect that the defendant had been given a fair trial.

179. Rideau v. Louisiana, 373 U.S. 723 (1963).

180. Groppi v. Wisconsin, 400 U.S. 505 (1971).

181. Sheppard v. Maxwell, 384 U.S. 333 (1966). A conviction was set aside in Billie Sol Estes v. Texas, 381 U.S. 532 (1965), in a 5-4 decision, because some of the proceedings had been televised over objection, on the ground that such activity denied the defendant a proper judicial atmosphere free from avoidable distraction.

182. Beck v. Washington, 369 U.S. 541 (1962). In Murphy v. Florida, 421 U.S. 794 (1975), the Court held that mere exposure of jurors to news accounts regarding the defendant does not create a presumption that due process has been violated.

things likely to have a prejudicial impact on the trial. Thus, on March 16, 1973, the Supreme Court of Pennsylvania reviewed the problem and came to the following conclusion:

In accordance with these views, we rule that in this Commonwealth policemen and members of the staffs of the office of District Attorneys shall not release to the news media: (a) the existence or contents of any statement or confession given by the accused, or his refusal to give a statement or to take tests; (b) prior criminal records of the accused, including arrests and convictions; (c) any inflamatory statements as to the merits of the case, or the character of the accused; (d) the possibility of a plea of guilty; (e) nor shall the authorities deliberately pose the accused for photographs at or near the scene of the crime, or in photographs which connect him with the scene of the crime.

We hold that anything short of compliance with these standards can operate to deprive an accused of due process of law. . . .[183]

Knowing Use of Perjured Testimony by the Prosecution

Another interesting element of federal due process was spelled out by the Supreme Court in 1935, in *Mooney* v. *Holohan*[184] where it was held that the knowing use by the prosecution of perjured testimony was a denial of due process. The requirements of justice, the Court declared, are not satisfied "by mere notice and hearing if a State has contrived a conviction through the pretense of a trial which in truth is but used as a means of depriving a defendant of liberty through a deliberate deception of court and jury by the presentation of testimony known to be perjured. Such a contrivance by a State to procure the conviction and imprisonment of a defendant is as inconsistent with the rudimentary demands of justice as is the obtaining of a like result by intimidation."[185] The Court reaffirmed this position in later cases.[186] This does not mean, however, that Mooney and the other defendants were given their freedom by the Supreme Court. All it held was that they were entitled to a chance, in some sort of state proceeding, to prove their claim that the prosecution had knowingly used perjured testimony.

The Court has not attempted to specify the kind of hearing they are

183. Com. v. Pierce, 451 Pa. 190, 200, 303 A.2d 209, 215 (1973).
184. 294 U.S. 103 (1935). See Richard H. Frost, *The Mooney Case* (Stanford: Stanford University Press, 1968).
185. 294 U.S. at 112.
186. See, e.g., Giles v. Maryland, 386 U.S. 66 (1967); Miller v. Pate, 386 U.S. 1 (1967); Napue v. Illinois, 360 U.S. 264 (1959); Alcorta v. Texas, 355 U.S. 28 (1957); Mesarosh v. United States, 352 U.S. 1 (1956); White v. Ragen, 324 U.S. 760 (1945); *Ex parte* Hawk, 321 U.S. 114 (1944); People *ex rel.* Whitman v. Wilson, 318 U.S. 688 (1943); Pyle v. Kansas, 317 U.S. 213 (1942).

entitled to under due process. As the Court once observed, "The Due Process Clause did not stereotype the means for ascertaining the truth" of such claims as this one.[187] But it is worth noting that the Supreme Court insists that a state prison rule abridging or impairing a prisoner's right to apply to the federal courts for a writ of habeas corpus is invalid.[188] A state prisoner also raises a federal question if he alleges that the prison officials suppressed his appeal documents.[189] There is a due process right of access to the courts, for otherwise the right to a fair hearing could be frustrated altogether. Furthermore, in a 1955 decision, the Court ruled that a state appellate court denies due process if it disposes of a criminal appeal on the basis of a transcript fraudulently prepared by the prosecutor.[190] While the defendant was not given his freedom, the Court held that he was entitled to be heard on the issue in a federal habeas corpus proceeding, and that the trial judge erred in dismissing the petition summarily as not stating a cause of action. As a matter of fact, in 1956 the Court went so far as to rule, though by a 5-4 vote, that a state denies due process if it refuses to provide a transcript, without cost, for an indigent defendant where the transcript is necessary to secure an adequate review of alleged trial errors.[191] "There can be no equal justice," said Justice Black, "where the kind of trial a man gets depends on the amount of money he has."

In 1963, in the important case of *Brady* v. *Maryland*,[192] the Court extended the thrust of the *Mooney* rule by holding that the prosecution's refusal of permission to defendant's counsel to inspect an accomplice's extrajudicial statements constituted, as in the case of the knowing use of false testimony, a denial of due process of law. "We now hold," wrote Justice Douglas, "that the suppression by the prosecution of evidence favorable to an accused upon request violates due process where the evidence is material either to guilt or to punishment, irrespective of the good faith or bad faith of the prosecution."[193] The underlying principle is not punishment of society for the misdeeds of the prosecutor, but avoidance of an unfair trial to the accused. The Court has indicated, however, that there is no constitutional requirement that the prosecution must make a complete and detailed accounting to the defense of all police

187. Hysler v. Florida, 315 U.S. 411, 417 (1942).
188. *Ex parte* Hull, 312 U.S. 546 (1941). See also White v. Regan, 324 U.S. 760, n. 1 (1945).
189. Cochran v. Kansas, 316 U.S. 255 (1942).
190. Chessman v. Teets, 350 U.S. 3 (1955).
191. Griffin v. Illinois, 351 U.S. 12 (1956).
192. 373 U.S. 83 (1963).
193. 373 U.S. 87. For a recent decision to the same effect, see Giglio v. United States, 405 U.S. 150 (1972). See Ronald N. Boyce, "Suppressed and Perjured Evidence: A Denial of Due Process," *Utah Law Review,* 5 (Spring 1956): 92-97.

investigatory work on a case, and that whether the prosecution unfairly suppressed evidence requested by the defense turns on the following factors: (1) suppression by the prosecution must have followed a defense request; (2) the evidence must be favorable to the defense; (3) the evidence must be material.[194]

An interesting variation on this theme was before the Court in 1973 in *Wardius v. Oregon*,[195] which dealt with a narcotics prosecution. At issue was a state statute which provided that a defendant may not introduce alibi evidence unless he first gives pretrial notice to the prosecution of his intention to introduce alibi evidence and identifies his alibi witnesses. The Court ruled that due process precludes enforcement of such a statute unless the defendant is given reciprocal discovery rights. Justice Marshall observed that discovery procedures are desirable in best serving the ends of justice, but that there must be a balance of forces between the accused and the accuser. Discovery must be a two-way street; otherwise, it is unfair. In a concurring opinion, Justice Douglas maintained that the notice-of-alibi statute was contrary to the rule against self-incrimination, since the defendant is compelled to aid the state in his prosecution.

The Prosecution and the Boundaries of Propriety

In a larger sense, the public prosecutor is not only obliged to refrain from using perjured testimony which he knows to be false and from suppressing evidence favorable to the accused. He is also obliged to refrain from overstepping the bounds of propriety and fairness in seeking convictions. He acts improperly if he misrepresents vital facts to the grand jury, or if he withholds evidence which might help the defendant, or if he persistently misstates the facts in his cross-examination of witnesses, or bullies and argues with the witnesses, or asserts personal knowledge of matters not proved, or if in his argument to the jury he indulges in "an appeal wholly irrelevant to any facts or issues in the case, the purpose and effect of which could only have been to arouse passion and prejudice."[196] Justice Sutherland once wrote on this subject,

---

194. Moore v. Illinois, 408 U.S. 786 (1972). The decision was 5-4, the dissenters arguing that evidence was withheld which might have been of substantial assistance to the defense.

195. 412 U.S. 470 (1973).

196. Viereck v. United States, 318 U.S. 236, 247 (1943). The Court is much more reluctant to overturn a state criminal conviction on the basis of the impropriety of the prosecutor's remarks, than in federal cases, on the theory that its general supervisory power over the lower federal courts provides a broader base for review than due process. Donnelly v. DeChristoforo, 416 U.S. 637 (1974). Speaking in dissent, Justice Douglas wrote, "The function of the prosecutor under the Federal Constitution is not to tack as many skins of victims as possible to the wall. His function is to vindicate the right of the people as expressed in the laws and give those accused of crime a fair trial." 416 U.S. 648-49.

The United States Attorney is the representative not of an ordinary party to a controversy, but of a sovereign whose obligation to govern impartially is as compelling as its obligation to govern at all; and whose interest, therefore, in a criminal prosecution is not that it shall win a case, but that justice shall be done. As such, he is in a peculiar and very definite sense the servant of the law, the twofold aim of which is that guilt shall not escape or innocence suffer. He may prosecute with earnestness and vigor—indeed, he should do so. But, while he may strike hard blows, he is not at liberty to strike foul ones. It is as much his duty to refrain from improper methods calculated to produce a wrongful conviction as it is to use every legitimate means to bring about a just one.[197]

The same view prevails in the state courts. In a fine statement Judge J. O. Waite of the Court of Common Pleas of Erie County, Pennsylvania, once made this point in the following words:

Under our jurisprudence a criminal prosecution is not a contest between the commonwealth doing all possible to secure a conviction and a defendant endeavoring to secure an acquittal. It is and should be an impartial investigation by the state to determine whether or not the accused is guilty of the offense charged against him. It is the duty of the District Attorney to present not only the facts against the accused but also those favoring him when the same have not been developed by his own counsel. The standard by which a District Attorney's office should be measured is not the proportion of the convictions secured but by the fairness with which each case is tried.[198]

A Note on Contempt of Court Procedure

The basic procedural principles applicable to the imposition of penalties by federal judges for criminal contempt are stated succinctly in Rule 42 of the Federal Rules of Criminal Procedure. Rule 42(a) provides that "a criminal contempt may be punished summarily if the judge certifies that he saw or heard the conduct constituting the contempt and that it was committed in the actual presence of the Court."[199] Under Rule 42(b) any other criminal contempt "shall be prosecuted on notice. The notice shall state the time and place of hearing, allowing a reasonable time for the

---

197. Berger v. United States, 295 U.S. 78, 88 (1935).

198. Com. of Pa. v. Ellis (Smith), 21 Erie County L. J. 216, 217 (1939).

199. Rule 42 derives from an act of Congress enacted on March 2, 1831, 4 Stat. 487, as construed by the Supreme Court in later cases. In *Ex parte* Robinson, 19 Wall. (U.S.) 505, 510 (1874), Justice Field wrote, "The power to punish for contempts is inherent in all courts; its existence is essential to the preservation of order in judicial proceedings, and to the enforcement of the judgments, orders and writs of the court and, consequently, to the due administration of justice. The moment the courts of the United States were called into existence and invested with jurisdiction over any subject, they became possessed of this power." See Walter F. Murphy, "The Contempt Power of the Federal Courts," *Federal Bar Journal*, 18 (January-March 1958): 34-55.

preparation of the defense, and shall state the essential facts constituting the criminal contempt charged and describe it as such." Furthermore, the Rule goes on to say, "If the contempt charged involves disrespect to or criticism of a judge, that judge is disqualified from presiding at a trial or hearing except with the defendant's consent."

The power of the judge to punish summarily—i.e., without notice of charges and a hearing—contempts committed in open court before his own eyes is, in the words of the first Justice Harlan, "absolutely essential to the protection of the courts in the discharge of their functions. Without it, judicial tribunals would be at the mercy of the disorderly and violent, who respect neither the laws enacted for the vindication of public and private rights, nor the officers charged with the duty of administering them."[200] Even so, the Court suggested in a 1925 case that where the contempt had in it "the element of personal criticism or attack upon the judge," the substitution of another judge to evaluate the contempt and pronounce sentence *may* be the proper course to follow.[201] In 1954, the Court strengthened this rule by, in effect, converting "may" to "shall," holding that a judge should not sit himself in judgment where the contempt charged is entangled with the judge's personal feelings toward a lawyer held in contempt.[202] The "vital point," said Justice Frankfurter, "is that in sitting in judgment on such a misbehaving lawyer the judge should not himself give vent to personal spleen or respond to a personal grievance."

The Supreme Court has held that the power to punish summarily under Rule 42(a) should be reserved for "exceptional circumstances," such as threatening a judge or actually disrupting court proceedings, since summary contempt applies only to misbehavior where speedy punishment is necessary to vindicate the dignity and authority of the court. Thus, it has ruled that notice and a hearing are the appropriate procedures where an individual refuses to reply to questions propounded before a grand jury on the ground of self-incrimination.[203] On the other hand, in a 6–3 decision rendered in 1975, the Court upheld a summary conviction for

200. *Ex parte* Terry, 128 U.S. 289, 313 (1888).
201. Cooke v. United States, 267 U.S. 517, 539 (1925).
202. Offutt v. United States, 348 U.S. 11, 14 (1945). In Cammer v. United States, 350 U.S. 399 (1956), the Court held that a lawyer is not an officer of the court within the meaning of a statute (18 U.S.C. §401(2)), which authorizes federal judges to punish the misbehavior of any of its officers. The Court noted that the purpose of the statute, derived from the Contempt Act of 1831, 4 Stat. 487, was to limit and not broaden the contempt power of federal courts, and that in addition all summary powers should, as a general rule, be construed narrowly.
203. Harris v. United States, 382 U.S. 162 (1965), overruling Brown v. United States, 359 U.S. 41 (1959). The Court was divided 5–4.

contempt where a witness who was granted immunity by the judge persisted in refusing to reply to questions at a trial.[204] The Court held that Rule 42(a) was never intended to be limited to situations where a witness uses scurrilous language or creates physical disorder. Said Chief Justice Burger, "The face-to-face refusal to comply with the court's order itself constituted an affront to the court, and when that kind of refusal disrupts and frustrates an ongoing proceeding, as it did here, summary contempt must be available to vindicate the authority of the court as well as to provide the recalcitrant witness with some incentive to testify."[205] On the other hand, the Court has sustained the power of a federal court to punish, under Rule 42(b), the failure of an individual out on bail to obey a surrender order.[206]

Of course, Rule 42 applies only to the federal courts; whether a state court has abused its contempt power, if reviewable at all by the Supreme Court, is determined on the basis of the commitment of Fourteenth Amendment due process to the concept of a fair trial. Even so, recent decisions of the Supreme Court seem to point in the direction of applying the principles of Rule 42 to the state courts. For example, in a 1971 case, the Court noted that when a state judge has been repeatedly vilified by an abusive defendant to such an extent that he became embroiled in a bitter running controversy and was not likely to maintain calm detachment, due process required that the contemnor be given a public trial before another judge.[207] In the same year, the Court held that where it is not clear from the record that the judge personally witnessed the contemptuous conduct, there must be a hearing on this issue, and since the issue involved charges that the judge was biased, the hearing must be conducted by another judge, since, as the Court explained, "trial before an 'unbiased judge' is essential to due process."[208] In fact, the Supreme Court will set aside a conviction for criminal contempt in a state court if it is convinced that the conduct upon which the conviction was based was not in fact contemptuous. For example, in a recent case appealed from the highest court of North Carolina, a defendant was obliged to proceed *pro se*, since the judge had refused to grant a continuance requested because of the unavailability of the defendant's counsel, and in his summation the accused stated that

---

204. United States v. Wilson, 44 L. Ed. 2d 186 (1975).
205. 44 L. Ed. 2d 193.
206. Green v. United States, 356 U.S. 165 (1958). The decision was 5-4, the debate being over the availability of jury trial in a situation where the penalty was three years in jail. In Cheff v. Schnackenberg, 384 U.S. 373 (1966), the Court finally ruled that a sentence exceeding six months for criminal contempt may not be imposed without a jury trial.
207. Mayberry v. Pennsylvania, 400 U.S. 455 (1971).
208. Johnson v. Mississippi, 403 U.S. 212, 216 (1971).

the judge was biased and had prejudged his case, and that he was a political prisoner. The judge summarily sentenced this defendant to thirty days in jail for contempt. Noting that he had not spoken in a boisterous tone, and had in no way disrupted the court proceedings, a unanimous Supreme Court ruled that the defendant's statements did not constitute criminal contempt.[209] Since he was compelled to proceed *pro se,* he was clearly entitled to as much latitude in conducting his defense as an attorney would have. Furthermore, to constitute contempt, there must be an imminent threat to the administration of justice; the danger must not be remote or even merely probable. Trial judges were admonished not to confuse offenses to their sensibilities with obstruction of the administration of justice.

209. *In re* Little, 404 U.S. 553 (1972).

5 / The Writ of Habeas Corpus

Significance

The writ of habeas corpus is a legal process one may use to vindicate summarily his right to personal liberty when he is detained illegally.[1] It holds a high place in the Anglo-American world of law and government. Blackstone described the Habeas Corpus Act as "that great bulwark of our Constitution."[2] Another eighteenth-century Tory, Samuel Johnson, once said, according to Boswell, that "the habeas corpus is the single advantage which our government has over that of other countries."[3] It has been observed that the writ has been one of the most fought over of our heritages. "To it, in large measure, the English speaking people owe their reputation as a liberty-loving people."[4] Professor Chafee called it "the most important human right in the Constitution," the one right which safeguards most of the others.[5] The English legal historian Holdsworth has said, "This writ has a great place in the history of our constitutional law because it has come to be the most efficient protection ever invented for the liberty of the subject."[6] Chief Justice Chase once declared that "the great writ of habeas corpus has been for centuries esteemed the best and only sufficient defence of personal freedom,"[7] and Chief Justice Hughes described it as "the precious safeguard of personal liberty."[8]

English Origins

The historical origins of habeas corpus are not clear. The roots of the concept have been traced to Section 39 of Magna Carta, which provided

---

1. See Rollin C. Hurd, *A Treatise on Habeas Corpus*, 2d ed. (Albany: Little & Co., 1876). For a convenient collection of original materials on habeas corpus, see Zechariah Chafee, Jr., *Documents on Fundamental Human Rights* (Cambridge: Harvard University Press, 1951), second pamphlet.

2. 4 Com. *438.

3. James Boswell, *Life of Johnson* (New York: Modern Library [1952]), p. 348.

4. Rex A. Collings, Jr., "Habeas Corpus for Convicts—Constitutional Right or Legislative Grace?" *California Law Review*, 40 (Fall 1952): 335–61.

5. Zechariah Chafee, Jr., "The Most Important Human Right in the Constitution," *Boston University Law Review*, 32 (April 1952): 143–61, 144.

6. William S. Holdsworth, *A History of English Law*, 3d ed. (Boston: Little, Brown & Co., 1923), 1: 227.

7. *Ex parte* Yerger, 8 Wall. (U.S.) 85, 95 (1868).

8. Bowen v. Johnston, 306 U.S. 19, 26 (1939).

that "no free man shall be taken or imprisoned or disseised or exiled or in any way destroyed except by the lawful judgment of his peers or by the law of the land." This came to mean that no man should be imprisoned without due process of law, and the judges invented specific writs to implement this concept.[9] There were early medieval writs whose purpose was to protect the liberty of the subject, though in various ways they were all inadequate. One was *De Homine Replegiando,* which did not apply to prisoners arrested on special order of the Crown, when the need was apt to be most acute. Another was *De Manucaptione,* which was limited to larceny cases in the sheriff's court, and fell into disuse when sheriffs were forbidden in 1354 to take indictments. A third writ was *De Odio et Atia,* which was limited to the question of whether a homicide accusation had been based on grounds of "hatred and malice," and also fell into disuse.[10]

Technically, the writ of habeas corpus is a device by which a man is brought into court, but there are various types of such writs. He may be summoned to appear in order to be required to testify, or to reply to a complaint, or to stand trial for a crime. Thus, habeas corpus *ad respondendum* is used in civil cases to take a person out of the custody of one court into the custody of another, where he may be sued, and it also lies to bring up a person who is in jail to answer a criminal charge. Habeas corpus *ad deliberandum et recipiendum* is granted to remove a man jailed in one jurisdiction to the place where the offense was committed that he may stand trial there. Habeas corpus *ad prosequendum* issues when it is necessary to remove a prisoner in order that he may be prosecuted in the proper jurisdiction.[11] The purpose of habeas corpus *ad testificandum* is to bring up a prisoner so that he may testify before a proper court. Thus, originally, the writ of habeas corpus was used to get people into jail, rather than out of it. But "the great writ of liberty," habeas corpus *ad subjiciendum et recipiendum,* has so overshadowed all the others that it has preempted the general title as "the writ of habeas corpus."

The history of the writ, both in England and in the United States, has been one of gradual but steady expansion. In the medieval period it was used by the common law courts, along with the writs of certiorari and

---

9. Holdsworth, *History of English Law,* 9: 104–25.

10. *Ibid.,* pp. 105–8; Edward Jenks, "The Story of Habeas Corpus," *Law Quarterly Review,* 18 (January 1902): 64–77.

11. The territorial limitation in the federal habeas corpus statute, 28 U.S.C. §2241 (a) (1970) authorizing federal district courts to grant writs of habeas corpus "within their respective jurisdiction," applies only to the Great Writ, and not to a writ of habeas corpus *ad prosequendum.* Accordingly, under the "all writs" statute, 28 U.S.C. §1651 (a) (1970), a federal district court in California has jurisdiction to issue a writ of habeas corpus *ad prosequendum* to a prison official in New York ordering the delivery of a prisoner for trial in California. Carbo v. United States, 364 U.S. 611 (1961).

privilege, to extend their jurisdiction over the local and franchise courts. In the latter part of the fifteenth century and throughout the sixteenth the common law judges used it to defend their jurisdiction in their long contest with rival courts, Chancery (equity), the Council and Star Chamber, and Admiralty.[12] Apparently the first use of habeas corpus as a constitutional remedy against the Crown in behalf of men committed to jail came in the reign of Henry VII (1485-1509). By the time of Charles I it had become an established constitutional remedy.[13] The Petition of Right of 1627[14] complained that the King had imprisoned subjects without any cause shown, and that when they were brought up on habeas corpus, no cause was shown except the special command of the King. Such imprisonment was forbidden. Then the act of 1640 which abolished Star Chamber[15] specifically authorized the writ to test the validity of a commitment on order of the King or the Privy Council. But this act did not go far enough, since only a few judges had the right to issue the writ, and most judges were unwilling to grant it in vacation. In those days the courts were in session for only about half of each year.

Following directly upon the case of Francis Jenkes, a London trader who in 1676 had extraordinary trouble in getting his freedom on bail, after his arrest for making an allegedly subversive speech (he had urged that Parliament be called into session), Parliament finally adopted the landmark Habeas Corpus Act of 1679.[16] This statute, which is wholly procedural in character, is one of the classic illustrations of the central importance of procedure. Its main purpose was to provide for a speedy inquiry by the judge into the legality of any imprisonment on a criminal charge, and for a speedy trial on the charge. It provided that any of the judges of the superior courts could issue the writ, either in term or vacation. Severe penalties were imposed on any judge who refused without good cause to entertain the writ, and on any official failing to comply with the writ. A time was specified within which the return of the writ had to be made, and within which an adjudication had to be made. Any person indicted for treason or felony had to be tried at the next term of court or bailed. If the government's witnesses were not then ready, the accused could be committed to the next term, at which time he would either have to be tried or given his freedom. Jailers were required to deliver to

---

12. See Holdsworth, *History of English Law,* 9: 109-12.
13. See the great cases: Five Knights' Case, 3 St. Tr. 1-235 (1627); Six Members' Case, 3 St. Tr. 235-94 (1629). See Chafee, *Documents on Fundmental Human Rights,* pp. 295-305. See also Bushell's Case, 6 St. Tr. 951, 999 (1670). Chafee, pp. 306-26.
14. 3 Car. I, c. 1.
15. 16 Car. I, c. 10.
16. 31 Car. II, c. 2. See Chafee, *Documents on Fundamental Human Rights,* pp. 327-40.

prisoners a true copy of the warrant of commitment. No prisoner released by habeas corpus could be again committed for the same offense.

There were several defects in the Habeas Corpus Act of 1679 which were remedied by later legislation. For one thing, the court had no power to examine the truth of any return made by the jailer, and the statute did not apply to any detention not on a criminal charge. These defects were remedied by a statute adopted in 1816.[17] Furthermore, under the 1679 act only the prisoner himself could apply for the writ. A court decision in 1704 authorized one's agent or friends to apply for him.[18] This is important, for the prisoner may be sick, or mentally incompetent, or illiterate, or he may be held incommunicado.

American Origins

For the most part, the privilege of habeas corpus was part of American colonial law, usually resting on common law foundations. But the colonies also put habeas corpus provisions in their court laws and adopted very strict bail laws, with heavy penalties for violations.[19] There were well-known cases in the colonial period involving the uses of the writ. Massachusetts Judge Dudley's refusal of the writ, in 1689, to John Wise, who had been jailed for resisting collection of an illegal tax, was publicly denounced and led to a civil action against the judge. In 1707, in New York, the ministers Makemie and Hampton secured their release after being arrested on the order of Governor Cornbury for unlicensed preaching. A New Jersey judge was denounced by the assembly in 1710 for denying the writ to Thomas Gordon. The Maryland assembly declared in 1725 that the privilege of the Habeas Corpus Act was a "birthright of the inhabitants" quite independently of any royal grant. The status enjoyed by the writ is reflected in the Continental Congress's *Letter to the People of Quebec,* October 26, 1774, which bracketed habeas corpus with representative government, jury trial, free ownership of land, and free press as the great rights enjoyed by Americans.[20]

While there was no mention of the writ in either the Declaration of Independence or the Articles of Confederation, habeas corpus clauses

17. 56 Geo. III, c. 100.
18. Ashby v. White, 14 St. Tr. 695 (1704), 4th Resol., H.L., at 825.
19. See A. H. Carpenter, "Habeas Corpus in the Colonies," *American Historical Review,* 8 (1902): 18-27; Hurd, *A Treatise on Habeas Corpus,* Book I, chap. 5. South Carolina re-enacted the English statute in 1692.
20. The *Letter* said, "If a subject is seized and imprisoned, tho' by order of Government, he may, by virtue of this right, immediately obtain a writ, termed a Habeas Corpus, from a Judge, whose sworn duty it is to grant it, and thereupon procure any illegal restraint to be quickly enquired into and redressed." Chafee, *Documents on Fundamental Human Rights,* pp. 168-69.

were incorporated in seven of the revolutionary state constitutions, beginning with the North Carolina Constitution of December 1776. Thus the New York Constitution of 1777 provided, "The writ of habeas corpus shall be enjoyed in the most free, easy, cheap, expeditious and ample manner, and shall not be suspended by the legislature except in the most urgent and pressing occasions and for a limited time, not exceeding twelve months." The Northwest Ordinance of July 13, 1787, declared that the inhabitants of the territory "shall always be entitled to the benefits of the writ. ..." All the United States Constitution says on the subject (Art. I, §9, 1. 2) is that "the Privilege of the Writ of Habeas Corpus shall not be suspended, unless when in Cases of Rebellion or Invasion the public Safety may require it." Most state constitutions have a similar provision, though a few forbid any suspension. The very first federal statute dealing with the courts, the Judiciary Act of 1789, authorized all federal courts "to grant writs of habeas corpus for the purpose of an inquiry into the cause of commitment."[21]

The Uses of the Writ

Depending on the circumstances, there are various methods available to a person who has been convicted of committing a crime to vindicate legal rights. The most common is an appeal from a judgment, but other remedies include the suit for damages, the injunction, the declaratory judgment, and, above all, the writ of habeas corpus. There are many clauses in the federal habeas corpus statute which make it very clear that to be eligible to apply for the writ, the petitioner must be "in custody."[22] Thus, as Justice Fortas said of the writ, "Its province, shaped to guarantee the most fundamental of all rights, is to provide an effective and speedy instrument by which judicial inquiry may be had into the legality of the detention of a person."[23] The writ is therefore available only on a showing by the applicant that he is actually restrained of his freedom in some way,[24] and it is conventional to say that the only relief the habeas corpus court can give is discharge from the restraint. Actually, the Supreme Court, especially in recent years, has given the concept of "custody" an increasingly broader meaning. In addition, it should be noted that the statute provides that the habeas corpus court "shall . . . dispose of the matter as law and justice require."[25] Furthermore, Congress

21. 1 Stat. 73, 81, §14.
22. 28 U.S.C. §§2241, 2242, 2243, 2244, 2245, 2249, 2252, 2254 (1970).
23. Carafas v. LaVallee, 391 U.S. 234, 238 (1968).
24. Wales v. Whitney, 114 U.S. 564, 572 (1885): "Something more than moral restraint is necessary to make a case for habeas corpus. There must be actual confinement or the present means of enforcing it."
25. 28 U.S.C. §2243.

amended the statute in 1966 to authorize the habeas corpus court to order "release from custody *or other remedy,*"[26] and, in the words of Justice Fortas, this seems "specifically to contemplate the possibility of relief other than immediate release from physical custody."[27]

The expanding nature of the writ is reflected in the changing position of the Supreme Court with respect to the availability of the writ to test the legality of a sentence scheduled to be served in the future. In 1934, in *McNally* v. *Hill,*[28] the Court held that where a person has been convicted on two separate counts, and was sentenced to two terms in jail to be served concurrently, a court will not inquire in a habeas corpus proceeding into the validity of only one of the sentences, on the ground that a decision in favor of the petitioner would not result in immediate release from custody. This case was specifically overruled by a unanimous decision rendered in 1968 in which the Court ruled that a prisoner serving one of two consecutive sentences is eligible to apply for a writ of habeas corpus to attack the sentence scheduled to be served in the future.[29] The writ of habeas corpus, Chief Justice Warren noted, as both the symbol and the guardian of individual liberty, has three characteristics: since the Civil War its major purpose has been to provide postconviction relief; there must be a prompt adjudication of the challenged restraint; and, the district court is authorized to look behind the bare record of a trial proceeding and conduct a factual hearing to determine the merits of the alleged deprivation of constitutional rights. The decisive point on which the Court relied was that the postponement of adjudication hurts the petitioner. Thus, the *McNally* decision defeats the principal purpose of the writ, which is to provide for swift judicial review of alleged unlawful restraints on liberty. Arguing that remedial statutes should be construed liberally, the Chief Justice concluded that the habeas corpus court may fashion some other remedy than immediate release.

In any event, some sort of custody or detention or loss of liberty must be involved to permit a judicial determination through habeas corpus. Thus, except in rare and exceptional cases, habeas corpus is not available before trial to an accused who is free on bail, and not being in custody he cannot use the writ to get a judicial inquiry into the size of the bail.[30] Further-

26. 28 U.S.C. §2244 (b).
27. 391 U.S. 234, 239.
28. 293 U.S. 131 (1934).
29. Peyton v. Rowe, 391 U.S. 54 (1968). Similarly, in Walker v. Wainright, 390 U.S. 335 (1968), the Court held that a prisoner could attack the first of two consecutive sentences in a federal habeas corpus proceeding even though he would still be confined under the second sentence if he succeeded.
30. Johnson v. Hoy, 227 U.S. 245 (1913); Walmer v. Tittemore, 61 F.2d 909 (7th Cir. 1932); Matysek v. United States, 339 F.2d 389 (9th Cir. 1964).

The Writ of Habeas Corpus / 137

more, it should be stressed that a prisoner who has been awarded habeas corpus is entitled to immediate discharge, even though the state appeals the court's decision to grant the writ, for otherwise, by mere notice of appeal, the custodian could prolong the term of an imprisonment already adjudged to be illegal "and frustrate the operation of the historic writ of liberty."[31]

Restraint may take various forms. One may be in jail pursuant to legal process emanating from a court. One may be in custody of the police following an arrest. A fugitive from justice is held for either international or interstate extradition. One may be restrained of his liberty by commitment to a mental institution. Restraint may be imposed by private authority, as in the case of custody of children. One may be in the custody of military or naval authorities. Aliens marked for exclusion or deportation may be held in custody. One may be detained under health or quarantine regulations. One may be jailed by a court for contempt, in the course of a civil action. The writ of habeas corpus is available for inquiry into the legality of all these forms of restraint.[32] It operates to free a person who is held by the police without charges, or who has been denied bail wrongfully or required to supply excessive bail. It can be used to test the sufficiency of the charge against one accused of crime, and above all, to challenge the jurisdiction of the court to try him. It will free a man if the court which tries him loses jurisdiction during the course of the proceedings. Courts have broad powers of inquiry where aliens are held for deportation. The jurisdiction of courts and legislative committees to commit for contempt can be tested by habeas corpus. It can be used to test the validity of some state or federal law or of some legal process.

The purpose of the ancient common law writ of habeas corpus is to free quickly one who has been detained illegally. It is known as a writ of right, because it issues automatically on a showing of cause. It is a writ of inquiry. It is also known as a high prerogative writ because it issues in the name of the sovereign power. It may be issued by any judge in chambers; the court does not have to be in session. The proceeding is summary, since it requires the immediate production of the person detained. There is no

---

31. People *ex rel.* Sabatino v. Jennings, 246 N.Y. 258, 260 (1927). Said Chief Judge Cardozo, "The writ may not be thwarted at the pleasure of the jailer. A statute suspending the effect of the discharge by the mere force of an appeal would be at war with the mandate of the Constitution whereby the writ of habeas corpus is preserved in all its ancient plenitude. . . . Little would be left of 'this, the greatest of all writs,' . . . if a jailer were permitted to retain the body of his prisoner during all the weary processes of an appeal begun without leave and languidly continued."

32. "The writ of habeas corpus is a procedural device for subjecting executive, judicial, or private restraints on liberty to judicial scrutiny." Chief Justice Wareen, in Peyton v. Rowe, 391 U.S. 54, 58 (1968).

time limit, no statute of limitations, so far as the writ of habeas corpus is concerned. The right to personal freedom from illegal restraint never lapses.

The essential elements of habeas corpus procedure may be stated briefly. The prisoner or a friend or agent petitions a judge. The judge issues the writ at once, and sends it to the jailer, whoever he is, and commands him to bring the prisoner to court at an early and specific hour together with the return, which is an explanation of the cause of the detention. Disregard of this order, though this rarely happens, is subject to severe punishment. Then the judge examines the return, hears evidence and argument if necessary, and decides whether the confinement is authorized by law. If it is lawful, the man goes back to custody; if it is not lawful, he is freed by the judge at once.

The Supreme Court, as well as Congress, has emphasized the basic importance of the writ of habeas corpus. Thus, the Court has ruled that a state may not make the writ available only to prisoners who can pay the filing fee,[33] and that a state is obliged to furnish a transcript or equivalent recordation of prior habeas corpus hearings for use in further proceedings.[34] Similarly, the Court has ruled invalid a state regulation which required submission of petitions for habeas corpus to the prison authorities before going to court.[35] More recently, the Court held invalid a state prison regulation which forbade any inmate from aiding another in the preparation of petitions for writs, whether with or without fee.[36] It was noted that the effect of this regulation, in the absence of any other sort of assistance, was to deny assistance to the many illiterate or poorly educated prisoners. The writ is much too important to permit such interference.[37]

That the writ of habeas corpus is not "a static, narrow, formalistic remedy" was emphasized in 1963 by a unanimous Court in *Jones* v. *Cunningham*.[38] Here the Court held that a state prisoner who was on parole, under an order significantly restricting his freedom, was "in custody" within the meaning of the federal habeas corpus statute, and that while

33. Smith v. Bennett, 365 U.S. 708 (1961).
34. Long v. District Court, 385 U.S. 192 (1966).
35. *Ex parte* Hull, 312 U.S. 546 (1941).
36. Johnson v. Avery, 393 U.S. 483 (1969).
37. See Marshall W. Krause, "A Lawyer Looks at Writ-Writing," *California Law Review,* 56 (April 1968): 317-77; Herman C. Spector, "A Prison Librarian Looks at Writ-Writing," *ibid.,* pp. 365-70; Note, "Prisoner Assistance on Federal Habeas Corpus Petitions," *Stanford Law Review,* 19 (April 1967): 887-94; Note, "Prison 'No-Assistance' Regulations and the Jailhouse Lawyer," *Duke Law Journal,* 1968 (April 1968): 343-61; Note, "Legal Services for Prison Inmates," *Wisconsin Law Review,* 1967 (Spring 1967): 514-31.
38. 371 U.S. 236, 243 (1963).

being on parole mooted the proceeding against the prison superintendent, the writ could issue against the members of the parole board. Under the terms of the parole order, the petitioner was required to live with designated relatives, he needed the permission of his parole officer to leave the community, change his residence, or own or operate a motor vehicle, and he had to make monthly reports to the parole officer. The officer was permitted to visit the petitioner at his home or place of employment at any time. Finally, the petitioner could be rearrested whenever the parole officer or the board believed he had violated a term or condition of the parole. Under these circumstances the Court held that the petitioner was under such restraint as to place him constructively "in custody," and thus he was entitled to petition for a writ of habeas corpus.

Five years later, in *Carafas* v. *LaVallee*,[39] a New York state prisoner, while still in custody pursuant to a conviction for burglary and grand larceny, and after exhausting his state remedies, applied to a federal district court, in June 1963, for a writ. His sentence expired in March 1967, and he was discharged from his parole status by the time the Supreme Court granted a writ of certiorari on October 16, 1967. Reversing a previous 5-4 decision,[40] the Court held that once the federal district court has taken jurisdiction, the petitioner is not defeated in his quest because he was released prior to the completion of proceedings on his application. The Court ruled that the case was not moot because, as a result of his conviction, the petitioner was unable to engage in certain businesses, such as the liquor trade, he was for a period of time ineligible to serve as a labor union official, and he could not vote or serve on juries in New York. Because of these collateral disabilities flowing from his conviction, it was decided that he had a substantial stake in the judgment of conviction which survived the satisfaction of the sentence. Said Justice Fortas, "He is suffering, and will continuing to suffer, serious disabilities because of the law's complexities and not because of his fault, if his claim that he has been illegally convicted is meritorious. There is no need in the statute, the Constitution or sound jurisprudence for denying to petitioner his ultimate day in court."[41] Under the statute the Court has a broad mandate to "dispose of the matter as law and justice require," and it speaks of "release from custody or other remedy." It follows that immediate release

---

39. 391 U.S. 234 (1968).
40. Parker v. Ellis, 362 U.S. 574 (1960). This case held that after a state prisoner is dismissed from prison, the case is moot so far as the jurisdiction of the Supreme Court is concerned with respect to a review of a previous denial of habeas corpus by the lower federal courts.
41. 391 U.S. 239.

from physical custody is not an indispensable precondition for granting relief under the federal habeas corpus act.

Similarly, in a 1973 decision, the Court held that after a person has been convicted in a state court, and has been released on his own recognizance pending execution of sentence, he was "in custody" within the meaning of the federal habeas corpus act.[42] Under California law he was subject to restraints not shared by the public generally; for example, he had to appear at all times and places ordered by the court, and he had to keep in force the stay of execution of sentence, described by Justice Brennan as in "itself an unusual and substantial impairment of his liberty."[43] Justice Brennan pointed out that the functions of habeas corpus "have undergone dramatic changes," and that the Court has "consistently rejected interpretations of the habeas corpus statute that would suffocate the writ in stifling formalisms or hobble its effectiveness with the manacles of arcane and scholastic procedural requirements."[44] The Court could discover no interference with any significant state interest since after he begins his sentence, the petitioner can surely ask for the writ.[45]

Habeas Corpus and Appeal

It is fundamental that habeas corpus is not a substitute for an appeal.[46] An appeal from a judgment is a direct review, and can raise many issues not permissible in a petition for habeas corpus, which is at best a form of indirect review, or what lawyers call a collateral attack on the judgment.[47] There are also procedural differences. Thus there are always time limits for appeals, whereas the right to file a petition for the writ never lapses. An appeal is limited to the trial record, but evidence outside the record is admissible in a habeas corpus proceeding. An appellant must raise all his objections in his appeal, but a petitioner for the writ need not raise all of

42. Hensley v. Municipal Court, 411 U.S. 345 (1973).
43. 411 U.S. 352.
44. 411 U.S. 345-50.
45. Justice Blackmun wrote a concurring opinion to question the wisdom of equating custody with almost any restraint, however tenuous. Three dissenting Justices argued that the petitioner was in neither actual or constructive custody, and complained that "the Court apparently feels, like Faust, that it has in its previous decisions already made its bargain with the devil, and it does not shy from this final step in the rewriting of the statute." 411 U.S. 355 (Rehnquist, J.).
46. Adams v. U.S. *ex rel.* McCann, 317 U.S. 269, 274 (1942); Glasgow v. Moyer, 225 U.S. 420, 428 (1912); *In re* Gregory, 219 U.S. 210, 213 (1911).
47. See Alexander Holtzoff, "Collateral Review of Convictions in Federal Courts," *Boston University Law Review,* 25 (January 1945): 26-55; Frank A. Peters, "Collateral Attack by Habeas Corpus upon Federal Judgments in Criminal Cases," *Washington Law Review,* 23 (May 1948): 87-115.

his objections in the same petition, though he may get into difficulties if he doesn't. An appeal always goes to a higher court than the trial court, whereas the prisoner's first petition for the writ of habeas corpus is filed in a court of coordinate jurisdiction. Furthermore, the findings of fact of the court in which the first habeas corpus proceeding is had are not final, and may be considered on appeal *de novo*. This is not true for most appeals.

In a larger sense, it is to be noted that the doctrine of *res judicata*—that once a cause of action has been finally determined between the parties on the merits by a competent court, it cannot be litigated again in any court—does not apply to habeas corpus. That is to say, if a prisoner has once applied for a writ and has been denied relief, he is not precluded from petitioning once more for the writ. The Supreme Court, however, has taken the position that while *res judicata* does not apply to a decision on habeas corpus refusing to discharge the prisoner, "it does not follow that a refusal to discharge on one application is without bearing or weight when a later application is being considered."[48] A federal court may, "according to a sound judicial discretion guided and controlled by a consideration of whatever has a rational bearing on the subject," dismiss a petition where the ground has been considered in a previous application.[49] When Congress revised the habeas corpus law in 1948, this principle was put in statutory form which now reads as follows: "No circuit or district judge shall be required to entertain an application for a writ of habeas corpus to inquire into the detention of a person pursuant to a judgment of a court of the United States if it appears that the legality of such detention has been determined by a judge or court of the United States on a prior application for a writ of habeas corpus and the petition presents no new ground not theretofore presented and determined, and the judge or court is satisfied that the ends of justice will not be served by such inquiry."[50]

The next paragraph of the federal habeas corpus act applies the same principle to state prisoners who apply for writs in federal courts.[51] Here again, after a federal court or judge has denied the writ to a state prisoner, "a subsequent application for a writ of habeas corpus . . . need not be entertained by a court of the United States or a justice or judge of the United States unless the application alleges and is predicated on a factual or other ground not adjudicated on the hearing of the earlier application for the writ, and unless the court, justice, or judge is satisfied that the

---

48. Salinger v. Loisel, 265 U.S. 224, 230 (1924).
49. Wong Doo v. United States, 265 U.S. 239, 240 (1924).
50. 28 U.S.C., §2444 (a) (1970).
51. 28 U.S.C. §2444 (b).

applicant has not on the earlier application deliberately withheld the newly asserted ground or otherwise abused the writ."[52]

So far as prisoners are concerned, the writ of habeas corpus is mainly concerned with jurisdictional questions. In attempting to attack his conviction collaterally by habeas corpus, the prisoner may properly make such objections as these: that the trial court lacked jurisdiction over the offense or over the person of the defendant, that the statute under which he was prosecuted was unconstitutional, or that the indictment charged an offense unknown to the law. Other permissible objections will be noted later. But objections which do not affect jurisdiction, and which may be advanced in an appeal, do not fall within the scope of habeas corpus. For example, a court will not, in a habeas corpus proceeding, inquire into the question as to whether the evidence was sufficient to sustain the verdict, since "upon habeas corpus the court examines only the power and authority of the court to act, not the correctness of its conclusions."[53] Similarly, a court will not, in a habeas corpus proceeding, consider such objections as that the court erred in its charge to the jury, or in the admission or exclusion of evidence, or in failing to acquit.

An Expanding Writ

The writ of habeas corpus has been far from static. Over the years, both as a result of legislation and court decisions, it has gradually expanded far beyond the common law of the eighteenth century. Under the English Habeas Corpus Act of 1679 the writ was not available to any person convicted of a crime in a court of competent jurisdiction. This principle was adopted by John Marshall in 1830 in *Ex parte Watkins,* where he asserted that "the judgment of a court of record whose jurisdiction is final, is as conclusive on all the world as the judgment of this court would be. It is as conclusive on this court as it is on other courts. It puts an end to inquiry concerning the fact by deciding it."[54] In other words, the object of habeas corpus is the liberation of persons imprisoned without sufficient

---

52. See Smith v. Yeager, 393 U.S. 122 (1968), which held that a state prisoner's relinquishment of the right to an evidentiary hearing in a federal habeas corpus proceeding does not prevent him from getting an evidentiary hearing in a later application for federal habeas corpus so long as it is established that the petitioner did not deliberately withhold any newly asserted ground in the prior proceeding, or otherwise abuse the writ. See also Neil v. Biggers, 409 U.S. 188 (1972), in which the Court held that its affirmance by an equally divided vote of an appeal from a conviction in a state court settles no issue of law and is therefore entitled to no precedential weight; it follows that such a judgment of the Supreme Court is not an adjudication which would bar a later habeas corpus proceeding in a federal court.

53. Harlan v. McGourin, 218 U.S. 442, 448 (1910).

54. 3 Pet. (U.S.) 193, 203. See also *Ex parte* Kearney, 7 Wheat. (U.S.) 38 (1822).

cause, and the judgment of a court of record having final jurisdiction is sufficient cause.

The first great change in federal law on this subject occurred with the enactment of the Judiciary Act of February 5, 1867,[55] adopted to help enforce the Reconstruction Acts. This statute made federal habeas corpus available to state as well as federal prisoners, and provided that federal judges, "in addition to the authority already conferred by law, shall have power to grant writs of habeas corpus in all cases where any person may be restrained of his or her liberty in violation of the constitution, or of any treaty or law of the United States." The statute also provided that "the petitioner may deny any of the material facts set forth in the return, or may allege any fact," to show that his detention was illegal, and the court to which the petition was addressed was required to determine the facts by hearing testimony and argument. This gave the prisoner a right to have the court consider the truth and substance of the causes of his detention. This, clearly, was a broader review than the bare review which common law practice permitted, for it opened the door to a more searching inquiry by the judge into the actual facts. The first case in which the Supreme Court used certiorari to bring up the record of a trial court in a habeas corpus case where the petitioner was under sentence was *Ex parte Lange,*[56] decided in 1873. The sentence was declared void and Lange's release was ordered. This case made it clear that the judgment of a court of competent jurisdiction was not conclusive, since the court's power to render the judgment may be inquired into by habeas corpus. It was also established that in deciding the matter the appellate court considers the record as well as the petition and return. The Supreme Court has never entertained any doubt of the power of Congress thus to liberalize the common law procedure on habeas corpus.[57]

Chief Justice Hughes once observed that "it must never be forgotten that the writ of habeas corpus is the precious safeguard of personal liberty and there is no higher duty than to maintain it unimpaired."[58] Thus, while the rule is that ordinarily where the trial court has determined its own jurisdiction over an offense, that decision must be reviewed by appeal, it is equally true that this rule is not so inflexible as to preclude habeas corpus where there are exceptional circumstances. One such circumstance would be where there is a conflict between state and federal authorities on an important question of law regarding their respective jurisdictions.[59]

55. 14 Stat. 385.
56. 18 Wall. (U.S.) 163 (1873).
57. Frank v. Mangum, 237 U.S. 309, 331 (1915).
58. Bowen v. Johnston, 306 U.S. 19, 26 (1939).
59. 306 U.S. 19, 26.

The most important decisions which have expanded the scope of habeas corpus have been those dealing with the denial or violation of constitutional rights. The power of the federal courts in this area is based upon the section of the 1867 act which provides for relief where a person is held "in violation of the constitution." On this issue judgments are examined and evidence is taken outside the original criminal trial record. The theory of the Supreme Court has been that even if the trial court originally had jurisdiction, it may be lost subsequently because of the denial of some constitutional right in the course of the trial. One of the best explanations of this development will be found in Justice Black's opinion in *Johnson* v. *Zerbst*,[60] decided in 1938. It was held here that the denial to a defendant in a federal trial court of the Sixth Amendment right to representation by counsel was remediable by habeas corpus. While Justice Black agreed that habeas corpus cannot be used as a substitute for an appeal as a way of reviewing errors of law not involving the issue of jurisdiction, he also pointed out, "The scope of inquiry in habeas corpus proceedings has been broadened—not narrowed—since the adoption of the Sixth Amendment." Compliance with the constitutional mandate of the Sixth Amendment, he held, is an essential jurisdictional prerequisite to a federal court's authority to try a person for a crime. "A court's jurisdiction at the beginning of trial may be lost 'in the course of the proceedings' due to failure to complete the court—as the Sixth Amendment requires—by providing Counsel for an accused who is unable to obtain Counsel, who has not intelligently waived this constitutional guaranty, and whose life or liberty is at stake. If this requirement of the Sixth Amendment is not complied with, the court no longer has jurisdiction to proceed. The judgment of conviction pronounced by a court without jurisdiction is void, and one imprisoned thereunder may obtain release by habeas corpus."

It is clear that a prisoner may present in a habeas corpus hearing the allegation that he was convicted under an unconstitutional statute or ordinance,[61] or that he was convicted twice for the same offense.[62] Similarly, a charge that the prisoner had been deceived or coerced into pleading guilty[63] is admissible in a habeas corpus proceeding. In a case[64] where the petitioner alleged that he had been coerced, by intimidation and threats of a federal law enforcement officer, to enter a plea of guilty, the Court said, "The issue here was appropriately raised by the habeas corpus petition. The facts relied on are dehors the record and their effect on the

---

60. 304 U.S. 458 (1938).
61. Yick Wo v. Hopkins, 118 U.S. 356 (1886); *Ex parte* Siebold, 100 U.S. 371 (1879).
62. *Re* Hans Nielson, 131 U.S. 176 (1889).
63. Walker v. Johnston, 312 U.S. 275 (1941).
64. Waley v. Johnston, 316 U.S. 101, 104 (1942).

judgment was not open to consideration and review on appeal. In such circumstances the use of the writ in the federal courts to test the constitutional validity of a conviction for crime is not restricted to those cases where the judgment of conviction is void for want of jurisdiction of the trial court to render it. It extends also to those exceptional cases where the conviction has been in disregard of the consititutional rights of the accused, and where the writ is the only effective means of preserving his rights."

Perhaps the most striking expansion of the scope of habeas corpus has been in the field of federal review of petitions filed by prisoners held in state institutions pursuant to the judgment of state courts.[65] The constitutional weapon has been the Due Process Clause of the Fourteenth Amendment, to which the Supreme Court has given an ever broader construction over the years. Thus a state denied due process if it permitted a criminal trial to be held under the domination of a mob, so "that counsel, jury and judge were swept to the fatal end by an irresistible wave of public passion, and . . . the State Courts failed to correct the wrong";[66] or if the prosecution knowingly made use of perjured testimony;[67] or if the prosecutor tricked the defendant into pleading guilty;[68] or if the prosecutor suppressed evidence favorable to the accused and coerced witnesses to testify falsely;[69] or if the prosecutor prepared a fraudulent transcript;[70] or if proper representation by counsel had been denied;[71] or if there had been discrimination in the selection of the jury;[72] or if coerced confessions had been used.[73] In all such cases, if the state courts fail to act, federal courts may grant the writ of habeas corpus because the due process right to fair procedure has been denied.

The expanding character of the writ of habeas corpus is also reflected in the willingness of the Supreme Court to permit federal habeas corpus courts to fashion suitable modes of procedure. Thus, in 1969, in *Harris* v. *Nelson*,[74] the Court ruled that in appropriate circumstances, when a federal district court is confronted by a petition for habeas corpus which

65. See Note, "Federal Habeas Corpus for State Prisoners," *Columbia Law Review,* 55 (February 1955): 196-209.
66. Moore v. Dempsey, 261 U.S. 86, 91 (1923). See also Frank v. Mangum, 237 U.S. 309, 335 (1915).
67. Mooney v. Holohan, 294 U.S. 103, 112 (1935).
68. Smith v. O'Grady, 312 U.S. 329 (1941).
69. Pyle v. Kansas, 317 U.S. 213 (1942).
70. Chessman v. Teets, 350 U.S. 3 (1955).
71. Gibbs v. Burke, 337 U.S. 773 (1949); Wade v. Mayo, 334 U.S. 672 (1948).
72. Brown v. Allen, 344 U.S. 443, 467-74, 477-82 (1953).
73. Leyra v. Denno, 347 U.S. 556 (1954).
74. 394 U.S. 286 (1969).

establishes a *prima facie* case for relief, the court may authorize the use of suitable discovery procedures, including interrogatories, reasonably fashioned to elicit facts necessary to help the court to "dispose of the matter as law and justice require," even though such a procedure is not authorized by any specific statute. Said Justice Fortas, "The writ of habeas corpus is the fundamental instrument for safeguarding individual freedom against arbitrary and lawless state action. . . . The scope and flexibility of the writ—its capacity to reach all manner of illegal detention—its ability to cut through barriers of form and procedural mazes—have always been emphasized and jealously guarded by courts and lawmakers. The very nature of the writ demands that it be administered with the initiative and flexibility essential to insure that miscarriages of justice within its reach are surfaced and corrected."[75] Since a court has no higher duty than to process carefully petitions for habeas corpus, its power of inquiry is plenary.

Some Limiting Factors

It must not be forgotten that the writ of habeas corpus is an extraordinary remedy. In fact, no lower federal court can grant the writ unless authorized to do so by statute. It is also settled that the appellate jurisdiction of the Supreme Court in habeas corpus cases is subject to exception and regulation by Congress.[76] In the famous *McCardle* case[77] the Court bowed to the will of Congress and actually yielded jurisdiction over a case which had already been argued, in obedience to a later statute which withdrew the jurisdiction. Furthermore, while federal courts may free state prisoners who are held in violation of some federal right, this rule doesn't work both ways. Since under Article VI of the Constitution the national government is always supreme within the scope of its delegated authority, state courts have no power to discharge federal prisoners[78] or members of the armed forces of the United States[79] from custody by habeas corpus.

The character of the writ of habeas corpus is further illustrated by the proposition that it is altogether exceptional to grant it when the law has

---

75. 394 U.S. 290–91.
76. See Chief Justice John Marshall, in *Ex parte* Bollman, 4 Cranch (U.S.) 75, 94 (1807): ". . . power to award the writ by any of the courts of the United States, must be given by written law."
77. *Ex parte* McCardle, 7 Wall. (U.S.) 506 (1868). The Act of March 27, 1868, 15 Stat. 44, withdrew the appellate jurisdiction in habeas corpus cases granted to the Supreme Court by the Act of February 5, 1867, 14 Stat. 385. This jurisdiction was restored in 1885, 23 Stat. 437.
78. Ableman v. Booth, 21 How. (U.S.) 506 (1858).
79. Tarble's Case, 13 Wall. (U.S.) 397 (1872).

provided some other remedy in regular course. The writ is "usually confined to situations where there is peculiar and pressing need for it. . . ."[80] Thus a federal prisoner must exhaust his federal remedies before seeking the writ. "The usual rule," Justice Holmes once wrote, "is that a prisoner cannot anticipate the regular course of proceedings having for their end to determine whether he shall be held or released, by alleging want of jurisdiction and petitioning for a habeas corpus."[81] In fact, the prisoner must first exhaust even his administrative remedies, if any are available, as in deportation proceedings.[82]

When Congress revised the federal judicial code in 1948, a new alternative to habeas corpus (§2255) was provided for in respect to federal prisoners. Hitherto such a prisoner, wherever he may have been tried, had to petition for habeas corpus in the court sitting in the district in which his place of incarceration was located. This had two disadvantages. First, the habeas corpus hearing usually had to be held in a court in which the records were not readily available. If the petitioner was in a federal penitentiary in California, but had been convicted in New York, the records were in New York, even though the suit could be brought only to California. Second, the few district courts in whose jurisdiction the major federal penitentiaries are located were required to handle unusually large numbers of petitions, often far from the scene of the facts, the witnesses, and the records. Accordingly, after extensive consideration, the Judicial Conference of the United States recommended a change in procedure to permit collateral attack on convictions in the sentencing courts. The new remedy is in the nature of the ancient writ of error *coram nobis*. It provides that federal prisoners claiming the right to be released because of a violation of the Constitution or laws, or because the trial court lacked jurisdiction, or because the sentence was in excess of the authorized maximum, or is otherwise subject to collateral attack, may at any time file a motion in the court which imposed sentence to vacate or correct the sentence.[83] In its discretion the court may act *ex parte,* it is not required to entertain a second motion for similar relief, and its decision may be appealed to the court of appeals. The statute also provides that an application for a writ of habeas corpus in behalf of a prisoner who is authorized to apply for relief by motion shall not be entertained if it appears that the petitioner has failed to seek relief by motion to the

80. Goto v. Lane, 265 U.S. 393, 402 (1924).
81. *Ex parte* Simon, 208 U.S. 144, 147 (1908).
82. United States v. Sing Tuck, 194 U.S. 161, 168 (1904): "It is one of the necessities of the administration of justice that even fundamental questions should be determined in an orderly way."
83. 28 U.S.C. §2255 (1970).

sentencing court, unless the remedy by motion is inadequate or ineffective to test the legality of the detention.[84] The Supreme Court has ruled unanimously that this statute does not impinge upon the prisoner's right to attack his conviction collaterally, and that its sole purpose is "to minimize the difficulties encountered in habeas corpus hearings by affording the same rights in another and more convenient forum."[85] Thus, the Court has held that a federal prisoner has a right to raise issues in a postconviction proceeding under §2255 which state prisoners may raise in federal habeas corpus proceedings.[86] Similarly, the Court has ruled that just as a denial of an application for habeas corpus by a judge or court is not *res judicata,* since conventional ideas concerning finality of litigation do not apply where liberty is involved and violation of constitutional rights is alleged, so too, in enacting §2255, Congress did not intend to change preexisting law relating to successive applications.[87] Accordingly, the Court held that where a second §2255 motion is filed which is not based on a ground previously presented and determined, the sentencing court is obliged to hold a hearing on the second motion. It was noted that §2255 is as broad as habeas corpus, and was designed to safeguard the same rights in another and more convenient forum. Thus, a ruling in the first §2255 motion that the pleadings were deficient does not preclude a second motion which turns on the merits.

Furthermore, the Supreme Court has long taken the position,[88] now reinforced by the 1948 revision of the habeas corpus statute,[89] that a state prisoner must litigate his federal claim in the state courts at least once, pursuant to available state remedies, before being eligible to apply for the writ in a federal district court.[90] The federal courts should not and do not

84. Some states have similar procedures. See, e.g., Wis. Stat. 1973, §974.06.
85. United States v. Hayman, 342 U.S. 205, 219 (1952).
86. Kaufman v. United States, 394 U.S. 217 (1969).
87. Sanders v. United States, 373 U.S. 1 (1963).
88. *Ex parte* Royall, 117 U.S. 241 (1886); *Ex parte* Hawk, 321 U.S. 114 (1944); Sweeney v. Woodall, 344 U.S. 86 (1952); Jennings v. Illinois, 342 U.S. 104 (1951).
89. 28 U.S.C. §2254(b) (1970).
90. Wade v. Mayo, 334 U.S. 672 (1948); Brown v. Allen, 344 U.S. 443, 447-51 (1953); Picard v. Connor, 404 U.S. 270 (1971); Murch v. Mottram, 409 U.S. 41 (1972). The rule is otherwise if state remedies are not available. Mattox v. Sacks, 369 U.S. 656 (1962). A state prisoner may resort to a federal district court for habeas corpus where a federal constitutional issue was appealed to the state supreme court and adjudicated there, even though the state court could have based its decision on a state ground; this meets the exhaustion of state remedies rule. Irvin v. Dowd, 359 U.S. 394 (1959). Furthermore, while ordinarily a plea of guilty precludes federal habeas corpus on such an issue as discrimination in the selection of the grand jury, Tollett v. Henderson, 411 U.S. 258 (1973), when a state law permits a defendant to plead guilty without forfeiting his right to judicial review of specified constitutional issues, the defendant is not foreclosed from pursuing those constitutional claims in a federal habeas corpus proceeding. Lefkowitz v. Newsome, 420 U.S. 283 (1975).

assume that the state courts will refuse to do what law and justice require. But the rule that state remedies must first be exhausted does not operate where no appropriate state remedy exists,[91] or when the state arbitrarily bars access to its remedies.[92] In addition, the Court ruled, in 1950, that state remedies are not exhausted until an attempt has been made to secure a review of the highest state court in the United States Supreme Court by means of certiorari, even though the Supreme Court denies the overwhelming majority of applications for certiorari, and almost never gives reasons for doing so.[93] In 1953, however, the Court ruled that it was error for a federal district court to give any weight to the fact that certiorari was denied, since all the denial means is that four Justices did not think the case ought to be reviewed.[94] Finally, in 1963, in the leading case of *Fay* v. *Noia*,[95] the Court abandoned the position it took in 1950, holding that a petition to it for certiorari is not a state remedy. The Court pointed out that the old rule was unduly burdensome, since most petitions for certiorari are refused; it clogged the Court's calendar and consumed a great deal of its time. In addition, Justice Brennan made the obvious point that since the United States Supreme Court is not a state court, a request for a remedy there is not subsumed under the heading of exhaustion of state remedies. It should be noted, in this connection, that many state judicial authorities keenly resent the freeing of state prisoners by federal judges,[96] although in fact this happens very rarely. Of 541 petitions filed by state prisoners in federal courts in 1952, for example, only 1.8 percent were successful. In the ten-year period 1945–55, of 5,337 petitions for habeas corpus filed by state prisoners in federal courts, only 82 (about 1.5 percent) were granted.[97] In 1964, out of a total of 3,220 petitions filed, only 125 such applications were successful.[98]

91. Young v. Ragen, 337 U.S. 235 (1949). Cf. Preiser v. Rodriguez, 411 U.S. 475 (1973).
92. Dowd v. Cook, 340 U.S. 206 (1951).
93. Darr v. Burford, 339 U.S. 200 (1950).
94. Brown v. Allen, 344 U.S. 443 (1953).
95. 372 U.S. 391 (1963).
96. See Report of the Committee on Habeas Corpus of the Conference of Chief Justices, and the Report of the Conference, in 1953, *State Government,* 26 (October 1953): 241–45; James A. Emmert, Attorney General of Indiana, "Use and Misuse of Habeas Corpus Writ by Prisoners," *Proceedings of the Conference of the National Association of Attorneys General* (1946), pp. 53–59; Melvin E. Beverly, "Federal-State Conflicts in the Field of Habeas Corpus," *California Law Review,* 41 (Fall 1953): 483–98; Louis H. Pollak, "Proposals to Curtail Federal Habeas Corpus for State Prisoners: Collateral Attack on the Great Writ," *Yale Law Journal,* 66 (November 1956): 50–66.
97. Walter V. Schaefer, "Federalism and State Criminal Procedure," *Harvard Law Review,* 70 (November 1956): 1–26, 19.
98. "Developments in the Law: Federal Habeas Corpus," *Harvard Law Review,* 83 (March 1970): 1038–1280, 1041.

The 1948 changes in the federal judicial code, authorizing a federal judge to give weight to a previous denial of the writ by a federal judge, codifying the principle of the exhaustion of state remedies, and requiring federal prisoners to seek relief by motion in the sentencing court before trying for the writ, are all responses to abuses of the writ. For there can be no doubt of the fact that there have been abuses. For example, the Court's decision in the *Zerbst* case[99] promptly led to the filing of a flood of applications for writs in the judicial districts containing federal penal institutions. Between 1938 and 1941 no fewer than 75 petitions were filed in the Northern District of California by prisoners incarcerated in Alcatraz Penitentiary on the basis of the rule of the *Zerbst* case. Writing in 1948, Judge Louis E. Goodman noted that during the preceding ten years twenty-six inmates in Alcatraz filed a total of 167 petitions, and he observed that the writ is "an historic right established by the state to effectuate a public policy to protect liberty, . . . not a plaything of penitentiary inmates to accomplish temporary vacation visits to the federal courts. . . ."[100] A computation by another federal judge shows that during the years 1943, 1944, and 1945, 1,556 petitions were filed by federal prisoners in the lower federal courts, and 1,570 by state prisoners. Relief was granted in only 76 of these 3,126 cases, and of these 76, 57 involved federal prisoners.[101]

In this connection a New Jersey court once declared,

In our desire to aid any indigent prisoner in our penal institutions whose incarceration might be discovered to be unlawful, our courts have in recent years encouraged a current flow of petitions for writs of habeas corpus which are sham and baseless and in which the fictitious factual allegations are falsely verified. Prisoners have become a distinctive class of litigants to whom special and exceptional privileges are accorded. The payment of filing fees is excused. The court rules are uniformly relaxed in such cases. Counsel is sometimes appointed to represent a prisoner without compensation. Experience has now revealed that the benevolent opportunities so afforded most of these prisoners with the best of intentions are being notoriously abused by too many who are manifestly unworthy of such leniencies.

Many of the briefs submitted *pro se* by the appellants contain scandalous aspersions impugning the motives and integrity of the trial judge and prosecuting officials. . . . Defamation is not argumentation.[102]

99. Johnson v. Zerbst, 304 U.S. 458 (1938).
100. "Use and Abuse of the Writ of Habeas Corpus," 7 F.R.D. 313, 314 (1947).
101. Judge John J. Parker, "Limiting the Abuse of Habeas Corpus," 8 F.R.D. 171 (1948). On the abuse of the writ, see the remarks of Circuit Judge Miller in Dorsey v. Gill, 148 F.2d 857, 862, n. 42 (D.C. Cir. 1945), cert. denied, 325 U.S. 890 (1945), and the dissenting opinion of Justice Jackson in Price v. Johnston, 334 U.S. 266, 295–301 (1948).
102. State v. Bey, 26 N.J. Super. 331, 102 A.2d 684, 685 (1954).

Several Supreme Court Justices have expressed doubts about the extent to which federal habeas corpus is now available to state prisoners. For example, writing in 1973, and with the concurrence of Chief Justice Burger and Justice Rehnquist, Justice Powell argued that federal collateral review of a state prisoner's Fourth Amendment claim "should be confined solely to the question of whether the petitioner was provided a fair opportunity to raise and have adjudicated the question in state courts," since search and seizure issues rarely bear on the question of innocence.[103] He maintained that the expanded writ defeats the most effective utilization of limited judicial resources, weakens the principle of finality in criminal trials, exacerbates friction between the federal and state systems of justice, and impairs the constitutional balance upon which American federalism is founded.[104]

However much the writ has been abused, the Supreme Court has insisted that if the allegations of the petitioner raise issues of fact, they should be resolved by testimony rather than merely by affidavits. It disapproves of the district court's disposing of petitions on the basis of *ex parte* affidavits without taking testimony, since nothing less than a hearing "will satisfy the command of the statute that the judge shall proceed 'to determine the facts of the case, by hearing the testimony and arguments.'"[105] It has been held that courts should lean over backwards to give petitioners a hearing, since prisoners who are unlearned in the law and unfamiliar with the complicated rules of pleading often act as as their own counsel in habeas corpus proceedings.[106] Furthermore, the responsibility of the district judge to hold a hearing is one which he cannot delegate to a court commissioner; the judge must himself, pursuant to the federal habeas corpus statute, hear the prisoner's testimony and dispose of the petition in the light of all the evidence.[107] Similarly, when the office of court commissioner was abolished, and the U.S. Magistrate was created to take his place, the Court ruled that the federal habeas corpus statute

103. Schneckloth v. Bustamonte, 412 U.S. 218, 250 (1973) (concurring opinion).
104. 412 U.S. 259-66. See George C. Doub, "The Case against Modern Federal Habeas Corpus," *American Bar Association Journal,* 57 (April 1971): 323-28; Henry J. Friendly, "Is Innocence Irrelevant? Collateral Attack on Criminal Judgments," *University of Chicago Law Review,* 38 (Fall 1970): 142-72; Curtis R. Reitz, "Federal Habeas Corpus: Post-conviction Remedy for State Prisoners," *University of Pennsylvania Law Review,* 108 (February 1960): 461-532; D. J. Meador, "The Impact of Federal Habeas Corpus on State Trial Procedures," *Virginia Law Review,* 52 (March 1966): 286-300. See addendum at p. 159, below.
105. Walker v. Johnston, 312 U.S. 275, 285 (1941). The prisoner does not, however, have a right to appear personally in the Court of Appeals to argue on appeal from a district court's order denying the writ, although the Court of Appeals, in its discretion, may permit his appearance. Price v. Johnston, 334 U.S. 266 (1948).
106. Price v. Johnston, 334 U.S. 266 (1948).
107. Holiday v. Johnston, 313 U.S. 342 (1941).

(28 U.S.C. §2243) requires that the district judge hold the evidentiary hearing personally; he cannot delegate that function to his magistrate, nor does it satisfy the statute if the hearing before the magistrate is recorded electronically and the judge then listens to the playback, since listening to a recording is not a substitute for actually conducting a hearing.[108]

The Problem of Military Detention

The habeas corpus power of our civil courts also extends to persons held in custody pursuant to judgments of courts-martial, but its scope is necessarily quite limited.[109] For the law which governs the members of our armed forces, the Articles of War, has always been regarded as an independent body of jurisprudence, administered by a separate system of military justice. This law is wholly statutory, adopted by Congress under its constitutional grant of power "to make Rules for the Government and Regulation of the land and naval Forces."[110] Under the modernized Uniform Code of Military Justice,[111] adopted in May 1950, the procedures of the courts-martial were seriously overhauled, and a new review court was established, the United States Court of Military Appeals. American courts-martial have always exercised jurisdiction only over criminal matters. Since the armed forces are a responsibility of the national government, and their law is national in character, it has long been established that a state court has no jurisdiction to entertain petitions for writs of habeas corpus filed by persons held under federal military authority.[112]

The scope of judicial review of military commitments that is obtainable by way of habeas corpus in civilian courts is limited in several ways.[113] For one thing, an American court will refuse to rule on the decision of an international military court, such as the International Military Tribunal which sat in Japan, for lack of jurisdiction.[114] Nor will a civilian court give

---

108. Wingo v. Wedding, 418 U.S. 461 (1974). Chief Justice Burger and Justice White dissented, maintaining that the Federal Magistrates Act was intended to confer a new and more significant status to magistrates in order to save on the judge's time and energy.

109. See Seymour W. Wurfel, "Military Habeas Corpus," *Michigan Law Review,* 49 (February 1951): 493–528, 699–722; "Symposium on Military Justice," *Vanderbilt Law Review,* 6 (March 1953): 161–369, and especially James Snedeker, "Habeas Corpus and Court-Martial Prisoners," pp. 288–304; "Developments in the Law: Federal Habeas Corpus," *Harvard Law Review,* 83 (March 1970): 1038–1280, 1208–38.

110. Art. I, §8, cl. 14.

111. 64 Stat. 108.

112. Tarble's Case, 13 Wall. (U.S.) 397 (1872).

113. It is well settled that the judgment of a military tribunal is not subject to direct review by a civil court. *Ex parte* Vallandingham, 1 Wall. (U.S.) 243 (1863); Dynes v. Hoover, 20 How. (U.S.) 65, 79 (1858).

114. Hirota v. MacArthur, 338 U.S. 197 (1949).

relief to a nonresident enemy alien, for the same reason.[115] This limitation is important, since as a consequence of our far-flung military operations during and after World War II all over the world, many people have been convicted by military courts or commissions for war crimes or other offenses. Several hundred of their petitions for writs of habeas corpus have been denied by American courts.

Another limitation is found in the general rule that one must first exhaust all available remedies before seeking the extraordinary remedy of habeas corpus. This is now especially important for military cases, because when Congress revised the Articles of War in 1948, a new Article 53 was added, which provides that on application of the accused the Judge Advocate General may in his discretion grant a new trial in any court-martial case, or vacate a sentence, or restore rights and privileges, within one year after final disposition of the case. For offenses committed during World War II the application for a new trial may be made within one year after termination of the war, or after their final disposition upon initial appellate review, whichever is later. In the revised Uniform Code of Military Justice of 1950, this provision, now Article 73, states that "at any time within one year after approval by the convening authority of a court-martial sentence which extends to death, dismissal, dishonorable or bad-conduct discharge, or confinement for one year or more, the accused may petition the Judge Advocate General for a new trial on grounds of newly discovered evidence or fraud on the court."

The Supreme Court has ruled that a court cannot entertain a habeas corpus proceeding until the new remedy afforded by the Articles of War has first been exhausted.[116] An analogy was drawn with the rule that a state prisoner must exhaust all available state remedies before being eligible to file a petition in a federal court challenging the jurisdiction of a state court. The reason is the same in both instances. If the remedy is taken, then interference by the federal court may turn out to be wholly needless. The Court pointed out, however, that the provision in Article 53 that the action of the Judge Advocate General shall be "final and conclusive," and "binding upon all departments, courts, agencies, and officers of the United States," did not deprive courts of jurisdiction to

---

115. Johnson v. Eisentrager, 338 U.S. 877 (1949). Similarly, in Ludecke v. Watkins, 335 U.S. 160 (1948), the Court held that an enemy alien interned under the authority of the Enemy Alien Act of 1798, and held for deportation, was not entitled to the writ of habeas corpus.

116. Gusik v. Schilder, 340 U.S. 128 (1950); Noyd v. Bond, 395 U.S. 683 (1969). A federal district court is not required to stay habeas corpus proceedings brought by a serviceman where no relief has been possible through the military judicial system. Parisi v. Davidson, 405 U.S. 34 (1972).

review the military judgments later by habeas corpus. "We read the finality clause of Article 53," the Court said, "as doing no more than describing the terminal point for proceedings within the court-martial system." If Congress had intended thereby to suspend the writ of habeas corpus, which has been available since the beginning of our history, it would have expressed its purpose in "plain and unmistakable" language.[117]

Above all, the Supreme Court has insisted that with regard to military courts the only ground for relief is that the sentencing court lacks jurisdiction. "It is well settled that 'by habeas corpus the civil courts exercise no supervisory or correcting power over the proceedings of a court-martial. . . . The single inquiry, the test, is jurisdiction.' *Re Grimley*, 137 U.S. 147 (1890)."[118] Thus the court will not review on habeas corpus such matters as the sufficiency of evidence, the competence of counsel, and the adequacy of the pretrial investigation. The correction of these errors is for the military authorities who are authorized by law to review the decisions of courts-martial. Habeas corpus will be used to inquire only into the question of jurisdiction in the technical sense. Whether the military court was legally constituted, whether it had jurisdiction over the defendant and the offense, and whether the sentence was within the maximum limit for the offense, are the allowable questions.[119] In a recent decision the Supreme Court ruled that a statute permitting the army to try an ex-soldier for an offense committed while in the service, in a court-martial, was unconstitutional as denying the fair trial rights of the Fifth and Sixth Amendments.[120] But habeas corpus has no concern for questions of guilt or innocence.[121] Similarly, so long as the law governing court-martial procedure affords a defendant at some point of time an opportunity to tender the issue of insanity, any error by the military in evaluating the evidence on this question will not go to jurisdiction, the only

---

117. 340 U.S. 132-33.

118. Hiatt v. Brown, 339 U.S. 103 (1950). The Court so held in the first case to reach it on the subject. *Ex parte* Reed, 100 U.S. 13 (1879).

119. In Madsen v. Kinsella, 343 U.S. 341 (1952) the Court sustained the jurisdiction of the U.S. Court of the Allied High Commission for Germany over the wife of an officer who committed murder while living in the American Zone of Germany. Similarly the Court once ruled that a court-martial had jurisdiction to try for crimes dependents of U.S. troops stationed overseas in military installations. Kinsella v. Krueger, 351 U.S. 470 (1956); Reid v. Covert, 351 U.S. 487 (1956). But on reconsideration the following term the Court reversed itself, six Justices holding that civilian dependents of members of the armed forces overseas cannot constitutionally be tried by a court-martial in peace time for capital offenses committed abroad. Reid v. Covert, 354 U.S. 1 (1957). In U.S. *ex rel.* Hirschberg v. Cooke, 336 U.S. 210 (1949), a naval court-martial was held to lack jurisdiction.

120. U.S. *ex rel.* Toth v. Quarles, 350 U.S. 11 (1955).

121. *Ex parte* Quirin, 317 U.S. 1, 25 (1942); *In re* Yamashita, 327 U.S. 1, 8, 17 (1946).

issue before the court in a habeas corpus proceeding.[122] It is only a denial of an opportunity to tender the issue that goes to the question of jurisdiction.

The Supreme Court reviewed this problem in the leading case of *Burns v. Wilson*.[123] Two soldiers had been convicted in Guam, by army courts-martial, of the crimes of rape and murder, and sentenced to death. After exhausting all remedies available under the Articles of War for review by military tribunals, the accused petitioned the district court of the District of Columbia for habeas corpus, charging that they had been denied due process at the trial, alleging suppression of favorable evidence and use of perjured testimony by the prosecution, an atmosphere of terror, ineffective counsel, use of coerced confessions, and illegal detention. In denying the writ Chief Justice Vinson pointed out that in military habeas corpus the scope of matters open for review has always been more narrow than in civil cases. This is so because of the peculiar relationship between the civil and military law. Like state law, military law is a separate jurisprudence, geared to the needs of discipline and duty. Congress, to whom the whole matter is entrusted by the Constitution, has defined the rights of those subject to military law, and has provided a complete system of review within the military system. The new Uniform Code of Military Justice and the completely revised Articles of War have careful guarantees for fair trial and review, including a special postconviction remedy for collateral attacks on judgments. Like the state courts, the military courts have the same responsibilities as the federal courts to protect constitutional rights. While civil courts do have jurisdiction over an application for habeas corpus from a military prisoner, "when a military decision has dealt fully and fairly with an allegation raised in that application, it is not open to a federal civil court to grant the writ simply to re-evaluate the evidence." Thus, if the military courts have refused to consider the serious due process claims of the petitioners, a federal district court is empowered to review them *de novo*. But since the record shows that the military courts heard the petitioners on every allegation, "it is not the duty of the civil courts simply to repeat the process—to re-examine and reweigh each item of evidence. . . . It is the limited function of the civil courts to determine whether the military have given fair consideration to each of these claims."[124]

It is clear, therefore, in the light of this decision, that habeas corpus is in fact available to test the validity of a judgment of a court-martial where

---

122. Whelchel v. McDonald, 340 U.S. 112 (1951).
123. 346 U.S. 137 (1953).
124. 346 U.S. 142, 144.

the attack is grounded on a claim that the constitutional rights of the accused have been disregarded.[125]

It remains to be noted that habeas corpus may be available to one who challenges his draft classification, but the amount of judicial review is very limited. In *Estep* v. *United States*[126] the Court ruled that while the statutory provision that classification orders of the selective service authorities shall be "final" precludes the customary scope of judicial review, and forbids courts to weigh the evidence to determine whether the classification was justified, a board may not act without jurisdiction, and it lacks jurisdiction "if there is no basis in fact for the classification which it gave the registrant." The Court went a step further in *Dickinson* v. *United States*,[127] which held that once the registrant has demonstrated that he falls *prima facie* within the exempted class of ministers of the gospel, the board cannot make an adverse decision merely by refusing to believe his evidence, but must develop other evidence to support its conclusion. The scope of review, however, is narrower for conscientious objectors than for ministers, because one can make out a *prima facie* case for a ministerial status by means of objective facts alone, whereas sincerity and good faith belief, which are the ultimate issues in conscientious objector cases, are purely subjective considerations.[128]

Finally, after one has been lawfully inducted into the army, the question of the propriety of his particular assignment to duty is not subject to judicial review by ways of habeas corpus.[129] Pointing out that judges are not given the task of running the army, Justice Jackson said, "The military constitutes a specialized community governed by a separate discipline from that of the civilian. Orderly government requires that the judiciary be as scrupulous not to interfere with legitmate Army matters as the Army must be scrupulous not to intervene in judicial matters."

Suspension of the Writ

In England the writ of habeas corpus can be suspended only by act of Parliament. The writ was suspended in the revolutionary year 1688, in 1696, in 1714, 1722, and 1744 in connection with Jacobite difficulties, and

125. See Schita v. King, 133 F.2d 283 (8th Cir. 1943); U.S. *ex rel.* Innes v. Hiatt, 141 F.2d 664 (3d Cir. 1944); Hunter v. Wade, 169 F.2d 973 (10th Cir. 1948), aff'd., 336 U.S. 684 (1949). In *Ex parte* Endo, 323 U.S. 283 (1944) habeas corpus was secured to get out of a relocation center operated by the War Relocation Authority, a civilian agency.
126. 327 U.S. 114 (1946). See Note, "Habeas Corpus and Judicial Review of Draft Classifications," *Indiana Law Journal,* 28 (Winter 1953): 244–56.
127. 346 U.S. 389 (1953).
128. Witmer v. United States, 348 U.S. 375 (1955).
129. Orloff v. Willoughby, 345 U.S. 83 (1953).

in the years 1794-1801 by annual statutes, and again in 1817, all growing out of the Napoleonic upheavals. The writ was also suspended by annual statutes from 1777 to 1782, the years of the American Revolution, for the crimes of treason and piracy. Occasionally there were suspensions for named individuals. In the United States, the question of suspension of the writ of habeas corpus is largely a national one. The Massachusetts state legislature suspended the writ, during Shays' Rebellion, from November 1786 to July 1787,[130] but this was the only such action by a state. The Confederate states suspended the writ during the Civil War.[131]

The principal episode of suspension of the writ occurred during the Civil War. Thomas Jefferson had attempted to persuade Congress to suspend the writ in 1807, during the Burr conspiracy, but after the bill passed the Senate, it failed in the House of Representatives. In the same year Chief Justice John Marshall intimated that whether the writ should be suspended was for the legislative body to decide.[132] But when Lincoln was faced, at the very beginning of his term, with the overwhelming crisis of the Civil War, he proceeded forthwith to suspend the writ, and thousands of people were arrested and held without formal charges or regular trials, without being able to secure their liberty by habeas corpus.[133] The legality of this action was hotly debated, since the Constitution is not at all clear on this point. Article I, §9, merely says, "The Privilege of the Writ of Habeas Corpus shall not be suspended, unless when in Cases of Rebellion or Invasion the public Safety may require it."[134] It should be noted that a suspension statute is always aimed at persons suspected of crime and not at people who have been convicted. Such a statute operates only to deny prisoners a speedy accusation and a speedy trial.

When Congress met in special session on July 4, 1861, President Lincoln insisted, in his message, that he had acted within the Constitution.[135] He noted that the Constitution is silent as to whether the suspension must be by Congress. Plainly the pertinent clause was made "for a dangerous emergency," and he could not believe that the danger had to run its course until Congress could be assembled. Noting that it was his duty to execute

130. Mass. Laws 1786, c. 42.
131. *In re* Cain, 60 N.C. 525 (1864); State v. Sparks, 27 Tex. 705 (1864).
132. *Ex parte* Bollman, 4 Cranch (U.S.) 75, 101 (1807): "If . . . the public safety should require the suspension it is for the legislature to say so."
133. See J. G. Randall, *Constitutional Problems under Lincoln,* rev. ed. (Urbana: University of Illinois Press, 1951), chaps. VI-VIII.
134. This Clause applies only to the federal government, not to the states. Gasquet v. Lapeyre, 242 U.S. 367, 369 (1917).
135. James D. Richardson, *A Compilation of the Messages and Papers, of the Presidents, 1789-1897,* 10 vols. (Washington: Government Printing Office, 1896-99), VI: 24.

the laws, he asked the famous question, "Are all the laws but one to go unexecuted, and the government itself go to pieces lest that one be violated?" The venerable Chief Justice Taney protested, in the *Merryman* case,[136] that only Congress can suspend the writ in loyal sections of the country where the courts were still functioning. Appealing to English and colonial precedents, and to the authority of Story and Marshall, he denounced the President's action as one of military usurpation which brought to an end a government of laws. Admitting he could not enforce his order, the Chief Justice declared it was up to the President "to cause the civil process of the United States to be respected and enforced." This was not, it should be noted, a decision of the Supreme Court, but only of one Justice sitting as a circuit judge.

But the President stood his ground, and after considering the problem many times Congress finally passed the Act of March 3, 1863,[137] which declared, "That, during the present rebellion, the President of the United States, whenever, in his judgment, the public safety may require it, is authorized to suspend the privilege of the writ of habeas corpus in any case throughout the United States, or any part thereof." In *Ex Parte Milligan*,[138] decided in 1866, the Supreme Court, in ruling that a civilian could not be tried by a military commission in Indiana, which was not a theater of war, and where the regular courts were functioning, assumed that the 1863 statute was valid. The Court held that the suspension of the writ did not authorize the arrest of anyone, but merely denied to one arrested the privilege of the writ to obtain his liberty.

The writ of habeas corpus has been suspended several times since the events of the Civil War. By the Act of April 20, 1871,[139] commonly known as the Ku Klux Act, Congress authorized the President to suspend the writ in the case of unlawful combinations which amount to rebellions against the United States. For a brief period of time in the fall in 1871, President Grant suspended the writ, under this statute, in nine South Carolina counties. Habeas corpus was also suspended in 1905 in the Philippine provinces of Cavite and Batangas.[140] Finally the writ was suspended in Hawaii in 1941, but shortly after the war was over, the Supreme Court held, without ruling on any constitutional question, that there had been

---

136. Ex parte Merryman, Fed. Cas. No. 9487 (1861); Chafee, *Documents on Fundamental Human Rights*, pp. 370–83.

137. 12 Stat. 755.

138. 4 Wall. (U.S.) 2, 114. See Chafee, *Documents on Fundamental Human Rights*, pp. 384–412.

139. 17 Stat. 13.

140. Pursuant to the Act of July 1, 1902, 32 Stat. 691, §5. See Fisher v. Baker, 203 U.S. 174 (1906).

no legal authority for the suspension.[141] The Court did not look with favor upon any interpretation which would sanction total military rule of a civilian community where normal governmental institutions were functioning. "We have always been especially concerned," said Justice Black, "about the potential evils of summary criminal trials. . . ."

141. Duncan v. Kahanamoku, 327 U.S. 304 (1946). The suspension was previously upheld in *Ex parte* Zimmerman, 132 F.2d 442 (9th Cir. 1942), but see the dissenting opinion of Judge Haney.

Addendum on Fourth Amendment Claims

With reference to the subject discussed in the first paragraph on page 151, it should be noted that on July 6, 1976, by a 6-3 vote, the Supreme Court ruled that a state prisoner who has had a chance to litigate his Fourth Amendment claim fully and fairly in the state courts is not entitled to consideration by a federal habeas corpus court of his allegation that evidence secured in an illegal search and seizure was introduced at his trial. *Stone* v. *Powell,* 44 U.S.L.W. 5313. The Court majority argued that the possible deterrent effect upon unlawful police conduct was outweighed by the detriment to the criminal justice system. Speaking in dissent, Justice Brennan protested that the Court's ruling in this case "portends substantial evisceration of federal habeas corpus jurisdiction. . . ."

6 / Trial by Jury

Constitutional Origins

Our system of trial by jury—one of the distinctive features of Anglo-American justice—is the end result of the experience of a number of centuries. It has changed in the past, in many different ways, and like all dynamic institutions, it is still in a state of flux.

Originally jurors were witnesses, called to decide disputed questions of fact because they were already acquainted with the facts or could readily acquire the necessary information. But they were, even in the primitive days of English justice, more than witnesses, for they were also a method of proof which parties had to accept.[1] It was clear by the fourteenth century that the principal function of the jury was the judicial function of judging. Similarly, in the earliest days, the jury which made the charges or the presentment also decided the issue of guilt or innocence. While the precise details are not known, it seems to be agreed that the distinction between the grand jury, which made the presentment, and the petit jury, which sat in judgment on the charges, was well established by the middle of the fourteenth century.[2] Why the common law jury came to consist of twelve men is not known, though it should be noted that for a long time the number varied from one figure to another. The rule that the jury must decide by unanimous vote seems to date from a case decided in 1367, which held unacceptable a verdict agreed to by eleven jurors.[3] The right of jurors to reach a conclusion freely, without coercion on the part of the judge or other governmental authority, was established in *Bushell's Case*[4] in 1670, one of the landmarks of English law.

1. William S. Holdsworth, *A History of English Law,* 3d ed. (Boston: Little, Brown & Co., 1923), I: 317.
2. James Bradley Thayer, *A Preliminary Treatise on Evidence* (Boston: Little, Brown & Co., 1898), pp. 82–83.
3. Anon. Case, 41 Lib. Assisarum 11 (1367).
4. Vaughan's Rep. 135, 6 St. Tr. 999 (1670). See W. G. Mason, "The Four Jurors in Bushell's Case," *American Bar Association Journal,* 51 (June 1965): 543–47. Cf. R. v. McKenna, [1960] 1 All E.R. 326, 329, where, in setting aside a conviction because the trial judge had hurried the jury, Justice Cassels of the Court of Criminal Appeals said, "It is a cardinal principle of our criminal law that in considering their verdict, a jury shall deliberate in complete freedom, uninfluenced by any promise, unintimidated by any threat. They still stand between the Crown and the subject, and they are still one of the main defenses of personal liberty."

The authors of the Constitution were thoroughly familiar with the jury system, and made careful provision on the subject. Article III, §2, declares, "The Trial of all Crimes, except in Cases of Impeachment,[5] shall be by Jury; and such Trial shall be held in the State where the said Crimes shall have been committed; but when not committed within any State, the Trial shall be at such Place or Places as the Congress may by Law have directed." Many critics of the Constitution at the time of its submission to the states for ratification insisted that this was not an adequate guaranty of the right to trial by jury, and further assurances were quickly added by amendment. Thus, the Fifth Amendment provides that no one shall be held to answer "for a capital, or otherwise infamous crime" unless upon a grand jury indictment, except in cases arising in the armed forces. The principal additions were made in the Sixth and Seventh Amendments. The Sixth declares that "in all criminal prosecutions, the accused shall enjoy the right to a speedy and public trial, by an impartial jury of the State and district wherein the crime shall have been committed, which district shall have been previously ascertained by law. . . ." In addition, the accused is guaranteed the right to be informed of the accusation, to confront adverse witnesses, to have compulsory process for obtaining witnesses in his favor, and to have the assistance of counsel. The Seventh Amendment guarantees the right of jury trial in civil actions where the amount in controversy is over twenty dollars.[6]

5. Impeachment trials are heard by the Senate, after charges are brought by the House of Representatives.
6. In Capital Traction Co. v. Hof, 174 U.S. 1 (1899), the Court held that a civil case in the District of Columbia can first be tried by a Justice of the Peace without a jury, if upon appeal a jury trial, as prescribed by the Seventh Amendment, may be had. The theory is that the trial before the Justice of the Peace is not a trial within the meaning of the common law. The Court ruled that the Seventh Amendment merely guarantees the right to jury trial at some stage of an action. It is well established that the Seventh Amendment right to trial by jury "in suits at common law" does not apply to equity cases, Barton v. Barbour, 104 U.S. 126 (1881), or to cases in the admiralty or maritime jurisdiction, The Sarah, 8 Wheat. (U.S.) 391 (1823), or to suits filed to enforce the order of an administrative agency, involving statutory proceedings unknown to the common law, N.L.R.B. v. Jones & Laughlin Steel Corp., 301 U.S. 1, 48 (1937), or to suits to enforce claims against the United States, McElrath v. United States, 102 U.S. 426, 440 (1880), or to a suit to cancel a certificate of naturalization for fraud, Luria v. United States, 231 U.S. 9, 27 (1913), or to other actions unknown to the common law. It should be noted, however, that the Seventh Amendment right to jury trial extends beyond the common law forms of action recognized in 1791, and does apply to causes of action based on statutes, the test being whether the statute creates legal rights and remedies enforceable in an action for damages in the ordinary courts of law, Curtis v. Loether, 415 U.S. 189 (1974), Pernell v. Southall Realty, 416 U.S. 363 (1974). Futhermore, where both legal and equitable issues are presented in a single case, ordinarily the right to jury trial of the legal issues is not lost because of prior determination of equitable claims, Beacon Theatres, Inc. v. Westover, 359 U.S. 500 (1959); Dairy Queen, Inc. v. Wood, 369 U.S. 469

While the Supreme Court had never ruled on the issue directly prior to 1968, it left the impression, in several well-known dicta,[7] that Fourteenth Amendment due process did not include the right to trial by jury, so that a denial of jury trial by a state was thought not to present a federal issue over which the Supreme Court could take jurisdiction. In the important case of *Duncan* v. *Louisiana*,[8] however, which specifically rejected the earlier dicta to the contrary, the Supreme Court ruled in 1968 that trial by jury in criminal cases is so fundamental to the American scheme of justice that it is a requirement of due process which is binding on the states. Duncan had been convicted in a Louisiana state court of the misdemeanor of simple battery (a battery committed without a dangerous weapon), an offense punishable by up to two years' imprisonment and a fine up to $300. A request for a jury trial having been rejected, the trial judge proceeded to convict Duncan, and sentenced him to sixty days in the parish prison and fined him $150. By a 7-2 vote the Supreme Court ruled that the denial of jury trial constituted a violation of due process. Pointing out that trial by jury in criminal cases has "impressive credentials" going back to Magna Carta, and that it was cherished by the Founding Fathers of the nation, Justice White based his conclusion primarily on the proposition that jury trial serves to prevent oppression by the government. He described this right as "an inestimable safeguard against the corrupt or overzealous prosecutor and against the compliant, biased, or eccentric judge."[9] He maintained that we have always been reluctant to entrust plenary powers over life and liberty to the judges because we fear the dangers of unchecked power.[10] The dissenters, Justices Harlan and Stewart, thought that since the administration of criminal justice is primarily a state matter, all the Fourteenth Amendment requires is that procedures be fundamentally fair, and they regarded the imposition of nationwide uniformity in this area as being unwise and unnecessary. Since most case triable by jury are settled by guilty pleas, and many by waiver,

---

(1962); Ross v. Bernhard, 369 U.S. 531, 539 (1970); "Actions are no longer brought as actions at law or suits in equity. Under the Rules there is only one action—a 'civil action'—in which all claims may be joined and all remedies are available." See Fleming James, Jr., "Rights to a Jury Trial in Civil Actions," *Yale Law Journal,* 72 (March 1963): 655-93.

7. The leading cases most frequently cited were Maxwell v. Dow, 176 U.S. 581, 603 (1900), which merely dealt with a jury of less than twelve in a noncapital case, Palko v. Connecticut, 302 U.S. 319, 325 (1937), which was concerned with a double jeopardy issue, and Snyder v. Massachusetts, 291 U.S. 97, 105 (1934), which involved the question as to the validity of a view of the scene of the crime by the jury without the presence of the defendant.

8. 391 U.S. 145 (1968).

9. 391 U.S. 156.

10. The rule of the Duncan case was held not to be retroactive in De Stefano v. Woods, 392 U.S. 631 (1968).

they insisted that it is simply not true that a trial by the court alone defeats justice.

The Court noted, however, that the *Duncan* rule did not apply to petty cases, but without defining the term, it merely held that a crime carrying a possible two-year sentence was not a petty offense. Finally, in 1970, in *Baldwin* v. *New York*,[11] it decided that no offense is petty, so far as the right to trial by jury is concerned, where the possible punishment authorized by the statute is imprisonment for more than six months. Baldwin had been convicted in a New York court of violating a "jostling" statute (aimed at pickpocketing) for which he was given the maximum sentence of one year. He was tried in the New York City Criminal Court, in which all trials are, by force of statute, without jury. The Court leaned heavily on the fact that in the federal courts and in most state courts offenses are classified as petty if the maximum penalty is no more than six months. The Court rejected the argument that the line should coincide with the line which the state draws between felonies and misdemeanors, pointing out that some misdemeanors are in fact serious offenses. In a separate concurring opinion, Justices Black and Douglas insisted that imprisonment for less than six months is also serious, and that the Court's position constituted a judicial mutilation of the written Constitution, but this view has never been accepted by the Court. Three Justices dissented, Chief Justice Burger arguing that the jury provisions of the Constitution are not addressed to the states, and lamenting the Court's tendency to force the states to conform to a common pattern of judicial procedure.

The importance which the Supreme Court attaches to the right of trial by jury was reflected in its 1968 decision in *United States* v. *Jackson*.[12] The Federal Kidnaping Act made kidnaping an offense which is punishable by death "if the verdict of the jury shall so recommend."[13] The other possible penalty was imprisonment for any term of years up to life. Accordingly, the only sure way to avoid the death penalty was to waive jury trial or plead guilty, since the statute permitted a verdict of death only by jury decision, and the trial judge had no discretion to set aside a jury recommendation of death. Under these circumstances, the Court ruled, the inevitable effect of the statute was to discourage utilization of the Sixth Amendment right to demand a jury trial, as well as the Fifth Amendment right not to plead guilty. Thus, said Justice Stewart, the statute has the effect of chilling "the assertion of constitutional rights by penalizing those who choose to exercise them. . . ."[14] As for the argument that federal trial

11. 399 U.S. 66 (1970).
12. 390 U.S. 570 (1968).
13. 18 U.S.C. §1201(a) (1970).
14. 390 U.S. 581.

judges can be relied upon to reject involuntary waivers of jury trial or coerced pleas of guilty, the Court responded that the issue is not a matter of coercion, but arises from the fact that the statute needlessly *encourages* waivers of jury trial or pleas of guilty.[15]

Again, the significance of trial by jury was reaffirmed the following year in *O'Callahan* v. *Parker*.[16] This case involved an army sergeant who, while on leave with a pass, and dressed in civilian clothes, broke into a girl's hotel room and attempted to rape her. Apprehended by the city police, he was delivered to the military police, and tried and convicted by a court-martial for violating several articles of the Uniform Code of Military Justice. He was required to forfeit all pay, given a dishonorable discharge and sentenced to ten years' imprisonment at hard labor. Following exhaustion of his military remedies, he applied for a writ of habeas corpus in a federal district court, and when this action eventually reached the Supreme Court, the Justices, dividing 5-3, held that he was entitled to the writ, because to be under military jurisdiction, the crime must be service-connected. The power granted to Congress by the Constitution "to make Rules for the Government and Regulation of the land and naval Forces,"[17] the Court majority insisted, must be exercised in harmony with the express guarantees of the Bill of Rights. In this case there was not the remotest connection between the defendant's military duties and the crime in question, and no issue involving military authority, or security of the post, or the integrity of military property. Since the crimes were not service-connected, the Court concluded that the defendant could not be tried by a court-martial, but rather, that he was entitled to trial by a civilian court. The Court saw a great deal of difference between a court-martial and trial by jury in a civil court. In a court-martial a defendant is not tried by a jury of his peers who must decide by unanimous vote, but rather by a panel of officers empowered to act by a two-thirds vote. The presiding officer of a court-martial is not a judge with tenure and a protected salary nurtured by judicial tradition, but is, rather, a military law officer. In addition, the convening officer has direct command authority over the members of the court-martial, and the rules of evidence and procedure are substantially different. Specialized military courts are undoubtedly needed to meet the special needs of the military, but their jurisdiction must be limited to what

---

15. In Brady v. United States, 397 U.S. 742 (1970) and Parker v. North Carolina, 397 U.S. 790 (1970), the Court upheld a guilty plea to a kidnaping charge the voluntariness of which was supported by substantial evidence. These cases are discussed in the section of chapter 7 in this book devoted to plea bargaining.

16. 395 U.S. 258 (1969). The rule of this case was held not to be retroactive, in Gosa v. Mayden, 413 U.S. 665 (1973).

17. U.S. Constitution, Art. I, §8, cl. 14.

is absolutely essential to maintain discipline; to expand military discipline beyond its proper domain carries with it a threat to liberty. Furthermore, the Court thought that courts-martial are singularly inept in dealing with the nice subtleties of constitutional law.[18] The three dissenting Justices—Harlan, Stewart and White—thought there were vital interests which supported the exercise of court-martial jurisdiction over nonmilitary crimes of servicemen, such as preservation of the reputation, morale, integrity, order, and safety of the Armed Services.[19]

The Requirement of Twelve Members

What is a jury trial? The term is not defined by the Constitution, but it has always been supposed that it drew its meaning from the usages of the common law. In a leading opinion on jury trial, Justice Sutherland wrote, in 1930,

That it means a trial by jury as understood and applied at common law, and includes all the essential elements as they were recognized in this country and England when the Constitution was adopted, is not open to question. These elements were: (1) That the jury should consist of twelve men, neither more nor less; (2) that the trial should be in the presence and under the superintendence of a judge having power to instruct them as to the law and advise them in respect of the facts; and (3) that the verdict should be unanimous.[20]

Since the English jury, in 1789, when the Constitution was ratified, consisted of twelve jurors, it was assumed by the Supreme Court that the number twelve is, in effect, a constitutional requirement. On the other hand, since the Supreme Court held to the view that the jury provision of the Sixth Amendment does not apply to the states, a position which it abandoned only in 1968,[21] it ruled in a leading decision in 1900, *Maxwell v. Dow,*[22] that so far as the federal Constitution is concerned, the states are not bound to have juries of twelve. In sustaining a conviction in a Utah court after a trial by a jury of eight members, the Court ruled that jury trial was not a privilege or immunity of federal citizenship within the

---

18. The Court relied upon various precedents: Toth v. Quarles, 350 U.S. 11 (1955) (discharged soldier cannot be court-martialed for offenses committed while in service); McElroy v. Guagliardo, 361 U.S. 281 (1960), Grisham v. Hagan, 361 U.S. 278 (1960) (overseas civilian employees of the Armed Forces may not be tried by courts-martial); Kinsella v. Singleton, 361 U.S. 234 (1960), Reid v. Covert, 354 U.S. 1 (1957) (civilian dependents accompanying military personnel overseas may not be tried by courts-martial).

19. Cf. Relford v. Commandant, 401 U.S. 355 (1971), which held that a rape by a serviceman, on active duty, on a military base was "service-connected," and therefore triable by a court-martial.

20. Patton v. United States, 281 U.S. 276, 288 (1930).

21. Duncan v. Louisiana, 391 U.S. 145 (1968).

22. 176 U.S. 581 (1900).

meaning of the Fourteenth Amendment, and that the use of a jury of less than twelve did not deny due process.

Many states employ juries with fewer than twelve members for various purposes, such as the trial of minor crimes or certain types of civil cases. In fact, so far as the federal Constitution is concerned, states are free to dispense with jury trial altogether in civil cases. So the Court ruled in *Walker* v. *Sauvinet*,[23] which upheld a Louisiana statute which authorized suits for damages against any person who had to have a license to do business and who discriminated on the grounds of race or color. In all such cases, if the jury failed to agree, or failed to render a verdict either for the plaintiff or the defendant, the statute empowered the judge to decide the case alone on the pleadings and evidence already on file. Again the Court ruled that trial by jury in suits at common law in a state court was not a privilege or immunity of national citizenship protected by the Fourteenth Amendment, and that due process does not mean that all state trials must be by jury.

Rule 23(b) of the Federal Rules of Criminal Procedure incorporates the traditional common law principle, "Juries shall be of 12 but at any time before verdict the parties may stipulate in writing with the approval of the court that the jury shall consist of any number less than 12." This does not really mean, however, that by agreement a federal criminal jury may have fewer than twelve. As will be pointed out later, a stipulation for a jury of less than twelve is regarded as a waiver of jury trial. This can be accomplished before as well as during the trial.

As soon as the Supreme Court ruled that in criminal cases, involving imprisonment for more than six months, trial by jury is a Fourteenth Amendment requirement which is binding upon the states, then the Court was confronted with the question of the validity of state criminal juries having fewer than twelve members. In 1970, in *Williams* v. *Florida*,[24] the Court upheld the constitutionality of a Florida statute which provided for six-man juries in all but capital cases. On trial for robbery, Williams's pretrial motion for a jury of twelve was denied, and following conviction by a jury of six, he was sentenced to a life term in the penitentiary. Eight Justices agreed that a jury of exactly twelve persons was not mandated by the Constitution. Justice White, after reviewing the history of the matter, concluded that the number twelve was a historical accident, and therefore was not immutably codified into the Constitution. He argued that the history of the adoption of the Sixth Amendment indicates that it was not intended that the Constitution automatically embodied every common law

23. 92 U.S. 92 (1876).
24. 399 U.S. 78 (1970).

aspect of jury trial. As a matter of fact, actually little thought was given to this matter by the authors of the Constitution. Justice White also pointed out that there have always been wide variations among the states; as of the time he was writing, five states provided for juries under twelve in felony cases, and nine states provided for juries of less than twelve for offenses carrying a maximum penalty of one year in jail. The twelve-man requirement, it was argued, cannot be regarded, in terms of purpose and function, as an indispensable component of the Sixth Amendment guaranty. Since the purpose of the jury is to prevent governmental oppression, community participation and shared responsibility are required, but this does not depend upon any particular number. It suffices if the number is large enough to promote group deliberation and a fair representative cross-section of the community, and Justice White thought that in these terms six would do as well as twelve. Thus he concluded, "To read the Sixth Amendment as forever codifying a feature so incidental to the real purpose of the Amendment is to ascribe a blind formalism to the Framers which would require considerably more evidence than we have been able to discover in the history and language of the Constitution or in the reasoning of our past decisions."[25] This is not to say, Justice White noted, that juries of twelve are unwise, or that there are no good reasons for having them, but these considerations are within the judgment of Congress and the states.

In a concurring opinion Justice Harlan argued that a six-man jury would not satisfy the requirement of the Sixth Amendment so far as federal courts are concerned, but he insisted, as he had often done in the past, that the Sixth Amendment should not be incorporated into the Fourteenth. Due process is a requirement of fundamental fairness, said Justice Harlan, and the New York six-man jury system is valid because it is not unfair. Thus, he maintained that the Court's preference for selective incorporation instead of due process was wrong, since that puts a constitutional straightjacket on the states, and tends to distort the essentially federal nature of our system of government, which is based on diversity and experimentation. Justice Marshall dissented alone on this issue, arguing that the proposition that the Sixth Amendment guarantees a jury of twelve was supported by an unbroken line of precedents going back seventy years.

Having decided that the number twelve is not enshrined in the Constitution, a great many federal district courts, all of whom have considerable local rule-making powers on their own, began to provide for juries of six in

---

25. 399 U.S. 102-3.

at least some civil cases. In 1973, in *Colegrove* v. *Battin*,[26] a rule promulgated by the U.S. District Court for Montana calling for six-man juries in the trial of civil cases was upheld by a 5-4 vote. By this time, fifty-four other federal district courts had adopted six-man juries for at least some civil cases. The Court majority ruled that jury performance is not a function of size, and that there is no constitutional history which reveals an intention on the part of the Framers to equate the constitutional and common-law characteristics of the jury. References in earlier Supreme Court opinions to juries of twelve were described as mere dicta. In addition, the Court could not find in this six-man jury any violation of any statute (28 U.S.C. §2072) or Rule of Court (Rule 48). Two dissenting Justices argued that under Rule 48 the only way to get a jury of less than twelve was by stipulation, whereas the other two dissenters regarded the Court's decision as a frontal assault on the very nature of a civil jury as it was understood for seven hundred years.

It is of interest to note that while the general rule in Great Britain is a jury of twelve, juries of eight sit in the county courts and other inferior courts,[27] and in the higher criminal courts, if one or more jurors die or are discharged for illness, the jury may proceed provided that it has no less than nine.[28]

Thus, today states are free, so far as the federal Constitution is concerned, to have juries with fewer than twelve members in both civil and criminal cases. The trial courts of the national government, the federal district courts, are free to have juries with fewer than twelve members, and a majority of them do, in at least some civil cases, but in criminal cases Rule 23(b) requires a jury of twelve, unless the parties stipulate otherwise with the approval of the Court. This means that the twelve-member jury in the federal courts is not mandated by the Constitution, and smaller juries could be created if the Supreme Court and Congress, which has review powers over Court Rules, so decide.

The Requirement of Unanimity

Rule 31(a) of the Federal Rules of Criminal Procedure restates familiar common law when it declares, "The verdict shall be unanimous. It shall be returned by the jury in open court." This requirement of unanimity, the Supreme Court recently held, applies in federal courts to all issues which are left to the jury, so that if the jury is authorized to determine the

---

26. 413 U.S. 149 (1973). For an earlier decision upholding the use of a six-man jury in civil cases in a federal district court see Cooley v. Strickland Transportation Co., 459 F.2d 779 (5th Cir. 1972). The Court of Appeals argued that the term "common law" in the Seventh Amendment was intended merely to distinguish between law and equity.

27. County Courts Act of 1959, s. 96, 7 & 8 Eliz. II, ch. 22.

28. Criminal Justice Act of 1965, s. 1, 13 & 14 Eliz. II, ch. 26.

nature of the punishment as well as the question of guilt, it must be unanimous in making both determinations.[29] Similarly, the Court has ruled that no civil suit can be decided by a jury in a federal court by other than a unanimous vote, in conformity with the Seventh Amendment.[30]

The wisdom of the rule of unanimity has long been the subject of considerable dispute. Thus the Advisory Committee on the Rules of Criminal Procedure suggested in 1943 the following rule: "A verdict shall be unanimous, but by written stipulation of the parties approved by the court it may be by a stated majority of the jurors."[31] But the Supreme Court would not accept this change, and continued the traditional unanimity principle in Rule 31(a).

The requirement of unanimity is defended largely on two grounds. It is said that unanimity is required by the doctrine that the prosecution must prove guilt beyond a reasonable doubt, and that it stimulates discussion in the jury room. As a practical matter, it is pointed out that mistrials due to the inability of a jury to arrive at a unanimous verdict (hung juries, they are called) are very rare. On the other hand, those who oppose the rule of unanimity stress the fact that majority rule prevails everywhere else, in the legislatures, appellate courts, city councils, and corporate boards of directors. They also argue that the requirement of unanimity often leads to undesirable compromise, and entails delay and expense. Of course, a single stubborn or corrupt juror can lead to a mistrial.

Many states authorize jury verdicts in various types of cases by less than a unanimous vote. For example, the New York Constitution authorizes the legislature to provide for verdicts by a five-sixths vote in any civil case.[32] The Missouri Constitution provides for verdicts by a two-thirds vote in civil cases heard in courts not of record, and by a three-fourths vote in courts of record.[33] The Idaho Constitution authorizes the legislature to

---

29. Andres v. United States, 333 U.S. 740 (1948).

30. American Publ. Co. v. Fisher, 166 U.S. 464 (1897). Here the Court set aside a statute of the Territory of Utah providing for a verdict by nine jurors in civil cases. Said Justice Brewer, ". . . unanimity was one of the peculiar and essential features of trial by jury at the common law. No authorities are needed to sustain this proposition." For a similar holding in regard to a statute of the Oklahoma Territory, see Bradford v. Territory *ex rel.* Woods, 1 Okla. 371, 34 Pac. 66 (1893).

31. Advisory Committee on Rules of Criminal Procedure, *First Preliminary Draft* (Washington, D.C.: Government Printing Office, 1943), p. 127.

32. N.Y. Const., Art. I, §2. See also Nebr. Const., Art. I, §6; Wisc. Const., Art. I, §5.

33. Mo. Const., Art. I, §22(a). For other provisions authorizing verdicts by three-fourths of the jurors in civil cases see Ark. Const., Art. II, §7; Miss. Const., Art. III, §31; Nev. Const., Art. I, §3; Ohio Const., Art. I, §5; S.D. Const., Art. VI, §6; Utah Const., Art. I, §10. The Washington Constitution, Art. I, §21, authorizes a jury of any number less than twelve in courts not of record that the legislature may provide for, and for verdicts of nine jurors in civil cases in any court of record.

provide that in all cases of misdemeanors five-sixths of the jury may render a verdict.[34] In noncapital cases the Louisiana Constitution authorizes a verdict by nine jurors.[35] The Minnesota Constitution empowers the legislature to provide for a five-sixths vote in any civil action after six hours of deliberation.[36] The Montana Constitution permits the jury to render a verdict by a two-thirds vote in all civil actions, and in all criminal cases not amounting to a felony.[37] The Oklahoma Constitution says the same thing, except that the vote must be by at least three-fourths of the jurors.[38] The New Mexico Constitution merely authorizes the legislature to provide for verdicts by less than a unanimous vote of the jury in civil cases.[39] The Oregon Constitution permits verdicts in criminal cases by a vote of ten jurors, except for a verdict of guilty of first-degree murder, and verdicts by three-fourths of the jury in civil cases.[40] The Texas Constitution authorizes verdicts by a vote of nine members of the jury in civil cases and in criminal cases below the grade of felony.[41]

So long as the Supreme Court held that the provisions of the federal Constitution dealing with jury trial did not apply, the states were perfectly free to permit verdicts by less than a unanimous vote. Indeed, the Supreme Court once ruled that the federal requirement of jury trial by unanimous vote did not control the state courts even when they were enforcing rights under a federal statute, such as the Employers' Liability Act of 1908.[42]

Again, the problem was complicated when in 1968 the Supreme Court read the jury provision of the Sixth Amendment into the Due Process Clause of the Fourteenth Amendment.[43] Since the unanimity rule prevails in federal courts, does it follow that the same rule must be observed in state courts? In two cases decided by 5–4 votes in 1972, the Supreme Court ruled constitutional the conviction of a defendant in Louisiana for armed robbery by a 9–3 vote of the jury, and of several defendants in Oregon for assault with a deadly weapon, burglary of a dwelling, and grand larceny, by votes of 11–1 (in two cases) and 10–2 (in the third

---

34. Ida. Const., Art. I, §7.
35. La. Const., Art. III, §41.
36. Minn. Const., Art. I, §4.
37. Mont. Const., Art. III, §23.
38. Okla. Const., Art. II, §19.
39. New Mex. Const., Art. II, §12. For a similar provision, see Ariz. Const., Art. II, §23.
40. Ore. Const., Art. I, §§11, 17.
41. Tex. Const., Art. V, §13.
42. Minn. & St. Louis R.R. Co. v. Bombolis, 241 U.S. 211 (1916). In this instance the state authorized the jury, in civil cases, to render a verdict by a five-sixths vote after twelve hours of deliberation.
43. Duncan v. Louisiana, 391 U.S. 145 (1968).

case).⁴⁴ The Court rejected the argument that unanimity is required to give substance to the reasonable doubt standard, and declared that the fact that three jurors disagreed with the other nine does not prove existence of a reasonable doubt. There was no proof that the nine jurors voting to convict failed to follow the judge's instructions, or that *their* minds were clouded by a reasonable doubt. In a concurring opinion, Justice Powell argued that unanimity is one of the indispensable features of a federal jury trial, and that the Sixth Amendment was intended to guaranty the right of jury trial as it was known at the common law, but he rejected the incorporation theory. Accordingly, as a straight due process issue, Justice Powell argued that unanimity is not fundamental to justice, and that the high purpose of jury trial is served by a nonunanimous verdict. Thus, on the one hand, Justice Powell did not want to dilute federal rights; on the other hand, he was unwilling to inhibit state experimentation by forcing the states into a common pattern. The dissenting Justices lamented what they characterized as a radical departure from American tradition and two centuries of history. They argued that the same rule should prevail at both the state and federal levels of government, and that the reliability of a less than unanimous verdict is diminished. They insisted that a unanimous verdict is required by the reasonable doubt standard of proof. Thus, it would seem that five Justices believe that the unanimity principle is constitutionally required in federal courts, whereas only four believe that the federal Constitution imposes that principle upon the states.

Again, it is worth noting that the Parliament of Great Britain abandoned the unanimity requirement for criminal cases in 1967.⁴⁵ Where there are not fewer than eleven jurors, ten may agree on a verdict, and where there are ten jurors, nine may agree on a verdict; but a nonunanimous verdict may not be accepted by the court unless the jury has deliberated for at least two hours, "or such longer period as the court thinks reasonable having regard to the nature and complexity of the case."⁴⁶

As in the case of jury size, unanimity of the jury is required in all federal civil and criminal cases, and a majority of the sitting Justices believe that is required by the Constitution. On the other hand, there is no federal

---

44. Johnson v. Louisiana, 406 U.S. 356 (1972); Apodaca v. Oregon, 406 U.S. 404 (1972). Under Louisiana law, capital cases and cases where the punishment is necessarily at hard labor must be decided by unanimous vote of the jury. In Oregon the statute requires a unanimous vote in cases where the charge is first degree murder. For a vigorous criticism of the decisions which sanctioned juries with less than twelve and nonunanimous verdicts, see Leonard W. Levy, *Against the Law* (New York: Harper & Row, 1974), chap. 5.

45. Criminal Justice Act of 1967, 15 & 16 Eliz. II, c. 80, §13.

46. 15 & 16 Eliz. II, c. 80, §§13 (1)(a), 13 (1)(b), 13 (3).

constitutional barrier to nonunanimous jury verdicts in state courts, whether in civil or criminal cases. Most states still follow the rule of unanimity, but there is no longer any federal constitutional compulsion to do so.

The Supervisory Responsibility of the Judge

A classic element of jury trial is that it is held under the supervision of a judge who instructs the jury as to the law and advises as to the facts. In a leading opinion on this subject, the first Justice Harlan emphasized the importance of the rule that it is the duty of juries in criminal cases to take the law from the court, and apply that law to the facts as they find them from the evidence. Justice Harlan wrote,

> Any other rule . . . would bring confusion and uncertainty in the administration of the criminal law. Indeed, if a jury may rightfully disregard the direction of the court in matter of law, and determine for themselves what the law is in the particular case before them, it is difficult to perceive any legal ground upon which a verdict of conviction can be set aside by the court as being against law. If it be the function of the jury to decide the law as well as the facts—if the function of the court be only advisory as to the law—why should the court interfere for the protection of the accused against what it deems an error of the jury in matter of law?
>
> Public and private safety alike would be in peril, if the principle be established that juries in criminal cases may, of right, disregard the law as expounded to them by the court and become a law unto themselves. Under such a system, the principal function of the judge would be to preside and keep order while jurymen, untrained in the law, would determine questions affecting life, liberty, or property according to such legal principles as in their judgment were applicable to the particular case being tried. If because, generally speaking, it is the function of the jury to determine the guilt or innocence of the accused according to the evidence, of the truth or weight of which they are to judge, the court should be held bound to instruct them upon a point in respect to which there was no evidence whatever, or to forbear stating what the law is upon a given state of facts, the result would be that the enforcement of the law against criminals and the protection of citizens against unjust and groundless prosecutions, would depend entirely upon juries uncontrolled by any settled, fixed, legal principles. . . . Under the contrary view—if it be held that the court may not authoritatively decide all questions of law arising in criminal cases—the result will be that when a new trial in a criminal case is ordered, even by this court, the jury, upon such trial, may of right return a verdict based upon the assumption that what this court has adjudged to be law is not law. We cannot give our sanction to any rule that will lead to such a result.[47]

---

47. Sparf v. United States, 156 U.S. 51, 101–3 (1895). Justice Gray filed a 73-page dissenting opinion. In the early days of the nation juries were generally free to decide issues of law as well as of fact in most states, but this is no longer true. See Mark De Wolfe Howe, "Juries as Judge of the Criminal Law," *Harvard Law Review,* 52 (February 1939): 582–616.

In many states the judge has very limited scope for commenting on the evidence to the jury, but in all federal courts the judge has a wide latitude in this respect. While the authority of the judge in the courtroom varies a great deal from state to state, it may be said, in a general way, that on the whole the federal judge has greater control over the trial than do most state judges. "In a trial by jury in a federal court," Chief Justice Hughes once wrote, "the judge is not a mere moderator, but is the governor of the trial for the purpose of assuring its proper conduct and of determining questions of law. . . . In charging the jury, the trial judge is not limited to instructions of an abstract sort. It is within his province, whenever he thinks it necessary, to assist the jury in arriving at a just conclusion by explaining and commenting upon the evidence, by drawing their attention to the parts of it which he thinks important; and he may express his opinion upon the facts, provided he makes it clear to the jury that all matters of fact are submitted to their determination."[48]

The federal judge's privilege of comment, however, is not unlimited. His discretion is not arbitrary but judicial, and he may not assume the role of a witness. He may analyze the evidence, but not add to it. Thus a judge committed reversible error when he told the jury that everything the defendant said was a lie, except when he agreed with the government's testimony, and that the defendant's habit of wiping his hands during the trial was always evidence of lying.[49] In addition, it is reversible error for the federal district judge to tell the jury, "It is my opinion that this defendant has been proven guilty beyond a reasonable doubt."[50] This went well beyond the permissible limits of a federal judge's right to comment on the evidence. Since the jury must be free to arrive at a verdict free from coercion by the judge, it is also reversible error for a judge to tell a jury which after two hours of deliberation reported that it was unable to reach agreement, "You have got to reach a decision in this case."[51] The Supreme Court thought that the judge's statement had a coercive effect.

Similarly, it is the judge's duty to keep the prosecutor within the limits required by a fair trial. This problem often arises in connection with the prosecutor's closing argument to the jury. Invariably prosecutors speak last to the jury, because the prosecution has the burden of proof, and many have a habit of overreaching themselves. Appeals which are wholly irrelevant to the facts and issues, made only for the purpose of arousing

---

48. Quercia v. United States, 289 U.S. 466, 469 (1933).
49. 289 U.S. 466.
50. United States v. Smith, 399 F.2d 896, 898 (6th Cir. 1968). For a collection of authorities which examine the propriety and prejudicial effect of a federal judge's expressing his opinion as to the defendant's guilt in criminal cases, see 7 A.L.R. Fed. 377.
51. Jenkins v. United States, 380 U.S. 445 (1965).

passion and prejudice, should not be allowed by the judge.[52] For, as Justice Sutherland once tellingly pointed out, the function of the public prosecutor is to see to it that justice is done, and not primarily to win cases.[53]

It is equally important for the judge to afford the defendant's counsel every legitimate opportunity to participate in the trial, from the examination of jurors and witnesses to the closing argument. While the judge has a reasonable discretion in limiting the amount of time necessary for argument, depending upon the nature of the evidence and the complexity of the issues involved, the lawyer has a fundamental right to argue his client's case to the jury. It is an important function of the lawyer to aid the court and jury not only in the presentation of the facts, but also in their analysis. Thus it is reversible error for the judge to tell the jury to pay no attention to the arguments of counsel.[54]

It remains to be noted that a jury must decide a case on the basis of evidence presented in court, and must not be tampered with or given information in any other way. In a leading case on this point, after the defendant was convicted by a jury on a charge of evasion of income taxes, he learned for the first time that an unnamed person had communicated with the juror who later became the foreman, and told him he could profit by bringing in an acquittal.[55] The juror reported this to the judge, who told the prosecuting attorney, and the latter arranged for an FBI investigation. The FBI report, which was submitted only to the judge and the prosecutor, concluded that the reported remark to the juror had been made in jest. The Supreme Court held that under these circumstances the defendant was entitled to a hearing to determine the nature of the incident and its effect on the jury. Said Justice Minton, for a unanimous Court, "In a criminal case, any private communication, contact, or tampering, directly or indirectly, with a juror during a trial about the matter pending before the jury is, for obvious reasons, deemed presumptively prejudicial, if not made in pursuance of known rules of the court and the instructions

---

52. Viereck v. United States, 318 U.S. 236 (1943).
53. Berger v. United States, 295 U.S. 78, 88 (1935).
54. State v. Gutterman, 20 N.D. 432, 433, 128 N.W. 307, Ann. Cas. 1912C, 816, 817 (1910): "Parties have a right to appear by counsel, and it is the privilege of counsel to address the jury. If the jury are to disregard the arguments of counsel altogether, if they are to shut their ears to the illustrations, comments, and reasonings, how unmeaning, indeed how absurd, is the appearance of counsel. It is a most valuable right to be represented by learned and eloquent counsel, not only before the court, as to the law, but also before the jury, as to the facts." In Rogers v. United States, 422 U.S. 35 (1975) the Court ruled that it is reversible error for a trial judge to respond to the jury's inquiry without informing the defense and giving defense counsel an opportunity to be heard.
55. Remmer v. United States, 347 U.S. 227 (1954).

and directions of the court made during the trial, with full knowledge of the parties. The presumption is not conclusive, but the burden rests heavily upon the Government to establish, after notice to and hearing of the defendant, that such contact with the juror was harmless to the defendant."[56]

In another case involving a three-day trial for murder in a Louisiana state court, a conviction was set aside because two deputy sheriffs who were the principal prosecution witnesses had been in continuous and intimate association with the jurors, eating and conversing with them, and doing errands for them.[57] The Court ruled that in the constitutional sense trial by jury in a criminal case necessarily implies at the very least that the evidence developed against the defendant shall come from the witness stand in a public court-room where there is full judicial protection for the defendant's rights of cross-examination and of the assistance of counsel. The continual association of the witnesses with the jurors was inherently and extremely prejudicial to the defendant, the Court ruled, even if they did not talk about the case itself, since his fate depended upon how much confidence the jury placed in these two witnesses.

Scope of the Right to Jury Trial in Federal Courts

Not every criminal prosecution falls within the requirement of jury trial. As suggested by the specific language of the Fifth Amendment, and the vesting in Congress of the power "to make Rules for the Government and Regulation of the land and naval Forces,"[58] Congress has a special system of justice for the armed forces which does not use the jury system in its traditional form.[59] Similarly, it was once held that a U.S. Consular Court, sitting in a foreign country, did not have to give the accused a jury trial, since the Constitution established a government only for the United States, and not for countries outside its limits.[60] The Court alluded to the impossibility of obtaining competent juries in the places where alone consular courts are likely to function. Such courts no longer exist. In addition, the Court ruled in 1971 that states may deny jury trial to

---

56. 347 U.S. 229. For a holding that FBI contacts with the families of jurors, during the course of a trial, are inherently prejudicial, see Ben Gold v. United States, 352 U.S. 985 (1957). The Court condemned "official intrusion into the privacy of the jury," and held that it was immaterial that the intrusion had been unintentional.

57. Turner v. Louisiana, 379 U.S. 466 (1965).

58. U.S. Const., Art. I, §8, cl. 14.

59. The power to provide for the punishment of military and naval offenses is given to Congress "without any connection between it and the 3d article of the Constitution defining the judicial power of the United States; indeed . . . the two powers are entirely independent of each other." Justice Wayne in Dynes v. Hoover, 20 How. (61 U.S.) 65, 79 (1858).

60. *In re* Ross, 140 U.S. 453 (1891).

juveniles,[61] and as a matter of fact most states deny jury trial in juvenile courts.[62]

In addition, the Supreme Court has ruled many times that the Constitution does not require jury trial for petty offenses, but it has never been very clear as to just where to draw the line between petty and serious offenses. The Court has refused to say that all misdemeanors are petty offenses, holding, on the contrary, that the term "crimes" within the meaning of Article III also extends to some misdemeanors involving a deprivation of liberty.[63] The decisive factor, it has been held, is the nature of the offense. Thus, the offense of buying unstamped oleomargarine for sale, for which the penalty was fifty dollars, was held to be a petty offense for which jury trial was not constitutionally necessary.[64] On the other hand, the Court ruled that the crime of conspiracy to interfere with a man's calling, for which the penalty was a twenty-five dollar fine or thirty days in jail, was a serious offense triable only by jury, on the theory that conspiracy is, generally speaking, a serious matter.[65] The offense of reckless driving and speeding was also held to be a serious offense since it was "in its very nature *malum in se,*" because it was an indictable offense at common law, and because driving a car speedily and recklessly was an act of "obvious depravity."[66]

On the other hand, more recently the Court ruled that dealing in secondhand goods without a license, for which the penalty was a $300 fine or ninety days in jail, was a petty offense not demanding jury trial.[67] Here it was noted that the offense was not indictable at the common law, and today was at most "an infringement of local police regulations." The moral quality of the act was described as "relatively inoffensive." But the Court also stressed the fact that the penalties were not severe enough to require calling this a jury offense. It was pointed out that in 1787 confinement for ninety days was not unusual for petty offenses tried without a jury, and many English and colonial statutes before the Revolution authorized summary punishment for petty offenses by imprisonment for as much as six months.[68] Finally, it was pointed out that many state and English laws

61. McKeiver v. Pennsylvania, 403 U.S. 528 (1971).
62. See, e.g., *In re* Fucini, 44 Ill. 2d 305, 255 NE 2d 380 (1970).
63. Callan v. Wilson, 127 U.S. 540 (1888).
64. Schick v. United States, 195 U.S. 65 (1904).
65. Callan v. Wilson, 127 U.S. 540 (1888).
66. District of Columbia v. Colts, 282 U.S. 63, 73 (1930).
67. District of Columbia v. Clawans, 300 U.S. 617 (1937).
68. This is fully documented in an exhaustive study of English common law and American colonial precedents by Felix Frankfurter and Thomas G. Corcoran, "Petty Federal Offenses and the Constitutional Guaranty of Trial by Jury," *Harvard Law Review,* 39 (June 1926): 917-1019. They concluded, at pp. 980-81, that the distinction between serious and minor

provide for such trials. Thus in one of the most recent cases on the subject the Court did stress the relative severity of the punishment as at least one of the criteria for determining whether an offense was petty or not.

It remains to be noted that a judge may punish a contempt committed in the presence of the court, without affording the individual concerned a jury trial. Rule 42(a) of the Federal Rules of Criminal Procedure is clear on this point. "A criminal contempt may be punished summarily if the judge certifies that he saw or heard the conduct constituting the contempt and that it was committed in the actual presence of the court."[69] In the case of *Sacher* v. *United States,*[70] the Court held that it was proper for the trial judge to wait until the end of the trial, though the defense lawyers were guilty of contemptuous behavior from time to time in the course of a nine-months trial, and then sentence them to jail without jury trial. The word "summarily" was construed as referring not to the timing of the action in reference to the offense, but to a procedure which dispenses with the formalities of a customary trial.[71]

While judges must have the power to punish summarily for any contempt committed in their presence, to protect the integrity of the judicial process, Rule 42(b) provides that "the defendant is entitled to a trial by jury in any case in which an act of Congress so provides." To cite an example, Congress provided that in cases of criminal contempt arising out of injunctive proceedings under the labor sections of the Clayton Act, where the acts committed in violation of a district court's orders were also crimes under federal or state law, the accused on demand could secure a jury trial. The Court upheld the statute since it did not interfere with the judge's power to deal summarily with contempts in his presence.[72] Congress went even further in the Norris–La Guardia Act of 1932 to provide that "in all cases of contempt arising under the laws of the United States governing the issuance of injunctions or restraining orders in any case involving or growing out of a labor dispute, the accused shall enjoy

---

misdeeds rested upon a moral judgment, and that "the gravity of danger to the community from the misconduct largely guided the moral judgment. . . . Broadly speaking, acts were dealt with summarily which did not offend too deeply the moral purposes of the community, which were not too close to society's danger, and were stigmatized by punishment relatively slight."

69. This follows the language of the Act of March 2, 1831, c. 99, 4 Stat. 487, 488, now 18 U.S. §401 (1970).

70. 343 U.S. 1 (1952).

71. Two of the three dissenting Justices in this case thought that the lawyers who were convicted of contempt were entitled to trial by jury.

72. Michaelson v. United States, 266 U.S. 42 (1924). See, for existing statute law, 18 U.S.C. §3691 (1970).

178 / *The Defendant's Rights Today*

the right to a speedy and public trial by an impartial jury. . . ."[73] But this statute does not apply to contempts "committed in the presence of the court or so near thereto as to interfere directly with the administration of justice nor to the misbehavior, misconduct or disobedience of any officer of the court in respect to the writs, orders or process of the court."[74] To cite another example, the Civil Rights Act of 1957 provides that in all cases of criminal contempt arising under the statute, where the penalty imposed by the judge is a fine of over $300 or imprisonment for more than forty-five days, the accused has a right to a trial *de novo* before a jury.[75] Similarly, the more extensive Civil Rights Act of 1964 provides for jury trial "in any proceeding for criminal contempt," but the statute also stipulates that this provision "shall not apply to contempts committed in the presence of the court, or so near thereto as to obstruct the administration of justice. . . ."[76]

In 1964, in the case involving the refusal of the Governor of Mississippi to obey a federal court order directing the admission of a Negro to the state university, the Court ruled, by a 5–4 vote, that in the absence of a statute requiring trial by jury, there is no constitutional right to such a trial.[77] The Court noted that a claim to trial by jury in cases of criminal contempt had often been made in the past, and as often rejected.[78] It was noted that the power to punish for contempt was given to the federal courts by the Judiciary Act of 1789,[79] and that it has always been the law of the land that one charged with criminal contempt of court does not have a constitutional right to trial by jury. The four dissenters noted that Article 3, Section 3, of the Constitution assures one of a jury in the "trial of all crimes," and argued, as Justice Black put it, that it is sheer fiction to say that a criminal contempt is not a crime. They maintained that criminal contempts are not essentially different from other crimes, except that the former involve the violation of a court order, whereas the latter involve the violation of a statute.

Soon thereafter, however, the Court ruled, in *Cheff* v. *Schnackenberg*,[80] that in criminal contempt cases, a federal court may not impose a sentence exceeding six months' imprisonment unless a jury trial has been received or waived. Four Justices rested the conclusion on the Court's supervisory

73. 18 U.S.C. §3692 (1970).
74. This proviso dates from the Act of March 2, 1831, 4 Stat. 487, now 18 U.S.C. §401(1) (1970). On the strict construction of this language in favor of defendants, see Nye v. United States, 313 U.S. 33, 47 (1941).
75. 71 Stat. 634, §151, 42 U.S.C. §1995 (1970).
76. 78 Stat. 268, §1101, 42 U.S.C. §2000h (1970).
77. United States v. Barnett, 376 U.S. 681 (1964).
78. This issue, it was noted, was fully reviewed in Green v. United States, 356 U.S. 165 (1958).
79. 1 Stat. 83, §17.
80. 384 U.S. 373 (1966).

power over the lower federal courts, whereas two others believed that jury trials are constitutionally required in all but "petty" criminal contempts.[81] The three dissenting Justices argued that the length of sentence was immaterial, and that the Court's distinction between serious and petty contempts was "mechanical." In short, they insisted that the crime of criminal contempt is a crime like other crimes.

After deciding, in 1968, in *Duncan* v. *Louisiana*[82] that trial by jury in state courts is a federally protected due process right, the Court, on the same day, in *Bloom* v. *Illinois*,[83] held that one convicted of criminal contempt in a state court, without jury trial, and sentenced to jail for twenty-four months, was denied due process.[84] A two-year sentence, the Court held, indicated that this was not a petty offense. In other words, the Court held that the traditional rule that there is no right to jury trial in criminal contempt cases is wrong except as to petty offenses. Serious contempts, said Justice White, are so nearly like other crimes that they are subject to the jury trial provisions of the Constitution. Later decisions have underscored the proposition that the denial of jury trial in state and federal courts is unlawful—indeed unconstitutional—where the sentence exceeds six months' imprisonment, even though the contempt took place in open court.[85]

---

81. Attention was drawn to 18 U.S.C. §1 (1970), which provides that "any misdemeanor, the penalty for which does not exceed imprisonment for a period of six months," is a "petty offense." While the Court has not yet formulated a general rule as to the necessity for jury trial where the punishment is a large fine, it did hold, in Muniz v. Hoffman, 422 U.S. 454 (1975), by a 5-4 vote, that the imposition of a fine of $10,000 on a union local with 13,000 members was not of such magnitude as to require a jury trial for contempt.

82. 391 U.S. 145 (1968).

83. 391 U.S. 194 (1968). The offense was wilfully petitioning the court to admit to probate a will falsely prepared and executed after the death of the putative testator.

84. The Court indicated that a six-months sentence was short enough to be regarded as a petty punishment in Dyke v. Taylor Implement Mfg. Co., 391 U.S. 216 (1968).

85. Codispoti v. Pennsylvania, 418 U.S. 506 (1974) (sentence was over three years); Frank v. United States, 395 U.S. 147 (1969) (three years probation, where six months in jail is the maximum penalty for violation of the probation, petty offense rule applies). See also Taylor v. Hayes, 418 U.S. 488 (1974), which again ruled that the contempt is petty if the penalty does not exceed six months in jail. But the Court also ruled that a summary procedure was not needed when the judge postpones the contempt proceeding against the defendant's lawyer until the end of the trial, and that the matter should have been turned over to be tried by another judge. As Justice Rehnquist pointed out in a dissenting opinion, this decision was squarely contrary to the rule established in Sacher v. United States, 343 U.S. 1 (1952).

Presumably, earlier cases holding that a contempt proceeding for violation of an injunction is not a criminal prosecution within the meaning of the Sixth Amendment, no longer state a proper rule of law. See, e.g., Gompers v. United States, 233 U.S. 604, 610 (1914); Myers v. United States, 264 U.S. 95, 104 (1924); In re Debs, 158 U.S. 564, 596 (1895) (". . . in brief, a court, enforcing obedience to its orders by proceedings for contempt, is not executing the criminal laws of the land, but only securing to suitors the rights which it has adjudged them entitled to").

In rare cases the Supreme Court will review the nature of the conduct which is the basis of a contempt conviction by a state judge to determine whether the conduct was in fact contemptuous, since punishment for contempt where undeserved violates due process. Thus, the Court has ruled that where a lawyer has been convicted for contempt because he filed a motion asking the trial judge to disqualify himself, and failing in that, moved for a change of venue, he has been denied due process, since the lawyer has a right to file motions and pleadings essential to present claims and raise relevant issues.[86] It was not alleged that the lawyer disobeyed any valid order of the court, or talked loudly, or acted boisterously, or otherwise attempted to prevent the judge or any other officer of the court from carrying on his judicial duties. Furthermore, the Court once set aside the conviction for contempt of a lawyer who advised the union he was representing to continue picketing in violation of an *ex parte* injunction, without a hearing at which he would have had an opportunity to establish that the court had no power to issue the injunction because the issue arose in a field reserved exclusively by Congress for the National Labor Relations Board.[87] While the Court did not discuss the jury question, it did hold that procedural due process requires that one who is charged with contempt of court be advised of the charges and have a reasonable opportunity to defend himself at a hearing.

Finally, it should be noted that jury trial is not required in civil contempt proceedings, since the purpose of punishment is remedial rather than punitive.[88] In cases of civil contempt, the contemnor is always free to purge himself of the contempt by obeying the court's order. As the saying goes, he holds the keys to the jail in his pocket. On the other hand, where the purpose is to impose punishment in order to vindicate the authority of the court for some past dereliction, the contempt is criminal in nature. In addition, actions to recover statutory penalties from transportation companies for bringing immigrants into the country in violation of the immigration laws, are not regarded as criminal prosecutions, but rather as civil in character.[89] Deportation proceedings are also regarded as not being criminal proceedings within the meaning of the jury provisions of

---

86. Holt v. Virginia, 381 U.S. 131 (1965). Cf. *In re* McConnell, 370 U.S. 230, 236 (1962), where the Court held that it was not contemptuous for a lawyer to persist in asking questions barred by the judge, saying "An independent judiciary and a vigorous, independent bar are both indispensable parts of our system of justice."

87. *Re* Green, 369 U.S. 689 (1962).

88. Shillitani v. United States, 384 U.S. 364 (1966).

89. Hepner v. United States, 213 U.S. 103 (1909) (the trial judge may direct a verdict in favor of the government, the complaining party); Oceanic Navigation Co. v. Stranahan, 214 U.S. 320 (1909) (the penalties may be imposed by administrative action alone); United States v. Regan, 232 U.S. 37 (1914) (reasonable doubt doctrine does not apply).

the Constitution.⁹⁰ In summary, as Justice Harlan once remarked, "The Sixth Amendment relates to a prosecution of an accused person which is technically criminal in its nature."⁹¹

Waiver

The general rule of law in the United States is that in the absence of statutory or constitutional permission, a defendant charged with a felony cannot waive his right to jury trial, on pleading not guilty.⁹² Perhaps the most important argument against waiver is that public policy forbids it, since the public as well as the accused has an interest in the outcome of the trial and is concerned with preserving the citizen's liberties.⁹³ In a few states the courts have held that the constitutional language on jury trial is phrased in such imperative language as to preclude waiver.⁹⁴ Today, however, waiver is permitted at least in some criminal cases in all state courts and in the federal courts.

That defendants in federal courts may waive jury trial was established in 1930 by the Supreme Court in *Patton* v. *United States.*⁹⁵ The Court took the position that jury trial is not part of the structure of government essential to the jurisdiction of the trial court, but rather a valuable personal privilege designed to safeguard the accused. To deny the defendant the power to waive a personal privilege would convert it into an imperative requirement. Furthermore, the Court concluded that waiver was not contrary to public policy, since it was well established that an accused can plead guilty and dispense with a trial altogether. But the

90. U.S. *ex rel.* Turner v. Williams, 194 U.S. 279, 290 (1904); Zakonaite v. Wolf, 226 U.S. 272 (1912).

91. United States v. Zucker, 161 U.S. 475, 481 (1896). This case held that since the Sixth Amendment does not apply in an action brought by the government against importers to recover from them the value of merchandise imported into the country fraudulently, there was no constitutional right to confront and cross-examine a government witness, in this instance a Frenchman whose testimony was submitted by deposition.

92. Michaelson v. Beemer, 72 Neb. 761, 101 N.W. 1007 (1904).

93. State v. Talken, 316 Mo. 596, 292 S.W. 32 (1927); Cancemi v. People, 18 N.Y. 128, 137 (1858).

94. Jackson v. Com., 221 Ky. 823, 299 S.W. 983 (1927).

95. 281 U.S. 276 (1930). What happened was that towards the end of a nine-day trial one of the jurors became severely ill and was unable to serve further. All parties agreed to go ahead with eleven jurors. But the Supreme Court treated this not as a trial by eleven jurors, but as a waiver of jury trial, since the Constitution was then thought to guarantee a common law jury of twelve. See Erwin N. Griswold, "The Historical Development of Waiver of Jury Trial in Criminal Cases," *Virginia Law Review,* 20 (April 1934): 655-69. The Court previously approved of the waiver of jury trial in connection with petty offenses in Schick v. United States, 195 U.S. 65, 72 (1904). It has been held that a defendant in a federal court who is charged with having committed a petty offense may waive trial by jury without the government's consent. United States v. Young, 142 F. Supp. 666 (D. Hawaii, 1956).

Court held that since jury trial is important, and as a rule preferable, the waiver cannot go into effect without the consent of both the prosecutor and the trial judge, as well as "the express and intelligent consent of the defendant."[96]

In accordance with this decision, Rule 23(a) of the Federal Rules of Criminal Procedure provides that "cases required to be tried by jury shall be so tried unless the defendant waives a jury trial in writing with the approval of the court and the consent of the government." It will be noted that this applies to all criminal cases, including capital cases, that the waiver must be in writing, and that both the judge and prosecutor must agree to it. In *Singer* v. *United States,*[97] decided by a unanimous Court in 1965, it was ruled that if the government refuses to consent to the defendant's request for a waiver of jury trial, then the trial must proceed with a jury. Pointing out that in our early history the ability to waive a jury trial was never considered to be of equal importance to the right to demand one, Chief Justice Warren asserted that there has never been, under Article III of the Constitution, a federally recognized right to a criminal trial before a judge sitting alone. He noted that the ability to waive a constitutional right does not ordinarily carry with it the right to insist upon the opposite of that right. Furthermore, trial by jury for crimes is the normal procedure, and in the light of the Constitution's emphasis upon the right to trial by jury, it is difficult to understand the proposition that to compel a man in a criminal case to be tried by jury against his will defeats his right to a fair trial or due process. Here the accused was given the very thing the Constitution guarantees. In our adversary system, the Chief Justice noted, the government as a litigant has a legitimate interest in seeing to it that cases in which it believes conviction is warranted should be tried by the tribunal which the Constitution regards as most likely to produce a fair result. On the other hand, some state courts hold that a defendant's request for a waiver cannot be denied.[98]

In addition, the Supreme Court has ruled that an accused may waive jury trial without the advice of counsel.[99] Said Justice Frankfurter, ". . . the procedural safeguards of the Bill of Rights are not to be treated as mechanical rigidities. What were contrived as protections for the accused should not be turned into fetters. To assert as an absolute that a

---

96. Waiver of jury trial must be made "expressly, knowingly and intelligently." Dranow v. United States, 325 F.2d 481, 482, 485 (8th Cir. 1963), cert. denied, 376 U.S. 912 (1964).
97. 380 U.S. 24 (1965).
98. See, e.g., People v. Spegal, 5 Ill. 2d 211, 125 N.E. 2d 468 (1955).
99. Adams v. U.S. *ex rel.* McCann, 317 U.S. 269, 279 (1942). Three Justices dissented, arguing that it could not be assumed that a layman is competent to waive jury trial without a lawyer.

layman, no matter how wise or experienced he may be, is incompetent to choose between judge and jury as the tribunal for determining his guilt or innocence, simply because a lawyer has not advised him on the choice, is to dogmatize beyond the bounds of learning or experience." He also pointed out that the vast majority of criminal cases in the state courts are tried before a judge without a jury.[100]

Today all states permit defendants to waive trial by jury,[101] although under various rules. Some states permit waiver only in felony cases; some states authorize waiver in all cases, and a few states in all cases except where the offense is punishable by death. Some states permit waiver only in the case of misdemeanors.[102] Many state constitutions now authorize waiver. For example the New York Constitution provides, "A jury trial may be waived by the defendant in all criminal cases, except those in which the crime charged may be punishable by death, by a written instrument signed by the defendant in person in open court before and with the approval of a judge or justice of a court having jurisdiction to try the offense."[103] In a few states statutes do not permit an uncounseled defendant to waive jury trial.[104]

The Representative Jury

"Our notions of what a proper jury is," Justice Murphy once observed, "have developed in harmony with our basic concepts of a democratic society and a representative government."[105] This being so, a jury cannot by "the organ of any special group or class." Similarly, when Congress adopted the Jury Selection Act of March 27, 1968, it included a "Declaration of Policy" in which it stated, "It is the policy of the United States that all litigants in Federal courts entitled to trial by jury shall have the right to grand and petit juries selected at random from a fair cross section of the community in the district or division wherein the court convenes. It

---

100. The fact that the defendant had the assistance of counsel in deciding to waive jury trial tends to negate an allegation of coercion. Roseman v. United States, 364 F.2d 18, 27 (9th Cir., 1966), cert. denied, 386 U.S. 918 (1967).

101. Harry Kalven, Jr., and Hans Zeisel, *The American Jury* (Boston: Little, Brown & Co., 1966), p. 24.

102. See *Report of the Judicial Council of New York* (Albany, 1939), pp. 153–78, for an account of the situation as of 1938.

103. N.Y. Const., Art. I, §2. See People v. Carroll, 3 N.Y. 2d 686, 171 N.Y.S. 2d 812, 148 N.E. 2d 875 (1958).

104. For example, in Texas and Virginia an uncounselled defendant may not waive a jury in any felony case. Tex. Code Crim. Proc. Ann., Art. 1-13 (Vernon 1966); Va. Code Ann. §§19.1-192, 19.1-193 (Cum. Supp. 1963). See Wilson v. State, 157 Tex. Cr. Rep. 642, 252 S.W. 2d 197 (1952).

105. Glasser v. United States, 315 U.S. 60, 85 (1942).

is further the policy of the United States that all citizens shall have the opportunity to be considered for service on grand and petit juries in the district courts of the United States, and shall have an obligation to serve as jurors when summoned for that purpose."[106] And Congress added, "No citizen shall be excluded from service as a grand or petit juror in the district courts of the United States on account of race, color, religion, sex, national origin, or economic status."[107]

The concept of a representative jury, however, does not and cannot mean that every jury must include a cross section of the community, since the community is made up of too many diverse elements, and the actual makeup of a particular jury is largely the result of chance. But the requirement of representativeness does mean that no significant element of the population should be excluded altogether from jury service. Thus a socialist has not been denied any constitutional right because he was tried by a jury composed exclusively of members of other political parties and of property owners.[108] But it would have been a violation of his constitutional right to a properly-constituted jury if socialists or persons not owning property had been barred from service on juries summoned to sit in the court in which he was tried. This was just the point litigated in *Thiel* v. *Southern Pacific Co.*[109] The federal district court in California in which Thiel had brought his action had adopted the practice of deliberately excluding all persons who work for a daily wage, apparently on the theory that they cannot afford to serve on juries. This the Supreme Court held improper, since our tradition of jury trial "necessarily contemplates an impartial jury drawn from a cross-section of the community. . . . This does not mean, of course, that every jury must contain representatives of all the economic, social, religious, racial, political and geographical groups of the community; frequently such complete representation would be impossible. But it does mean that prospective jurors shall be selected by court officials without systematic and intentional exclusion of any of these groups. Recognition must be given to the fact that those eligible for jury service are to be found in every stratum of society. Jury competence is an individual rather than a group or class matter. That fact lies at the very heart of the jury system." Since daily earners are a substantial part of the community, they cannot be excluded intentionally and systematically "without doing violence to the democratic nature of the jury system." Of course, the judge may in his discretion excuse a wage earner for whom jury service would entail an undue financial hardship, but it cannot be assumed that all daily wage earners are eligible to be excused, without a

106. 28 U.S.C. §1861 (1970).
107. 28 U.S.C. §1862 (1970).
108. Ruthenberg v. United States, 245 U.S. 480 (1918).
109. 328 U.S. 217 (1946).

showing of actual hardship. Furthermore, "jury service is a duty as well as a privilege of citizenship; it is a duty that cannot be shirked on a plea of inconvenience or decreased earning power."[110] Some years later a federal Court of Appeals applied this reasoning to invalidate the makeup of a state jury.[111]

The question of excluding women from jury service in federal courts presents a comparable issue. In 1948 Congress revised the statute law describing the qualifications of jurors to prescribe uniform standards for jurors in federal courts instead of making qualifications depend upon state laws, and these standards were revised in 1968. Prior to 1948, Congress provided that jurors in a federal court should have the same qualifications as those of the highest trial court in the state. Since in California, as in most states, women were eligible for jury service under local law, the Supreme Court ruled, in *Ballard* v. *United States*,[112] that a federal court in California could not bar women from jury service. The Court rejected the argument that an all-male panel will be as truly representative of the community as if women were included. "The truth is," said Justice Douglas, "that the two sexes are not fungible; a community made up exclusively of one is different from a community composed of both; the subtle interplay of influence one on the other is among the imponderables."[113] Furthermore, the Court made the important ruling that in such cases the appellant does not have to prove that the makeup of his particular jury actually prejudiced his case.[114] "The evil lies in the admitted exclusion of an eligible class or group in the community in disregard of the prescribed standards of jury selection. The systematic and intentional exclusion of women, like the exclusion of a racial group, . . . or an economic or social class, . . . deprives the jury system of the broad base it was designed by Congress to have in our democratic society. . . . The injury is not limited to the defendant—there is injury to the jury system, to the law as an institution, to the community at large, and to the democratic ideal reflected in the processes of our courts."[115]

---

110. 328 U.S. 220, 223, 224.

111. See Labat v. Bennett, 365 F.2d 698 (5th Cir. 1966), cert. denied, 386 U.S. 991 (1967), wherein the Court of Appeals held that the exclusion of manual workers and similar "daily wage earners" from parish juries in Louisiana was "unacceptable." Pointing out that the manual working class contains a disproportionately large number of Negroes, the Court ruled that this principle of exclusion violated the Equal Protection Clause of the Fourteenth Amendment. Judge Wisdom said, ". . . a jury system without daily wage earners simply is not representative of the community." 365 F.2d 720.

112. 329 U.S. 187 (1946).

113. 329 U.S. 193-94.

114. Many state courts also hold that actual prejudice need not be proved or will be presumed. See Walter v. State, 208 Ind. 231, 195 N.E. 268, 98 A.L.R. 607 (1935).

115. 329 U.S. 195.

Women are now fully eligible for jury service in federal courts by virtue of federal statute law, but whether the national Constitution imposes such a rule upon the states was finally decided in their favor only very recently. In *Hoyt* v. *Florida*,[116] decided in 1961, a unanimous Court upheld a conviction of a woman for second-degree murder by an all-male jury. Under Florida law no woman was called for jury service unless she had registered her desire to be placed on the list with the clerk of the circuit court, while of course no such requirement applied to men. The Court ruled that this arrangement violated neither the due process nor the equal protection clauses of the Fourteenth Amendment, since it could find in the challenged system of jury selection no arbitrary and systematic exclusion of women; the differential treatment of women was based, in the Court's judgement, on a reasonable classification, because "woman is still regarded as the center of home and family life."[117]

Considering the strength of the movement towards equal rights for women in recent years, it is not at all surprising that in 1975 the Supreme Court, by an 8-1 vote, overruled a unanimous precedent only thirteen years old. In *Taylor* v. *Louisiana*[118] the Court ruled unconstitutional, as a violation of the Sixth Amendment, made fully applicable to the states in 1968 in *Duncan* v. *Louisiana*,[119] a state statute which excluded women from jury service unless they had previously filed a written declaration of their desire so to serve. In Taylor's case, 53 percent of all persons eligible for jury service in the judicial district were women, whereas no more than 10 percent were on the jury wheel. The Court held that this method of jury selection denied the defendant the right to a representative jury drawn from a fair cross section of the community, a right essential to the fulfilment of the Sixth Amendment guaranty. It was noted that 54 percent of all women between eighteen and sixty-four were in the labor force in 1974, and that it was untenable to say that it would be a special hardship for every woman to perform jury service, or that society cannot spare any woman from her present duties.[120] Finally, it is worth noting that the Court ruled that though a male, the defendant had standing to object to the exclusion of women, since the injury is to the jury system itself, just as the Court ruled in 1972 that a white defendant may challenge a jury from which Negroes were systematically excluded.[121]

116. 368 U.S. 57 (1961).
117. 368 U.S. 62. Justice Harlan said this.
118. 419 U.S. 522 (1975).
119. 391 U.S. 148 (1968).
120. The rule of this case was held not retroactive in Daniel v. Louisiana, 420 U.S. 31 (1975).
121. Peters v. Kiff, 407 U.S. 493 (1972).

An Impartial Jury

The Sixth Amendment declares, as do most state constitutions, that the accused shall enjoy in all criminal prosecutions the right to "an impartial jury." This is in accord with the common law, for as Lord Mansfield said in 1764, "A juror should be as white Paper, and know neither plaintiff nor defendant, but judge of the issue merely as an abstract proposition upon the evidence produced before him. He should be superior even to a suspicion of partiality."[122] But complete impartiality is hard to find, and the law does not demand the impossible. Chief Justice Marshall once had occasion to reject counsel's argument that jurors must be "perfectly indifferent and free from prejudice."[123] He distinguished between jurors with "light" impressions and those with "deep" ones. The former "may fairly be supposed to yield to the testimony," whereas the latter "will close the mind against the testimony," which is a sufficient objection.

In order to secure an impartial jury, prospective jurors are questioned by the lawyers on both sides. Very often this *voir dire* examination, as it is called, is very lengthy and costly, and many objections have been made on this score. The remedy is to give the judge authority to control the examination of jurors, as is provided for in Rule 24(a) of the Federal Rules of Criminal Procedure. If he wishes to, the federal judge may himself conduct the examination, although he must permit counsel on both sides to put supplementary questions, either directly or through him. Prospective jurors found to be lacking in impartiality are subject to challenge. An unlimited number of challenges for cause are allowed or disallowed by the judge, in his sound discretion. But both sides also have a limited number of peremptory challenges. A peremptory challenge is an objection to a juror for which no reason has to be given, and upon which the judge must exclude. The number of peremptory challenges is regulated by law. Although the Supreme Court has ruled that there is a constitutional right to challenge for cause, and no such right to peremptory challenges,[124] the latter are allowed by a rule of court. Rule 24(b) of the Federal Rules of Criminal Procedure allows twenty peremptory challenges to each side if the offense charged is punishable by death; if the offense is punishable by imprisonment for more than one year, the government is entitled to six peremptory challenges and the defendant to ten; if the offense is punishable by imprisonment for not more than one year or by fine or both, each side gets three peremptory challenges. The number of peremptory challenges in other courts varies a great deal from state to state. Thus, the New

---

122. Mylock v. Saladine, 1 Wm. Blackstone Rep. 480, 481 (1781), 96 Eng. Rep. 278.
123. United States v. Burr, 25 Fed. Cas. 49 (Nos. 14,692g and 14,693) (C.C.D. Va. 1807).
124. Stilson v. United States, 250 U.S. 583 (1919).

York statute allows twenty for class A felonies, fifteen for class B or C felonies, if punishment is ten year of imprisonment or more, and ten in all other cases.[125]

The trial judge has a wide discretion in determining the competency of jurors in a criminal case, and an appellate court will very rarely set aside his judgment as an abuse of discretion.[126] Before a juror is dismissed for having an opinion, it must be shown to be more than a mere impression, and must be founded on some evidence, since not every opinion is indicative of lack of impartiality. For, as Chief Justice Waite once observed, "In these days of newspaper enterprise and universal education, every case of public interest is almost, as a matter of necessity, brought to the attention of all the intelligent people in the vicinity, and scarcely any one can be found among those best fitted for jurors who has not read or heard of it, and who has not some impression or some opinion in respect to its merits."[127] Thus it is well established that the mere fact that a juror has read a newspaper account of a criminal charge is not in itself sufficient grounds for excusing the juror.[128] The grounds upon which jurors may be challenged for cause are often spelled out in state statutes. For example, the Illinois statute lists the following grounds for challenges for cause: (1) lack of statutory qualifications; (2) service on a jury during the previous year; (3) being a party to any suit pending for trial in the same court; (4) possession of a preconceived opinion on the merits of the case, though a mere opinion based on newspaper reading is not enough to disqualify if the juror states on oath that he believes he can render a verdict fairly and impartially.[129]

Qualifications for jury service are listed in the statute books. Federal law declares that any United States citizen who is over eighteen and has resided in the judicial district for at least one year is competent to serve on any grand or petit jury unless (1) he has been convicted in any court of a crime punishable by imprisonment for more than one year, and his civil rights have not been restored by a pardon or amnesty, or (2) he is unable to read, write, speak, and understand the English language, or (3) he is incapable, by reason of mental or physical infirmities, of rendering satisfactory jury service.[130] Members of the armed forces, members of fire and

125. N.Y. Code of Crim. Proc., §270.25 (McKinney 1971).
126. Bratcher v. United States, 149 F.2d 742 (4th Cir. 1945), cert. denied, 325 U.S. 885 (1945).
127. Reynolds v. United States, 98 U.S. 145, 155–56 (1878).
128. Finnegan v. United States, 204 F.2d 105 (8th Cir. 1953), cert. denied, 346 U.S. 821 (1953); Allen v. United States, 4 F.2d 688 (7th Cir. 1925).
129. Ill. Ann. Stat., c. 78, §14 (Cum. Supp. Smith-Hurd 1974).
130. U.S.C.A. §1861 (Cum. Supp. 1975). Before 1948, the statute merely provided that federal jurors had to have the same qualifications and were eligible for the same exemptions

police departments, and federal and state public officers "who are actively engaged in the performance of official duties," are exempt from jury service in federal courts.[131] In addition, the district judge may "for good cause" excuse or exclude from jury service any person called as a juror, particularly on "a showing of undue hardship or extreme inconvenience," or where there is danger that it is likely that the proceedings will be obstructed.[132]

While there are variations in the language used, state laws follow a similar pattern. For example, the Illinois statute declares that jurors must be local residents, of the age of eighteen or over, "in the possession of their natural faculties and not infirm or decrepit," and that they must be "free from all legal exceptions, of fair character, of approved integrity, of sound judgment, well informed, and who understand the English language."[133]

Jurors are paid *per diem* fees, usually very modest ones. In 1968 Congress raised the fee for federal jurors from ten to twenty dollars a day, fixed the travel allowance at ten cents per mile, and provided that if a trial goes over thirty days, the judge may allow, in his discretion, up to twenty-five dollars per day for every day over thirty.[134] Some states have adopted legislation providing that an employee who is excused from his employment for jury duty must be paid his usual compensation, less the compensation received for serving as a juror. A unanimous Court held such a state statute constitutional, in 1973, ruling that it is not a denial of property without due process of law to require an employer to pay wages for time spent as a juror, since the public welfare is involved.[135]

Whether employees of the national government should be eligible to sit on juries in criminal cases in the federal courts, where the government itself is, of course, the complaining party, has long been disputed. In 1909

---

as state jurors. The 1948 revision was designed to establish uniform rules for federal jury selection, and also provided for fewer exemptions. The most recent federal statute on the subject is the Jury Selection Act of March 27, 1968, 28 U.S.C.A. §§1861-71, 82 Stat. 54. See Note, "An Analysis of Alternative Constructions of the Requirement that Federal Jurors Be Competent under State Law," *Yale Law Journal*, 64 (June 1955): 1059-69; William Wicker, "Jury Panels in Federal Courts," *Tennessee Law Review*, 22 (February 1952): 203-19.

131. 28 U.S.C.A. §1863(6) (Cum. Supp. 1975). For a decision upholding the exclusion of lawyers, ministers, doctors, dentists, railway engineers, and firemen from a state's juries, see Rawlins v. Georgia, 201 U.S. 638 (1906). Justice Holmes stressed that "the exclusion was not the result of race or class prejudice."

132. 28 U.S.C.A. §1866(c) (Cum. Supp. 1975).

133. Ill. Ann. Stat., c. 78, §2 (Cum. Supp. Smith-Hurd 1974).

134. 28 U.S.C.A. §1871 (Cum. Supp. 1975).

135. Dean v. Gadsen Times Publishing Corp., 412 U.S. 543 (1973). The Court relied upon Day-Bright Lighting, Inc. v. Missouri, 342 U.S. 421 (1952), which held valid a state statute requiring an employee to be given four hours in which to vote, without loss of any pay.

the Supreme Court ruled on common law grounds that government employees in the District of Columbia were not eligible to serve as jurors in any criminal or other case in which the government itself is a party, since they might tend to be biased, however unconsciously, in favor of their employer.[136] But this made it difficult to secure properly qualified jurors in the District, where such a large part of the population is employed by the government. Finally, Congress passed an act in 1935 declaring that government employees were eligible for jury service in any case in which the government was a party.[137] The following year the Supreme Court sustained this statute, holding that when a government employee is called for jury service, he may be examined for actual bias, but that bias will not necessarily be implied.[138] "Impartiality," said Chief Justice Hughes, "is not a technical conception. It is a state of mind. For the ascertainment of this mental attitude of appropriate indifference, the Constitution lays down no particular tests and procedure is not chained to any ancient and artificial formula."[139] He could not see why a governmental employee was any more interested in the enforcement of the penal laws than any other citizen. The notion that a government worker may fear for his job if he votes in favor of the accused he characterized as "far-fetched and chimerical," not rising to the dignity of an argument.[140]

The issue was back in the Court in 1948, in *Frazier v. United States*,[141] in which the accused had been convicted, in a District of Columbia court, of violating the Harrison Narcotics Act, by a jury composed entirely of employees of the federal government. In fact, one juror and the wife of another were employed by the Treasury, which was responsible for enforcing the Act. Frazier had used up his peremptory challenges against persons privately employed, and thus, as the Court noted, the composition of the jury was largely his own doing. The final makeup of the jury, the Court held, was due to chance. If, said Justice Rutledge, a panel is lawfully selected, with no invalid exclusions, there is no cause for complaint merely because it turns out that the jury finally chosen happens not to be representative of the community. The only ground for challenge of these jurors was for actual bias, which had not been made at the trial. Four Justices dissented, Justice Jackson remarking, "On one proposition I should expect trial lawyers to be nearly unanimous: that a jury, every member of

---

136. Crawford v. United States, 212 U.S. 183 (1909). See Francis H. Heller, "Justice, Jury Trials, and Government Service," *Cornell Law Quarterly*, 35 (Summer 1950): 814–23.
137. Act of August 22, 1935, c. 605, 49 Stat. 682.
138. United States v. Wood, 299 U.S. 123 (1936). Three Justices dissented.
139. 299 U.S. 145–46.
140. 299 U.S. 150.
141. 335 U.S. 497 (1948).

which is in the hire of one of the litigants, lacks something of being an impartial jury." Particularly in recent years, he argued, the government is using its power as never before "to pry" into the lives and thoughts of its employees "upon the slightest suspicion of less than complete trustworthiness. It demands not only probity but unquestioning ideological loyalty."[142] It is unreasonable to assume, he maintained, that every clerk in the bureaucracy feels so secure that he can put his dependence upon the government out of mind.

The same issue was again litigated in 1950 in *Dennis* v. *United States*,[143] in which the secretary of the Communist Party of the United States was convicted by a jury in the District of Columbia of contempt of a congressional committee. Seven of the jurors in his case were government employees, each of whom had expressed his belief that he could render a fair and impartial verdict. By a 5-2 vote the Court held that he was not entitled to a new trial because his challenge to the government employees for cause was not sustained. The Court ruled that an absence of any showing of actual bias was decisive. While the trial judge, in exercising his discretion, must be zealous to protect the rights of the accused, a member of an unpopular minority group is not entitled to exceptions not available to all defendants. The Court found that there was no evidence to support the view that there was a climate of opinion among government employees which led them to feel that they would jeopardize their tenure or provoke investigation if they reached a verdict in favor of the accused. Finally, the Court refused to fashion a special rule applicable to Communists. The opportunity of every defendant to prove actual bias is his guaranty of the right to an impartial jury.

Justice Black dissented in this case on the theory that, given the then prevailing pattern of loyalty investigations and purges, government employees could not meet an objective test of complete impartiality. That is to say, he felt that under existing conditions an average government employee was not free to vote to acquit Communists or any others accused of being subversive. Justice Frankfurter, who also dissented, developed the theory that government employees in the District of Columbia should be disqualified in any prosecutions that are concerned with security. Indeed, he maintained that in any case involving security a government employee should not even be asked whether he feels free to decide against the government, for his answer would require him to announce publicly that he is either brave or weak.

Since actual bias is the key to the problem of exclusion for cause from

---

142. 335 U.S. 514, 515.
143. 339 U.S. 162 (1950).

192 / *The Defendant's Rights Today*

the jury, the Court held soon afterwards, however, that it is error for the trial judge to refuse to permit counsel to interrogate government employees upon *voir dire* examination with specific reference to the possible influence of the loyalty program upon their ability to render a just and impartial verdict.[144] This accords with an earlier holding that a Negro on trial in the District of Columbia for the murder of a white man is entitled to have the jurors asked on their *voir dire* examination whether they have any racial prejudice that would prevent a fair and impartial verdict.[145] Such also is the rule in many state courts.

In respect to the concept of an impartial jury, special attention should be given to the 5–4 decision of the Supreme Court in 1968, in *Witherspoon v. Illinois*.[146] Witherspoon had been tried on a charge of murder in the state court, and convicted by a jury which prescribed the death penalty. At the time of his trial, an Illinois statute provided, "In trials for murder it shall be a cause for challenge of any juror who shall, on being examined, state that he has conscientious scruples against capital punishment, or that he is opposed to the same." This gave the prosecution unlimited challenges for cause to exclude jurors who, in the words of the Illinois Supreme Court, "might hesitate to return a verdict inflicting [death]."[147] At Witherspoon's trial, the prosecution eliminated nearly half the venire of prospective jurors by challenge under this statute, thus getting rid of all who had expressed any qualms about capital punishment. A bare majority of the Supreme Court held that on the issue of guilt, the jury was a proper one, but that on the issue of the sentence—imprisonment or death—it was self-evident that the jury "fell woefully short of that impartiality to which the petitioner was entitled under the Sixth and Fourteenth Amendments."[148] The Court stated that on the issue of death the jury should express the conscience of the community, and that in a nation in which fewer than half of the people believe in the death penalty, the State produced a jury "uncommonly willing to condemn a man to die."[149] To put it differently, the state may not leave the fateful issue of life or death in

---

144. Morford v. United States, 339 U.S. 258 (1950).
145. Aldridge v. United States, 283 U.S. 308 (1931). In Ham v. South Carolina, 409 U.S. 524 (1973), the rule of this case was applied to a state case where a Negro defendant was denied the right to ask prospective jurors questions regarding racial prejudice. The defendant was also bearded, but the Supreme Court upheld the propriety of the judge's refusal to inquire into prejudice against beards, on the ground that while the issue of racial prejudice had constitutional dimensions, the beard question did not rise to such a level of significance. Two Justices dissented on the latter issue.
146. 391 U.S. 510 (1968).
147. People v. Carpenter, 13 Ill. 2d 470, 476, 150 N.E. 2d 100, 103 (1958).
148. 391 U.S. 518.
149. 391 U.S. 521.

the hands of a tribunal "organized to return a verdict of death." Through the imposition of "a hanging jury," said Justice Stewart, "the State of Illinois has stacked the deck against the petitioner," thus denying him due process of law.[150]

The dissenters argued that the state as well as the defendant has a right to an impartial jury, and that if the Court wants to hold capital punishment unconstitutional, it ought to do so forthrightly, not by making it impossible for the state to get a jury that will enforce the death penalty. Actually, the Court majority did not go as far as the dissenters suggested, since it seemed to approve of the right of the prosecution to challenge for cause those prospective jurors who state that their reservations about capital punishment would prevent them from making an impartial decision, or who say that they would never, whatever the facts may be, vote to impose the death penalty. Thus it would seem that *Witherspoon* does not go very far, and does not inhibit the state from challenging for cause in capital cases very much.[151]

Exclusion of Negroes from Jury Service

For many years an act of Congress has squarely forbidden the exclusion of citizens from jury service in any federal court on account of race or color.[152] In addition, since 1875 the federal penal code has included the following provision: "No citizen possessing all other qualifications which are or may be prescribed by law shall be disqualified for service as grand or petit juror in any court of the United States, or of any State on account of race, color, or previous condition of servitude; and whoever, being an officer or other person charged with any duty in the selection or summoning of jurors, excludes or fails to summon any citizen for such cause, shall be fined not more than $5,000."[153] It will be noted that here, for the first time, Congress undertook to punish state officials for discrimination against Negroes as regards jury service in state courts. The constitutional power of Congress to do so was upheld in the leading case of *Ex parte Virginia*,[154] where the Court sustained an indictment of a Virginia judge who was accused of excluding Negroes from juries in his court. The statute was based on the Fourteenth Amendment's provision that "no

---

150. 391 U.S. 523.
151. In Bumper v. North Carolina, 391 U.S. 543 (1968) the Court held that the rule of the Witherspoon case did not apply because the jury recommended a life sentence, even though the same question had been put to prospective jurors.
152. Now 28 U.S.C.A. §1862 (Cum. Supp. 1975).
153. Civil Rights Act of March 1, 1875, 18 Stat. 335, §4, now 18 U.S.C. §243 (1970). The original language has been altered only very slightly since 1875.
154. 100 U.S. 339 (1880).

State shall . . . deny to any person within its jurisdiction the equal protection of the laws," and the power vested in Congress by Section 5 of this amendment, "to enforce, by appropriate legislation," its various provisions.

But direct federal prosecution of state officials to discourage discrimination against Negroes in regard to jury service has been a very rare thing. The principal federal weapon has always been the power of the Supreme Court to set aside the conviction or dismiss the indictment of a Negro who had been indicted or tried in a state court which practiced such discrimination. That is to say, a state denies a Negro the equal protection of the laws, contrary to the Fourteenth Amendment, if it puts him on trial before a jury from which Negroes were systematically and arbitrarily excluded. Another federal remedy is to sue for a writ of habeas corpus, provided of course that all requirements of the federal habeas corpus act are met. In addition, it is possible for Negroes, as members of the excluded class, and even though they are not defendants in criminal cases, to sue in a federal court to enjoin state officials responsible for the selection of jurors from engaging in arbitrary, discriminatory practices.[155] The Supreme Court has taken the position that people who are excluded from juries because of race are as much aggrieved as defendants.

The principle of direct review was first established in 1880, in *Strauder* v. *West Virginia,*[156] which set aside the conviction of a Negro for murder on the ground that, pursuant to a state statute, Negroes were barred altogether from jury service. Perhaps the best-known case of this type was *Norris* v. *Alabama,*[157] which reversed the conviction of the so-called Scottsboro boys on the ground that Negroes had long been excluded, systematically and arbitrarily, from juries sitting in the county in which the trial was held. Here Chief Justice Hughes emphasized that when a claim to a federal right is made, the federal court's function is to determine not merely whether a right was denied in express terms, but also whether it was denied in substance and effect. It follows, as the Court held, that although a state statute may be fair on its face, the protection of the Fourteenth Amendment extends to the action of administrative officers who actually effected the prohibited discrimination. Formerly state statutes frankly barred Negroes from jury service by limiting such service to white people. Today such crude statutes no longer exist. The problem, therefore, is to look behind the face of the statute into its actual enforce-

---

155. The first case of this sort not brought by a defendant challenging a conviction was Carter v. Jury Commission of Greene County, 396 U.S. 320 (1970). The same sort of action was approved in a companion case, Turner v. Fouche, 396 U.S. 346 (1970).

156. 100 U.S. 303 (1880). So held also in Neal v. Delaware, 103 U.S. 370 (1881).

157. 294 U.S. 587 (1935).

ment or administration. Thus Justice Black once observed, "The fact that the written words of a state's laws hold out a promise that no such discrimination will be practiced is not enough. The Fourteenth Amendment requires that equal protection to all must be given—not merely promised."[158]

It is clear, of course, that a Negro does not have a right to be tried only by Negro jurors. Nor does he have a right to have a number of Negroes on his jury which would be proportioned to the Negro population of the district.[159] In fact, he is not, as a matter of constitutional law, entitled to have any Negroes at all on his jury. He may have to stand trial before an all-white jury as a result of all sorts of factors, such as challenges or chance. But what the Negro is entitled to is a jury system which does not exclude Negroes arbitrarily and systematically. That is why the facts are so important in these cases.

Take the *Norris* case as an example. The total population of Jackson County, Alabama, where the indictment was returned, was 36,881, of whom 2,688 were Negroes. No Negro, it was shown, had served on any jury in the county within the memory of witnesses who had lived there all their lives, and who ranged in age from fifty to seventy-six. The clerk of the jury commission, the clerk of the court, the court reporter, who had not missed a session in twenty-four years, and two jury commissioners all testified that they had never known of a Negro serving on a grand jury in the county. In addition, by direct testimony defense counsel was able to identify in the record some thirty specific Negroes who were qualified for jury service. Similar facts were brought out in connection with conditions in the county in which the trial was had. Such facts create a strong *prima facie* case of discrimination, and the burden then shifts to the state to prove that discrimination did not take place. This burden of proof is not met merely by denying that discrimination actually occurred. "If," said Chief Justice Hughes, "in the presence of such testimony as defendant

---

158. Smith v. Texas, 311 U.S. 128, 130 (1940). See also Turner v. Fouche, 396 U.S. 346 (1970).

159. Akins v. Texas, 325 U.S. 398 (1945). Said Justice Reed, "Fairness in selection has never been held to require proportional representation of races upon a jury. . . . Purposeful discrimination is not sustained by a showing that on a single grand jury the number of members of one race is less than that race's proportion of the eligible individuals. The number of our races and nationalities stands in the way of evolution of such a conception of due process or equal protection. Defendants under our criminal statutes are not entitled to demand representatives of their racial inheritance upon juries before whom they are tried." See also Carter v. Jury Commission of Greene County, 396 U.S. 320 (1970), which held that the mere absence of Negroes from the county jury commission is not *prima facie* evidence of discriminatory exclusion, that Negroes are not constitutionally entitled to proportional representation by race on the jury commission any more than on any particular jury.

adduced, the mere general assertions by officials of their performance of duty were to be accepted as an adequate justification for the complete exclusion of negroes from jury service, the constitutional provision—adopted with special reference to their protection—would be but a vain and illusory requirement."[160]

In 1939 the Supreme Court by unanimous vote rejected the suggestion that since an indictment is not evidence of guilt, but merely brings the accused before the court for prosecution, a subsequent conviction should not be set aside on the ground that Negroes had been arbitrarily and systematically excluded from the grand jury.[161] The Court regarded it as settled law that exclusion from either grand or petit jury service on account of race is forbidden by the Fourteenth Amendment.

A *prima facie* case of discrimination may be established in several ways. Usually it is a matter of numbers. Where one-third of the population of the county is Negro, and 70 percent of the Negroes over ten are literate, and no Negro is called for jury service in a period of forty years, a *prima facie* case of forbidden discrimination has been made out.[162] A conviction will be set aside if there has been discrimination, "whether accomplished ingeniously or ingenuously."[163] Thus, the use by the jury commissioners of differently colored pieces of paper for white people and Negroes has been regarded as *prima facie* evidence of discrimination.[164] While it is true that the absence of Negroes from one particular jury may not be enough to make out a *prima facie* case, when that jury is viewed in the context of the practice of thirty years or more, during which no Negro ever served in a county with a large Negro population, a very strong showing of systematic exclusion has been made.[165] Furthermore, in establishing his case the defendant does not have to prove actual discrimination in the drawing of his particular jury; all he is obliged to do is to make out a *prima facie* case of the discriminatory exclusion of Negroes as a general policy.[166] On the other hand, it is not absolutely necessary to give evidence of long-contin-

---

160. 294 U.S. 598. See also Hollins v. Oklahoma, 295 U.S. 394 (1935); Hale v. Kentucky, 303 U.S. 613 (1938); Whitus v. Georgia, 385 U.S. 545 (1967); Alexander v. Louisiana, 405 U.S. 625 (1972).
161. Pierre v. Louisiana, 306 U.S. 354 (1939). In a dissenting opinion in Cassell v. Texas, 339 U.S. 282 (1950), Justice Jackson argued that the absence of Negroes on the grand jury did not prejudice a Negro defendant, though he conceded that there is prejudice if Negroes are barred from the trial juries.
162. Pierre v. Louisiana, 306 U.S. 354 (1939).
163. Smith v. Texas, 311 U.S. 128, 132 (1940).
164. Avery v. Georgia, 345 U.S. 559 (1953). In a concurring opinion Justice Frankfurter observed that these slips of paper could serve no other purpose but discrimination.
165. Patton v. Mississippi, 332 U.S. 463 (1947).
166. Hill v. Texas, 316 U.S. 400 (1942); Avery v. Georgia, 345 U.S. 559 (1953).

ued discriminatory practices, since it may be possible to prove discrimination in the defendant's particular case.[167] The constitutional requirement is not satisfied by a mere token appointment of Negroes, such as one to each grand jury, for while proportional representation of the races is not requisite, neither is proportional limitation permissible.[168] An accused is entitled to have the charges against him considered by a jury in the selection of which there has been neither inclusion nor exclusion because of race. In addition, it is incumbent upon the state court to permit the defendant to offer evidence in support of his claim that Negroes had been arbitrarily and systematically excluded from serving on his jury.[169]

It is settled law, however, that since a Negro is not entitled to a jury containing members of his race, but only freedom from a system of purposeful or deliberate denial of jury service to Negroes on account of race, if the use of peremptory challenges by the prosecutor results in an all-white jury, there has been no denial of equal protection of the laws.[170] The peremptory challenge system, Justice White has observed, has very old credentials; peremptories are freely used all over the country today and are regarded as a necessary part of trial by jury, and the whole point of the system is that anyone may be challenged without cause. He noted that to limit the power to make these challenges by virtue of the Equal Protection Clause would entail a radical departure from the operation of the system, and the challenge would no longer be peremptory.[171]

The doctrine which has emerged in the cases dealing with the systematic and arbitrary exclusion of Negroes from jury service can be extended to other substantial groups in the population. Thus in *Hernandez v. Texas*[172] a unanimous Court ruled that where 14 percent of the population of the county is of Mexican or Latin-American descent, the barring of all such persons from the juries violates the Equal Protection Clause of the Fourteenth Amendment. In this instance it was proved that no person with a Mexican or Latin-American name had served on a jury within the past twenty-five years. This established a strong *prima facie* case which is not rebutted by a mere denial of discrimination. The Court rejected the argument that within the contemplation of the Fourteenth Amendment

167. Cassell v. Texas, 339 U.S. 282 (1950).
168. 339 U.S. 282.
169. Coleman v. Alabama, 377 U.S. 129 (1964). The Supreme Court has ruled that, as required by the plain language of the Jury Selection Act of 1968, a defendant in a criminal case, or any litigant in a civil case, has an unqualified right to inspect the jury lists, in order to challenge jury selection procedures. Test v. United States, 420 U.S. 38 (1975).
170. Swain v. Alabama, 380 U.S. 202 (1965).
171. Three Justices dissented, arguing that there is no constitutional right to peremptory challenges, and that the command of the Fourteenth Amendment should prevail.
172. 347 U.S. 475 (1954).

there are only two classes, white and Negro, although it is true that historically differences in race and color have defined the most easily identifiable groups requiring the aid of the courts to get equal treatment under the law. But, as Chief Justice Warren pointed out, "community prejudices are not static," and whether a particular group is sufficiently well defined to stand out as a group is a question of fact. He ruled that the appellant had succeeded in proving, on the basis of community attitudes and local practices, that persons of Mexican descent constituted a separate class in the county distinct from "whites."

It may be concluded that we are now committed to the proposition that the jury, as an instrument of public justice, must be fairly representative of the community. Exclusion of racial or other identifiable, substantial groups is violative of both the Constitution and of statute law adopted to implement it. In addition, in the words of Justice Black, racial discrimination in the selection of jurors "is at war with our basic concepts of a democratic society and a representative government."[173]

The "Blue-Ribbon" Jury

Whether the so-called "blue-ribbon" jury is consistent with accepted principles has been a matter of sharp debate. Twice the Supreme Court has ruled that the New York blue-ribbon jury system squares with the Constitution, but on both occasions the decision was reached by a 5–4 vote.[174] It should be noted that the New York statute—now repealed—was by no means a novel one of recent date, having first been adopted in 1896. It must also be recalled that there is a tremendous amount of diversity in jury practices in the states, with which the Supreme Court has traditionally been loathe to interfere. "The function of this federal Court under the Fourteenth Amendment in reference to state juries," Justice Jackson wrote in the first of the blue-ribbon jury cases, "is not to prescribe procedures but is essentially to protect the integrity of the trial process by whatever method the state sees fit to employ."[175]

The blue-ribbon system represented an effort to use special panels of jurors for difficult cases. Under the New York law, on the application of either party in a civil or criminal case the judge could, in his sound

173. Smith v. Texas, 311 U.S. 128, 130 (1940).
174. Fay v. New York, 332 U.S. 261 (1947); Moore v. New York, 333 U.S. 565 (1948). Justice Jackson spoke for the Court in both cases, and Justice Murphy spoke for the dissenters. The New York statute was first upheld, without opinion, in Hall v. Johnson, 186 U.S. 480 (1902). Special juries were by no means unknown at the common law of England. See, e.g., Anonymous, 1 Salk 405, 91 Eng. Rep. 351 (1696); Rex v. Edmonds, 4 B. & A. 471, 106 Eng. Rep. 1009 (1821).
175. 332 U.S. 294.

discretion, order trial by a special jury on a showing that because of the importance or complexity of the case, such a jury was required. He could also decide to use a special jury if he found that the issue in a pending case had been so widely commented upon that an ordinary jury could not be obtained without delay and difficulty, or for any other reason which would advance the efficient and impartial administration of justice. In New York County there were about 60,000 persons on the general jury panel, and about 3,000 on the special or blue-ribbon panel. Special jurors were selected by the county clerk from those accepted for the general panel, but only after each had been subpoenaed for personal appearance, and had testified under oath as to his fitness. The statute did not exclude or authorize exclusion of anyone from the special panels because of race, creed, color, or occupation. There were no economic qualifications.

In upholding New York's blue-ribbon system, the Court took note of the fact that a mere showing that some class is not represented in a particular jury is not enough. It must be clearly established that the absence of this class was caused by persistent discrimination, and the burden of proving purposeful and intentional discrimination rests, in the first instance, with the defendant. Thus the absence of Negroes on a particular special panel is not conclusive evidence of unconstitutionality; there must be proof of systematic and intentional exclusion of Negroes as a class. Furthermore, the Court concluded that it was not established that there was, as alleged, a great disparity in the ratio of convictions as between general and special juries. All the accused is entitled to, so far as due process is concerned, is a fair trial, and a verdict on the evidence. He is not entitled to a setup that will give him a chance to escape after he is properly proven guilty. For, said Justice Jackson, "society also has a right to a fair trial. The defendant's right is a neutral jury. He has no constitutional right to friends on the jury."

The minority of the Court protested that a blue-ribbon jury, by its very nature, is not drawn impartially from a cross section of the community. "Under our Constitution," Justice Murphy insisted, "the jury is not to be made the representative of the most intelligent, the most wealthy or the most successful, nor of the least intelligent, the least wealthy or the least successful. It is a democratic institution, representative of all qualified classes of people."[176] He did not believe it was essential to prove exclusion of any economic, racial, or social group, or that blue-ribbon juries convict more often than others, since he thought the very concept was bad—"the systematic and intentional exclusion of all but the 'best' or the most learned or intelligent of the general jurors. . . . One is constitutionally

176. 332 U.S. 299.

entitled to be judged by a fair sampling of all one's neighbors who are qualified, not merely those with superior intelligence or learning."[177]

Right to a Trial in the Locality by a Local Jury

American public law is committed to the proposition that a defendant is entitled to a trial in the locality where the alleged offense was committed. So far as federal practice is concerned, the Constitution is quite clear, and even emphatic. A clause of the article dealing with the judicial branch of the national government declares, "The trial of all Crimes, except in Cases of Impeachment, shall be by Jury; and such Trial shall be held in the State where the crimes shall have been committed; but when not committed within any State, the Trial shall be at such Place or Places as the Congress may by Law have directed."[178] Thus Congress has discretion to prescribe the place of trial only for offenses not committed within any state, and in such instances it may designate any place.[179] Technically, this article refers to venue, or the place of trial. Questions of venue in criminal cases, the Supreme Court has emphasized, "are not merely matters of formal legal procedure. They raise deep issues of public policy in the light of which legislation must be construed."[180]

In addition, the Sixth Amendment provides that one who is charged with a crime is entitled to trial by a jury "of the State and district wherein the crime shall have been committed, which district shall have been previously ascertained by law...." Be it noted that the Sixth Amendment deals only with the place from which the jury can be called. This is known, technically, as vicinage. The principle of trial by a jury in the vicinage became a serious bone of contention between the British government and the colonies as they drifted towards war. In 1769 Parliament approved an act providing for the trial in England of persons accused of treason in Massachusetts, and the Virginia legislature protested a few months later against this derogation of "the inestimable Privilege of being tried by a Jury from the Vicinage."[181] Other colonial assemblies joined in the protest,

---

177. Moore v. New York, 333 U.S. 565, 570 (1948). For a scholarly defense of the blue-ribbon jury, see Grant P. DuBois, Jr., "Desirability of Blue Ribbon Juries," *Hastings Law Journal*, 13 (May 1962): 479-89.

178. U.S. Const., Art. III, §2, cl. 3. Though the constitutional rule is clear enough, it is sometimes very difficult to decide where the crime was committed. See the division of the Court in Johnston v. United States, 351 U.S. 215 (1956).

179. Jones v. United States, 137 U.S. 202, 211 (1890); United States v. Dawson, 15 How. (U.S.) 467, 488 (1853). Congress may determine the place of trial by a statute passed after the commission of the offense. Cook v. United States, 138 U.S. 157, 182 (1891).

180. United States v. Johnson, 323 U.S. 273, 276 (1944).

181. William Wirt Blume, "The Place of Trial of Criminal Cases," *Michigan Law Review*, 43 (August 1944): 59-94, 64-65. See also Henry G. Connor, "The Constitutional

and in 1774 the First Continental Congress drew attention once more to this "great and inestimable privilege of being tried by their peers of the vicinage," according to the course of the common law. Other parliamentary statutes authorized trials in revenue cases by vice-admiralty courts located outside the colony where the offense occurred, and some offenses against the King's property could be tried in England.[182] Accordingly, one of the "Repeated injuries and usurpations" of which the King was accused in the Declaration of Independence was "transporting us beyond Seas to be tried for pretended Offences."

The constitutional requirement as to vicinage presents difficulties. Since we now have eighty-nine federal judicial districts within the country, as compared with the fifteen created by the Judiciary Act of 1789, a great deal of inconvenience results in the administration of justice, for an accused can be tried by a jury drawn only from the district where the crime was committed, wherever he may be apprehended. Federal vicinage has therefore been aptly described by a competent scholar as "an anachronism unsuited to modern conditions and productive of neither better justice nor greater liberty."[183] Furthermore, whereas jurors were originally chosen for what they knew about the case, but are now chosen for what they don't know—the Sixth Amendment guarantees an "impartial jury"—there is no compelling reason for insisting upon a jury drawn from a fairly small neighborhood. However, many districts have been subdivided by Congress into divisions, and it is settled law that a federal jury need not necessarily be drawn from the whole district, but may be taken from a division or part thereof.[184] On the other hand, juries need not be limited to the divisions.[185] This accords with congressional policy. About all the vicinage requirement amounts to today is that jurors cannot be drawn from outside the district.

The state requirements on the subject of vicinage present a somewhat different problem. It has been demonstrated that in the earliest state constitutions adopted prior to 1800, such provisions as there were on this subject did not guarantee trial by a jury drawn from such a small vicinage as the county, and that some rather vague sections were merely designed to prevent transportation outside the state, or to some distant place, for

---

Right to a Trial by a Jury of the Vicinage," *University of Pennsylvania Law Review*, 57 (January 1909): 197–215.

182. See Edward Dumbauld, *The Declaration of Independence* (Norman: University of Oklahoma Press, 1950), pp. 133–37.

183. Francis H. Heller, *The Sixth Amendment* (Lawrence: University of Kansas Press, 1951), p. 95.

184. Ruthenberg v. United States, 245 U.S. 480, 482 (1918).

185. Barrett v. United States, 169 U.S. 218 (1898).

trial.[186] Accordingly, some courts agree with a holding of the Supreme Court of Connecticut that in the absence of a state constitutional provision on the subject, the right to a fair trial "has never been regarded as involving as a necessary element the requirement that in all cases an accused be tried within the county or other territorial jurisdiction within which the offense was committed."[187] But most state constitutions have vicinage provisions today, stipulating either the county or district as the area from which juries must be drawn. There are some states, however, which have no provision on the subject, and in a few states the provisions are indefinite.[188] Of course, if the state constitution or an otherwise valid statute designates the county as the vicinage, the courts have no choice but to obey such a command. But where the constitution is silent or indefinite, the tendency of the state courts is to hold that the county is not necessarily the area from which juries must be drawn. Furthermore, the trend is in the direction of permitting legislative flexibility. This is the situation in such large states as Texas, California, and New York. This accords with Sir James Stephen's suggestion that the place of trial ought to be determined "by the convenience of the court, the witnesses, and the person accused."[189]

The Merits of Trial by Jury

It is clear to any observer that our jury system has defects. In contrast with the judge, who is a known and educated person holding a conspicuous public position, the jury consists of twelve unknown individuals, "a group just large enough to destroy even the appearance of individual responsibility."[190] Unlike the judges, juries give no reasons for their decisions. Juries are said to be more influenced by currents of strong prejudice than judges.[191] Typical jurors lack the training, education, and intelligence that typical judges have. Even though jurors are, for the most part, untrained people, they are often called upon to decide complex and extremely difficult problems. Jurors are generally selected in a haphazard manner; the judges are liberal in excusing many if not most of the potentially best people called; and challenges remove many of those who

186. Blume, "The Place of Trial of Criminal Cases," pp. 67–78.
187. State v. Pace, 129 Conn. 570, 572, 29 A.2d 755, 756 (1943). The Supreme Court of Maine has ruled that "vicinity" does not mean "county." State v. Longley, 119 Me. 535, 112 A. 260 (1921).
188. Blume, "The Place of Trial of Criminal Cases," p. 78.
189. James Fitzjames Stephen, *A History of the Criminal Law of England* (London: Macmillan & Co., 1883), I: 278.
190. *Ibid.*, p. 568.
191. See Note, "Community Hostility and the Right to an Impartial Jury," *Columbia Law Review*, 60 (March 1960): 349–80.

survive to be drafted for trial service. Thus, Herbert Spencer once described a jury as a group of twelve people of average ignorance. The jury system most certainly adds to the costs which society must pay for the administration of justice, and is one reason why court calendars are crowded and often heavily in arrears. The mere possibility of jury trial is often a bludgeon in the hands of litigants to discourage the opposing side. The biases of jurors are a matter of frequent comment.[192] There is an old saw to the effect that juries are prejudiced in favor of pretty women and against big corporations.

It cannot be gainsaid that the jury system can be improved. Indeed, the jury system has always been flexible and dynamic, and has changed in many ways during the course of the centuries of its evolution. That it is still changing is suggested by the great number of variations that are to be found in the patterns of jury trial among the various states. Many improvements are now being urged.[193] It is argued by some that aptitude tests or some educational attainment ought to be required of jurors. Judges should tighten up, it is said, on their present practice of excusing from service the very people who are best suited for the juries. Often too much time is spent in selecting jurors, in connection with which the lawyers are too much in control. It is maintained that juries should be more closely confined to making only factual determinations, the application of the law to the facts being left entirely to the judge.[194] Judges often lack adequate powers to assist juries by commenting on the facts. Jurors should be given handbooks of basic instructions and provided with better facilities. They should, some say, be allowed to take notes. The National Commission on Law Observance and Enforcement (the Wickersham Commission) concluded, on this subject, "The remedy for the conspicuous

---

192. See William Dienstein, *Are You Guilty?* (Springfield, Ill.: Chas. C. Thomas, 1954), chap. 9; Stanley F. Brewster, *Twelve Men in a Box* (Chicago: Callaghan & Co., 1934); Roscoe Pound, *Criminal Justice in America* (New York: Henry Holt, 1930); Morris J. Bloomstein, *Verdict: The Jury System,* rev. ed. (New York: Dodd, Mead, 1972). See the remarks of the eminent English scholar, Glanville Williams, *The Proof of Guilt,* 2d. ed. (London: Stevens & Sons, 1958), pp. 236-37: "There is no guarantee that members of a particular jury may not be quite unusually ignorant, credulous, slow-witted, narrow-minded, biased or temperamental. The danger of this happening is not one that can be removed by some minor procedural adjustment; it is inherent in the English notion of a jury as a body chosen from the general population at random." For a stirring defense of the jury system by an eminent English judge, see Lord Justice Patrick Devlin, *Trial by Jury* (London: Stevens & Sons, 1956).

193. Judge J. F. McLaughlin, "Needed Improvements to Our Jury System," 16 F.R.D. 481-88 (1954);American Bar Association Project on Standards for Criminal Justice, *Trial by Jury* (New York: Institute of Judicial Administration, 1968).

194. See Jerome Frank, *Courts on Trial* (Princeton, N.J.: Princeton University Press, 1949).

abuses of jury trials in American criminal justice is to be found in less use and more rational use of the jury, in confining the jury to the work of fact-finding, in vigorous judicial direction and control of the selection of trial jurors, and above all, in strong trial judges free from politics and empowered and inclined to make the trial an effective instrument for its purpose."[195]

While it may be conceded that the jury system, like most human contrivances, can be improved, its defects should not be so magnified as to obscure its solid virtues. Wigmore once summarized a great deal on this subject when he wrote,

We are good friends of jury trial. We believe in it as the best system ever invented for a free people in the world's history. In spite of all suggestions to substitute the trained judge of fact, we believe that a system of trying facts by a regular judicial official, known beforehand and therefore accessible to all the arts of corruption and chicanery, would be fatal to justice. The grand solid merit of jury trial is that the jurors of fact are selected at the last moment from the multitude of citizens. They cannot be known beforehand, and they melt back into the multitude after each trial.[196]

Wigmore advanced four principal arguments in favor of trial by jury.[197] First, it prevents popular distrust of official justice. The administration of justice must command the respect and confidence of the people, and "bureaucratic, purely official justice, can never receive such confidence." The jury system gives the citizen a necessary political share in daily justice. Secondly, jury trial provides for necessary flexibility in legal rules. Law is more general than justice. The judge is expected to and must enforce the law in the same way for all. The jury, however, "adjusts the general rule of law to the justice of the particular case." Thirdly, the jury system educates the citizenry in the administration of law. Thus the great legal historian Holdsworth once wrote: "The jury itself is educated by the part which it is required to take in the administration of justice. The jury system teaches the members of the jury to cultivate a judicial habit of mind. It helps to create in them a respect for law and order. It makes them feel that they owe duties to society, and that they have a share in its government."[198]

Finally, Wigmore maintained that the jury system improves the quality of a verdict because it is based on the reconciliation of varied temperaments and minds; the best way to apply generalities to concrete cases is to

---

195. *Report on Criminal Procedure,* Report no. 8 (Washington: Government Printing Office, June 9, 1931), p. 28.

196. John H. Wigmore, "To Ruin Jury Trial in the Federal Courts," *Journal of the American Judicature Society,* 9 (1925): 61.

197. "A Program for the Trial of Jury Trial," *Journal of the American Judicature Society,* 12 (April 1929): 166-71.

198. Holdsworth, *A History of English Law,* I: 348-49.

get an average judgment, that is to say, "the reconciliation of several judgments taken at random." Holdsworth added that the jury system "tends to make the law intelligible by keeping it in touch with the common facts of life. . . . The jury system has for some hundreds of years been constantly bringing the rules of law to the touchstone of common sense."[199]

In his classic study of American democracy Alexis de Tocqueville took the position that jury trial was one of the principal elements of republicanism, "as direct and as extreme a consequence of the sovereignty of the people as universal suffrage." Through it the people are also judges and thus are invested with the direction of society. For the jury is not only a judicial institution; it is even more important to understand it as a political institution profoundly affecting the destinies of society. The jury penetrates into every usage of life, and exerts a powerful influence upon the national character. It "serves to communicate the spirit of the judges to the minds of all the citizens, and this spirit, with the habits which attend it, is the soundest preparation for free institutions. It imbues all classes with a respect for the thing judged and with the notion of right. . . . It teaches men to practice equity; every man learns to judge his neighbor as he would himself be judged. . . . The jury teaches every man not to recoil before the responsibility of his own actions and impresses him with that manly confidence without which no political virtue can exist. . . . By obliging men to turn their attention to other affairs than their own, it rubs off that private selfishness which is the rust of society. The jury contributes powerfully to form the judgment and to increase the natural intelligence of a people; and this, in my opinion, is its greatest advantage."[200]

The opening lines of the report of the University of Chicago Law School jury project are well worth quoting: "The Anglo-American jury is a remarkable political institution. We have had it with us for so long that any sense of surprise over its main characteristics has perhaps somewhat dulled. It recruits a group of twelve laymen, chosen at random from the widest population; it convenes them for the purpose of the particular trial; it entrusts them with great official powers of decision; it permits them to carry on deliberations in secret and to report out their final judgment without giving reasons for it; and, after their momentary service to the state has been completed, it orders them to disband and return to private life. The jury thus represents a deep commitment to the use of laymen in the administration of justice. . . . It opposes the cadre of professional,

---

199. *Ibid.*, p. 349. Sir James Fitzjames Stephen, who was a judge of Queen's Bench, maintained that trial by jury is more important to judges than to anyone else. "It saves judges from the responsibility—which to many men would appear intolerably heavy and painful—of deciding simply on their own opinion upon the guilt or innocence of the prisoner." *A History of the Criminal Law of England,* I: 573.

200. *Democracy in America,* Phillips Bradley, ed. (New York: Knopf, 1948), I: 283.

experienced judges with this transient, ever-changing, ever-inexperienced group of amateurs. The jury is thus by definition an exciting experiment in the conduct of serious human affairs, and it is not surprising that, virtually from its inception, it has been the subject of deep controversy, attracting at once the most extravagent praise and the most harsh criticism."[201]

The Chicago jury project made a number of important findings. For one thing, in both criminal and civil cases judges expressed agreement with jury verdicts in about 80 percent of the cases surveyed. Furthermore, the study concluded that, on the whole, jurors understand their job, take it very seriously, perform their task competently and want to do so, are able to interpret legal rules, and feel that the experience was both interesting and worthwhile. Many studies also show that persons who have served on juries are not in favor of abolishing the jury system.[202] In addition, a national poll of trial judges, who of course had a great deal of experience with juries, indicated that a large majority of them were satisfied with the jury system.[203] Thus, while the jury system, like most human institutions, works imperfectly, and requires continuous attention, it is deeply rooted in the American legal culture, and plays a very important role in the criminal justice system. A jury may react in many different ways. It may acquit a guilty man because it believes that he has already suffered enough, or because it disapproves of the law the violation of which was the basis of the prosecution, or because it believes that the victim of the crime was at least partly at fault, or because it concludes that conviction will do more harm than good, as for example, in disrupting the life of a family.[204] In short, the members of the jury react in terms of their moral values and social experience. In this rather rough and unsystematic way, juries give support to Thomas Jefferson's observation that juries have been "the firmest bulwarks of English liberty," and that if he had to decide whether

201. Kalven and Zeisel, *The American Jury*, pp. 2-3.
202. See, e.g., David W. Moffat, "As Jurors See a Lawsuit," *Oregon Law Review*, 24 (April 1945): 199-207; Dale W. Broeder, "The University of Chicago Law Project," *Nebraska Law Review*, 38 (May 1959): 744-60.
203. Harry Kalven, Jr., "The Dignity of the Civil Jury," *Virginia Law Review*, 50 (October 1964): 1055-75. For the similar views of an experienced trial judge, see Joseph N. Ulman, *A Judge Takes the Stand* (New York: Knopf, 1933).
204. See United States v. Berrigan, 417 F.2d 1002, 1006 (4th Cir. 1969): "We recognize . . . the undisputed power of the jury to acquit, even if its verdict is contrary to the law as given by the judge and contrary to the evidence. This is a power that must exist as long as we adhere to the general verdict in criminal cases, for the courts cannot search the minds of the jurors to find the basis upon which they judge. If the jury feels that the law under which the defendant is accused is unjust, or that exigent circumstances justified the actions of the accused, or for any reason which appeals to their logic or passion, the jury has the power to acquit, and the courts must abide by that decision."

it be best to omit the people from the legislative, or judicial departments, he would better leave them out of the legislative, since "the execution of laws is more important than the making of them."[205]

205. Letter to the Abbé Arnoud, July 19, 1789, quoted in Saul K. Padover, ed., *Thomas Jefferson on Democracy* (New York: Penguin Books, Pelican ed., 1946), p. 62.

7 / The Right to Counsel

Growth of the Right[1]

One of the most important rights of one who is accused of having committed a crime is that of being represented by an attorney. It is important for the rather obvious reason that most laymen know little or nothing about law, and particularly about legal procedure. Without the assistance of counsel most persons accused of crimes are not likely to have an adequate defense. A defendant needs a lawyer as urgently as a sick man needs a doctor, and in many instances even more urgently, for while nature often heals the sick without outside aid, it seems to have little concern for the plight of the accused.

Justice Schaefer of the Illinois Supreme Court has observed, "Of all the rights that an accused person has, the right to be represented by counsel is by far the most pervasive, for it affects his ability to assert any other rights he may have."[2] Indeed, it must be recalled that our system of justice is an adversary one in which charges are brought and prosecuted by lawyers employed by government. As a noted legal scholar once wrote, "Without the assistance of counsel, the defendant is practically powerless to challenge the prosecution. It is the lesson of human experience that, even in the case of the most well-intentioned prosecutors, the absence of such a challenge can result in carelessness and failure to review the evidence and properly prepare the case, which makes it easier to convict the innocent."[3]

1. I have drawn heavily upon my own studies of this problem: "The Constitutional Right to Counsel in Federal Courts," *Nebraska Law Review,* 30 (May 1951): 559-99; "The Federal Right to Counsel in State Courts," *ibid.,* 31 (November 1951): 15-54; "The Right to Counsel under State Law," *Wisconsin Law Review,* 1955 (March 1955): 281-328. For an excellent, full-length study see William M. Beaney, *The Right to Counsel in American Courts* (Ann Arbor: University of Michigan Press, 1955). For a very recent survey of this subject by Professor Beaney, see Stuart S. Nagel, ed., *The Rights of the Accused* (Beverly Hills: Sage Publications, 1972), chap. 5. See also Leonard W. Levy, *Against the Law* (New York: Harper & Row, 1974), chap. 4, for a thorough analysis of right-to-counsel cases decided by the Burger Court.

2. Walter V. Schaefer, "Federalism and State Criminal Procedure," *Harvard Law Review,* 70 (November 1956): 1-26, 8.

3. Samuel Dash, "The Emerging Role and Function of the Criminal Defense Lawyer," *North Carolina Law Review,* 47 (April 1969): 598-632, 603. See the remarks of Charles V. Laughlin, "The Place and Function of the Lawyer," *Washington & Lee Law Review,* 8, no. 1 (1951): 1-16, 5: "Advocacy . . . has the merit of equalizing parties to a controversy . . . Advocacy also has a tendency to equalize influence."

American constitutional law has always been concerned with the plight of one who is accused of having committed a crime. The Sixth Amendment, which was ratified in 1791, stipulates that "in all criminal prosecutions, the accused shall enjoy the right . . . to have the assistance of counsel for his defense." Since the Congress which submitted this provision to the states adopted it without debate, its wisdom must have been taken for granted. And the constitution of every state but Virginia now has some sort of explicit provision to the same effect. The state constitutions have a rather standardized statement on the subject, much like the clause of the Michigan Constitution: "In every criminal prosecution, the accused shall have the right . . . to have the assistance of counsel for his defense."[4] Some nine state constitutions throw in for good measure an additional clause guaranteeing this right in civil cases as well. While the Virginia Constitution alone is silent on the matter, the Virginia Supreme Court of Appeals has construed the constitutional provision forbidding the deprivation of life or liberty "except by the law of the land" as including the right to counsel, and it is also protected by statute.[5] It follows that the national government and all of the states are in accord to the extent that they consider representation by counsel a fundamental right of one who has been accused of crime. It has been characterized as a "vital and fundamental right" which should be strictly protected.[6] "The purpose of the guarantee of the right to counsel," it has been asserted, "is to protect accused from a conviction resulting from his own ignorance of legal and constitutional rights. . . . Without the benefit of counsel, the accused, ignorant of his rights, would in effect stand deprived of the protective mantle of due process of law."[7]

Since, generally speaking, our legal system grew from the English common law, it is not without interest to note that as regards the right to counsel American practice moved forward at a swifter pace. While at the common law a defendant always had the right to counsel when charged with a misdemeanor, until a surprisingly recent date in England he had no right to be represented by a lawyer in cases of treason or felony, precisely when he needed help most.[8] The accepted theory was that the judge

---

4. Mich. Const., Art. I, §20.
5. Barnes v. Com., 92 Va. 794, 803, 23 S.E. 784, 787 (1895); Cottrell v. Com., 187 Va. 351, 46 S.E. 2d 413 (1948); Whitley v. Cunningham, 205 Va. 251, 135 S.E. 2d 823 (1964); Va. Code, §§19.2-157-63 (1975).
6. Walker v. State, 194 Ga. 727, 734, 22 S.E. 2d 462, 466 (1942).
7. State *ex rel.* Baker v. Utecht, 221 Minn. 145, 151, 21 N.W. 2d 328, 332 (1946), cert. denied, 327 U.S. 810 (1946).
8. Theodore F. T. Plucknett, *A Concise History of the Common Law,* 5th ed. (Boston: Little, Brown, 1956), pp. 434-35.

would see to it that the accused had a fair trial,[9] and it was also believed by no less a jurist than Lord Coke that the Crown would not charge the commission of a serious crime unless the evidence was "so clear and manifest" that there could be no defense.[10] While noted lawyers like Blackstone criticized this harsh rule, it persisted for a long time. The first great change came in 1695, as a result of many abuses of judicial process that occurred during the Restoration period, when Parliament adopted a statute permitting representation by counsel in cases of treason,[11] and finally, the right to a full defense was extended to all felony cases in 1836.[12]

The American colonies took a somewhat more generous position. Early statutes guaranteed the right to counsel, and it found its way into many of the revolutionary state constitutions. When the Supreme Court first looked into this matter thoroughly, Justice Sutherland concluded that in at least twelve of the thirteen colonies the English common law rule had been rejected.[13] Certainly Congress has always regarded the right as worthy of protection, since the assistance of counsel was assured in the original Judiciary Act of 1789 and in the first federal criminal code, adopted in April 1790.[14]

Scope of the Right to Counsel

So far as proceedings in the federal courts are concerned, the right to counsel is secured by the Sixth Amendment, by acts of Congress, rules of court, and judicial decisions. State constitutions, statutes, rules of court, and judicial decisions guarantee the enjoyment of this valuable right in the local courts. The most difficult question has been whether there is any federal remedy when the right has been denied by the states. It is elementary, as already noted, that the federal Bill of Rights does not, as such, apply to the states. But it is now equally elementary that the due process clause of the Fourteenth Amendment has been construed more and more generously to include most of the guarantees of the Bill of Rights. Since it is now established that due process secures the essentials of a fair trial, it is not surprising that the Court finally got around to saying that the right to

9. Joseph Chitty, *A Practical Treatise on the Criminal Law,* 1st Am. ed. (Philadelphia: Edward Earle, 1819), I: 406.

10. Sir Edward Coke's *The Third Part of the Institutes of the Laws of England* (London: Earl R. Brooks, 1797), chap. 2, p. 29.

11. 7 & 8 Wm. III, c. 3, §1 (1695).

12. 6 & 7 Wm. IV, c. 114, §1 (1836).

13. Powell v. Alabama, 287 U.S. 45, 64 (1932). Beaney, *The Right to Counsel in American Courts,* chap. II, expresses the view that Justice Sutherland's opinion exaggerated the colonial position on this question.

14. 1 Stat. 73, 92 (1789); 1 Stat. 112, 118 (1790), now 18 U.S.C. §3005 (1970).

counsel is of such a fundamental character that its denial by a state, at least under some circumstances, constitutes a violation of the Fourteenth Amendment. This happened in 1932, in the celebrated Scottsboro case.[15]

Before looking into the present scope of the due process rule, dealing with the extent to which there is a federally protected right to counsel in the states, it would be well to inquire into the meaning of the right to counsel in the federal courts under the Sixth Amendment, and in the state courts under state law. A concise summary of the federal law is Rule 44 of the Rules of Criminal Procedure for the United States District Courts, as adopted by the Supreme Court in 1944, and as amended in 1966. It now reads as follows: "Every defendant who is unable to obtain counsel shall be entitled to have counsel assigned to represent him at every stage of the proceedings from his initial appearance before the commissioner (now U.S. Magistrate) or the court through appeal, unless he waives such appointment." This rule, which is a distillation of a great deal of experience and adjudication, describes the end result of an evolving doctrine. In all probability, the original meaning of the Sixth Amendment merely was that a defendant could not be tried without representation by a lawyer if he had one, but the principle has come to mean that if an unrepresented defendant appears in court, the judge must take the initiative in advising him of his right to have a lawyer, and must also offer to appoint one if he cannot secure one. It should be noted that the scope of the Sixth Amendment is most sweeping, since it refers to "*all* criminal prosecutions." It follows that the right is enforceable even in cases involving petty offenses.[16]

Until the Sixth Amendment guaranty of the right to counsel was fully nationalized by decisions of the Supreme Court, the situation was otherwise in the states. While some state statutes or rules of court stipulated that a person accused of a misdemeanor had a right to appointed counsel, the general rule was that in the absence of statute the court had no duty to appoint counsel in misdemeanor cases. The statutes of all the states provided for the appointment of counsel in capital cases, and those of at least thirty-four states required such appointment on request in noncapital felony cases.[17] But in the absence of statutory directives, many state courts took the position that in noncapital cases, even those involving felonies, no constitutional duty rested upon the court to supply counsel for indigent defendants, particularly where the defendants, by reason of age,

---

15. Powell v. Alabama, 287 U.S. 45 (1932).
16. See Evans v. Rives, 126 F.2d 633 (D.C. Cir. 1942); James v. Headley, 410 F.2d 325, 328 (5th Cir. 1969) ("Any loss of liberty would be serious").
17. Beaney, *The Right to Counsel in American Courts*, pp. 84–86.

experience, and familiarity with legal procedure, were thought to be capable of looking after themselves.

In addition, many state appellate courts took the position that if the record showed that the defendant did not suffer prejudice for lack of counsel, or that the presence of counsel would have made no difference in the outcome, then no constitutional right had been denied. The appellate court would review the record to see if the accused had had a fair trial. If it appeared that the defendant understood the nature of the charge against him, that there was sufficient evidence to support a conviction, that the trial judge was careful in safeguarding the defendant's rights, and saw to it that all the issues were developed properly, and that the issues were not particularly complex, then it was concluded that a fair trial was given. Some convictions were set aside, or writs of habeas corpus were awarded, where the uncounselled defendant was very young and immature, or especially ignorant, or was otherwise incapable of looking after his own interests.

The distinction between capital and noncapital offenses which many state courts made was encouraged by the meaning which the Supreme Court initially read into the due process requirement of the Fourteenth Amendment. When in 1932 the Court first held that due process included the right to counsel, that is to say, that a denial of counsel by a state violated the Fourteenth Amendment, it was careful to limit its decision to capital cases. This case involved a trial for rape of nine illiterate, uneducated, friendless, and inexperienced Negro boys ranging in age from thirteen to twenty-one.[18] These boys had no lawyer at all during the critical interval between the arraignment and the beginning of the trial, but just before the actual trial began the judge appointed a local lawyer to represent them. Taking the position that the aid of counsel is essential for a fair hearing, because most men, even educated men, lack the skill and knowledge to present a defense, the Court concluded that these boys had been denied due process. But the Court very carefully limited its rule to capital cases. Since the two dissenting Justices in the Scottsboro case emphasized that these defendants had in fact had a lawyer when put to trial, it should be noted that the Court went beyond the statement of a bare rule to hold that the right is not merely formal, but includes "effective and substantial aid." Such aid cannot be given ordinarily without some time being allowed to prepare the defense. How much time is

---

18. Powell v. Alabama, 287 U.S. 45 (1932). For accounts of this case see Quentin Reynolds, *Courtroom* (N.Y.: Farrar & Strauss, 1950), pp. 248-314: Allan K. Chalmers, *They Shall be Free* (New York: Doubleday, 1951).

necessary to enable the lawyer to prepare properly, as later decisions have shown, is a relative matter depending upon the nature of the case.[19]

The extent to which a federal court should review a state criminal proceeding or inquire into the validity of an incarceration of a prisoner in a state penal institution pursuant to the mandate of a state court always presents a delicate issue of which federalism is an important ingredient. It should be remembered that the states operate under constitutions and laws of their own, and that state as well as federal judges take an oath to support the United States Constitution. Furthermore, all the states provide for various corrective processes, whether by appeal or special writ, for the review of their courts. All of them have postconviction remedies available. The Supreme Court is understandably reluctant to overrule the highest state courts, especially where the issues are largely issues of fact of which the state courts must perforce have greater and more immediate knowledge. The United States district courts are also understandably reluctant to give state prisoners their freedom by way of the writ of habeas corpus, since they have already had their chance to prove their point in the state courts. Indeed, a state prisoner may not apply at all to a federal court for habeas corpus unless he has first exhausted his state remedies. All this means that most litigants must be content with recourse to the state courts.

Following the Scottsboro decision, for a time a majority of the Justices of the Supreme Court took a conservative view of their function in construing the due process clause of the Fourteenth Amendment as it related to the right to counsel. The leading case, *Betts* v. *Brady*,[20] was decided in 1942. Dividing 6-3, a majority of the Justices ruled that the conclusion did not automatically follow that due process had been violated from the fact that a state trial judge refused to appoint a lawyer for an uncounselled defendant in a noncapital felony case. The due process clause, said Justice Roberts, "formulates a concept less rigid and more fluid" than the more specific command of the Sixth Amendment. Whether due process has been violated depends upon "an appraisal of the totality of facts in a given case," the test being whether under the circumstances there had been a denial of "fundamental fairness, shocking to the universal sense of justice." It follows that the Fourteenth Amendment does not embody "an inexorable command that no trial for any offense, or in any court, can be fairly conducted and justice accorded a defendant

---

19. See Avery v. Alabama, 308 U.S. 444 (1940); Tucker v. Howard, 177 F.2d 494 (7th Cir. 1949); Jones v. Kentucky, 97 F.2d 335 (6th Cir. 1938).
20. 316 U.S. 455 (1942).

who is not represented by counsel." For example, the Court ruled that a mature person who fully understood the charge against him, a charge couched in plain language of "devastating frankness," could be allowed to plead guilty to a noncapital felony without the aid of a lawyer.[21]

The federal due process rule came to this: so far as the cases involving capital offenses were concerned, the Fourteenth Amendment required of state courts that they observe the strict rule prevailing in the federal courts by virtue of the explicit command of the Sixth Amendment.[22] But in noncapital cases the absence of counsel vitiated the proceedings only if there were special circumstances present which resulted in injustice. The approach was a case-to-case method in which an attempt was made to weigh degrees of prejudicial error. While this was not a clear-cut rule, and was criticized as not giving adequate guidance to the state courts, Justice Reed explained that there could be no panacea for the difficulty, and that "the due process clause is not susceptible of reduction to a mathematical formula."[23] A minority of the Court rejected this distinction between capital and noncapital cases, a distinction for which they could find not the slightest warrant in any constitutional language. Furthermore, as Justice Douglas once pointed out, the considerations which require counsel in capital cases are equally relevant in all other cases, since "due process shows no less solicitude for liberty than for life."[24] He argued that the need for counsel and not the nature of the charge should determine the basic issue of fairness.

Since lack of counsel in noncapital cases was not in and of itself indicative of a violation of due process, some additional factor showing fundamental injustice had to be shown. The Court refused to find a violation of due process even in cases where very young and inexperienced defendants had no counsel at the arraignment, on the ground that counsel appointed for the trial were free under state practice to change the plea or present whatever defense there may have been.[25] It was unwilling to rule

21. Bute v. Illinois, 333 U.S. 640 (1948).
22. See Williams v. Kaiser, 323 U.S. 471 (1945); Tomkins v. Missouri, 323 U.S. 485 (1945); De Meerleer v. Michigan, 329 U.S. 663 (1947). But as in the federal courts, a grown person who knows what he is doing can waive counsel in capital cases. Carter v. Illinois, 329 U.S. 173 (1946); Quicksall v. Michigan, 339 U.S. 660 (1950).
23. Gibbs v. Burke, 337 U.S. 773, 781 (1949). For Justice Frankfurter's statement that the due process clause protects only the "ultimate dignities of man," see Carter v. Illinois, 329 U.S. 173, 175 (1946). For a powerful criticism of the rule of Betts v. Brady, see Yale Kamisar, "The Right to Counsel and the Fourteenth Amendment: A Dialogue on 'The Most Pervasive Right' of an Accused," *University of Chicago Law Review,* 30 (Autumn 1962): 1–77.
24. Bute v. Illinois, 333 U.S. 640, 681 (1948) (dissenting opinion).
25. Canizio v. New York, 327 U.S. 82 (1946).

against the states where it could not find that lack of counsel resulted in a miscarriage of justice.[26] But there were some noncapital cases where the Court discovered sufficiently exceptional circumstances—such as youth— to warrant the correction of state proceedings.[27] Certainly the Court looked with a jaundiced eye upon any attempt to impute to an inexperienced youth a capacity to waive the right to counsel competently and intelligently. Furthermore, the Court did not believe that either a failure of the defendant to ask for an assignment of counsel or his entering of a plea of guilty was necessarily acceptable proof of a waiver.[28] The Court also found that uncounselled defendants had been denied due process where the plea of guilty was induced by trickery on the part of the authorities,[29] or where serious prejudicial errors occurred at the trial.[30]

This search for plus factors indicating that lack of counsel resulted in fundamental unfairness to the defendant continued until 1963, when a unanimous Court, in the leading case of *Gideon* v. *Wainwright*,[31] overruled *Betts* v. *Brady* by extending the rule previously announced as applying only to capital cases to include noncapital felony cases as well. Gideon had been tried in a Florida state court on the felony charge of breaking and entering a poolroom. Alleging poverty, Gideon had requested the trial judge to appoint defense counsel to represent him, but this request had been denied with the explanation that under Florida law only a defendant charged with a capital offense is entitled to such an appointment. Accordingly, Gideon conducted his own defense; he was convicted and sentenced to five years in prison. Pointing out that Fourteenth Amendment due process includes all guarantees of the Bill of Rights which are fundamental safeguards of liberty, Justice Black held that the *Betts* decision was wrong in holding that the right to counsel was

---

26. Foster v. Illinois, 332 U.S. 134 (1947); Gryger v. Burke, 334 U.S. 728 (1948).

27. Uveges v. Pennsylvania, 335 U.S. 437 (1948); Wade v. Mayo, 334 U.S. 672 (1948). It was said that whether injustice occurred depended upon such circumstances as "the age of the accused, his education, intelligence and experience, whether the offense charged was simple of comprehension or complicated, the occurrences at the trial, such as how effectively the trial judge interposed to protect the rights of the accused, and whether or not the proceeding turned upon intricacies of substantive law or procedure." Buchanan v. O'Brien, 181 F.2d 601, 603 (1st Cir. 1950). See also Cash v. Culver, 358 U.S. 633 (1959) (defendant young and uneducated); McNeal v. Culver, 365 U.S. (1961) (defendant mentally disturbed).

28. Rice v. Olson, 324 U.S. 786 (1945); Gibbs v. Burke, 337 U.S. 773, 780 (1949).

29. Smith v. O'Grady, 312 U.S. 329 (1941).

30. Gibbs v. Burke, 337 U.S. 773 (1949); Townsend v. Burke, 334 U.S. 736 (1948).

31. 372 U.S. 335 (1963). For a lively account of this case see Anthony Lewis, *Gideon's Trumpet* (New York: Random House, 1964). For a superb analysis of this case, see also J. H. Israel, "Gideon v. Wainwright: The 'Art' of Overruling," in *The Supreme Court Review, 1963*, Philip B. Kurland, ed. (Chicago: University of Chicago Press), pp. 211–72.

not one of these fundamental rights. He asserted that not only precedents, "but also reason and reflection require us to recognize that in our adversary system of criminal justice, any person haled into court, who is too poor to hire a lawyer, cannot be assured a fair trial unless counsel is provided for him. This seems to us to be an obvious truth. Governments, both state and federal, quite properly spend vast sums of money to establish machinery to try defendants accused of crime. Lawyers to prosecute are everywhere deemed essential to protect the public's interest in an orderly society. Similarly, there are few defendants charged with crime, few indeed, who fail to hire the best lawyers they can get to prepare and present their defenses. That government hires lawyers to prosecute and defendants who have the money hire lawyers to defend are the strongest indications of the widespread belief that lawyers in criminal courts are necessities, not luxuries."[32] Thus, the Court concluded that *Betts* was "an anachronism" when it was decided, and should be overruled.[33]

The Supreme Court took another giant step in applying to the states the Sixth Amendment guaranty of the right to counsel as it is understood in federal practice, in 1972, in *Argersinger v. Hamlin*,[34] where by another unanimous vote due process was construed as requiring counsel even in misdemeanor cases, so long as the possible punishment is imprisonment for any period of time. Argersinger, an indigent, was convicted by a Florida court of the offense of carrying a concealed weapon, and sentenced to ninety days in jail. The Supreme Court of Florida had ruled that the right to court-appointed counsel extends only to nonpetty offenses punishable by more than six months in jail.[35] Holding that basic rights have never been limited to serious offenses, Justice Douglas applied the rationale of *Gideon,* namely, that the assistance of counsel is a requisite to the very existence of a fair trial because a layman can't defend himself. He pointed out that legal issues can be as complex in the case of a petty offense as in that of serious offenses—for example, vagrancy cases present many constitutional issues—and he complained of the "assembly-line justice" which characterizes the handling of many misdemeanor cases.

32. 372 U.S. 344.

33. It is of interest to note that following his release from jail on the writ of habeas corpus, Gideon was tried again, this time with representation by a competent appointed lawyer, and was acquitted.

34. 407 U.S. 25 (1972).

35. State *ex rel.* Argersinger v. Hamlin, 236 So. 2d 442 (Fla. 1970). In a dissenting opinion, Justice Boyd wrote, "There is no magic yardstick by which we can determine liberty is more precious to one person than to another. From the inside all jails look alike." 236 So. 2d 445.

Misdemeanor courts, he asserted, are obsessed with speed; there is too much rush, too little individual attention, and not enough preparation. Justice Douglas cited statistics which indicate that misdemeanants with attorneys are five times more likely to get off than those who are uncounselled. Thus, the Court announced a clear ruling that no imprisonment may be imposed, for any length of time, for any offense, whether classified as petty, a misdemeanor or a felony, unless the defendant has counsel at his trial, absent a knowing and intelligent waiver.[36]

It should be noted that a number of state supreme courts had ruled, prior to *Argersinger,* that the right to counsel applies to any indigent misdemeanor offender who may be given any jail sentence,[37] although in 1965 the New York Court of Appeals drew the line at traffic violations.[38] Furthermore, since the Supreme Court has decided that the rules of law pronounced in *Gideon*[39] and *Argersinger*[40] were retroactive, these decisions had a profound impact in the many states which formerly drew the line between felonies and misdemeanors. Thus, in Florida, between April 1, 1963, and April 1, 1966, 6,403 of the 8,000 inmates of the state prison system filed postconviction motions, 2,506 were given new trials, and 1,311 were released with no further charges.[41] Finally, it remains to be noted that a defendant has an unqualified right to the assistance of his

---

36. In a concurring opinion, Justice Brennan suggested that law students could be used, under supervision, to represent indigents in cases involving minor offenses. In a separate concurring opinion, Justices Powell and Rehnquist took the position that the rule of the Court was too rigid, and that it would have a serious impact both on the already overburdened courts and the legal profession. They would prefer to permit trial courts to exercise discretion on a case-by-case basis, with weight attached to three factors, the complexity of the offense charged, the probable sentence on conviction, and such individualized factors as the competence of the accused to present his own case and community attitudes to a particular defendant or incident.

37. See State v. Borst, 278 Minn. 388, 154 N.W. 2d 888 (1967), and the numerous state citations gathered together in the opinion. See also *In re* Johnson, 62 Cal. 2d 325, 398 P.2d 420, 42 Cal. Rptr. 228 (1965); State *ex rel.* May v. Boles, 149 W.Va. 155, 139 S.E. 2d 177 (1964); People v. Agnew, 114 Cal. App. 2d 841, 250 P.2d 369 (1952); Bolkovac v. State, 229 Ind. 294, 98 N.E. 2d 250 (1951); Decker v. State, 113 Ohio St. 512, 150 N.E. 74 (1925). For statutes to this effect, see N.H. Rev. Stat. Ann. §§604-A:1:2 (Supp. 1967); Tex. Code Crim. Proc. Ann., Art. 26.04 (Vernon 1966). See John M. Junker, "The Right to Counsel in Misdemeanor Cases," *Washington Law Review,* 43 (April 1968): 685-734.

38. People v. Letterio, 16 N.Y. 2d 307, 266 N.Y.S. 2d 368, 213 N.E. 2d 670 (1965), cert. denied, 384 U.S. 911 (1966). Since there are millions of traffic cases, the Court said that any other rule would lead to "chaotic" results.

39. Burgett v. Texas, 389 U.S. 109 (1967); Kitchens v. Smith, 401 U.S. 847 (1971).

40. Berry v. City of Cincinnati, 414 U.S. 29 (1973).

41. See Gene D. Brown, "Collateral Post Conviction Remedies in Florida," *University of Florida Law Review,* 20 (Winter 1968): 306-43, 308.

own counsel in connection with any kind of offense, including traffic offenses.[42]

Effective Representation by Counsel

If the right to counsel is to be more than a mere formality, a defendant is entitled to effective representation. Thus, it is reversible error for a judge to appoint a single lawyer to represent two or more defendants who have conflicting interests.[43] If there is such a state of disagreement between the accused and his counsel as to create a conflict of interests between them, and this is brought to the court's attention, it is the duty of the judge to inquire into the nature or seriousness of the differences.[44] Of course, ordinarily, a defendant who asks the court to appoint counsel for him must take whoever is offered to him.[45] In addition, to the end that the accused may enjoy the effective assistance of counsel, the lawyer, whether selected by the accused or appointed by the court, should have adequate time to prepare a defense properly. Again, the right would be reduced to a mere formality if the defendant were rushed to trial without giving his attorney a fair opportunity to confer with his client—an opportunity secured in many states by carefully drawn statutes—examine the evidence, and study the other elements of the case.[46] On the other hand, a defendant cannot claim an indefinite amount of time, for society has a legitimate interest in the expeditious dispensation of justice. It is impossible to draw a line between too little time and too much, outside the context of concrete situations.

42. See Tacoma v. Heater, 67 Wash. 2d 733, 409 P.2d 867 (1966); State v. Krozel, 24 Conn. Supp. 266, 190 A.2d 61 (1963). These two cases held that the refusal of the police to permit a motorist to contact his counsel until four hours after his arrest for drunken driving violated his constitutional right to counsel, since such refusal resulted in irreparable prejudice to his defense.

43. Glasser v. United States, 315 U.S. 60 (1942); Hudson v. North Carolina, 363 U.S. 697 (1960); People v. Robinson, 42 Cal. 2d 741, 269 P.2d 6 (1954); People v. Rose, 348 Ill. 214, 180 N.E. 791 (1932). The Federal Criminal Justice Act provides, "The United States magistrate or the court shall appoint separate counsel for defendants having interests that cannot properly be represented by the same counsel, or when other good cause is shown." 18 U.S.C. §3006A (b) (1970).

44. McDonald v. Johnston, 62 F. Supp. 830 (N.D. Calif. 1945), rev'd., 157 F.2d 275 (9th Cir. 1946), cert. denied, 329 U.S. 795 (1946).

45. United States v. Gutterman, 147 F.2d 540 (2d Cir. 1945); Schuble v. Youngblood, 225 Ind. 169, 73 N.E. 2d 478 (1947).

46. In Reynolds v. Cochran, 365 U.S. 525 (1961), the Court ruled that a refusal by the trial judge of a two-day continuance so that the defendant's lawyer could be present deprived the accused of his constitutional right to counsel. Said Justice Black for a unanimous Court, "... even in the most routine-appearing proceedings the assistance of able counsel may be of inestimable value." 365 U.S. 532–33. The Court relied heavily upon Chandler v. Fretag, 348 U.S. 3 (1954), which involved much the same point of law.

It is clear that an attorney must be allowed time to confer with the accused, and that he is entitled to a continuance if the circumstances warrant. Many matters are relevant to a consideration of the merits of a request for a continuance: the seriousness of the charges, the mental competence of the accused, the number and availability of witnesses, the nature of the public atmosphere, the complexity of the legal and factual issues involved, the effect of the denial, the diligence of the accused, the illness or preoccupation of counsel with other business. It is familiar law, however, that a judge exercises a sound discretion in ruling on motions for continuances, and will not be overruled by a reviewing court unless he abused his discretion by making an arbitrary decision. To cite rather obvious instances, it is error for a judge to deny a motion for a continuance where he has allowed no time at all for counsel to prepare,[47] or only one minute,[48] or ten minutes.[49] On the other hand, five months may be enough.[50] In addition, the right of counsel to prepare his case includes a right to confer in private with his client. Furthermore, communications between lawyer and client are confidential, and the government impairs the effective aid of counsel by tapping the telephone and listening in on such communications.[51]

It is generally agreed that effective representation means that a defendant is entitled to the aid of a lawyer at "every step of the proceedings." Until a rather recent date, courts generally ruled that the right to counsel related primarily to the trial, so that the absence of counsel at a police interrogation did not invalidate a confession.[52] Three important decisions of the Supreme Court, however, rendered in 1964 and 1966, extended the right to counsel to many proceedings which precede the actual trial. In *Massiah v. United States*,[53] a divided Court ruled inadmissible incriminating statements made by the accused to government agents, after indictment and while free on bail, in the absence of retained counsel. The

47. Walleck v. Hudspeth, 128 F.2d 343 (10th Cir. 1942); Zasada v. State, 19 N.J. Super. 589, 89 A.2d 45 (1952).
48. United States v. Helwig, 159 F.2d 616 (3d Cir. 1947).
49. Schita v. King, 133 F.2d 283 (8th Cir. 1943); Edwards v. State, 204 Ga. 384, 50 S.E. 2d 10 (1948).
50. United States v. Hartenfeld, 113 F.2d 359 (7th Cir. 1940), cert. denied, 311 U.S. 647 (1940).
51. Coplon v. United States, 191 F.2d 749 (D.C. Cir. 1951), cert. denied, 342 U.S. 926 (1952).
52. See, e.g., Linkins v. State, 202 Md. 212, 96 A.2d 246 (1953); State v. Tune, 13 N.J. 203, 98 A.2d 881 (1953); Com. v. Agoston, 364 Pa. 464, 72 A.2d 575 (1950), cert. denied, 340 U.S. 844 (1950); Com. v. Bryant, 367 Pa. 135, 147, 79 A.2d 193, 198 (1951), cert. denied, 341 U.S. 954 (1951) (due process does not require that a person be protected "against his own natural desire to unburden himself").
53. 377 U.S. 201 (1964).

Court majority stressed the fact that a defendant needs the assistance of counsel during the most critical period after arraignment and before trial.[54] The Court went a step further a month later, in *Escobedo* v. *Illinois,*[55] when by a 5-4 vote, it ruled that a confession was inadmissible if made to the police at the station house in the course of an interrogation, after the police had repeatedly refused the defendant's lawyer, who was waiting outside the door of the interrogation room, permission to see his client and advise him of his rights. The Court held that the interrogation at the station house was precisely the stage when legal advice was most critical to the accused, and that it would exalt form over substance to make the right to counsel depend upon whether the interrogation occurred before or after indictment. The right to counsel would become hollow and merely formal, Justice Goldberg pointed out, where for all practical purposes a conviction was already assured by an in-custody pretrial examination. It may well be that a lawyer will advise his client not to answer questions, but, said Justice Goldberg, "Our Constitution, unlike some others, strikes the balance in favor of the right of the accused to be advised by his lawyer of his privilege against self-incrimination."[56] He added that we should not have to fear that if the accused is allowed to see his lawyer, he will become aware of his constitutional rights and exercise them. Indeed, if the exercise of these rights thwarts the justice system, then something is very wrong with the system.[57]

Finally, in 1966, in *Miranda* v. *Arizona,*[58] again by a 5-4 vote, the Court set aside convictions secured in three state courts and one federal court which involved the use of confessions secured by the police in the absence of counsel, or without an effective waiver of counsel. Here the Court made it clear that the right to the assistance of counsel accrues as soon as one is in custody, or is "otherwise deprived of his freedom of action in any significant way," unless he has "voluntarily, knowingly and intelligently" waived this right. Prior to any questioning the accused must be told that he has a right to remain silent, that he has a right to the presence of an attorney, and that if he cannot afford to retain counsel, one will be appointed for him. Furthermore, if at any stage of the questioning process the accused indicates that he wishes to consult a lawyer before speaking, all questioning must stop. In short, the Court ruled that a

---

54. Three Justices dissented on the ground that a pretrial statement should be admissible in evidence if made voluntarily, and that the absence of counsel was only one of several factors to be considered in judging the issue of voluntariness.

55. 378 U.S. 478 (1964).

56. 378 U.S. 488.

57. Four Justices dissented, insisting that the only issue was whether the confession was voluntary, and that the Ecobedo decision would cripple law enforcement.

58. 384 U.S. 436 (1966).

person who is in custody, and subject to interrogation, needs the assistance of a lawyer if the privilege against self-incrimination is to achieve its purpose.

Furthermore, in two cases decided in 1967,[59] and again by 5-4 votes, the Court held that a postindictment pretrial lineup at which the accused is exhibited to identifying witnesses is a critical stage in a criminal prosecution at which the accused has a right to counsel. Arguing that the framers of the Bill of Rights envisaged a broad role for counsel, who must be concerned with fact as well as law questions, Justice Brennan, speaking for the Court majority, noted that it was well established that the right to counsel accrues before the trial, and applies to all critical stages of the proceedings. *Escobedo* and *Miranda* both emphasized that the period from arraignment to trial is of critical importance. The basic principle is that the accused should not have to stand alone at any stage of the prosecution, whether formal or informal, in court or out, where counsel's absence may derogate from the defendant's right to a fair trial. Many vagaries are involved in eyewitness identification, and Justice Brennan noted that there have been many cases of mistaken identification. Thus, at this stage the assistance of counsel protects the accused in an important measure at a critical time. Furthermore, while some courts have taken the position that "adversary judicial proceedings" begin with the filing of the complaint and the issuance of a warrant, so that the right to counsel applies to any planned confrontation with witnesses after that,[60] the more orthodox view has been that the right to counsel, so far as an identification process is concerned, begins only after the filing of formal charges, whether by indictment or information.[61] In 1972 the U.S. Supreme Court went along with the orthodox view in holding, by a 5-4 vote, that the right to counsel does not attach for lineup purposes until formal charges have been filed.[62] The majority view was that the right to counsel accrues only after adversary judicial proceedings have been initiated. The dissenting Justices argued that it is immaterial whether the identification confrontation takes place before or after indictment; what matters is that, having been arrested, the accused needs protection from the dangers inherent in eyewitness identification. Finally, in 1973 the Court ruled, in a 6-3

---

59. United States v. Billy Joe Wade, 388 U.S. 218 (1967); Gilbert v. California, 388 U.S. 263 (1967). See also Foster v. California, 394 U.S. 440 (1969), where the Court held a lineup identification to constitute a denial of due process, wholly apart from the counsel issue, because of the highly suggestive nature of the identification procedure. See Comment, "The Right to Counsel during Pretrial Identification Proceedings—An Examination," *Nebraska Law Review,* 47, no. 4 (1968): 747-61.
60. See, e.g., Arnold v. State, 484 S.W. 2d 248 (Mo. 1972).
61. See, e.g., Com. v. Lopes, 287 N.E. 2d 118 (Mass. 1972).
62. Kirby v. Illinois, 406 U.S. 682 (1972).

decision, that the Sixth Amendment does not guarantee the right to counsel at photographic displays conducted by the government allowing witnesses to attempt to identify the offender.[63] The Court majority thought that this is not a critical stage in the proceedings, and that the right to counsel does not include the prosecutor's preparations for trial through the interviewing of witnesses. The dissenters regarded this decision to be a serious departure from the rule established in the lineup cases, because they thought that the same dangers of mistaken identification exist.

For a long time American courts disagreed as to whether the accused has a constitutionally protected right to have a lawyer at the preliminary hearing, though the better view was that this stage of the proceedings was sufficiently important to require the assistance of counsel.[64] A unanimous Supreme Court finally came to grips with this issue in 1963, in *White* v. *Maryland*,[65] where it was decided that since, under state law, the accused enters a plea, the preliminary hearing is a critical stage in the proceedings which requires the assistance of counsel. The Court took the position that only the presence of counsel would have enabled the defendant to know what defenses were available to him, and how to plead intelligently. In 1970, in *Coleman* v. *Alabama*,[66] the Court held that the preliminary hearing is a critical stage in the state's procedure because at this point defense counsel may expose weaknesses in the state's case through skillful cross-examination, lay the groundwork for impeachment of witnesses at the trial, prepare a better defense through effective discovery of the state's case, and make early argument for bail or a psychiatric examination.[67] Similarly, in 1961, in *Hamilton* v. *Alabama*,[68] a unanimous Court ruled that a defendant has a right to counsel at the arraignment, since under Alabama procedure the defense of insanity must be made at this point or be lost, and since the arraignment is the point in time when pleas in abatement, or a motion to quash on the ground that the grand jury was

---

63. United States v. Ash, 413 U.S. 300 (1973). To the same effect was the *en banc* decision of the Court in Reed v. Anderson, 461 F.2d 739 (3rd Cir. 1972).

64. See, e.g., Wood v. United States, 128 F.2d 265 (D.C. Cir. 1942). See William M. Beaney, "Right to Counsel before Arraignment," *Minnesota Law Review,* 45 (April 1961): 771–82.

65. 373 U.S. 59 (1963).

66. 399 U.S. 1 (1970). See also Dancy v. United States, 361 F.2d 75 (D.C. Cir. 1965). In Adams v. Illinois, 405 U.S. 278 (1972), the Court held that the Coleman rule was not retroactive.

67. Chief Justice Burger dissented, arguing that while it may be sound policy to make a lawyer available at the preliminary hearing, it is not a command of the Constitution. He insisted that the Constitution refers only to "criminal prosecutions," and that a preliminary hearing is not a criminal prosecution.

68. 368 U.S. 52 (1961). See also Walton v. Arkansas, 371 U.S. 28 (1962).

improperly drawn, must be made. State courts have long been practically unanimous in agreeing that the right to counsel accrues at the arraignment, since defendants need the advice of counsel on the crucial question of how to plead. While it has been argued that a plea can usually be changed at a later date, the better view is that once a plea of guilty has been entered, a very damaging admission has been made, and counsel may be understandably reluctant to try to undo the harm later by changing the plea.

Certainly all agree that a defendant is entitled to have his lawyer with him during the entire trial, and that the lawyer has a right to do all things necessary to present a proper defense, such as participate in the selection of jurors, put witnesses on the stand, file motions, and present arguments within reasonable time limits fixed by the judge. It is also incumbent upon the judge not to instruct or otherwise communicate with the jury in the absence of counsel. For example, in 1960 a case reached the Supreme Court from the highest court of Georgia which called attention to the importance of permitting counsel to do his job.[69] Georgia still has the old common law rule that in a criminal case the defendant is incompetent to testify under oath in his own behalf, but he does have a statutory right to make an unsworn statement to the court and jury. In a murder trial the judge refused to permit defense counsel to question the defendant in order to elicit this statement, and this, the Supreme Court ruled, was in effect a denial of the defendant's right to the assistance of his lawyer.

Federal and state courts have differed as to the propriety of the judge pronouncing sentence in the absence of counsel, but in 1948,[70] and again in 1962,[71] the Supreme Court ruled that where sentence was pronounced on the basis of untrue assumptions, on a habitual criminal charge, without the presence of counsel, the defendant had been denied a constitutional right. It was noted that when, under Virginia law, one faces a charge of being a habitual criminal, the validity of any prior conviction may be inquired into, and this involves legal issues much too intricate for a layman to be expected to master. Thus, at least where the circumstances are such as to invite potential prejudice because of the complexity of the legal issues involved, the rules relating to the right of counsel at the trial apply at the sentencing as well.

Finally, it remains to be noted that one who has been convicted of a crime has postconviction remedies available to him, and that the utilization of these remedies involves questions relating to the right to the assis-

---

69. Ferguson v. Georgia, 365 U.S. 570 (1961).
70. Townsend v. Burke, 334 U.S. 736 (1948).
71. Chewning v. Cunningham, 368 U.S. 443 (1962).

tance of counsel. The Court broke new ground in 1963, in *Douglas* v. *California*,[72] when it held that the denial of counsel to help an indigent on an appeal constitutes an invidious discrimination based upon poverty in violation of the Equal Protection Clause. While later cases reiterated and strengthened the right of counsel for the appeal,[73] the Court took a step back, in 1974, when by a 6-3 vote it decided that the *Douglas* rule applies only to a first appeal as of right, but not to a later discretionary appeal.[74] Justice Rehnquist, speaking for the Court, held that all that is required is that the defendant have meaningful access to the system of justice, and that the briefs prepared for the first appeal can be used for later discretionary appeals. The three dissenters could see no logical distinction between appeals of right and permissive review procedures, so far as the right to counsel is concerned.

In addition, in 1972, the Court ruled that a state prisoner who petitions a federal district court for a writ of habeas corpus is entitled to an evidentiary hearing in that court on the issue as to whether he had been denied counsel in a previous habeas corpus proceeding in a state court.[75] Finally, in the important case of *Mempa* v. *Rhay*,[76] decided by a unanimous Court in 1967, it was held that before a person's probation may be revoked, he is entitled to the assistance of counsel, at least in a situation where sentence was originally deferred. In effect, the Court treated this case as one involving the sentencing stage of a criminal proceeding. On the basis of this decision, some lower federal and state courts have ruled that the right to counsel applies to all state probation or parole revocation hearings.[77] On the other hand, some state courts have ruled that the *Mempa* case went the way it did because sentencing had been deferred, but that otherwise a probation revocation is not a critical stage in the criminal justice process for which counsel is essential.[78] So the Supreme Court ruled in

---

72. 372 U.S. 353 (1963). The Court relied upon the rule in Griffin v. Illinois, 351 U.S. 12 (1956), which required the state to supply free transcripts to indigents seeking to appeal. See B. Boskey, "The Right to Counsel in Appellate Proceedings," *Minnesota Law Review*, 45 (April 1961): 783-802.

73. See Swenson v. Bosler, 386 U.S. 258 (1967); Entsminger v. Iowa, 386 U.S. 748 (1967); Anders v. California, 386 U.S. 738 (1967) (right to counsel on appeal cannot be denied merely because appointed counsel advised the court that the appeal was without merit).

74. Ross v. Moffitt, 417 U.S. 600 (1974).

75. Boyd v. Dutton, 405 U.S. 1 (1972).

76. 389 U.S. 128 (1967).

77. See, e.g., Gunsolus v. Gagnon, 454 F.2d 416 (7th Cir. 1971); Earnest v. Willingham, 406 F.2d 681 (10th Cir. 1969); Perry v. Williard, 247 Ore. 145, 427 P.2d 1020 (1967); People *ex rel.* Menechino v. Warden, 27 N.Y. 2d 376, 267 N.E. 2d 238 (Crt. of App. 1971).

78. See, e.g., Smith v. Warden, 450 P.2d 356 (Nev. 1969); Riggins v. Rhay, 450 P.2d 806 (Wash. 1969).

1973, in *Gagnon* v. *Scarpelli*,[79] holding that a state is not under a constitutional duty to provide counsel for indigents in all probation revocation cases, that a revocation is not a criminal trial, and that a decision as to the need for counsel must be made on a case-by-case basis in the exercise of a sound discretion on the part of those who administer the state probation system. Counsel is required, the Court held, only if there is a disputed issue which can be represented fairly only by a lawyer.

Competence of Counsel

Since, in the words of Justice Sutherland, the defendant's right to the assistance of counsel is not merely *pro forma,* but implies a right to "effective aid,"[80] it follows that he has a right to have a reasonably competent lawyer acting in his behalf. But this proposition raises many awkward questions. On the one hand, there is no agreed-upon standard of competence below which the accused has been in effect denied a valuable constitutional right. On the other hand, convicted persons are all too eager to seize the opportunity of putting their lawyers on trial.[81] Furthermore, indigent defendants are often represented by over-worked public defenders, or so-called "regulars" who hang around court-houses waiting for low-fee, high-volume appointments by the judge, or by neophytes who do not object to serve as court-appointed counsel, and are often eager to get something to do. The experience of David L. Bazelon, Chief Justice of the Court of Appeals of the District of Columbia, over a period of twenty-three years, led him to conclude that most indigent defendants did not receive effective assistance of counsel.[82]

The United States Supreme Court has never directly confronted the issue of counsel ineffectiveness, but the question has frequently been reviewed in lower federal courts and in many state courts. To begin with, it should be noted that lawyers are all officers of the courts, "licensed to practice, upon proof of character and fitness to perform professional duties. There is a presumption of proper performance of duty by each of them. . . ."[83] The presumption, of course, is rebuttable,[84] but it is established doctrine that in order to warrant relief on the ground of incompe-

---

79. 411 U.S. 778 (1973).
80. Powell v. Alabama, 287 U.S. 45, 71 (1932).
81. See J. D. Casper, *American Criminal Justice* (Englewood Cliffs, N.J.: Prentice-Hall, 1972), chap. 4, "The Defendant and his Attorney."
82. David L. Bazelon, "The Defective Assistance of Counsel," *University of Cincinnati Law Review,* 42, no. 1 (1973): 1–46, 2. See Patricia M. Wald, *Law and Poverty: 1965* (Report to the National Conference on Law and Poverty, Washington, D.C., June 23–25, 1965).
83. Dorsey v. Gill, 148 F.2d 857, 876 (D.C. Cir. 1945), cert. denied, 325 U.S. 890 (1945). See, to the same effect, U.S. *ex rel.* Feeley v. Ragen, 166 F.2d 976, 980 (7th Cir. 1948).
84. Achtien v. Dowd, 117 F.2d 989, 992 (7th Cir. 1941).

tence of counsel, the defendant must carry the burden of bringing forth "strong and convincing proof."[85] Courts are very reluctant to liberalize rules relating to the adequacy of counsel. As the Court of Appeals for the District of Columbia once remarked, "To allow a prisoner to try the issue of the effectiveness of his counsel under a liberal definition of the phrase is to give every convict the privilege of opening a Pandora's box of accusations which trial courts near large penal institutions would be compelled to hear."[86] But aside from the liberality of the definition of incompetence, it cannot be asserted that the courts have spelled out standards with any particular clarity.[87]

Of course, it is well understood that the Constitution does not assure an indigent defendant the assistance of any particular lawyer, nor that of the most brilliant counsel in the area, for in that event "preeminence at the bar would be the surest road to bankruptcy."[88] In addition, a defendant is usually permitted to conduct his own defense. Since the Judiciary Act of 1789, a federal statute has provided that "parties may plead and conduct their own cases personally or by counsel. . . ."[89] Indeed, the right of an accused to proceed *pro se* has been described by the Court of Appeals for the Second Circuit as an "absolute and primary right."[90] On the other hand, the Supreme Court of California has taken the position that there is no constitutional compulsion to allow the accused the right of self-representation,[91] and more recently the New York Court of Appeals ruled that

---

85. Schmittler v. State, 228 Ind. 450, 467, 93 N.E. 2d 184, 191 (1950). A few courts have shifted the burden of proof to require the state to show that counsel's mistakes did not amount to serious prejudicial error. See, e.g., Peyton v. Coles, 389 F.2d 224 (4th Cir. 1968), cert. denied, 393 U.S. 849 (1968).

86. Diggs v. Welch, 148 F.2d 667, 670 (D.C. Cir. 1945), cert. denied, 325 U.S. 889 (1945).

87. See Comment, "Federal Habeas Corpus—A Hindsight View of Trial Attorney Effectiveness," *Louisiana Law Review,* 27 (June 1967): 784-96. It may be noted that the fifth of the Canons of Professional Ethics of the American Bar Association states that in criminal cases counsel should use "all fair and honorable means to present every defense that the law permits to the end that no person may be deprived of life or liberty, but by due process of law."

88. U.S. *ex rel.* Mitchell v. Thompson, 56 F. Supp. 683, 688 (S.D.N.Y. 1944).

89. 28 U.S.C. §1654 (1970); 1 Stat. 73, §35 (1789). See also Rule 44, Federal Rules of Criminal Procedure.

90. United States v. Plattner, 330 F.2d 271, 274 (2nd Cir. 1964). So the Supreme Court ruled in Farretta v. California, 422 U.S. 806 (1975). See also Adams v. U.S. *ex rel.* McCann, 317 U.S. 269, 279 (1942), where Justice Frankfurter said, ". . . the Constitution does not force a lawyer upon a defendant." See also Carter v. Illinois, 329 U.S. 173, 174 (1946); People v. Coaley, 11 Mich. App. 602, 162 N.W. 2d 110 (1968); State v. Johnson, 74 Wash. 2d 567, 445 P.2d 726 (1968); U.S. *ex rel.* Maldonado v. Denno, 239 F. Supp. 851, 854 (S.D.N.Y. 1965); Reynolds v. United States, 267 F.2d 235, 236 (9th Cir. 1959).

91. People v. Sharp, 7 Cal. 3d 448, 103 Cal. Rptr. 233, 499 P.2 489 (1972).

while a defendant has a right to proceed *pro se,* it is not an absolute right.[92] The request must be made unequivocally and in good time, the right to appointed counsel must be waived intelligently and knowingly, and the accused must not engage in disruptive conduct or otherwise interfere with the fair and orderly exposition of the issues. The Court recognized that a *pro se* defense may have certain advantages: it may evoke the jury's sympathy; it permits the accused to demonstrate his faith both in his innocence and in the justice system; and it may be appropriate where the defendant lacks confidence in the ability or commitment of assigned counsel. Nevertheless, the right to proceed *pro se* cannot be absolute, because the overriding consideration is the determination of the issues in a manner consistent with fundamental fairness.[93]

Incompetence rising to the level of a denial of a constitutional right has not been proved merely because it can be shown, by going through the trial record, that mistakes were made, since very few trials indeed, of any duration or complexity, are wholly free from mistakes. As a federal appeals court once observed, "[L]awyers are not required to be infallible. If they were, law practice would soon totally disappear."[94] The fact that appointed counsel was young and inexperienced does not necessarily prove incompetence, although many judges exercise good judgment in refusing to appoint such lawyers in cases involving very serious offenses.[95] Similarly, the conclusion of incompetence does not follow from the fact that counsel advised the defendant to plead guilty, or failed to make certain objections or motions or defenses, or because counsel lost his case.

There have been a few cases where a reviewing court has been convinced that counsel was so grossly and wretchedly incompetent as to support the inference that the defendant had not had at least a minimum measure of adequate representation.[96] Convictions have been set aside where an appellate or habeas corpus court has concluded that appointed counsel

92. People v. McIntyre, 43 U.S. L.W. 2284 (N.Y. Ct. App. Dec. 20, 1974).

93. Most courts hold that whether a defendant may proceed *pro se* rests in the sound discretion of the trial court. See Comment, "Self-Representation in Criminal Trials," *California Law Review,* 59 (November 1971): 1479-1513; Note, "The Right of an Accused to Proceed without Counsel," *Minnesota Law Review,* 49 (May 1965): 1133-53.

94. Williams v. Beto, 354 F.2d 698, 705 (5th Cir. 1965).

95. See Note, "The Right to Counsel and the Neophyte Attorney," *Rutgers Law Review,* 24 (Winter 1970): 378-402, 392.

96. See, e.g., Johnson v. United States, 110 F.2d 562 (D.C. Cir. 1940); Jones v. Huff, 152 F.2d 14 (D.C. Cir. 1945); Abraham v. State, 228 Ind. 179, 91 N.E. 2d 358 (1950); State v. Bouse, 199 Ore. 676, 264 P.2d 800 (1953). For a thorough canvass of the precedents and experience with this problem, see J. R. Waltz, "Inadequacy of Trial Defense Representation as a Ground for Post-Conviction Relief in Criminal Cases," *Northwestern University Law Review,* 59 (July-August 1964): 289-342.

was so inexperienced in criminal matters that he failed utterly to do such obvious things as to challenge the validity of a confession or of a search and seizure or take other steps which a competent lawyer would routinely pursue,[97] or where counsel was appointed but a few minutes before trial, and thus had no time to prepare a defense,[98] or where appointed counsel simply made no effort at all to present any sort of defense.[99] In addition, it has been held that the right to the effective assistance of counsel applies to an appeal as well as to the trial,[100] and that failure to advise a convicted person of his right to appeal is strong evidence of incompetence.[101]

From the very nature of the problem, American courts have not been able to devise a clearly articulated standard of judgment to describe the sort of incompetence which would warrant the conclusion that the defendant had been denied his constitutional right to the "effective assistance" of counsel. The Court of Appeals for the District of Columbia once ruled, as have others, that the incompetence must be so great that the whole trial was a "mockery of justice,"[102] but some years later this Court rejected this standard for a fundamental unfairness test, holding that the question is "whether gross incompetence blotted out the essence of a substantial defense."[103] It has been suggested that a proper standard

97. U.S. v. Hammonds, 425 F.2d 597 (D.C. Cir. 1970); Smotherman v. Beto, 276 F. Supp. 579 (N.D. Tex. 1967); Coles v. Peyton, 389 F.2d 224 (4th Cir. 1968), cert. denied, 393 U.S. 849 (1968); People v. Ibarra, 60 Cal. 2d 460, 34 Cal. Reptr. 863, 386 P.2d 487 (1963); People v. Blevins, 251 Ill. 381, 96 N.E. 214 (1911); People v. Nitti, 312 Ill. 73, 143 N.E. 448 (1924); McLaughlin v. Royster, 346 F. Supp. 297 (E.D. Va. 1972); Brubaker v. Dickson, 310 F.2d 30 (9th Cir. 1962), cert. denied, 372 U.S. 978 (1963); Goodwin v. Swenson, 287 F. Supp. 166 (W.D. Mo. 1968).

98. U.S. ex rel. Williams v. Brierley, 291 F. Supp. 912 (E.D. Pa. 1968); Moore v. United States, 432 F.2d 730 (3rd Cir. 1970).

99. State v. Merchant, 10 Md. App. 545, 271 A.2d 752 (1970); Stewart v. State, 229 So. 2d 53 (Miss. 1969); People v. Morris, 3 Ill. 2d 437, 121 N.E. 2d 810 (1954). See Comment, "The Right to Effective Assistance of Counsel," *Mississippi Law Journal,* 42 (Spring 1971): 213-25.

100. In re Smith, 3 Cal. 3d 192, 90 Cal. Rptr. 1, 474 P.2d 969 (1970). See Note, "Adequate Appellate Review for Indigents," *Iowa Law Review,* 52 (April 1967): 902-29.

101. Smotherman v. Beto, 276 F. Supp. 579 (N.D. Tex. 1967); Coffman v. Bomar, 220 F. Supp. 343 (M.D. Tenn. 1963).

102. Edwards v. United States, 256 F.2d 707 (D.C. Cir. 1958), cert. denied, 358 U.S. 847 (1958) (". . . mere improvident strategy, bad tactics, mistake, carelessness or inexperience do not necessarily amount to ineffective assistance of counsel, unless taken as a whole the trial was a 'mockery of justice'. . . ."), per Burger, Cir. J., 256 F.2d 708. For other holdings that the test is whether the trial was "a farce or a mockery of justice," see Williams v. Beto, 354 F.2d 698, 704 (5th Cir. 1965); Mitchell v. Illinois, 411 Ill. 407, 408, 104 N.E. 2d 285 (1952), cert. denied, 343 U.S. 969 (1952); People v. Ibarra, 60 Cal. 2d 460, 34 Cal. Rptr. 863, 386 P.2d 487 (1963). For an argument that the "mockery of justice" formulation is overly vague and places too great a burden on the defendant, see Joel J. Finer, "Ineffective Assistance of Counsel," *Cornell Law Review,* 58 (July 1973): 1077-1120.

103. Scott v. United States, 427 F.2d 609, 610 (D.C. Cir. 1970).

would require that counsel should perform as well as a lawyer of ordinary training and skill who seeks conscientiously to protect his client's interests, and that due allowance should be made for harmless error.[104] The Supreme Court of Wisconsin, in 1973, held that "the representation must be equal to that which the ordinarily prudent lawyer, skilled and versed in criminal law, would give to clients who had privately retained his services."[105] Thus, the Wisconsin Court also said, "an accused is not entitled to the ideal, perfect defense or the best defense but only to one which under all the facts gives him reasonably effective representation."

A trial judge has denied a constitutional right if he appoints a lawyer who is involved in a conflict of interests,[106] or if he has intimidated and demeaned counsel to the point where he is utterly ineffective.[107] Courts often hold that poor representation by a lawyer of the defendant's own choosing will not be reviewed, on an agency theory according to which a lawyer speaks for his client, and the client is bound thereby.[108] The Supreme Court of Illinois once took this position,[109] but a few years later rejected the double standard,[110] as have other courts.[111]

There are very good reasons why appellate and habeas corpus courts are reluctant to give relief where the issue of the lawyer's competence is pressed. For one thing, the law is by no means an exact science, and lawyers must have great latitude as to strategy and tactics. Since, as it has been observed, "the practice of law is an art as well as a science,"[112] the competence of counsel should not be judged by what some other lawyer would have done, and surely not on the basis of the outcome of the case. Furthermore, it has been asserted that to give defendants relief because of the gross mistakes of their lawyers would be an invitation to the making of mistakes, thus opening the door to collusion and endless confusion in the administration of justice.[113] If the rule were otherwise, one state court has

104. Comment, "Effective Assistance of Counsel for the Indigent Defendant," *Harvard Law Review,* 78 (May 1965): 1434-51. See People v. Odom, 71 Ill. App. 2d 480, 487, 218 N.E. 2d 116, 119-20 (1966) (test is deprivation of "a fair trial").

105. State v. Harper, 57 Wis. 2d 543, 557, 205 N.W. 2d 1, 9 (1973) (per Hallows, C.J.).

106. The leading case on this point of law is Glasser v. United States, 315 U.S. 60 (1942). See also Goodson v. Peyton, 351 F.2d 905 (4th Cir. 1965).

107. United States v. Davis, 442 F.2d 72 (10th Cir. 1971), noted critically in *Utah Law Review,* 1972 (Winter 1972): 127-32.

108. See, e.g., Hendrickson v. Overlade, 131 F. Supp. 561 (N.D. Ind. 1955). For a criticism of this rule, see Sam Polur, "Retained Counsel, Assigned Counsel: Why the Dichotomy?" *American Bar Association Journal,* 55 (March 1969): 254-56.

109. People v. Ventura, 415 Ill. 587, 590, 114 N.E. 2d 710, 712 (1953).

110. People v. Cox, 12 Ill. 2d 265, 146 N.E. 2d 19 (1957).

111. See, e.g., Bell v. Alabama, 367 F.2d 243 (5th Cir. 1966); Wilson v. Rose, 366 F.2d 611 (9th Cir. 1966).

112. Williams v. Beto, 354 F.2d 698, 706 (5th Cir. 1965).

113. State v. Dreher, 137 Mo. 11, 38 S.W. 567 (1897).

asserted, "a lawyer with a desperate case would have only to neglect it in order to ensure reversal or vacation of the conviction."[114] Few judges or scholars accept this argument as valid, since it would be a very rare lawyer indeed who would deliberately advertise his incompetence, or risk a court rebuke, possibly a disbarment proceeding. But it is a very serious matter for a reviewing court to sustain the defendant's contention that his lawyer was grossly incompetent, and this must be an important element in the reluctance of courts to pass judgment on such a delicate point. An appellate court would be passing on a vital aspect of the lawyer's professional standing without giving him a hearing.

Judge Bazelon, the presiding judge of the Court of Appeals of the District of Columbia, has suggested that lawyers should not be permitted to represent defendants in criminal trials unless they are certified as having the specialized skill and knowledge required for this sort of practice, just as medical specialists must be certified by examining bodies.[115] He also suggests that counsel for indigents should be appointed by someone other than the trial judge. This is a valuable suggestion, since many lawyers trim their sails to please the appointing judge in order to be in line for more appointments. It has also been suggested that in addition to special certification, courts should supply defense counsel with a checklist of functions he must perform before trial.[116] Increased compensation for appointed counsel might encourage better service. Where public defenders are used, there ought to be a limit on the number of cases one lawyer can be assigned in a year. It has been asserted that some public defenders must handle as many as 500 cases a year.[117] The National Legal Aid and Defenders Association suggests an upper limit of 150 felony cases per year. Finally, the adequacy of defense of indigents would be greatly improved if appointed counsel were given expert and investigational assistance. At the federal level, the first significant grant of federal aid to indigents to secure the assistance of experts and investigational facilities was authorized by the Federal Criminal Justice Act of 1964.[118] But the upper limit of $300 was inadequate, and now the Act, as amended in 1970 and 1974, permits payments in excess of $300 if certified by the court "as necessary to provide fair compensation for services of an unusual character or duration," and approved by the chief judge of the circuit. In most states the granting of investigational aid is discretionary with the trial

---

114. Mitchell v. Illinois, 411 Ill. 407, 408, 104 N.E. 2d 285 (1952), cert. denied, 343 U.S. 969 (1952).
115. Bazelon, "The Defective Assistance of Counsel," pp. 18–19.
116. Finer, "Ineffective Assistance of Counsel," pp. 1077–1120.
117. *Ibid.*
118. U.S.C. §3006 A (1964).

judge, and most courts will not do so in the absence of an authorizing statute. As of 1970, 14 states had statutes providing for some aid of this sort, but often only in capital cases.[119]

Plea Bargaining

The indispensability of the lawyer to one who is accused of crime is reflected in the significant role of plea bargaining in the criminal justice system. It is generally agreed that about 90 percent of all felony convictions are obtained from guilty pleas; a little over a third of these pleas are negotiated, and the process of negotiation almost invariably requires the assistance of a lawyer. The essence of the plea bargain is that in return for sparing the government the expense and expenditure of human time and energy involved in a trial, the defendant pleads guilty to a lesser offense than that which was originally charged, or some charges are dismissed altogether. Thus, even guilty people need lawyers to help them negotiate the most favorable possible settlement. This was acknowledged by the Supreme Court in the *Argersinger* case,[120] where Justice Douglas wrote, "Beyond the problem of trials and appeals is that of the guilty plea, a problem which looms large in misdemeanor as well as in felony cases. Counsel is needed so that the accused may know precisely what he is doing, so that he is fully aware of the prospect of going to jail or prison, and so that he is treated fairly by the prosecution."[121]

In a cluster of three important cases decided in 1970, the Supreme Court upheld pleas of guilty entered as a result of plea bargaining where it concluded that the pleas were made voluntarily and intelligently, on the advice of counsel.[122] The Court rejected the argument that the pleas were induced unconstitutionally simply because the defendants were motivated by a desire to avoid stiffer penalty, for the whole point of plea bargaining is that the accused settles the case by pleading guilty to a lesser charge carrying a less severe penalty. Even where the accused asserted his

---

119. See Note, "The Indigent's Right to an Adequate Defense: Expert and Investigational Assistance in Criminal Proceedings," *Cornell Law Review,* 55 (April 1970): 632–45.

120. Argersinger v. Hamlin, 407 U.S. 25 (1972).

121. 407 U.S. 34.

122. Brady v. United States, 397 U.S. 742 (1970); Parker v. North Carolina, 397 U.S. 790 (1970); McMann v. Richardson, 397 U.S. 759 (1970). See also Dukes v. Warden, 406 U.S. 250 (1972); Tollett v. Henderson, 411 U.S. 258 (1973). There is a large literature on plea bargaining. The leading book on this subject is Donald J. Newman, *Conviction* (Boston: Little, Brown, & Co., 1966). See also Abraham S. Blumberg, *Criminal Justice* (Chicago: Quadrangle Books, 1967); Arnold S. Trebach, *The Rationing of Justice* (New Brunswick, N.J.: Rutgers University Press, 1964); Richard M. Cohen and Jules Witcover, *A Heartbeat Away* (New York: Viking Press, 1974) (on the plea bargaining of Vice President Spiro T. Agnew).

innocence, after entering a plea of guilty, arguing that his plea was designed to avoid facing the death penalty, the Supreme Court upheld the conviction, declaring that the standard is whether the plea represented an intelligent and voluntary choice, and that the fact that the defendant was trying to limit the possible penalty does not prove that the plea of guilty was not the product of a free and rational choice, especially where he was represented by competent counsel.[123] The Court noted that state and lower federal courts were divided on the question as to whether a plea of guilty can be accepted when it is accompanied by protestations of innocence, but in this case the Court said that the evidence against the accused was so overwhelming that it substantially negated the claim of innocence, and gave the judge another means of testing whether the plea was entered intelligently. Three Justices dissented, arguing that the previous 1970 cases were wrongly decided, and that the influence of the threat of death must be given great weight in determining the question of the voluntariness of the plea.

The Court came to further grips with the problem of plea bargaining in 1971, in the important case of *Santobello* v. *New York*.[124] Charged with two felony counts of gambling, after negotiations, the district attorney agreed to permit the defendant to plead guilty to the lesser included offense of possession of gambling records, which carried a maximum sentence of one year in jail. The prosecutor also agreed to make no recommendation to the court with respect to the sentence. The Court accepted the plea, in June 1969, and set a date for sentencing. For various reasons, much delay ensued, and Santobello did not appear for sentencing until the following January. By this time the judge in the original proceeding had retired, and another prosecutor had replaced the original one. Being ignorant of the promise made by the first prosecutor, the second prosecutor recommended the maximum one-year sentence. The sentencing judge declared that since he was not at all influenced by what the district attorney said, there was no need to adjourn the sentencing. Holding that he had plenty to go on in the probation report, which showed that Santobello was a professional criminal, he gave him the maximum one-year sentence. Describing this record as another example of "an unfortunate lapse in orderly prosecutorial procedures," due to the heavy work load of an understaffed prosecutor's office, the Court held that what happened constituted a breach of agreement.

Chief Justice Burger pointed out that plea bargaining "is an essential component of the administration of justice. Properly administered, it is to

123. North Carolina v. Alford, 400 U.S. 25 (1970).
124. 404 U.S. 257 (1971).

be encouraged. If every criminal charge were subjected to a full-scale trial, the States and the Federal Government would need to multiply by many times the number of judges and court facilities."[125] He went on to cite other reasons for approving of plea bargaining. "It leads to prompt and largely final disposition of most criminal cases; it avoids much of the corrosive impact of enforced idleness during pretrial confinement for those who are denied release pending trial; it protects the public from those accused persons who are prone to continue criminal conduct even while on pretrial release; and, by shortening the time between charge and disposition, it enhances whatever may be the rehabilitative prospects of the guilty when they are ultimately imprisoned." However, said the Chief Justice, all this presupposes fairness in securing agreement between a defendant and a prosecutor. He stressed that under the Federal Rules of Criminal Procedure relating to pleas in federal courts, the judge must develop the factual basis for the plea *on the record.* Furthermore, the plea must be voluntary and knowing, and if induced by a promise, that must be made known. Thus, Chief Justice Burger concluded, "when a plea rests in any significant degree on a promise or agreement of the prosecutor, so that it can be said to be part of the inducement or consideration, such promise must be fulfilled,"[126] and the fact that the breach of the agreement was inadvertent was no excuse.

Not only is it important for the prosecution to adhere to the terms of the bargain arrived at; it is also vital that the judge make the effort to explore the acceptability of a guilty plea. Thus, Rule 11 of the Federal Rules of Criminal Procedure declares that "[t]he court may refuse to accept a plea of guilty, and shall not accept such a plea. . . . without first addressing the defendant personally and determining that the plea is made voluntarily with understanding of the nature of the charge and the consequences of the plea. . . . The court shall not enter a judgment upon a plea of guilty unless it is satisfied that there is a factual basis for the plea."[127] After all, on a plea of guilty a defendant waives many precious rights, including trial by jury, the right to confront and cross-examine his accusers, the right to offer witnesses and testimony in his own behalf, and the privilege against self-incrimination. This explains why many state courts have ruled that plea bargaining agreements must be disclosed to the trial court and

---

125. 404 U.S. 260.
126. 404 U.S. 261-62. On the binding quality of the bargained plea, see Bryan v. United States, 492 F.2d 775 (1st Cir. 1974); United States v. Gilligan, 256 F. Supp. 244 (S.D. N.Y. 1966); State v. Wolski, 160 N.W. 2d 146 (Minn. 1968).
127. Many state statutes say as much. See, e.g., Wis. Stat. §971.08 (1971); Mich. Stat. Ann., §28.1058 (1972); Minn. Stat. Ann., §630.30 (1947).

incorporated in the trial record.[128] In addition, plea bargaining is likely to yield more accurate results if the accused has the assistance of a lawyer, and if an adequate presentence report is made available to the judge. Above all, the court must determine whether the plea of guilty is voluntary, and whether the accused is in fact guilty of the crime to which the plea is made.[129] The President's Commission on Law Enforcement and Administration of Justice, reporting in 1967, pointed out that "the negotiated plea of guilty can be subject to serious abuses. In hard-pressed courts, where judges and prosecutors are unable to deal effectively with all cases presented to them, dangerous offenders may be able to manipulate the system to obtain unjustifiably lenient treatment. There are also real dangers that excessive rewards will be offered to induce pleas or that prosecutors will threaten to seek a harsh sentence if the defendant does not plead guilty. Such practices place unacceptable burdens on the defendant who legitimately insists upon his right to trial. They present the greatest potential abuse when the sentencing judge becomes involved in the process as a party to the negotiations, as in some places he does."[130]

Thus, plea bargaining involves many problems relating to the prosecutor's unchecked discretion and the judge's role. Accordingly, it has been suggested that the responsibility for negotiating guilty pleas should be vested in one or more assistant prosecutors who specialize in bargaining at the earliest possible stage in the proceedings, by imposing limits on the prosecutor's discretion through the formulation of general policies in the office, and by imposing limits on the judge's sentencing power where a plea has been bargained.[131] For example, if the judge feels bound to impose a sentence greater than that recommended by the prosecutor, the defendant should be permitted to withdraw his plea. Clearly, plea bargaining serves very useful—indeed essential—purposes in the operation of the criminal justice system, but both the interests of society and of defendants will be best served if the process is brought under the control of established general policies. In most jurisdictions, the plea bargaining

---

128. See, e.g., People v. West, 91 Cal. Rptr. 385, 477 P.2d 409 (1970); Austin v. State, 49 Wis. 2d 727, 183 N.W. 2d 56 (1971); State v. Ward, 112 W. Va. 552, 165 S.E. 803 (1932). Judge Tobriner of the Supreme Court of California wrote, ". . . the plea bargain can be viable only if it is candidly disclosed to the trial court and incorporated in the record of the case. Through that procedure the murky fog of subterfuge that now suffuses the plea bargain can be swept away." 477 P.2d 421.

129. See Walter E. Hoffman, "Plea Bargaining and the Role of the Judge," 53 F.R.D. 499 (1971).

130. *The Challenge in a Free Society*, p. 135. For an argument that plea bargaining is unconstitutional, see Note, "The Unconstitutionality of Plea Bargaining," *Harvard Law Review*, 83 (April 1970): 1387–1411.

131. See Welsh S. White, "A Proposal for Reform of the Plea Bargaining Process," *University of Pennsylvania Law Review*, 119 (January 1971): 439–65.

process takes the form of *ad hoc* improvisation, to a very considerable extent. The substitution of known general rules for unchannelled discretion would be a considerable improvement.

Waiver

While a defendant may waive his right to counsel, it is established now that the waiver must be "intelligent and competent," that ordinarily a waiver is "an intentional relinquishment or abandonment of a known right or privilege," and that the judge has a "serious and weighty responsibility" to make sure that the defendant knew what he was doing when he waived this valuable right.[132] The Supreme Court has also taken the position that failure to comply with the mandate of the Sixth Amendment means that the district court loses jurisdiction over the case. Thus, in the absence of a competent and intelligent waiver, the lack of counsel stands as a jurisdictional defect which renders subsequent proceedings invalid, and which may therefore be remedied by means of habeas corpus.[133] While the Court is reluctant to infer waiver by implication, it is even more reluctant to set aside the trial court's judgment, which as a rule carries with it a presumption of regularity. Ordinarily, therefore, the burden of proof is upon the defendant. But if the defendant presents serious charges of denial of counsel in his petition for habeas corpus, the Supreme Court prefers that the district court should hold a hearing and hear testimony rather than dispose of the matter by affidavits alone.[134]

What constitutes an intelligent and competent waiver in the federal courts poses a complex problem. While some federal courts have held that a defendant who does not request counsel and pleads guilty has waived his right,[135] the better and prevailing view, consistent with Rule 44, is that whether a defendant actually waived his right depends upon an evaluation

---

132. Johnson v. Zerbst, 304 U.S. 458 (1938). In Faretta v. California, 422 U.S. 806 (1975) the Court held, in a 6–3 decision, that a defendant in a state criminal trial has a constitutional right to proceed without counsel when he voluntarily and intelligently elects to do so.

133. 422 U.S. 806.

134. Walker v. Johnston, 312 U.S. 275 (1941). The judge cannot devolve this duty upon his commissioner, but must hold the hearing himself. Holiday v. Johnston, 313 U.S. 342 (1941). In Wingo v. Wedding, 418 U.S. 461 (1974) the Court held that the Federal Magistrates Act of 1968, which substitutes magistrates for the former commissioners, did not change the requirement of the Habeas Corpus Act, 18 U.S.C. §2243, that a federal judge must personally conduct the habeas corpus evidentiary hearing. The Court thought that the statute plainly accords a prisoner a right to testify before a judge. A federal appeals court has suggested that allowing a U.S. magistrate to evaluate the petitioner's claims to a writ of habeas corpus "could raise serious constitutional questions." Ellis v. Buchkoe, 491 F.2d 716, 717 (6th Cir. 1974). See Comment, "Masters and Magistrates in the Federal Courts," *Harvard Law Review*, 88 (February 1975): 779–803.

135. See, e.g., Macomber v. Hudspeth, 115 F.2d 114 (10th Cir. 1940), cert. denied, 313 U.S. 558 (1941).

of all the circumstances.[136] Thus an uneducated and inexperienced man doesn't waive his right if it can be shown that he did not know that he had any right to waive.[137] Where the record does not show affirmatively that the defendant was properly informed of his right to counsel, and he asserts that he knew nothing about it, then the very least a court can do, even where a plea of guilty had been entered, is to inquire into the evidence.[138] Various factors carry weight in determining whether there had been a competent waiver: the defendant's previous contacts with the criminal law, his age, maturity, and experience in life, his education and intelligence. The defendant's youth and inexperience have weighed heavily against the conclusion that there had been a competent waiver.[139] A misrepresentation by the district attorney as to when the accused is entitled to counsel negatives the inference of a proper waiver.[140] Waiver will not be inferred on the part of insane persons, since they are incompetent to make this decision.[141] It is clear, however, that a grown man who knows what he is doing may waive his right.[142] But it is equally well established that "it is the solemn duty of a federal judge before whom a defendant appears without counsel to make a thorough inquiry and to take all steps necessary to insure the fullest protection of this constitutional right at every stage of the proceedings. . . . This duty cannot be discharged as though it were a mere procedural formality."[143]

In 1966, in the *Miranda* case,[144] (which is discussed more thoroughly in chapter 9, dealing with self-incrimination) the Court spelled out in very precise language the basic rules with respect to the defendant's waiver of his right to counsel. Speaking for the Court, Chief Justice Warren stated, in very clear language, that after a person has been taken into custody, "or otherwise deprived of his freedom of action in any significant way," he must be warned, before questioning, "that he has a right to remain silent, that any statement he does make may be used as evidence against him, and that he has a right to the presence of an attorney, either retained or appointed. The defendant may waive effectuation of these rights,

---

136. The Court held in Carnley v. Cochran, 369 U.S. 506 (1962), that failure to request counsel does not constitute a waiver. Justice Brennan wrote, "Presuming waiver from a silent record is impermissible." 369 U.S. 516.

137. Evans v. Rives, 126 F.2d 633 (D.C. Cir. 1942).

138. U.S. *ex rel.* Nortner v. Hiatt, 33 F. Supp. 545 (M.D. Pa. 1940); Levine v. Hudspeth, 102 F.2d 691 (10th Cir. 1939).

139. See, e.g., Moore v. Michigan, 355 U.S. 155 (1957); Williams v. Huff, 146 F.2d 867 (D.C. Cir. 1944); Com. of Pennsylvania *ex rel.* Herman v. Claudy, 350 U.S. 116 (1956).

140. Michener v. Johnston, 141 F.2d 171 (9th Cir. 1944).

141. Honaker v. Cox, 51 F. Supp. 829 (W.D. Mo. 1943).

142. Adams v. U.S. *ex rel.* McCann, 317 U.S. 269 (1942).

143. Von Moltke v. Gillies, 332 U.S. 708, 722 (1948).

144. 384 U.S. 436 (1966).

provided the waiver is made voluntarily, knowingly and intelligently."[145] The Chief Justice went on to explain that counsel is indispensable at the interrogation; his presence mitigates the dangers of untrustworthiness, reduces the likelihood of coercion, and offers an assurance that statements made by the accused are reported correctly at the trial. Furthermore, the Chief Justice restated the point that failure to ask for a lawyer does not constitute a waiver, pointing out that the person who does not request counsel is the one who most needs one.

In general, state appellate courts agree that the constitutional right to counsel is a personal right which the accused may waive. It is also agreed that the waiver must be made voluntarily and understandingly, that the defendant must have known what he was doing when he made his decision, and that he was competent in terms of maturity and intelligence to make such a decision. State appellate courts are reluctant to accept waivers from the very young, the mentally incompetent, and the very ignorant. Where the record is unclear or silent on the point, state courts often prefer to assume that the trial judge did his full duty, indulging in a strong presumption in favor of the regularity of judicial proceedings, and requiring convincing proof to overcome it. It has been said that all doubts must be resolved "in favor of the integrity, competency and proper performance of the duties of the judge and the state's attorney."[146]

A special problem of proof is involved, however, in situations where a prisoner seeks to establish, many years after the event, that he had not enjoyed his constitutional right to counsel. The privilege of habeas corpus, it should be remembered, is never eroded by time alone. In such cases, where the records are incomplete and direct testimony may be impossible to get, the state courts seem to agree that to set aside an old judgment one must present very clear and convincing evidence, and establish his case by a substantial preponderance of evidence. In other words, the petitioner carries a heavy burden of proof.[147] Much of the difficulty in connection with the problem of proof arises from the fact that many trial courts keep

---

145. 384 U.S. 444.

146. Edgemon v. State, 195 Tenn. 496, 500, 260 S.W. 2d 262, 264 (1953).

147. See *Ex parte* Snow, 84 Okla. Cr. 423, 435, 183 P.2d 588, 594 (1947), where the Oklahoma Court of Criminal Appeals said, "Timely relief . . . should be given to a right timely asserted but when permitted to become clouded by time, with attendant lapse of memory, dislocation of witnesses, the loss of records and the grim hand of death, justice may require the denial of such rights; because, under such circumstances, the rights sought to be asserted may become mere matters of speculation based upon faulty recollection or figments of imagination, if not outright falsification." For the difficulties involved in dealing with the problem of ordering a retrial for an offense that occurred twenty-five years previously, see Loper v. Beto, 405 U.S. 473 (1972). In a dissenting opinion, Justice Blackmun argued that ordering a new trial under such circumstances amounted in fact to an enforced state acquittal and release.

faulty records of their proceedings. It would help a great deal if the legislature or state supreme court would specify that a complete written record must be prepared in every case. This has happened in a few states. In this manner later argument as to who said what to whom can be avoided.

The Question of Compensation

Until recently, lawyers appointed by federal judges to represent indigent defendants in criminal prosecutions were not allowed compensation by the government, and Congress refused to enact legislation authorizing the payment of even modest fees, until it adopted the Criminal Justice Act of 1964.[148] Until a fairly recent date, many states as well as the federal government operated on the old common law rule that an attorney, as an officer of the court, is obliged to accept a court appointment to represent an indigent, without compensation, and an unreasonable refusal on the part of the lawyer to serve was punishable under the court's contempt powers.[149] This was a curious rule since, even if one accepts the oft-repeated fiction that a lawyer is an officer of the court, he has always been the only court official who was obliged to work without being paid for his services. Furthermore, it was expecting too much to hope that, unlike other average people, an average lawyer would be motivated to do his very best if he were not to be compensated for his work. There is a very strong presumption that people are likely to function more effectively if they are paid for the work they do than if they are compelled to work for nothing. In addition, judges were reluctant to appoint big-income lawyers, whose time was very valuable and who would resent an appointment, and were therefore inclined to appoint neophytes who didn't have much to do, and were eager to get some courtroom experience. But, over the years, more and more state supreme courts ruled that an appointment of a lawyer to serve without fee in defense of indigents in criminal cases was unconstitutional as an illegal taking of private property without compensation, or as a denial of a property right without due process of law, or as a species of involuntary servitude.[150]

148. As amended in 1968 and 1970 the statute is in 18 U.S.C. §3006A (1970).

149. The leading federal case was Nabb v. United States, 1 Ct. Cl. 173 (1864). For a recent case to the same effect, see Dolan v. United States, 351 F.2d 671 (5th Cir. 1965). Many state courts ruled that in the absence of a statute, appointed counsel assigned to represent an indigent defendant could not recover compensation from the public treasury. See, e.g., Posey v. Mobile County, 50 Ala. 6 (1873); Lamont v. Solano County, 49 Cal. 158 (1874); Johnson v. Whiteside County, 110 Ill. 22 (1884); People *ex rel.* Ransom v. Niagara County, 78 N.Y. 622 (1879). For a full list of authorities, see 130 A.L.R. 1440.

150. See, e.g., County of Dane v. Smith, 13 Wis. 585, 80 Am. Dec. 754 (1861); Knox County Council v. State *ex rel.* McCormick, 217 Ind. 493, 29 N.E. 2d 405, 130 A.L.R. 1427

It cannot be asserted that under the traditional dispensation poor defendants received adequate help. Writing in 1951, a leading authority asserted, "In 1947 an estimated 97,000 persons who could not afford a lawyer faced prosecution on serious criminal charges of a type classified in many states as felonies. Not more than 22,000 were assisted by public or voluntary defender organizations. Approximately 36,000 received the frequently inadequate services of assigned private counsel, and at least 38,000 went without any form of Legal Aid whatever."[151] Since this was written the situation has improved a great deal. At the federal level, under the terms of the Criminal Justice Act of 1964, as amended, each United States district court, with the approval of the judicial council of the circuit, must put into operation a plan for furnishing representation for all defendants (except in the case of petty offenses) "who are financially unable to obtain an adequate defense." The plan may involve representation by private attorneys, or by a bar association or legal aid agency, or a combination of both. The statute also fixes a modest fee schedule at a rate not exceeding $30 per hour for time spent in court, and $20 per hour for time reasonably expended out of court, though as an alternative the judicial council of the circuit may adopt the minimum hourly scale established by a bar association in the district. The maximum is $1,000 for each attorney in a felony case, and for misdemeanors the maximum is $400. The maximum fee for representation of a defendant in an appellate court is $1,000 for each attorney. For work in connection with posttrial motions or probation revocation proceedings the maximum fee is $250. Payments in excess of these maxima may be made for "extended or complex representation" if the court certifies that an excess payment is necessary to provide fair compensation. In addition, payment for investigative services up to a maximum of $300 per case is permitted, though here again a judge has discretion to allow a larger fee "for services of an unusual character or duration." Finally, the statute permits the establishment of public defender organizations in any district where at least 200 persons annually require the appointment of counsel. The compensation of the full-time salaried attorneys attached to these organizations is fixed by the judicial council of the circuit at a rate not to exceed that received by the United States attorney for the district. Provision is also made for community defender organizations with support coming from public funds.

(1940) (well-reasoned, leading decision); State v. Rush, 46 N.J. 339, 217 A.2d 401 (1966); Bradshaw v. Ball, 487 S.W. 2d 294 (Ky. Ct. App. 1972). On the need for compensation of assigned counsel, see the excellent note in *Northwestern University Law Review*, 60 (May–June 1965): 212–23.

151. Emery A. Brownell, *Legal Aid in the United States* (Rochester, N.Y.: Lawyers Co-Operative Publ. Co., 1951), p. 86.

240 / *The Defendant's Rights Today*

The scale on which the federal statute functions is reflected in a statement made to the American Law Institute in May 1966, by Chief Justice Warren, in which he noted that under the Criminal Justice Act, from the day it went into effect on August 20, 1965, to April 30, 1966, the number of counsel appointed to represent indigents reached 12,383.[152] According to the 1972 *Report* of the Administrative Office of the U.S. Courts, during fiscal year 1972 about 50,000 persons were represented under the Criminal Justice Act, and of this total about 7,000 (14 percent) were assigned to defender organizations. The average cost per case was $206. During the year, seventy-nine claims for compensation in excess of $1,000 in felony cases were allowed; the average payment for extended or complex representation was $2,133, and the highest amount paid to any one attorney in a felony case was $7,500. The sum of $830,708 was paid out in 1972 for transcripts, investigative and other expert services. There were eight Federal Public Defender Organizations in fiscal year 1972, and the cost of their operations was approximately $1,300,000. Federal Public Defenders were assigned in 5,614 cases. Grants aggregating $672,040 were made to five Community Defender Organizations in San Diego, Chicago, Detroit, New York, and Philadelphia, and these organizations received 1,550 cases during the year. The average cost per case for Federal Public Defenders was approximately $250, and for Community Defender Organizations $340. The lower cost for Federal Public Defenders is due in part to the fact that they are housed in rent-free federal buildings.[153]

Most states now provide by statute for some compensation for appointed counsel. In some instances, very modest fees are stipulated, but in others the statute permits a "reasonable compensation" as determined by the court. In addition there are salaried full-time public defenders in some states (Alaska, New Jersey, and Colorado), in some large municipalities (e.g. Chicago, St. Louis, Memphis, Omaha, San Francisco, Milwaukee), and in about 10 percent of the counties, with over half in California and Illinois. Perhaps the best-known public defender system is that of Los Angeles County. Created in 1914, it is the largest full-time system in the country with a staff of over 360 defense attorneys, selected by civil service examination, and it has received a great deal of favorable attention.[154]

152. 34 U.S.L.W. 2643.

153. *Annual Report of the Director of the Administrative Office of the U.S. Courts, 1972* (Washington: U.S. Government Printing Office, 1973), pp. 483–87. For a broad analysis of the costs involved, see Note, "Dollars and Sense of an Expanded Right to Counsel," *Iowa Law Review,* 55 (June 1970): 1249–67.

154. See L. T. David, "Institutional or Private Counsel: A Judge's View of the Public Defender System," *Minnesota Law Review,* 45 (April 1961): 753–69; E. E. Cuff, "Public Defender System: The Los Angeles Story," *ibid.,* pp. 715–35.

There has been a long debate in the country over the relative merits of appointed counsel and public defenders. Certainly the system of appointed counsel has grave flaws. The appointment of defense counsel by judges is generally done in an altogether haphazard way. Very often a lawyer is designated for this service merely because he happens to be in the courtroom at the time the judge has to make his decision. Many judges seem to prefer to appoint young and inexperienced lawyers whose time is not very valuable, and who will not resent being asked to serve. Frequently, lawyers who know very little about the special complexities of the criminal law are appointed. Furthermore, in many big cities a group of lawyers hang around the courtroom waiting for appointments, and build up fairly good incomes through sheer volume, giving most cases very little attention. Being dependent upon the good will of the judge they are strongly inclined to humor him and not make any trouble by offering a very vigorous defense. Indeed, the appointed counsel system would work much better if defense counsel were not appointed by the judge presiding over the case. The most promising solution to the problem lies in the hands of the local bar associations, which should be encouraged, as some do, systematically to prepare panels of lawyers experienced in criminal law work, and willing to accept appointments, from which judges or court administrators could make selections.

On the other hand, the public defender concept is strongly preferred by many students of the American criminal justice system. For one thing, it is argued that the public defender system is less expensive than the appointed counsel system, though such comparative figures as are available are not conclusive on this point, and in any event, where human liberty is at stake the relatively small element of increased expense should not be permitted to carry much weight. It is also argued that the public defender system is apt to supply defendants with better criminal lawyers, since they are specialists in the field. Mr. James V. Bennett, a former Director of the Federal Bureau of Prisons, and a respected penologist, once made the point that the public defender is very valuable in shaping the attitudes of the prisoner, since by providing competent and fair representation, the bitterness engendered by the legal process is reduced, and thus rehabilitation is encouraged.[155] In addition, public defender offices usually have sufficient investigative and clerical staff to improve the quality of the defense work.

There are two criticisms often made of the public defender system, however, which cannot be ignored. One is that much too frequently the

155. James V. Bennett, "To Secure the Right to Counsel," *Journal of the American Judicature Society*, 32 (April 1949): 177–81. See also, H. L. Pollock, "Equal Justice in Practice," *Minnesota Law Review*, 45 (April 1961): 737–52.

public defender lawyer handles too many cases, and thus many defendants get only a bare minimum of rather perfunctory representation. The other is that since the public defender is, like the prosecutor, a public official, there are public officials on both sides of the counsel table. Many believe that this is inconsistent with the adversary character of American criminal justice, and that a defendant is likely, therefore, to receive more effective representation through the services of an independent appointed lawyer. This argument carries weight, as an abstract proposition, but in actual fact much depends upon who is appointed, and who does the appointing.

Whether defense counsel is an appointed lawyer or a public defender, his services are available without cost to the defendant only if he is indigent. A committee made up of members of the Judicial Conference of the United States and of the Department of Justice pointed out, in 1969, that to be eligible for appointed counsel or other defense services under the Criminal Justice Act, a person accused of a federal crime does not have to be utterly destitute; in the words of the statute, he need only be "financially unable" to obtain an adequate defense.[156] If the defendant is able to pay part of the cost of his defense, he should be required to do so, and only the balance will be provided out of public funds. As a matter of fact, there is considerable case law which is to the effect that one does not have to be a complete pauper in order to qualify for legal assistance at public expense.[157] Similarly, in a civil action, the U.S. Supreme Court once ruled that a party does not have to be absolutely destitute to enjoy the benefit of the *in forma pauperis* statute.[158]

Many states have recoupment statutes which provide that a person who has been convicted of a criminal offense must repay the state the costs of providing him with counsel if he subsequently acquires the means to bear the costs of his legal defense. In a recent case coming up from Oregon's highest court, the Supreme Court upheld the constitutionality of a recoupment statute, it being noted that repayment, under state law, is never mandatory, that there is no repayment if the defendant is convicted, that it must be shown that he is able to repay, and that the court may remit if payment will impose a manifest hardship on the defendant or his family.[159] The Court refused to believe that a requirement of repayment by

---

156. Quoted in Dallin H. Oaks, "Improving the Criminal Justice Act," *Journal of the American Bar Association,* 55 (March 1969): 217–22, 219.

157. See, e.g., Anaya v. Baker, 427 F.2d 73 (10th Cir. 1970); State v. Vallejos, 87 Ariz. 119, 348 P.2d 554 (1960); People v. Eggers, 27 Ill. 2d 85, 188 N.E. 2d 30 (1963). On the problems involved in defining indigency, see Comment, "The Definition of Indigency: A Modern-Day Legal Jabberwocky?" *St. Mary's Law Journal,* 4 (Spring 1972): 34–47.

158. Adkins v. E. I. Dupont de Nemours, 335 U.S. 331 (1948).

159. Fuller v. Oregon, 417 U.S. 40 (1974). There were two dissents, Justice Marshall arguing that since repayment could be made a condition of probation, failure to repay could send a person to prison, which amounts to imprisonment for debt.

a defendant who subsequently gains the ability to pay the expenses of legal representation without hardship chilled the exercise of the constitutional right to counsel. On the other hand, the Supreme Court held the Kansas recoupment statute invalid as a denial of the equal protection of the laws because it denied to the defendant debtor most of the protective exemptions which are available to all other debtors.[160]

Representation of Unpopular Defendants

Lawyers have a group responsibility to see to it that politically unpopular defendants are represented by counsel when they are accused of crimes. At the present time, persons accused of crimes against national security, or who are labelled as subversive or are regarded as political radicals, often experience great difficulties in getting lawyers to represent them, even though they are prepared to pay the required fees. There are very persuasive reasons which explain the reluctance of lawyers to represent such defendants: social pressures, far of loss of clients, fear of endangering later pursuit of public office, even the fear in some instances of contempt proceedings or disbarment. The American Bar Association is strongly committed to the proposition that it is the duty of the bar to represent all defendants, however unpopular.[161] President Truman called attention to this matter late in 1951 when he said,

> The Bar has a notable tradition of willingness to protect the rights of the accused. It seems to me that if this tradition is to be meaningful today it must extend to all defendants, including persons accused of such abhorrent crimes as conspiracy to overthrow the Government by force, espionage, and sabotage. Undoubtedly, some uninformed persons will always identify the lawyer with the client. But I believe that most Americans recognize how important it is to our tradition of fair trial that there be adequate representation by competent counsel. Lawyers in the past have risked the obloquy of the uninformed to protect the rights of the most degraded. Unless they continue to do so in the future, an important part of our rights will be gone.[162]

Remedies

In cases where a defendant believes or claims that his constitutional right to counsel has been denied, he has a choice among a variety of remedies available to him.[163] But most remedies are ineffectual and even

160. James v. Strange, 407 U.S. 128 (1972). On this case, see the Note in the *Kansas Law Review*, 20 (Winter 1972): 344-51.
161. See Joseph E. Downs and Alvin L. Goldman, "The Obligation of Lawyers to Represent Unpopular Defendants," *Howard Law Journal*, 9 (Winter 1963): 49-67, for a fine analysis of this problem.
162. *New York Times*, Sept. 19, 1951, p. 10, col. 4. See also the remarks of Dean Erwin N. Griswold, of the Harvard Law School, in *Harvard Law School Record*, 15, October 30, 1952.
163. See Beaney, *The Right to Counsel in American Courts*, pp. 74-76, 129-35.

worthless, and in both federal and state courts the remedy most commonly used is the writ of habeas corpus. There is never any time limit after which the writ may not be filed, and there is no limit to the number of times a prisoner may file his petitions. The traditional view has been that the writ will be granted if he can show that the court which sentenced him had no jurisdiction or lost it in the course of the proceedings. As already noted, the Supreme Court is committed to the view that denial of the constitutional right to counsel, or failure of the judge to protect it properly, results in the trial court losing jurisdiction.[164] As a matter of fact, however, the expanding concept of habeas corpus now goes beyond the classic limits of jurisdiction. Thus the federal habeas corpus statute states flatly that the writ extends to any prisoner who "is in custody in violation of the Constitution . . . of the United States."[165] Since a trial without counsel violates either the Sixth or the Fourteenth Amendments, the statute makes the writ available without regard to the traditional, technical meaning of the term "jurisdiction."

One of the great inadequacies of such postconviction remedies as the motion for a new trial or the motion in arrest of judgment is that they must be made within a very short period of time (ten days in the federal courts), and an uncounselled defendant usually loses the right to offer these motions through inaction. Furthermore, in most states the trial court's denial of these motions is not appealable, so that it hardly does any good to make them. In both state and federal courts the writ of *coram nobis* is available, through which the trial court is asked to correct its judgment on the basis of facts not in the record, that is, facts not previously known to the judge. But in most right-to-counsel cases such facts do not exist.

In 1948, mainly to relieve federal courts located in districts where federal penitentiaries exist of a heavy burden of habeas corpus work, Congress passed a statute authorizing federal prisoners, at any time, to "move the court which imposed the sentence to vacate, set aside or correct the sentence" wherever it is claimed that a constitutional or statutory right had been violated.[166] If a colorable claim is asserted, the court must hold a hearing, and a denial of the motion is appealable. But the sentencing court is not required to entertain a second or successive motion for similar relief on behalf of the same prisoner, and above all, the prisoner may not apply for a writ of habeas corpus until he has applied for relief, by motion, to the court which sentenced him, "unless it also appears that the remedy by motion is inadequate or ineffective to test the legality of his detention."

In both state and federal courts the defendant may seek to take his case

164. Johnson v. Zerbst, 304 U.S. 458 (1938).
165. 28 U.S.C. §2241 (c) (3) (1970).
166. 28 U.S.C. §2255 (1970).

up by appeal or the common law writ of error. But here again there are rigid time limits which are quickly reached (ten days in the federal courts), and since an appeal deals only with errors in the record, the defendant must file a bill of exceptions, something which is rarely possible where an uncounselled defendant failed to make exceptions in the course of the trial.

On rare occasions, as in the Scottsboro case, the issue of the constitutional right to counsel is examined by the Supreme Court in a direct review of the highest state court's affirmance of the trial court. But the issue is usually raised in the course of a habeas corpus proceeding, which reaches the federal courts in one of two ways. An application for the writ of habeas corpus may be initiated in the state courts, and following its denial by the state court of last resort, get to the Supreme Court by way of a petition for a writ of certiorari. The granting of this writ is wholly within the Court's discretion, and is reserved for cases which in the opinion of at least four Justices deserve its attention in the public interest. The vast majority of petitions for certiorari are turned down. Alternatively, a state prisoner may file application for habeas corpus in a federal district court, and if he is turned down there, and loses in the court of appeals, he may again apply to the Supreme Court for certiorari.

But it is well established that one who is imprisoned for violation of a state criminal law must first exhaust his state remedies before applying to a federal court for relief.[167] The federal courts should not and do not assume that the state courts will refuse to do what the Constitution and justice require. The necessity of first exhausting available state remedies was underscored by the 1948 revision of the federal habeas corpus statute, which now states, "An application for a writ of habeas corpus in behalf of a person in custody pursuant to the judgment of a State court shall not be granted unless it appears that the applicant has exhausted the remedies available in the courts of the State, or that there is either an absence of available State corrective process or the existence of circumstances rendering such process ineffective to protect the rights of the prisoner."[168]

While a state prisoner must exhaust all of his state remedies before petitioning a federal court for the writ, this requirement is premised on the assumption that effective state remedies are available. This important point was driven home in the course of a prolonged tussle between the Supreme Court and the State of Illinois, which reached its climax in 1947, when Justice Rutledge castigated the state for its "procedural labyrinth . . . made up entirely of blind alleys," which he described as a

---

167 Woods v. Nierstheimer, 328 U.S. 211 (1946).
168. 28 U.S.C. §2254 (b) (1970).

"merry-go-round."[169] The Illinois legislature finally clarified the situation by passing a statute in August 1949, which provides for an adequate post-conviction remedy through which such issues as the right to counsel can be raised.[170]

It remains to be noted that while the matter has been the subject of lively dispute among the Justices, it is now held that the concept of the exhaustion of state remedies does not include an application for certiorari to the Supreme Court of the United States.[171] In 1950 the Court ruled that after one has lost in his highest state court, he must try his luck with a petition for certiorari to the United States Supreme Court, which was treated as part of his state remedy, even though his chances of getting the writ are very small indeed, and even though the denial of the writ, the Court insisted, had no legal significance.[172] The 1963 decision in *Fay* v. *Noia*[173] eliminated this largely useless procedural gesture.

Right to Counsel in Military Justice

From the very beginning of the American government under the Constitution, the armed forces have had their own system of justice, and at an early date the Supreme Court ruled that the judgment of a military tribunal was not subject to direct review by a civil court.[174] But court-martial proceedings may be challenged in habeas corpus actions in a civil court,[175] after military remedies, if available, have been exhausted, and the habeas corpus court may go beyond traditional issues of a strictly jurisdictional character to inquire into the denial of constitutional rights,[176] though the scope of review tends to be more narrow than in cases decided by civilian courts.[177] It is also possible to get some review of a decision of the military courts by means of a suit in the Court of Claims for back pay,[178] though such suits are quite rare.

Although a few civil courts took the position, early on, that the accused

---

169. Marino v. Ragen, 332 U.S. 561 (1947). See also Loftus v. Illinois, 334 U.S. 804 (1948); Young v. Ragen, 337 U.S. 235 (1949).

170. Ill. Ann. Stat., c. 38, §§122-1–7 (Smith-Hurd 1964).

171. Fay v. Noia, 372 U.S. 391, 435–38 (1963).

172. Darr v. Burford, 339 U.S. 200 (1950), overruling Wade v. Mayo, 334 U.S. 672 (1948).

173. 372 U.S. 391 (1963).

174. *Ex parte* Vallandigham, 1 Wall. (U.S.) 243 (1863); Dynes v. Hoover, 20 How. (U.S.) 65 (1857).

175. *Ex parte* Reed, 100 U.S. 13 (1879). See 28 U.S.C. §2241 (1970).

176. Burns v. Wilson, 346 U.S. 137 (1953).

177. Hiatt v. Brown, 339 U.S. 103 (1950).

178. See, e.g., Begalke v. United States, 286 F.2d 606 (Ct. Cl. 1960).

had a right to counsel in a court-martial,[179] the first positive grant to the defendant of a right to counsel appeared in the *Manual for Courts-Martial* for 1916 (at p. 51), and it has been in the *Manual,* which has the force of law, ever since. The subject is now dealt with in considerable detail in the Uniform Code of Military Justice,[180] which Congress adopted in 1950, and which, among other things, created the three-judge Court of Military Appeals. In the words of Chief Justice Warren, "The Code represents a diligent effort by Congress to insure that military justice is administered in accord with the demands of due process."[181] Thus, Section 827 (a) of the Uniform Code stipulates, "For each general and special court-martial the authority convening the court shall detail trial counsel and defense counsel, and such assistants as he considers appropriate."

There are three types of court-martial, general, special, and summary. For a general court-martial, which deals with the most serious crimes, the court must be assisted by a military judge and counsel on both sides must be qualified lawyers. In a special court, which has jurisdiction over less serious crimes, defense counsel must be a lawyer only if trial counsel is a qualified attorney. In either a general or special court-martial the accused has a right to be represented by a civilian lawyer of his own choosing if he can secure one. In summary courts, which are concerned with petty offenses, counsel is unnecessary on both sides.[182] One who appeals to the U.S. Court of Military Appeals is entitled to be represented by a civilian lawyer of his own choosing or by assigned counsel. Under Article 32 of the Uniform Code the accused also has a right to counsel during the pretrial investigation of the charges. Today there exists a considerable body of precedents, developed by the U.S. Court of Military Appeals and federal civilian courts, dealing with the right to counsel in military courts.

One bone of contention in this area of military justice is that a serviceman may be put to trial before a special court-martial without being represented by a qualified lawyer, a fact which is often deplored.[183] The

---

179. One of the first cases to hold that there is a right to counsel in courts-martial in the National Guard was People *ex rel.* Garling v. Van Allen, 55 N.Y. 31 (Ct. of App. 1873).

180. 10 U.S.C.§§801–940 (1970). See Alfred Avins, "Accused's Right to Defense Counsel before a Military Court," *University of Detroit Law Journal,* 42 (October 1964): 21–53.

181. Earl Warren, "The Bill of Rights and the Military," *New York University Law Review,* 37 (April 1962): 181–203, 188.

182. For surveys of this subject, see S. Sidney Ulmer, *Military Justice and the Right to Counsel* (Lexington: University Press of Kentucky, 1970); Note, "The Uniform Code of Military Justice and the Right to Counsel," *University of Cincinnati Law Review,* 36 (Summer 1967): 472–86; Comment, "Right to Counsel and the Serviceman," *Catholic University Law Review,* 15 (May 1966): 203–33.

183. See Edward F. Sherman, "The Right to Competent Counsel in Special Courts-Martial," *American Bar Association Journal,* 54 (September 1968): 866–71.

248 / The Defendant's Rights Today

U.S. Court of Military Appeals has made it clear that the use of non-lawyers in special courts-martial violates neither the Uniform Code nor the Sixth Amendment.[184] In the case of *In re Staley,*[185] decided by the U.S. District Court for Utah in 1965, and widely noted in law journals,[186] it was ruled that an officer is not qualified to act as defense counsel, in a special court-martial trying a charge of issuing fraudulent checks, merely because he is an officer. While the Court did not insist that defense counsel must be a qualified lawyer, it declared that at the very least appointed defense counsel ought to know something about the law. While it is within the competence of Congress to control military due process, minimal constitutional law due process requirements must be met, for, the Court declared, the military service is not a "constitutionally uninhabitable wasteland."[187]

Speaking more generally, the U.S. Court of Military Justice, like the civilian courts, regards the right to counsel as a guaranty of effective representation.[188] When this Court first confronted the issue of competence, it adopted a very rigid test, insisting that to prove incompetence it must be demonstrated that the proceedings were "so erroneous as to constitute a ridiculous and empty gesture, or were so tainted with negligence or wrongful motives on the part of his counsel as to manifest a complete absence of judicial character."[189] On further reflection, however, the Court backed away from such a harsh rule;[190] and today it has been asserted by a noted scholar, "[R]ecent decisions of the Court of Military Appeals have insisted on high standards of behavior for appointed counsel."[191] As in the case of the civil courts, however, the Court of

---

184. United States v. Culp, 14 U.S.C.M.A. 199, 33 C.M.R. 411 (1963). For court decisions to the same effect, see Le Ballister v. Warden, 247 F. Supp. 349, 352 (D. Kan. 1965); Kennedy v. Commandant, 258 F. Supp. 967, 970 (D. Kan. 1966). Of course, the appointment of qualified defense counsel is an indispensable prerequisite to the jurisdiction of a general court-martial, Butler v. United States, 8 C.M.R. 692 (1953). For such a court both trial and defense counsel must be certified as professionally competent by the judge advocate general.

185. 246 F. Supp. 316 (1965).

186. See, e.g., *U.C.L.A. Law Review,* 13 (August 1966): 1419-31; *University of Pittsburgh Law Review,* 27 (March 1966): 695-700; *California Western Law Review,* 2 (Spring 1966): 121-26.

187. 246 F. Supp. 322.

188. See Paul E. Wilson, "The Right of the Accused to Effective Counsel: The Military View," *Kansas Law Review,* 14 (May 1966): 593-611.

189. United States v. Hunter, 2 U.S.C.M.A. 37, 6 C.M.R. 37 (1952).

190. See, e.g., United States v. Parker, 6 U.S.C.M.A. 75, 19 C.M.R. 201 (1955); United States v. McMahan, 6 U.S.C.M.A. 709, 21 C.M.R. 31 (1956).

191. Ulmer, *Military Justice,* p. 96. See, e.g., United States v. Huff, 29 C.M.R. 213, 11 U.S.C.M.A. 397 (1960); Oakley v. United States, 25 C.M.R. 624 (1958); United States v.

Military Appeals has been unable to work out a formula for the measurement of unacceptable incompetence, and decides each case on its own facts.[192] Overall, the level of competence insisted upon by the Court of Military Appeals compares very favorably with the position taken by the civilian courts. In addition, a serviceman is entitled to appointed counsel without regard to any question of indigency.

Right to Counsel in Non-criminal Cases

Since the Sixth Amendment applies only to "criminal prosecutions," the cluster of rights now attached to the constitutional guaranty of the right "to have the assistance of counsel" does not apply to civil cases. It follows that, as a general rule, an indigent person involved in civil litigation does not have a right to have counsel appointed to represent him.[193] A few state statutes, however, authorize the judge to appoint attorneys in cases involving indigent parties,[194] and the federal judicial code permits the judge to appoint counsel for a poor person, but he "may dismiss the case if the allegation of poverty is untrue, or if satisfied that the action is frivolous or malicious."[195] Furthermore, in March 1972, the federal District Court for the Northern District of California went so far as to rule that due process and equal protection require that a juvenile court must appoint counsel to represent indigent parents in state welfare proceedings in which the court may find their child to be neglected and remove the child from the parents' home.[196] The Court refused to determine the rights of persons threatened with fundamental deprivations on the basis of the fact that the California Code called these proceedings "civil." Whatever the label, the Court held that it was fundamentally unfair to remove a child from an indigent parent without giving the parent

---

McFarlane, 23 C.M.R. 320, 8 U.S.C.M.A. 96 (1957). In United States v. Tempia, 37 C.M.R. 249, 16 U.S.C.M.A. 629 (1967), the Court of Military Appeals ruled that the Miranda rules apply to people in the military service.

192. See Note, "The Right to Competent and Effective Counsel under the Uniform Code of Military Justice," *Tulane Law Review,* 46 (December 1971): 293-308, for an excellent survey of the problem of counsel incompetence.

193. Sandoval v. Rattikin, 395 S.W. 2d 889 (Tex. Civ. App. 1965), cert. denied, 385 U.S. 901 (1966). See Note, "The Indigent's Right to Counsel in Civil Cases," *Yale Law Journal,* 76 (January 1967): 545-62.

194. See Board of Commissioners v. Pollard, 153 Ind. 371, 55 N.E. 87 (1899).

195. 28 U.S.C. §1915 (d) (1970). See U.S. *ex rel.* Gardner v. Madden, 352 F.2d 792 (9th Cir. 1965) (such an appointment is a privilege within the discretion of the district court); Weller v. Dickson, 314 F.2d 598 (9th Cir. 1963) (appointed counsel should be allowed only in exceptional cases); De Maris v. United States, 187 F. Supp. 273 (S.D. Ind. 1960).

196. Cleaver v. Wilcox, 40 U.S.L.W. 2658 (N.D. Calif. March 22, 1972).

the assistance of counsel appointed and compensated by the state. In this sort of case, in contrast with divorce cases, the state itself is the adversary party, and there is therefore a gross inherent imbalance in experience and expertise if the parents are not represented by counsel. The Court also ruled that the desire of the state to save money is not such a compelling state interest as to justify the classification of parties in child neglect cases on the basis of ability to afford a private attorney.

Similarly, the New York Court of Appeals ruled in 1972 that the failure of the Family Court to advise an indigent parent charged with child neglect that he is entitled to assigned counsel constituted a denial of both due process and equal protection.[197] The Court held that the parent's interest in the care and control of the child was too fundamental an interest and right[198] to be relinquished to the state without a hearing, with assigned counsel if the parent lacks the means to retain a lawyer of his own choosing. In addition, it was noted that the parent faces the danger of criminal charges as well as the possible loss of his child's society. In the following year, the Supreme Judicial Court of Maine also ruled that in child neglect cases parents must be advised of their right to counsel, and offered appointed counsel at the state's expense, if they are indigent, since a finding of neglect could be the basis for a later criminal prosecution.[199] The Court held that the fact that Maine calls this a civil action was not dispositive of the issue, since the proceeding is basically accusatory, and the average parent knows nothing about legal problems.

In addition, in child abuse cases the child needs legal representation, and this is often provided for by statute or court-made rules. A computation published in 1972 indicated that seventeen states provided an absolute right to counsel for the abused child, and seventeen states gave the courts discretion in the matter; the remaining states had no legal provision on the subject.[200] Thus, the New York Family Court Act of 1962, as amended in 1970, requires notice of the right to counsel, whether retained or appointed, to all children who are involved in an abuse case.[201] In adopting this statute, the legislature declared that the guaranty of counsel was premised upon a "finding that counsel is often indispensable

---

197. *In re* B, 30 N.Y. 352, 285 N.E. 2d 288 (1972). See Note, "Child Neglect: Due Process for the Parent," *Columbia Law Review,* 70 (March 1970): 465–85.

198. Parents have a substantive constitutional right to raise their children. Stanley v. Illinois, 405 U.S. 645 (1972); May v. Anderson, 345 U.S. 528 (1953); Skinner v. Oklahoma, 316 U.S. 535 (1942); Meyer v. Nebraska, 262 U.S. 390 (1923).

199. Danforth v. State Department of Health and Welfare, 303 A.2d 794 (Me. 1973).

200. See Note, *Cornell Law Review,* 58 (November 1972): 177–90.

201. N.Y. Family Court Act, art. 10 (McKinney Supp. 1972).

to a practical realization of due process of law and may be helpful in making reasoned determinations of fact and proper orders of disposition."[202]

In addition, the Supreme Court of Alaska ruled in 1974 that an indigent person involved in a nonsupport proceeding which can result in incarceration has a due process right to court-appointed counsel.[203] The Court took the position that even though a nonsupport contempt proceeding is not normally considered a "criminal action," the possibility of being jailed is the same, and anyone facing a deprivation of liberty must be afforded all fundamental constitutional rights, including the right of representation by counsel.

While holdings that the Court must appoint counsel in civil cases are quite rare, it is well established that the due process guaranty of a fair and meaningful hearing assures to litigants representation by counsel of their own choosing.[204] Similarly, wherever there is a right to an administrative hearing, as a general rule that implies the right to representation by counsel.[205] Thus, the federal Administrative Procedure Act provides, "A person compelled to appear in person before an agency or representative thereof is entitled to be accompanied, represented and advised by counsel or, if permitted by the agency, by other qualified representative. A party is entitled to appear in person or by or with counsel or other duly qualified representative in an agency proceeding."[206] Accordingly, many courts have ruled that one has a right to be represented in such administrative proceedings as one involving the discharge of a civil service employee,[207] or a hearing before an NLRB trial examiner,[208] or the cease and desist order of an air pollution control board.[209] It is equally well established, however, that in such administrative proceedings there is no obligation on the part

---

202. *Ibid.*, §241.
203. Otton v. Zaborac, 525 P.2d 537 (Alaska 1974).
204. See Note, "The Right to Counsel in Civil Litigation," *Columbia Law Review*, 66 (November 1966): 1322–39, 1327.
205. See K. C. Davis, *Administrative Law Treatise*, vol. 1, §8.10 (St. Paul: West Publ. Co., 1958; Suppl., 1970); Note, "Representation by Counsel in Administrative Proceedings," *Columbia Law Review*, 58 (March 1958): 395–407.
206. 5 U.S.C. §555 (b) (1970).
207. Fusco v. Moses, 304 N.Y. 424, 107 N.E. 2d 581 (1952).
208. Great Lakes Screw Corp. v. N.L.R.B., 409 F.2d 375 (7th Cir. 1969).
209. Brown v. Air Pollution Control Board, 37 Ill. 2d 450, 227 N.E. 2d 754, 33 A.L.R. 3d 222 (1967). The Court said, "Even if the statute did not provide a right to counsel, in a proceeding such as here, which could affect one's property rights, the right to counsel would be undeniable. Administrative as well as judicial proceedings are governed by the fundamental principles and requirements of due process of law." 37 Ill. 2d 454.

of the government to appoint counsel for any of the parties.[210] In an important 1970 decision holding that a recipient of Aid to Families with Dependent Children is entitled to a pretermination hearing, the Supreme Court of the United States remarked, in a *dictum,* "We do not say that counsel must be provided at the pretermination hearing, but only that the recipient must be allowed to retain an attorney if he so desires."[211] Similarly, Congress stipulated in the Immigration and Naturalization Act of 1952 that in deportation cases, "the alien shall have the privilege of being represented (at no expense to the Government) by such counsel, authorized to practice in such proceedings, as he shall choose."[212] The denaturalization statute is silent on the subject of the right to counsel;[213] now although a denaturalization case is not a criminal proceeding, but one in equity,[214] it is not, on the other hand, an ordinary civil action, and as in criminal matters, the government is limited to matters charged in the complaint,[215] and the reasonable doubt standard applies.[216] It would not require much movement on the part of the courts to recognize the essentiality of counsel in such proceedings.[217]

There are some administrative proceedings where the courts have taken the position that the denial of representation by counsel is not prejudicial legal error. For example, the Adminstrative Procedure Act does not apply

---

210. See, e.g., Nees v. S.E.C., 414 F.2d 211 (9th Cir. 1969) (revocation of license of securities salesman for fraud); Boruski v. S.E.C. 340 F.2d 991 (2nd Cir. 1965), cert. denied, 381 U.S. 943 (1965) (revocation of registration of a broker-dealer); Bancroft v. Board of Governors of Registered Dentists, 202 Okla. 108, 109, 210 P.2d 666, 668 (1949) (revocation of dentist's license).

211. Goldberg v. Kelly, 397 U.S. 254, 270 (1970). As Chief Justice Berger pointed out in his dissenting opinion, HEW regulations were soon to go into effect under which the Department recognized the welfare recipient's right to appointed counsel. 45 CRF §220.25 (effective July 1970).

212. 8 U.S.C. §1252 (b) (2) (1970). See C. Gordon, "Right to Counsel in Immigration Proceedings," *Minnesota Law Review,* 45 (April 1961): 875-96.

213. 8 U.S.C. §1451 (1970).

214. Luria v. United States, 231 U.S. 9 (1913); United States v. Fischer, 48 F. Supp. 7 (S.D. Fla. 1942).

215. United States v. Stromberg, 227 F.2d 903 (5th Cir. 1955); United States v. Jackson, 55 F. Supp. 517 (E.D. Mich. 1944).

216. United States v. Wezel, 49 F. Supp. 16 (S.D. Ill. 1943). The U.S. Supreme Court has ruled that the evidence supporting a denaturalization decision must be "clear, unequivocal, and convincing." Schneiderman v. United States, 320 U.S. 118, 125 (1943); Baumgartner v. United States, 322 U.S. 665, 670 (1944); Knauer v. United States, 328 U.S. 654, 657 (1946).

217. In Klapprott v. United States, 335 U.S. 601 (1949), four Justices ruled that the lack of counsel in a denaturalization proceeding was a major flaw which, along with other procedural shortcomings, justified a reversal.

to the Selective Service System,[218] whose regulations are silent with reference to the registrant's right to be represented before the local board by legal counsel.[219] It has been repeatedly held by the courts that a selective service classification proceeding is not a criminal trial, and that the registrant is not guaranteed the right to be represented by a lawyer.[220] Similarly, in 5-4 decisions, the U.S. Supreme Court has ruled that the Constitution does not assure the right to be represented by counsel in an investigatory proceeding before a state fire marshall,[221] or in a preliminary fact-finding inquiry of a judge into alleged unethical practices of attorneys.[222] Similarly, it has been ruled that there is no legally protected right to counsel on the part of students involved in the investigative phase of a college disciplinary procedure,[223] and the Supreme Court ruled in 1975 that while a high school student must be given some sort of hearing at which he can respond to charges, before being suspended, he does not have under these circumstances a constitutional right to counsel.[224] However, while juvenile proceedings are supposed to be nonadversary in character, the Supreme Court ruled, in 1967, in the landmark case of *In re Gault*,[225] that among other basic rights, the alleged juvenile offender must be advised of his right to retained or appointed counsel.

218. 50 U.S.C. §463 (b) (1970).

219. See 32 CFR §1624.1.

220. United States v. Willis, 409 F.2d 830 (5th Cir. 1969), cert. denied, 396 U.S. 864 (1969); Nickerson v. United States, 391 F.2d 760 (10th Cir. 1968), cert. denied, 392 U.S. 907 (1968); United States v. Capson, 347 F.2d 959 (10th Cir. 1965), cert. denied, 382 U.S. 911 (1965). *Contra:* United States v. Weller, 309 F. Supp. 50 (N.D. Calif. 1969). See Note, "Right to Counsel and the Selective Service System," *William and Mary Law Review,* 10 (Spring 1969): 721-38.

221. *In re* Groban, 352 U.S. 330 (1957). See also F.C.C. v. Schreiber, 201 F. Supp. 421 (S.D. Calif. 1962). In United States v. Smith, 87 F. Supp. 293 (D. Conn. 1949), the Court ruled that one involved in a Bureau of Internal Revenue tax return investigation by a special agent has a right to counsel, but the general rule is to the contrary. See Note, "The Constitutional Right to Counsel in Tax Investigations," *University of Chicago Law Review,* 33 (Autumn 1965): 134-50. See also Note, "The Right to Counsel in an Administrative Investigatory Proceeding," *Administrative Law Review,* 16 (Summer 1964): 325-32.

222. Anonymous v. Baker, 360 U.S. 287 (1959). The four dissenters objected to what they called Star Chamber proceedings which could lay the groundwork for a later criminal prosecution.

223. Barker v. Hardway, 283 F. Supp. 228 (S.D. W. Va. 1968), aff'd. per cur., 399 F.2d 638 (4th Cir. 1968), cert. denied, 394 U.S. 905 (1969).

224. Goss v. Lopez, 419 U.S. 565 (1975). The Court was divided 5-4, the minority taking the position that the decision constituted an unwise and unwarranted interference with the local school authorities.

225. 387 U.S. 1 (1967).

8 / Searches and Seizures

Rights of Privacy

American law in many ways seeks to protect certain rights of privacy. This is the purpose of the Fourth Amendment to the U.S. Constitution, which declares, "The right of the people to be secure in their persons, houses, papers, and effects, against unreasonable searches and seizures, shall not be violated, and no Warrants shall issue, but upon probable cause, supported by Oath or affirmation, and particularly describing the place to be searched, and the persons or things to be seized." Closely allied to this guaranty is the Fifth Amendment's provision that no person "shall be compelled in any criminal case to be a witness against himself."

In a broader sense the common law has grown, in an evolving civilization, to protect other rights of privacy against invasion. Systematic attention was drawn to this aspect of the law by Samuel D. Warren and Louis D. Brandeis in a notable article published in 1890.[1] Here they described the "general right of the individual to be let alone" as an expanding concept.[2] Many years later, discussing the import of the Fourth and Fifth Amendments in an eloquent dissenting opinion, Justice Brandeis returned to this early theme: "The makers of our Constitution undertook to secure conditions favorable to the pursuit of happiness. They recognized the significance of man's spiritual nature, of his feelings and of his intellect. They knew that only a part of the pain, pleasure, and satisfactions of life are to be found in material things. They sought to protect Americans in their beliefs, their thoughts, their emotions and their sensations. They conferred, as against the government, the right to be let

---

1. "The Right to Privacy," *Harvard Law Review,* 4 (December 15, 1890): 193–220.
2. See *Restatement, Torts* §867 (1939): "A person who unreasonably and seriously interferes with another's interest in not having his affairs known to others or his likeness exhibited to the public is liable to the other." This doctrine now prevails in some sixteen jurisdictions. Leon R. Yankwich, "The Right of Privacy," *Notre Dame Lawyer,* 27 (Summer 1952): 499–528, 505. The first case squarely to recognize the right to privacy was Pavesich v. New England Life Insurance Co., 122 Ga. 190, 50 S.E. 68 (1905). The Georgia court asserted that "the right of privacy has its foundations in the instincts of nature." For an excellent general survey, see William M. Beaney, "The Constitutional Right to Privacy in the Supreme Court," in *Supreme Court Review, 1962,* Philip B. Kurland, ed. (Chicago: University of Chicago Press), pp. 212–51.

alone—the most comprehensive of rights and the right most valued by civilized men."³

Writing at a much later date concerning the underlying philosophy of the rights protected by the Fourth Amendment, Justice Jackson declared,

> These, I protest, are not mere second-class rights but belong in the catalog of indispensable freedoms. Among deprivations of rights, none is so effective in cowing a population, crushing the spirit of the individual and putting terror in every heart. Uncontrolled search and seizure is one of the first and most effective weapons in the arsenal of every arbitrary government. And one need only briefly to have dwelt and worked among a people possessed of many admirable qualities but deprived of these rights to know that the human personality deteriorates and dignity and self-reliance disappear where homes, persons and possessions are subject at any hour to unheralded search and seizure by the police.
>
> But the right to be secure against searches and seizures is one of the most difficult to protect. Since the officers are themselves the chief invaders, there is no enforcement outside of court.⁴

It is important to emphasize that like all other rights, the Fourth Amendment right to privacy belongs to everyone, the humble as well as the mighty, the bad as well as the good. Judge Thomas F. McAllister of the Sixth Circuit drew attention to this elementary proposition when he wrote, "The Fourth Amendment does not exclude from its protection a woman of the underworld. Police officers can no more violate her rights under the Constitution than they can violate those of any other person. We have heard enough in these last years, throughout the world, of the knock on the door in the nighttime, the arrest, the ransacking search, and the prison cell, to take warning. The constitutional rights of everyone are immediately imperiled when the rights, of even the outcast, the disdained, and the powerless, are trampled over with impunity."⁵ Similarly, Justice Brennan once observed, "Every householder, the good and the bad, the guilty and the innocent, is entitled to the protection designed to secure the common interest against unlawful invasion of the house."⁶

The broad scope of contemporary governmental activities invites the steady growth of information which government must gather. Enforcement of the criminal law, especially in a period of widespread concern, even alarm, with the crime rate, requires that governmental agencies engage in an enormous amount of information-gathering. The millions of people who apply for welfare, social security, medical, and other comparable services, must submit evidence regarding eligibility and entitlement.

---

3. Olmstead v. United States, 277 U.S. 438, 478 (1928).
4. Dissenting in Brinegar v. United States, 338 U.S. 160, 168 (1949).
5. Worthington v. United States, 166 F.2d 557, 568 (6th Cir. 1948).
6. Miller v. United States, 357 U.S. 301, 313 (1958).

Business people who borrow money from the government, e.g. the Small Business Adminstration, must disclose a great deal of information to public officials. The same is true for students or veterans who borrow money, or those who apply for FHA mortgages. Employers must submit detailed and voluminous reports to satisfy the requirements of the social security statutes, the income tax laws, and such regulatory statutes as the Fair Labor Standards (Wages and Hours) Act, which is policed by the Labor Department. Over 80,000,000 persons must supply detailed information to the Internal Revenue Service touching upon income, contributions, and deductions. Those who wish to sell securities must file voluminous registration statements witht the Securities and Exchange Commission. Candidates for public office must submit reports of sources of financial support. In almost countless ways, the right of privacy must yield to the requirements of government for more and more information. Of course, there is a right to privacy, but it is a mere truism to point out that it is by no means absolute in character.

In fact, the Fourth Amendment does not forbid all searches and seizures, but only "unreasonable" ones. And, as Justice Minton once observed, "what is a reasonable search is not to be determined by any fixed formula. The Constitution does not define what are 'unreasonable' searches and, regrettably, in our discipline we have no ready litmus-paper test. The recurring questions of the reasonableness of searches must find resolution in the facts and circumstances of each case."[7]

Historical Origins

The ancient maxim of the English common law that every man's home is his castle conveyed the idea of the right to privacy. Lord Chatham (Pitt), in a celebrated address in Parliament in 1766 on general warrants, declared that "the poorest man may, in his cottage, bid defiance to all the forces of the Crown. It may be frail; its roof may shake; the wind may blow through it; the storm may enter; the rain may enter; but the King of England may not enter; all his force dares not cross the threshold of the ruined tenement."[8] Though the common law gradually took a position opposed to the use of general warrants, in the turbulent sixteenth and seventeenth centuries the government often issued general warrants in proceedings in the courts of Star Chamber or High Commission in order to

---

7. Rabinowitz v. United States, 339 U.S. 56, 63 (1950).
8. Quoted in T. M. Cooley, *Constitutional Limitations*, 8th ed. (Boston: Little, Brown & Co., 1927), I: 611. For the history of the search and seizure problem, see Nelson B. Lasson, *The History and Development of the Fourth Amendment to the United States Constitution* (Baltimore: Johns Hopkins Press, 1937); Osmond K. Fraenkel, "Concerning Searches and Seizures," *Harvard Law Review*, 34 (February 1921): 361-87.

get evidence of sedition. Since the authorities did not know what would turn up, they could not be specific, as in searching for stolen goods. Particularly in actions for seditious libel against authors and printers did the resort to general warrants become quite common, though they were also utilized in the customs service, in trade regulation, and in tax collections.

The problem came to a head in the celebrated case of John Wilkes, a member of Parliament, who in 1762 began to publish anonymously the famous *North Briton* pamphlets, which tellingly criticized the current policies of the government.[9] Stung especially by Number 45, the secretary of state, Lord Halifax, issued a general warrant to search for the authors, printers, and publishers, and having found them, to seize their papers. This "fishing expedition" resulted in the arrest of forty-nine people, including Wilkes, who defied the warrant as "a ridiculous warrant against the whole English nation," and had to be carried bodily from his home. His papers were then seized, and he was locked up in the Tower for a few days. Wilkes and his associates then brought suit in the courts for false imprisonment, and received substantial verdicts. The printers were awarded judgments ranging from £200 to £400 each, and Wilkes got a judgment of £1,000 against the undersecretary who had been responsible for the execution of the warrant. Later he received a judgment of £4,000 against Lord Halifax himself. The government paid all the judgments, and Wilkes and Chief Justice Pratt, who had presided over the cases and who soon became a member of the peerage as Lord Camden, became popular heroes of liberty.

At about the same time the papers of another author, John Entick, were seized under the authority of a general warrant, and a successful suit for damages was instituted. On appeal, Lord Camden delivered an opinion which is regarded as a milestone in the history of the right of privacy.[10] He condemned the general character of the warrants, but went on to point out that they had been issued to search for evidence. Thus he connected the privilege against unreasonable searches with the privilege against self-incrimination. "It is very certain," he declared, "that the law obligeth no man to accuse himself; because the necessary means of compelling self accusation, falling upon the innocent as well as the guilty, would be both cruel and unjust; and it should seem, that search for evidence is disallowed upon the same principle." Thus Lord Camden held, first, that

---

9. See George Rudé, *Wilkes and Liberty* (Oxford: Clarendon Press, 1962).

10. Entick v. Carrington, 19 How. St. Tr. 1029 (1765). Justice Bradley has described this case as "one of the landmarks of English liberty. . . . It is regarded as one of the permanent monuments of the British Constitution. . . ." Boyd v. United States, 116 U.S. 616, 626 (1886).

general warrants were bad because they were uncertain, and that the search for evidence violated the principle against self-incrimination. Finally, the decisions of the judges were ratified by the House of Commons when it adopted a resolution in 1766, under the vigorous prodding of Pitt, condemning general warrants.

In the American colonies the big controversy arose from the fact that the customs authorities resorted to the use of general warrants, called writs of assistance, in their search for goods smuggled into the country in violation of the trade laws. One of the first great disputes between the colonies and the mother country was precipitated when the advocate general of Massachusetts Bay, James Otis, resigned his office to argue a case in which the writ of assistance was at issue. In a stirring presentation Otis argued that the general warrant was "the worst instance of arbitrary power, the most destructive of English liberty." For, he declared, "it is a power, that places the liberty of every man in the hands of every petty officer."

The resort to writs of assistance, or general warrants, to enforce the tax laws, was the basis for one of the most deeply felt objections to the policy of the British government on the part of the American colonies in the period just prior to the outbreak of organized warfare. For example, a Boston Town meeting, under the leadership of Samuel Adams, adopted "A List of Infringements and Violations of Rights" in November 1772, in which protest was expressed against the appointment by the Crown of new tax officers armed with powers of general search and seizure without specific warrants. The meeting went on to declare,

> These officers are by their commission invested with powers altogether unconstitutional, and entirely destructive to that security which we have a right to enjoy; and to the last degree dangerous, not only to our property, but to our lives. . . . Thus our houses and even our bed chambers are exposed to be ransacked, our boxes, chests, and trunks broke open, ravaged and plundered by wretches, whom no prudent man would venture to employ even as menial servants; whenever they are pleased to say they *suspect* there are in the house wares, etc., for which the dutys have not been paid. Flagrant instances of the wanton exercise of this power, have frequently happened in this and other seaport towns. By this we are cut off from that domestick security which renders the lives of the most unhappy in some measure agreable. . . ."[11]

The rule against general warrants received its first formal constitutional statement in the Virginia Bill of Rights of June 12, 1776, the tenth section of which declared "that general warrants, whereby an officer or messenger

---

11. S. E. Morrison, ed., *Sources and Documents Illustrating the American Revolution, 1764-1788,* 2d ed. (Oxford: Clarendon Press, 1929), p. 92.

may be commanded to search suspected places without evidence of a fact committed, or to seize any person or persons not named, or whose offence is not particularly described and supported by evidence, are grievous and oppressive, and ought not to be granted." Thereafter, a clause on searches and seizures was included in every state bill of rights, though the language varied, especially in that some clauses required an oath or affirmation for the issuance of the warrants, and some did not. Article 14 of the Massachusetts Declaration of Rights of 1780 was the first to use the phrase "unreasonable searches and seizures," thus going beyond merely forbidding general warrants. The language of the Fourth Amendment is almost identical with that of the Massachusetts clause.

Searches and Seizures by Private Parties

While the law on searches and seizures has many growing edges, and at some crucial points is subject to deep divisions of opinion,[12] some propositions are well established. For one thing, the Supreme Court ruled in *Burdeau v. McDowell*[13] that the protection of the Fourth Amendment applies only to governmental action, and not to the action of private persons. In this instance McDowell's office was entered by representatives of a company by which he had been employed, and they broke the locks of his private desk, blew open the lock of his private safe, took his private papers and delivered them to the Department of Justice for use in a mail fraud investigation. The Supreme Court held that the papers could be used, since the Fourth Amendment was intended as a restraint only upon the activities of government, and in this instance no official had anything to do with the wrongful seizure, although it was also pointed out that the individual had a right of redress against those who took his private papers illegally. Justice Brandeis and Holmes protested in dissent that "respect for law will not be advanced by resort, in its enforcement, to means which shock the common man's sense of decency and fair play." They refused to believe that the action of a public official is necessarily lawful because it does not violate a constitutional prohibition. While this decision was

---

12. For surveys of the law, see J. W. Landynski, *Search and Seizure and the Supreme Court* (Baltimore: The Johns Hopkins Press, 1966); E. G. Trimble, "Search and Seizure under the Fourth Amendment as Interpreted by the United States Supreme Court," *Kentucky Law Journal,* 41 (January, May 1953): 196-215, 388-413, and 42 (January, March 1954): 197-231, 423-54; E. W. Machen, Jr., *The Law of Search and Seizure* (Chapel Hill: Institute of Government, University of North Carolina, 1950); John J. Cogan, Jr., *The Law of Search and Seizure* (Chicago: Office of State's Attorney, Cook County, 1950); Note, "The Federal Search and Seizure Exclusionary Rule," *Journal of Criminal Law, Criminology and Police Science,* 45 (May-June 1954): 51-61.

13. 256 U.S. 465 (1921).

promptly denounced as placing "a premium on lawlessness,"[14] it remains an authoritative interpretation of the Fourth Amendment.

A quite different situation was created where evidence was seized unlawfully by state officials and then turned over to federal officials to be used in a federal prosecution, before the Court applied the Fourth Amendment to the states. In several cases decided in the 1920s involving enforcement of the prohibition laws, the Supreme Court ruled that evidence secured illegally by state officials may not be used by federal officials who had cooperated with the state officials in the wrongful search and seizure.[15] But in 1949 the Court announced the so-called "silver platter" rule, which meant, as Justice Frankfurter phrased it, "that a search is a search by a federal official if he had a hand in it; it is not a search by a federal official if evidence secured by state authorities is turned over to the federal authorities on a silver platter."[16] The "silver platter" doctrine, however, was destined to enjoy a very short life, for in 1960, by a 5-4 vote, the Court repudiated it.[17] Having ruled, in *Wolf* v. *Colorado* (1949)[18] that the Fourteenth Amendment prohibits unreasonable searches and seizures by state officers, the Court majority felt that the underpinning for the admissibility rule as to state-seized evidence being used in a federal court had been removed. Justice Stewart could see no logical distinction between evidence obtained in violation of the Fourth Amendment, and evidence secured in violation of the Fourteenth, nor did he think it mattered to the victim whether his constitutional right had been invaded by a federal agent or by a state officer. He also noted that when a federal court admits evidence lawlessly seized by state agents, it frustrates state policy, in a particularly inappropriate and ironic way. He insisted that "the imperative of judicial integrity" forbade wilful disobedience by the federal judges of a Constitution they are sworn to uphold.[19]

Finally, it should be noted that in *Rea* v. *United States* (1956),[20] though again by a 5-4 vote, the Court ruled that a federal district court has the duty to enjoin a federal agent from testifying in a state court as to evidence secured unlawfully on the basis of an improper warrant. The Court

14. Forrest R. Black, "Burdeau v. McDowell: A Judicial Mile-Post on the Road to Absolutism," *Boston University Law Review,* 12 (January 1932): 32-40.

15. Gambino v. United States, 275 U.S. 310 (1927); Byars v. United States, 273 U.S. 28 (1927).

16. Lustig v. United States, 338 U.S. 74, 78 (1949).

17. Elkins v. United States, 364 U.S. 206 (1960). The dissenting opinion was filed with a companion case, Rios v. United States, 364 U.S. 253 (1960).

18. 338 U.S. 25 (1949).

19. For a later application of this rule see Preston v. United States, 376 U.S. 364 (1964).

20. 350 U.S. 214 (1956). See Note, *Columbia Law Review,* 56 (June 1956): 940-43.

avoided constitutional issues pressed upon it, preferring to rule on the basis of its supervisory powers over federal law enforcement agencies. Pointing out that no action was sought against a state official, "[T]o enjoin the federal agent from testifying," Justice Douglas wrote, "is merely to enforce the federal Rules against those owing obedience to them."[21] The four dissenting Justices rejected the proposition that federal courts share with the executive branch of the government responsibility for supervising law enforcement activities as such.[22]

The Fourth and Fifth Amendments

It is important to remember that the Fourth Amendment does not forbid all searches and seizures, but only unreasonable searches and seizures. While legislative bodies and executive agencies both define the range of permissible action in this area, in the first instance, in our system of government these matters are ultimately for the courts to decide. That the protection against unreasonable searches and seizures is closely related to the Fifth Amendment privilege against self-incrimination, so far as a determination of the question of reasonableness is concerned, was established by the Supreme Court in one of the earliest decisions on this subject, *Boyd* v. *United States*.[23] This decision also construed the meaning of search and seizure broadly, beyond the surface significance of the phrase. In this litigation the Court held unconstitutional an act of Congress adopted in 1874 which provided that in noncriminal proceedings for forfeiture under the customs laws, federal courts may require the production of invoices called for by the prosecutor, and that in the event of a failure to bring them in, the allegations of the government would be regarded as admitted.

The Court held that this statute was defective for two reasons: it authorized an unreasonable search, and it compelled the claimant of the property under forfeiture to testify against himself. The importance of the first point lies in the fact that the concept of a search and seizure was extended far beyond such obvious events as breaking into a house or opening boxes and drawers. Justice Bradley said that the Fourth Amendment guaranty applies "to all invasions, on the part of the Government and its employees, of the sanctity of a man's home and the privacies of life. . . . Any forcible and compulsory extortion of a man's own testimony or of his private papers to be used as evidence to convict him of crime or to

---

21. 350 U.S. 217.
22. See James A. Eichner, "Impact of the Rea Case on the Law of Illegal Search and Seizure," *University of Florida Law Review*, 9 (Summer 1956): 178-92. The Court limited the thrust of the Rea Case in Wilson v. Schnettler, 365 U.S. 381 (1961).
23. 116 U.S. 616 (1886).

forfeit his goods is within the condemnation" of the Constitution. And he added, "In this regard the Fourth and Fifth Amendments run almost into each other." He noted that the "unreasonable searches and seizures" condemned by the Fourth Amendment are almost always made for the purpose of compelling a man to give evidence against himself. He was "unable to perceive that the seizure of a man's private books and papers to be used in evidence against him is substantially different from compelling him to be a witness against himself."

Furthermore, the Court distinguished in the *Boyd* case between the search for things which are themselves prohibited and for books and papers sought as evidence. The law has long recognized as reasonable a search and seizure "of stolen or forfeited goods or goods liable to duties and concealed to avoid the payment thereof," but these "are totally different things from a search for and seizure of a man's private books and papers for the purpose of obtaining information therein contained, or of using them as evidence against him. . . . In the one case, the Government is entitled to the possession of the property; in the other it is not."[24]

Thus the *Boyd* decision established several propositions:

1. Any measure, regardless of its form, which accomplishes the same result as an unauthorized search, is deemed to be similarly repugnant to the Fourth Amendment.
2. The compulsory production of a man's private papers to establish a case for the forfeiture of property is as illegal as it would be to establish a criminal charge against him. At the very least, proceedings for the forfeiture of property were regarded as quasi-criminal.
3. A search and seizure of private papers in effect compels a man to testify against himself in violation of the Fifth Amendment privilege against self-incrimination, and therefore such a search and seizure is unreasonable, and repugnant to the Fourth Amendment.
4. There is a constitutional difference between a search for things which are themselves prohibited, such as stolen goods, and a search for books and papers sought as evidence, the latter being illegal.

The Search Warrant

Rule 41(a) of the Federal Rules of Criminal Procedure authorizes issuance of a search warrant, upon request of a federal law enforcement officer or government attorney, by a federal magistrate or a judge of a state within the district wherein the property sought is located. State statutes and rules of court have similar provisions authorizing various classes of judges or magistrates to sign search warrants. The underlying

---

24. 116 U.S. 630, 633, 623.

idea is that the decision to enter a home or other structure to search for evidence of crime is a serious matter which should ordinarily be decided upon by an independent judicial officer not directly involved in law enforcement. In a well-known statement, Justice Jackson explained the supporting rationale as follows:[25]

> The point of the Fourth Amendment, which often is not grasped by zealous officers, is not that it denies law enforcement the support of the usual inferences which reasonable men draw from evidence. Its protection consists in requiring that those inferences be drawn by a neutral and detached magistrate instead of being judged by the officer engaged in the often competitive enterprise of ferreting out crime. Any assumption that evidence sufficient to support a magistrate's disinterested determination to issue a search warrant will justify the officers in making a search without a warrant would reduce the Amendment to a nullity and leave the people's homes secure only in the discretion of police officers. Crime, even in the privacy of one's own quarters, is, of course, of grave concern to society, and the law allows such crime to be reached on proper showing. The right of officers to thrust themselves into a home is also a grave concern, not only to the individual but to a society which chooses to dwell in reasonable security and freedom from surveillance. When the right of privacy must reasonably yield to the right of search is, as a rule, to be decided by a judicial officer, not by a policeman or Government enforcement agent.

Since the basic objective of the search warrant procedure is that the decision to search should preferably be made by a "neutral and detached magistrate," the Supreme Court has ruled that it was improper for a state attorney general in active charge of a murder investigation, and later chief prosecutor at the trial, to sign the search warrant in his capacity as a justice of the peace.[26] On the other hand, the Court has decided that the clerk of a municipal court qualifies as a "neutral and detached magistrate" in issuing warrants of arrest for breaches of local ordinances.[27] In a unanimous decision, the Court noted that it has never been held that only a lawyer or judge can grant a warrant, and that the label is not determinative. What matters is that he who issues the warrant is neutral and detached, and is capable of determining probable cause. In this instance it was stressed that the clerk was not tied up with prosecutors or the police, but that he was attached to a judge, and that there was no showing that he lacked the capacity to handle the problems involved in making not too difficult decisions. Indeed, the Court thought that it should be recognized that the states have discretion and flexibility in dealing with this matter, and that since local judges are very busy, the clerk may well do a better job of it precisely because the judge is so preoccupied with his duties.

25. Johnson v. United States, 333 U.S. 10, 13-14 (1948).
26. Coolidge v. New Hampshire, 403 U.S. 443 (1971).
27. Shadwick v. City of Tampa, 407 U.S. 345 (1972).

Rule 41(b) of the Federal Rules of Criminal Procedure describes the property which may be seized with a warrant as follows: "(1) property that constitutes evidence of the commission of a criminal offense; or (2) contraband, the fruits of crime, or things otherwise criminally possessed; or (3) property designated or intended for use or which is or has been used as the means of committing a criminal offense." This definition of what may be searched for and seized under a search warrant is a distillation of the position asserted by the Supreme Court in 1921 in the landmark case of *Gouled v. United States.*[28] In holding that it would be unlawful to authorize a search for such evidence as personal papers—for that would violate the privilege against self-incrimination—the Court in *Gouled* limited the scope of search and seizure under warrant to "stolen or forfeited property, or property liable to duties, and concealed to avoid payment of them, excisable articles, and books required by law to be kept with respect to them, counterfeit coin, burglars' tools and weapons, implements of gambling, 'and many other things of like character'. . . ."[29] Basically, the Rule limits the classes of property which may be searched for and seized to either stolen property to which the holder has no legal claim, or property used to commit a crime, a search for such property being reasonable.

In 1967, in the important case of *Warden v. Hayden,*[30] the Court seriously modified the "mere evidence" rule by, in effect, overruling the *Gould* decision. Hayden had been convicted of armed robbery by a Maryland court, and in the course of his trial items of clothing (a cap, jacket, and trousers) which identified him, and which were seized during a search of his home, were admitted in evidence. After being denied habeas corpus by a federal district court, the court of appeals by divided vote reversed on the ground that the seized clothing was improperly admitted in evidence because these items had "evidential value only," and were therefore not lawfully subject to seizure. The Supreme Court reversed, holding that nothing in the language of the Fourth Amendment supports the distinction between "mere evidence" and the instrumentalities of crime, fruits of crime, or contraband. In fact, Justice Brennan characterized the distinction, however familiar, as "wholly irrational, since, depending on the circumstances, the same 'papers and effects' may be 'mere evidence' in one case and 'instrumentality' in another."[31] He maintained that the old distinction, resting on concepts of relative interests in property, has been discredited, and that the premise of *Gouled,* that the

28. 225 U.S. 298 (1921).
29. 225 U.S. 308.
30. 387 U.S. 294 (1967).
31. 387 U.S. 302.

government may not seize evidence for the mere purpose of proving crime, has also been discredited. He argued that the fact that the government may search to obtain evidence which would aid in apprehending and convicting criminals was settled in the *Schmerber* case,[32] involving the taking of blood-samples to establish alcoholic content. It has long been a fiction, said Justice Brennan, that the government must assert some property interest in the material it seizes; the main object of the Fourth Amendment is to protect privacy rather than property, and therefore all that is required is a nexus between the item seized and criminal behavior. While it is true that Congress has never authorized the issuance of search warrants for the seizure of mere evidence of crime, Justice Brennan maintained that in *Gouled* the Court needlessly concluded that the Constitution limits searches and seizures to the categories of fruits of crime, instrumentalities of crime, and contraband. At the same time, however, Justice Brennan very carefully noted that since the items of clothing were not "testimonial" or "communicative" in nature, their introduction did not compel the defendant to become a witness against himself in violation of the Fifth Amendment.

In a concurring opinion in which Chief Justice Warren joined, Justice Fortas argued that the Court's repudiation of the "mere evidence" rule was so unneccessarily broad as to constitute a dangerous step towards general searches. He thought that the introduction in evidence of identifying clothing worn in the commission of a crime, and seized during hot pursuit, was a reasonable and specific exception to the "mere evidence," rule, but he would not "drive an enormous and dangerous hole" in the constitutional guaranty to accommodate it. Justice Douglas dissented alone, arguing that the government may not seize "testimonial" evidence, such as clothing, and use it at the trial. He also repeated the objections he had previously put into the record when he dissented in the *Schmerber* case.

It should be noted that the *Hayden* case involved action by state police; the scope of federal searches and seizures would still be limited to what is authorized by federal statutes or rules of court. Some state laws are more specific, and often more sweeping than existing federal rules. For example, the statutes of North Carolina authorize warrants to search for and seize stolen property, false or counterfeit coins, notes, bills or bonds and instruments used to counterfeit them, personal property used in connection with gambling and lotteries, liquor illegally possessed for the purpose of sale, game taken in violation of game laws, reused beverage bottles, and deserting seamen.[33] Some states have more sweeping clauses on this subject. Thus Wisconsin statutes, in addition to listing certain

32. Schmerber v. California, 384 U.S. 757 (1966).
33. Machen, *The Law of Search and Seizure*, p. 4.

types of property, such as stolen property, obscene matter and forged instruments, provide that warrants may issue to search for and seize "anything which is the fruit of, has been used in the commission of, or which may constitute evidence of any crime."[34]

Rule 41 goes on to provide that a warrant shall issue only on an affidavit sworn to before a federal magistrate or state judge, who grants the warrant if satisfied "that grounds for the application exist or that there is probable cause to believe that they exist." The warrant must identify the property and name or describe the person or place to be searched. This is strictly in accord with the command of the Fourth Amendment, and such are the requirements also of state law. Further, the Rule provides that the finding of probable cause may be based in whole or in part on hearsay evidence, that is to say, on evidence which would not be legally admissible at a trial. The warrant must be executed and returned within ten days,[35] and it must be served in the daytime, unless "for reasonable cause shown" the issuing authority authorizes its execution at some other time. The officer taking property under a warrant must give the person involved a copy of the warrant and a receipt for the property taken. "The return shall be made promptly and shall be accompanied by a written inventory of any property taken."

The basic key to warrant procedure is that a neutral and detached magistrate makes a finding of "probable cause," and it is impossible to define with any precision the meaning of this phrase. It is certain, however, that the magistrate may rely upon facts based on the affiant's personal knowledge of what he saw. "In determining what is probable cause," Justice Stone once said, "we are not called upon to determine whether the offense charged has in fact been committed. . . . If the apparent facts set out in the affidavit are such that a reasonably discreet and prudent man would be led to believe that there was a commission of the offense charged, there is probable cause justifying the issuance of a warrant."[36] Thus a judge would be within bounds in granting a warrant on the basis of odors alone, such as the distinctive odors of burning opium, if the officer was qualified to identify the odor.[37] Certainly he may rely upon an experienced officer's testimony as to something he saw himself.[38] But

---

34. Wis. Stat. 1973, §968.13.

35. Some states have specific time limits of varying duration; others merely require that the warrant be executed "forthwith" or within a reasonable period of time. The Supreme Court has ruled that after the ten days have run a federal warrant cannot be redated and reissued. Sgro v. United States, 287 U.S. 206 (1932).

36. Dumbra v. United States, 268 U.S. 435, 441 (1925). See also United States v. Ventresca, 380 U.S. 102 (1965).

37. Johnson v. United States, 333 U.S. 10 (1948).

38. Steele v. United States, No. 1, 267 U.S. 498 (1925).

it is never sufficient for the officer merely to recite that he has cause to suspect a law violation, without more. The Supreme Court has declared, "Under the Fourth Amendment, an officer may not properly issue a warrant to search a private dwelling unless he can find probable cause therefor from the facts or circumstances presented to him under oath or affirmation. Mere affirmance of belief or suspicion is not enough."[39] It is well established, however, that a magistrate may issue a warrant based on information supplied to the affiant officer by an unidentified informer, so long as there is a substantial factual basis for believing the informer.[40] Of course, no federal warrant may be issued unless an offense as defined by an act of Congress is alleged to have been committed.[41]

The authority to search must be described with some precision by the language of the warrant. In one case, a warrant to search a dwelling was issued pursuant to a state sedition act, and under it the officers searched the home for five hours and seized about three hundred different publications, as well as many private documents, such as files of personal correspondence, insurance policies, a marriage certificate, and household bills and receipts. The Supreme Court held this clearly unconstitutional as a general warrant, the very thing the Fourth Amendment was intended to prohibit.[42]

It is important to understand, as Justice Goldberg once put it, that in determining probable cause the magistrate must not serve as a mere rubber stamp for the police, that the magistrate must not accept without question a mere conclusion, but must make sure that a finding of probable cause is supported by credible facts and circumstances.[43] Thus,

39. Nathanson v. United States, 290 U.S. 41, 47 (1933). See also Byars v. United States, 273 U.S. 28, 29 (1927); Go-Bart Co. v. United States, 282 U.S. 344 (1931). A well-recognized exception exists with reference to enforcement of the customs laws. A statute permits a customs officer to search any vehicle or person if he "shall suspect there is merchandise which is subject to duty." He may also search any trunk or other container "in which he may have reasonable cause to suspect there is merchandise which was imported contrary to law." 19 U.S.C. §482 (1970).

40. United States v. Harris, 403 U.S. 573 (1971); Jones v. United States, 362 U.S. 257 (1960); Draper v. United States, 358 U.S. 307 (1959). The informer plays a vital part in criminal law enforcement, and refusal of the police to identify the informer has been upheld as to state courts, McCray v. Illinois, 386 U.S. 300 (1967), and federal courts, Roviaro v. United States, 353 U.S. 53 (1957).

41. Grau v. United States, 287 U.S. 124 (1932); United States v. Berkeness, 275 U.S. 149 (1927).

42. Stanford v. Texas, 379 U.S 476 (1965). Especially where books and ideas are involved, said the Court, there is need for "scrupulous exactitude" in spelling out what may be seized. For another example of what the Court condemned as a general serarch, see Kremen v. United States, 353 U.S. 346 (1957), which involved the seizure of the entire contents of a house and their removal to FBI offices some two hundred miles away.

43. Aguilar v. Texas, 378 U.S. 108 (1964).

a supporting affidavit is inadequate where the affiants merely say that they "have received reliable information from a credible person," without any explanation as to why the information is reliable and why the informer is to be considered credible.[44]

The settled law in that states is to the same effect, that an affidavit made only on information and belief, without the support of facts, is insufficient to justify the issuance of a warrant.[45] Furthermore, now that the proscriptions of the Fourth Amendment are enforced against the states through the Fourteenth, the standard of reasonableness is the same for both federal and state authorities.[46]

Leaving out qualifying considerations or rules that prevail in some jurisdictions and not in others, the principal requirements for a valid search warrant are as follows:

1. There must be a showing of probable cause; mere affirmation or belief is not sufficient; underlying facts must be brought to the attention of the magistrate.
2. The statement of facts supporting probable cause must be made on oath or affirmation.[47]
3. The warrant must describe with certainty the place to be searched though this need not be the sort of precise legal description one finds in a deed. It is not necessary to give the name of the owner or occupant if the facts stated definitely describe the place.
4. "The goods to be seized under a search warrant must be described with such certainty that they may be identified and with such particularity that the officer charged with the execution of the warrant will be left with no discretion respecting the property to be taken."[48]

Generally speaking, the rule is that the searching officer may seize only the property described in the warrant. Whether he may also seize other

---

44. 378 U.S. 108. A similar decision was made on similar facts in Spinelli v. United States, 393 U.S. 410 (1969).

45. See People v. Moten, 233 Mich. 169, 206 N.W. 506 (1925).

46. Ker v. California, 374 U.S. 23 (1963).

47. In People v. Alfinito, 16 N.Y. 2d 181, 264 N.Y.S. 2d 243 (1965), the New York Court of Appeals broke new ground by holding that a criminal defendant has a right to challenge a search and seizure by attacking the facts on which a search warrant issued, though it also held that the burden of proof is on the person attacking the warrant, and that any fair doubt should be resolved in favor of the warrant. Most jurisdictions hold the other way. See, e.g., Kenney v. United States, 157 F.2d 442 (App. D.C. 1946); United States v. Brunett, 53 F.2d 219, 225 (W.D. Mo. 1931); Johnson v. State, 163 Tex. Cr. Rep. 101, 289 S.W. 2d 249 (1956); Armstrong v. State, 195 Miss. 300, 15 So. 2d 438 (1943); Burrell v. State, 207 Md. 278, 113 A.2d 884 (1955).

48. People v. Sovetsky, 343 Ill. 583, 588, 175 N.E. 844, 846 (1931).

property which he stumbles onto in the course of his search presents an issue which is not clearly defined in the reported cases. In a dissenting opinion, Justice Frankfurter once declared that "if, in the course of a valid search, materials are uncovered, the very possession or concealment of which is a crime, they may be seized."[49] While a federal circuit court once ruled that "it may be laid down as a principle that where a search is justifiable and legal for the purpose of obtaining the instrumentalities of the commission of a particular crime, the seizure of evidence that an entirely different crime may have been committed is not justified by the circumscribed authority for the legal search,"[50] many decisions hold the other way.[51] The Supreme Court and lower federal courts have often upheld convictions based on evidence not described in the search warrant. Thus, officers searching for canceled checks were allowed to seize draft cards which the accused had no legal right to possess,[52] and a seizure of counterfeit stamps by an officer searching for illegal liquor has been upheld.[53] While there seems to be some confusion of thought on this subject, the Criminal Division of the Department of Justice seems to have no doubts. In a *Handbook on the Law of Search and Seizure,* as revised in February 1971, it advised federal agents in the following unequivocal language (at p.10): "While conducting a search for the property described in the warrant, an agent may also seize property which is the subject matter of a different crime. For example, if an agent is searching for a roulette wheel and comes upon stolen fur coats, he may seize the coats, even though not authorized specifically to do so by the search warrant."

Scope of the Guaranty

The guaranty of the Fourth Amendment extends primarily to the person of the individual and his dwelling. While it may also extend to business places, the law has been consistently more fastidious about protecting the privacy of the home. "The search of a private dwelling without a warrant," the Supreme Court has said, "is in itself unreasonable and abhorrent to our laws. Congress has never passed an act purporting to authorize the search of a house without a warrant." Except in certain

---

49. Zap v. United States, 328 U.S. 624, 632 (1946).
50. Takahashi v. United States, 143 F.2d 118, 124 (9th Cir. 1944).
51. See, e.g., Paper v. United States, 53 F.2d 184 (4th Cir. 1931); Haverstick v. State, 196 Ind. 145, 147 N.E. 625 (1925); People v. Harter, 244 Mich. 346, 221 N.E. 302 (1928).
52. Harris v. United States, 331 U.S. 145 (1947).
53. United States v. Seltzer, 5 F.2d 364 (D. Mass. 1925). See also Milam v. United States, 296 Fed. 629 (4th Cir. 1924), cert. denied, 265 U.S. 586 (1924) (search for liquor turned up illegal aliens); United States v. Charles, 8 F.2d 302 (N.D. Calif. 1925) (search for narcotics turned up liquor).

cases incidental to arrest, "belief, however well founded, that an article sought is concealed in a dwelling house furnishes no justification for a search of that place without a warrant. And such searches are held unlawful notwithstanding facts unquestionably showing probable cause."[54] But the guaranty does not extend to searches and seizures in the open fields. Justice Holmes once declared that the distinction between houses and open fields is "as old as the common law."[55] Nor does the guaranty extend to personal papers no longer in the owner's possession, and lawfully in the hands of someone else. Thus when a man's records are in the hands of a court-appointed receiver, pursuant to a bankruptcy proceeding, he cannot object to the use of the records as evidence by the public prosecutor.[56] But the guaranty does extend to letters and sealed packages in the mail; while in the mail they can be opened and examined only by authority of a search warrant.[57]

While corporations are not entitled to the protection of the privilege against self-incrimination, which is wholly a personal right applying only to natural individuals, it is settled law, ever since the *Silverthorne* case,[58] that corporations enjoy the Fourth Amendment protection against unreasonable searches and seizures. But it is established that an officer of a corporation who has custody of its records may not refuse to produce them because they may disclose guilt on his part, since he does not hold them in his private capacity.[59] Similarly, one who serves as the representative of a

54. Agnello v. United States, 269 U.S. 20, 32, 33 (1925). While the Court has taken a broad view of the places as to which the constitutional immunity from unreasonable searches may be claimed—e.g., dwellings, business offices, stores, hotel rooms, apartments, and automobiles—it has drawn the line at jails, holding that a jail has none of the attributes of privacy which are at the basis of the general rule. Lanza v. New York, 370 U.S. 139 (1962). See also Stroud v. United States, 251 U.S. 15 (1919).

55. Hester v. United States, 265 U.S. 57 (1924). For more recent cases invoking the open fields doctrine, see Air Pollution Variance Board of Colorado v. Western Alfalfa Corp., 416 U.S. 861 (1974) (visual inspection of smoke pollution without entering the building); United States v. Brown, 473 F.2d 952 (5th Cir. 1973) (digging under a chicken coop in an open field); Care v. United States, 231 F.2d 22 (10th Cir. 1956), cert. denied, 351 U.S. 932 (1956) (still discovered about 125 yards from the house); People v. Bradley, 1 Cal. 3rd 80, 460 P.2d 129 (1969) (seizure of marijuana plants in the back yard). In all the open field cases search had been without warrant.

56. Dier v. Banton, 262 U.S. 147 (1923).

57. *Ex parte* Jackson, 96 U.S. 727 (1878). In United States v. Van Leeuwen, 397 U.S. 249 (1970), the Court held that detention of packages at the post office for twenty-nine hours after posting as first class mail while a search warrant was being obtained, was not unreasonable under the Fourth Amendment, where there were several suspicious circumstances justifying the delay.

58. Silverthorne Lumber Co. v. United States, 251 U.S. 385 (1920). This point had been assumed in Hale v. Henkel, 201 U.S. 43 (1906).

59. Essgee Co. v. United States, 262 U.S. 151 (1923).

collective group, such as a trade union or political association, may not refuse to produce papers which are not his own personal property. The reason for this rule, it has been explained, is that organizations, whether incorporated or not, must, because of their "scope and nature," submit to governmental regulation, and a cloak of privilege would make effective law enforcement impossible.[60]

Several very recent decisions of the Supreme Court have brought within the ambit of the Fourth Amendment problems not usually thought of as involving search and seizure questions. In *Davis* v. *Mississippi*[61] (1969), for example, the Court held that unlawful detention of a young arrestee for the sole purpose of obtaining his fingerprints was subject to the limits prescribed by the Fourth Amendment. The Court ruled that the Fourth Amendment applies to the investigatory stage of a criminal proceeding, and indeed, that detention of the defendant in itself constituted an unreasonable seizure of his person contrary to the Fourth Amendment. Justice Black argued in dissent that this was a wholly unnecessary expansion of the Fourth Amendment, and Justice Stewart protested that fingerprints are not evidence in the conventional sense, as are weapons or stolen goods. On the other hand, in *Cupp* v. *Murphy*[62] (1973), the Court held that the taking of fingernail scrapings from a strangulation suspect, over his protest and without a warrant, was not an unreasonable search and seizure where probable cause existed for an arrest. The Court thought that this limited search was reasonable in the effort to preserve highly evanescent evidence; the intrusion into the person was very limited, and the evidence readily destructible. Speaking in dissent, Justice Douglas maintained that the police should have been required to get a search warrant from a magistrate, and Justice Brennan would have remanded the case for a probable cause determination. Finally, in *United States* v. *Dionisio*[63] (1973), the Court held that an order of a federal grand jury requiring a witness to make voice exemplars for identification purposes, without a preliminary showing of reasonableness, did not violate the Fourth Amendment, since the exemplar compelled production of a physical characteristic which is constantly exposed to the public. In a companion case decided the same day, *United States* v. *Mara*,[64] a similar conclusion was reached with respect to a grand jury's requirement of handwriting exemplars. It was emphasized that since handwriting, like

60. United States v. White, 322 U.S. 694 (1944). See also Schenck v. United States, 249 U.S. 47 (1919).
61. 394 U.S. 721 (1969).
62. 412 U.S. 291 (1973).
63. 410 U.S. 1 (1973).
64. 410 U.S. 19 (1973).

speech, is repeatedly shown to the public, there is no more expectation of privacy in regard to the physical characteristics of a person's script than there is in the tone of his voice.

Administrative Searches

The question as to whether warrantless searches taking the form of administrative inspections can be squared with the Fourth Amendment has been litigated in the Supreme Court many times, particularly in recent years. In the field of health inspection the Court was confronted with this sort of issue in 1959, in *Frank* v. *Maryland*,[65] which was decided by a 5–4 vote. The issue was the constitutionality of a Baltimore ordinance of very ancient vintage which authorized health department inspectors to demand entry into any home where they have reason to believe a nuisance exists. In this instance, there was evidence of the presence of rats in a house which was obviously in a state of extreme decay. Speaking for the Court, Justice Frankfurter argued that there is a right to resist unauthorized (i.e. warrantless) entry only where the purpose is to get information relating to criminal activity, and in this instance the inspector was not searching for evidence usable in a criminal prosecution, but was merely trying to maintain minimum community standards of health and well-being. He also stressed that the power of inspection granted by the Baltimore Code was strictly limited: there had to be valid grounds to suspect the existence of a nuisance; the inspection had to be in the day time; and the use of force to gain entry was not authorized. Finally, Justice Frankfurter maintained that this inspection without warrant was part of a regulatory scheme for general welfare, not attached to the criminal law, and that it had deep historical antecedents. The ordinance in question had been adopted in 1801, and many thousands of inspections had been made under its authority.

Speaking in dissent, Justice Douglas asserted that this decision "greatly dilutes the right of privacy." He went so far as to assert that "we witness indeed an inquest over a substantial part of the Fourth Amendment."[66] He insisted that the Fourth Amendment does not distinguish between civil and criminal cases, and also pointed out that the health inspection could lay the groundwork for a criminal prosecution. He could see no excuse here for not insisting that the health inspector be required to secure a

---

65. 359 U.S. 360 (1959). The issue was first raised in the Supreme Court in District of Columbia v. Little, 339 U.S. 1 (1950), but a majority of the Court managed to avoid the constitutional issue through a rather technical interpretation of the controlling ordinance.

66. 359 U.S. 374.

warrant. "History shows," he declared, "that all officers tend to be officious; and health inspectors . . . are no exception."[67]

The dubious life expectancy of rules of law pronounced by a bare majority of the Court is reflected in the fact that in two cases decided in 1967, *Camara* v. *Municipal Court of San Francisco*,[68] and *See* v. *City of Seattle*,[69] the Court reversed the *Frank* holding by a vote of 6-3. Both cases involved inspections of buildings without warrant. In *Camara* an inspection of a dwelling by building inspectors, under the San Francisco Housing Code, was involved, whereas in *See* an inspector for the fire department had been denied admission to a commercial warehouse because he lacked a warrant. The Court overruled the *Frank* decision, holding that except in certain defined classes of cases, the general rule is that a search of private property without proper consent is unreasonable unless it has been authorized by a valid search warrant. Speaking for the Court, Justice White rejected the *Frank* contention that the Fourth Amendment applies only where criminal behavior is suspected, since the discovery of a violation of a fire or housing code may lead to a criminal complaint. He also rejected the *Frank* argument that inspections of this sort are surrounded by adequate safeguards, pointing out that the occupant has no way of knowing whether enforcement of the municipal code requires inspection of his premises; he has no way of knowing what the lawful limits of the inspector's power to search are; and he has no way of knowing whether the inspector is acting under proper authorization. These are questions which ought to be reviewed by a neutral magistrate. Justice White also rejected the argument that the public interest in health and safety demands a rule sanctioning searches without warrant, for the issue is not whether the inspections may be made, but rather whether they may be made without a warrant. At the same time, since the Court was apparently unwilling to weaken the inspection process too much, it ruled that it was not necessary for the inspector to secure a separate warrant for each search, but rather that warrants could lawfully be issued on an area basis. Probable cause to issue such warrants would be based on the age of the neighborhood, the nature of its buildings, and the general condition of the area. These warrants would fall within the ultimate standard of reasonableness. The Court reached a similar conclusion in *See*, which involved inspection of a commercial structure instead of a private

---

67. 359 U.S. 382. The Frank case was followed in Ohio *ex rel.* Eaton v. Price, 364 U.S. 263 (1960), though by an evenly divided Court.
68. 387 U.S. 523 (1967).
69. 387 U.S. 541 (1967).

residence. The three dissenting Justices, Clark, Harlan, and Stewart, accused the Court of discounting several centuries of municipal experience, and of striking down hundreds of city ordinances all over the country, thus jeopardizing the health, welfare, and safety of millions of people. They could see nothing unreasonable about the sort of searches sanctioned by the *Frank* decision. They also predicted that under the Court's newly fashioned rule relating to area inspections, warrants will be issued in broadcast fashion, thus reducing the whole matter to pretense, a mere ceremony involving unnecessary delay and expense.

Another important issue was litigated in the leading case of *Wyman* v. *James*[70] (1971), again by a 6-3 vote. The question was whether a beneficiary of the program for Aid to Families with Dependent Children (AFDC) could refuse a warrantless home visit by a caseworker without risking termination of benefits, as required by a New York statute. A three-judge federal district court held that the New York statute was invalid, on the ground that the home visitation is a search, and if not consented to, or not authorized by a warrant based on probable cause, violates the Fourth Amendment. On appeal, the Supreme Court reversed. In a rather remarkable opinion Justice Blackmun argued that this home visitation by the caseworker was not a search, but alternatively that if it was a search, it was not unreasonable. He described the search as a gentle and limited effort to safeguard the best interests of children, and to determine that aid was properly going to those for whom it was intended. As in the case of private charity, said Justice Blackmun, the public as provider has a right to know how its funds are utilized, where the purpose is assistance and rehabilitation. In short, the home visit is, in his view, an important part of welfare administration. He also noted that the procedure followed in this situation was proper, in that there was advance written notice of an intended visit on a specific date. There was, he noted, no search for information of criminal activity, at an awkward hour, no forcible entry, and no reprehensible conduct of any kind. Justice Blackmun also pointed out that what was involved was not a police visit, but a call by a welfare worker whose objective was the welfare of the aid recipient; the caseworker was not a sleuth but a friend in need. Finally, he maintained that a warrant would not improve the situation; it could be applied for *ex parte,* without notice to the party involved, and would justify entry by force at less limited hours. Thus he concluded that Mrs. James had a right to refuse the home visit, but could not avoid the consequence of cessation of aid. This home visitation was characterized, therefore, as a reasonable administrative tool, serving a valid purpose in the

---

70. 400 U.S. 309 (1971).

operation of the AFDC program, and was not an unwarranted invasion of personal privacy.

Speaking in dissent, Justice Douglas pointed out that there is now a vast amount of "new property" resulting from government largesse, such as aid to farmers, contractors, old people, etc. ($126 billions in 1969, according to his figures). Every beneficiary of government largesse, he asserted, has a "house" which is protected by the Fourth Amendment. He lamented the fact that welfare is an object of suspicion, arguing that home privacy is as important for the lowly as it is for the mighty. In another dissenting opinion, Justice Marshall argued that the protections of the Fourth Amendment cannot be limited to the criminal law in an age of growing governmental activities, with their inspectors, caseworkers, and researchers. He did not believe that this case was one of benevolent inspection, for he thought that caseworkers are required to be sleuths who have a duty under the law to report any evidence of fraud which a home visit uncovers. He could see no difference between the sort of inspections held invalid in *Camara* and *See* and the visitation in this case. He said that the Court had not explained why a commercial warehouse deserves more protection than a poor woman's home, and insisted that the usual rule, that a search without a warrant is generally constitutionally unreasonable, ought to be followed in this instance.

In *Abel* v. *United States*[71] (1960) the Court, by a 5-4 vote, upheld the validity of an administrative arrest by warrant of the Immigration and Naturalization Service, and a subsequent search of his hotel room and belongings, with FBI cooperation, where the purpose was to check up on an illegal entry. The seized material (e.g. forged birth certificates and a code booklet) was used to convict Abel of conspiracy to commit espionage. The Court held that administrative arrests are sanctioned by history and law, and that a search following an administrative arrest is as proper and may be as extensive as after an arrest for a crime. As for the argument that an administrative arrest on warrant is without the authority of a judge, it was noted that a criminal arrest on probable cause without a warrant is also without a judge's permission. Thus, it was concluded that government officers who effect a deportation arrest have a right of incidental search analogous to the search permitted criminal-law enforcement officers. Further, evidence secured by the government through a lawful search and seizure connected with an arrest pending deportation may be used as evidence in a criminal prosecution. Speaking in dissent Justice Douglas observed that "cases of notorious criminals—like cases of small, miserable ones—are apt to make bad law."[72] He argued that since the FBI

71. 362 U.S. 217 (1960).
72. 362 U.S. 241.

was the moving force behind this arrest and search, in their zeal the federal officers actually circumvented the Fourth Amendment. Justice Brennan maintained that the good faith of the administrative officers involved was beside the point; the Fourth Amendment protects everyone, not merely criminals, and its protection does not fluctuate with the intent of the officers.

On the other hand, in *Colonnade Catering Corp.* v. *United States*[73] (1970), the Court held, by a 5–3 vote, that federal agents, acting without a search warrant, are not authorized under the liquor laws forcibly to enter a locked storeroom. The basic reasoning of the Court was that the statute (26 U.S.C. §7342) imposes a fine for refusal by a building-owner or manager to permit entry or inspection of the premises by a Treasury agent, and that this was intended by Congress to be the exclusive sanction. Justice Douglas took the occasion to point out that we have a strong tradition against using force to break down doors without definite authority. The three dissenters disagreed with the argument that the statute in question excluded forcible entry if necessary, pointing out that for centuries places selling liquor have been subjected to strict governmental scrutiny.

A different conclusion was reached in *United States* v. *Biswell*[74] (1972), where the Court ruled valid a search and seizure without warrant, in the premises of a federally licensed pawnshop operator dealing in sporting weapons, on the ground that adequate permission was embodied in the Gun Control Act of 1968. It was noted that close scrutiny of traffic in firearms is of central importance in federal efforts to prevent violent crime, and that inspection is a crucial part of a comprehensive regulatory scheme. Since effective enforcement demands inspections without warrant, it follows that they constitute reasonable official conduct conformable with the Fourth Amendment. Soon afterwards, the Court upheld the constitutionality of provisions of the Bank Secrecy Act of 1970, and implementing regulations promulgated by the Secretary of the Treasury, which require federally insured banks to maintain records of the identities of their customers, and retain microfilm copies of checks over $100, and records of all transfers over $10,000 to a place, person, or account outside the United States.[75] Covered banks must report transportation into or out of the United States of instruments exceeding $5,000 in value, and make reports of domestic transactions having a high degree of usefulness in criminal, tax, or regulatory investigations. The statute was upheld over Fourth Amendment (and Fifth Amendment) objections. The plenary

73. 397 U.S. 72 (1970).
74. 406 U.S. 311 (1972).
75. California Bankers Assoc. v. Shultz, 416 U.S. 21 (1974).

power of Congress over foreign commerce was noted, and the domestic reporting requirements were regarded as reasonably and properly related to valid governmental purposes. Three dissenting Justices saw in this statutory scheme an unconstitutional invasion of privacy.

Search Without Warrant: Arrest

An ancient exception to the usual rule on searches and seizures is that a police officer may search the person of one who has been legally arrested without a warrant. A search of the person is not lawful if its purpose is to discover grounds as yet unknown for an arrest, and in such a situation the search does not become lawful because of what is found.[76] But if the individual has been arrested lawfully, the police officer may search his person, and this is based, as Judge Cardozo once said, upon a "shrewd appreciation of the necessities of government."[77] For an arresting officer must have the power to disarm the accused, in order to make an effective arrest, protect himself, preserve evidence of the crime, and prevent escape from custody, and if he may disarm, he may search. Since the search is lawful, he retains what he finds if connected with crime.[78]

The extent to which officers who have made a lawful arrest may go beyond searching the person to a search of the place in which the arrest occurred presents issues fraught with difficulties, and has long been the subject of great controversy. It is clear that for the same reasons that permit a search of the person following a lawful arrest, the law has long recognized that the officer may search the place in which the arrest was made and seize things used to carry on the criminal enterprise, which are in the immediate possession and control of the accused.[79] But it has been held that the authority to search a house or place of business incidental to a lawful arrest is certainly not greater than that conferred by a search warrant. It follows that private papers wanted solely as evidence which could not be seized even under a search warrant issued upon ample evidence may not be taken as incidental to an arrest.[80] It is also settled law that where the search is incidental to an arrest, the arrest must occur before the search, and the search must be completed at the time of the arrest.[81] The

76. Johnson v. United States, 333 U.S. 10 (1948).
77. People v. Chiagles, 237 N.Y. 193, 197, 142 N.E. 583, 584 (1923).
78. Chief Justice Vinson said, in Harris v. United States, 331 U.S. 145, 150 (1947), "The Fourth Amendment has never been held to require that every valid search and seizure be effected under the authority of a search warrant. Search and seizure incident to lawful arrest is a practice of ancient origin and has long been an integral part of the law-enforcement procedures of the United States and of the individual states."
79. Marron v. United States, 275 U.S. 192 (1927).
80. United States v. Lefkowitz, 285 U.S. 452 (1932).
81. People v. Conway, 225 Mich. 152, 195 N.W. 679 (1923).

debate in the courts has been largely over the meaning of such phrases as "the immediate surroundings" or "the premises within the control of the accused" as a description of how far beyond the person a search may go as an incident to arrest. To cite only one example, most courts hold that if a man is arrested in his yard, the yard may be searched, but not his house, except under unusual circumstances.

While the Supreme Court has frowned upon general and exploratory searches of places of business, following an arrest,[82] it ruled in 1950, in *United States* v. *Rabinowitz,*[83] that a thorough search of a shop in which the arrest was made is permissible if the search was specific and there was probable cause to believe that the accused had possession of illegal articles in the room searched. Furthermore, in the much-discussed case of *Harris* v. *United States,*[84] the Court, by a 5-4 vote, opened the door to even more extensive search. Five FBI agents, armed with a valid warrant of arrest, arrested Harris in the living room of a four-room apartment, for violating the mail fraud statute and the National Stolen Property Act. Looking for two cancelled checks, the agents proceeded to search all the rooms thoroughly for about five hours. Apparently they practically tore the place apart. In a bureau drawer one agent finally found a sealed envelope marked "personal papers," which was opened and found to contain a number of draft board cards and certificates Harris had no legal right to possess. The Court ruled that the search could validly extend beyond the room in which Harris was arrested because he was in exclusive possession of the whole apartment. It also held that the search was not, under the circumstances, too intensive, in view of the fact that the agents were looking for two cancelled checks, two little pieces of paper. In a dissenting opinion Justice Murphy charged that in this case the Court had "resurrected and approved, in effect, the use of the odious general warrant or writ of assistance, presumably outlawed forever from our society by the Fourth Amendment."

In 1969, in the leading case of *Chimel* v. *California,*[85] the Court, by a 6-2 vote, overruled both *Rabinowitz* and *Harris,* in holding that a warrantless search of an entire house cannot be justified constitutionally as incident to a valid arrest. In this instance, Chimel had been arrested on the authority a warrant of arrest, on the basis of which, over objection, the police searched the entire three-bedroom house in which the arrest occurred, including the attic, the garage, and a small workshop. The Court held that this went too far, that when an arrest is made, it is

82. Go-Bart Importing Co. v. United States, 282 U.S. 344 (1931).
83. 339 U.S. 56 (1950). The vote was 5-3.
84. 331 U.S. 145 (1947).
85. 395 U.S. 752 (1969). See also Von Cleef v. New Jersey, 395 U.S. 814 (1969).

reasonable to search the person arrested in order to remove weapons and seize evidence which might otherwise be concealed or destroyed. In addition, the Court ruled that the officer may search "the area into which an arrestee might reach in order to grab a weapon or evidentiary items must, of course, be governed by a like rule."[86] In other words, it is entirely reasonable to search the area within the arrestee's "immediate control," but the police may not go further without consent or a search warrant.

The *Chimel* case has since its enunciation been applied in a variety of situations.[87] Thus, if the police lawfully arrest a man *outside* his home, absent an emergency, he cannot thereafter be taken inside the house for the purpose of conducting a warrantless search.[88] Similarly, if the police arrest a man on the front steps of his home, they cannot thereafter conduct a warrantless search of the house.[89] It follows, of course, that if the police arrest a man at a point two blocks from his home, they may not thereafter, as incidental to the arrest, take him to his home and search it.[90] On the other hand, though by a 5-4 vote, the Court has ruled that after a man has been lawfully arrested, and taken to jail, his clothing may be searched there, the majority Justices being of the opinion that this search was a normal incident of custodial arrest.[91] Since the clothing search occurred ten hours after the arrest, the dissenters argued that the search could not be regarded as being incidental to the arrest.

The Court once ruled that even the seizure of contraband property violates the Fourth Amendment if it had been "reasonably practicable" for the law enforcement officers to secure search warrants.[92] Since the government agents had known every detail long before the raid was made, and the property was not readily movable, the Court held that they should have asked for a search warrant before making the seizure. But this was a 5-4 decision, and two years later, this rule was abandoned,[93] and it has not been followed. Officers are not legally obliged to get a search warrant even if they had had time to do so. What is regarded as decisive is the reasonableness of the search under all the circumstances, and not the practicality of procuring a search warrant.

---

86. 395 U.S. 763.
87. The Court has ruled that the rule of the Chimel case is not retroactive. Williams v. United States, 401 U.S. 646 (1971); Hill v. California, 401 U.S. 797 (1971).
88. Shipley v. California, 395 U.S. 818 (1969).
89. Vale v. Louisiana, 399 U.S. 30 (1970).
90. James v. Louisiana, 382 U.S. 36 (1965).
91. United States v. Edwards, 415 U.S. 800 (1974).
92. Trupiano v. United States, 334 U.S. 699 (1948). This was also the holding in McDonald v. United States, 335 U.S. 451 (1948).
93. United States v. Rabinowitz, 339 U.S. 56 (1950).

280 / *The Defendant's Rights Today*

Several states have what are known as stop-and-frisk laws which permit the police to make something less than a real search on a detention which is something less than a legal arrest. Thus, New York adopted a statute in 1964 which provides as follows:

1. A police officer may stop any person abroad in a public place whom he reasonably suspects is committing, has committed or is about to commit a felony or any of the crimes specified in section 552 of this Chapter, and may demand his name, address and an explanation of his actions.

2. When a police officer has stopped a person for questioning pursuant to this section and reasonably suspects that he is in danger of life or limb, he may search such person for a dangerous weapon. If the police officer finds such a weapon or any other thing the possession of which may constitute a crime, he may take and keep it until the completion of the questioning, at which time he shall either return it, if lawfully possessed, or arrest such person.[94]

This new and controversial stop-and-frisk law was quickly upheld as constitutional by the New York Court of Appeals, which declared that "prompt inquiry into suspicious or unusual street action is an indispensable police power in the orderly government of large urban communities."[95] In the important case of *Terry* v. *Ohio*[96] (1968), the Supreme Court, with only Justice Douglas dissenting, sustained the constitutionality of an Ohio stop-and-frisk statute. Though Chief Justice Warren, who spoke for the Court, made it clear that while such laws are well within the purview of the Fourth Amendment, and while stopping a man on the street and patting him down for weapons is by no means a petty indignity, and while the warrant procedure is to be preferred, the governmental interest in effective crime prevention and detection justifies giving the policeman authority to assure himself that the suspicious person with whom he is dealing is not armed. Thus, the police officer does not have to wait until the point where there is probable cause to make an arrest; he may make the limited search for weapons if there is "reasonable apprehension of danger." Said the Chief Justice, "[T]he issue is whether a

---

94. N.Y. Code of Criminal Procedure, §180-a.

95. People v. Rivera, 14 N.Y. 2d 441, 444, 201 N.E. 2d 32, 34 (1964). To the same effect was the decision of the New York Court of Appeals in People v. Peters, 18 N.Y. 2d 238, 219 N.E. 2d 595 (1966), where it was noted that since a frisk is a lesser invasion of privacy than a full search, "reasonable suspicion," as distinguished from probable cause, is adequate. A similar police procedure in California was sustained in People v. Martin, 46 Cal. 2d 106, 293 P.2d 52 (1956). See Note, "The Law of Arrest: Constitutionality of Detention and Frisk Acts," *Northwestern University Law Review*, 59 (November–December 1964): 641–59; Theodore Souris, "Stop-and-Frisk," *Journal of Criminal Law, Criminology and Police Science*, 57 (September 1966): 251–64.

96. 392 U.S. 1 (1968). See also the companion case, Sibron v. New York, 392 U.S. 40 (1968).

reasonably prudent man in the circumstances would be warranted in the belief that his safety or that of others was in danger."[97]

Search Without Warrant: Automobiles

The two situations where it may be reasonable to search without a warrant are in the case of arrest and in the case of movable vehicles, such as automobiles. The leading Supreme Court decision which held the search of automobiles without a warrant to be reasonable if made upon probable cause was *Carroll* v. *United States*.[98] Chief Justice Taft emphasized that Congress had always made a distinction between the search of a store, dwelling, or other building, and the search of a ship, wagon, or automobile, "where it is not practicable to secure a warrant because the vehicle can be quickly moved out of the locality or jurisdiction in which the warrant must be sought." But there must be probable cause for believing that the vehicle was carrying contraband or illegal merchandise. In such a situation the right to search has nothing to do with the right of arrest. The right to search and the validity of the seizure "are dependent on the reasonable cause the seizing officer has for belief that the contents of the automobile offend against the law."[99]

The *Carroll* decision was reviewed fully in 1949, and its doctrine was reaffirmed by the Supreme Court in *Brinegar* v. *United States*.[100] In addition, the Court made it clear that there is a great deal of difference between the amount of proof needed to establish guilt and proof sufficient to substantiate the existence of probable cause.[101] The strict rules of evidence which prevail at trials cannot be made requirements for estab-

---

97. 392 U.S. 27.

98. 267 U.S. 132 (1925). The same rule applies to boats. United States v. Lee, 274 U.S. 559 (1927). For another decision upholding the reasonableness of a warrantless search of an automobile, see Scher v. United States, 305 U.S. 251 (1938).

99. 267 U.S. 158-59. Quite apart from the question of arrest, the police may search an automobile if there is probable cause to search it, either on the spot of arrest, or later on at the police station. Chambers v. Maroney, 399 U.S. 42 (1970). Furthermore, by a 5-4 vote, the Court has ruled that the police may search an automobile held for possible forfeiture without a warrant. Cooper v. California, 386 U.S. 58 (1967). In addition, it has been held that the police may seize an object in an automobile that had been taken to the police parking lot which was in plain view, without a warrant. Harris v. United States, 390 U.S. 234 (1968).

100. 338 U.S. 160 (1949). It should be noted that there always was dissent to the rule about searching moving vehicles. In the Carroll case two Justices dissented, with Justice McReynolds denouncing the methods sanctioned by the Court as wholly unwarranted. Three Justices dissented in the Brinegar case, Justice Jackson developing the idea that the latitude of search should depend upon the gravity of the offense. He would allow great latitude of search to catch kidnappers, but not to catch bootleggers.

101. On this point, see Husty v. United States, 282 U.S. 694 (1931).

lishing probable cause for the search of moving vehicles; otherwise officers could rarely take effective action. Probable cause turns upon probabilities. "These are not technical," said Justice Rutledge, "they are the factual and practical considerations of everyday life on which reasonable and prudent men, not legal technicians, act." The difficulty lies in drawing a line between mere suspicion, which is not sufficient, and probable cause. "That line necessarily must be drawn by an act of judgment formed in the light of the particular situation and with account taken of all the circumstances." It should be added that the Court has ruled that the right to search a car does not confer the right to search the person of occupants of the car.[102]

While the police may, after lawfully arresting a person sitting in an automobile, search the automobile on probable cause, a search is unlawful if made at a later date at the police garage without a warrant.[103] On the other hand, the Court has applied the stop-and-frisk principle endorsed in the *Terry* case to a person sitting in an automobile, as to whom the police officer has reasonable grounds for the suspicion that he was armed, on the basis of the tip of a reliable informer.[104] Very recently, a closely divided Court made it clear that there is a distinction between the warrantless search of an automobile and the warrantless search of a person or a building, and that less stringent requirements apply to movable vehicles.[105] Thus, the warrantless search of a police officer's disabled rented automobile, in an effort to find his revolver, after he had been arrested for drunken driving and had been hospitalized, was held reasonable under the Fourth Amendment.[106] Four dissenters thought that since the automobile was wrecked and couldn't be moved, and the search was remote from the arrest, the police had ample opportunity to get a warrant, which is usually the preferred procedure.

Whether the police may stop an automobile, on the basis of probable cause, to search for one thing and discover something else which is evidence of crime has been litigated many times. *Almeida-Sanchez* v. *United States*[107] (1973), where the Court divided 5–4, involved a warrantless search by a border patrol of an automobile, thought to be transporting illegal aliens, which turned up with a large amount of illegally imported

102. United States v. Di Re, 332 U.S. 581 (1948).
103. Preston v. United States, 376 U.S. 364 (1964).
104. Adams v. Williams, 407 U.S. 143 (1972). Three Justices dissented, Justice Marshall warning that the Court's decision "invokes the specter of a society in which innocent citizens may be stopped, searched and arrested at the whim of police officers who have only the slightest suspicion of improper conduct." 407 U.S. 162.
105. Cardwell v. Lewis, 417 U.S. 583 (1974).
106. Cody v. Dombrowski, 413 U.S. 433 (1973).
107. 413 U.S. 266 (1973).

marijuana. The controlling statute permitted the border patrol to search automobiles "within a reasonable distance" from an international boundary, and in this instance the search took place about twenty-five miles from the border. In effect, a bare majority of the Court ruled that this was not a border search. The four dissenters thought that twenty-five miles was a reasonable distance in view of the difficult problems which confront the border patrol.[108]

This decision turned on the rather special issue as to what constitutes a border search. In other cases not presenting such an issue, the Court has upheld the validity of searches where the object seized was altogether unrelated to the original objective of the search. The leading case on this matter is *United States* v. *Robinson*[109] (1973), where the police, after making a full custody arrest of a man for operating an automobile after revocation of his operator's permit, conducted a full field search of his person and found some heroin capsules. Dividing 6–3, the Court upheld the introduction of the heroin as evidence at the trial on the ground that this was merely a search incident to a lawful arrest. Justice Rehnquist argued that having made a lawful arrest, the police officer may seize any evidence he finds which is probative of criminal conduct. The dissenters argued, citing several state decisions, that where a person has been lawfully arrested for violation of a motor vehicle regulation, the officer has no right to conduct a full field search. They were concerned with the danger of abuse of authority, where a policeman will use a traffic arrest as a pretext to conduct a full search. In a companion case the Court reached the same conclusion where a man was lawfully arrested for driving his automobile without having a driver's license in his possession, and after a full search the police officer found some marijuana.[110]

Of course, state courts are free to hold to higher standards than those required by the U.S. Constitution as construed by the Supreme Court, and a number of them have declined to follow the *Robinson* rule. Thus, the New York Court of Appeals has taken the position that where there is arrest for a traffic offense, the admissibility of the fruits of the ensuing search must be limited to evidence relating to the purpose of the arrest.[111] Similarly, the Supreme Court of California recently ruled that it was unlawful for a police officer to stop an automobile because it was being operated without lights, and after arresting the driver, search his person

---

108. In United States v. Peltier, 422 U.S. 531 (1975), and Bowen v. United States, 422 U.S. 916 (1975), the Court held, by 5-4 votes, that the Almeida-Sanchez decision was not applicable retroactively.
109. 414 U.S. 218 (1973).
110. Gustafson v. Florida, 414 U.S. 260 (1973).
111. People v. Marsh, 20 N.Y. 2d 98, 228 N.E. 2d 783 (1967).

and seize marijuana in his possession.[112] The Court argued that since most motorists are engaged in lawful business or innocent pleasure, a routine warrantless search of a minor traffic offender, in the absence of specific facts or circumstances that give the arresting officer a reasonable basis to conclude that the offender might be armed, violates the Fourth Amendment. Indeed, while police roadblocks to check all motorists for violations of traffic laws relating to such matters as drivers' licenses and motor vehicle registrations are regarded as reasonable in the effort to enforce valid statutes,[113] it does not follow that these efforts justify unlimited searches to seek for materials unrelated to the law-enforcement purpose involved.

Electronic Surveillance

The securing of information by government agents through eavesdropping is not in and of itself unlawful. An officer standing on a public sidewalk, for example, may peer into a house and testify as to what he saw and heard. In one well-known case the Supreme Court held evidence admissible which was secured by federal officers who reported on conversations overheard by means of a detectaphone, an instrument which, when placed against a partition wall, picks up and amplifies sound waves.[114] The Court stressed the absence of illegal trespass, and chose to regard this form of eavesdropping as no more objectionable than listening to conversations through a crack in a door. Similarly, in another case the Court held evidence admissible which was secured by means of a microphone secreted on the person of an undercover agent who walked into a shop and transmitted conversation with the accused to an agent stationed outdoors with a receiving set.[115] The Court ruled that this was a no greater invasion of privacy than eavesdropping outside an open window, or using field glasses or a telescope to magnify vision, all of which are permissible. The Court

---

112. People v. Simon, 7 Cal. 3rd 186, 101 Cal. Rptr. 837, 496 P.2d 1205 (1972).

113. City of Miami v. Aronovitz, 114 So. 2d 784 (Fla. 1959); Com. v. Mitchell, 355 S.W. 2d 686 (Ky. 1962); Mincy v. District of Columbia, 218 A.2d 507 (App. D.C. 1966).

114. Goldman v. United States, 316 U.S. 129 (1942). Three Justices dissented, Justice Murphy arguing that the absence of physical entry (trespass) was no longer a decisive factor, in view of the development of new and effective devices; what is decisive, he argued, is the unwarranted invasion of privacy. Where, however, the police have inserted a "spike mike" into a party wall, the physical intrusion involved goes beyond mere eavesdropping, even though there may have been no trespass in the technical sense of the common law. Silverman v. United States, 365 U.S. 505 (1961).

115. On Lee v. United States, 343 U.S. 747 (1952). The vote was 5-4. In a heated dissenting opinion Justice Frankfurter conceded that while a criminal prosecution is more than a game, in any event it is not, he insisted, a dirty game. He added, "Few sociological generalizations are more valid than that lawlessness begets lawlessness." 343 U.S. 760.

reaffirmed this decision later on when it held admissible in evidence a wire recording made by a Treasury agent, through use of a concealed device, while speaking to the accused in the latter's office.[116] Since the agent was in the defendant's office with his consent, there was, the Court declared, no violation of privacy. Finally, note may be made here of a decision of the Court of Appeals for the Ninth Circuit which held admissible evidence obtained through the use of a men's room peephole in a public park.[117] The Court ruled that it was reasonable for the police to engage in clandestine surveillance of such a place as a public toilet if, but only if, they have reasonable cause to believe that it was being used for the commission of a crime. Its position was that people who choose to commit crimes where they may be seen take the chance that they will be seen.

The principal problem relating to eavesdropping is that of wiretapping. The constitutional issue it presents was fully explored, for the first time, in the famous case of *Olmstead* v. *United States*,[118] decided in 1928. In this case the Court held, by a 5–4 vote, that the tapping of telephone lines did not contravene the Fourth Amendment. This Amendment, Chief Justice Taft declared, refers to search for material things, the person, his house, his papers, and effects. "The United States takes no such care of telegraph or telephone messages as of mailed sealed letters. The Amendment does not forbid what was done here. There was no searching. There was no seizure. There was no entry of the houses or offices of the defendants."[119] Furthermore, the Court held that unless required to do so by legislation, it would not exclude evidence secured unethically, which was in accord with the common law rule that the admissibility of evidence is not affected by the way it was obtained. Any other view, said the Chief Justice, "would make society suffer and give criminals greater immunity than has been known heretofore."[120]

Speaking in dissent, Justice Holmes described wiretapping as a "dirty business," and protested that apart from the Constitution, "the government ought not to use evidence obtainable, and only obtainable, by a

---

116. Lopez v. United States, 373 U.S. 427 (1963). Three dissenting Justices objected to the government's using the fruits of this sort of surreptitious electronic eavesdropping. See Hoffa v. United States, 385 U.S. 293 (1966), dealing with the testimony of a government informer, where the Court held that the Fourth Amendment does not protect a wrongdoer's misplaced belief that a person to whom he voluntarily confides will not reveal what he has heard and observed.

117. Smayda v. United States, 352 F.2d 251 (9th Cir. 1965), cert. denied, 382 U.S. 981 (1966).

118. 277 U.S. 438 (1928). For an exellent analysis of this case, see Walter F. Murphy, *Wiretapping on Trial* (New York: Random House, 1965).

119. 277 U.S. 464.

120. 277 U.S. 468.

criminal act." In this instance the act was defined as a crime by the law of the state in which the wiretapping occurred. And Justice Holmes went on to say that there were two conflicting objects of desire: to secure all possible evidence in order to catch criminals and to prevent the government from fostering other crimes in order to get the evidence. The Justice then went on to make the famous statement: "We have to choose, and for my part I think it a less evil that some criminals should escape than that the government should play an ignoble part."[121] In a separate dissenting opinion Justice Brandeis denounced wiretapping as being particularly pernicious since the privacy of persons at both ends of the line is invaded, and *all* conversations are overheard. "As a means of espionage," he said, "writs of assistance and general warrants are but puny instruments of tyranny and oppression when compared with wiretapping." And he argued that it was immaterial that the intrusion was in aid of law enforcement. "Experience should teach us to be most on our guard to protect liberty when the government's purposes are beneficent. Men born to freedom are naturally alert to repel invasion of their liberty by evil-minded rulers. The greatest dangers to liberty lurk in insidious encroachment by men of zeal, well-meaning, but without understanding." He went on to make the oft-quoted observation: "Crime is contagious. If the government becomes a law-breaker, it breeds contempt for law; it invites every man to become a law unto himself; it invites anarchy."[122]

In 1934, however, Congress wrote into the Federal Communications Act §605, which reads as follows: "No person not being authorized by the sender shall intercept any communication and divulge or publish the existence, contents, substance, purport, effect or meaning of such intercepted communication to any person." Soon afterwards the Supreme Court ruled that the term "no person" covers federal agents, and that §605 barred the admission in a criminal trial of testimony as to communications overheard as a result of a tapping of telephone wires.[123] As for the argument that Congress did not intend to hamper the activities of the government in apprehending and convicting criminals, the Court said, "Congress may have thought it less important that some offenders should go unwhipped of justice than that officers should resort to methods deemed inconsistent with ethical standards and destructive of personal

---

121. 277 U.S. 470.
122. 277 U.S. 476, 479, 485.
123. Nardone v. United States, 302 U.S. 379 (1937). Two Justices dissented, arguing with great vigor that a distinction ought to be made between wiretapping by private individuals and by responsible officials trying to enforce the criminal law. In Rathbun v. United States, 355 U.S. 107 (1957), the Court held that §605 did not apply where a policeman listened in on a telephone conversation by means of an extension phone, since no interception of a message was involved.

liberty."[124] In addition, the Court ruled soon afterwards that the interdiction of §605 applied to intrastate as well as interstate communications, noting that to protect interstate commerce Congress may reach intrastate transactions if necessary.[125] Furthermore, it has been held that not only does §605 interdict the introduction into evidence in a federal trial of intercepted telephone conversations; it also forbids the prosecution to make other use of the proscribed evidence.[126] Since it does not permit the government to enjoy the "fruit of the poisonous tree," a trial judge commits reversible error if he refuses to permit the defendant to question prosecution witnesses as to any use they may have made of information secured by wiretapping. On the other hand, the protection of §605 was greatly diluted by holding that a defendant cannot object to the admission of evidence derived from the wiretapping of communications to which he was not a party.[127] That is, A cannot object to evidence dealing with a conversation between B and C, since the statute protects only the sender of the intercepted messages. So far as the Fourth Amendment is concerned, it is well established that one may not validly object to the introduction of evidence secured by an illegal search and seizure of which he was not a victim.

Finally, the Supreme Court ruled in 1952 that §605 of the Federal Communications Act does not apply to the states.[128] This decision was specifically overruled in 1968, however, in *Lee* v. *Florida*,[129] where the Court held that in the light of all the decisions since 1952, if evidence secured in violation of the federal Constitution is inadmissible in a state court, which is the teaching of *Mapp* v. *Ohio*,[130] so is evidence secured in violation of a valid federal statute. This decision also rested on what Justice Stewart referred to as "the imperative of judicial integrity," which means that no court, federal or state, may serve as an accomplice in the wilful violation of the laws of the United States. The Court also drew attention to the *Benanti* case,[131] which held that communications intercepted by state officers contrary to §605 were inadmissible in a federal trial.

In 1966 and 1967 the Supreme Court came to grips more directly with

124. 302 U.S. 383.
125. Weiss v. United States, 308 U.S. 321 (1939).
126. Nardone v. United States, 308 U.S. 338 (1939).
127. Goldstein v. United States, 316 U.S. 114 (1942). Speaking for three dissenters, Justice Murphy argued that the statute should be interpreted broadly as a "congressional command that society shall not be plagued with such practices as wire-tapping."
128. Schwartz v. Texas, 344 U.S. 199 (1952).
129. 392 U.S. 378 (1968). Three Justices dissented, arguing that if §605 is to be rewritten, that is for Congress to do.
130. 367 U.S. 643 (1961). This case is analyzed in the next section.
131. Benanti v. United States, 355 U.S. 96 (1957).

the problems of electronic eavesdropping, and developed a considerable body of new doctrine. In *Osborn* v. *United States*[132] the Court held valid a tape recording made with a concealed recorder by an undercover agent of the FBI, a procedure which had been authorized by two local federal district judges. Since there was no indiscriminate use of a listening device, but only use under precise and discriminating circumstances carefully spelled out by the judges, the Fourth Amendment requirement of particularity was met.[133] Soon thereafter, in *Katz* v. *United States,*[134] the Court set aside a conviction for the offense of transmitting wagering information by telephone where the government was permitted to introduce evidence regarding the defendant's end of telephone conversations which had been overheard by FBI agents, who had attached an electronic listening and recording device to the outside of the public telephone booth from which the defendant had made his calls. The trial court ruled that the critical point was that there had been no physical entrance into the area occupied by the accused. The Supreme Court disagreed, holding that since the Fourth Amendment protects people, not places, it does not really matter whether a phone booth can be characterized as a constitutionally protected area. Justice Stewart pointed out that one who uses a public phone booth may rely on the protection of the Fourth Amendment; he is entitled to assume that what he says there will not be broadcast to the world. It was also noted that the Court has long since abandoned the view expressed in the *Olmstead* case that there must be some trespass to come within the scope of the Amendment. Thus, since the government's activities violated the privacy upon which the defendant justifiably relied while using the phone booth, there had been a search and seizure within the meaning of the Fourth Amendment. As established in the *Osborn* case, a duly authorized magistrate could constitutionally have authorized such a search and seizure, but except for such exceptions as cases involving moving vehicles, search incident to arrest, hot pursuit, or consent, a search without a warrant is *per se* unreasonable. Justice Black, dissenting alone, argued that the Fourth Amendment does not deal with eavesdropping, but only with tangible things.

Furthermore, in *Berger* v. *New York*[135] the Court held inadmissible, in a state trial on bribery charges, recordings made with a recording device authorized by a judge for the reason that the statute on which the warrant was based lacked the particularization required by the Fourth Amend-

---

132. 385 U.S. 323 (1966).

133. Justice Douglas dissented alone in an unusually eloquent opinion which lamented the increasing, aggressive breaches of privacy by the government.

134. 390 U.S. 347 (1967). In United States v. White, 401 U.S. 745 (1970), the Court declined to give the Katz case retroactive effect.

135. 388 U.S. 41 (1967).

ment. The warrant was a broadside authorization which did not specify the particular crime or place or person or conversation involved. In other words, the Court held the warrant defective because adequate judicial supervision and protective procedures were lacking; the statute was construed as giving a blanket grant of permission to eavesdrop. In a concurring opinion, Justice Douglas pointed out that this decision overruled the *Olmstead* case *sub silentio.* Clearly, the teaching of this case is that while a wiretap is not illegal *per se,* it must be authorized by a magistrate in a warrant which satisfies the normal requirements of the Fourth Amendment.

Congress responded promptly to the Berger decision by enacting Title III of the Omnibus Crime Control and Safe Streets Act of 1968.[136] This statute authorizes the use of electronic surveillance for carefully defined classes of crimes, on the basis of a court order, and in accordance with rules requiring detailed and particularized application. In 1972, the Court ruled that the Attorney General could not lawfully authorize electronic surveillance in internal security matters without prior judicial approval secured in accordance with the terms of the 1968 statute.[137] The Court recognized the need of the government to resort to wiretaps, to protect the country from subversion, but it also insisted upon the essentiality of Fourth Amendment safeguards. It rejected the government's contention that security problems involve complex and subtle problems beyond the competence of courts to evaluate, and the demand for secrecy. Justice Powell pointed out that courts regularly deal with the most difficult issues in our society, and that judges can be relied upon to keep confidences. Finally, the Court pointed out that its decision had nothing to do with regard to foreign agents and foreign powers. In the area of foreign affairs the constitutional powers of the President may well support warrantless searches, but alternatively, Congress may choose to spell out his powers in this respect by statute. So far it has not done so, and the Court has not been called upon to resolve the problem.[138]

136. 18 U.S.C. §§2510-20 (1970).
137. United States v. U.S. District Court, 407 U.S. 297 (1972).
138. The Court construed Title III of the 1968 statute broadly in United States v. Kahn, 415 U.S. 143 (1974), where the Court approved of a warrant covering telephone calls of a named individual "and others as yet unknown." Three Justices thought this amounted to approval of a virtual general warrant. A number of convictions have been set aside by the Court because of bugging or wiretapping without authorization. See, e.g., Black v. United States, 385 U.S. 26 (1966) (bugging of a hotel suite to listen in on conversations with defendant's attorney in connection with a tax evasion prosecution); O'Brien v. United States, 386 U.S. 345 (1967) (installation of microphone in a business establishment in connection with a customs violation); Gelhard v. United States, 408 U.S. 41 (1972) (witness may refuse to respond to questions based on illegal wiretapping, in accordance with 18 U.S.C. §2512).

In spite of the fact that most states have statutes forbidding wiretapping, and the enactment by Congress of §605 of the Federal Communications Act, and Title III of the Crime Control Act of 1968, and in spite of court decisions on the subject, wiretapping today "flourishes as a wide-open operation at the federal, state, municipal, and private levels."[139] Private parties as well as governmental agencies resort to wiretapping for a tremendously wide range of purposes.[140] Some government attorneys have maintained that there is a basic distinction between "intercepting" and "divulging" telephone communications, and that §605 forbids only the latter. Since the Department of Justice taps telephone wires regularly, it has steadfastly refused to prosecute other federal and state officials and private persons who do so.

Many observers, including several recent Attorneys General, have defended wiretapping at least for certain particularly heinous offenses, such as kidnapping, extortion, and crimes involving national security, such as espionage. Some have argued that in combatting the crimes of organized groups, as distinguished from individuals, wiretapping ought to be permitted. Furthermore, it is maintained that wiretapping is no worse than many methods now in use, such as the employment of informers, stool pigeons, spies, and eavesdroppers, and strongly preferable to such practices as the third degree. Most defenders of wiretapping today seem to agree that it should be controlled by carefully drawn legislation, and many who take this view, but by no means all, believe that officers should be required to get the permission of a judge to tap wires, upon a showing of probable cause. Other safeguards are needed to prevent tampering with the recordings, and appropriate sanctions for violation should be provided for.[141] Thus, in its final report the Special Senate Committee to Investigate Organized Crime stated, "Wiretapping is a powerful tool in the hands of law-enforcement officers. Federal agents are seriously handicapped in

---

139. Alan F. Westin, "The Wire-Tapping Problem: An Analysis and a Legislative Proposal," *Columbia Law Review,* 52 (1952): 165–208, 167. See also Samuel Dash, Richard F. Schwartz and Robert E. Knowlton, *The Eavesdroppers* (New Brunswick: Rutgers University Press, 1959); Symposium, "The Wiretapping-Eavesdropping Problem: Reflections on *The Eavesdroppers,"Minnesota Law Review,* 44 (April 1960): 813–940.

140. "Despite the great number of state statutes regulating or forbidding wire-tapping, and the interpretation by the highest court of Section 605 as a prohibition of the practice, there is abundant evidence that the practice is widespread by Federal officers, by state enforcement officials, and by private individuals." Charles T. McCormick, *Handbook of the Law of Evidence* (St. Paul: West Publishing Co., 1954), pp. 300–301. See also Alan F. Westin, *Privacy and Freedom* (New York: Atheneum, 1967).

141. For some sensible suggestions as to what a statute on this subject ought to say, see Westin, "The Wire-Tapping Problem," pp. 200–208.

their regular enforcement work by the legal restrictions which presently surround this valuable instrument of investigation. If properly safeguarded by the same restrictions that are imposed by law upon searches and seizures, wiretapping does not infringe upon the right of privacy of the honest citizen. Several States, notably New York, have laws which permit the use of wiretapping pursuant to court order and subject to reasonable safeguards."[142]

On the other hand, there are powerful objections to legalizing wiretapping. A distinguished legal scholar writes, "The chief difference between wire tapping and other forms of surveillance is the extent of its intrusion into the privacy of people who are not even suspected of crime.... Sometimes it is said that innocent people have nothing to fear from their conversations being overheard. But this ignores the nature of conversation as well as the fact that most people have some aspects of their lives that they do not wish to expose."[143] Unlike a search by authority of a warrant, which is specific and limited, he points out, "wire tapping is unavoidably a hunt for evidence, pure and simple, *i.e.*, for incriminating admissions. And since no one can forecast when the incriminating admission will be made, the hunt may have to go on for months, as against the specific and limited temporal authority granted by the ordinary search warrant for tangible things."[144]

Furthermore, wiretapping is more intrusive than the authorized search for tangible things because the subject is not usually aware of the intrusion. It has also been noted "that enforcement agencies do not exercise their power with restraint. Regulations have been side-stepped or ignored; wiretapping information has been used for personal or political benefit."[145] It may well be that indiscriminate wiretapping would help the police catch criminals, but so would listening in on confessions to priests, rifling of the mails, unrestricted search of private homes, the third degree, and many other practices which are now illegal.

Whatever case may be made for wiretapping in restricted areas by police officers, subject to the strict limitations of a carefully drawn statute,

---

142. Sen. Rep. 725, 82d Cong., 1st sess. (1951). See Herbert Brownell, Jr., "The Public Security and Wire Tapping," *Cornell Law Quarterly*, 39 (1954): 195-212; William P. Rogers, "The Case for Wire Tapping," *Yale Law Journal*, 63 (1954): 792-98.

143. Louis B. Schwartz, "On Current Proposals to Legalize Wire Tapping," *University of Pennsylvania Law Review*, 103 (1954): 157-67, 161-62.

144. *Ibid.*, p. 163. See Patrick Murphy Malin, "Is Wire Tapping Justified?" *Annals of the American Academy*, 300 (1955): 28-35. See also the perceptive dissenting opinion of Justice Brennan in Lopez v. United States, 373 U.S. 427, 475-90 (1963).

145. Westin, "The Wire-Tapping Problem," p. 188.

wiretapping by private individuals seems to be wholly inexcusable, and ought to be made illegal everywhere, and punished where indulged in.

The Exclusionary Rule

At the common law otherwise competent evidence has always been admissible even though it was secured by means of an illegal search and seizure. As recently as 1904 the Supreme Court held that a federal court may receive any competent evidence without inquiring into the means by which it had been procured.[146] But an imaginative lawyer had a bright idea when, in 1908, he filed a motion before trial to compel a federal district attorney to return papers alleged to have been seized unlawfully.[147] Though the court found on the merits that there had been no improper seizure, it decided that the filing of the motion was proper. In 1911 a lower federal court held that illegally seized papers may be returned,[148] and finally in 1914, in *Weeks* v. *United States,*[149] decided by unanimous vote, the Supreme Court ruled squarely that the denial by a federal trial court of a pretrial motion for the return of papers seized unlawfully was a prejudicial error. Speaking for the Court, Justice Day maintained that if the documents in question could be held and used in evidence in a criminal prosecution, then the protection of the Fourth Amendment might just as well be stricken from the Constitution.

The federal exclusionary rule is based on the proposition that there is no other effective protection against illegal searches and seizures. Justice Jackson once argued that this is not true for most other rights, in connection with which there are effective remedies, pointing out that "an illegal search and seizure usually is a single incident, perpetrated by surprise, conducted in haste, kept purposely beyond the court's supervision and limited only by the judgment and moderation of officers whose own interests and records are often at stake in the search. There is no opportunity for injunction or appeal to disinterested intervention. The citizen's choice is quietly to submit to whatever the officers undertake or to resist at risk of arrest or immediate violence."[150]

The federal exclusionary rule applies not only to the use of evidence seized unreasonably; it also operates to exclude the indirect or derivative use of such evidence. The leading decision on this point is the *Silverthorne* case.[151] In this instance federal officers seized certain papers illegally and

146. Adams v. New York, 192 U.S. 585 (1904).
147. United States v. Wilson, 163 F. 338 (Cir. Ct. S.D. N.Y. 1908).
148. Wise v. Mills, 185 F. 318 (Cir. Ct. S.D. N.Y. 1911), appeal dismissed, 220 U.S. 549 (1911).
149. 232 U.S. 383 (1914).
150. Brinegar v. United States, 338 U.S. 160, 182 (1949) (dissenting opinion).
151. Silverthorne Lumber Co. v. United States, 251 U.S. 385 (1920).

made copies of them. The property was returned on motion, but following an indictment, on the basis of the knowledge derived from the illegal search and seizure, the company was ordered by subpoena to produce the originals. The Supreme Court reversed a contempt conviction for refusal to bring in the papers, holding that the protection of the Constitution against illegal searches and seizures applies not only to physical possession, but also to the advantages that the government can gain over the object of its pursuit by doing the forbidden act. Said Justice Holmes, "The essence of a provision forbidding the acquisition of evidence in a certain way is that not merely evidence so acquired shall not be used before the court, but that it shall not be used at all. Of course this does not mean that the facts thus obtained become sacred and inaccessible. If knowledge of them is gained from an independent source they may be proved like any others, but the knowledge gained by the government's own wrong cannot be used by it in the way proposed."[152]

Most states have preferred to follow the common law rule that pertinent evidence is admissible, even if secured illegally.[153] A survey made in 1949 by Justice Frankfurter indicated that thirty states still adhered at that time to this rule.[154] He also noted that the United Kingdom and all the British Commonwealths took the same position. The influential John Henry Wigmore has always been among those opposed to the exclusionary rule. In his weighty treatise on evidence he writes, "Necessity does not require, and the spirit of our law does forbid, the attempt to do justice incidentally and to enforce penalties by indirect methods."[155] He argued that the rule of the *Weeks* case was a product of "misplaced sentimentality," and described it as "heretical."[156] In his opinion it makes justice inefficient, and coddles the law-evading classes of the population. The way to deal with an official who commits an illegal search or seizure is to prosecute him criminally or sue him for damages, which, says Wigmore, is the "direct" and "natural" way to proceed. But the example of the United States Supreme Court is a weighty one, and by the late 1950s about eighteen states had elected to follow the *Weeks* rule.[157]

The freedom of the states to follow or reject the *Weeks* rule, as they choose, was affirmed by the important decision of the Supreme Court in

---

152. 251 U.S. 392. Similarly, witnesses may not testify as to what they saw during an illegal search. Amos v. United States, 255 U.S. 313 (1921).

153. For a leading case, see People v. Defore, 242 N.Y. 13, 150 N.E. 585 (1926), Cardozo, J.

154. Wolf v. Colorado, 338 U.S. 25, 29 (1949).

155. *A Treatise on Evidence,* 3d ed. (Boston: Little, Brown & Co., 1940), 8; 4.

156. *Ibid.,* pp. 32–33.

157. For an example of a conversion to the federal rule, see Richards v. State, 77 A.2d 199 (Del. 1950).

Wolf v. *Colorado*[158] in 1949. Dividing 6-3, the Court ruled that a state had not denied due process solely because evidence had been admitted at the trial which had been obtained under circumstances which would have made the evidence inadmissible in a federal court because of an infraction of the Fourth Amendment. Pointing out once more that the Fourteenth Amendment does not apply to the states all the specific limitations of federal law, and that due process is an expanding concept guaranteeing basic rights essential to a free society, the Court held that the federal exclusionary rule was not such a right. It was noted that the *Weeks* rule dated only from 1914, that it was not derived from the explicit requirements of the Fourth Amendment or of legislation, but was merely "a matter of judicial implication." Since most of the English-speaking world does not follow the exclusionary rule, the Court refused to say that it was essential to justice. It was emphasized that other remedies are available, suits for damages and criminal prosecutions. At the same time the Court ruled that the right to privacy which the Fourth Amendment protects against arbitrary intrusion by the police is within the scope of due process. Thus presumably if a state should affirmatively sanction lawless police incursion into privacy, under this ruling it would violate due process. The dissenting Justices in the *Wolf* case insisted that by rejecting the exclusionary principle the Court was ruling out the only sanction that makes the right of privacy effective.

The Court reviewed this question a few years later in *Irvine* v. *California*[159] and by a 5-4 vote decided to stand by the rule of the *Wolf* case. The decisive break came in 1961, in the landmark case of *Mapp* v. *Ohio,*[160] where by a 5-4 vote the Court overruled *Wolf,* holding that the exclusionary rule of the *Weeks* case was not merely a rule of evidence, but was also based on the Constitution, binding upon the states by way of Fourteenth Amendment due process. In an exhaustive opinion, Justice Clark noted that many states had already chosen to follow the exclusionary rule without federal compulsion.[161] He also maintained that other possible remedies for unlawful searches and seizures, such as criminal prosecutions and suits for damages, were both "worthless and futile." It was time, said Justice Clark, to close the only door still remaining open, which permits the admission of evidence secured by official lawlessness in flagrant abuse of a basic right. He argued that it is logically and constitutionally necessary to hold that the exclusionary rule is an essential part of the right of privacy. In short, he concluded, the rule is that no person is to be convicted by unconstitutional

158. 338 U.S. 25 (1949).
159. 347 U.S. 128 (1954).
160. 367 U.S. 643 (1961).
161. By this time, twenty-three states had adopted the exclusionary rule.

evidence, whether in a state or federal court. This rule is also supported by common sense, since it does not make sense to permit the state prosecutor to use evidence which the federal prosecutor across the street may not use. Furthermore, to have one rule for federal officials and another for state officials stimulates federal-state conflict, and encourages federal officials to flout the law by finding a way of taking their evidence to state courts. It may well be the case, said Justice Clark, that a criminal may go free because a constable blundered, but there is another and overriding consideration, "the imperative of judicial integrity." And he added, "Nothing can destroy a government more quickly than its failure to observe its own laws, or worse, its disregard of the charter of its own existence."[162]

Three of the four dissenting Justices in *Mapp* regarded the exlusionary rule as a federal remedy only, which they would not impose on the states. They insisted that since about half the states still adhered to the old common law rule of nonexclusion, the issue is fairly debatable, and therefore the states should be free of federal compulsion in deciding upon the rule they prefer to follow. Justice Harlan also insisted that there is a great difference between the Supreme Court's supervisory responsibility over the lower federal courts and its responsibility as regards the state courts. Justice Stewart thought the case turned on a freedom of speech issue. (This case involved a seizure of literature alleged to be obscene.)

"The *Mapp* case," a distinguished legal scholar wrote soon after the decision was announced, "represents the Supreme Court's most ambitious effort to affect and determine the quality of state criminal justice."[163] He pointed out that this decision "seeks directly to influence the out-of-court conduct of state police personnel," that it imposes the prevailing federal standard upon all state officers, that it will involve "frequent and extensive assertions of federal power," and that it will intrude "farther into areas of local policy and self-determination than earlier decisions of the Court affecting state criminal procedures."

While this is a fair characterization of the *Mapp* decision, it cannot be denied that its basic rationale is a powerful one. As Donald E. Santarelli of the U.S. Department of Justice recently said, the exclusionary rule has two fundamental purposes: "to deter unlawful or undesirable or unconstitutional police conduct, and ... to insure some integrity in the judicial process by not having the judicial process sanction, approve and be party to constitutional violations or undesirable or unlawful police conduct in allowing

162. 367 U.S. 659.
163. Francis A. Allen, "Federalism and the Fourth Amendment: A Requiem for Wolf," *Supreme Court Review, 1961,* Philip B. Kurland, ed. (Chicago: University of Chicago Press), pp. 1–48, 47.

evidence to be used notwithstanding the manner in which it was seized."[164] In a more extended statement, Professor Oaks has vigorously defended the exclusionary rule in the following language:

> If constitutional rights are to be anything more than pious pronouncements, then some measurable consequence must be attached to their violation. It would be intolerable if the guarantee against unreasonable search and seizure could be violated without practical consequence. It is likewise imperative to have a practical procedure by which courts can review alleged violations of constitutional rights and articulate the meaning of those rights. The advantage of the exclusionary rule—entirely apart from any direct deterrent effect—is that it provides an occasion for judicial review, and it gives credibility to the constitutional guarantees. By demonstrating that society will attach serious consequences to the violation of constitutional rights, the exclusionary rule invokes and magnifies the moral and educative force of the law. Over the long term this may integrate some fourth amendment ideals into the value system or norms of behavior of law enforcement agencies.[165]

The Warren Court, which extended the exclusionary rule to the states, soon made it clear that state searches and seizures were to be evaluated according to federal standards as spelled out in the Fourth Amendment and the interpretive decisions of the Court.[166] While the Court said that the *Mapp* rule is not a "fixed formula," and that states are not precluded from having their own rules, they may do so provided that they do not violate federal constitutional standards. Furthermore, the Court quickly held that the admission of unconstitutionally obtained evidence is not to be regarded by a state court as mere harmless error, where there was a reasonable possibility that the evidence complained of might have contributed to the conviction.[167] In addition, the Court ruled that the exclusionary rule is not limited to criminal prosecutions, but applies to forfeiture proceedings as well, such proceedings being regarded as quasi-criminal in character.[168]

The departure of Chief Justice Warren from the scene, and the appointment of Warren E. Burger to the center chair on the Court, brought to this position of great influence a stern and seasoned critic of the exclusionary rule. Chief Justice Burger lost little time, and went out of his way, to announce, in a dissenting opinion, that the exclusionary rule "is both conceptually sterile and practically ineffective," and altogether too in-

---

164. 61 F.R.D. 273 (March 1974). For a symposium discussion of the exclusionary rule, see 61 F.R.D. 259-86.
165. D. H. Oaks, "Studying the Exclusionary Rule in Search and Seizure," *University of Chicago Law Review*, 37 (Summer 1970): 665-757, 756.
166. Ker v. California, 374 U.S. 23 (1963).
167. Fahy v. Connecticut, 375 U.S. 85 (1963). Four dissenting Justices took the position that a state should be free to apply its own harmless error rule in a criminal trial involving search and seizure issues.
168. One 1958 Plymouth Sedan v. Pennsylvania, 380 U.S. 693 (1965).

flexible, though he said that he would hesitate to abandon it until some "meaningful substitute" is developed.[169] The hostility of the Burger Court to the exclusionary rule found concrete expression in 1974, in *United States v. Calandra,*[170] where by a 6-3 vote it was decided that the rule does not apply to testimony before grand juries. The grand jury, Justice Powell explained, as an ancient and very important historic institution, has traditionally had wide latitude to inquire into violations of the criminal law. It sits in secret, without a presiding judge, and it is not restrained by technical procedural or evidentiary rules in its quest for evidence it deems appropriate. Furthermore, the grand jury hearing is not an adversary proceeding in which guilt or innocence is adjudicated; it may act on evidence which would be inadmissible at a court trial, and everyone has a duty to testify at its request. Justice Powell went on to argue that the prime purpose of the exclusionary rule is not to redress an injury to the privacy of the search victim, but rather, "to deter future unlawful police conduct." It follows that the exclusionary does not apply to all possible situations, but is limited to those situations where it will do the most good. In this instance, the Court must weigh the potential injury to the historic role and functions of the grand jury as against the benefits to be derived from the rule in this context. Extension of the exclusionary rule, said Justice Powell, would in this situation seriously impede the grand jury without yielding up correlative benefits. Speaking for the minority, Justice Brennan asserted that the Court's decision was based on the "startling misconception" that deterrence of police misconduct was the basic objective of the exclusionary rule. He insisted that it was mainly designed to enable the judiciary to avoid the taint of partnership in official lawlessness, and to assure the people that the government would not profit from its own lawless behavior. He asserted that this was the first time that the Court had discounted, to the point of extinction, the vital function of the exclusionary rule to insure that the judiciary would avoid even the slightest appearance of sanctioning illegal government conduct. He expressed the fear that this holding was a long step in the direction of abandoning the exclusionary rule altogether.

Whether the *Mapp* decision has had the desired effect, or, for that matter, any effect at all, with respect to the behavior of local police officers, prosecutors, and judges, is a much-debated question. Perhaps it is too soon to tell, for it does take time for a new, complex rule of law to sink in and to win acceptance. The few available studies on this point are inconclusive.[171]

169. Bivens v. Six Unknown Federal Narcotics Agents, 403 U.S. 388, 415 (1971).
170. 414 U.S. 338 (1974).
171. For the citations to available studies, and a brief review of the exclusionary rule in action, see Jacob W. Landynski, "Search and Seizure," in Stuart S. Nagel, ed., *The Rights of the Accused* (Beverly Hills: Sage Publications, 1972), pp. 29-57, esp. 49-53. See also Leonard W. Levy, *Against the Law* (New York: Harper & Row, 1974), chap. 2.

The Question of Remedies

It seems to be clear that the remedy of criminal liability for unreasonable searches and seizures is wholly ineffective.[172] Although the federal criminal code has made it a crime for over fifty years for anyone executing a search warrant to exceed his authority wilfully or to exercise it with unnecessary severity,[173] there is no record of a successful prosecution. The number of state prosecutions has been infinitesimally small. Obviously prosecuting attorneys are reluctant to prosecute officers who were doing what the prosecutors ordered or wanted them to do.

If a seizure has been made illegally, as, for example, under the authority of a defective warrant, the aggrieved person may, subject to certain qualifications, bring a suit for damages against the magistrate, or the police officer, or any affiant who swore falsely. The Supreme Court made it very clear, in a 1971 case, that an illegal search and seizure by federal agents is an actionable wrong for which a suit for damages lies.[174] "Historically," said Justice Brennan, "damages have been regarded as the ordinary remedy for an invasion of personal interests in liberty."[175] Successful civil suits for damages are so rare and so unsatisfactory, however, that, as Justice Murphy observed in his dissent in the *Wolf* case this remedy is "illusory."[176]

Under Rule 41(e) of the Federal Rule of Criminal Procedure, "a person aggrieved by an unlawful search and seizure may move the district court for the district in which the property was seized for the return of the property on the ground that he is entitled to lawful possession of the property which was illegally seized. The judge shall receive evidence on any issue of fact necessary to the decision of the motion. If the motion is granted the property shall be restored and it shall not be admissible in evidence at any hearing or trial." The admission of evidence may be challenged on various grounds, that the property was illegally seized without a warrant, that the warrant was insufficient on its face, that the property seized was not that described in the warrant, that there was not probable cause for believing the existence of the grounds on which the warrant was issued, that the person who signed the warrant was not lawfully empowered to do so, or that the warrant was executed illegally.

There are two important procedural limitations which the federal courts have imposed upon the exclusionary rule, and which have contrived to

---

172. See Richard A. Edwards, "Criminal Liability for Unreasonable Searches and Seizures," *Virginia Law Review,* 41 (June 1955): 621–32.

173. 18 U.S.C. §2234 (1970).

174. Bivens v. Six Unknown Agents of the Federal Bureau of Narcotics, 403 U.S. 388 (1971).

175. 403 U.S. 395.

176. Wolf v. Colorado, 338 U.S. 25, 42 (1949).

reduce its usefulness somewhat. One is the rule that no one has standing to move for the suppression of evidence unless he or his property or premises were involved; he cannot object to the use of illegally seized evidence if he is a mere "third party."[177] Thus, the Court has ruled that the codefendants of the owner of a store do not have standing to challenge the validity of a search of the store for stolen goods, since they were not on the premises at the time of the contested search and seizure, they had no proprietary or possessory interest in the premises, and were not charged with an offense which included, as an essential element of the offense charged, possession of the seized evidence at the time of the contested search and seizure.[178] Speaking more generally, the suppression of the product of a Fourth Amendment violation can be successfully urged only by those whose rights were violated by the search itself, and not by those who are aggrieved solely by the introduction of damaging evidence, from which it follows that codefendants and coconspirators lack standing, since Fourth Amendment rights are personal rights which may not be asserted vicariously.[179]

On the other hand, the owner of property which was seized unlawfully does not lack standing to object merely because the property was seized in someone else's hotel room, the Court noting that it could not isolate or separate the search from the seizure, and asserting that it would not permit "a quibbling distinction to overturn a principle which was designed to protect a fundamental right."[180] In addition, one has standing to object to the use of evidence seized unlawfully in his office, since the word "houses" in the Fourth Amendment extends to commercial premises, and the protection of the Fourth Amendment is not limited to those who have title to the searched premises.[181] Thus, a person has sufficient interest in the premises, to assert standing, if he was present in an apartment with the permission of the owner.[182] Said Justice Frankfurter, ". . . it is unnecessary and ill-advised to import into the law surrounding the constitutional right to be free from unreasonable searches and seizures subtle distinctions, developed and refined by the common law in evolving the body of private property law which, more than almost any other branch of law, has been shaped by distinctions whose validity is largely historical. Even in the area from which they derive, due consideration has led to the discarding of these distinctions in the homeland of the common law. . . . Distinctions such as those between

---

177. See Richard A. Edwards, "Standing to Suppress Unreasonably Seized Evidence," *Northwestern University Law Review,* 47 (September–October 1952): 471–91.
178. Brown v. United States, 411 U.S. 223 (1973).
179. Alderman v. United States, 394 U.S. 165 (1969).
180. United States v. Jeffers, 342 U.S. 48, 52 (1951).
181. Mancusi v. DeForte, 392 U.S. 364 (1968).
182. Jones v. United States, 362 U.S. 257 (1960).

'lessee,' 'licensee,' 'invitee' and 'guest,' often only of gossamer strength, ought not to be determinative in fashioning procedures ultimately referable to constitutional safeguards."[183]

Finally, it is worth noting that the Court has ruled that testimony as to possession, given to establish standing, may not thereafter be admitted against the defendant at the trial on the issue of guilt, for, as Justice Harlan observed, it is "intolerable that one constitutional right should have to be surrendered in order to assert another."[184]

There is another procedural limitation, in addition to that of standing, namely, that the constitutional issue must be asserted seasonably.[185] The Supreme Court insists that the individual concerned must raise the issue as soon as possible. Ordinarily this means that the challenge must be made before trial. It is usually too late if the accused waits until the seized evidence has been offered at the trial.[186] But if he did not know anything about the search until the evidence was offered at the trial, the Supreme Court has ruled that the objection is not too late, since it is made as soon as possible.[187]

Waiver

As in the case of other personal rights guaranteed by the Constitution, such as the right to jury trial or to representation by counsel, the Fourth Amendment right to privacy may be waived. One who permits a policeman to search his premises without a warrant has waived his right. The consent, however, must be voluntary, uncoerced, and given without trickery or fear or promise of reward.[188] It is not necessary, however, for the state to establish that the person who consented to the search knew that he had a right to refuse such consent.[189] In other words, the Supreme Court has declined to apply the *Miranda* warning rule to searches and seizures, on the theory that to do so would unduly burden police investigations. Further-

---

183. 362 U.S. 266.

184. Simmons v. United States, 390 U.S. 377, 394 (1968).

185. See Richard A. Edwards, "Seasonable Protests against Unreasonable Searches and Seizures," *Minnesota Law Review,* 37 (February 1953): 188-98.

186. Segurola v. United States, 275 U.S. 106 (1927).

187. Gouled v. United States, 255 U.S. 298 (1921). See also Amos v. United States, 255 U.S. 313 (1921); Agnello v. United States, 269 U.S. 20 (1925).

188. See Bumper v. North Carolina, 391 U.S. 543 (1963), where permission to search followed an assertion by the officer that he had a warrant in his pocket, when in fact he had no warrant. There is, however, no rule forbidding the use of undercover agents and decoys who are invited in by the accused. Lewis v. United States, 385 U.S. 206 (1966).

189. Schneckloth v. Bustamonte, 412 U.S. 218 (1973). Three Justices dissented, arguing that it is hard to believe that anyone has waived something as precious as a constitutional right without being aware of its existence.

more, if the warning rule were made applicable, all a defendant would have to testify to is that he didn't know he could refuse consent. The ultimate test is that of voluntariness, and this depends on "the totality of the circumstances." There is nothing constitutionally suspect, Justice Stewart argued, in a person voluntarily allowing a search, and indeed, the community has an interest in encouraging consent to solve its problems. However, mere acquiescence in the authority of the police or mere failure to object is not, without more, ordinarily regarded as an invitation to search. Similarly, one has not consented if he agrees to a search as the result of a display of a warrant which turns out to be invalid, since it is not presumed that one would consent to an unlawful search. But consent is regarded as voluntary if it is given upon the assertion by the officer that if it is not given he will secure a search warrant. In this situation the choice is up to the individual concerned. In a World War II case involving the search of the premises of a filling station for unlawful gasoline ration coupons, the Supreme Court held that the permissible limits of persuasion to induce consent to a search are not as narrow where the officers are seeking to inspect public documents as they are where private papers are sought in a private residence.[190]

It is an important rule of law that a valid consent to a search must be made by the person whose premises are to be searched. It follows that a landlord may not give permission to the police to conduct a warrantless search of the house of his renter.[191] Similarly, a hotel clerk cannot waive the privacy right of the occupier of a room.[192]

Consent to search may, in some instances, be a condition for dealing with the government. In the well-known case of *Zap* v. *United States*,[193] (1946), the defendant was convicted of knowingly making a fictitious claim against the government. Zap had contracts with the government which included a clause, pursuant to acts of Congress, stipulating that a contractor with the government must submit his "accounts and records" for inspection and audit, which "shall be open at all times to the Government and its representatives." In this case, agents of the FBI, in course of an audit of Zap's books and records, at his place of business and during business hours, found a check which was evidence of fraud against the government. No search warrant had been secured, and the Court held that a right to a warrant had been waived voluntarily as a condition of obtaining the government's business.

Similarly, the Supreme Court of California ruled, in 1971, that where a

190. Davis v. United States, 328 U.S. 582 (1946).
191. Chapman v. United States, 365 U.S. 610 (1961).
192. Stoner v. California, 376 U.S. 483 (1964).
193. 328 U.S. 624 (1946).

convicted person was given probation on the condition that he "submit his person, place of residence, vehicle, to search and seizure at any time of the day or night, with or without a search warrant, whenever requested to do so by the Probation Officer or any law enforcement officer," he has waived his right to a warrant.[194] To hold otherwise, the Court ruled, would defeat the purpose of the consent provision, which was to deter further offenses and to determine whether the probationer was complying with the terms of probation.[195]

Conclusion

Clearly, the law dealing with searches and seizures is very complex and often demanding, but there are persuasive reasons which explain and justify this body of law. As Chief Justice Hughes once asserted, "The proceeding by search warrant is a drastic one. Its abuse led to the adoption of the Fourth Amendment, and this, together with legislation regulating the process, should be liberally construed in favor of the individual."[196] The plain fact is that the Fourth Amendment right to privacy is important. Justice Douglas once pointed out that it does not deal with mere formalities. "The presence of a search warrant," he wrote, "serves a high function. Absent some grave emergency, the Fourth Amendment has interposed a magistrate between the citizen and the police. This was done not to shield criminals nor to make the home a safe haven for illegal activities. It was done so that an objective mind might weigh the need to invade that privacy in order to enforce the law. The right of privacy was deemed too precious to entrust to the discretion of those whose job is the detection of crime and the arrest of criminals. Power is a heady thing; and history shows that the police acting on their own cannot be trusted. And so the Constitution requires a magistrate to pass on the desires of the police before they violate the privacy of the home."[197]

In spite of the importance of this right, it is abundantly clear that it is often flouted, and usually with complete impunity. A study of the records of one Chicago court for one year revealed 4,593 violations of this right by the police.[198] It ought to be noted that Illinois was one of the minority of states which at the time followed the federal exclusionary rule. The law does not seem to deter police violations of the right in question, though it may be

194. People v. Mason, 5 Cal. 3d 759, 97 Cal. Rptr. 302, 488 P.2d 630 (1971).

195. The Court regarded Zap v. United States, 328 U.S. 624 (1946), as controlling authority for its decision.

196. Sgro v. United States, 287 U.S. 206, 210 (1932).

197. McDonald v. United States, 335 U.S. 451, 455 (1948).

198. Note, "The State Exclusionary Rule as a Deterrent against Unreasonable Search and Seizure," *Journal of Criminal Law, Criminology and Police Science,* 45 (March-April 1955): 697-707.

argued that without the law there would be even more frequent violations. Perhaps no other constitutional right is breached so often, and with such an absence of popular resentment. It has been suggested that the main reason for this apathy is that the victims of illegal searches are usually lawbreakers. Certainly they are rarely pillars of the community. Even the interest of the courts in the problem is a recent one, dating largely from the efforts to enforce the prohibition law after World War I.

9 / Self-Incrimination

Historical Roots

Closely allied to the freedom from unreasonable searches and seizures, as has been noted previously, is the privilege against self-incrimination. It is an ancient teaching of English and American law that it is improper to compel a man to convict himself of a crime by giving unwilling testimony. This is related, in turn, to the assumption of our criminal jurisprudence that one is innocent until proved guilty by competent evidence. That is to say, an individual accused of a crime does not have the burden of establishing his innocence. On the contrary, it is the duty of the state (the prosecution) to prove guilt, and to prove it beyond reasonable doubt.

The privilege against self-incrimination is deeply rooted in Anglo-American law and experience. But since it was not mentioned in the great English charters, such as Magna Carta, the Petition of Right, and the Bill of Rights, it has been argued that on this point the American colonists drew their inspiration from the pre-Revolutionary French agitation against the Ordinance of 1670, which provided for compulsory self-incrimination. The better view, however, is that since the privilege was put into the constitutions of seven states before 1789, it is more likely that the French took their cue from these constitutions, which were widely and eagerly read in pre-Revolutionary France.[1]

In all probability, the most important experience in England leading to the spelling out of the privilege was had in the period of the persecution of the Puritans during the reign of Charles I.[2] The government made much use of special prerogative courts, the Court of High Commission, which went after religious subversion, and the Court of Star Chamber, which specialized in the prosecution of political subverters. Both were interested in prying into men's minds, since both were largely concerned with dangerous

---

1. R. C. Pittman, "The Colonial and Constitutional History of the Privilege against Self-Incrimination in America," *Virginia Law Review*, 21 (May 1935): 763-89; Edward S. Corwin, "The Supreme Court's Construction of the Self-Incrimination Clause," *Michigan Law Review*, 29 (November, December 1930): 1-27, 191-207; Leonard Levy, *Origins of the Fifth Amendment* (New York: Oxford University Press, 1968).

2. See John A. Kemp, "The Background of the Fifth Amendment in English Law: A Study of its Historical Implications," *William and Mary Law Review*, 1, no. 2 (1958): 247-86.

thoughts. Ignoring such common law rules for the trial of cases as were then observed, these courts acquired a well-deserved reputation for highhanded, summary procedures. One such procedure was the use of the *ex officio* oath as a weapon for inducing people to give incriminating testimony. Developed by the ecclesiastical courts in the Stuart period as a means of running down the hidden enemies of the Established Church, the *ex officio* oath became a powerful weapon of persecution. In the common law courts a defendant was not put upon his oath until he was formally charged with having committed a crime, or unless he was at the very least under great suspicion. But since it was much more difficult to get evidence of dangerous thoughts, the judge in a special prerogative court could, simply by virtue of his office, that is to say, *ex officio,* and without a formal charge, put a defendant on oath. He would then proceed to interrogate him, and since in this religious age oaths were taken seriously, the *ex officio* oath exacted a terrible toll. In short, the *ex officio* oath was a method of judicial interrogation on mere suspicion, and thus, as Wigmore puts it, it degenerated "into a merely unlawful process of poking about in the speculation of finding something chargeable."[3]

The famous trials of "Freeborn John" Lilburne,[4] one of the true heroes of English liberty, held in the 1630s and 1640s, first vindicated the privilege against self-incrimination. Accused of importing subversive books from Holland, and later of treason, this stubborn and dedicated man refused to take the oath which required testimony and confession of wrongdoing. He was jailed and severely beaten, but finally won vindication for his position in Parliament. This important right had a place in American law from earliest colonial days, having been incorporated into the Massachusetts Body of Liberties of 1641 and the Connecticut Code of 1650. A Virginia statute adopted in October, 1677, resulting from Governor Berkeley's reign of terror following Bacon's Rebellion, declared that "noe man shall compell a man to sweare against himself in any matter wherein he is lyable to corporal punishment."[5] The practices of the prerogative courts of Governor and Council in the colonies, more than anything else, solidified opinion on the subject. Thus the Virginia Bill of Rights of 1776, which was copied by Pennsylvania, Vermont, and North Carolina, provided that no defendant "can ... be compelled to give evidence against himself."[6] Today all but two of the state constitutions include a specific provision securing the privilege

---

3. John H. Wigmore, *Treatise on Evidence,* 3d ed. (Boston: Little, Brown & Co., 1940), 8: 284.

4. See H. W. Wolfram, "John Lilburne: Democracy's Pillar of Fire," *Syracuse Law Review,* 3 (Spring 1952): 214–58.

5. 2 Henning 442.

6. The Massachusetts Constitution of 1780, Part I, Art. 12, provided, "No subject shall be ... compelled to accuse, or furnish evidence against himself."

against self-incrimination. In the two states which have no explicit constitutional provision on the subject—New Jersey and Iowa—the right is nevertheless held by their courts to be part of the existing law.[7] The federal guaranty is in the Fifth Amendment, which states that "no person . . . shall be compelled in any criminal case to be a witness against himself."

Thus, as Erwin N. Griswold, Dean of the Harvard Law School, has remarked, the Fifth Amendment privilege against self-incrimination is neither an alien nor a novel doctrine, but rather an old and good friend, "one of the great landmarks in man's struggle to make himself civilized."[8] Of this amendment Justice Douglas has written, "It is one of the great landmarks in man's struggle to be free of tyranny, to be decent and civilized. It is our way of escape from the use of torture. It protects man against any form of the Inquisition. It is part of our respect for the dignity of man."[9]

Scope of the Privilege

While it has been argued that the only purpose of the privilege was to prevent torture,[10] the Supreme Court has always taken a much more generous view of its scope. This was established in *Counselman* v. *Hitchcock*,[11] where the Court ruled that the privilege could be claimed by a

---

7. The general rule against self-incrimination is followed in Iowa as part of due process, State v. Height, 117 Iowa 650, 91 N.W. 935 (1902), and in New Jersey as a principle of the common law, State v. Zdanowicz, 69 N.J.L. 619, 55 A. 743 (1903).

8. *The Fifth Amendment Today* (Cambridge: Harvard University Press, 1955), p. 7. In Murphy v. Waterfront Commission of New York, 378 U.S. 52, 55 (1964), Justice Goldberg wrote of the privilege against self-incrimination: "It reflects many of our fundamental values and most noble aspirations: our unwillingness to subject those suspected of crime to the cruel trilemma of self-accusation, perjury or contempt; our preference for an accusatorial rather than an inquisitorial system of criminal justice; our fear that self-incriminating statements will be elicited by inhumane treatment and abuses; our sense of fair play which dictates 'a fair state-individual balance by requiring the government to leave the individual alone until good cause is shown for disturbing him and by requiring the government in its contest with the individual to shoulder the entire load,' . . . our respect for the inviolability of the human personality and of the right of each individual 'to a private enclave where he may lead a private life' . . . ; our distrust of self-deprecatory statements; and our realization that the privilege, while sometimes 'a shelter to the guilty,' is often 'a protection to the innocent.' . . ."

9. William O. Douglas, *An Almanac of Liberty* (Garden City, N.Y.: Doubleday & Co., 1954), p. 238. See also Sidney Hook, *Common Sense and the Fifth Amendment* (New York: Criterion Books, 1957); Lewis Mayers, *Shall We Amend the Fifth Amendment?* (New York: Harper, 1959); Fred E. Inbau, *Self-Incrimination* (Springfield, Ill.: Thomas, 1950).

10. Nathan April, "A Reappraisal of the Immunity from Self-Incrimination," *Minnesota Law Review*, 39 (December 1954): 75–92.

11. 142 U.S. 547 (1892). This was Chief Justice John Marshall's view, sitting as a circuit court judge in Aaron Burr's case, United States v. Burr, 1 Burr's Trial 244 (1807), quoted in 142 U.S. 565.

witness as well as by the accused. "The privilege is limited to criminal matters," Justice Blatchford wrote, "but it is as broad as the mischief against which it seeks to guard." The privilege protects a person against having to reveal a criminal fact in civil proceedings as well. Indeed, the privilege against self-incrimination extends to all sorts of proceedings in which testimony may be required, whether in the course of litigation or not, including all court actions, civil[12] as well as criminal, grand jury investigations, legislative investigations, and inquiries by administrative bodies. Although the Fifth Amendment speaks of "any criminal case," actually the interpretations of the Court have focused attention upon the type of information being sought, rather than upon the nature of the proceeding in which the individual is questioned.

There are, however, important limitations to the privilege. It does not protect a person from giving testimony merely because it would tend to expose him to public ridicule or disgrace, or bring him into disrepute. It must be shown that the testimony would expose the witness to a criminal prosecution. Furthermore, since the privilege is purely personal, one cannot refuse to give testimony on the ground that it would incriminate someone else.[13] Thus, it was ruled in 1973 that a taxpayer cannot invoke his Fifth Amendment privilege to prevent the enforcement of a summons issued by the Internal Revenue Service directing the taxpayer's accountant to produce books, records, bank statements, and cancelled checks in the latter's possession.[14] The Court thought it important to reiterate that the Fifth Amendment privilege is a personal one, adhering to the person and not to information which may incriminate. Said Justice Powell, "It is extortion of information from the accused himself that offends our sense of justice."[15] In this instance, it was only the accountant who was compelled to do something, and he did not claim self-incrimination. Furthermore, the Court noted that in federal law there is no confidential accountant-client privilege. Writing in dissent, Justice Douglas asserted that this decision sanctions "yet another tool of ever-widening governmental invasion and oversight of our private lives."[16]

Since the privilege is a personal right, it applies only to natural persons, and cannot be used on behalf of any organization, such as a corporation or

---

12. For the leading holding that the privilege applies in civil cases, see McCarthy v. Arndstein, 266 U.S. 34 (1924). Said Justice Brandeis, "The privilege is not ordinarily dependent upon the nature of the proceeding in which the testimony is sought or is to be used." See also Maness v. Meyers, 419 U.S. 449 (1975); Wigmore, *Treatise on Evidence*, vol. 8, §2252.
13. Rogers v. United States, 340 U.S. 367 (1951).
14. Couch v. United States, 409 U.S. 322 (1973).
15. 409 U.S. 328.
16. 409 U.S. 338. Justice Marshall also dissented.

labor union.[17] In fact, in 1974, with Justice Douglas dissenting alone, the Court ruled that since a three-man partnership was a collective entity, one partner posessing the entity's records in a representative capacity can't rely on the privilege to avoid producing the records, even though the records might incriminate him personally.[18] Like corporations and unions, partnerships are organized institutional entities controlled by law. Moreover, the papers and effects which the privilege protects must be the private property of the person claiming the privilege, or at least in his possession in a purely personal capacity. Persons holding the official records and documents of an organization in a representative capacity cannot claim the personal privilege against self-incrimination, even though the production of the papers might tend to incriminate them personally. The reason for this rule, the judges have explained, is that the scope of the economic activities of organizations, whether incorporated or not, is so great as to demand governmental regulation. If privileged, effective regulation and enforcement of many federal and state laws would be impossible.[19]

A shadow was cast over the old rule that one cannot be required to produce private business records held personally by the decision in *Shapiro v. United States.*[20] Here the Supreme Court ruled that the privilege did not include business records required by statute to be kept in order that regulatory laws may be enforced, in that instance the wartime Price Control Act. But this was a 5-4 decision, Justice Frankfurter protesting that "if records merely because required to be kept by law *ipso facto* become public records, we are indeed living in glass houses. Virtually every major public law enactment—to say nothing of State and local legislation—has record-keeping provisions." While the possible scope of the *Shapiro* decision is indeed sweeping, it should be noted that the doctrine has been invoked rather sparingly since it was first announced. It has not yet been applied with judicial approval in the important tax field, although federal tax legislation has extensive record-keeping provisions.[21] In fact, it has been

---

17. Campbell Painting Corp. v. Reid, 392 U.S. 286 (1968) (corporation); Curcio v. United States, 353 U.S. 118 (1957) (incorporated union); United States v. White, 322 U.S. 694 (1944) (unincorporated union); Wilson v. United States, 221 U.S. 361 (1911) (corporation).

18. Bellis v. United States, 417 U.S. 85 (1974).

19. United States v. White, 322 U.S. 694 (1944).

20. 335 U.S. 1 (1948). See Note, "Constitutional Limits on the Admissibility in the Federal Courts of Evidence Obtained from Required Records," *Harvard Law Review*, 68 (December 1954): 340-49.

21. See, e.g., Blumberg v. United States, 222 F.2d 496 (5th Cir. 1955). For cases decided by courts of appeal holding that income tax records are not altogether privileged, but where the issue arose indirectly, see Falsone v. United States, 205 F.2d 734 (5th Cir. 1953), cert. denied, 346 U.S. 864 (1953); Beard v. United States, 222 F.2d 84 (4th Cir. 1955), cert. denied, 350 U.S. 846 (1955).

noted that "the Internal Revenue Service has not attempted to compel production of an individual's record for use against him where the investigation involves possible criminal liability."[22]

That the "required records" exception of the *Shapiro* case is a very limited one is reflected in later decisions involving attempts by the federal government to compel persons to file registration statements which would expose the registrants to possible criminal prosecution in such areas as subversive activity and commercialized gambling. When the constitutionality of the Gambler's Occupational Tax Act of 1951, which required all persons "engaged in the business of accepting wagers" to pay a tax and register with the Collector of Internal Revenue, was first challenged, the Supreme Court upheld the statute in two cases on the theory that the privilege relates only to past acts, and not to future acts that may or may not be committed.[23] That is to say, the Court reasoned that under the wagering statute, one is not compelled to confess to acts already committed; he is merely informed by the act that in order to engage in the business of wagering in the future, he must fulfil certain conditions. This position, from which a minority of three Justices dissented vigorously, was abandoned by the Court in two cases decided upon in 1968.[24] The Court reasoned that since wagering is widely prohibited under both federal and state law, and since the information obtained under the federal wagering tax act was readily available to federal and state law enforcement authorities, the obligation to pay the occupational tax and register creates a real and appreciable, and not a merely imaginary, hazard of self-incrimination. The argument previously made that the law applies only to future acts was abandoned; if one registers, that in itself increases the likelihood that past offenses will be discovered and prosecuted. Thus the Court could see no warrant for holding that the privilege against self-incrimination was entirely inapplicable to prospective

---

22. Paul P. Lipton, "Record Keeping and the Privilege against Self-Incrimination," *Proceedings of the Fourteenth Annual Institute on Federal Taxation* (Albany: Matthew Bender & Co., 1956), pp. 1331–44, 1337. Of course, the privilege does not authorize a taxpayer to decline to file an income tax return, United States v. Sullivan, 274 U.S. 259 (1927), though the privilege might apply to portions of the return. See Note, "Constitutional Aspects of Federal Tax Investigations," *Columbia Law Review,* 57 (May 1957): 676–99.

23. United States v. Kahriger, 345 U.S. 22 (1953); Lewis v. United States, 348 U.S. 419 (1955). The vote in these cases was 6–3. Making a false statement in the form required by the wagering tax act was held to be a criminal offense as a violation of a general statute punishing the making of fraudulent statements to the government. United States v. Fox, 396 U.S. 77 (1969).

24. Marchetti v. United States, 390 U.S. 39 (1968); Grosso v. United States, 390 U.S. 62 (1968). These decisions were held to be nonretroactive in Mackey v. United States, 401 U.S. 667 (1971), unless there had been seizures of property. United States v. U.S. Coin and Currency, 401 U.S. 715 (1971).

acts. The basic principle is that he who claims the privilege must be confronted by a real, substantial hazard of incrimination, and this cannot be defined by an inflexible chronological formula. Finally, the "required records" doctrine of the *Shapiro* case was held not relevant to this situation; the *Shapiro* requirements were essentially noncriminal and in a regulatory area (price control), whereas here the activities in question were inherently suspect of criminality, in respect to which persons were not obliged to keep and preserve records. Thus, the underlying premises of the *Shapiro* doctrine were described by Justice Harlan as follows: "[F]irst, the purposes of the United States' inquiry must be essentially regulatory; second, information is to be obtained by requiring the preservation of records of a kind which the regulated party has customarily kept; and third, the records themselves must have assumed 'public aspects' which render them at least analogous to public documents."[25]

The Court has, in a series of decisions which began with the wagering tax cases, ruled unconstitutional several federal statutes which required the filing of registration statements in connection with the imposition of special taxes. A firearms control statute was held invalid on the ground that satisfaction of the obligation to register would have compelled the registrant to provide information of an incriminating character.[26] Similarly, a statute requiring members of the Communist Party to file registration statements with the Attorney-General was held unconstitutional by a unanimous vote of the Supreme Court, Justice Brennan pointing out that the risks of self-incrimination in registering were "obvious", since this information could be used as evidence in prosecutions under such federal criminal statutes as the Smith Act and the Subversive Activities Control Act.[27] The Court has also set aside a conviction under the Marijuana Tax Act, on the ground that the taxpayer had to supply incriminating information which was made available to law enforcement officials.[28]

---

25. Grosso v. United States, 390 U.S. 62, 67–68 (1968).

26. Haynes v. United States, 390 U.S. 85 (1968). An amended firearms act was upheld in United States v. Freed, 401 U.S. 601 (1971), on the ground that the act barred the use of registration data in a prosecution for prior or concurrent offenses, and because as a matter of practice registration data were not made available to local, state, or other federal authorities.

27. Albertson v. Subversive Activities Control Board, 382 U.S. 70 (1965). See Bernard D. Meltzer, "Required Records, the McCarran Act, and the Privilege against Self-Incrimination," *University of Chicago Law Review*, 18 (Summer 1951): 687–728.

28. Leary v. United States, 395 U.S. 6 (1969). In Minor v. United States, 396 U.S. 87 (1969), the Court upheld a conviction for selling marijuana without the official order form required by the Marijuana Tax Act, on the theory that there was no real and substantial possibility that the order form requirement would in any way incriminate sellers, it being improbable that buyers would be willing to comply with the requirement.

How the Privilege is Pleaded

There is no particular formula which must be employed or procedure which must be observed in order to plead the privilege against self-incrimination. The Supreme Court has taken the position that tribunals must be alert to notice when the privilege is relied upon, even though the witness uses ambiguous or evasive language. In several cases the Court has had occasion to rule on this point where witnesses who were called to testify before the House Committee on Un-American Activities attempted to plead the privilege in such an evasive way that they could enjoy the advantages of silence without incurring the public odium which might follow a forthright claim to the privilege. The tactic was to decline to answer "primarily on the basis of the first amendment, supplemented by the fifth," or to refuse to answer for the reason given by some previous witness, that reason also being couched in such language.[29] Chief Justice Warren declared that "no ritualistic formula or talismanic phrase" or orthodox statement is necessary to invoke the privilege.[30] He said that "a claim of the privilege does not require any special combination of words. Plainly a witness need not have the skill of a lawyer to invoke the protection of the Self-Incrimination Clause. If an objection to a question is made in any language that a committee may reasonably be expected to understand as an attempt to invoke the privilege, it must be respected both by the committee and by a court. . . ."[31] Any reference to the Fifth Amendment suffices, the Court ruled, since in common parlance today the Fifth Amendment has come to mean the privilege against self-incrimination. The Chief Justice added that especially today, when people fear the stigma that might result from a forthright claim of the constitutional right to refuse to testify, and "when the privilege is under attack by those who wrongly conceive of it as merely a shield for the guilty," it is incumbent upon governmental bodies to be most scrupulous to protect the exercise of the right.

What is Incrimination?

It is important to note that the privilege under discussion extends not only to evidence which actually incriminates the witness, but also to evidence which may *tend* to incriminate. It follows that testimony which would merely lend support to the charge of crime falls within the privilege. This was made abundantly clear in the case of Patricia Blau,[32] who appeared as a

---

29. Quinn v. United States, 349 U.S. 155 (1955); Emspak v. United States, 349 U.S. 190 (1955); Bart v. United States, 349 U.S. 219 (1955).
30. Emspak v. United States, 349 U.S. 194 (1955).
31. Quinn v. United States, 349 U.S. 162 (1955).
32. Patricia Blau v. United States, 340 U.S. 159 (1950). See also Hoffman v. United States, 341 U.S. 479 (1951).

witness before a federal grand jury in Denver and refused to say whether she knew the names of the state officers of the Communist Party, or the organization of the party, or whether she had ever been employed by it or had ever had custody of its records. The Supreme Court held unanimously that in view of the fact that the Smith Act was on the statute books, a statute forbidding the teaching or advocacy of the duty or desirability of overthrowing the government by violent or other lawless means, she reasonably could fear that criminal charges might be brought against her if she admitted employment by the Communist Party or intimate knowledge of its workings. And Justice Black went on to say, "Whether such admissions by themselves would support a conviction under a criminal statute is immaterial. Answers to the questions asked by the grand jury would have furnished a link in the chain of evidence needed in a prosecution of petitioner. . . ." under the Smith Act. Accordingly, many witnesses appearing before legislative investigating committees have refused to answer questions about present or past membership in the Communist Party on Fifth Amendment grounds, and their right to do so has been uniformly upheld by the courts.

It should be stressed that the answers elicited by the questions must tend to expose the witness to a prosecution for a crime to fall within the privilege. If the witness has already been tried for the offense, or has been pardoned, he cannot refuse to testify, since there is no possibility of punishment again. Or if the legislature has conferred immunity from prosecution by statute, the witness cannot refuse to reply to the questions put to him, since the only reason for the privilege no longer exists.

But people who do refuse to answer questions may suffer other consequences for which the Fifth Amendment supplies no protection. One who refuses to say, standing on his constitutional right not to incriminate himself, whether or not he is a member of the Communist Party, runs the risk that many people, rightly or wrongly, will draw an unfavorable inference from his silence. Such an inference, while not inevitable, is altogether natural, for ordinarily we expect people who are given the opportunity to proclaim their innocence of adverse charges. Innocent people will usually deny untrue charges. Said Wigmore, " 'Logic is logic,' ever since the days of the One-Hoss Shay; and it is on that score impossible to deny that the very claim of the privilege involves a confession of the fact. 'Were you assisting the defendant at the time of the affray?'; this may be answered 'yes' or 'no'; if 'no,' the fact is not criminating and the privilege is not applicable; if 'yes,' the fact is criminating and the privilege applies. The inference, as a mere matter of logic, is not only possible but inherent, and cannot be denied."[33]

---

33. Wigmore, *Treatise on Evidence*, 8: 409–10.

Furthermore, a number of state statutes, city ordinances, and school board regulations provide that public employees who refuse to answer questions put to them by legislative committees on grounds of the privilege against self-incrimination are automatically dismissed from public employment.[34] Several state courts have sustained such statutes and regulations against constitutional objections.[35] Their view has been that all the privilege protects the individual from is punishment, and that dismissal from public employment is not punishment, because there is no constitutional right to such employment. While they concede that refusal to testify does not prove guilt, they insist that no issue of guilt or innocence is involved, but only an issue of fitness for employment.

In the spring of 1956, however, the Supreme Court ruled by a 5-4 vote in *Slochower* v. *Board of Higher Education of New York City*[36] that automatic and summary dismissal of a teacher merely because he utilized the privilege against self-incrimination in the course of a committee hearing violated Fourteenth Amendment due process. Slochower was a professor at Brooklyn College who had twenty-seven years experience as a college teacher and was entitled to tenure under state law. Under this law he could be discharged only for cause after notice and a hearing and appeal. Slochower had invoked the Fifth Amendment before the Internal Security Subcommittee of the Senate Judiciary Committee. While he stated that he was not then a member of the Communist Party and was willing to answer all questions regarding memberships, associations, and beliefs since 1941, he refused to answer questions concerning his membership during 1940 and

---

34. See Note, "Mandatory Dismissal of Public Personnel and the Privilege against Self-Incrimination," *University of Pennsylvania Law Review,* 101 (June 1953): 1190-1204.

35. Daniman v. Board of Education of New York, 306 N.Y. 532, 119 N.E. 2d 373 (1954); Faxon v. School Committee of Boston, 331 Mass. 531, 120 N.E. 2d 772 (1954); Drury v. Hurley, 339 Ill. 33, 88 N.E. 2d 728 (1949). The state of New York has gone so far as to write this doctrine into its fundamental law. The New York Constitution was amended in 1949, 1959, and 1973, Article I, §6, so that the self-incrimination clause reads as follows: "No person shall be subject to be twice put in jeopardy for the same offense; nor shall he be compelled in any criminal case to be a witness against himself, providing, that any public officer who, upon being called before a grand jury to testify concerning the conduct of his present office or of any public office held by him within five years prior to such grand jury call to testify, or the performance of his official duties, in any such present or prior offices, refuses to sign a waiver of immunity against subsequent criminal prosecution, or to answer any relevant question concerning such matters before such grand jury, shall by virtue of such refusal, be disqualified from holding any other public office or public employment for a period of five years from the date of such refusal to sign a waiver of immunity against subsequent prosecution, or to answer any relevant question concerning such matters before such grand jury, and shall be removed from his present office by the appropriate authority or shall forfeit his present office at the suit of the attorney-general."

36. 350 U.S. 551 (1956).

1941 on the ground of self-incrimination. Under Section 903 of the Charter of the City of New York, the Court of Appeals of the state ruled that assertion of the privilege was equivalent to a resignation, and that since dismissal was therefore automatic, the teacher had no right to charges, notice, a hearing, etc. It is to be noted, however, that the Court of Appeals accepted the committee's determination that the privilege had been properly invoked, and held that no inference of membership in the Communist Party could be drawn from the refusal to testify. It found that the Charter merely imposed a condition on public employment.

The Supreme Court went about as far as it ever has in making it clear that while there is no constitutional right to public employment, the inference does not follow that the government may attach any conditions it pleases to such employment. "To state that a person does not have a constitutional right to government employment," said Justice Clark, "is only to say that he must comply with reasonable, lawful, and nondiscriminatory terms laid down by the proper authorities." He stressed the fact that in recent decisions dealing with the discharge of public employees the Court has always insisted that the state must conform with the requirements of due process.[37] Furthermore, said Justice Clark, "we must condemn the practice of imputing a sinister meaning to the exercise of a person's constitutional right under the Fifth Amendment. The right of an accused person to refuse to testify, which had been in England merely a rule of evidence, was so important to our forefathers that they raised it to the dignity of a constitutional enactment, and it has been recognized as 'one of the most valuable prerogatives of the citizen.' *Brown* v. *Walker,* 161 U.S. 591, 610. . . . The privilege against self-incrimination would be reduced to a hollow mockery if its exercise could be taken as equivalent either to a confession of guilt or a conclusive presumption of perjury. . . . A witness may have a reasonable fear of prosecution and yet be innocent of any wrongdoing. The privilege serves to protect the innocent who otherwise might be ensnared by ambiguous circumstances."[38]

Justice Clark noted that the Charter section operated automatically. "No consideration is given to such factors as the subject matter of the questions, remoteness of the period to which they are directed, or justification for exercise of the privilege. It matters not whether the plea resulted from mistake, inadvertence or legal advice conscientiously given, whether wisely or unwisely. The heavy hand of the statute falls alike on all who exercise their

---

37. Adler v. Board of Education, 342 U.S. 485 (1952); Garner v. Los Angeles Board, 341 U.S. 716 (1951); Wieman v. Updegraff, 344 U.S. 183, 192 (1952): ". . . constitutional protection does extend to the public servant whose exclusion pursuant to a statute is patently arbitrary or discriminatory."
38. 350 U.S. 557–58.

constitutional privilege, the full enjoyment of which every person is entitled to receive." Pointing out that the Board based Slochower's discharge entirely on events occurring before a federal committee, and that the questions which he declined to answer were admittedly asked for a purpose wholly unrelated to his college functions, the Court concluded that "since no inference of guilt was possible from the claim before the federal committee, the discharge falls of its own weight as wholly without support." In other words, the discharge was arbitrary. This does not mean that Slochower had a constitutional right to be a professor at Brooklyn College. Nor does it mean that the state does not have broad powers to select and discharge its employees. But it does mean that the state must conduct a "proper inquiry."[39]

The four dissenting Justices in this case maintained that "legally authorized bodies have a right to demand that citizens furnish facts pertinent to official inquiries," and that avoidance of the public duty to respond can properly be considered to stamp the employee as unfit to hold certain official positions, especially that of a teacher of the youth. They insisted that refusal to answer questions asked by public authorities relating to official conduct jeopardizes popular confidence in the schools.

Similarly, in a more recent decision the Court has ruled that the privilege against self-incrimination is available to a lawyer facing charges of professional misconduct who was disbarred after refusing to honor a subpoena *duces tecum* demanding production of financial records by invoking the privilege.[40] The Court held that the privilege should not be watered down by imposing the dishonor of disbarment and deprivation of a livelihood as a price for asserting it. The right of a person to remain silent means that he is to suffer no penalty for such silence, and in this context the concept of penalty is not limited to a fine or imprisonment. It refers, Justice Douglas argued, to any sanction which makes the assertion of the privilege "costly." At the same time, the Court ruled that a statute which requires a policeman to choose between his job and the privilege violates the constitution, Justice Douglas remarking that "policeman, like teachers and lawyers, are not relegated to a watered-down version of constitutional rights."[41]

39. 350 U.S. 558-59.
40. Spevack v. Klein, 385 U.S. 511 (1967). This case, decided by a 5-4 vote, overruled Cohen v. Hurley, 366 U.S. 117 (1961), which had also been decided by a 5-4 vote.
41. Garrity v. New Jersey, 385 U.S. 493, 500 (1967). To the same effect were the decisions in Stevens v. Marks, 383 U.S. 234 (1966); Gardner v. Broderick, 392 U.S. 273 (1968). In Lefkowitz v. Turley, 414 U.S. 70 (1973), the Court ruled unconstitutional a New York statute which provided that one who holds a public contract who takes the privilege if called to testify regarding the contract is ineligible for further state contracts for a period of five years. The underlying rationale was that a waiver of immunity secured under the threat of a substantial economic sanction cannot be characterized as voluntary.

To a considerable extent, the Court's decision in the *Slochower* case was diluted in 1958, in *Beilan* v. *Board of Education of Philadelphia,* [42] where by a 5-4 vote the Court upheld the dismissal of a public school teacher who had refused to reply to questions put to her by the superintendent regarding Communist activity. The only ground given for the discharge was professional incompetency, no reference being made to the privilege. The Court majority held that the question was relevant to the issue of fitness and suitability to serve as a teacher, and that the ultimate finding on which the dismissal was based was not disloyalty, but rather insubordination, lack of frankness and candor. In a companion case, *Lerner* v. *Casey,* [43] again by a 5-4 vote, the Court reached a similar conclusion in upholding the dismissal of a subway conductor in New York who had also refused to answer questions regarding Communist activity on self-incrimination grounds. The Court held that the dismissal was not due to the invocation of the privilege, but was based on a reasonable belief that the employee was of "doubtful trust and reliability," which is well within the requirements of due process of law. The dissenting Justices argued that Beilan had in fact been dismissed for refusing to testify on Fifth Amendment grounds, and that no inference of wrongdoing should be permitted to flow from the invocation of any constitutional right.

Whether a particular situation involves the issue of self-incrimination reaches the Supreme Court in many different forms. For example, the Court has ruled that it is reversible error for the trial judge to permit the government, for the purpose of impeaching a defendant's credibility, to cross-examine him at the trial with regard to his assertion of the privilege against self-incrimination before the grand jury, where the assertion of the privilege was not inconsistent with the defendant's later testimony at the trial. [44] Four concurring Justices argued that under no circumstances would it be justifiable to make use of a person's assertion of a constitutional privilege to discredit or convict him. Similarly, the Court has ruled that it is highly prejudicial for the prosecutor to tell the jury of the defendant's failure to take the stand at previous trials on the same charges, for this amounts to using his silence against him. [45] In an appeal of a state conviction, the Court held unconstitutional a statute which required the defendant to testify before any other defense witness is heard, on the ground that this rule was an inpermissible restriction on the defendant's right to remain silent unless he chooses to speak in the unfettered exercise of his own will. [46] The state's interest in preventing testimonial influence does not

42. 357 U.S. 399 (1958).
43. 357 U.S. 468 (1958).
44. Grunewald v. United States, 353 U.S. 391 (1957).
45. Stewart v. United States, 366 U.S. 1 (1961). The decision was 5-4.
46. Brooks v. Tennessee, 406 U.S. 605 (1972). The decision was 6-3.

justify overriding the defendant's right to remain silent at the trial. On the other hand, the Court held valid a Florida rule of criminal procedure which, on written demand of the prosecutor, requires the defendant, if he intends to claim an alibi, to serve notice in advance of trial, giving the prosecutor information about the place where he will claim to have been, and the names and addresses of his alibi witnesses.[47] The Court held that at most this is a limited form of pretrial discovery, justified by the state's interest in protecting itself against an eleventh-hour defense of alibi. The Court noted that whenever the defendant presents his defense, he must present witnesses who will then be subject to cross-examination, and refused to consider the alibi defense "compelled," since the defendant does not have to offer alibi as a defense, and nothing prevents him from abandoning it. Justices Black and Douglas thought this was a clear violation of the defendant's fundamental right to remain silent, arguing that the state must prove its case without any kind of assistance from the defendant himself. In another recent decision, the Court held that compelling a grand jury witness to furnish voice exemplars for identification purposes, without a preliminary showing of reasonableness, does not violate the Fourth or Fifth Amendments, on the theory that nothing testimonial is involved.[48] Finally, to cite a quite different problem, in *California* v. *Byers,*[49] decided in 1971 by a 5–4 vote, the Court held constitutional a California hit-and-run statute which requires every motorist who has been involved in a property damage accident to stop and identify himself, by giving his name and address to the police and the owner of the property. The Court majority thought that no substantial risk of self-incrimination is involved in complying with a mainly regulatory statute designed to promote satisfaction of civil liabilities for automobile accidents. Chief Justice Burger stressed that the statute was directed at the public at large, rather than at a selected group suspected of crime. Furthermore, he maintained that the required information is not testimonial in the Fifth Amendment sense, and that all the statute demands is "an essentially neutral act." In a vehement dissenting opinion, Justice Black argued that this decision practically wipes out the Fifth Amendment provision against compelled self-incrimination.

Waiver

Freedom from self-incrimination, like many other personal rights, may be waived. A defendant in a criminal prosecution may, if he chooses, refuse to testify, but he is at liberty to waive his privilege by taking the stand. Similarly, a witness may voluntarily testify, and merely by not asserting the

---

47. Williams v. Florida, 399 U.S. 78 (1970).
48. United States v. Dionisio, 410 U.S. 1 (1973).
49. 402 U.S. 424 (1971).

privilege, he waives it. But one who, claiming the privilege, testifies voluntarily, does not waive his privilege unless he gives testimony which is in fact incriminating. Once a witness has given incriminating testimony, however, he cannot plead the privilege with respect to further testimony on the same subject, since he has already incriminated himself. This was the substance of the Court's decision in *Rogers* v. *United States*,[50] which was concerned with the appearance of a witness, in response to a subpoena, before a federal grand jury. After testifying that she had held the position of treasurer of the Communist Party of Denver until a certain recent date, that she had been in possession of the party's records, and that she had turned them over to another person, she refused to identify that person, asserting the privilege. The Supreme Court upheld a conviction for contempt, pointing out that the witness had voluntarily testified to incriminating facts, and that having done so she was not free to select any stopping place in the testimony. Said Chief Justice Vinson, "Since the privilege against self-incrimination presupposes a real danger of legal detriment arising from the disclosure, petitioner cannot invoke the privilege where response to the specific question in issue here would not further incriminate her. Disclosure of a fact waives the privilege as to details."[51] Having admitted as much as she did, the Court felt that disclosure of acquaintance with her successor presented no more than a mere imaginary possibility of increasing the danger of prosecution. For the Chief Justice maintained that naming other officers could not incriminate her further, since she could be convicted of conspiracy with persons whose names are not even known.

That this aspect of the doctrine of waiver is debatable is reflected in the 5–3 division of the Court in the *Rogers* case. Speaking for the dissenters, Justice Black lamented the fact that some people are hostile to the Self-Incrimination Clause "as an outmoded relic of past fears generated by ancient inquisitorial practices that could not possibly happen here," and therefore as "more or less of a constitutional nuisance." He noted that the Court has almost always construed the Amendment broadly, on the theory that compelling a person to convict himself of crime is contrary to the principles of free government, and abhorrent to the instincts of an American. He regarded the doctrine of waiver as a device for whittling away the protection afforded by the privilege. While he conceded that a

---

50. 340 U.S. 367 (1951). To the same effect is Brown v. United States, 356 U.S. 148 (1958). In England a witness who replies to some questions does not waive his right to refuse to answer later questions; he may claim his privilege at any time. Halsbury, *Laws of England*, vol. 13, §804; Regina v. Garbett (1847), 1 Denison's Crown Cases 236. On the other hand, under English law a bankrupt can be required to give incriminating evidence.

51. 340 U.S. 372–73.

constitutional right can be relinquished intentionally, he insisted that an inference to this effect should not be made lightly, nor be supported by vague and uncertain evidence. In this instance the dissenters could find no evidence that the witness intended to give up her privilege of silence concerning the persons in possession of the Communist records. Justice Black thought that the Court's decision posed this dilemma for witnesses: that they must either risk imprisonment for contempt by asserting the privilege prematurely, or lose the privilege by answering a single question. "The Court's view," he said, "makes the protection depend on timing so refined that lawyers, let alone laymen, will have difficulty in knowing when to claim it."[52]

The *Rogers* case does not stand for the proposition that any answer to an incriminating question opens the door to unrestricted further questioning, for additional questions which add new elements of guilt are not permissible. For example, in a later case[53] a witness answered "yes" to the question, "Are you a well-known member of the Communist Party?" A federal judge in the district court of the District of Columbia held that this reply did not constitute a waiver of the privilege when the witness was then asked, "Have you ever held office in the Communist Party?" For the second question was directed to a new element of the crime pointed up by the first. Furthermore, it has been held that mere denial of an incriminating fact, as contrasted with an affirmative admission, does not require the witness to answer further questions relating to that fact.[54] This is in accord with the view of the Supreme Court, previously declared, that "waiver of constitutional rights ... is not lightly to be inferred. A witness cannot properly be held after claim to have waived his privilege and consequent immunity upon vague and uncertain evidence."[55]

The Issue of Comment

Until 1965, most states followed the rule prevailing in federal courts, that it is not permissible for the judge or the prosecutor to comment to the jury on the failure of the defendant to take the stand and testify in his own behalf.[56] For the most part, the theory has been that comment forces the defendant to take the stand by making it more hazardous for him to remain

52. 340 U.S. 376, 378.
53. United States v. Nelson, 103 F. Supp. 215 (D.D.C. 1952).
54. McCarthy v. Arndstein, 262 U.S. 355 (1923). So held also in People *ex rel.* Taylor v. Forbes, 143 N.Y. 219, 38 N.E. 303 (1894).
55. Smith v. United States, 337 U.S. 137, 150 (1949).
56. For leading cases see *In re* Opinion of the Justices, 300 Mass. 620, 15 N.E. 2d 662 (1938); State v. Wolfe, 64 S.D. 178, 266 N.W. 116 (1936).

silent. Indeed, for many years a federal statute has provided that a defendant's failure to testify "shall not create any presumption against him."[57] The Supreme Court has ruled that this language gives the criminal accused an "indefeasible right" to have the jury instructed by the trial judge that his failure to testify does not create any presumption against him.[58] It was held that the statute must be contrued as an "implied direction" to judges to so instruct the juries, since this was the only way that the congressional policy could be implemented. In reply to the familiar argument that it is psychologically impossible for the jury to avoid an unfavorable inference from the failure of the defendant to testify in his own behalf, "the short answer is that Congress legislated on a contrary assumption and not without support in experience." In addition to state constitutional self-incrimination clauses, many state statutes forbid comment.

It is pertinent to note that before 1864 no state permitted a defendant in a criminal case to testify at all. When states began to enact statutes making it competent for him to testify, beginning with Maine in 1864, this legislation almost always provided that failure of the accused to testify should not create a presumption against him. The act of Congress on this subject was adopted in 1878. Wigmore explains that the long delay in making defendants competent to testify was due to a reluctance to deprive the defendant of a supposed advantage. "His failure to use the right of testifying would (it was believed) damage his cause more seriously than if he were able to claim that his silence was enforced by law."[59] But the main reason for the perseverance of the old rule was, according to Wigmore, the fear of subjecting the defendant to the ordeal of cross-examination.

In the celebrated case of *Twining* v. *New Jersey* (1908),[60] however, the Supreme Court ruled that a state does not deny due process of law by permitting the trial judge to draw an unfavorable inference against a defendant who has refused to testify in a criminal court. In a well-drawn opinion Justice Moody reasoned that while settled common law procedures in use in England at the time of the settlement of America were an important index to the meaning of due process, they were not the only measure of that concept, for if usage alone were the determining factor, "the procedure of the first half of the seventeenth century would be fastened upon the American jurisprudence like a straight-jacket. . . ." On the contrary, the

---

57. U.S.C. §3481 (1970). The present language dates from the 1948 revision. The statute was originally adopted March 16, 1878, 20 Stat. 30. This statute was held to forbid unfavorable comment by the court or the district attorney in Wilson v. United States, 149 U.S. 60 (1892).

58. Bruno v. United States, 308 U.S. 287 (1939).

59. *Treatise on Evidence*, 2: 703.

60. 211 U.S. 78 (1908).

touchstone of due process is not age but justice. Reviewing the history of the self-incrimination concept, Justice Moody concluded that it was not an essential part of due process. While it may be a salutary principle, "it cannot be ranked with the right to hearing before condemnation, the immunity from arbitrary power not acting by general laws, and the inviolability of private property." It was not, he said, "an unchangeable principle of universal justice," and indeed doesn't exist outside the common law.[61]

The Supreme Court reviewed this issue fully in 1947, in the important case of *Adamson* v. *California*,[62] and reached the same conclusion, though four Justices dissented, Justice Black arguing that the due process clause of the Fourteenth Amendment was intended to apply all the provisions of the federal Bill of Rights to the states. This theory of total incorporation has never been accepted by a majority of the Court.

At the time of the *Adamson* decision, six states still permitted comment either by virtue of constitutional provision or statute or both—Iowa, New Jersey, California, Connecticut, Ohio, and Vermont.[63] This practice came to an end in 1965, when in *Griffin* v. *California*,[64] by a 7–2 vote, the Supreme Court ruled that if a state court permits comment on the failure of the defendant to testify, it violates due process. Speaking for the Court, Justice Douglas asserted that comment "is a remnant of the 'inquisitorial system of criminal justice,' . . . which the Fifth Amendment outlaws. It is a penalty imposed by courts for exercising a constitutional privilege. It cuts down on the privilege by making its assertion costly." Justice Douglas rejected the argument that comment makes no difference. He asserted that there is a great deal of difference between what a jury may think without help, and what it may infer "when the court solemnizes the silence of the accused into evidence. . . ."[65]

The two dissenters, Justices Stewart and White, took the position that a jury will note that the accused did not testify even if not reminded of it, and pointed out that the jury was properly instructed that failure of the defendant to testify does not create a presumption of guilt. They also maintained that the Supreme Court has no general supervisory power over the state courts in the formulation of procedural rules for the administration of justice.

There are several well-known objections to comment. One is that it is

---

61. 211 U.S. 101, 113.
62. 332 U.S. 46 (1947).
63. See State v. Ferguson, 226 Iowa 361, 283 N.W. 917 (1939); State v. Kisik, 99 N.J.L. 385, 125 A. 239 (1924); People v. Modesto, 62 Cal. 2d 436, 398 P.2d 753 (1965); Ohio Const., Art. I, §10; Cal. Const., Art. I, §13.
64. 380 U.S. 609 (1965).
65. 380 U.S. 614.

feared that if comment is permitted the prosecution may be tempted to use it as a substitute for proof, thus also encouraging careless police work. The burden of proof, it is believed, will be shifted at the expense of the presumption of innocence. It is also maintained that comment tends to force the accused to take the stand because of the fear of the consequences of not doing so. To compel him to testify then exposes him to unwanted cross-examination. On the other hand, it is invariably pointed out that since jurors draw their own inferences from the fact that the accused did not testify, comment does not in fact make much difference. It is "quite natural" for people to believe that if the accused is innocent, he has every reason to testify, since the truth will protect him. Finally, it is argued that the true purpose of the guaranty against self-incrimination is to forbid direct coercion, which is altogether unaffected by comment. The American Bar Association and the American Law Institute adopted resolutions in 1931 in favor of comment by both the judge and the prosecutor.[66]

The Supreme Court's present position clearly runs in the other direction. Accordingly, it has decided several times that violation of the rule against comment cannot be regarded as harmless error.[67]

Self-Incrimination and Federalism

Having ruled that various aspects of self-incrimination are elements of due process binding upon the states through the Fourteenth Amendment, the Supreme Court went all the way, in 1964, in the leading case of *Malloy* v. *Hogan*,[68] in deciding that the Fourteenth Amendment made the Fifth Amendment privilege against self-incrimination fully applicable to the states, and that therefore federal standards are controlling in state cases. Speaking for a bare majority of five, Justice Brennan, beginning with the premise that the privilege against self-incrimination is an essential mainstay of the American system of accusatorial justice, declared that "it would be incongruous to have different standards determine the validity of a claim of privilege based on the same feared prosecution, depending on whether the claim was asserted in a state or federal court. Therefore, the same standards must determine whether an accused's silence in either a federal or state proceeding is justified."[69] Speaking in dissent, Justice Harlan argued that the incongruity of having different standards prevail in

---

66. See Robert P. Reeder, "Comment upon Failure of Accused to Testify," *Michigan Law Review*, 31 (November 1932): 40–58.

67. Chapman v. California, 386 U.S. 18 (1967); Anderson v. Nelson, 390 U.S. 523 (1968); Fontaine v. California, 390 U.S. 593 (1968).

68. 378 U.S. 1 (1964).

69. 378 U.S. 11.

federal and state courts is at the heart of the American federal system. He insisted, as he did consistently, that the test of due process is fundamental fairness and not federal standards. Two other dissenting Justices argued that Malloy's claim should have been rejected even if judged by federal standards.

The questions as to whether one may refuse to testify in a federal proceeding because the testimony would incriminate under state law, whether one who has been given immunity in a federal proceeding also has immunity in subsequent state proceedings, and whether one who has been given immunity in a state proceeding is therefore immune in a later federal proceeding, have been the subject of extensive review in Supreme Court litigation. The Court once ruled that one could not refuse to testify in a federal proceeding because the testimony would incriminate him under state law, in accordance with the theory of federal supremacy, which in this context meant that the enforcement of a national statute could not be made to depend upon state law or state policy.[70] By the same token, the Court also ruled that testimony given in a state court under a state statute granting immunity could be admitted in a federal court,[71] the theory being that a state cannot decide when to relieve an individual from a federal prosecution. Similarly, the Court ruled that a state may compel a witness to give testimony which might incriminate him under federal law.[72]

Since the national government is supreme within the range of its delegated authority, however, it may bar the use of evidence in any court, state as well as federal, in order to secure testimony for proper federal purposes. When a witness who had been summoned to testify before a U.S. Senate investigating committee was given immunity by a federal statute which barred the use of his testimony as evidence "in any court," the

---

70. United States v. Murdock, 284 U.S. 141 (1931).

71. Feldman v. United States, 322 U.S. 487 (1944). The vote was 4–3. The Court had previously ruled that the due process clause does not prevent a state from compelling testimony by granting immunity from prosecution for any state offense, although incrimination under federal law was possible. Jack v. Kansas, 199 U.S. 372 (1905).

72. Knapp v. Schweitzer, 357 U.S. 371 (1958). The Court was divided 6–3. Said Justice Black in dissent, "I cannot agree that we must accept this intolerable state of affairs as a necessary part of our federal system of government." 357 U.S. 385. However, a state court was always free to hold that a state immunity law is deficient if it does not exclude a federal prosecution. It was so held in People v. Den Uyl, 318 Mich. 645, 29 N.W. 2d 284, 2 A.L.R. 2d 625 (1947); State ex rel. Mitchell v. Kelly, 71 So. 2d 887 (Fla. 1954). The Michigan Supreme Court pointed out that it was aware that its holding was at variance with the position taken by federal and other state courts, but it added, "It seems like a travesty on verity to say that one is not subjected to self-incrimination when compelled to give testimony in a State judicial proceeding which testimony may forthwith be used against him in a Federal criminal prosecution." 318 Mich. 651, 29 N.W. 2d 287.

Supreme Court ruled that the phrase "any court" included state as well as federal courts.[73] In other words, in conformity with the federal supremacy doctrine, Congress can say to a witness, "[Y]ou must testify, but the evidence will not be used against you in any court, state or federal."

In the important case of *Murphy* v. *Waterfront Commission of New York*,[74] decided in 1964, the Court finally decided that the rule works both ways. That is to say, just as a federal grant of immunity protects a witness from state prosecution, so a state grant of immunity will protect the individual from a later federal prosecution. On the general theory that a grant of immunity is valid only if it is coextensive with the scope of the privilege against self-incrimination, the Court overruled three well-known precedents[75] on the basis on the holding in *Malloy* v. *Hogan*,[76] which was decided on the same day, and which held that the Fifth Amendment privilege was fully applicable to the states. "We hold," said Justice Goldberg, "that the constitutional privilege against self-incrimination protects a state witness against incrimination under federal as well as state law and a federal witness against incrimination under state as well as federal law."[77] This means, of course, that a state may grant a person immunity from a federal prosecution, a proposition which is difficult to reconcile with the general concept of federal supremacy. That the Court was willing to make such a concession suggests the great weight which it now attaches to the privilege against self-incrimination.

The Problem of Immunity

The emphasis in our time upon the right of an individual to refuse to give testimony which will convict him of crime has tended to obscure the fact that this right to remain silent is altogether limited and exceptional. For the general rule is that one has a duty to testify, and to testify truthfully, subject to prosecution for perjury, about matters in which grand juries, courts, or investigating committees have legitimate interests. As Chief Justice Hughes once remarked, "[I]t is . . . beyond controversy that one of the duties which the citizen owes to his government is to support the administration of justice by attending its courts and giving his testimony whenever he is properly

---

73. Adams v. Maryland, 347 U.S. 179 (1954). The same rule applies to testimony given to a federal grand jury under the immunity of a national statute. Reina v. United States, 364 U.S. 507 (1960).

74. 378 U.S. 52 (1964).

75. United States v. Murdock, 284 U.S. 141 (1931); Feldman v. United States, 322 U.S. 487 (1944); Knapp v. Schweitzer, 357 U.S. 371 (1958).

76. 378 U.S. 11 (1964).

77. 378 U.S. 77–78.

summoned."[78] Even as to self-incrimination, while one may plead the privilege, he does not have to do so. The testimony of people who have knowledge of the facts is essential if many of the processes of government are to function at all. Indeed, the duty to testify is so great that grand juries, courts, legislative committees, regulatory administrative agencies, and other bodies having the responsibility of getting information may require people to attend by subpoena. Violation of a subpoena is punishable as contempt. Perhaps the best-known example of the duty to testify is reflected in the legal right of an accused to compel persons to appear, through court order, in order to give testimony. Thus the Sixth Amendment declares that in all criminal prosecutions the accused has the right "to have compulsory process for obtaining witnesses in his favor," and the Supreme Court has ruled that this principle is so important that it is a requirement of Fourteenth Amendment due process which is binding upon the states.[79]

State constitutions and legal codes so provide, in the same or similar language.[80] "For more than three centuries," says Wigmore, "it has now been recognized as a fundamental maxim that the public (in the words sanctioned by Lord Hardwicke) has a right to every man's evidence."[81] The giving of testimony may involve a sacrifice of time, labor, or profits, or of privacy, or it may lead to disgrace and ridicule, but nevertheless, says Wigmore, "he who will live by society must let society live by him, when it requires to.... From the point of view of society's *right* to our testimony, it is to be remembered that the demand comes, not from any one person or set of persons, but from the community as a whole,—from justice as an institution, and from law and order as indispensable elements of civilized life."[82]

Clearly there is a duty to speak, for contrary to a widespread impression, there is no absolute right to silence. There is only a limited privilege of refusing to testify as to matters which may lead the testifier to jail. Since the

---

78. Blackmer v. United States, 284 U.S. 421, 438 (1932). Cf. the statement of Justice Pitney in Blair v. United States, 250 U.S. 273, 281 (1919): "It is clearly recognized that the giving of testimony and the attendance upon court or grand jury in order to testify are public duties which every person within the jurisdiction of the government is bound to perform upon being properly summoned.... The personal sacrifice involved is a part of the necessary contribution of the individual to the welfare of the public." See also United States v. Bryan, 339 U.S. 323, 331 (1950). Lord Bacon said in 1612 that all subjects owed the King their "knowledge and discovery." Countess of Shrewsbury's Case, 2 How. St. Tr. 769, 778 (1612).

79. Washington v. Texas, 388 U.S. 14 (1967).

80. Thus the Virginia Constitution, Art. I, §8, provides that in criminal prosecutions the defendant has the right "to call for evidence in his favor."

81. *Treatise on Evidence*, 8: 64.

82. *Ibid.*, p. 66.

only consequence which the privilege against self-incrimination avoids is a criminal prosecution, if government promises in advance not to prosecute, then one has no right to remain silent. Thus if one is given a pardon in advance, or an amnesty by legislative decree, he cannot refuse to testify, except upon pain of punishment for contempt. As early as 1857 Congress adopted an immunity statute, and today most major federal regulatory enactments have immunity provisions.[83] There are many similar laws in the state statute books. For example, the New York State Crime Commission found that there were in that state in 1953 some forty-six different statutory provisions under which a witness may obtain immunity by giving testimony.[84] While most of these provisions dealt with criminal proceedings before a magistrate, grand jury, or court, a few were applicable to civil proceedings and to inquiries before legislative committees or executive officers. A very few states have provisions in their constitutions on this subject. The constitutions of California and Alabama extend immunity to selected types of cases,[85] but the Oklahoma Constitution goes all the way in regard to crimes by providing as follows: "Any person having knowledge or possession of facts that tend to establish the guilt of any other person or corporation charged with an offense against the laws of the State, shall not be excused from giving testimony or producing evidence, when legally called upon so to do, on the ground that it may tend to incriminate him under the laws of the State; but no person shall be prosecuted or subjected to any penalty or forfeiture for or on account of any transaction, matter, or thing concerning which he may so testify or produce evidence."[86] In short, the state has traded the right to prosecute for what it regards as the more valuable right to find out the facts of life in the community.

The Supreme Court ruled, in the *Counselman* case, the earliest litigation on the subject, that the legislative body cannot abridge the constitutional privilege unless the statute affords an "absolute immunity against future prosecution for the offence to which the question relates."[87] A provision that the evidence or testimony should not be used against the witness in any criminal trial was held to be inadequate. But this particular statute was

83. For a list, see Shapiro v. United States, 335 U.S. 1, 6 (1948). Robert G. Dixon, Jr., has summarized the history of federal immunity statutes in a series of articles in the *George Washington Law Review,* 22 (March, April 1954): 447–80, 554–81, and 23 (April, June 1955): 501–34, 627–57.

84. *Third Report of the New York State Crime Commission,* May 4, 1953, Leg. Doc. No. 68 (1953), p. 15. For an immunity case coming up from New York, see Ragen v. New York, 349 U.S. 58 (1955).

85. Calif. Const., Art. IV, §35 (bribery or corrupt solicitation of members of the legislature); Ala. Const., Art. VIII, §189 (violation of election laws).

86. Okla. Const., Art. II, §27.

87. Counselman v. Hitchcock, 142 U.S. 547, 586 (1892).

revised by Congress to declare that "no person shall be prosecuted or subjected to any penalty or forfeiture for or on account of any transaction, matter or thing, concerning which he may testify or produce evidence," and this, the Court held, sufficed to meet the test of complete immunity.[88] For, as the Court suggested, if a witness cannot be prosecuted on facts concerning which he testified, he cannot fairly say he has been compelled in a criminal case to be witness against himself. "He might suffer disgrace and humiliation but such unfortunate results to him are outside of constitutional protection."[89] Furthermore, although it is established that one must claim the Fifth Amendment privilege in order to enjoy its protection, the Supreme Court ruled in 1943 that the witness did not have to claim his privilege under this type of compulsory testimony statute, since as it stood the witness secured immunity merely by testifying.[90] But Congress is free to say in an immunity statute that if a witness desires immunity he must assert his constitutional privilege, and this has been the practice since 1933.

In the important case of *Kastigar* v. *United States,*[91] decided in 1972, the Court ruled that the absolute immunity spelled out in 1892 in the *Counselman* case was not constitutionally required, and that something less than complete immunity sufficed. Subpoenaed to appear before a federal grand jury in California, Kastigar was granted immunity under the Organized Crime Control Act of 1970, which provides that "no testimony or other information compelled under the order (or any information directly or indirectly derived from such testimony or other information) may be used against the witness in any criminal case, except a prosecution for perjury. . . ."[92] Kastigar refused to testify on the ground that he had not been granted transactional immunity from prosecution for any offense to which the compelled testimony might relate. In upholding a conviction for contempt, the Supreme Court ruled that transactional immunity was not required by the Constitution. Justice Powell asserted that the privilege "protects against any disclosures that the witness reasonably believes could be used in a criminal prosecution or could lead to other evidence that might be so used."[93] But that is as far as the privilege goes, for, Justice Powell noted, immunity statutes must be understood as seeking "a rational accommodation between the imperatives of the privilege and the legitimate demands of government to compel citizens to testify."[94] He pointed out that

88. Brown v. Walker, 161 U.S. 591 (1896).
89. Smith v. United States, 337 U.S. 137, 147 (1949).
90. United States v. Monia, 317 U.S. 424 (1943).
91. 406 U.S. 441 (1972).
92. 18 U.S.C. §6002 (1970).
93. 406 U.S. 445.
94. 406 U.S. 446.

many offenses are of such a character that the only persons who can give useful testimony are those implicated in the crime. While Congress got into the habit of conferring transactional immunity in its statutes, following the *Counselman* decision in 1892, Congress reconsidered the matter in 1970 on the theory that immunity from the use of compelled testimony and evidence derived therefrom was coextensive with the scope of the privilege. The Court agreed, Justice Powell maintaining that transactional immunity is considerably broader than the Fifth Amendment privilege. The privilege, he asserted, has never been construed to mean that one who invokes it cannot later be prosecuted, provided that the evidence used against him is not derived from the compelled testimony. It follows, as the Court noted, that once a defendant has been granted immunity, the government in a later prosecution would have the affirmative duty to prove that it had an independent, legitimate source for its evidence, wholly independent of the compelled testimony. Neither the 1970 statute nor the Fifth Amendment grants a pardon or amnesty; both allow the government to prosecute, using evidence from legitimate independent sources.

The vote in this case was 5-2, with two Justices not participating. Speaking in dissent, Justice Douglas argued that transactional immunity had always been part of the fabric of our constitutional law, and that mere use immunity permits the government to grant far less than it has taken away. "Government acts in an ignoble way," he declared, "when it stoops to the end which we authorize today."[95] In his dissenting opinion, Justice Marshall asserted that it was not enough to say that the burden of proof is on the government, for this decision leaves the witness dependent upon the integrity and good faith of the prosecuting authorities, since the necessary information is uniquely within their knowledge, and it would be extremely difficult for the witness to prove otherwise.

The enactment of an immunity statute turns upon the resolution of several important questions. For one thing, the legislative body will want to avoid giving "immunity baths" to people who do not deserve them.[96] It will also want to make sure that the information which will thereby be secured is sufficiently important to make the price of immunity one worth paying. In addition, the immunity must be as broad as the privilege. The House Judiciary Committee once declared, "The power to grant immunity is one of tremendous responsibility, the exercise of which must be guarded by

---

95. 406 U.S. 467.

96. The first immunity statute relating to congressional investigations was enacted by Congress in 1857, 11 Stat. 155. It resulted in giving immunity to so many people who were not entitled to it that it was drastically reduced in 1862, 12 Stat. 333. All a criminal had to do to get immunity from prosecution for any crime was to contrive in some fashion to get himself investigated by a committee.

discretion and wisdom. All possibility of abuse must be obviated lest it become a loophole for the escape from punishment of the guilty. It must at all times be the perfect medium whereby a true balance [is achieved] between the need and the right of the Government to obtain the necessary information to carry out its constitutional functions and the constitutional right of an individual not to incriminate himself."[97]

So many people have refused in recent years to testify before congressional committees looking into security questions—during 1953, for example, 317 witnesses invoked the privilege before these committees—that Congress adopted an immunity statute late in 1954 to cover this area.[98] While this statute was extensively amended in 1970, especially to substitute use for transactional immunity, in its original form it led to important litigation. So far as Congressional proceedings are concerned, some interesting procedural safeguards were spelled out: (1) In the case of proceedings in either house of Congress, an affirmative vote of a majority of those present is required. (2) In the case of committees, a vote of two-thirds of the members of the full committee is required. (3) The immunity originally extended to "the transactions, matters, or things" concerning which the witness is required to testify or produce evidence. (4) The witness does not acquire immunity automatically by testifying, but must claim his privilege against self-incrimination. (5) An order of a United States district court must be secured to require testimony. (6) Testimony so compelled cannot be used as evidence in any criminal proceeding "in any court," which the House Judiciary Committee declared included any state as well as any federal court. The statute now bars the use of the required testimony "in any criminal case." (7) Before either house of Congress or any of its committees votes to grant immunity, the Attorney General must be notified. He must also be notified of any proposed application to a United States district court, and be given an opportunity to be heard before the court enters it order.

In addition, the Act provides that any federal district attorney, upon the approval of the Attorney General, may request the district court to grant immunity to any witness in any case or proceeding before grand juries or courts. Finally, the statute provides that no witness who acquires the immunity secures any exemption from prosecution for perjury or contempt

---

97. Report of the Committee on the Judiciary, H.R. Rep. 2606, 83d Cong., 2d sess. (1954), p. 5.

98. Act of August 20, 1954, 68 Stat. 745, 18 U.S.C. §3486 (1970). The Act was amended on October 15, 1970, 84 Stat. 926, and is now 18 U.S.C. §§6001–6005. See Samuel H. Hofstadter, *The Fifth Amendment and the Immunity Act of 1954* (New York: Fund for the Republic, 1955); O. John Rogge, "The New Federal Immunity Act and the Judicial Function," *California Law Review,* 45 (May 1957): 109–33.

committed while giving testimony or producing evidence under the compulsion of the statute.

In the first proceeding involving this immunity statute, the federal district attorney for the southern district of New York filed an application in November 1954, for an order to require one Ullmann to testify before a grand jury investigating matters concerned with attempts to endanger the national security by espionage. He refused to answer questions regarding his knowledge of such activities, and regarding his alleged participation and membership in the Communist Party, and the membership of others, on Fifth Amendment grounds. He was convicted of contempt for this refusal and sentenced to six months in jail.[99] The United States Court of Appeals for the Second Circuit unanimously sustained the lower court, though all three judges expressed regret that they did not feel free to reexamine the basic rule that the privilege against self-incrimination applies only to testimony that might lead to a prosecution for a crime.[100] Judge Frank said that he was not prepared to assert that the request for a modification of this rule, in the light of contemporary conditions, lacked all merit, but he felt that it would be improper for an inferior court to undertake to modify existing Supreme Court doctrine. Judge Clark concurred "regretfully," lamenting "the steady and now precipitate erosion of the Fifth Amendment." For, he declared, "practically, as we know, no formal immunity can protect a minority deviator from society's dooms when he departs from its norms. And realistically viewed there is much in the defendant's contention that at the end of the road is a charge of perjury supported by the oath of a renegade or paid informer."

By a 7–2 vote the Supreme Court affirmed, holding that the Immunity Act of 1954 was constitutional.[101] Conceding that the privilege against self-incrimination is "an important advance in the development of our liberty" which "must not be interpreted in a hostile or niggardly spirit," Justice Frankfurter held that the basic issue was settled, and settled properly, in the earlier case of *Brown* v. *Walker*.[102] He rejected Ullmann's attempt to distinguish the *Brown* case on the ground that today there are new disabilities which did not then exist, such as loss of job, expulsion from trade unions, loss of passport, and public opprobrium, arguing that all the

---

99. *In re* Ullman, 128 F. Supp. 617 (S.D. N.Y. 1955).

100. United States v. Ullmann, 221 F.2d 760 (2d Cir. 1955).

101. Ullmann v. United States, 350 U.S. 422 (1956). See Maxwell Brandwen, "Reflections on Ullmann v. United States," *Columbia Law Review,* 57 (April 1957): 500–17.

102. 161 U.S. 591 (1896). This decision upheld, by a 5–4 vote, the constitutionality of a similar statute, the Act of February 11, 1893, 27 Stat. 443, which dealt with testimony before the Interstate Commerce Commission.

privilege protects against is a criminal charge. Thus he concluded, "Immunity displaces the danger. Once the reason for the privilege ceases, the privilege ceases."

Justices Douglas and Black, who dissented, were for overruling the *Brown* decision, and for adopting "the view of the minority in that case that the right of silence created by the Fifth Amendment is beyond the reach of Congress." Since the Immunity Act does not protect against many disabilities, such as loss of jobs, passports, etcetera, they insisted that it grants only partial and not complete immunity. They maintained that the loss of a job or a passport is a penalty that ought to fall within the ambit of the constitutional privilege. For it not only protects against prosecution or conviction for crime; it is also "a safeguard of conscience and human dignity and freedom of expression. . . ." Indeed, they argued that the right of silence is designed to protect against infamy and disgrace. Such a view, however, though strongly supported by historical and analytical arguments, has never commended itself to a majority of the Court.

The Problem of Motive

Whatever inference people may draw from the refusal of a person to answer questions on the ground of self-incrimination,[103] the question of motivation still remains to be explored. Why do so many insist on the privilege? In discussing this matter, a distinction must be drawn between defendants in criminal cases and mere witnesses. A defendant does not have to offer a reason for not testifying, since he has a right not to testify merely because he is a defendant. This is not true of witnesses, who are obliged to proffer an independent justification. Of course, the defendant may be guilty in fact, and this may be a very persuasive reason for not taking the stand, since his testimony may merely strengthen the case against him. But even if he is not guilty as charged, a defendant may have very good reasons for not testifying. Perhaps the most important is that he may be entangled in circumstances that make him look guilty, and thus he fears that his testimony will further entrap him. Another common reason is the fear of exposing one's self to cross-examination, which, in exploring the issue of the defendant's credibility, may bring to the jury's attention facts about past criminal or immoral behavior which will strengthen the case against him. To be sure, it is frequently possible for a skillful prosecutor to get evidence of an evil past before the jury by seeking to establish a pattern concerning the defendant's habits or skills. Nevertheless, a defendant often

103. See the excellent article by John T. Noonan, Jr., "Inferences from the Invocation of the Privilege against Self-Incrimination," *Virginia Law Review,* 41 (April 1955): 311–42. See also Laurent B. Frantz and Norman Redlich, "Does Silence Mean Guilt?" *The Nation,* 176 (June 6, 1953): 471–77.

runs great risks in exposing himself to cross-examination. Furthermore, he may decline to take the stand because of a desire to protect friends, or because he fears getting involved in a perjury charge he may not be able to disprove.

Finally, a defendant may, for a variety of reasons—personal unattractiveness, stupidity, timidity, neuroticism, and the like—be advised by his lawyer not to testify for fear of making a bad impression. Justice Field explained all this when he wrote, "It is not everyone who can safely venture on the witness stand though entirely innocent of the charge against him. Excessive timidity, nervousness when facing others and attempting to explain transactions of a suspicious character, and offenses charged against him, will often confuse and embarrass him to such a degree as to increase rather than remove prejudices against him. It is not every one, however honest, who would therefore willingly be placed on the witness stand."[104]

Witnesses apparently refuse to testify for a variety of reasons. One, of course, is fear of prosecution for crimes. Presumably many of the notorious gangsters who declined to testify during the nationally televised hearings of the Kefauver Committee investigating organized crime—and who indelibly impressed upon the country the existence of the Fifth Amendment—had sound reasons for anticipating prosecutions if they answered the questions put to them. Apparently many of those who have refused to answer questions about membership in the Communist Party have feared prosecutions for conspiracy under the Smith Act. It must be recognized that we live today at a time when more and more political crimes are being spelled out by law. But there seem to be other reasons for not testifying: the desire to protect friends or to protest against the methods or purposes or validity of the tribunal asking the questions, or the fear of committing perjury. It would seem, too, that a witness may be so entangled in circumstantial evidence of guilt that he fears entrapment. Federal Circuit Judge Magruder has observed that the witness "might not be unreasonable in believing that the question was asked for a purpose, and that the purpose was to lead him into a booby trap in which he would make some disclosures useful to the prosecution in weaving a case against him. Just where the line should be drawn in such a case, in the application of the privilege, might be a question; but it is certainly clear that it should be drawn well short of the point where the interrogator might have a substantial chance of striking pay dirt."[105]

It should be clear that the constitutional privilege against self-incrimination serves important purposes. The government, with all its enormous inquisitorial powers, may not force a man, by torture or other compulsion,

104. Wilson v. United States, 149 U.S. 60, 66 (1892).
105. Maffie v. United States, 209 F.2d 225, 229 (1st Cir. 1954).

to give testimony which will contribute to his conviction for crime. The existence of the privilege requires the prosecution, including the police, to make an independent search for evidence, instead of relying upon the fruits of compulsory interrogation. Sir James Fitzjames Stephen, in his history of English criminal law, tells a now-famous story which illustrates the significance of this point. He relates that during the discussions of the Indian Code of Criminal Procedure in 1872, some comments were made as to why native police officers applied torture to prisoners. An experienced civil servant made the following observation: "There is a great deal of laziness in it. It is far pleasanter to sit comfortably in the shade rubbing red pepper into a poor devil's eyes than to go about in the sun hunting up evidence."[106]

It cannot be gainsaid that there have been abuses of the privilege in recent years, but weapons are available to limit these abuses without sacrificing the constitutional principle. One is the discharge from public service of government employees who decline to answer questions on the ground of self-incrimination. By executive order President Eisenhower made refusal to testify before a congressional committee one of the criteria of security bearing on the question of suitability for government employment.[107] Similarly, a police officer may not be forced to testify about his activities as a policeman, but the community has a legal right to fire him if he does refuse to testify, on the ground that he is not qualified for a position in the public service.[108] The other great weapon is the immunity statute. If it is more important to have a man's testimony than it is to try him for crime—and often such is the case—then our governments may get the information they need by pardoning the witness in advance. If proper safeguards are provided for, the immunity statute can go far in reducing the abuse of a valued constitutional principle.

Other Privileged Communications

The right of silence on grounds of self-incrimination is by no means the only privilege recognized by the law. Under the common law, and more recently through statutes, most American jurisdictions accept the proposition that communications between husband and wife, lawyer and client, and priest and penitent, are privileged, which means that such parties cannot be compelled to testify as to communications between them. In most states a doctor-patient privilege is also recognized by law, though the rule is limited by various exceptions. Governmental military and diplomatic

---

106. James Fitzjames Stephen, *A History of the Criminal Law of England* (London: Macmillan & Co., 1883), I: 442.
107. Executive Order 10491, October 13, 1953, 18 Fed. Reg. 6583.
108. See Drury v. Hurley, 339 Ill. App. 33, 88 N.E. 2d 728 (1949).

secrets are privileged. During the past century the judges have been extremely reluctant to multiply the categories of privileged communications, and therefore the extension of the concept of privilege has been the product of statutes.[109] Thus, some fifteen states have made communications with one's accountant privileged, and eleven states have adopted statutes extending the privilege to communications with one's psychologist. As of 1972, nineteen states have enacted some sort of statute permitting a journalist to refuse to reveal confidential sources of information.

It is in connection with the newsman's privilege that there has been the greatest amount of debate. Most courts have been unwilling to create such a privilege on constitutional grounds, in the absence of a statute.[110] The debate came to a head in 1972, in the case of *Branzburg* v. *Hayes*,[111] when by a 5-4 vote the Supreme Court held that denial of the privilege to newsmen refusing to testify before grand juries as to matters they regarded as derived from confidential sources was not in violation of the First Amendment guaranty of freedom of the press. Justice White had no doubts regarding the significance of a free press, but, speaking for the Court, he pointed out that this case involved no intrusions upon speech, no prior restraint upon publication, no command that the press publish something it wants to withhold, no tax on the privilege of publishing, and no penalty based on the content of published material. The only issue was whether reporters had an obligation to respond, as other citizens do, to questions relevant to an investigation into the commission of a crime. Justice White called attention to the fact that the First Amendment does not invalidate every incidental burden on the press which may result from the enforcement of civil or criminal laws of general applicability. It has been established, for example, that the press is subject to the National Labor Relations Act, the Fair Labor Standards Act, the Sherman Act, nondiscriminatory taxation, the law of libel, and the contempt power. Thus, it is not surprising, said Justice White, that the great weight of authority holds that newsmen are not exempt from the normal duty of the citizen to appear before a grand jury and answer questions relevant to a criminal investigation. The First

---

109. For a thorough survey of the law on privilege, see Charles T. McCormick's *Handbook of the Law of Evidence*, ed. Edward W. Cleary, 2d ed. (St. Paul: West Publishing Co., 1972), pp. 151–242.

110. Garland v. Torre, 259 F.2d 545 (2d Cir. 1958), cert. denied, 358 U.S. 910 (1958); State v. Knops, 49 Wis. 2d 647, 183 N.W. 2d 93 (1971); State v. Buchanan, 250 Ore. 244, 436 P.2d 729 (1968), cert. denied, 392 U.S. 905 (1968); *In re* Pappas, 266 N.E. 2d 297 (Mass. 1971). See Note, "Reporters and their Sources: The Constitutional Right to a Confidential Relationship," *Yale Law Journal*, 80 (December 1970): 317–71; Harold L. Nelson, "The Newsmen's Privilege against Disclosure of Confidential Sources and Information," *Vanderbilt Law Review*, 24 (May 1971): 667–81.

111. 408 U.S. 665 (1972).

Amendment interest, he concluded, was outweighed by the general obligation of a citizen to appear before a grand jury or at a trial and give whatever information he possesses. The general rule is that the public has a right to every man's evidence except for those people who are protected by privilege, and in this instance the Court thought that the public interest in law enforcement and effective grand jury proceedings must prevail over an uncertain burden on news gathering.

Justice Douglas, speaking in dissent, argued that the First Amendment confers upon the press a complete, absolute immunity. He feared that the Court's decision would weaken the freedom of the press, to which he ascribed a preferred position in our constitutional law. Justice Stewart complained, in his dissenting opinion, of what he characterized as "the Court's crabbed view of the First Amendment," which he thought reflected "a disturbing insensitivity to the critical role of an independent press in our society." He feared that the Court's decision would invite the undermining of the historic freedom of the press "by attempting to annex the journalistic profession as an investigative arm of government." The right to publish, Justice Stewart insisted, must include the right to gather news, for which the promise of confidentiality may be essential. At the very least, he thought that when a reporter is asked to appear before a grand jury and reveal confidences, the government should be required (1) to show probable cause that the newsman has information clearly relevant to a specific probable crime, (2) to show that the information cannot be obtained by means less destructive of First Amendment rights, and (3) to demonstrate a compelling and overriding interest in the information.

Actually, it is quite possible to accommodate the needs of the press in large measure without going all the way by creating a new legal privilege. For example, in August 1970, the U.S. Attorney General announced that in respect to federal subpoena policy regarding the news media, the Department of Justice would observe certain guidelines. He declared that the Department did not consider the press "an investigative arm of the government," and recognized that all reasonable efforts should be made to obtain information from nonpress sources before any consideration is given to subpoenaing the press. If a subpoena is considered, negotiations with the press should be attempted first, and if they fail, no subpoena to the press should be requested without the express authorization of the Attorney General. He declared that he would not authorize a subpoena unless there was sufficient reason to believe that a crime had occurred, from disclosures by nonpress sources, and unless there was sufficient reason to believe that the information sought was essential to a successful investigation. In addition, the government should have unsuccessfully attempted to obtain the information from alternative nonpress sources, and normally requests should be limited to the verification of published information. Finally, the subpoena should be directed, wherever possible, to a limited subject matter, and should cover a reasonably limited period of time. While the Attorney General recognized the possibility that "emergencies and other unusual situations" might develop, he expressed the hope that these general rules would cover the great majority of cases.

The Problem of Confessions

A problem closely related to self-incrimination, and often incorrectly identified with it, is that of the use of confessions in criminal cases. Though there is some resemblance between the rule that a person cannot be compelled to testify against himself and the rule that a coerced confession is inadmissible as evidence in a criminal case, they are, in law, quite distinct concepts. Thus, coerced confessions are barred in federal courts not on the basis of the Fifth Amendment, but rather according to a rule of the law of evidence which federal judges have adopted. Wigmore has emphasized the distinctions between the rule which excludes untrustworthy confessions and the privilege against compulsory testimonial self-incrimination.[112] For one thing, they developed independently in history; whereas the privilege was well established by 1680, the rule on confessions was not created until about a century later. The privilege extends only to statements made in a court or some other official body, whereas the confession rule covers statements made out of court as well. The confession rule extends to statements made both with and without compulsion, as in the case of trickery, whereas the privilege requires a showing of compulsion. Even where the privilege is waived, or nullified by an immunity statute, the confession rule still operates. Testimony under oath which would not violate the confession rule might still be barred by the privilege. The privilege can be claimed by any witness in any civil or criminal case, and indeed in any proceeding, such as a grand jury or legislative committee hearing, where testimony under oath may be required, whereas the confession rule can be invoked only by defendants in criminal cases. Furthermore, the purpose of the confession rule is to exclude statements which are false, whereas the privilege operates to exclude statements which may be true. The only relationship between the two doctrines, say Wigmore, "is found in the general spirit of protection and caution which our legal system shows towards an accused."

Rightly or wrongly, and the point is debated by experts, American law embodies some suspicion concerning the trustworthiness of confessions. This is probably due mainly to the widespread use of "third degree" methods by the police. This suspicion is reflected in the rule prevailing in the federal courts and almost all state courts that where the prosecution

---

112. *Treatise on Evidence*, vol. 8, §2266.

relies upon a confession in a criminal case, it must also present independent evidence to establish the fact that the crime charged has been committed (the *corpus delicti*).[113] Thus the New York Code of Criminal Procedure (§395) provides that a confession is not enough to warrant a defendant's conviction "without additional proof that the crime charged has been committed." As the Supreme Court once declared, the purpose of the requirement of corroboration of confessions is to prevent "errors in convictions based upon untrue confessions alone."[114]

Justice Clark has explained in some detail the underlying reasons for the corroboration rule, the foundation of which, he declared, "lies in a long history of judicial experience."[115] There is "the realization that sound law enforcement requires police investigations which extend beyond the words of the accused." Confessions may be unreliable because they are coerced or induced. Caution is also warranted "because the accused may be unable to establish the involuntary nature of his statements." Furthermore, a man's confession is often given under the pressure of a police investigation, and his words "may reflect the strain and confusion attending his predicament rather than a clear reflection of his past." And finally, said Justice Clark, "the experience of the courts, the police and the medical profession recounts a number of false confessions voluntarily made."[116]

The general rule is that a confession must be voluntary, and must not have been induced by force, or threats, or promises of leniency. This does not mean that the police may not interrogate a prisoner, or that a prisoner's confession must be "a spontaneous utterance" to relieve the conscience.[117] A confession is not bad merely because it was made by someone who had been arrested and questioned while in custody. It must be understood that wholly voluntary confessions are quite common, either because of the natural desire to tell the truth or to relieve the conscience of the burden of guilt.[118] In addition, there are many statutes or rules of court which are designed to safeguard the use of confessions. Rule 5 of the Federal Rules of Criminal Procedure provides that when an officer makes an arrest, he shall take the arrested person "without unnecessary delay" to the nearest

---

113. Judge Learned Hand once said, "It must be conceded that there has been a very general concordance of judicial opinion in the United States that some sort of corroboration of a confession is necessary to conviction. . . ." Daeche v. United States, 250 F. 566, 571 (2d Cir. 1918).

114. Warszower v. United States, 312 U.S. 342, 347 (1941).

115. Smith v. United States, 348 U.S. 147, 153 (1954).

116. See Note, "Voluntary False Confessions," *Indiana Law Journal,* 28 (Spring 1953): 374-92.

117. People v. Mummiani, 258 N.Y. 394, 397, 180 N.E. 94, 95 (1932).

118. See Theodore Reik, *The Compulsion to Confess* (New York: Farrar, Straus and Cudahy, 1959); O. John Rogge, *Why Men Confess* (New York: Thomas Nelson, 1959).

available official empowered to commit persons charged with offenses against federal law, generally a federal magistrate. The magistrate is then required to inform the defendant of the complaint against him, of his right to retain counsel or to have assigned counsel, and of his right to a preliminary examination. He must also inform the accused "that he is not required to make a statement and that any statement made by him may be used against him." Most states have statutes which seek to accomplish these purposes.

The admissibility of confessions secured as a result of police interrogation is now governed by the rules pronounced by the Supreme Court in the landmark case of *Miranda* v. *Arizona,* [119] decided in 1966. Dividing 5-4, the Court ruled that "after a person has been taken into custody or otherwise deprived of his freedom of action in any significant way," prior to any questioning by the police, the person must be warned of his right to remain silent, that any statement he makes may be used as evidence against him, and that he has a right to a lawyer, either retained or appointed. He may waive these rights, but only if that is done "voluntarily, knowingly and intelligently." If at any time and in any manner he indicates that he wishes to consult an attorney, there can be no questioning, and if he is alone and indicates in any manner that he does not want to be interrogated, the police may not question him. Finally, the mere fact that he may have answered some questions, or volunteered some statements on his own, does not deprive him of the right to refrain from answering further questions until he has consulted with a lawyer and thereafter consents to be questioned. These rules regarding police interrogation were based upon the constitutional privilege against self-incrimination. The Court was impressed by the inherently coercive character of police custody, and wished to protect individuals from being subjected to police methods of questioning which are aimed at exploiting the suspect's weaknesses. [120]

It is to be noted that the Court made it clear that the police may freely ask questions of persons not under restraint, and that confessions given voluntarily, or volunteered statements, are not barred. Of course, the *Miranda* rules apply to all sorts of statements against interest, and not merely confessions, but so far as confessions are concerned they pronounce principles which are fully available to challenge their admissibility in later court proceedings.

---

119. 384 U.S. 436 (1966).

120. The dissenters in this case thought that the Court was going too far too rapidly, arguing that, as an essential tool in effective law enforcement, custodial interrogation should not be weakened. Justice Clark was of the opinion that there is very little police brutality in the country. Justice Harlan characterized the Court's decision as "heavy-handed and one-sided." Justice White did not agree that custodial interrogation is inherently coercive.

The *Miranda* decision was strongly critized by various state appellate courts.[121] In fact, in June 1972, the Criminal Law Revision Committee in Great Britain published a report which argued that "the law of evidence should not be less tender to criminals generally," and recommended serious changes in the Judges' Rules, after which the *Miranda* rules were modelled.[122] But various empirical studies indicate that confessions were not as essential in as many cases as was formerly assumed, that there has been no sharp decline in the number of usable confessions as a result of *Miranda*, and that the *Miranda* rules have not weakened law enforcement in any significant way.[123] In fact, there is some credible evidence which indicates that the *Miranda* rules have had a desirable effect so far as improper police practices are concerned.[124]

The *Miranda* decision, which the Court has ruled to be nonretroactive,[125] gave rise, as might be expected, to all sorts of questions. What, for example, is meant by the concept of custody? In a 1969 decision, the Court held that where the police were admitted into the home lawfully, and surrounded the suspect in his bedroom, and he responded to questions while still in bed without first being informed of his right to remain silent, the *Miranda* rules were violated because the suspect was in custody; he had been arrested at the time he gave his name, and he was not free to leave the room.[126] Furthermore, one who gives information to an Internal Revenue Service agent, without the benefit of the *Miranda* warnings, while in jail on another charge, is in custody within the meaning of that decision.[127] In addition, the

121. See Bradley C. Canon, "Organizational Contumacy in the Transmission of Judicial Policies: The *Mapp, Ecobedo, Miranda* and *Gault* Cases," *Villanova Law Review*, 20 (November 1974): 50–79.

122. Criminal Law Revision Committee, *Eleventh Report: Evidence (General)*, Comnd. 4991 (June 1972), p. 12.

123. See E. J. Younger, "Results of a Survey conducted by the District Attorney's Office of Los Angeles County Regarding the Effect of the Miranda Decision upon the Prosecution of Felony Cases," *American Criminal Law Quarterly*, 5 (Fall 1966): 32–39; Note "Interrogations in New Haven: The Impact of Miranda," *Yale Law Journal*, 76 (July 1967): 1519–648; Richard H. Seeburger and R. S. Wettick, Jr., "Miranda in Pittsburgh—A Statistical Study," *University of Pittsburgh Law Review*, 29 (October 1967): 1–26; Richard J. Medalie, Leonard Zeitz, and Paul Alexander, "Custodial Police Interrogation in Our Nation's Capital: The Attempt to Implement Miranda," *Michigan Law Review*, 66 (May 1968): 1347–422; Cyril D. Robinson, "Police and Prosecutor Practices and Attitudes Relating to Interrrogation as Revealed by Pre- and Post-Miranda Questionnaires: A Construct of Police Capacity to Comply," *Duke Law Journal*, 1968 (June 1968): 425–524.

124. See the pioneering study by Bradley C. Canon, "Is the Exclusionary Rule in Failing Health? Some New Data and a Plea Against a Precipitous Conclusion," *Kentucky Law Journal*, 62, no. 3 (1973–74): 681–730. See also Neal A. Milner, *The Court and Local Law Enforcement* (Beverly Hills: Sage, 1971); Otis H. Stephens, Jr., *The Supreme Court and Confessions of Guilt* (Knoxville: University of Tennessee Press, 1973).

125. Jenkins v. Delaware, 395 U.S. 213 (1969).

126. Orozco v. Texas, 394 U.S. 324 (1969).

127. Mathis v. United States, 391 U.S. 1 (1968).

Court rejected the contention that tax investigations are immune from the *Miranda* rules, since they frequently lead to criminal prosecutions.

There is some evidence, however, which suggests that under the leadership of Chief Justice Burger, the Court is gradually weakening the *Miranda* rules. Thus, where a suspect was given all the required warnings by the police, except that he was not told that he had a right to appointed counsel if he could not afford counsel of his own choosing, the Court ruled that this was not a sufficiently serious omission to warrant a reversal.[128] Justice Rehnquist argued that just as the law does not require that the defendant receive a perfect trial, but only a fair one, so it must not insist that policemen make no errors whatsoever. Furthermore, the Court has ruled that while admissions secured without the *Miranda* warnings may not be admitted to establish the prosecution's case in chief, if the defendant takes the stand, he may, on cross-examination, be asked about such admissions, not as evidence of guilt, but as relating to the issue of his credibility.[129] Chief Justice Burger proceeded on the premise that no defendant has a right to take the stand and commit perjury, and in seeking the truth, the prosecution has a right to confront him with prior inconsistent utterances.[130]

In 1943, in the important *McNabb* case,[131] the Supreme Court ruled that in federal courts a confession is inadmissible if it was secured while the defendant was unlawfully detained. But the Court did not announce this rule as one required by the Constitution, but simply as a rule of court adopted in the course of its supervision of the administration of justice in the federal courts, where it seeks to establish and maintain "civilized standards of procedure and evidence." The admission of confessions

---

128. Michigan v. Tucker, 417 U.S. 433 (1974).

129. Harris v. New York, 401 U.S. 222 (1971). The decision was had by a 5–4 vote. In Brown v. Illinois, 45 L. Ed. 2d 416 (1975), the Court held that statements made by the defendant which were the fruit of an illegal arrest without probable cause and without a warrant, were inadmissible as evidence even though he had been given Miranda warnings; to say that the Miranda warnings wash out the taint of an unconstitutional arrest would substantially dilute the Fourth Amendment.

130. A similar decision was made in Oregon v. Hass, 420 U.S. 714 (1975). In United States v. Hale, 422 U.S. 171 (1975), the Court held that it was prejudicial error for the trial judge to deny a motion for a mistrial where the prosecutor, on cross-examination, caused the defendant to admit that after his arrest, and after he was warned of his right to remain silent, he refused to offer exculpatory evidence to the police.

131. McNabb v. United States, 318 U.S. 332 (1943). So also held in a companion case, Anderson v. United States, 318 U.S. 350 (1943). See James E. Hogan and Joseph M. Snee, "The McNabb-Mallory Rule: Its Rise, Rationale and Rescue," *Georgetown Law Review,* 47 (Fall 1958): 1-46; John B. Waite, "Police Regulation by Rules of Evidence," *Michigan Law Review,* 42 (February 1944): 679-93. Waite was very critical of a decision which "propounds once again the wisdom of a judicial policy which turns known criminals loose upon society as a means of punishing the police."

obtained during a period of illegal confinement, while not forbidden by act of Congress, would, the Court argued, stultify the policy of Congress as expressed in statutes which require the prompt commitment of arrested persons.[132] A few years later, by a 5–4 decision in *Upshaw* v. *United States*,[133] the Court clarified the *McNabb* rule by holding that if the confession was secured during illegal detention, its inadmissibility does not depend upon whether or not torture or other coercion was used. In 1957, in the *Mallory* case,[134] the Court reaffirmed the *McNabb* rule by setting aside a rape conviction in the District of Columbia on the ground that the defendant's confession had been secured during a period of illegal confinement, the police after arrest having failed to take him to a committing magistrate without unnecessary delay.

The Supreme Court has refused to apply the *McNabb* rule to state criminal procedure by making it a requirement of due process of law. Its position is that it has no power of general supervision over the trial of criminal cases in state courts, and that so far as confessions are concerned the due process test is voluntariness.[135] That is to say, a confession in a state court must be declared inadmissible only when the fundamental principles

132. In United States v. Mitchell, 322 U.S. 65 (1944), the Court ruled that a voluntary confession is not invalidated by the fact that *after* it was made the accused was held illegally.

133. 335 U.S 410 (1948).

134. Mallory v. United States, 354 U.S. 449 (1957).

135. Gallegos v. Nebraska, 342 U.S. 55 (1951); Brown v. Allen, 344 U.S. 443 (1953). Many state courts have rejected the McNabb rule, holding that the fact that the confession was given during a time of illegal detention does not affect the admissibility of the confession, the test being its voluntariness. For citations, see Francis Wharton's *Criminal Evidence*, 12th Ed. (Rochester, N.Y.: Lawyers Cooperative Publ. Co., 1955), vol. 2, §366; Fred E. Inbau and John E. Reid, *Lie Detection and Criminal Interrogation*, 3d ed. (Baltimore: Williams and Wilkins, 1953), p. 210, n. 157. See, e.g., People v. Elmore, 277 N.Y. 397, 14 N.E. 2d 451 (1938); Com. v. Turner, 358 Pa. 350, 58 A.2d 61 (1948); State v. Gardner, 119 Utah 579, 230 P.2d 559 (1951); State v. Browning, 206 Ark. 791, 178 S.W. 2d 77 (1944); Fry v. State, 147 P.2d 803 (Okla. Cr. App. 1944); State v. Folkes, 174 Ore. 568, 150 P.2d 17 (1944). See the remarks of Judge Jennings in State v. Zukauskas, 132 Conn. 450, 460, 45 A.2d 289, 293 (1945): "Society, as well as this defendant, is entitled to equal protection of the law and to due process of law. . . . There is a respectable body of opinion which holds that the rule . . . goes too far in favoring criminals." English courts hold that a confession is not to be excluded merely because the police violated the Judges' Rules, the test being trustworthiness. See The King v. Voisin [1918] 1 K.B. 531, 538: "It is desirable in the interests of the community that investigations into crime should not be cramped." The Canadian courts rule the same way: Boudreau v. The King, [1949] Can. Sup. Ct. 262, 270, 3 D.L.R. 81, 88 (1949). Said Justice Rand, "It would be a serious error to place the ordinary modes of investigation of crime in strait-jacket of artificial rules. . . . Rigid formulas can be both meaningless to the weakling and absurd to the sophisticated or hardened criminal; and to introduce a new rite as an inflexible preliminary condition would serve no genuine interest of the accused and but add an unreal formalism to that vital branch of the administration of justice."

of liberty and justice which are the substance of due process are violated, and if the confession was voluntary, due process is satisfied even if it was secured during a period of illegal detention. This, of course, applies only to Fourteenth Amendment due process, and does not prevent a state supreme court from adopting the stricter *McNabb* approach, under its own supervision of criminal justice in the state courts.

Congress wrote into the Crime Control Act of 1968 a provision which purported to modify the *McNabb-Mallory* rule.[136] The statute provides that a confession in the District of Columbia "shall be admissible in evidence if it is voluntarily given." In determining the issue of voluntariness, however, the judge is required to take into consideration five enumerated factors, including "the time elapsing between arrest and arraignment," but also taking into account whether the defendant understood the nature of the offense with which he was charged, whether he was advised or knew that he was not required to make a statement, and whether he had the assistance of counsel. But the statute declares that the judge is not to regard any one factor as conclusive. In fact, in the next paragraph the statute declares that a confession is not inadmissible "solely because of delay in bringing such persons before a magistrate," if the delay was less than six hours, unless the judge finds that a delay of over six hours was reasonable under the circumstances. In effect, then, the statute restates the *McNabb-Mallory* rule by defining delay in terms of six hours; thus it is still the law in federal courts that too much delay, as so defined, renders a confession suspect.

That the use in a state criminal trial of a coerced confession violates the due process clause of the Fourteenth Amendment was first announced by a unanimous vote of the Supreme Court in 1936 in *Brown* v. *Mississippi*.[137] In this case three Negroes accused of murder confessed, but only after having been severely whipped and otherwise subjected to brutal violence. The convictions rested entirely upon the confessions, and there was no doubt of the fact that the confessions had been coerced. Speaking for the Court, Chief Justice Hughes observed that while a state is free to regulate the procedure of its courts in accordance with its own conceptions of policy, it may not offend "some principle of justice so rooted in the traditions and conscience of our people as to be ranked as fundamental."[138] He went on to say, "Because a State may dispense with a jury trial, it does not follow that it may substitute trial by ordeal. The rack and torture chamber may not be substituted for the witness chair." But the Chief Justice made it clear that the principle of self-incrimination was not involved in the case. Compulsion

---

136. 18 U.S.C. §3501 (1970).
137. 297 U.S. 278 (1936). See M. G. Paulsen, "The Fourteenth Amendment and the Third Degree," *Stanford Law Review*, 6 (May 1954): 411-37.
138. Quoted from Snyder v. Massachusetts, 291 U.S. 97, 105 (1934).

by torture to extort a confession is a different matter, a question of justice. And a trial where a conviction rests solely upon confessions obtained by methods of violence, which are "revolting to the sense of justice," is a mere pretense, and not a fair trial as required by due process.

The doctrine of the *Brown* case was reinforced by another unanimous decision of the Court in 1940 in *Chambers* v. *Florida*.[139] In spite of the fact that the jury found that the confessions had been made voluntarily, the Supreme Court made an independent search of the record, since a federal (due process) right had been seasonably asserted, and concluded that the evidence supported the conclusion that the confessions had been induced by compulsion.[140] While there was sharp conflict on the issue of physical violence and mistreatment, the record did show the use of such methods as arrest on suspicion without warrant and protracted questioning for six days by relays of officers, without the assistance of friends or counsel. Speaking for the Court, Justice Black denounced the use of "secret inquisitorial processes" to extort confessions, pointing out that tyrannical governments have always used dictatorial criminal procedure to make scapegoats of the weak or helpless, of members of political, religious or racial minorities, or of nonconformists. Those who have suffered most have always been "the poor, the ignorant, the numerically weak, the friendless, and the powerless." Justice Black asserted that the Court was not impressed by the argument that law enforcement methods such as those then under review were necessary to uphold our laws. "The Constitution proscribes such lawless means," he said, "irrespective of the end." Furthermore, the argument "flouts the basic principle that all people must stand on an equality before the bar of justice in every American court."

The most difficult problem now before the Supreme Court, so far as the use of coerced confessions in state trials in concerned, has to do with assessing the coerciveness inherent in prolonged interrogation. This issue

---

139. 309 U.S. 227 (1940). See also White v. Texas, 310 U.S. 530 (1940); Ward v. Texas, 316 U.S. 537 (1942); Malinski v. New York, 324 U.S. 401 (1945).

140. The reluctance of the Supreme Court to set aside the state court's finding on the issue of coercion is reflected in Lisenba v. California, 314 U.S. 219 (1941); Cicenia v. LaGay, 357 U.S. 504 (1958); LaVallee v. Rose, 410 U.S. 690 (1973). In the latter case five Justices concluded that the state trial court's decision on the issue of voluntariness was adequate, whereas four Justices thought that the state trial court had failed to offer any reasoned explanation for its action. In Brooks v. Florida, 389 U.S. 431 (1967), the Court held that the record of the case documented "a shocking display of barbarism." On the other hand, in Greenwald v. Wisconsin, 390 U.S. 519 (1968), the Court divided 6-3, the majority holding that under the totality of circumstances (no counsel, lack of food, sleep and medication, inadequacy of warning) the state court erred in regarding a confession to be voluntary.

was raised squarely in the *Ashcraft* case in 1944.[141] Here the confession of a grown man was held to have been coerced because the accused had been questioned continuously for thirty-six hours by various officials working in relays. The Court held that under such circumstances the accused did not possess mental freedom when he confessed. But three Justices disagreed, and Justice Jackson wrote for the minority a long and brilliant discussion of the whole problem. He emphasized that interrogation, unlike violence, is not illegal *per se.*[142] And in a sense, he maintained, most confessions are coerced. Not only is interrogation for thirty-six hours coercive; even custody and examination for one hour are coercive. Indeed, "arrest itself is inherently coercive, and so is detention." Furthermore, he argued that the fact that the defendant had been questioned for thirty-six hours was not in itself conclusive. Some men are overborne in a few hours; others are tougher, and can stand up for days. Thus in his view the ultimate question was not, How long was the accused questioned? but rather, Did he possess his own will and self-control at the time of the confession? Finally, he insisted that an appellate court should give great weight to the judgment of the trial judge and jury, who are the triers of fact.

There have been a number of cases following the *Ashcraft* decision in which the Supreme Court held that state courts had denied due process of law by admitting confessions secured by various forms of psychological coercion.[143] In one of these cases Justice Frankfurter made the following informative statement: "A confession by which life becomes forfeit must be the expression of free choice. A statement to be voluntary of course need not be volunteered. But if it is the product of sustained pressure by the police it does not issue from a free choice. When a suspect speaks because he is overborne, it is immaterial whether he has been subjected to a physical or mental ordeal. Eventual yielding to questioning under such circumstances is plainly the product of the suction process of interrogation and therefore the reverse of voluntary."[144] The Court has been especially

---

141. Ashcraft v. Tennessee, 322 U.S. 143 (1944).

142. See, on this point, Stroble v. California, 343 U.S. 181 (1952); Taylor v. Alabama, 335 U.S. 252 (1948).

143. See, e.g., Harris v. South Carolina, 338 U.S. 68 (1949); Turner v. Pennsylvania, 338 U.S. 62 (1949); Fikes v. Alabama, 352 U.S. 191 (1957); Payne v. Arkansas, 356 U.S. 560 (1958); Davis v. North Carolina, 384 U.S. 907 (1966); Lynum v. Illinois, 372 U.S. 528 (1963); Blackburn v. Alabama, 361 U.S. 199 (1960); Haynes v. Washington, 373 U.S. 503 (1963).

144. Watts v. Indiana, 338 U.S. 49, 53 (1949). See the remarks of Judge Frank in U.S. *ex rel.* Caminito v. Murphy, 222 F.2d 698, 701 (2d Cir. 1955). In this case the accused had been questioned continuously from 6 P.M. to 2 A.M., then locked up in an unheated cell, and interrogated for eleven hours the following day. Said the Judge, "It has no significance that in this case we must assume there was no physical brutality. For psychological torture may be far more cruel, far more symptomatic of sadism. Many a man who can endure

quick to reverse convictions where the confession which followed protracted interrogation was wrung from young people under twenty years of age.[145] Thus a boy of fifteen "cannot be judged by the more exacting standards of maturity. That which would leave a man cold and unimpressed can overawe and overwhelm a lad in his early teens."[146]

The Supreme Court has set aside many state convictions based on confessions, as, for example, where there had been "massive official interrogation" of an uneducated and emotionally unstable young man,[147] or where the police held a man incommunicado and threatened to bring his wife in for questioning,[148] or where a feeble-minded illiterate was questioned repeatedly while held in protective police custody for five days,[149] or where the accused has been injected with a "truth serum."[150] Of course, it should be noted that the Supreme Court has often concluded that on the facts considered as a whole the challenged confession was admissible.[151]

Until very recently the Supreme Court tended to follow the rule that a second confession, if voluntary, is admissible, even though it followed a confession that had been coerced.[152] But in 1954, in *Leyra v. Denno,*[153] the Court began to hedge when it ruled that where the second confession is made immediately after the first, so that both are in fact simply parts of one continuous process, occurring in the same place, within a few hours, the lack of mental freedom in respect to the first confession will be imputed to the second.[154] The three dissenting Justices in this case

---

beatings will yield to fatigue. To keep a man awake beyond the point of exhaustion, while constantly pummelling him with questions, is to degrade him, to strip him of human dignity, to deprive him of the will to resist, to make him a pitiable creature mastered by a single desire—at all costs to be free of torment. . . . Indeed, the infliction of such psychological punishment is more reprehensible than a physical attack: It leaves no discernible marks on the victim."

145. See, e.g., Haley v. Ohio, 332 U.S. 596 (1948); Lee v. Mississippi, 332 U.S. 742 (1948).

146. Haley v. Ohio, 332 U.S. 596, 599 (1948). See also Gallegos v. Colorado, 370 U.S. 49 (1962), which expressed disapproval of a confession made by a fourteen-year-old boy after five days of detention without any adult protection.

147. Spano v. New York, 360 U.S. 315 (1959).

148. Rogers v. Richmond, 365 U.S. 534 (1961).

149. Culombe v. Connecticut, 367 U.S. 568 (1961). See also Reck v. Pate, 367 U.S. 433 (1961).

150. Townsend v. Sain, 372 U.S. 293 (1963).

151. See, e.g., Thomas v. Arizona, 356 U.S. 390 (1958); Ashdown v. Utah, 357 U.S. 426 (1958).

152. See United States v. Bayer, 331 U.S. 532 (1947); Lyons v. Oklahoma, 322 U.S. 596 (1944).

153. 347 U.S. 556 (1954).

154. A similar conclusion was reached in Beecher v. Alabama, 408 U.S. 234 (1972) and in Clewis v. Texas, 386 U.S. 707 (1967).

protested that they knew of no previous case where this Court has ruled that an invalid confession *ipso facto* invalidates a later confession as a matter of law.

On what theory does the use of coerced confessions deny due process of law? At the common law such confessions were inadmissible because they were inherently untrustworthy. That is to say, there is a high probability that a coerced confession may be false.[155] In *Brown* v. *Mississippi*[156] and other early confession cases arising under the Fourteenth Amendment the Court proceeded on the theory that it was seeking to protect the right to a fair trial. Thus Justice Roberts once wrote, "As applied to a criminal trial, denial of due process is the failure to observe that fundamental fairness essential to the very concept of justice. In order to declare a denial of it we must find that the absence of that fairness fatally infected the trial; the acts complained of must be of such quality as necessarily prevent a fair trial. Such unfairness exists when a coerced confession is used as a means of obtaining a verdict of guilt."[157] But beginning with the *Ashcraft* case in 1944,[158] the Court began to put forward the rationale that the federal coerced confessions rule had as its purpose to discourage illegal police practices. Accordingly, Justice Frankfurter wrote in 1949, "In holding that the Due Process Clause bars police procedure which violates the basic notions of our accusatorial mode of prosecuting crime and vitiates a conviction based on the fruits of such procedure, we apply the Due Process Clause to its historic function of assuring appropriate procedure before liberty is curtailed or life is taken."[159] Thus, there seem to be two different standards. On the one hand, a confession is bad if it is untrustworthy in the light of the confessor's power to resist the methods used to induce him to confess. On the other hand, a confession may be regarded as inadmissible if it was obtained by methods offensive to due process, without regard to the question of the probable falsity of the confession. The first test is concerned with the danger of erroneous convictions, the second with the danger of tolerating uncivilized police methods.

It is clear that the Supreme Court disapproves of the use of strong-arm methods by the local police to secure evidence. This was reflected in the case of *Rochin* v. *California*.[160] On information that the accused was selling narcotics the police unlawfully broke into his dwelling, whereupon he swallowed two capsules containing morphine. He was then handcuffed,

---

155. See Wigmore, *Treatise on Evidence,* vol. 3, §815.
156. 297 U.S. 278 (1936).
157. Lisenba v. California, 314 U.S. 219, 236 (1941).
158. Ashcraft v. Tennessee, 322 U.S. 143 (1944).
159. Watts v. Indiana, 338 U.S. 49, 55 (1949).
160. 342 U.S. 165 (1952).

taken to a hospital, and his stomach was pumped against his will. He was convicted on the basis of this regurgitated evidence. The Court set aside the conviction, Justice Frankfurter declaring that "the proceedings by which this conviction was obtained do more than offend some fastidious squeamishness or private sentimentalism about combatting crime too energetically. It is conduct that shocks the conscience. . . . This course of proceedings by agents of government to obtain evidence is bound to offend even hardened sensibilities. They are methods too close to the rack and the screw to permit of constitutional differentiation." While the states have much leeway in their conduct of prosecutions, still they must respect "certain decencies of civilized conduct." Said Justice Frankfurter, "It would be a stultification of the responsibility which the course of constitutional history has cast upon this Court to hold that in order to convict a man the police cannot extract by force what is in his mind but can extract what is in his stomach." Justices Black and Douglas concurred separately to argue that the state had violated the self-incrimination rule of the Fifth Amendment, since they preferred to base the protection of human rights upon the specific provisions of the Bill of Rights rather than upon what they call the "nebulous standards" of due process. Since all but four states would apparently admit this evidence, Justice Douglas could not agree that it could be said that this state had violated the decencies of civilized conduct. He preferred to invoke the "unequivocal, definite and workable rule of evidence" decreed for all courts by the Self-Incrimination Clause.

It is difficult to believe that a procedure which is routine in hospitals is such brutal conduct that it shocks the conscience. In fact, the Court backed away from the full implications of the *Rochin* case in two later cases involving compulsory blood-testing in a search for evidence. In *Breithaupt* v. *Abram* (1957),[161] by a 6–3 vote, the Court ruled that where a doctor, on the direction of the police, withdrew a blood sample, by use of a hypodermic needle, from the body of an unconscious man who, while driving a truck, had been involved in a collision with a passenger car whose three passengers were killed, the community's "sense of justice" had not been violated. The Court thought that nothing "brutal" or "offensive" had occurred when measured by the yardstick of common experience. This, said Justice Clark, was admittedly a scientifically accurate method of detecting alcoholic content in the blood, and he argued that this very slight intrusion in the person of the individual is outweighed by society's interest in the increasing slaughter on the highways. The three dissenting Justices thought that this decision could not be reconciled with *Rochin,* and regarded the event as an unwarranted police

---

161. 352 U.S. 432 (1957).

assault on an unconscious man. Some years later, in *Schmerber* v. *California*,[162] by a 5–4 vote, the Court took the same position where the needle was inserted over the objections of a fully conscious man. The majority held that the evidence at issue was not testimonial in nature and that it was important to note that the individual concerned was not compelled to say anything. The dissenters argued that what happened was a clear violation of the constitutional right against self-incrimination.

The view which prevails in most state and federal courts—what may be called the "orthodox" view—is that the judge alone decides whether the confession was voluntary or not.[163] If he concludes that the confession was involuntary, it does not go to the jury; if he finds it was voluntary, it is considered by the jury. But when the confession goes to the jury, evidence regarding the circumstances under which the confession was made may be presented to the jury on the issue of its credibility. That is to say, the jury cannot rule on the competency of the confession (the issue of voluntariness), but only on its weight. Furthermore, at the request of the accused, the jury is usually excluded from the preliminary hearing on the issue of the competency of the confession, at which the defendant may testify. The Supreme Court has ruled that when the admissibility of a confession is in issue in a federal criminal trial, the accused is entitled to testify out of the presence of the jury.[164]

Whether a state judge is constitutionally required to decide on the voluntariness of a confession before it goes to the jury has been the subject of extensive litigation involving New York procedures. In *Stein* v. *New York*,[165] decided in 1953 by a 6–3 vote, the Supreme Court gave its approval to a procedure according to which the issue of coercion was left to the jury, but where, since the jury rendered a general verdict, it could conclude that the confession was coerced and still convict. It was impossible to tell whether the jury has found the confession coerced and convicted on other evidence, or whether the jury had concluded that the confession was voluntary and relied upon it. The Court majority ruled that the Fourteenth Amendment did not forbid jury trial of the issue. In fact, the Court held that the trial judge had not acted unlawfully in refusing to instruct the jury that if it found that the confession had been coerced, it must return a verdict of acquittal, since the jury could convict on the basis of other evidence.

162. 384 U.S. 757 (1966).
163. See Bernard D. Meltzer, "Involuntary Confessions: The Allocation of Responsibility between Judge and Jury," *University of Chicago Law Review*, 21 (Spring 1954): 317–54.
164. United States v. Carignan, 342 U.S. 36, 38 (1951).
165. 346 U.S. 156 (1953).

The decision was overruled in 1964, by a 5-4 vote, in the important case of *Jackson* v. *Denno*.[166] After Jackson shot and killed a policeman, he, who was also shot, was taken to a hospital, where he soon made an oral confession to the police. Two hours later he made another confession, soon after he was given demerol and scopolamine. In accordance with New York practice, the trial judge submitted the issue of the voluntariness of the confession to the jury. The jury was told that if it found the confession involuntary, it was to disregard it, and determine innocence or guilt solely from the other evidence; but if the jury found the confession voluntary, then it was instructed to determine its truth or reliability and afford its weight accordingly. The court majority found this procedure unconstitutional, Justice White arguing that it was axiomatic that a defendant in a criminal case was denied due process if his conviction was founded, in whole or in part, upon an involuntary confession, without regard for the truth or falsity of the confession, and even though there was ample evidence aside from the confession to support the conviction. He also ruled that it is equally well established that at some stage in the proceedings, the defendant has a constitutional right to object to the use of the confession, and to have a fair hearing and a reliable determination of the issue of voluntariness, uninfluenced by the truth or falsity of the confession. Under the New York rule, the trial judge had to make a preliminary determination with regard to a confession offered by the prosecution, and exclude it if he concluded that under no circumstances could it be deemed voluntary; but if the evidence presents a fair question as to its voluntariness, as where reasonable men may differ over facts or inferences from certain facts, then the judge must receive the confession, and leave the issue of its voluntariness, as well as its truthfulness, to the jury, with proper instructions. Again, since a New York jury returns only a general verdict, it is impossible to discover whether the jury found the confession voluntary and relied on it, or involuntary and ignored it. Accordingly, the Court held that this procedure had a significant impact upon the defendant's Fourteenth Amendment rights, for under the New York procedure, the evidence given to the jury inevitably injects irrelevant and impermissible considerations of the truthfulness of the confession into the assessment of its voluntariness. It cannot now be determined how the jury decided the issue, and it cannot be assumed that it did so properly. That is to say, it cannot be assumed that the jury has not been influenced by the confession, even if it held it involuntary. The four dissenting Justices

---

166. 378 U.S. 368 (1964). See W. L. Swanson and R. W. Eichmeier, "The Role of Judge and Jury in Determining a Confession's Voluntariness," *Journal of Criminal Law, Criminology and Police Science,* 48 (May-June 1957): 59-65.

argued that, as held in the *Stein* case, the states are free, under the Fourteenth Amendment, to allocate the trial of issues between judge and jury as they deem best. They saw nothing improper in submitting the question of voluntariness to the jury without first having a definitive ruling from the judge.[167]

It remains to be noted that in 1972, by a 4-3 vote, the Court held it is not unlawful for a state court to make a judgment on the issue of voluntariness on the basis of a preponderance of the evidence.[168] That is to say, it is not a requirement of due process that voluntariness must be supported by proof beyond a reasonable doubt, since neither the confession nor its voluntariness are elements of the crime for which the accused is tried. The three dissenters argued that the same considerations which apply the reasonable doubt standard to the issue of guilt or innocence ought to apply to the confession issue. Justice Brennan asserted that it is just as critical in our system of justice, when an individual's words are used against him, that there should be no reasonable doubt that he has spoken of his own free will.

The Supreme Court's decisions on confessions have undoubtedly had their effect upon the course of state law. Some state courts are beginning to hold that coercion may take the form of psychological pressure resulting from protracted interrogation as well as physical duress. While the *McNabb* rule, that confessions secured during illegal detention are not admissible in federal courts, has not been applied by the Supreme Court to the states as a requirement of due process of law, a few state courts are beginning to take note of its desirability. But both our national and our state courts will admit confessions made in response to police questioning, if the *Miranda* rules have been observed, on the conviction that interrogation serves a justifiable purpose in apprehending violators of the law. Certainly the police in this country take this view. Accordingly, we have been unwilling to go as far as England, where the police may not question suspects after arrest at all, on the theory that police interrogation is

---

167. The Court reiterated, in Boles v. Stevenson, 379 U.S. 43 (1964) and Sims v. Georgia, 385 U.S. 538 (1967), that the federal due process rule requires the trial judge to decide the issue of voluntariness before submitting the confession to the jury. While it is preferable that a voluntariness hearing be held outside the presence of the jury, this is not an inflexible rule, especially where the defendant has consented to having the judge hear the issue before the jury. Pinto v. Pierce, 389 U.S. 31 (1967). That mere procedural flaws which made no difference do not entitle the defendant to a new hearing on the issue of voluntariness was decided in Procunier v. Atchley, 400 U.S. 446 (1971). If one testifies to overcome the impact of confessions illegally obtained and improperly introduced, such testimony may not be used against him in a later trial. Harrison v. United States, 392 U.S. 219 (1968).

168. Lego v. Twomey, 404 U.S. 477 (1972).

inherently coercive. There only a magistrate may interrogate. Commenting on this fact, a distinguished scholar has written, "Desirable as such a reform would be in the interest of liberty of the citizen, it could only be maintained in a community where the crime rate is relatively low, where the police are highly efficient and trained to a strong sense of professional ethics, and where the community has a regard for civil rights so strong that it will insist upon the maintenance of these rights even in favor of the 'least of these,'—the disreputable and the outcast."[169] It should be added that guilty defendants are usually convicted in England, and with relative ease. There are not so many jury trials, appeals are much more expensive and thus fewer in number, and the judge controls the courtroom. In short, the system operates efficiently.

Supreme Court review of confessions heard in state courts draws attention to the problems involved in police interrogation, even if conducted under the *Miranda* rules. All too often, interrogation leads to the use of the third degree, which is a wholly evil thing. It has a brutalizing effect upon the police, and encourages the falsehoods which must be employed in making the necessary denials; it undermines public confidence in the police and in the administration of justice, and it sharpens the victim's antipathy to society. Officials' lawlessness feeds on itself and breeds vengeful reprisals. But there is no simple remedy, and the exclusion of coerced confessions, when coercion can be proved, is a sanction of only limited value. In the long run, at least, the remedy lies in the accomplishment of basic changes in our society which will reduce the crime rate, increase the efficiency of the police through better recruitment, higher qualifications, and better training, improve the courts, and develop greater public confidence in the administration of justice. For the basic cause of the use of the third degree in this country, a leading student of the subject has written, "is the inability of our law enforcement officers to protect society without resort to it."[170]

169. Charles T. McCormick, *Handbook of the Law of Evidence,* 1st ed. (St. Paul: West Publishing Co., 1954), p. 250.
170. Sam Bass Warner, "How Can the Third Degree Be Eliminated?" *Bill of Rights Review,* (Summer 1940): 24–33, 33.

10 / Double Jeopardy

Nature of the Right

The Fifth Amendment of the U.S. Constitution provides that no person shall be "subject for the same offence to be twice put in jeopardy of life or limb." The constitutions of all states but five have a double jeopardy clause also, and in the five states without such clauses common law rules against double jeopardy are applied by the courts.[1] The language of thirty-five state constitutions follows that of the Fifth Amendment. The Mississippi Constitution stipulates that "there must be an actual acquittal or conviction on the merits to bar another prosecution."[2] The constitutions of seven states provide that no person "after acquittal" shall be tried again for the same offense.[3]

The double jeopardy concept of our criminal law is found in all modern legal systems, and has its counterpart, in the civil law, in the doctrine of *res judicata*. This doctrine means that once a cause of action has been finally determined on the merits by a competent tribunal, and appeal rights have been used up, the same matter cannot be litigated again.[4] One major purpose of *res judicata*, like that of the double jeopardy concept, is to avoid burdensome multiplicity of actions, and thus to economize on the time of the courts. But it has been observed that "the broader and even more important aspect of the public policy of *res judicata* is its promotion of peace and quiet in the community through the creation of certainty in the relations of men."[5]

---

1. These states are Connecticut, Maryland, Massachusetts, North Carolina, and Vermont. See, for appropriate citations, the dissenting opinion of Chief Justice Vinson in Brock v. North Carolina, 344 U.S. 424, 435 (1953).

2. Miss. Const., Art. III, §22.

3. Mich. Const., Art. III, §14; Mo. Const., Art. I, §19; N.H. Const., Part I, §16; N.J. Const., Art. I, §11; Okla. Const., Art. II, §21; R.I. Const., Art. I, §7; Tex. Const., Art. I, §14.

4. See Robert Von Moschzisker, "Res Judicata," *Yale Law Journal*, 38 (January 1929): 299–334, 300: "Speaking broadly, the rule of res judicata means that when a court of competent jurisdiction has determined, on its merits, a litigated cause, the judgment entered, until reversed, is forever and under all circumstances, final and conclusive as between the parties to the suit and their privies, in respect to every fact which might properly be considered in reaching a judicial determination of the controversy, and in respect to all points of law there adjudged, as those points relate directly to the cause of action in litigation and affect the fund or other subject-matter then before the court."

5. *Ibid.*

In the common law the double jeopardy principle was expressed in the maxim *"nemo debet bis vexari pro una et eadem causa,"* which means that "no one shall be twice vexed for the same cause." In the common law at the time the Constitution was adopted the double jeopardy principle was recognized by four pleas in bar which were available to an accused: *autrefois acquit, autrefois convict, autrefois attaint,* and former pardon. The term "former jeopardy," however, was known to the common law and was used by Blackstone.[6]

Justice Frankfurter has asserted that the double jeopardy doctrine "is part of the protection of the Constitution against pressures and penalties that offend civilized notions of justice."[7] It has been said that "this great principle forms one of the strong bulwarks of liberty," without which the guilty would be subjected "to the unnecessary costs and vexations of repeated prosecutions," and the innocent to the danger of erroneous convictions.[8] For without "this salutary rule, one obnoxious to the government might be harassed and run down by repeated attempts to carry on a prosecution against him."[9] The principle is founded in "the humanity of the law, and in a jealous watchfulness over the rights of the citizen," which is so necessary because of the inequality of the parties in a criminal case.[10] As the Georgia court said over a century ago, "It is a salutary precaution in favor of the citizen against an abuse of the sovereign authority; for history teaches the melancholy truth, that however fenced and guarded, limited and defined, by laws or usages, it sometimes breaks over all these barriers, defies the sentiment of the world, and in the name of the law violates justice and outrages humanity. The reign of the Stuarts in England illustrates these views. . . ."[11] Similarly, Justice Black once explained the philosophy of the double jeopardy rule as follows:

> The underlying idea, one that is deeply ingrained in at least the Anglo-American system of jurisprudence, is that the State with all its resources and power should not be allowed to make repeated attempts to convict an individual for an alleged offense, thereby subjecting him to embarrassment, expense and ordeal and com-

---

6. 4 Com. *335.
7. Concurring in U.S. *ex rel.* Marcus v. Hess, 317 U.S. 537, 555 (1943). For an excellent analysis of the law of double jeopardy often cited by the Supreme Court, see Jay A. Sigler, *Double Jeopardy* (Ithaca: Cornell University Press, 1969).
8. State v. Cooper, 1 Green (N.J.L.) 361, 370 (1833).
9. State v. Reynolds, 4 Haywood (Tenn.) 110 (1817).
10. State v. Jones, 7 Ga. 422, 425 (1849).
11. 7 Ga. 426. See also Com. v. Olds, 5 Littell (Ky.) 137, 139 (1824): "Every person acquainted with the history of governments, must know, that state trials have been employed as a formidable engine in the hands of a dominant administration. . . ."

354 / The Defendant's Rights Today

pelling him to live in a continuing state of anxiety and insecurity, as well as enhancing the possibility that even though innocent he may be found guilty.[12]

The Nationalization of the Double Jeopardy Concept

In the landmark case of *Palko* v. *Connecticut*[13] the Supreme Court held that the Fourteenth Amendment due process has not been violated where a state gives the prosecution the right to appeal on questions of legal error. In other words, the Court refused to read the double jeopardy concept of the Fifth Amendment into the Fourteenth. In this case Palko was found guilty of murder in the second degree and sentenced to life imprisonment. The state won an appeal on the ground that certain errors of law had occurred at the trial (such an improper exclusion of testimony and improper instructions to the jury); at the second trial Palko was found guilty of first degree murder and sentenced to death.

Justice Cardozo noted that some of the guarantees of the Bill of Rights, such as freedom of speech and religion and the right to counsel, have been absorbed into due process, while others, such as grand jury indictment and trial by jury, have not. The "rationalizing principle," he said, is whether the right is "of the very essence of a scheme of ordered liberty." Certain rights have been taken into the Fourteenth Amendment "in the belief that neither liberty nor justice would exist if they were sacrificed." The kind of double jeopardy which takes the form of a state appeal from an acquittal does not violate our fundamental principles of liberty and justice. It is not cruel, said Justice Cardozo, for the state to ask that the case shall go on until there is a trial "free from the corrosion of substantial legal error." If errors had been made adverse to the defendant, he could have appealed. "A reciprocal privilege, subject at all times to the discretion of the presiding judge, . . . has now been granted to the state. There is here no seismic innovation. The edifice of justice stands, in its symmetry, to many, greater than before."

In the case of Willie Francis[14] the Court held by a 5-4 vote that where a prisoner was put in the electric chair, and through inadvertent mechanical difficulty death did not result, it would not be double jeopardy to proceed a second time with the execution. The *Palko* case was held to be decisive. "For," said Justice Reed, "we see no difference from a constitutional point of view between a new trial for error of law at the instance of the state that results in a death sentence instead of imprisonment for life and an execution that follows a failure of equipment. When an accident, with

---

12. Green v. United States, 355 U.S. 184, 187-88 (1957). See also the remarks of Justice Harlan in United States v. Jorn, 400 U.S. 470, 479 (1970).
13. 302 U.S. 319 (1937).
14. Louisiana *ex rel.* Willie Francis v. Resweber, 329 U.S. 459 (1947).

no suggestion of malevolence, prevents the consummation of a sentence, the state's subsequent course in the administration of its criminal law is not affected on that account by any requirement of due process under the Fourteenth Amendment."

Since the states were not bound by the double jeopardy rule of the Fifth Amendment, as construed by the Supreme Court, they were at liberty to permit procedures which at the federal level were regarded as unlawful.[15] For example, while the vast majority of the states followed the federal rule that the state has no right to appeal from an acquittal,[16] and indeed in most jurisdictions the state cannot even appeal from rulings on issues arising before jeopardy has attached, such as a judgment on a demurrer to the indictment, some states have permitted appeals in such situations by statute.[17] In fact, in a very few jurisdictions the state could appeal, following a verdict of not guilty, if error of law prejudicial to the prosecution was made.[18] The theory was that the jeopardy is continuous until a result is reached which is free of legal error, and that the state had the same right to a proper legal trial that the defendant has.[19] The Connecticut court once said, "The end is not reached, the cause is not finished, until both the facts, and the law applicable to the facts, are finally determined. The principle of finality is essential; but not more essential than the principle of justice. A final settlement is not more vital than a right settlement."[20] But in no state could the state appeal from a finding of not guilty in a proceeding free from legal error, even though the finding was clearly against the weight of the evidence.[21]

In 1969, in the leading case of *Benton* v. *Maryland,*[22] the power of the states to fashion rules on double jeopardy law which are inconsistent with prevailing federal rules came to a rather abrupt end. Overruling the *Palko* case, the Court ruled squarely "that the double jeopardy prohibition of the

15. On the other hand, a state was always free to hold that it was bound by the federal Double Jeopardy Clause. So the Supreme Court of New Jersey ruled in State v. Farmer, 48 N.J. 145, 224 A. 2d 481 (1966).
16. See, e.g., *Ex parte* Bornee, 76 W. Va. 360, 85 S.E. 529, L.R.A. 1915F 1093 (1915); People *ex rel.* Hodson v. Miner, 144 Ill. 308, 33 N.E. 40, 19 L.R.A. 342 (1893).
17. See, e.g., Ill. Rev. Stat. 1945, c. 38, §747: "The People may sue out writs of error to review any order or judgment quashing or setting aside an indictment or information." This statute has been repealed. For a more elaborate statute see Calif. Penal Code, 1970, §1238.
18. See, e.g., Wis. Stat. §358.12 (1953). There were similar statutes in Connecticut and Vermont.
19. State v. Witte, 243 Wis. 423, 10 N.W. 2d 117 (1943); State v. Felch, 92 Vt. 477, 105 A. 23 (1918).
20. State v. Lee, 65 Conn. 265, 30 A. 1110, 27 L.R.A. 498, 48 Am. St. Rep. 202 (1894).
21. State v. Evjue, 254 Wis. 581, 37 N.W. 2d 50 (1948).
22. 395 U.S. 784 (1969).

Fifth Amendment represents a fundamental ideal in our constitutional heritage, and that it should apply to the States through the Fourteenth Amendment."[23] Benton had been tried in a Maryland state court on charges of burglary and larceny. The jury acquitted him of the larceny charge, but convicted him on the burglary count. On the ground that both the grand jury and the petit jury had been selected improperly, Benton won his appeal, and he was reindicted and retried. At the second trial, he was again charged with both larceny and burglary, over double jeopardy objection, and this time the jury convicted him on both counts. The second trial was clearly inconsistent with a long-standing rule of federal double jeopardy law.[24] Speaking for the Court, Justice Marshall pointed out that *Palko* rested upon an approach to basic constitutional rights which the Court had rejected in recent decisions. For example, *Betts* v. *Brady*,[25] dealing with the right to counsel, was overruled by *Gideon* v. *Wainwright*,[26] and the holding of *Twining* v. *New Jersey*,[27] relating to self-incrimination, was overruled in *Malloy* v. *Hogan*.[28] Recent cases, said Justice Marshall, have thoroughly rejected the *Palko* notion that basic constitutional rights can be denied by states so long as the totality of circumstances do not disclose a denial of fundamental fairness. It is now established that once it is decided that a particular Bill of Rights guaranty is fundamental to the American system of justice, the same constitutional standards apply against both the state and the federal governments. Accordingly, he asserted, "Palko's roots had thus been cut away years ago. We today only recognize the inevitable."[29] Of course, the major premise of the *Benton* case was the fundamental nature of the guaranty against double jeopardy. Tracing the doctrine back to ancient Greek and Roman times, Justice Marshall noted that it was established in the English common law long before our independence, and is today part of the constitutional or common law of every state. The underlying rationale is that the state should not take advantage of its power to subject a defendant to avoidable embarrassment, expense, and ordeal, and should not require him to live in a continuing state of anxiety and insecurity which enhances the chances of convicting the innocent.[30]

---

23. 395 U.S. 794. See Jay A. Sigler, "The New Broom: The Federalization of Double Jeopardy," in Stuart S. Nagel, ed., *The Rights of the Accused* (Beverly Hills: Sage Publications, Inc., 1972), chap. 10.

24. United States v. Ball, 163 U.S. 662 (1896). See also Green v. United States, 355 U.S. 184 (1957).

25. 316 U.S. 455 (1942).

26. 372 U.S. 335 (1963).

27. 211 U.S. 78 (1908).

28. 378 U.S. 1 (1964).

29. 395 U.S. 795.

30. Justice Harlan filed a dissenting opinion, with which Justice Stewart concurred,

The federalizing of the Fifth Amendment's double jeopardy rule opened the door to both Supreme Court development of doctrines applicable in federal courts and invited review of inconsistent state policies. Accordingly, there has been an unusual amount of decision-making in this area by the Supreme Court since 1969.

Scope of the Right

The courts have construed the double jeopardy principle to apply to multiple punishments as well as prosecutions. It means, of course, that no one should be harassed by successive prosecutions for a single wrongful act, thus saving the defendant and the public from the expense of prolonged and unnecessary litigation, and safeguarding the accused from the stigma and harassment of repeated criminal prosecutions.[31] But it has also come to mean that one should not be punished more than once for the same offense, for, as the Supreme Court asked in its leading decision on this matter, "of what avail is the constitutional protection against more than one trial if there can be any number of sentences pronounced on the same verdict?"[32] In fact, the trial court cannot impose a second punishment for a single offense, even to correct an erroneous and voidable sentence, if the sentence has been executed.[33] It is established, however, that before sentence is executed, the judge may correct an inadvertent error in passing sentence, since, as Justice Black has explained, "the Constitution does not require that sentencing should be a game in which a wrong move by the judge means immunity for the prisoner."[34]

The problem of multiple punishments was thoroughly reviewed in 1969 in the important case of *North Carolina* v. *Pearce*,[35] decided on the same day as *Benton*. Two men had been convicted of crimes, and after spending several years in jail, succeeded in having their convictions set aside in postconviction proceedings. Thereupon they were retried and convicted a

---

expressing his strong opposition to overruling the Palko case, which he characterized as one of the Court's truly great decisions. He expressed his opposition, as he had previously, to the whole doctrine of selective incorporation, arguing that it was eroding many basic elements of the American federal system. At the same time, he said he would hold that if a state retries a person previously acquitted, after an errorless trial, it had denied due process.

31. See State v. Hoag, 36 N.J. Super. 555, 114 A.2d 573, 577 (App. Div. 1955): "The concept of double jeopardy is designed to prevent the government from unduly harassing an accused. . . ." It has also been pointed out that it encourages rehabilitation of the wrongdoer. United States v. Candelaria, 131 F. Supp. 797 (S.D. Cal. 1955).

32. *Ex parte* Lange, 18 Wall. (U.S.) 163, 173 (1874).

33. 18 Wall. (U.S.) 163, 173.

34. Bozza v. United States, 330 U.S. 160, 166 (1947). See also Forman v. United States, 361 U.S. 416 (1960).

35. 395 U.S. 711 (1969).

second time, after which they were given more severe sentences than had been imposed the first time. The Supreme Court made two important rulings in passing judgment on their petitions for federal habeas corpus. First of all, the Court ruled that where sentence is imposed for the same offense after retrial, the Constitution requires that credit must be given for the punishment already endured; otherwise there would be multiple punishments, which are forbidden by the Double Jeopardy Clause. Secondly, while neither the Double Jeopardy Clause nor the Equal Protection Clause imposes an absolute bar to a more severe sentence after reconviction, a state trial court would be violating due process if it followed a regular practice of imposing a heavier sentence upon a reconvicted defendant for the purpose of punishing him for succeeding in getting his original conviction set aside. Due process forbids putting such a price on the exercise of the right of appeal; due process rules out vindictiveness as to the second sentence. It follows, therefore, that whenever a judge imposes a more severe sentence upon a defendant after a new trial, the reasons for doing so must appear affirmatively in the record. Furthermore, these reasons must be based upon objective information regarding the conduct of the defendant occurring after the original sentencing proceeding, and the factual data must be part of the record, so that the resentencing decision can be reviewed on appeal.[36]

Concurring separately, Justices Douglas, Marshall, and Harlan argued that in their judgment, the second penalty should never exceed the first, on the theory that since a defendant risks the maximum permissible punishment when first tried, he should never have to face it again, since that amounts to double punishment. Dissenting in part, Justice Black maintained that in subjecting the sentencing process to detailed rules of procedure, the Court was engaged in impermissible legislation. He would prefer to leave trial judges free to exercise their discretion in sentencing. In a separate concurring opinion, Justice White declared that he would hold that following retrial, an increased sentence must be based on objective and factual data not known to the trial judge at the time of the original sentence.

The impact of the *Pearce* case was reflected in the Court's decision in *Blackledge* v. *Perry*[37] (1974). While serving a term of imprisonment in a North Carolina penitentiary, Perry got involved in an altercation with another inmate, on the basis of which he was convicted in the state district

---

36. This rule was held not to be retroactive in Michigan v. Payne, 412 U.S. 47 (1973).
37. 417 U.S. 21 (1974). See also North Carolina v. Rice, 404 U.S. 244 (1971), where a similar issue was presented, but where the appeal was dismissed on grounds of mootness.

court of the misdemeanor of assault with a deadly weapon, after trial without a jury, and sentenced to six months' imprisonment, to be served after completion of his prior prison term. Under North Carolina law, a person convicted in a district court has an absolute right of appeal to the superior court, without even alleging error, which takes the form of a trial *de novo*. Prior to the second trial, however, the prosecutor secured an indictment charging Perry with the felony of assault with a deadly weapon with intent to kill, though the indictment covered the same conduct for which he had been previously tried and convicted in the lower court. This time, following a plea of guilty, Perry was given a sentence of 5–7 years. Seven Justices joined in holding that this was a violation of the double jeopardy rule. While the teaching of the *Pearce* decision is that due process is not offended by all possibilities of increased punishment upon retrial after appeal, but only those that pose a realistic likelihood of "vindictiveness," in this instance they felt that the prosecutor had a considerable stake in discouraging convicted misdemeanants from appealing and getting trials *de novo* in the superior court. This raises the price for one who chooses to brave the hazards of a second trial. While there was no evidence that the prosecutor acted in bad faith or with malice, the point is that the defendant must be freed from the fear of retaliatory motivation. A person convicted of an offense is entitled to pursue his statutory right to a trial *de novo* without apprehension that the state will retaliate by substituting a more serious charge for the original one. Due process forbids such a potential for vindictiveness. Finally, the Court ruled that the plea of guilty to the second charge did not prevent the defendant from making his constitutional claim in a federal habeas corpus proceeding, since the issue relates to the very power of the state to bring the defendant into a court to answer a charge against him. Speaking in dissent, Justice Rehnquist argued that there was no showing of vindictiveness on the part of the prosecutor, and that a guilty plea constitutes a waiver of the constitutional issue. Otherwise plea bargaining would be discouraged, to the detriment of everyone involved in the criminal justice system. Justice Powell agreed that the guilty plea was a waiver of any claim to a constitutional deprivation.

Finally, the Court fashioned a variation of the *Pearce* rule, though by a 5–4 vote, in *Chaffin* v. *Stynchcombe*[38] (1973). Here the Court ruled that the imposition *by a jury* of a greater sentence on a retrial, following reversal of a prior state conviction, does not violate due process, so long as the jury was not informed of the prior sentence. The Court attached great

---

38. 412 U.S. 17 (1973).

weight to its earlier decision in *Stroud* v. *United States*,[39] which upheld the jury's imposition of the death penalty in a second trial conducted after the defendant has been successful in his appeal from a conviction in respect to which that jury had imposed a life sentence. The Court had no doubt concerning the constitutionality of the practice prevailing in twelve states of permitting juries to pronounce sentence, and also had no doubt of the right of a state to retry a defendant who succeeds in getting his first conviction set aside, and to impose any sentence legally authorized, whether greater or less than the first, provided that the resentencing was not motivated by vindictiveness or retaliation. Justice Powell declared that the potential for abuse of the sentencing process by the jury is *de minimis* in a properly controlled retrial where the jury has not been informed of the prior sentence. The jury, unlike the judge, he explained, consists of different people who are not likely to have motives of self-vindication. Finally, the Court did not accept the contention that this decision would "chill" the exercise of the right of appeal. After all, the district attorney may choose not to prosecute again; the defendant may be acquitted at the second trial; or a second appeal may succeed. The dissenting Justices objected to fashioning one rule for judges and another for juries with respect to resentencing, for in either event the taking of appeals is discouraged, and juries may also be animated by vindictiveness. Furthermore, as Justice Marshall pointed out, any effort to find out whether there was vindictiveness in the jury would require a sacrifice of the traditional secrecy of jury deliberations.

The basic meaning of the double jeopardy doctrine is that if an accused has been convicted of a crime, he cannot be tried a second time for the same crime. But if there has been legal error in the trial, the defendant may appeal and secure a new trial. "It is elementary in our law," Justice Clark has written, "that a person can be tried a second time for an offense when his prior conviction for that same offense has been set aside by his appeal."[40] On the other hand, if the accused is acquitted by the trial court,[41] the prosecution (the government) may not appeal, even though

---

39. 251 U.S. 15 (1919). In Williams v. Oklahoma, 358 U.S. 576 (1959), the Court held that it was not a violation of the Double Jeopardy Clause's prohibition of multiple punishments for a trial judge, in pronouncing the sentence of death on a plea of guilty to the crime of kidnapping, to take into account a previous conviction for murder, for which a life sentence had been imposed. The Court rejected the contention that this amounted to punishing the defendant a second time for the same offense, since under Oklahoma law murder and kidnapping are separate and distinct offenses, and in this instance neither charge mentioned the other. Justice Douglas dissented alone, arguing that in substance this defendant was tried twice for murder.

40. Forman v. United States, 361 U.S. 416, 425 (1960).

41. Fong Foo v. United States, 369 U.S. 141 (1962); Sapir v. United States, 348 U.S. 373 (1955), especially the concurring opinion of Justice Douglas. After the court accepts a

the trial court committed legal errors detrimental to the prosecution's side in the case, and even if the indictment had been defective.[42]

This does not mean that government may never appeal in a criminal case which has gone in favor of the defendant at the trial court level. The federal code of criminal procedure on this point is very explicit. It provides as follows:

> In a criminal case an appeal by the United States shall lie to a court of appeals from a decision, judgment, or order of a district court dismissing an indictment or information as to any one or more counts, except that no appeal shall lie where the double jeopardy clause of the United States Constitution prohibits further prosecution.
>
> An appeal by the United States shall lie to a court of appeals from a decision or order of a district court suppressing or excluding evidence or requiring the return of seized property in a criminal proceeding, not made after the defendant has been put in jeopardy and before the verdict or finding on an indictment or information, if the United States attorney certifies to the district court that the appeal is not taken for purpose of delay and that the evidence is a substantial proof of a fact material in the proceeding.[43]

In other words, the government may appeal a preliminary ruling made by the district court in favor of the accused if the matter appealed from occurred before he was placed in jeopardy. But whether in fact the action of the trial court constituted an acquittal, which, of course, is not appealable by the government, has often posed serious problems of construction for the Court. Thus, the Court ruled very recently that where, following a man's conviction for illegal conversion of union funds, the federal district judge granted a postverdict motion for dismissal of the indictment on the ground that the delay between the occurrence of the offense and the indictment had prejudiced the defendant, there has been no double jeopardy which would forbid the government to appeal.[44] Pointing out that Congress intended to allow government appeals whenever the Constitution would permit, Justice Marshall argued that current legislation permits the government to appeal any ruling by a judge terminating a prosecution, except a verdict of acquittal by a jury or judge. It has never been suggested, said Justice Marshall, that the Double Jeopardy Clause imposed any general ban on appeals by the prosecution; it was aimed at multiple prosecutions, and not at government appeals, at least where the appeal would not require a new trial. In this instance, a reversal of the trial court's order arresting judgment after verdict would merely reinstate

---

plea of not guilty there can be no later prosecution for the same crime unless the defendant withdraws his plea. State *ex rel.* Hunt v. Warden, 107 N.Y.S. 2d 136 (1951).

42. United States v. Ball, 163 U.S. 662, 669 (1896).
43. 18 U.S.C. §3731 (1970).
44. United States v. Wilson, 421 U.S. 309 (1975).

the jury's verdict. Clearly this is not a violation of the policy against multiple prosecutions. In other words, the defendant has no legitimate claim to benefit from an error of law when that error can be corrected without subjecting him to a second trial before a second trier of fact.[45]

On the other hand, where a juvenile court has conducted a jurisdictional or adjudicatory hearing, and after taking testimony from two prosecution witnesses, has found the accused guilty as charged, he is subjected to impermissible jeopardy if thereafter the juvenile court turns him over to another court to be prosecuted as an adult.[46] In effect, the young man was subjected to the burden of two trials for the same offense. It follows that the juvenile court must make its transfer decision prior to the holding of an adjudicatory hearing. Similarly, where the record shows that a district court "dismissed" an indictment and "discharged" the defendant after bench trial, the ruling is not appealable by the government.[47] There was no general finding of guilt by the judge, and a decision now in favor of the government would not justify a reversal with instructions to reinstate a general finding of guilt, since there was no such finding. While it was not clear that the district judge acquitted the defendant, a reversal and remand would require a retrial of factual issues already adjudicated, and this is contrary to the Double Jeopardy Clause.

Although the Constitution of the United States, as well as most state constitutions, speak of jeopardy of "life or limb," it is well established that the principle applies to minor offenses or misdemeanors as well as felonies.[48] But the principle applies only in criminal cases, and there are marginal situations where there is some question as to the nature of the proceeding. On one occasion, the Supreme Court ruled that an action to recover a penalty for an act declared to be a crime is a punitive proceeding, even though it takes the form of a civil action and the statute calls the penalty a tax.[49] A government suit for special "taxes" imposed on those selling liquor in violation of state law was held to be barred by a previous conviction for violating the National Prohibition Act. On the other hand, it has decided that an *in rem* proceeding for the forfeiture of the property used by a distillery corporation was a civil procedure against the property, and no part of the punishment for the criminal offense, for which the corporation had been previously convicted.[50] Contempt proceedings, such as those resulting from refusal to answer grand jury

---

45. Justices Douglas and Brennan dissented on the theory that the ruling of the trial court was based in part on evidence adduced at the trial.
46. Breed v. Jones, 421 U.S. 519 (1975).
47. United States v. Jenkins, 420 U.S. 358 (1975).
48. Jarl v. United States, 19 F.2d 891 (8th Cir. 1927); Berkowitz v. United States, 93 F. 452 (3d Cir. 1899).
49. United States v. La Franca, 282 U.S. 568, 575 (1931).
50. Various Items of Personal Property v. United States, 282 U.S. 577, 581 (1931).

questions,[51] or to obey an injunction,[52] are regarded as civil in character, on the theory that the object is not to punish a public offense, but to compel that respect for and obedience to the proper orders of a court which are necessary for the orderly and effectual administration of justice.

Furthermore, since loyalty hearings in the civil service are not regarded as criminal trials, and charges of subversiveness as criminal accusations, the principle of double jeopardy has no application. Thus, in the case of Dr. Peters, the same charges were aired formally three times, and the accused was dismissed after having been cleared twice.[53] In the civil service it appears that a new doctrine of perpetual jeopardy has taken the place of the old legal principle which forbids double jeopardy. In one instance a high State Department official was dismissed after being cleared eight times. But in contemplation of law these are not criminal proceedings, and therefore the double jeopardy doctrine does not apply.

When Does Jeopardy Attach?

"It is settled law, everywhere, that jeopardy means the danger of conviction."[54] But at what point has the danger been reached? It is, of course, clear that there has been jeopardy when there has been a trial before a court of competent jurisdiction under a valid indictment, and a verdict of acquittal or conviction has been rendered. But jeopardy may be reached before the case has gone to a final judgment. If the trial is heard by the court without a jury, it is the general rule that jeopardy attaches when the first witness is sworn or when the court has begun to hear evidence.[55] If the trial is before a jury, it is established that jeopardy attaches when the jury has been impaneled and sworn.[56] The usual explanation for this rule is that under early English common law, a jury, once sworn, had to be kept together until it rendered a verdict. It is also suggested that jeopardy attaches at this point to prevent the danger of the state's experimenting with jury after jury in order to get a favorable jury, or to stall for time while searching for adequate evidence. In fact, the

---

51. Yates v. United States, 355 U.S. 66 (1957); State v. Kasherman, 177 Minn. 200, 224 N.W. 838 (1929), cert. denied, 280 U.S. 602 (1929).

52. Gibson v. Hutchinson, 148 Iowa 139, 126 N.W. 790, Ann. Cas. 1912B 1007 (1910).

53. Peters v. Hobby, 349 U.S. 331 (1955). See Adam Yarmolinsky, *Case Studies in Personnel Security* (Washington: Bureau of National Affairs, 1955), case no. 51, pp. 60-69. This case involved a civil service employee who answered charges in 1948, and then the same charges in 1952 and 1954.

54. Rosser v. Com., 159 Va. 1028, 167 S.E. 257 (1933).

55. Clawans v. Rives, 104 F.2d 240, 242 (D.C. Cir. 1939); Rosser v. Com., 159 Va. 1028, 167 S.E. 257, 259 (1933); People v. Garcia, 120 Cal. App. 767, 7 P.2d 401 (1931); State v. Yokum, 155 La. 846, 99 So. 621 (1923).

56. Cornero v. United States, 48 F.2d 69 (1931); Green v. State, 147 Tenn. 299, 247 S.W. 84, 28 A.L.R. 842 (1923); State v. Sommers, 60 Minn. 90, 61 N.W. 907 (1895); State v. Snyder, 98 Mo. 555, 12 S.W. 369 (1889).

Supreme Court ruled in 1975 that in a case of jury trial, jeopardy attaches when the court begins to hear evidence.[57] It follows that jeopardy had not attached where the district court granted the defendant's motion to dismiss the indictment, since he had not been put to trial before the trier of facts. It is a fundamental principle, Chief Justice Burger observed, "that an accused must suffer jeopardy before he can suffer double jeopardy." Actually, it has been argued by some critics that it would be better to say that jeopardy attaches only after the prosecution has introduced enough evidence to make out a *prima facie* case, since there is no danger of conviction until this has happened. Such a position would permit greater flexibility in correcting mistakes made prior to that point in the trial.

Before there can be jeopardy, the proceedings must have been in a court having jurisdiction.[58] It has often happened that defendants have pleaded a conviction in a justice of the peace court as a bar to a later prosecution for the same offense. But if the justice court lacked jurisdiction, a court having jurisdiction may proceed to try the accused.[59] One who has merely been arrested and discharged by a magistrate after a preliminary examination has not been put in jeopardy, for neither a preliminary examination nor a discharge for want of probable cause constitutes such an adjudication as to bar a later prosecution for the offense in question.[60] Similarly, mere arraignment and pleading to an indictment do not put the accused in jeopardy.[61] Dismissal of an indictment on motion of the prosecuting attorney is not jeopardy,[62] nor is there jeopardy even if the indictment was set aside after the jury was impaneled because the indictment was insufficient.[63] But even though the indictment is defective, if there has been an acquittal on the merits then there has been jeopardy.[64]

57. Serfass v. United States, 420 U.S. 377 (1975).
58. Johnsen v. United States, 41 F.2d 44 (9th Cir. 1930); Scalf v. Com., 195 Ky. 830, 243 S.W. 1034 (1922); Rector v. State, 6 Ark. 187 (1845). In the absence of a lawful jury the trial court lacks jurisdiction. State v. Bates, 22 Utah 65, 61 P. 905, 83 Am. St. Rep. 768 (1900).
59. See, e.g., State v. Goetz, 65 Kan. 125, 69 P. 187 (1902); Drake v. State, 68 Ala. 510 (1881).
60. Collins v. Loisel, 262 U.S. 426 (1923); U.S. *ex rel.* Rutz v. Levy, 268 U.S. 390 (1925); Com. v. Rice, 216 Mass. 480, 104 N.E. 347 (1914); People v. Dillon, 197 N.Y. 254, 90 N.E. 820, 18 Ann. Cas. 552 (1910); State v. Jones, 16 Kan. 608 (1876).
61. Bassing v. Cady, 208 U.S. 386 (1908).
62. Collins v. Loisel, 262 U.S. 426 (1923). See also Taylor v. United States, 207 U.S. 120, 127 (1907), holding that the quashing of an indictment occurs before jeopardy is reached.
63. Bennett v. Com., 150 Ky. 604, 150 S.W. 806, 43 L.R.A. (N.S.) 419 (1912); State v. Holton, 88 Minn. 171, 92 N.W. 541 (1902).
64. United States v. Ball, 163 U.S. 662 (1896).

Offenses Against Two Sovereigns

Over a century ago a man who was brought to trial in a state court for violation of a fugitive slave law set up the defense that he would also be liable under the federal law on the same subject. The Supreme Court unanimously ruled that this would not be double jeopardy, since every American citizen owes allegiance to two sovereignties, and may be liable for punishment for an infraction of the laws of either.[65] "The same act may be an offense or transgression of the laws of both." In fact, the Court said that the offender is not punished twice for the same offense; by one act he committed two offenses, for each of which he is punishable.

But the Court ruled squarely on this question for the first time in 1922, in *United States* v. *Lanza*,[66] which held that one who had been convicted in a state court for violating the local prohibition law could also be tried in a federal court under the National Prohibition Act, even though the same liquor was involved in both cases. Said Chief Justice Taft, ". . . an act denounced as a crime by both national and state sovereignties is an offense against the peace and dignity of both and may be punished by each." Since the Bill of Rights applies only to the national government, "the double jeopardy therein forbidden is a second prosecution under authority of the Federal Government after a first trial for the same offense under the same authority."[67] One immediate result of the *Lanza* decision was that New York repealed its own prohibition law. The rationale of the *Lanza* decision has been severely criticized as tending to water down an important liberty through the "metaphysical subtlety" of the two sovereignties doctrine,[68] and as being an overly literal interpretation of the Constitution.[69] Both the Supreme Court[70] and state appellate courts[71] have persisted in following this rule.

Consider, for example, the sad case of Mr. Bartkus and his tussle with

---

65. Moore v. Illinois, 14 How. (U.S.) 13 (1852).
66. 260 U.S. 377 (1922).
67. 260 U.S. 382.
68. See J. A. C. Grant, "The *Lanza* Rule of Successive Prosecutions," *Columbia Law Review*, 32 (December 1932): 1309-31.
69. See the comments of Judge Tolin in United States v. Candelaria, 131 F. Supp. 797, 802 (S.D. Calif. 1955): the *Lanza* rule "overlooks the Biblical truth that '. . . the Letter of the Law Kills but the spirit gives life.' The Spirit of the rule against double jeopardy is certainly violated by allowing the State prosecution of this defendant, but the letter of the law permits it."
70. See Hebert v. Louisiana, 272 U.S. 312 (1926).
71. Gilbert v. State, 19 Ala. App. 104, 95 So. 502 (1923); Little v. Com., 197 Ky. 320, 247 S.W. 2d 2 (1923); Rambo v. State, 38 Okla. Cr. 192, 259 P. 602 (1927); State v. Jewett, 120 Wash. 36, 207 P. 3 (1922).

the State of Illinois.⁷² Bartkus was first tried for robbery of a federally insured bank in a federal district court in Illinois, before a jury, and *acquitted.* Then he was indicted on the same facts, and tried and convicted in a state court for violating a state law making bank robbery a criminal offense. Under the Habitual Offender State of Illinois, this conviction resulted in a life sentence. Dividing 5–4, the Court ruled that what happened here did not violate the double jeopardy principle. It was held that the federal and state prosecutions were conducted separately, that the Illinois officials had discretionary responsibility to undertake a prosecution, and that the state prosecution was not a sham and cover for a federal prosecution. Justice Frankfurter, speaking for the Court, leaned heavily on the argument that its decision in this case was consistent with previous federal and state decisions extending over a century of time, and giving support to the belief that to permit successive state and federal prosecutions for different crimes arising from the same acts was not offensive to the concept of due process. For the Court to rule now that due process bars a second trial "would be disregard of a long, unbroken, unquestioned course of impressive adjudication. . . ."⁷³ Finally, Justice Frankfurter advanced the practical objection that prosecution and the imposition of a very light penalty in one court would prevent the other jurisdiction from enforcing its own proper policies. Thus the propriety of the second trial in the case of Bartkus was supported by "precedent, experience, and reason."

Speaking in dissent, Justice Black complained that this was the first time in the history of the double jeopardy guaranty that the Court has upheld the conviction of a defendant who had been previously *acquitted* of the same offense in a federal court. If double jeopardy is bad, he argued, it is equally bad where two sovereigns inflict the punishment rather than one. He could see no justification for the view that individual rights deemed essential by both the states and the nation are lost through the combined operations of the two governments. Justice Brennan argued in his dissenting opinion that the state prosecution was so dominated by federal officials as to be in effect a second federal prosecution. He declared, "What happened here was simply that the federal effort which failed in the federal courthouse was renewed a second time in the state courthouse across the street."⁷⁴

On the same day, though by a 6–3 vote, the Court took a similar

72. Bartkus v. Illinois, 359 U.S. 121 (1959). See Note, "Double Prosecution by State and Federal Governments: Another Exercise in Federalism," *Harvard Law Review,* 80 (May 1967): 1538–65.
73. 359 U.S. 136.
74. 359 U.S. 169.

position in *Abbate* v. *United States*.[75] After Abbate was *convicted* in an Illinois court of the crime of destroying some facilities of a telephone company, he was indicted in the federal district court, on the same facts, for the crime of destroying part of a system of communications controlled by the United States. In holding the second trial constitutionally proper, the Court was content to say that it was not writing on a clean slate, that the *Lanza* rule had been reaffirmed and applied by the Court in a number of cases, and that it would not overrule such a firmly established rule. The three dissenting Justices thought that the *Lanza* rule was a bad rule which ought to be rejected. Justice Black was not convinced that a state and the nation can be considered two wholly separate sovereignties for the purpose of allowing them to do together what neither can do separately.

The *Lanza* rule is manifestly a very harsh one, but it should be noted that a state is free to provide by statute, as New York has, that prior acquittal or conviction in a federal court will bar a state prosecution for the same act.[76] In the spirit of the *Lanza* rule, however, it has been ruled that there is no double jeopardy if a man is tried by the courts of two states where the offense was committed in both states in violation of the laws of both.[77] Here again, however, some states have adopted statutes providing that an acquittal or conviction in another state or country will bar a prosecution therein.[78] Furthermore, many state courts had ruled that prosecution by both the state and a municipality for the same offense is not double jeopardy, though on this point there was a minority view.[79] By a unanimous decison rendered in 1970, however, the Supreme Court put a stop to this argument by holding that the two-sovereignties rule of the *Lanza* case does not apply to states and their subdivisions, since political subdivisions of the state are not sovereign entities, and their relationship is quite unlike that of states to the federal government.[80] Thus, one who has

75. 359 U.S. 187 (1959).

76. People *ex rel.* Liss v. Superintendent, 282 N.Y. 115, 25 N.E. 2d 869 (1940); People v. Lo Cicero, 14 N.Y. 2d 374, 251 N.Y.S. 2d 953, 200 N.E. 2d 622 (1964). A similar position was taken in State v. Fletcher, 22 Ohio App. 2d 83, 259 N.E. 2d 146 (1970).

77. Strobhar v. State, 55 Fla. 167, 47 So. 4 (1908).

78. See, e.g., Minn. Stat. 1953, §610.23. The Supreme Court once ruled that if conduct is a crime against the law of nations, a prior conviction in one country will bar another prosecution for the same offense. United States v. Furlong, 5 Wheat. (U.S.) 184, 197 (1820).

79. See, e.g., State v. Lee, 29 Minn. 445, 13 N.W. 913 (1882). This subject was canvassed by Charles M. Kneier, "Prosecution under State Law and Municipal Ordinance as Double Jeopardy," *Cornell Law Quarterly,* 16 (February 1931): 201–11.

80. Waller v. Florida, 397 U.S. 387 (1970). In Robinson v. Neil, 409 U.S. 505 (1970), the Court held unanimously that the rule of the Waller case was retroactive, since double jeopardy does not involve mere procedural matters, but prevents a trial from taking place at all.

been convicted of violating a municipal ordinance is not thereafter triable, on the same facts, for violating a state statute.

Finally, it remains to be noted that an acquittal of a member of the United States armed forces by a court-martial is a bar to a later prosecution in the federal civil courts for the same conduct.[81] But an acquittal by a federal court-martial is not a bar to a later prosecution in a state court,[82] though the state court may lack jurisdiction for some other reason, such as federal supremacy with regard to the activity in question. Conversely, acquittal by a state court does not free the accused from a later trial by a court-martial.[83]

Right of the Government to Appeal

It is settled law in the federal courts that the government has no right to appeal from an acquittal in a criminal case. So the Supreme Court ruled in *Kepner* v. *United States,*[84] although a minority of four took the position that the jeopardy should be regarded as a single and continuing jeopardy from the beginning of the proceeding to the end of the appeal. The majority thought the common law settled the matter the other way. In an earlier case, the Court relied upon long-established principles of common law, the overwhelming weight of state authority, and considerations of humanity arising from the danger of government persecution and unnecessary vexation where the contest is between parties of such unequal strength, to support the proposition that a writ of error does not lie in behalf of the United States in a criminal case.[85] In fact, Congress once sought by statute to give the government the right of appeal in the District of Columbia, except that a verdict in favor of the defendant should not be set aside, but the Court held the act unconstitutional as requiring advisory opinions, that is to say, the performance of a nonjudicial function.[86] Now that federal jeopardy law applies to the states, it may be presumed that the same rule will be applicable, namely, that a state may not constitutionally appeal from an acquittal in a criminal case.

81. Grafton v. United States, 206 U.S. 333 (1907). See also Sanford v. Robbins, 115 F.2d 435 (5th Cir. 1940), cert. denied, 312 U.S. 697 (1941).
82. See *dicta* in Coleman v. Tennessee, 97 U.S. 509, 513 (1878); *In re* Fair, 100 F. 149, 151 (D. Neb. 1900); United States v. Clark, 31 F. 710, 715 (E.D. Mich. 1887); State v. Rankin, 4 Coldw. (Tenn.) 145 (1867).
83. *In re* Stubbs, 133 F. 1012 (D. Wash. 1905). See J. A. Crane, "Double Jeopardy and Courts-Martial," *Minnesota Law Review,* 3 (February 1919): 181–87; H. A. Meriam and J. V. Thornton, "Double-Jeopardy and the Court-Martial," *Brooklyn Law Review,* 19 (December 1952): 62–80.
84. 195 U.S. 100 (1904).
85. United States v. Sanges, 144 U.S. 310 (1892).
86. United States v. Evans, 213 U.S. 297 (1909).

Some Exceptions to the General Rule of Jeopardy

A fraudulent acquittal or conviction, obtained by the accused for the purpose of protecting himself from further prosecution and adequate punishment, is not a bar to a second prosecution. This rule is acquiesced in "as just and necessary to the proper administration of public justice."[87] In a case where the accused connived to have a friend on the jury, the court said: "Fraud vitiates every transaction into which it enters; and whenever it is of such a character and extent as necessarily to prevent a valid conviction, there is no jeopardy, and the prisoner may be held for another trial."[88] A common form of fraud occurs where an accused contrives to secure a conviction on an assault and battery charge before a justice of the peace in order to avoid a later prosecution on a more serious charge. Since this practice would make "a travesty" of criminal prosecutions, such convictions are often set aside.[89] As one court has said, "If the whole case is controlled and managed by the accused, there are no adverse parties, and where this is so there can not, in the true sense of the term, be a former conviction or acquittal."[90]

Another exception to the general rule that a former jeopardy bars a second prosecution is that the defendant may waive his protection against double jeopardy. It is a personal privilege which he may waive either expressly or by implication, and it is usually waived by implication through failure to claim it before the second trial.[91] The most common form of waiver occurs when a defendant has a verdict set aside on his own motion to the trial court, or by way of an appeal he himself has taken. In such instances it is universally held that he may be tried a second time, usually on the theory that the motion[92] or appeal[93] constituted a waiver of the guaranty. Furthermore, it makes no difference whether the first judg-

---

87. State v. Simpson, 28 Minn. 66, 9 N.W. 78, 41 Am. Rep. 269 (1881).
88. State v. Bell, 81 N.C. 591, 594 (1879).
89. De Bord v. People, 27 Colo. 377, 61 P. 599, 83 Am. St. Rep. 89 (1900); State v. Smith, 57 Kan. 673, 47 P. 541 (1897); State v. Caldwell, 70 Ark. 74, 66 S.W. 150 (1902).
90. Halloran v. State, 80 Ind. 586, 590 (1881).
91. State v. White, 71 Kan. 356, 360, 80 P. 89 (1905).
92. Thus a motion for a new trial is a waiver of the right to plead former jeopardy. State v. Austin, 318 Mo. 859, 300 S.W. 1083 (1927). See J. P. Bishop, *Criminal Law,* 9th ed. (Chicago: Flood Publ. Co., 1923), §998, p. 740: "Whenever the defendant for any cause moves in arrest of judgment or applies to the court to vacate a judgment already entered . . . he will be presumed to waive any objection to being put a second time in jeopardy." This point is spelled out in several state constitutions: Colo. Const., Art. II, §18; Wyo. Const., Art. I, §11; Ga. Const., Art. I, §1, Par. 8; La. Const., Art. I, §9; Mo. Const., Art. I, §19.
93. United States v. Ball, 163 U.S. 662 (1896); United States v. Jones, 31 F. 725 (5th Cir. 1887); Sanders v. State, 85 Ind. 318, 44 Am. Rep. 29 (1882).

ment is invalidated through the defendant's collateral attack, as by habeas corpus, instead of by direct attack.[94]

Termination of Proceedings

As already noted, jeopardy attaches when the jury has been impaneled and sworn. If, for example, after a trial has gone this far, the prosecutor should decide that he did not have sufficient evidence and asks the court to discharge the jury, a second prosecution for the same offense would be forbidden by the double jeopardy principle. There are, however, certain exceptional situations where a judge may discharge a jury, before it reaches a verdict, without any jeopardy resulting that will bar a second prosecution. The leading decision on this subject was *United States* v. *Perez*,[95] decided by the Supreme Court in 1824. It held that the judge's discharge of a jury which was unable to agree on a verdict would not bar a future trial for the same offense. "We think," said Justice Story, "that in all cases of this nature, the law has invested Courts of justice with the authority to discharge a jury from giving any verdict, whenever, in their opinion, taking all the circumstances into consideration, there is a manifest necessity for the act, or the ends of public justice would otherwise be defeated. They are to exercise a sound discretion on the subject. . . . To be sure, the power ought to be used with the greatest caution, under urgent circumstances, and for very plain and obvious causes. . . ."

The rule that termination of proceedings may not necessarily result in jeopardy so as to bar a second prosecution is usually explained on the theory that jeopardy did not attach. But this flies in the face of the obvious fact that it did. Perhaps a better explanation, offered by some courts, is that jeopardy depends upon there being a regular and complete proceeding. The Vermont court once explained that jeopardy depends upon the presumption that the tribunal will continue legally organized to the end of the trial, and that if anything happens in the course of the trial which conclusively rebuts this presumption it also rebuts the presumption of the jeopardy of the prisoner by reason of the commencement of the trial.[96]

It is universally agreed that the discharge of a "hung jury" is one of the reasons of "manifest necessity" which would not operate to bar a second trial.[97] Several state constitutions say as much.[98] The Alabama Constitution goes farther in saying that "courts may, for reasons fixed by law,

---

94. Bryant v. United States, 214 F. 51 (8th Cir. 1914); *Ex parte* Longoria, 280 S.W. 2d 743 (Tex. Cr. App. 1955).

95. 9 Wheat. (U.S.) 579 (1824).

96. State v. Emery, 59 Vt. 84, 88, 7 A. 129, 131 (1886).

97. Logan v. United States, 144 U.S. 263, 298 (1892); Dreyer v. Illinois, 187 U.S. 71, 85 (1902); State v. Farne, 190 S.C. 75, 1 S.E. 2d 912 (1939); Harlan v. State, 190 Ind. 322, 130 N.E. 413 (1921); Dreyer v. People, 188 Ill. 40, 58 N.E. 620, 59 N.E. 424, 58 L.R.A. 869 (1900).

98. Ark. Const., Art. II, §8: ". . . if, in any criminal prosecution, the jury be divided in

discharge juries from the consideration of any case, and no person shall gain any advantage by reason of such discharge of the jury."[99] Several other state constitutions make it clear that a mistrial shall not bar a second prosecution.[100] Appellate courts have approved of the discharge of juries for various physical reasons of "manifest necessity": illness and death in a juror's family,[101] incapacitation of a juror,[102] illness of the judge,[103] or serious illness of the judge's wife.[104] Judges have acted within permissible discretion in discharging juries because of the occurrence of various forms of prejudicial misconduct on the part of judges, prosecutors, and jurors: where a juror was found to have sworn falsely on the *voir dire* examination as to his acquaintance with the accused,[105] where it was learned that one of the jurors was related to one of the defendants,[106] where a juror was disqualified because it was learned that he had served on the grand jury which brought in the indictment,[107] where a juror was discovered to have served on the jury of a former trial of the same cause,[108] where improper evidence was brought to the jury's attention,[109] where the district attorney referred in the presence of the panel of prospective jurors to another criminal case pending against the accused,[110] or presented evidence of a previous conviction,[111] where the judge himself was guilty of misconduct by questioning the good faith of the prosecutor in front of the jury,[112] where a juror was noticed shaking hands during a trial recess with the widow of the deceased,[113] or where the judge failed to allow the defendant his full number of peremptory challenges.[114]

---

opinion, the court before which the trial shall be had may, in its discretion, discharge the jury, and commit or bail the accused for trial at the same or the next term of said court." Similar provisions are Colo. Const., Art. II, §18; Wyo. Const., Art. I, §11.

99. Ala. Const., Art. I, §9.

100. Ga. Const., Art. I, §1, Par. 8; La. Const., Art. I, §15; Mo. Const., Art. I, §19.

101. Salistean v. State, 115 Neb. 838, 215 N.W. 107, 53 A.L.R. 1057 (1927); *Ex parte* Earle, 316 Mich. 295, 25 N.W. 2d 202 (1946).

102. United States v. Potash, 118 F.2d 54 (2d Cir. 1941), cert. denied, 313 U.S. 584 (1941).

103. Freeman v. United States, 237 F. 815 (2d Cir. 1916).

104. State v. Tatman, 59 Iowa, 471, 13 N.W. 632 (1882).

105. Simmons v. United States, 142 U.S. 148 (1891). A discharge was approved in Com. v. McCormick, 130 Mass. 61, 39 Am. Rep. 423 (1881), where one of the jurors was found to have gone bail for a defendant.

106. United States v. McCunn, 36 F.2d 52 (S.D. N.Y. 1929).

107. Thompson v. United States, 155 U.S. 271 (1894).

108. Martin v. State, 163 Ark. 103, 259 S.W. 6, 33 A.L.R. 133 (1924).

109. People v. Davis, 233 Mich. 29, 206 N.W. 522 (1925).

110. Himmelfarb v. United States, 175 F.2d 924 (9th Cir. 1949).

111. Blair v. White, 24 F.2d 323 (8th Cir. 1928).

112. United States v. Giles, 19 F. Supp. 1009 (W.D. Okla. 1937).

113. Golden v. State, 63 Ga. App. 765, 12 S.E. 2d 108 (1940).

114. State v. Helm, 66 Nev. 286, 209 P.2d 187 (1949). The necessity to discharge the jury

A judge may also, in extreme situations, declare a mistrial because of the publication of articles in the newspapers which are likely to prejudice the jury.[115] Where a court dismisses an indictment as not charging a crime, after the jury was sworn, there is no jeopardy because the court in the first proceeding lacked jurisdiction.[116] The Supreme Court returned to consider this issue in a 1973 case decided by a 5-4 vote, the majority upholding the declaration of a mistrial by a state judge, for reasons of "manifest necessity," where, after the jury had been impaneled, but before any evidence had been presented, the judge terminated the proceeding because he concluded that the indictment was fatally deficient under state law.[117] Justice Rehnquist noted that there is no mechanical formula by which to measure the requirements of public justice, and that the trial judge must be conceded to have a broad discretion. Since an obvious error would have made reversal on appeal a certainty, and the delay was only minimal, a mistrial under these circumstances implemented a reasonable state policy. The dissenting Justices preferred to follow the general rule that jeopardy attaches when the jury has been selected and sworn, and argued that as a result of the declaration of a mistrial the defendant lost the option of securing an acquittal from the first jury.

The entry of a *nolle prosequi* after jeopardy has attached, without the defendant's consent, amounts to an acquittal which bars a later trial.[118] Speaking more generally, it is clear that the discharge of a defendant, after the jury has been sworn and before a verdict, without his consent and in the absence of special circumstances, is a bar to a later trial for the same offense.[119] Thus, a discharge because of the government's failure to secure the attendance of material witnesses does not fall within the "urgent necessity" rule.[120] Furthermore, in a recent case the Court ruled a second trial improper where the judge had aborted the first trial, after the jury was chosen and sworn, because he did not believe that the govern-

---

is "both manifest and over-ruling" where the court knows that the defect will require a verdict of guilty to be set aside, if the trial is permitted to go to a conclusion.

115. Simmons v. United States, 142 U.S. 148 (1891); United States v. Montgomery, 42 F.2d 254 (S.D. N.Y. 1930).

116. United States v. Rogoff, 163 F. 311 (S.D. N.Y. 1908). Cf. Lovato v. New Mexico, 242 U.S. 199 (1916) for a broad view as to the limits of judicial discretion.

117. Illinois v. Somerville, 410 U.S. 458 (1973).

118. Clawans v. Rives, 104 F.2d 240 (D.C. Cir. 1939); Rosser v. Com., 159 Va. 1028, 167 S.E. 257 (1933).

119. *Ex parte* Glenn, 111 F. 257 (N.D. W.Va. 1901).

120. Downum v. United States, 372 U.S. 734 (1963); Cornero v. United States, 48 F.2d 69, 74 A.L.R. 797 (9th Cir. 1931).

ment's witnesses in a tax fraud case fully understood the nature of the self-incrimination privilege, even though they had been warned about it by the Internal Revenue Service.[121] The holding of the trial judge that these witnesses must first consult attorneys was ruled by the Court to be an abuse of discretion, since the judge always had the simple option of ordering a continuance. Three Justices dissented on the ground that except for the inconvenience of delay, the judge's ruling could not possibly have hurt the defendant.

The scope of discretion which the Supreme Court now accords to the trial judge was underscored in the case of *Wade* v. *Hunter*.[122] A soldier who was in an outfit moving into Germany was put on trial before a general court-martial for rape. After hearing evidence and argument of counsel the court-martial decided to continue the case in order to hear witnesses not then available because of the continuing advance of the troops. A week later, the General of the Division withdrew the charges and directed the court-martial to take no further proceedings, because the mother and father of the victim were unable to be present on account of illness and because of the tactical situation. A majority of six Justices held that the accused could at a later date be tried by another court-martial. Said Justice Black,

> The double-jeopardy provision of the Fifth Amendment . . . does not mean that every time a defendant is put to trial before a competent tribunal he is entitled to go free if the trial fails to end in a final judgment. Such a rule would create an insuperable obstacle to the administration of justice in many cases in which there is no semblance of the type of oppressive practices at which the double-jeopardy prohibition is aimed. There may be unforeseeable circumstances that arise during a trial making its completion impossible, such as the failure of a jury to agree on a verdict. In such event the purpose of law to protect society from those guilty of crimes frequently would be frustrated by denying courts power to put the defendant to trial again. And there have been instances where a trial judge has discovered facts during a trial which indicated that one or more members of a jury might be biased against the Government or the defendant. It is settled that the duty of the judge in this event is to discharge the jury and direct a retrial. What has been said is enough to show that a defendant's valued right to have his trial completed by a particular tribunal must in some instances be subordinated to the public's interest in fair trials designed to end in just judgments.[123]

Whether a particular trial should be discontinued, Justice Black pointed out, is a question to be decided within the sound discretion of

---

121. United States v. Jorn, 400 U.S. 470 (1971).
122. 336 U.S. 684 (1949).
123. 336 U.S. 688–89.

those who know most about the relevant factors. No rigid formula is possible. All that can be said is that "a trial can be discontinued when particular circumstances manifest a necessity for so doing, and when failure to discontinue would defeat the ends of justice." The Court refused to say that the absence of witnesses can never justify a discontinuance of a trial. Such a position would entail "the mechanical application of an abstract formula." Here the tactical situation, the fact that the officers were needed for military functions, and the absence of any charge of bad faith, supported the Court's conclusion that discretion had not been abused. The three dissenting Justices expressed the fear that with such holdings as this the double jeopardy guaranty of the Constitution might "be eroded away by a tide of plausible-appearing exceptions."

That the Court is equally reluctant to interfere with the state courts is suggested by another case, *Brock* v. *North Carolina*.[124] Here the state trial court had granted the prosecution's motion for a mistrial because its two most essential witnesses refused to testify on grounds of self-incrimination. These two witnesses had been tried previously themselves, but judgments had not been entered on their convictions, and they declined in this posture to testify in Brock's trial, since they intended, if adverse judgments were entered against them, to appeal. Under these circumstances the trial court thought that since the ends of justice required their testimony, Brock's case should be dismissed so that the previous case against the two witnesses could be brought to a conclusion. The highest court of North Carolina said that there was no double jeopardy because the trial court, under the long-standing common law of the state, has discretion to declare a mistrial if it is in the interests of justice to do so. Leaning heavily, on the *Palko* precedent, the Supreme Court found here no denial of due process, declaring that it has long favored the view that the trial judge has a broad discretion to declare a mistrial if that will best serve the ends of justice to either or both parties. As Justice Frankfurter declared, in a concurring opinion, under these circumstances it could not be said that the mistrial request was unfair or oppressive to the accused. Chief Justice Vinson dissented, protesting that this was the first time in the history of the Court that it was urged that a state could grant a mistrial in order to present a stronger case at some later trial. He thought it highly undesirable to permit the prosecutor, if he thinks he cannot win a conviction, to stop the trial and try again on another day. A defendant could not ask for a mistrial because the state had done well, and the defense poorly, and he argued the same rule ought to apply to the prosecution. Of course, it

124. 344 U.S. 424 (1953).

should be borne in mind that this decision was made before *Palko* was overruled.

Closely Related Offenses

The question of double jeopardy often arises where a person has, with one act, committed closely related offenses defined by different statutes. Speaking generally, the rule is that there is no double jeopardy if the second statute requires proof of an additional fact which the other does not. For example, one convicted of insulting a public officer may also be tried for disorderly conduct, though both prosecutions arose from the same act.[125] A defendant convicted of selling illicit liquor may later be tried for possessing the same liquor, since possessing and selling are distinct offenses.[126] One may possess without selling, or sell something he does not possess. "There is nothing in the Constitution," Justice Brandeis has noted, "which prevents Congress from punishing separately each step leading to the consummation of a transaction which it has power to prohibit and punishing also the completed transaction."[127] On the basis of a single sale of narcotics, the offender may be prosecuted both for selling unstamped drugs, and for selling drugs not in pursuance of a written order.[128] An acquittal of the offense of stealing government property does not bar a later trial for receiving and concealing government property known to be stolen.[129] Agreeing to receive forbidden compensation and receiving such compensation have been held to be separate crimes, since either could occur without the other.[130] Making a false entry in the books of a bank showing a credit, and making a false statement later in a report on the bank's condition showing the same credit, have been held to be separate offenses.[131] Congress may punish a person for being in contempt of Congress and also make this conduct a crime.[132] Breaking into a post office with intent to commit larceny and committing the larceny are separate offenses.[133] A conviction for conspiracy to restrain trade in

125. Gavieres v. United States, 220 U.S. 338 (1911). But if the basic facts are the same, a second prosecution is inadmissible. Sealfon v. United States, 332 U.S. 575 (1948).
126. Albrecht v. United States, 273 U.S. 1 (1927). Cf. United States v. Michener, 331 U.S. 789 (1947), holding that causing a plate to be made for counterfeiting purposes and possession of the plate with intent to counterfeit are separate offenses.
127. 273 U.S. 11.
128. Blockburger v. United States, 284 U.S. 299 (1932); Gore v. United States, 357 U.S. 386 (1958).
129. *Ex parte* Rhinelander, 11 F. Supp. 298 (W.D. Tex. 1935).
130. Burton v. United States, 202 U.S. 344 (1906).
131. United States v. Adams, 281 U.S. 202 (1930).
132. *In re* Chapman, 166 U.S. 661, 672 (1897).
133. Morgan v. Devine, 237 U.S. 632 (1915).

violation of §1 of the Sherman Act will not stand in the way of a later prosecution for a conspiracy to monopolize trade forbidden by §2 of the same statute.[134] Nor will a conviction or acquittal on substantive charges bar a later prosecution for perjury committed at the trials for the substantive offenses.[135]

The Supreme Court has gone even farther in upholding the claims of the prosecution. It is well established that the commission of a crime and a conspiracy to commit the crime are separate offenses. For example, the Court has upheld an indictment for conspiracy to violate the Internal Revenue Code, though there were also indictments for a series of substantive offenses, each of which was found to have been committed pursuant to the conspiracy.[136] Said Justice Douglas, "It has been long and consistently recognized by the Court that the commission of the substantive offense and a conspiracy to commit it are separate and distinct offenses.... A conspiracy is a partnership in a crime.... It has ingredients, as well as implications, distinct from the completion of the unlawful project."[137] Furthermore, it is established that an acquittal or conviction for violating a criminal statute does not bar a later civil action for penalties, even for punitive penalties. In the leading case of *Helvering* v. *Mitchell*,[138] after the defendant was acquitted by a jury of a charge of tax fraud, the Court held that the criminal action did not prohibit a later civil action for penalties. The decisive fact was that the penalty was a civil and not a criminal sanction. Similarly, an acquittal in a criminal prosecution for conspiracy to violate the Sherman Act has been held to be no

---

134. American Tobacco Co. v. United States, 328 U.S. 781 (1946).

135. United States v. Williams, 341 U.S. 58 (1951).

136. Pinkerton v. United States, 328 U.S. 640 (1946). See also Ianneli v. United States, 420 U.S. 770 (1975).

137. 328 U.S. 643–44. See also Carter v. McClaughry, 183 U.S. 365 (1902); United States v. Bayer, 331 U.S. 532 (1947) ("... the agreement to do the act is distinct from the act itself."); Pereira v. United States, 347 U.S. 1, 11 (1954), where Chief Justice Warren wrote, "It is settled law in this country that the commission of a substantive offense and a conspiracy to commit it are separate and distinct crimes, and a plea of double jeopardy is no defense to a conviction for both."

138. 303 U.S. 391 (1938). For a later decision on this point, see U.S. *ex rel.* Marcus v. Hess, 317 U.S. 537 (1943), holding that conviction for defrauding the government, and the payment of a large fine, did not bar a later informer action for even larger penalties. Again punitive damages were held to fall within the concept of a civil remedy. The Court held in Rex Trailer Co. v. United States, 350 U.S. 148 (1956), that after conviction for violating the Surplus Property Act, the government could bring a civil action for the recovery of penalties, in the nature of liquidated damages, based on the same transactions. The Court ruled unanimously that the latter recovery was civil in nature, and that it is clearly established that Congress may impose both a criminal and civil sanction regarding the same act or omission without running afoul of the double jeopardy doctrine.

bar to a civil suit to enjoin the same conspiracy.[139] The Court relied upon the difference in the degree of the burden of proof in civil and criminal cases.

Most state courts follow the "same evidence" test. Long ago, the Massachusetts court ruled that a conviction for lewd and lascivious cohabitation does not bar a conviction for adultery based on the same association, the test being not whether the defendant has already been tried for the same act, but whether he has been put in jeopardy for the same offense.[140] The court said, "A single act may be an offence against two statutes; and if each statute requires proof of an additional fact which the other does not, an acquittal or conviction under either statute does not exempt the defendant from prosecution and punishment under the other."

This problem attains its most exaggerated form when the same offense is committed against more than one victim in a single transaction or event. In 1958, in *Hoag* v. *New Jersey*[141] the Supreme Court ruled, by a 5-3 vote, that after a man has been acquitted of the charge of robbing three individuals, double jeopardy would not stand in the way of a second trial on a charge of having robbed a fourth person. It was stressed that the New Jersey statute, according to the state's highest court, made each of the robberies a separate offense, though they took place on the same occasion, and the state court had ruled that double jeopardy does not apply unless the same evidence necessary to sustain a second indictment would have been sufficient to secure a conviction on the first.[142] It is better practice for a state normally to try the several offenses in a single prosecution, but Justice Harlan ruled that due process does not demand it. To put it somewhat differently, the Court refused to make the doctrine of collateral estoppel a constitutional requirement binding on the states. The three dissenting Justices protested that in fact the main defense of the accused, an alibi, was adjudicated twice, and a jury verdict of acquittal at the first trial ought to be conclusive.[143]

This decision came down before the *Benton* case was decided, and in the leading case of *Ashe* v. *Swenson*[144] (1970), the Court in effect overruled

139. United States v. National Assoc. of Real Estate Boards, 339 U.S. 485 (1950). In One Lot Emerald Cut Stones v. United States, 409 U.S. 232 (1972), the Court held that an acquittal on a smuggling charge would not prevent the government from instituting a forfeiture action.

140. Morey v. Com., 108 Mass. 433 (1871).

141. 356 U.S. 464 (1958).

142. State v. Hoa, 35 N.J. Super. 555, 114 A.2d 573 (1955).

143. For similar decisions, see United States v. Raudenbush, 8 Pet. (U.S.) 288 (1834); Burton v. United States, 202 U.S. 344 (1906).

144. 397 U.S. 436 (1970).

the *Hoag* decision. Ashe was tried in a Missouri court on a charge of participating with several confederates in the robbery of one of several persons engaged in a poker game, and was acquitted. A few weeks later, he was tried for the robbery of a second participant, and on the testimony of the same witnesses, was convicted, after a plea of former jeopardy was rejected. The Supreme Court held that the second trial was constitutionally improper, on the basis of the important principle of collateral estoppel, which, said Justice Stewart, "means simply that when an issue of ultimate fact has once been determined by a valid and final judgment, that issue cannot again be litigated between the same parties in any future lawsuit."[145] He pointed out that although collateral estoppel was first developed in civil litigation, it has been a rule of federal criminal law at least since 1916.[146] Clearly, since the first jury found that the accused was not one of the robbers, that made the second trial wholly impermissible. The question was not whether Missouri could validly charge Ashe with six separate offenses, and not whether he could have received six punishments if he had been convicted in a single trial of robbing the six victims. "It is simply whether, after a jury determined by its verdict that the petitioner was not one of the robbers, the State could constitutionally hale him before a new jury to litigate that issue again."[147] In a concurring opinion, Justice Brennan protested that the "same evidence" test was deficient, since it virtually annuls the guaranty by permitting multiple prosecutions where a single transaction is divisible into discrete crimes. He would prefer to hold that normally the Double Jeopardy Clause requires, in the interest of justice, economy, and convenience, that the prosecution join at one trial all charges growing out of a single criminal act.

It is clear that by one act a person may commit a number of offenses, and therefore expose himself to multiply punishments.[148] This is not, however, the nub of the problem. The question of justice relates to the propriety of permitting separate trials for several offenses committed in the same transaction. For multiple prosecutions are contrary to the policy of the double jeopardy concept of avoiding multiple vexations or the harassment of an unnecessary multiplicity of prosecutions.[149] The remedy lies in the "same transaction" rule, according to which the prosecution

---

145. 397 U.S. 443.

146. The Court relied upon United States v. Oppenheimer, 242 U.S. 85 (1916), which is not altogether in point.

147. 397 U.S. 446.

148. See Otto Kirchheimer, "The Act, the Offense and Double Jeopardy," *Yale Law Journal*, 58 (March 1949): 513–44.

149. Frank E. Horack, Jr., "The Multiple Consequences of a Single Criminal Act," *Minnesota Law Review*, 21 (June 1937): 805–22; M. E. Lugar, "Criminal Law, Double Jeopardy and Res Judicata," *Iowa Law Review*, 39 (Winter 1954): 317–47.

must test, in a single trial, the defendant's criminal liability on all issues that may, logically and conveniently, be tried in one proceeding.[150] It is now the general policy of the federal government that several offenses arising out of a single transaction should be alleged and tried together, in the interest of fairness and orderly law enforcement,[151] and in a series of cases the Court has applied the principle of collateral estoppel to various fact situations in state cases appealed to it.[152]

Included Offenses

An acquittal or an unreversed conviction of a lesser offense included within a greater offense prevents a later trial for the greater offense. Thus an acquittal for larceny bars a later prosecution for robbery of the same house for the same money, because robbery could not have been committed without the commission of a larceny as an included inferior offense.[153] By the same token, acquittal for manslaughter is a bar to an indictment for murder, because it is a judicial determination that the accused did not unlawfully take the life of the deceased, and therefore he is not guilty of any offense of which unlawful killing is a necessary element. To put the matter somewhat differently, conviction or acquittal of an offense which has several degrees, as to any degree, bars later prosecution for the same offense in any other degree. Where the defendant has been acquitted or convicted of the greater offense, he has been in jeopardy for all included crimes. Thus an acquittal for robbery bars a prosecution for larceny.[154] Similarly, where the first prosecution was for a lesser offense than the one charged later, there would be double jeopardy if the later prosecution puts the accused in jeopardy for the lesser offense. For example, a conviction for battery bars a later prosecution for assault with intent to murder.[155] To put the matter still differently, if the facts put in

150. See, for example, Harris v. State, 193 Ga. 109, 17 S.E. 2d 573 (1941). Here a man was acquitted of a murder charge and later tried for robbery by open force. The appellate court held that by acquitting the defendant in the murder trial the jury necessarily found that he did not participate in the transaction, and that this issue could not be tested again. He couldn't be guilty of the robbery charge without being guilty also of the murder charge.
151. Petite v. United States, 361 U.S. 529 (1960).
152. For example, in Turner v. Arkansas, 407 U.S. 366 (1972), an acquittal on a murder charge was held to bar a later trial for robbery based on the same facts. See also Simpson v. Florida, 403 U.S. 384 (1971); Harris v. Washington, 404 U.S. 55 (1971). It is a fair assumption that Ciucci v. Illinois, 356 U.S. 571 (1958), which was decided by a 5-4 vote, has lost its vitality. Accused of murdering his wife and three children, Ciucci was tried three different times, on the same evidence, until the prosecution finally secured a jury willing to impose the death penalty.
153. State v. Mikesell, 70 Iowa 176, 30 N.W. 474 (1886).
154. State v. Brannon, 55 Mo. 63, 17 Am. Rep. 643 (1874).
155. People v. McDaniels, 137 Cal. 192, 69 P. 1006, 59 L.R.A. 578, 92 Am. St. Rep. 81 (1902).

the second indictment would have justified a conviction under the first, the second offense is the same as the first. Thus a conviction for the manufacture of liquor bars a later prosecution for possession, since manufacture necessarily connotes possession.[156] A previous conviction for unlawful cohabitation bars a later prosecution for adultery.[157] The general view, then, is that a lesser offense is necessarily included in a charge of the greater if the proof necessary to establish the greater offense will of necessity establish every element of the lesser offense. It does not matter whether the offenses are felonies, misdemeanors, or both.[158]

There is one well-recognized exception to the general rule. It is usually held that where a defendant has been convicted of an assault, following which the victim dies, the defendant may later be tried for murder or manslaughter.[159] It has been explained that no murder had occurred at the time of the first trial, and that the state does not have to postpone the trial for the assault indefinitely to wait and see whether the victim will die.[160]

A special problem arises when a defendant who has been tried for murder and convicted of manslaughter is granted a new trial. The question then arises, For which offense is he triable the second time? The preferable view is that the first conviction for manslaughter is the equivalent of an acquittal for murder, and thus the new trial can be for manslaughter only. It has been explained that otherwise an innocent man would be afraid to appeal, since he would have to pay too great a premium for the privilege of asserting his innocence.[161] But some courts have taken the opposite view, that a new trial reopens the whole proceeding.[162] Such was the position of the Supreme Court in *Trono* v. *United States*,[163]

156. Tritico v. United States, 4 F.2d 664 (5th Cir. 1925). See also State v. Switzer, 65 S.C. 187, 43 S.E. 513 (1903); Scalf v. Com., 195 Ky. 830, 243 S.W. 1034 (1922). Illegal importation and concealment of liquor are separate offenses. Krench v. United States, 42 F.2d 354 (6th Cir. 1930).

157. *Ex parte* Nielson, 131 U.S. 176 (1889).

158. See, e.g., La. Rev. Stat. 15:406 (1950): "When the crime charged includes another of lesser grade, a verdict of guilty of the lesser crime is responsive to the indictment, and it is of no moment that the greater offense is a felony and the lesser a misdemeanor."

159. Diaz v. United States, 223 U.S. 442 (1912).

160. Com. v. Ramunno, 219 Pa. St. 204, 68 A. 184, 14 L.R.A. (N.S.) 209, 123 Am. St. Rep. 653, 12 Ann. Cas 818 (1907). Cf. Com. v. Evans, 101 Mass. 25, 26 (1869): "As the death occurred after that conviction, the offence now prosecuted was not then complete; and was not capable of judicial determination."

161. People v. Gilmore, 4 Cal. 376, 60 Am. Dec. 620 (1854).

162. State v. Gillis, 73 S.C. 318, 53 S.E. 487, 5 L.R.A. (N.S.) 571 (1906).

163. 199 U.S. 521, 531 (1905). See also Stroud v. United States, 251 U.S. 15 (1919), where the defendant was first convicted of first degree murder and given a life sentence, following which he appealed and got a new trial. He was convicted again and given a death sentence. The Court held that there was no double jeopardy since each conviction was for the same offense, first degree murder.

wherein it was ruled that if the defendant is successful on the appeal, he thereby waives his right to avail himself of the former acquittal of the greater offense, since in appealing from the judgment the "accused necessarily appeals from the whole thereof, as well as that which acquits as that which condemns." But it ought to be noted that four Justices dissented on the ground that the Court's position was contrary to the great weight of authority. In 1957, in *Green* v. *United States,* [164] though again by a 5-4 vote, the Court in effect overruled the *Trono* case, although Justice Black chose to say that *Trono* was being distinguished and limited to its "peculiar factual setting." Green was charged with both arson and first degree murder by means of the alleged arson, and the jury found him guilty of arson and of second degree murder, the verdict being silent on the first degree murder charge. The second degree murder conviction was successfully appealed, following which Green was tried again and convicted of first degree murder under the original indictment. The Supreme Court held that the second trial for first degree murder placed Green in jeopardy twice for the same offense, because the first jury's verdict was an implicit acquittal on the first degree murder charge. The Court rejected the argument that Green's appeal was a waiver of his right to the constitutional defense of former jeopardy, and the alternative argument that by appealing Green prolonged his original jeopardy was brushed aside as "untenable." Justice Black said that the government's contention amounted to saying that a defendant must be willing to barter his constitutional protection against a second prosecution for an offense punishable by death as the price of a successful appeal from an erroneous conviction for a lesser offense. This, Justice Black wryly observed, puts this man in "an incredible dilemma." The four dissenting Justices thought that this case was governed by *Trono,* and that actually the Court was overruling *Trono.* Of course, this is what happened. In fact, by 1970 the Court was in a position to reaffirm the *Green* decision by a unanimous vote, when it held that after a trial for murder, and a conviction for the lesser included crime of voluntary manslaughter, the defendant could not, after a successful appeal, be put on trial again for murder.[165] Acquittals may be either express or implied, and the conviction for manslaughter at the first trial must be regarded as an implied acquittal on the murder charge.

It remains to be noted that an accused may not be convicted for two offenses which require inconsistent findings of fact. For example, one cannot be convicted of both grand theft and driving a vehicle without the consent of the owner, since the first offense requires a showing of specific felonious intent to deprive the owner of his property permanently, while the other requires a finding that the accused intended to use the auto-

164. 355 U.S. 184 (1957).
165. Price v. Georgia, 398 U.S. 323 (1970).

mobile temporarily.[166] It is evident, the court noted, that these crimes cannot coexist, since the first intent negatives the existence of the second. One can be convicted of either offense, therefore, but not of both.

Conclusion

It cannot be denied that the double jeopardy guaranty doctrine is still in a state of considerable confusion, though *Benton* and the subsequent decisions represent a considerable improvement in double jeopardy law. The guaranty has been characterized as "moribund," and its protection as largely "illusory."[167] Indeed, it has been asserted that the doctrine is not even a rule of law, but "nothing more than a declaration of an ancient and well established public policy," often disregarded when an overruling consideration of public policy intervenes.[168] Reform by statute as well as by court decision is long overdue. It is encouraging to note, however, that American courts are increasingly committed to the proposition that, absent unusual circumstances, the prosecutor should be required to try a defendant at one time for all offenses growing out of the same transaction or event. The prosecutor's discretionary powers are very great indeed, but it is not consistent with the spirit and purpose of the Double Jeopardy Clause to permit him to harass defendants through successive prosecutions for technically separate offenses growing out of the same facts. Furthermore, the nationalization of the Double Jeopardy Clause in the *Benton* case opens the door, at long last, to some measure of improvement and standardization of double jeopardy principles in the states. On the other hand, the two-sovereignties principle still prevails, and one can only hope that the Court will eliminate this harsh rule in the near future. After all, if a state's grant of immunity to a witness must be respected by federal agencies, and federal grants of immunity by state agencies, it would seem eminently proper and reasonable to apply the same logic to double prosecutions for the same offense.

166. State v. Parsons, 70 Ariz. 399, 222 P.2d 637 (1950). Cf. Bargesser v. State, 95 Fla. 404, 116 So. 12 (1928) (larceny of an auto and receiving the auto as stolen property); People v. Koehn, 207 Cal. 605, 279 P. 646 (1929) (attempt to commit murder by use of explosives and malicious use of explosives).

167. See Comment, "Statutory Implementation of Double Jeopardy Clauses: New Life for a Moribund Constitutional Guarantee," *Yale Law Journal,* 65 (January 1956): 339–68.

168. Note, "Double Jeopardy," *Minnesota Law Review,* 24 (March 1940): 522–63.

11 / Cruel and Unusual Punishments

The Constitutional Rule

The Eighth Amendment provides, "Excessive bail shall not be required, nor excessive fines imposed, nor cruel and unusual punishments inflicted." This prohibition of cruel and unusual punishments is a universal rule of constitutional law in the United States.[1] Every state constitution but those of Connecticut and Vermont has a comparable clause. Vermont's highest court has ruled that the prohibition is a part of the common law of the state, and a Connecticut statute makes the infliction of cruel or unlawful punishment a crime.[2] The concept has deep roots in English experience. Thus Section 20 of Magna Carta (1215) provided that "a freeman shall be amerced for a small offence only according to the degree of the offence; and for a grave offence he shall be amerced according to the gravity of the offence." The same principle of proportionality was expressed for merchants and villeins.[3]

The classic statement of this principle, from which the American phraseology is derived, was in the English Bill of Rights of 1689, Section 10 of which declared "That excessive bail ought not to be required, nor excessive fines imposed; nor cruel and unusual punishments inflicted."[4]

---

1. See Note, "The Effectiveness of the Eighth Amendment: An Appraisal of Cruel and Unusual Punishment," *New York University Law Review,* 36 (April 1961): 846–75; Note, "The Constitutional Prohibition against Cruel and Unusual Punishment—Its Present Significance," *Vanderbilt Law Review,* 4 (April 1951): 680–88; Thomas M. Cooley, *A Treatise on the Constitutional Limitations . . . ,* 8th ed. (Boston: Little, Brown & Co., 1927), 1: 692–96. For a recent scholarly survey, see Larry C. Berkson, *The Concept of Cruel and Unusual Punishment* (Lexington, Mass.: D. C. Heath, 1975).

2. State v. O'Brien, 106 Vt. 97, 170 A. 98 (1934); Conn. Gen. Stat. Ann. §53-20 (1968).

3. The Laws of Edward the Confessor (1042–66) provided in §41, "We do forbid that a person shall be condemned to death for a trifling offence. But for the correction of the multitude, extreme punishment shall be inflicted according to the nature and extent of the offence. For that ought not for a trifling matter to be destroyed which God has made after His own image, and has redeemed with the price of His own blood." Boyd C. Barrington, *The Magna Charta and other Great Charters of England,* 2d ed. (Philadelphia: William J. Campbell, 1900), p. 199. While this code is generally regarded to be a fourteenth century forgery (*ibid.,* p. 181), these laws reflect the thinking of the age.

4. This clause is traceable to the events connected with the "Popish Plot" (1678–79) and the conviction of Titus Oates, in 1685, for perjury, for which he was fined 2,000 marks, sentenced to life imprisonment, defrocked, and ordered to be whipped and to be pilloried four times a year. Following the Glorious Revolution, Oates petitioned Parliament for

But this sentiment was articulated even before this date in earlier colonial documents. Section 46 of the Massachusetts Body of Liberties of 1641 declared that "for bodilie punishments we allow amongst us none that are inhumane Barbarous or cruell." The bill of rights of the earliest constitutions of five of the original states had provisions forbidding excessive bail or fines, or cruel and unusual punishment. Article 2 of the Northwest Ordinance of 1787 provided, "All fines shall be moderate; and no cruel or unusual punishments shall be inflicted." The universality of this principle is reflected in its inclusion in the Universal Declaration of Human Rights (Article 5) which the General Assembly of the United Nations adopted on December 10, 1948: "No one shall be subjected to torture or to cruel inhuman or degrading treatment or punishment."

There were some very cruel and degrading punishments in English practice which American constitutional law obviously bans: dragging through the streets to the place of execution, embowelling alive, mutilation by cutting of the hands or ears, branding on the face or hand, slitting the nostrils, public dissection, beheading and quartering, burning alive, the pillory, stocks, and the ducking stool, the thumb screw and the rack. But Blackstone said in 1765 that "the humanity of the English nation has authorized, by a tacit consent, an almost general mitigation of such part of these judgments as savor of torture or cruelty. . . ."[5]

Scope of the Guaranty

The basic problem of interpretation with respect to clauses forbidding cruel and unusual punishments has been whether they refer only to the mode of punishment, or whether they also authorize judicially enforceable limits to the severity of the punishment in respect to the seriousness of the crime. While some courts have taken the position that these clauses have

---

release from judgment, denouncing it as "inhumane and unparalleled." Thus, just prior to the enactment of the Bill of Rights in 1689, Parliament was confronted with this issue. See Anthony F. Granucci, "'Nor Cruel and Unusual Punishments Inflicted': The Original Meaning," *California Law Review,* 57 (October 1969): 839–65. Granucci does not believe, as is often alleged, that this clause is derived from the "Bloody Assize" of Chief Justice George Jeffreys of King's Bench (1685). Justice Joseph Story, in his *Commentaries on the Constitution of the United States,* 3d ed. (Boston: Little, Brown & Co., 1858), II: 680–81, was not this specific. He wrote that the Eighth Amendment was "adopted as an admonition to all departments of the national govenment to warn them against such violent proceedings, as had taken place in England in the arbitrary reigns of some of the Stuarts. . . . Enormous fines and amercements were . . . sometimes imposed, and cruel and vindictive punishments inflicted."

5. 4 Com. *376. See Alice Morse Earle, *Curious Punishments of Bygone Days* (Chicago: H. S. Stone, 1896); E. G. Black, "Torture under English Law," *University of Pennsylvania Law Review,* 75 (February 1927): 344–48.

to do only with the method of punishment,[6] even they will generally go on to consider its severity as well. For example, where a defendant was given a life sentence for robbery,[7] or a death sentence for an attempt to commit a train robbery,[8] or three to fifteen years for horse-stealing,[9] the court, while asserting that the constitutional clause applied only to the method of punishment, insisted on going on to discuss how serious these crimes were in order to justify the severity of the punishment. Actually the great weight of authority sustains the propriety of the court's inquiring into the severity of the sentence, so that a sentence which is clearly excessive is in most jurisdictions said to constitute a cruel and unusual punishment.

Writing in 1970, a federal district court judge stated what may now be characterized as a generally accepted view of the basic meaning of the constitutional clause forbidding cruel and unusual punishments. "It is flexible and tends to broaden as society tends to pay more regard to human decency and dignity. . . . Generally speaking, a punishment that amounts to torture, or that is grossly excessive in proportion to the offense for which it is imposed, or that is inherently unfair, or that is unnecessarily degrading, or that is shocking or disgusting to people of reasonable sensitivity is a 'cruel and unusual' punishment."[10]

Similarly, Chief Justice Warren once called attention to the elasticity of the concept. "The Amendment," he wrote, "must draw its meaning from the evolving standards of decency that mark the progress of a maturing society."[11] And, he noted, "the basic concept underlying the Eighth Amendment is nothing less than the dignity of man. While the State has the power to punish, the Amendment stands to assure that this power be exercised within the limits of civilized standards."[12]

The Death Penalty

The method of executing a death sentence has often been the subject of constitutional litigation. Of course, death by hanging is of ancient origin, and has not been regarded as a cruel or unusual punishment.[13] In holding

---

6. State v. Griffin, 84 N.J.L. 429, 87 A. 138 (Sup. Ct. 1913), aff'd., 85 N.J.L. 613, 90 A. 259 (1914). Here the court upheld a law which provided for a fine of $1,000 to $5,000 and a jail sentence of one to five years for the crime of keeping a disorderly house where gambling is permitted.
7. Franklin v. Brown, 73 W.Va. 727, 81 S.E. 405, L.R.A. 1915C, 557 (1915).
8. Territory v. Ketchum, 10 N.M. 718, 65 P. 169, 55 L.R.A. 90 (1901).
9. People v. Morris, 80 Mich. 634, 45 N.W. 591 (1890).
10. Chief Judge Henley, in Holt v. Sarver, 309 F. Supp. 362, 380 (E.D. Ark. 1970).
11. Trop v. Dulles, 356 U.S. 86, 101 (1958).
12. 356 U.S. 100.
13. State v. Burris, 194 Iowa 628, 190 N.W. 38 (1922); State v. Butchek, 121 Ore. 141, 253 P. 367 (1927).

death by shooting to be permissible, the Supreme Court said that while it is difficult to define the scope of the Eighth Amendment, it rules out punishments by torture or other "unnecessary cruelty."[14] It is clearly established that the legislature may change the manner of inflicting the death penalty. Novelty is not *per se* cruelty, and no method can spare the suffering due to the fear of death. If the end is reached as swiftly and painlessly as possible, the method used is permissible. On such a theory, death by electrocution was universally approved by American courts when introduced.[15] The constitutional clause "cannot be taken so broadly as to prohibit every humane improvement not previously known."[16] Said Chief Justice Fuller, in a leading case, "Punishments are cruel when they involve torture or a lingering death; but the punishment of death is not cruel, within the meaning of that word as used in the Constitution. It implies there something inhuman and barbarous, something more than the mere extinguishment of life."[17] Similarly death by lethal gas was sustained as being more humane and less painful than hanging.[18]

But what about the validity of capital punishment in terms of contemporary moral standards? Former Justice Goldberg argued strongly in 1970 for the proposition that the death penalty should be declared unconstitutional by the Supreme Court on the basis of the Eighth Amendment.[19] He declared that in spite of the fact that the federal government and thirty-eight states still had capital punishment, it is "highly suspect under the standards of degrading severity and wanton imposition."[20] It has often been asserted that all forms of execution involve torture.[21] Furthermore, as the President's Commission on Law Enforcement and Administration of Justice pointed out in its notable 1967 Report, "there is evidence that

---

14. Wilkerson v. Utah, 99 U.S. 130 (1878). The fact that soldiers convicted of desertion or other capital military offenses were usually sentenced to be shot was regarded as persuasive.

15. People *ex rel.* Kemmler v. Durston, 119 N.Y. 569, 24 N.E. 6 (1890), aff'd., 136 U.S. 436 (1890); State v. Tomasi, 75 N.J.L. 739, 69 A. 214 (1908). For an interesting account of the Kemmler case by an electrical engineer, see Theodore Bernstein, "A Grand Success," *Institute of Electrical and Electronics Engineers,* 10 (February 1973): 54–58.

16. *In re* Storti, 178 Mass. 549, 60 N.E. 210, 52 L.R.A. 520 (1901), per Holmes, C.J.

17. *In re* Kemmler, 136 U.S. 436, 447 (1890). In McElvaine v. Brush, 142 U.S. 155 (1891), the Court also upheld a death sentence by electrocution which in addition stipulated that the prisoner had to be kept in solitary confinement until the punishment of death was inflicted.

18. Hernandez v. State, 43 Ariz. 424, 32 P. 2d 18 (1934); State v. Gee Jon, 46 Nev. 418, 211 P. 676, 30 A.L.R. 1443 (1923).

19. See Arthur J. Goldberg and Alan M. Dershowitz, "Declaring the Death Penalty Unconstitutional," *Harvard Law Review,* 83 (June 1970): 1773–819.

20. *Ibid.,* p. 1784.

21. See Comment, "The Death Penalty Cases," *California Law Review,* 56 (October 1968): 1268–490, 1337–43.

the imposition of the death sentence and the exercise of dispensing power by the courts and the executive follow discriminatory patterns. The death sentence is disproportionately imposed and carried out on the poor, the Negro, and the members of unpopular groups."[22] In addition, it is frequently argued that capital punishment is cruel in the constitutional sense because it does not accomplish the main purposes which punishment is supposed to serve, such as deterrence and rehabilitation. The statistics clearly show that capital punishment does not affect the homicide rate, and of course it defeats rehabilitation altogether. That leaves retribution as the objective, hardly a highly prized attribute in a civilized society.

While not confronting the issue directly, the Supreme Court on several occasions stated in *dicta* that there was no question about the constitutionality of the death penalty as such. Chief Justice Fuller said as much in 1890.[23] Justice Reed repeated this thought in 1947 when he wrote, "The cruelty against which the Constitution protects a convicted man is cruelty inherent in the method of punishment, not the necessary suffering involved in any method employed to extinguish life humanely."[24] And in 1958 Chief Justice Warren declared, "Whatever the arguments may be against capital punishment, both on moral grounds and in terms of accomplishing the purposes of punishment—and they are forceful—the death penalty has been employed throughout our history, and, in a day when it is still widely accepted, it cannot be said to violate the constitutional concept of cruelty."[25]

Accordingly, in 1952, the federal courts upheld the death sentence in the case of the Rosenbergs, Judge Jerome N. Frank of the Court of Appeals for the Second Circuit ruling that death for the two atom spies did not shock and outrage the moral sense of the community, and that Congress has the power to prescribe the death penalty for wartime espionage.[26] Indeed, all through the 1960s federal and state courts upheld the imposition of the death penalty for such heinous offenses as murder[27]

22. *The Challenge of Crime in a Free Society* (Washington: U.S. Government Printing Office, 1967), p. 143.
23. *In re* Kemmler, 136 U.S. 436, 447 (1890).
24. Louisiana *ex rel.* Francis v. Resweber, 329 U.S. 459, 464 (1947).
25. Trop v. Dulles, 356 U.S. 86, 99 (1958).
26. United States v. Rosenberg, 195 F.2d 583, 608 (2nd Cir. 1952), cert. denied, 344 U.S. 838 (1952).
27. State v. Forcella, 52 N.J. 263, 245 A.2d 181 (1968); People v. Walcher, 42 Ill. 2d 159, 246 N.E. 2d 256 (1969). In England, the Murder (Abolition of Death Penalty) Act of 1965, which was confirmed by Parliament after a trial period in 1970, abolished the death penalty for murder. The death penalty is still available, however, for high treason (Treason Act, 1814), piracy with violence (Piracy Act, 1837), and setting fire to Her Majesty's ships or stores (Dockyards Protection Act, 1772).

and rape,[28] and even when, in rape cases, the life of the victim was neither taken nor endangered,[29] or the criminal act was the result of uncontrollable impulse.[30] Repeatedly, reviewing courts ruled that the decision to abolish the death penalty was within the discretion of the legislature, and that constitutional provisions forbidding cruel and unusual punishments could not be construed to mean that capital punishment was illegal. And in the face of mounting criticism and agitation, many state appellate courts held as the country moved into the 1970s, that our constitutional principles did not forbid the imposition of the death penalty for such serious offenses as murder,[31] rape,[32] and armed robbery.[33]

In 1963, the Supreme Court denied a writ of certiorari which would have given it an opportunity to decide whether the imposition of the death penalty for a rape, where human life was neither taken nor endangered, could be squared with the Eighth Amendment.[34] Three dissenting Justices thought that at the very least the Court should review the question. Justice Goldberg made three observations on the subject. First, he pointed out, the trend throughout the world is against punishing rape by death; only five of sixty-six countries responding to a UN survey—the United States, Nationalist China, Northern Rhodesia, Nyasaland and South Africa—still retain the death penalty for this offense, and thirty-three of the American states do not. Secondly, the punishment may be greatly disproportionate to the offense charged. Finally, said Justice Goldberg, it is worth considering whether the permissible aims of punishment—e.g. deterrence, isolation, rehabilitation—can be achieved as effectively by punishing rape less severely.

This line of thought finally bore fruit in an important decision of the

---

28. Maxwell v. Stephens, 229 F. Supp. 205, 217 (E.D. Ark. 1964); Sims v. Balkcom, 220 Ga. 7, 11, 136 S.E. 2d 766, 769 (1964) ("no more reprehensible crime"); Gordon v. State, 160 So. 2d 73, 76–77 (Miss. 1964); State v. Crook, 253 La. 961, 221 So. 2d 473 (1969).

29. Ralph v. Pepersack, 335 F.2d 128, 141 (4th Cir. 1964), cert. denied, 380 U.S. 925 (1965).

30. Jackson v. Dickson, 325 F.2d 573 (9th Cir. 1963), cert. denied, 377 U.S. 957 (1964). The Supreme Court held in Leland v. Oregon, 343 U.S. 790 (1951), that the Constitution does not bar use of the old right-wrong (M'Naghten) test, nor does it require adoption of the irresistible impulse test.

31. State v. Cripps, 259 La. 403, 250 So.2d 382 (1971); Bartholomey v. State, 260 Md. 504, 273 A.2d 164 (1971); State v. Kremens, 57 N.J. 309, 272 A.2d 537 (1971); Steigler v. State, 277 A.2d 662 (Del. 1971); Curry v. State, 468 S.W.2d 455 (Tex. Cr. App. 1971); Williams v. Com., 464 S.W.2d 244 (Ky. 1971); State v. Coleman, 460 S.W.2d 719 (Mo. 1970); State v. Cerny, 480 P.2d 199 (Wash. 1971).

32. State v. Atkinson, 278 N.C. 168, 179 S.E.2d 410 (1971); Liddell v. State, 251 So.2d 601 (Ala. 1971).

33. Hart v. State, 227 Ga. 171, 179 S.E.2d 346 (1971).

34. Rudolph v. Alabama, 375 U.S. 889 (1963).

Court of Appeals of the Fourth Circuit rendered in 1970 which held that the Eighth Amendment bars execution for a rape in which the victim's life was neither taken nor endangered, because death is an excessively disproportionate penalty for such an offense.[35] The court noted that both the National Commission on Reform of Federal Criminal Laws and the Model Penal Code have recommended repeal of the death penalty for rape, and that Congress abolished it for the District of Columbia in 1970.[36] The court also pointed out that the death penalty is imposed infrequently, which indicates that it is not only excessive but also that it is meted out arbitrarily.

The capital punishment issue was brought into a new focus in 1971 in *McGautha* v. *California*.[37] This appeal involved a joinder of two cases coming up from California and Ohio. In the California case McGautha was convicted of first degree murder in a state court, and after a separate penalty trial before the same jury, was sentenced to death. In the Ohio case the defendant was convicted of murder, with no jury recommendation of mercy, and accordingly sentenced to death. Dividing 6-3, the Supreme Court held that the absence of standards to guide the jury's discretion whether to impose or withhold the death penalty did not violate due process, and further, that Ohio's single-verdict procedure for determining both guilt and punishment in capital cases was not unconstitutional. Speaking for the Court, Justice Harlan noted that the absence of criteria was settled policy, and argued that it was beyond the present human ability to spell out criteria. When jurors are confronted with the truly awesome responsibility of decreeing death for a fellow human being, Justice Harlan maintained, we are entitled to assume that they will act with due regard for the consequences of their decision, and consider a variety of factors. In a concurring opinion Justice Black merely noted that the Eighth Amendment cannot be read to outlaw capital punishment, which, he pointed out, was very common when the Amendment was adopted. The dissenters, Justices Douglas, Brennan, and Marshall, urged that courts should not be reluctant to change the law, and that legislatures are not incapable of spelling out the criteria. The choice, Justice Brennan asserted, is between government by rule of law and government by whim.

35. Ralph v. Warden, Maryland Penitentiary, 438 F.2d 786 (4th Cir. 1970). The court noted that a similar decision was made in Calhoun v. State, 214 S.W. 335, 338 (Tex. Cr. App. 1919). See comments in *George Washington Law Review,* 40 (October 1971): 161-72; *Minnesota Law Review,* 56 (November 1971): 95-110; *University of Cincinnati Law Review,* 40 (Summer 1971): 396-401; *University of Richmond Law Review,* 5 (Spring 1971): 392-400.

36. 84 Stat. 473, 600 (1970). Rape is punishable by death under military law, 10 U.S.C. §920 (1970), but not in Indian country, 18 U.S.C. §1153 (1970).

37. 402 U.S. 183 (1971).

Due process forbids, he argued, "such an unguided, unbridled, unreviewable exercise of naked power."[38]

The debate over capital punishment took a dramatic turn on February 18, 1972, when the Supreme Court of California, currently one of the nation's most innovative appellate courts, held by a 6-1 vote that capital punishment violated Article I, §6, of the state Constitution, which provides, "nor shall cruel or unusual punishments be inflicted."[39] The Court held that the purpose of this clause was to assure that the state's power to punish will be exercised within the limits of civilized standards, and that capital punishment offends "contemporary standards of decency."[40] Chief Justice Wright noted that the death penalty was rarely used—only twice in the whole country in 1967—and that the lengthy imprisonment prior to execution had dehumanizing effects amounting to "psychological torture."[41] Furthermore, he maintained that capital punishment was not necessary for the accomplishment of any valid state interest. Retribution, or vengeance, he ruled out as incompatible with the dignity of an enlightened society. Offenders can be isolated from society in less onerous ways. Whether capital punishment has a deterrent effect is basically a speculative point at best. "We have concluded," wrote the Chief Justice, "that capital punishment is impermissibly cruel. It degrades and dehumanizes all who participate in its processes. It is unnecessary to any legitimate goal of the state and is incompatible with the dignity of man and the judicial process."[42] This decision was quickly overruled, however, through popular ratification of a constitutional initiative on November 7, 1972; by a 2-1 margin the voters of California reinstated a mandatory death penalty for four offenses: killing a prison guard, train-wrecking, treason against the state, and perjury which leads to the execution of an innocent person.[43]

In the same year, however, in *Furman* v. *Georgia*,[44] a bare majority of

38. 402 U.S. 252.

39. People v. Anderson, 100 Cal. Rptr. 152, 6 Cal. 3rd 628, 493 P. 2d 880 (1972) cert. denied, 406 U.S. 958 (1972).

40. 493 P. 2d 891.

41. See Note, "Mental Suffering under Sentence of Death: A Cruel and Unusual Punishment," *Iowa Law Review,* 57 (February 1972): 814-33.

42. 493 P. 2d 899. The lone dissenting judge thought that capital punishment is a deterrent, and that in any event this is the sort of issue which ought to be decided by the legislature or the electorate.

43. Calif. Const., Art. I, §27. This amendment also bars the state Supreme Court from declaring capital punishment invalid again, and authorizes the legislature to enact new legislation making the death penalty mandatory.

44. 408 U.S. 238 (1972). See Michael Meltsner, *Cruel and Unusual: The Supreme Court and Capital Punishment* (New York: Random House, 1973); Charles L. Black, Jr., *Capital Punishment: The Inevitability of Caprice and Mistake* (New York: Norton, 1974).

the U.S. Supreme Court set aside the death penalty for three Negroes, two of whom had been convicted of rape, and one of murder, after trial by jury in state courts. A judgment was concurred in by five Justices, but there was no majority opinion. Two Justices, Brennan and Marshall, favored a holding that the death penalty was *per se* unconstitutional because it is cruel and unusual within the meaning of the Eighth Amendment. But three Justices, Douglas, Stewart, and White, wrote separate concurring opinions in which they refused to rule the death penalty unconstitutional *per se*, preferring to limit their holding to the proposition that capital punishment is invalid because of the arbitrary and capricious manner in which the death sentence is actually meted out. Justice Stewart made the interesting remark that "these death sentences are cruel and unusual in the same way that being struck by lightning is cruel and unusual."[45] Similarly, Justice White argued that the death penalty is imposed so infrequently that it is not a credible threat, and that it is now so attenuated that it cannot be of any substantial service to criminal justice. More specifically, Justice Douglas maintained that the death penalty is "unusual" because it is imposed discriminatorily or arbitrarily by reason of race, religion, wealth, social position or class. Arguing that the Eighth Amendment concept is not static, but draws its meaning from evolving standards of decency, Justice Brennan maintained that the death penalty is an uncivilized and inhuman punishment. It uniquely degrades man's dignity; it is inflicted arbitrarily; it is not acceptable to contemporary society; and it is unnecessarily excessive, because it does not serve any penal purpose more effectively than some less severe punishment. He agreed with Justice Marshall in accepting the contention that there is no persuasive evidence which establishes that the death penalty has any deterrent value.[46] Justice Marshall characterized the death penalty as excessive and unnecessary. He ruled out retribution as an intolerable purpose in a free society, and argued that statistics do not support either the objective of deterrence or the prevention of recidivism. Finally, he maintained that capital punishment is morally unacceptable to the American people at the present time, at least to those people who are informed on the subject and care about it.

As Chief Justice Burger was quick to point out in his dissenting opinion, only two members of the Court ruled capital punishment unconstitutional *per se;* the other three who made up the majority based their votes on

45. 408 U.S. 309. Said Justice Brennan, at 408 U.S. 293, "Indeed, it smacks of little more than a lottery system."
46. See Daniel Polsby, "Death of Capital Punishment? *Furman* v. *Georgia,*" *Supreme Court Review*, 1972 (1972): 1–40, at 34, for a summary of various studies relating to the deterrence issue. Polsby concludes that all available data indicate that the rate of criminal homicide does not depend on the presence or absence of capital punishment.

present sentencing procedures and practices. Thus the basic question remained unsettled. All four dissenters expressed their personal distaste for capital punishment, but argued that its abolition is a matter for legislative determination. The Chief Justice pointed out that forty states and the District of Columbia still had capital punishment, and that indeed during the past decade Congress had created several new federal crimes punishable by death, e.g., air piracy (1961)[47] assassination of the President (1965)[48] or of members of Congress (1971).[49] Chief Justice Burger thought that the Eighth Amendment does not necessarily mandate enlightened principles of penology, that retribution is a legitimate objective, that the evidence regarding deterrence is inconclusive, and that there was no empirical proof of discrimination. Justice Blackmun thought that it would be regressive to deny jury discretion and make the death penalty mandatory. Justice Powell noted that the language of the Fifth and Fourteenth Amendments, with their references to the taking of life without due process, assumes the validity of capital punishment. If, he maintained, discriminatory impact makes capital punishment unconstitutional, then that would be equally true for all crimes of violence. If capital punishment falls more heavily on the have-nots, said Justice Powell, that is because they commit more crimes. Justice Rehnquist argued that this decision raises basic issues regarding the role of judicial review in a democratic society.

According to Justice Powell, this decision nullified the capital punishment laws of thirty-nine states and the District of Columbia. In addition, on the same day the Supreme Court vacated death sentences in over 120 other cases coming up from twenty-six states.

Of course, states are free to abolish capital punishment if they so desire. Michigan did so in 1846, Rhode Island in 1852, Wisconsin in 1853, and Maine in 1876. In 1967, New York restricted capital punishment to murder of a police officer or murder by one serving a life sentence. Now, of course, states had to confront the implications of the *Furman* decision, and they were quick to do so. By mid-June, 1974, twenty-eight states had adopted laws making the death penalty mandatory for certain serious crimes, and 103 persons were in some death row.[50] On March 15, 1972, the Texas Court of Criminal Appeals upheld the constitutionality of the death penalty by a 4–1 vote,[51] but after the *Furman* decision the sentence

47. 49 U.S.C. §1472(i) (1970).
48. 18 U.S.C. §1751 (1970).
49. 18 U.S.C. §351 (1970). There have been three other federal capital offenses since 1897, treason, murder, and rape.
50. Washington *Star-News,* June 13, 1974, p. A-14.
51. Tezeno v. State, 484 S.W. 2d 374 (Tex. Cr. App. 1972).

was commuted, thus mooting the issue of constitutionality. Indeed, as a result of the *Furman* decision, the highest courts of twenty-six states found it necessary, by the end of 1973, to invalidate death sentences, and in most instances a life sentence was substituted.[52]

All nine Justices who participated in the *Furman* decision agreed that capital punishment was an unwise public policy. They agreed that when the Eighth Amendment was ratified in 1791 the abolition of capital punishment was not intended, and all of them also agreed that the Amendment should be interpreted in a flexible manner. As the arguments advanced by the Justices are pieced together, it is clear that capital punishment as such was not outlawed, but that certain guidelines must be followed. It would seem that more of those who are legally eligible for execution must be put to death; those who are executed must be rationally distinguishable from those who are spared; and the penalty must not discriminate against the "lower castes." It is also a fair inference that the *McGautha* decison was overruled *sub silentio,* and accordingly, juries who have the authority to pick between life and death must be given standards to guide their exercise of judgment, or alternatively, the death penalty must be made mandatory.

State legislatures responded in different ways to the implications of the *Furman* decision. For example, the Wyoming legislature enacted a statute in 1973 making the death penalty mandatory where first degree murder involved the killing of a police officer or fireman, or where the killing was for a reward, or where explosives were used, or where the defendant has previously been convicted of murder, or where the murder occurred in the course of a rape, kidnapping, or hijacking of a public conveyance.[53] Similarly, the Nevada legislature, while abolishing the death penalty for some offenses, made the death penalty mandatory for the killing of a police officer or fireman, for a killing pursuant to a contract, for a killing through use of a bomb, or where the murder was part of a common

---

52. See, e.g., Sullivan v. State, 229 Ga. 731, 194 S.E. 2d 410 (1972); State v. Sinclair, 263 La. 377, 268 So. 2d 514 (1972); Capler v. State, 268 So. 2d 338 (Miss. 1972); Hodges v. Com., 213 Va. 316, 191 S.E. 2d 794 (1972); Donaldson v. Sack, 265 So. 2d 499 (Fla. 1972); Bartholomey v. State, 267 Md. 175, 297 A.2d 696 (1972); State v. Waddell, 282 N.C. 431, 194 S.E. 2d 19 (1973); State v. Dickerson, 298 A. 2d 761 (Del. 1973). See, C. W. Ehrhardt and others, "The Aftermath of Furman: The Florida Experience," *Journal of Criminal Law, Criminology and Police Science,* 64 (March 1973): 2-21; Note, "Capital Punishment in Virginia," *Virginia Law Review,* 58 (January 1972): 97-142; Laughlin McDonald, "Capital Punishment in South Carolina: The End of an Era," *South Carolina Law Review,* 24, no. 5 (1972): 762-94; Note, "Capital Punishment after Furman," *Journal of Criminal Law, Criminology and Police Science,* 64 (September 1973): 281-89.

53. Wyo. Stat. Ann. §6-54 (1973). For a similar statute see Mont. Laws 1973, ch. 513, §94-5-105.

scheme or design.[54] The Nevada legislature stated in the preamble to this statute, "It is hereby declared as a matter of legislative determination that the availability of capital punishment serves as a deterrent to the commission of certain offenses against the state and as a deterrent to the aggravation of certain crimes against the state." A number of state legislatures have adopted statutes which provide that in deciding whether to impose the death penalty, the jury shall take into consideration and weigh both aggravating and mitigating circumstances. The Florida statute is a good example.[55] Florida was the first state to reinstate the death penalty, and the new statute was promptly upheld by the state Supreme Court in the first post-*Furman* case of its kind.[56] The statute provides for a bifurcated trial; after conviction there must be a second trial before the same judge and jury to determine whether the death penalty should be imposed. If the defendant pleaded guilty or waived jury trial, then the judge must empanel a jury to hold a sentencing hearing. In any case, the jury may recommend either death or life imprisonment, but the jury's decision is merely advisory to the judge, who determines the penalty, but only after considering the presence or absence of eight aggravating circumstances and seven mitigating circumstances. The aggravating circumstances involve the following: whether the defendant was under a sentence of imprisonment at the time of the offense, the commission by the defendant of previous felonies, whether there had been great risk of death to many persons, whether the homicide occurred in the course of a robbery, a rape, arson, or airplane piracy, whether the crime was for pecuniary gain, whether the crime was especially cruel and atrocious, etcetera. Among circumstances deemed mitigating to which the judge must give weight are the absence of prior crimes, the existence of extreme mental or emotional imbalance, the factor of youth, the existence of extreme duress, minor participation with others, etcetera. The judge may impose the death sentence if he finds that the aggravating circumstances are not outweighed by the mitigating circumstances, but if he decides upon the death penalty, he must make written findings which are subject to review by the state Supreme Court. The Supreme Court may reduce a

54. Nev. Laws 1973, ch. 798.
55. Fla. Capital Punishment Act of Dec. 1, 1972, Fla. Laws 1973, ch. 72-724, §9. See Note, "Florida's Legislative and Judicial Responses to *Furman* v. *Georgia:* An Analysis and Criticism," *Florida State University Law Review,* 2 (Winter 1974): 108–52. For a similar statute, see Ariz. Laws 1973, ch. 138.
56. State v. Dixon, 283 So. 2d 1 (Fla. 1973). The Court held that all the Furman case requires is that the jury's discretion should be "reasonable" and "controlled." 283 So. 2d 10. In Jurek v. State, 522 S.W.2d 934 (Tex. Cr. App. 1975), the Court upheld the Texas death penalty statute on the ground that the guidelines for the jury were adequate, and that it is not contrary to Furman to give the jury some discretion provided it is reasonable and controlled.

death sentence to life imprisonment, but may not change a life sentence to a sentence of death. Other recently enacted statutes authorize the jury to weight the aggravating and mitigating circumstances.[57] It should be noted, in addition, that as the states have been reenacting capital punishment statutes, the general tendency has been to reduce, often quite drastically, the number of crimes for which the death penalty may be imposed at all.[58] This movement against capital punishment is in accord with world-wide tendencies, and is supported by a huge body of published scholarly data and opinion.[59]

Other Forms of Punishment

Punishment by flogging or whipping has often been sustained, generally on the ground that it has long been used, and on the drawing of an

---

57. See, e.g., Ark. Acts 1973, ch. 438; Tenn. Laws 1973, ch. 192. Cf. Ga. Code Ann., §27-2534.1 (1973). On Georgia's statutory response to Furman, see the note in *Mercer Law Review*, 24 (Summer 1973): 891-937.

58. The U.S. Senate passed "a bill to establish rational criteria for the mandatory imposition of the sentence of death," S. 1401, on March 13, 1974, by a vote of 54-33. The bill provides for a separate sentencing hearing before the jury which determined guilt, or if there has been a plea of guilty, before a jury impanelled for this purpose, or before the judge alone if both sides agree. Capital offenses include destruction of aircraft or motor vehicles where death results, assassination or kidnapping of members of Congress, homicide occurring during an escape from custody, espionage, transportation of explosives resulting in death, or malicious damage by explosives resulting in death. The bill lists a number of mitigating factors: whether the defendant was under eighteen, whether there was significant impairment of his capacity to appreciate the wrongfulness of his conduct, whether there had been unusual and substantial duress, whether the defendant's role had been a minor one where some one else committed the offense, or whether the defendant could not reasonably have foreseen that his conduct might result in a death. If no mitigating factor at all is found, and one or more aggravating factors are identified, then the death penalty is to be imposed. The aggravating factors include previous conviction for a capital offense, knowing creation of a grave risk to national security, or to the death of another person, crimes involving major elements of national defense, such as nuclear weapons or aircraft, and crimes which are especially heinous, cruel, and depraved. Arguing that the death penalty is a deterrent, Senator McClellan, the chief spokesman for the bill, said, "The death penalty must be restored if our criminal justice system is to combat effectively the ever-increasing tide of violent crimes—crimes of terror—that threaten to engulf our Nation and if the confidence of the American people in our system of justice is to be restored." *Cong. Rec.* (daily ed. March 12, 1974), p. S 3508.

59. See, e.g., H. L. A. Hart, *Punishment and Responsibility* (New York: Oxford University Press, 1968); J. A. McCafferty, *Capital Punishment* (Chicago: Aldine-Atherton, 1972); Hugo A. Bedau, *The Death Penalty in America* (Chicago: Aldine, 1968); S. E. Grupp, *Theories of Punishment* (Bloomington: Indiana University Press, 1972); R. Gerber and P. McAnany, *Contemporary Punishment* (Notre Dame: University of Notre Dame Press, 1972); E. L. Pincoffs, *The Rationale of Legal Punishment* (New York: Humanities Press, 1966); W. H. Moberly, *The Ethics of Punishment* (Hamden, Conn.: Archon Books, 1968). See addendum at pp. 419-20, below.

analogy with the parents' right to whip their children.[60] "The punishment of offences by stripes is certainly odious," the Virginia court said over a century ago, "but cannot be said to be *unusual.*"[61] Today flogging has almost disappeared. Congress abolished flogging for all federal courts in 1839.[62] Flogging is still permitted in Delaware by statute,[63] and in 1963 the Supreme Court of Delaware held lawful a sentence of thirty lashes (plus three years in jail) for the crime of grand larceny.[64] The Court pointed out that whipping had been authorized by the legislature continuously since 1719, and it argued that while the law is not static, neither may history properly be ignored. If whipping is to be abolished, the Court declared, legislative action is necessary. Similarly, a federal district court recently ruled that the infliction of corporal punishment upon school children is not a cruel and unusual punishment in the constitutional sense, providing that it is not so excessive as to amount to child abuse.[65]

The weight of opinion is clearly opposed to flogging as a form of punishment. The North Carolina Supreme Court ruled in 1914 that flogging prisoners to enforce discipline is not lawful, because, "in view of the enlightenment of this age" it is not reasonable, for "that which degrades and embrutes a man cannot be either necessary or reasonable."[66] Similarly, the Court of Appeals for the Eighth Circuit condemned

60. *In re* Candido, 31 Hawaii 982 (1931) (whipping of an incorrigible prisoner with a cat-o'-nine-tails for violation of prison rules held not contrary to Eighth Amendment); Foote v. Maryland, 59 Md. 264 (1883) (seven lashes for wife-beating); Garcia v. Territory, 1 N.M. 415 (1869) (thirty lashes for larceny).

61. Com. v. Wyatt, 6 Rand. (Va.) 694, 701 (1828).

62. Act of Febr. 28, 1839, 5 Stat. 322 c. 36, §5.

63. Del. Code Ann., Tit. 11, §332 (larceny of a horse, twenty lashes, plus fine up to $200 and prison sentence up to five years); §354 (burning a court house or any building containing public records, sixty lashes, $1,000, twenty years); §355 (arson of ships, mills, business establishments, twenty lashes, $500, twenty years); §391 (breaking and entering a dwelling at night, twenty to forty lashes, $500, twenty years); §811 (robbery by violence or putting in fear, up to forty lashes, $500, three to twenty-five years).

64. State v. Cannon, 190 A.2d 514 (Del. 1963).

65. Ware v. Estes, 328 F. Supp. 657 (N.D. Tex. 1971). The punishment consisted of striking the buttocks one or several times with a wooden paddle; it was used sparingly, and only as a last resort. The common law does not protect students from all corporal punishment. See Comment, "Corporal Punishment in the Public Schools," *Harvard Civil Rights-Civil Liberties Law Review,* 6 (May 1971): 583-94. See Ingraham v. Wright, 498 F.2d 248 (5th Cir. 1974), holding that the imposition of severe physical and psychological injuries, systematically administered to junior high students, and inflicted without giving students a chance to explain the circumstances, violated the Eighth Amendment. Judge Rives, in his opinion, canvassed the whole issue of the punishment of students at great length.

66. State v. Nipper, 166 N.C. 272, 275, 81 S.E. 164, 165 (1914).

flogging in the Arkansas State Penitentiary as violative of the Eighth Amendment, because it "offends contemporary concepts of decency and human dignity and precepts of civilization which we profess to possess; and . . . violates . . . standards of good conscience and fundamental fairness. . . ."[67] Speaking for the Court, Judge Blackmun, who was later appointed to the Supreme Court, maintained that corporal punishment cannot be confined within enforceable rules which cannot readily be circumvented by the sadistic and the unscrupulous; it generates hate and degrades both the punisher and the punished; it frustrates the achievement of rehabilitative goals. Accordingly, it has been held that a charge that a prison official whipped certain prisoners as a disciplinary matter states an offense within the meaning of a federal civil rights act[68] which makes it a crime for any one under color of law to deny a federal right or privilege.[69]

The sterilization of criminals by vasectomy has been condemned as an unusual punishment which is "ignominious and degrading, and in that sense is cruel."[70] While the physical suffering is not very great, that is not the only test of cruel punishment; "shame and humiliation and degradation and mental torture" also fall within the constitutional prohibition.[71] On the other hand, several courts have upheld the power of the legislature to decree sterilization by vasectomy for sex offenders on the ground that the operation is minor, safe, and quite painless.[72]

In addition, many states now have habitual offender laws, under which one who commits a second, or third, or fourth felony, as the case may be, is given a much heavier punishment for the last offense. Such statutes have invariably been sustained against the charge that they impose cruel and unusual punishments.[73] In a leading case the Massachusetts court once said, "The penalty was determined, no doubt, by the view that in such a case the criminal habit has become so fixed, and the hope of refor-

67. Jackson v. Bishop, 404 F.2d 571, 579 (8th Cir. 1968).
68. 18 U.S.C. §242.
69. United States v. Jones, 207 F.2d 785 (5th Cir. 1953).
70. Mickle v. Henrichs, 262 F. 687 (D. Nev. 1918).
71. Davis v. Berry, 216 F. 413 (S.D. Iowa 1914).
72. State v. Feilen, 70 Wash. 65, 126 P. 75, 41 L.R.A. (N.S.) 418, Ann. Cas. 1914B, 512 (1912); *In re* Opinion of the Justices, 230 Ala. 543, 162 So. 123 (1935).
73. Graham v. West Virginia, 224 U.S. 616 (1912); Moore v. Missouri, 159 U.S. 673 (1895); State *ex rel.* Drexel v. Alvis, 153 Ohio 244, 91 N.E. 2d 22 (1950); *Ex parte* Hibbs, 86 Okla. Cr. 113, 190 P.2d 156 (1948), cert. denied, 335 U.S. 835 (1948); Hanson v. State, 48 Wis. 2d 203, 179 N.W. 2d 909 (1970) (indeterminate sentence up to three years for theft of two boxes of candy by a repeater); Cipolla v. State, 207 Kan. 822, 486 P.2d 1391 (1971) (forty to sixty years for grand larceny committed by a habitual offender).

mation is so slight, that the safety of society requires and justifies a long-continued imprisonment of the offender."[74]

The Issue of Severity

It is clear that the United States Supreme Court interprets the Eighth Amendment as applying to the issue of the severity of the punishment as well as to the question of the method of punishment. It has reviewed and upheld several sentences as not being excessive,[75] and in the famous case of *Weems* v. *United States*[76] it set aside a sentence made under a statute of the Philippine Islands. Weems had been convicted of the crime of falsifying a public record, for which he was sentenced to fifteen years in prison at hard labor, with chains at the ankle and wrist, fined 4,000 pesos, deprived of political rights, and subjected to police surveillance after completion of sentence. "No circumstance of degradation," Justice McKenna observed, was omitted. It is a precept of justice, he argued, that punishment should be proportioned to the offense. The Eighth Amendment was not designed solely against acts of cruelty practiced in Stuart days. A constitution is concerned with future evils, and not merely with those of the past. The clause in question is progressive; it "is not fastened to the obsolete but may acquire meaning as public opinion becomes enlightened by a humane justice."[77] Justice McKenna also pointed out that crimes much worse than that of Weems were not punished so severely. Similarly the Court of Appeals for the District of Columbia once held that it was cruel and unusual punishment to imprison or fine a man ($40 fine or four months in jail) merely because some people happened to regard him, in the language of the statute, as a "suspicious" person.[78] Such a statute would today be held invalid on the due process ground of vagueness.[79]

The United States Supreme Court gave added significance to the Eighth

---

74. McDonald v. Com., 173 Mass. 322, 53 N.E. 874, 875 (1899).

75. *Ex parte* Watkins, 7 Pet. (U.S.) 568, 574 (1833) (fine of $3,050 on three indictments); Howard v. Fleming, 191 U.S. 126, 136 (1903) (ten years for "gold-brick" swindle); Badders v. United States, 240 U.S. 391 (1916) (five years and $7,000 for mail fraud).

76. 217 U.S. 349 (1910). See Note, "What is Cruel and Unusual Punishment," *Harvard Law Review,* 24 (November 1910): 54–56.

77. 217 U.S. 378. Justice White dissented on the ground that the Court's holding casts on the judiciary the duty of determining when the punishment is proportionate to the crime, which he regarded as wholly a legislative function.

78. Stoutenburgh v. Frazier, 16 App. D.C. 229, 48 L.R.A. 220 (1900).

79. Palmer v. Euclid, 402 U.S. 544 (1971). See also Coates v. Cincinnati, 402 U.S. 611 (1971), holding unconstitutionally vague a city ordinance which made it an offense for a person to conduct himself "in a manner annoying to persons passing by." In Lanzetta v. New Jersey, 306 U.S. 451 (1939), the Court ruled that a statute making it a crime to be a "gangster" was invalid because it lacked an ascertainable standard of guilt.

Amendment in 1958, when, by a 5-4 vote, in *Trop* v. *Dulles*,[80] it ruled that loss of citizenship, upon conviction for wartime desertion from the armed forces, was an impermissible cruel and unusual punishment. Chief Justice Warren pointed out that convictions for desertion were by no means rare; that all desertion means is absence from duty plus the intention not to return, and that it includes a great range of conduct prompted by many different things, such as fear, laziness, hysteria, or emotional imbalance. The offense may occur anywhere, not only in combat, but even in training camps. During World War II there were about 21,000 convictions for desertion in the Army alone; of these about 7,000 of those convicted were actually separated from the service, within the discretion of the Army authorities, and thus rendered stateless. The Chief Justice stressed the fact that the statute was not limited to desertion to the enemy, and that no such element was present in *Trop*. Holding that this denationalization was inflicted as punishment, the Court ruled that it went beyond "the limits of civilized standards," because it involves "the total destruction of the individual's status in organized society." Chief Justice Warren argued that this is punishment more primitive than torture, for it destroys the individual's political existence; "the expatriate has lost the right to have rights." Since this punishment subjects the individual to "a fate of ever-increasing fear and distress,"[81] because as a stateless person he never knows what to expect, and since statelessness is deplored in all democratic countries, it is offensive to a cardinal principle of the Constitution. The four dissenting Justices argued that it was not the business of the Court to pronounce upon a policy question which was for Congress to decide under the war power. Since wartime desertion has always been a capital offense, and therefore subject to the death penalty, denationalization must be regarded as a lesser penalty. "Is constitutional dialectic so empty of reason," Justice Frankfurter asked, "that it can be seriously urged that loss of citizenship is a fate worse than death?"[82] Chief Justice Warren conceded that this offense may be punished by the death penalty, but he did not believe that this is a license for the government to devise any punishment short of death within the limit of its imagination.

State appellate courts are very reluctant to hold criminal statutes unconstitutional on the ground that the punishment is too severe. The presumption is normally in favor of the statute, and it is conceded that the legislature is usually the best judge of what the penalties should be. The legislature must have a wide latitude of discretion, and a severe punishment is not necessarily a cruel one. Courts will therefore upset legislative standards in these matters only in very extreme cases. "In order to justify a

80. 356 U.S. 86 (1958).
81. 356 U.S. 100, 101, 102.
82. 356 U.S. 125.

court in declaring any punishment to be cruel and unusual with reference to its duration," the Kentucky court has said, "it must be so proportioned to the offense committed that it shocks the moral sense of all reasonable men as to what is right and proper under the circumstances."[83] Or, as the South Dakota court once asserted, "the courts can reasonably interfere only when the punishment is so excessive or so cruel as to meet the disapproval and condemnation of the conscience and reason of men generally . . . where the punishment is so severe and out of proportion to the offense as to shock public sentiment and violate the judgment of reasonable people."[84]

American courts almost invariably sustain the constitutionality of very severe sentences for such heinous offenses as murder,[85] kidnapping,[86] armed robbery[87] burglary with explosives,[88] and bank robbery.[89] In fact, many courts are content to say merely that if the sentence is within the statutory limit, it cannot be regarded as a cruel and unusual punishment unless the statute itself is invalid.[90] The usual justifying rationale is that the court should not usurp a legislative function, that the reviewing court should not interfere with the trial judge's discretion, and that other remedies are available, such as executive clemency. This means that the appealing party must challenge the statute rather than the sentence.

This approach is especially noteworthy in areas of criminal activity where public feelings of aversion and concern are especially strong, such

---

83. Weber v. Com., 303 Ky. 56, 64, 196 S.W. 2d 465, 469 (1946).

84. State v. Becker, 3 S.D. 29, 40–41, 51 N.W. 1018, 1022 (1892).

85. See U.S. *ex rel.* Bongiorno v. Ragen, 54 F. Supp. 973, 980 (N.D. Ill. 1944), aff'd. 146 F. 2d 349 (7th Cir. 1945), cert. denied, 325 U.S. 865 (1945) (199 years); People v. Rodgers, 186 N.W. 2d 840 (Mich. App. Div. 3, 1971) (ninety-nine to a hundred years for second degree murder).

86. See State v. Taylor, 82 Ariz. 289, 312 P.2d 162 (1957) (life sentence without possibility of parole).

87. See Mallon v. State, 49 Wis. 2d 185, 181 N.W. 2d 364 (1970) (up to twenty-five years); U.S. *ex rel.* Clark v. Zelker, 321 F. Supp. 1085 (S.D. N.Y. 1971) (fifteen to twenty years).

88. See People v. Mire, 173 Mich. 357, 138 N.W. 1066 (1912) (fifteen to thirty years). Cf. State v. Quintana, 92 Ariz. 308, 376 P.2d 773 (1962) (nine to ten years for first degree burglary).

89. See State v. Colcord, 170 Minn. 504, 212 N.W. 894 (1927) (life imprisonment).

90. See, e.g., Brown v. State, 152 Fla. 853, 13 So. 2d 458 (1943), where the Court upheld a seven-year sentence for concealment of a half gallon of moonshine whiskey simply on the ground that the penalty was within the statutory limit. For precisely the same sort of rationale, see also United States v. Collins, 432 F.2d 1136 (7th Cir. 1971) (eight years for unlawful transportation of firearms); United States v. Dawson, 400 F.2d 194, 200 (2nd Cir. 1968), cert. denied, 393 U.S. 1023 (1969) (two years for filing a false income tax return); Hemans v. United States, 163 F.2d 228, 237 (6th Cir. 1947), cert. denied, 332 U.S. 801 (1947) (four years plus $1,000 fine for travelling interstate to avoid giving testimony in a felony proceeding).

as those dealing with sexual crimes and drug abuse. Very severe punishments, including the death penalty, even for an attempted rape,[91] have almost invariably been upheld by appellate courts. Of course, there is a special abhorrence attached to the crime of rape, but our culture apparently tolerates very severe penalties for sex offenses which in many circles are not regarded as offenses at all. For example, two consenting homosexual male adults were recently convicted in North Carolina of fellatio; one entered a plea of *nolo contendere,* and received a five-to-seven year sentence, whereas the other chose to stand trial, and on conviction was given a sentence of twenty to thirty years. In a postconviction proceeding the federal district court upheld these sentences with the bland observation that the statutory limit was sixty years.[92] In a 1971 case decided in New Mexico, two consenting adults were sentenced to the penitentiary for an indeterminate sentence of one year to life for the crime of sodomy.[93] Similarly, the Minnesota Supreme Court recently upheld a sentence of a year in jail for the crime of prostitution.[94] In addition, commitment of deviates under sex crimes laws has often been sustained.[95]

Similarly, appellate courts in the United States find little difficulty in upholding the validity of extremely severe penalties where offenses involving the narcotics laws are concerned. Undoubtedly this is a reflection of intense public anxiety about the drug problem. Thus, federal and state reviewing courts in all sections of the country have registered acceptance of ten-year sentences for the mere possession of very small amounts of marijuana,[96] and much longer sentences where marijuana was sold.[97]

---

91. Walker v. State, 186 Md. 440, 47 A.2d 47 (1946). See also Dutton v. Smart, 222 Ga. 35, 148 S.E. 2d 396 (1966) (forty years for assault to commit rape); State v. Atkinson, 278 N.C. 168, 179 S.E. 2d 410 (1971) (death); State v. Brownridge, 459 S.W. 2d 317 (Mo. 1970) (ninety-nine years).

92. Perkins v. North Carolina, 234 F. Supp. 333 (W.D. N.C. 1964).

93. Washington v. Rodriguez, 82 N.M. 428, 483 P.2d 309 (1971).

94. State v. Anderson, 280 Minn. 461, 159 N.W. 2d 892 (1968). In the case of *In re Lynch,* 105 Cal. Rptr. 217, 503 P.2d 921 (1973), the Supreme Court of California ruled that a statute providing for an indeterminate one-year to life sentence for a second offense of indecent exposure violated the state constitution's probibition of cruel and unusual punishments.

95. See, e.g., Howland v. State, 51 Wis. 2d 162, 186 N.W. 2d 319 (1971).

96. Miller v. State, 458 S.W. 2d 680 (Tex. Cr. App. 1970) (three and a half grams); People v. Sinclair, 30 Mich. App. 473, 186 N.W. 2d 767 (1971) (two cigarettes). Suspension of the driver's license of a convicted user of marijuana was upheld in State v. Smith, 58 N.J. 202, 276 A.2d 369 (1971).

97. Smith v. United States, 273 F.2d 462 (10th Cir. 1959) (fifty-two years on fourteen counts involving three sales and two possessions); People v. White, 27 Mich. App. 432, 183 N.W. 2d 606 (1971) (twenty years for one unlawful sale); People v. White, 26 Mich. App. 35, 181 N.W. 2d 803 (1970) (twenty to twenty-five years for unlawful sale); United States v. Kellerman, 432 F.2d 371 (10th Cir. 1971) (twenty years for unlawful transference).

All sorts of severe penalties have also been sustained where heroin and other hard drugs were involved.[98] The Court of Appeals of the District of Columbia recently upheld a conviction and sentence of one year in jail for mere possession of narcotics paraphernalia (e.g., hypodermic syringes), on the theory that it is unlawful to administer drugs.[99] A flat prohibition of parole for certain narcotics offenses was also recently upheld.[100]

In 1962, however, the Supreme Court of the United States drew some sort of line with regard to punishment for violation of narcotics laws in the important case of *Robinson* v. *California*.[101] Robinson has been convicted in a Los Angeles court for violating a California statute which made it a criminal offense to "be addicted to the use of narcotics." Two policemen testified at the jury trial that Robinson had needle marks and scabs on his arms, and the jury was instructed that he could be convicted even if there was no proof of the actual use of narcotics within the state. On an appeal from a ninety-day sentence, the Supreme Court held that this statute does not punish a person for the use, purchase, sale, or possession of narcotics, or for any antisocial conduct, but for merely having the "status" of being an addict. Since the Court concluded that narcotic addiction is an illness, one, in fact, which may be contracted innocently or involuntarily, the statute inflicts a cruel and unusual punishment in the constitutional sense. While it was conceded that as an abstract matter a sentence of ninety days is not very cruel, "even one day in prison," said Justice Stewart, "would be a cruel and unusual punishment for the 'crime' of having a common cold."[102] It is well worth noting that it was in the *Robinson* case that the Court first ruled squarely that the Eighth Amendment applies to the states by way of Fourteenth Amendment due process.[103]

---

98. Ormento v. United States, 328 F. Supp. 246 (S.D. N.Y. 1971) (forty years for conspiracy to import a vast amount of heroin); State v. James, 474 P.2d 779 (Ore. App. 1970) (up to ten years for illegal possession of heroin); United States v. Holman, 436 F.2d 863 (9th Cir. 1970) (eight years); McWilliams v. United States, 394 F.2d 41 (8th Cir. 1968), cert. denied, 393 U.S. 1044 (1969) (twenty-five years on four counts).

99. Wheeler v. United States, 276 A.2d 722 (D.C. App. 1971). See Note, "Punishment of Narcotics Addicts for Possession: A Cruel and Unusual Punishment," *Iowa Law Review,* 56 (February 1971): 578-97.

100. Halprin v. United States, 295 F.2d 458 (9th Cir. 1961).

101. 370 U.S. 660 (1962). On this case, see Note, "Revival of the Eighth Amendment: Development of Cruel-Punishment Doctrine by Supreme Court," *Stanford Law Review,* 16 (July 1964): 996-1015; Note, "The Cruel and Unusual Punishment Clause and the Substantive Criminal Law," *Harvard Law Review,* 79 (January 1966): 635-55.

102. 370 U.S. 667. Two dissenters, Justices Clark and White, argued that this is a policy question for legislative bodies to deal with, and that drug addiction alone may pose a threat of serious crime.

103. In O'Neil v. Vermont, 144 U.S. 323 (1892), and Collins v. Johnston, 237 U.S. 502,

Lower courts promptly followed suit, as indeed they had to, in holding, invalid statutes making mere drug addiction a crime.[104] But they were equally quick and consistent in ruling that the *Robinson* doctrine did not apply if the convictions were for *use* of narcotics.[105] Similarly, the New York Court of Appeals ruled in 1967 that the constitutional ban on cruel and unusual punishments would not prevent the imprisonment of narcotics addicts convicted of larceny even though they stole solely to finance their addiction.[106] On the other hand, in 1968, the Court of Appeals for the District of Columbia set aside as a cruel and unusual punishment a mandatory ten-year sentence imposed upon a narcotics recidivist for unlawful possession of heroin which was the direct result of his addiction.[107] Since the Supreme Court regards narcotics addiction to be a disease, it was argued that it follows that the Eighth Amendment barely permits any punishment at all for the offense. The Court ruled that mere possession is not in itself a grave offense, and that in this instance it was but a symptom of the addiction. Resentencing was therefore called for.[108]

If drug addiction is a disease which may not be punished as a crime, how about the status of being an alcoholic? The Court of Appeals for the Fourth Circuit ruled in 1966 that the conviction of a chronic alcoholic for public drunkenness, under a North Carolina statute, violated the Eighth Amendment because his acts were compulsive and symptomatic of his disease.[109] But in 1968 the Supreme Court declined to push the *Robinson* doctrine quite that far. By a 5–4 vote, in *Powell* v. *Texas*,[110] the Court affirmed a state court conviction of a chronic alcoholic for public drunkenness, on the theory that the conviction was not for being a chronic

---

510 (1915), the Court had ruled squarely that the Eighth Amendment does not apply to the states. Clearly these holdings were overruled *sub silentio* in *Robinson.*

104. See, e.g., State v. Bridges, 360 S.W. 2d 648 (Mo. 1962); People v. Davis, 27 Ill. 2d 57, 188 N.W. 2d 225 (1963); *Ex parte* Rogers, 366 S.W. 2d 559 (Tex. Cr. App. 1963).

105. State *ex rel.* Blouin v. Walker, 244 La. 699, 154 So. 2d 368 (1963), cert. denied, 375 U.S. 988 (1964); Browne v. State, 24 Wis. 2d 491, 129 N.W. 2d 175 (1964), cert. denied, 379 U.S. 1004 (1965); U.S. *ex rel.* Swanson v. Reincke, 344 F.2d 260 (2nd Cir. 1965); Bruno v. State of Louisiana, 316 F. Supp. 1120 (E.D. La. 1970).

106. People v. Borrero, 19 N.Y. 2d 332, 280 N.Y.S. 2d 109 (1967).

107. Watson v. United States, 439 F.2d 442 (D.C. App. 1968, 1970).

108. The Supreme Court of Michigan has set aside a ten-year sentence for mere possession of marijuana, though it was within the statutory maximum, as being a cruel and unusual punishment, People v. Sinclair, 387 Mich. 91, 194 N.W. 2d 878 (1972), and a twenty-year sentence for a first offender convicted of selling marijuana, even though the sentence was the required mandatory minimum sentence provided by the statute, People v. Lorentzen, 387 Mich. 167, 194 N.W. 2d 827 (1972).

109. Driver v. Hinnant, 356 F.2d 761 (4th Cir. 1966). A similar decision was rendered in Easter v. District of Columbia, 124 App. D.C. 33, 361 F.2d 50 (1966).

110. 392 U.S. 514 (1968).

alcoholic, but for being in public while drunk. Thus, argued Justice Marshall, the state had not sought to punish a mere status, but only to deal with public behavior which may create substantial health and safety hazards and may offend "the moral and esthetic sensibilities of a large segment of the community." He insisted that his position rested upon "traditional common-law concepts of personal accountability," and that "essential considerations of federalism" counseled against the formulation of a rigid constitutional rule which would reduce or eliminate experimentation by the states and freeze into a rigid mold developing ideas relating to the relationship between law and psychiatry. Two concurring members of the Court, Justices Black and Harlan, pointed out that public drunkenness has been a crime throughout the nation's history, in every state, and was explicitly proscribed by statute in England in 1606. They thought that jailing alcoholics may well have some therapeutic as well as deterrent value, and that at the very least it gets drunks off the street, where they may harm others. Furthermore, they maintained that to hold that a state may not constitutionally punish if the conduct resulted from compulsion would have a revolutionary impact, and that it was not wise to fasten upon the states any particular test of criminal responsibility. The four dissenters argued that the medical profession agrees that alcoholism is a disease, and that conviction in this case was contrary to the fundamental teaching of *Robinson,* that "criminal penalties may not be inflicted upon a person for being in a condition he is powerless to change."[111] They could think of no drearier example of the futility of using penal sanctions to solve a psychiatric problem than that supplied by the history of jailing chronic alcoholics.[112]

Since the line which courts draw in deciding whether or not particular punishments are excessive is imprecise, and since the supporting rationale is stated in highly unspecific terms, it might serve a useful purpose to cite a few additional concrete examples drawn from a variety of segments of the criminal law.

The following are instances of stiff punishments which appellate courts have upheld:

Four years in jail and a $5,000 fine for assault and battery[113]

Imprisonment in the state penitentiary up to one year, or in the county jail for fifteen days to six months, of which ten days may, in the court's discretion, be on a bread and water diet, for a husband wilfully

---

111. 392 U.S. 532, 535, 567.

112. Justice Fortas pointed out in his dissenting opinion that the appellant had been convicted of public intoxication approximately a hundred times since 1949.

113. Weber v. Com., 303 Ky. 56, 196 S.W. 2d 465 (1946).

abandoning his wife, leaving her in a destitute condition and unreasonably refusing to support her[114]

A jail sentence of sixty days to six months and a fine of $100 to $500 for maintaining a common nuisance[115]

Sixty days in jail, with the first and last twenty days on a bread and water diet, for liquor law violations[116]

A $200 fine and ninety days in jail for violating a restraining order forbidding the sale of liquor without a license[117]

Two to ten years in jail and a fine up to $2,000 for violating a "White Cap Act" forbidding groups of three or more to go about at night, or to do any unlawful act, while wearing white caps, masks or other disguise[118]

Five years in jail and a fine of $10,000 for mutilation of a draft card[119]

Up to three years in jail for the theft of two boxes of candy[120]

One to five years for issuing a check against insufficient funds[121]

Ten years in jail plus a $10,000 fine for bribery in an athletic contest[122]

One to twenty years for operating a motor vehicle without the owner's consent[123]

Two to four years for larceny of a jacket valued at $55.95[124]

On the other hand, the following are examples of sentences which reviewing courts have regarded as cruel and unusual punishments in the constitutional sense:

Thirty years in jail at hard labor for a burglary without weapons or tools on the part of a man without a previous criminal record, and in face of a jury recommendation of clemency[125]

Three years in jail for unlawful concealment of one gallon of moonshine whiskey[126]

114. Spencer v. State, 132 Wis. 509, 112 N.W. 462 (1907).
115. State v. Becker, 3 S.D. 29, 51 N.W. 1018 (1892).
116. State *ex rel.* Nelson v. Smith, 114 Neb. 653, 209 N.W. 328 (1926).
117. *Ex parte* Keeler, 45 S.C. 537, 23 S.E. 865, 31 L.R.A. 678, 55 Am. St. 785 (1896).
118. Hobbs v. State, 133 Ind. 404, 32 N.E. 1019, 18 L.R.A. 774 (1893).
119. United States v. Weissman, 434 F.2d 175 (8th Cir. 1970).
120. Hanson v. State, 48 Wis. 2d 203, 179 N.W. 2d 909 (1970).
121. State v. Nance, 20 Utah 2d 372, 438 P.2d 542 (1968).
122. State v. Di Paglia, 247 Iowa 79, 71 N.W. 2d 601, 49 A.L.R. 2d 1223 (1955).
123. McDougle v. Maxwell, 1 Ohio St. 2d 68, 203 N.E. 2d 334 (1964). The Court stressed the fact that the prisoner would be eligible for parole after serving ten months.
124. People v. Jackson, 29 Mich. App. 654, 185 N.W. 2d 608 (1971).
125. State v. Kimbrough, 212 S.C. 348, 46 S.E. 2d 273 (1948).
126. Nowling v. State, 151 Fla. 584, 10 So. 2d 130 (1942).

A fine of $720, or in default thereof 2,160 days (nearly six years), in jail for trespass on a public park and destroying plants[127]

Twenty-one months in jail for bigamy where the accused remarried in the innocent belief he had been divorced from his previous wife[128]

Five years in prison and a fine of $576,853, in default of which 288,426 days in jail for larceny by a bank president of $288,426 of state money[129]

Five years in prison and a surety of $500 to keep the peace for five additional years, for assault and battery upon the wife[130]

Banishment from the state for a period of years or permanently for various offenses[131]

Thirty-six years in jail for passing eight bad checks in a single day totalling $1,384.35[132]

Life sentence without benefit of parole for two fourteen-year-old boys convicted of an especially shocking rape of an elderly woman[133]

Thirty years in jail or a fine of $24,600 for owning an automatic gum vending machine[134]

---

127. State *ex rel.* Garvey v. Whitaker, 48 La. Ann. 527, 19 So. 457, 35 L.R.A. 561 (1896).

128. Stephens v. State, 73 Okla. Cr. 349, 121 P.2d 326 (1942).

129. State v. Ross, 55 Ore. 450, 104 P. 596, 42 L.R.A. (N.S.) 601 (1909), rehearing, 55 Ore. 474, 106 P. 1022, 42 L.R.A. (N.S.) 601 (1910), writ of error dismissed, 227 U.S. 150 (1913). Here the court held that imprisonment for life for nonpayment of a fine is cruel and unusual punishment.

130. State v. Driver, 78 N.C. 423 (1878). Remarking that the judge's power to punish is limited, the Court said, "What the precise limit is, cannot be prescribed. The Constitution does not fix it, precedents do not fix it, and we cannot fix it, and it ought not to be fixed." 78 N.C. 429.

131. People v. Baum, 251 Mich. 187, 231 N.W. 95 (1930); State v. Baker, 58 S.C. 111, 36 S.E. 501 (1900).

132. Faulkner v. State, 445 P.2d 815 (Alaska, 1968). The Court accepted what is admittedly the minority view, "that the bare fact that a sentence is within the maximum prescribed by the legislature does not prevent it from violating the constitutional ban against cruel and unusual punishment." 445 P.2d at 818.

133. Workman v. Com. of Kentucky, 429 S.W. 2d 374, 33 A.L.R. 3d 326 (Ky. Ct. App. 1968). The Court held that to determine that fourteen-year-old boys are to be judged incorrigible for the rest of their lives is shocking to the conscience of modern society. "We believe . . . ," said the Court, "that it is impossible to make a judgment that a fourteen-year-old youth, no matter how bad, will remain incorrigible for the rest of his life." 429 S.W. 2d at 378. Protesting that the underlying policy question is for the legislature to decide, a dissenting judge wrote, "At this time the lack of law and order is especially of prime concern. Our courts must bear their share of blame and shame for this condition. . . . Until our courts quit coddling criminals, disobedience and disrespect for law and order will contine." 429 S.W. 2d at 379. On this case, see Note, *Wayne Law Review,* 15 (Spring 1969): 882–94.

134. Mayor and Council of Hoboken v. Bauer, 55 A.2d 883 (Record. Crt. 1947).

Deportation for knowingly making false representation to the Immigration and Naturalization Service[135]

While these two lists of examples of cases falling on both sides of the line of excessivity are of about equal length, this fact should not mislead the reader. The law reports contain hundreds of cases where reviewing courts upheld what seemed to be unusually severe penalties. On the other hand, cases in which sentences were set aside on grounds of excessiveness are very hard to find.

Fines and Penalties

The question as to whether particular fines or penalties are excessive has been before the courts a great many times. In one well-known case the Supreme Court declined to set aside the assessment, under the Texas antitrust laws, of penalties of $5,000 a day, which, over a period of some three hundred days, amounted to a fine in excess of $1,600,000.[136] It was emphasized that the corporation which was fined this amount had assets of about $40,000,000, and had declared dividends amounting to as much as 700 per cent a year. The Court declared that it would interfere only when the fine is "so grossly excessive as to amount to a deprivation of property without due process of law."[137] Cases where reviewing courts have set aside fines on grounds of being excessive have been extremely rare.[138]

135. Dear Wing Jung v. United States, 312 F.2d 73 (9th Cir. 1962). In Ho Ah Kow v. Nunan, 12 Fed. Cas. 252 (No. 6,546) (C.C.D. Cal. 1879), Justice Field, sitting as a circuit judge, held that cutting off the pig tails of a Chinese was a cruel and unusual punishment because of the ignominy involved.

136. Waters-Pierce Oil Co. v. Texas (No. 1), 212 U.S. 86 (1909).

137. 212 U.S. 111. For other cases where stiff fines have been upheld, see Everson v. State, 66 Neb. 154, 92 N.W. 137 (1902) (fine of double the amount embezzled, to operate as a judgment at law for use of the damaged party); Southern Express Co. v. Com. *ex rel.* Walker, 92 Va. 59, 22 S.E. 809, 41 L.R.A. 436 (1895) (fine of $100 against an express company for violating a statute forbidding excessive charges); People v. Jenkins, 64 Misc. 2d 826, 316 N.Y.S. 2d 475 (N.Y. Sup. Ct. 1st Dep't. 1970) ($100 fine imposed upon a welfare recipient for resisting arrest and third degree assault. For a famous protest against excessive fines, see the dissenting opinion of Justice Brandeis in U.S. *ex rel.* Milwaukee Social Democratic Publishing Co. v. Burleson, 255 U.S. 407, 435 (1921).

138. See People v. Saffore, 271 N.Y.S. 2d 972, 18 N.Y. 2d 101, 218 N.E. 2d 686 (1966), where, on a plea of guilty to third degree assault, the accused was given a year in jail for each unpaid dollar. The sentencing court knew that the defendant was unable to pay the fine when it was levied upon him. In Williams v. Illinois, 399 U.S. 235 (1970), the Supreme Court held that such a sentence violated the equal protection of the laws if the total amount of time to be spent in jail exceeded the maximum prison term spelled out in the statute. See also Freidus v. Leary, 66 Misc. 2d 70, 320 N.Y.S. 2d 122 (Sup. Ct. N.Y. Co. 1971), which ruled that a $50 fine for removing an illegally parked car was unreasonable, arbitrary and capricious. The Court concluded from the evidence that a charge of $10 would be adequate to reimburse the city for the costs of removal.

Due Process and the States

While the Supreme Court formerly took the position that the Eighth Amendment does not apply to the states,[139] it once clearly implied that an excessive state fine would deny due process,[140] and a similar inference was suggested by its position in the remarkable case of *Louisiana ex rel. Francis* v. *Resweber.*[141] Willie Francis, sentenced to death after due trial, was strapped into the electric chair, but due to a mechanical failure nothing happened when the switch was turned on, although he claimed he received a slight shock. The Court held, by a 5-4 vote, that the Fourteenth Amendment did not forbid the state to proceed to electrocute Francis, by strapping him into the chair a second time at a later date, because the first failure had been an accident, with no showing of malevolence. Speaking for the majority, Justice Reed said that he was examining the circumstances "under the assumption, but without so deciding," that violation of the principle of the Eighth Amendment as to cruel and unusual punishments would violate Fourteenth Amendment due process. But he went on to say, "The traditional humanity of modern Anglo-American law forbids the infliction of unnecessary pain in the execution of the death sentence. Prohibition against the wanton infliction of pain has come into our law from the Bill of Rights of 1688. The identical words appear in our Eighth Amendment. The Fourteenth would prohibit by its due process clause execution by a state in a cruel manner." But he did not believe that the execution on the second attempt would be any worse than any other execution. "The cruelty against which the Constitution protects a convicted man is cruelty inherent in the method of punishment, not the necessary suffering involved in any method employed to extinguish life humanely."[142] The four dissenting Justices took the position that while the failure of the first attempt was accidental, the reapplication of the current would be intentional. They protested that "death by installments" was cruel torture, and that electrocution had been sustained originally only because it produced death instantaneously. They had no doubt that the taking of life "by unnecessarily cruel means shocks the most fundamental instincts of civilized man," and violates due process.

At long last, in 1962, as already noted, in *Robinson* v. *California,*[143] the Supreme Court squarely ruled that the Eighth Amendment prohibition of

---

139. O'Neil v. Vermont, 144 U.S. 323 (1892); Collins v. Johnston, 237 U.S. 502, 510 (1915).

140. Waters-Pierce Oil Co. v. Texas (No. 1), 212 U.S. 86, 111 (1909). See also the dissenting opinion of Justice Field in O'Neil v. Vermont, 144 U.S. 323, 337 (1892).

141. 329 U.S. 459 (1947). On this case, see Barrett Prettymen, Jr., *Death and the Supreme Court* (New York: Harcourt, Brace & World, 1961).

142. 329 U.S. 462, 463, 464.

143. 370 U.S. 660 (1962).

cruel and unusual punishment applies as a limitation upon the states through Fourteenth Amendment due process, and actually reversed a state criminal conviction on this ground.

The Treatment of Prisoners

The issue of cruel and unusual punishment arises not only with respect to the sentence, but also in regard to the treatment of the prisoner in the jail. Courts have traditionally refused to interfere with the treatment of prisoners out of deference to the concept of separation of powers, for fear of subverting prison discipline, and because judges have felt that they lack the necessary expertise. Called the "hands-off" doctrine,[144] it was restated as recently as 1962 by the federal Court of Appeals for the Eighth Circuit: "Courts have uniformly held that the supervision of inmates of federal institutions rests with the proper administrative authorities and that courts have no power to supervise the management and disciplinary rules of such institutions."[145] In addition, for reasons of comity federal judges have been extremely reluctant to interfere with prison discipline in state penal institutions. While it is theoretically possible for a prisoner to seek injunctive relief or to sue for damages, neither of these remedies is actually available or effective. For example, many statutes prevent convicts from suing, and such doctrines as those of administrative discretion and sovereign immunity bar recoveries.[146] The "hands-off" doctrine clearly ended in the 1960s, but even at an earlier date the federal courts were confronted with the issue in a group of cases arising from the escape in 1943 of some 175 convicts from custody in Georgia and the later efforts of the Georgia authorities to get them back from other states.[147]

The leading case involved one Leon Johnson, who was arrested in Pennsylvania on a warrant of the Governor of Pennsylvania at the request of the Governor of Georgia. Alleging that he had been mistreated in a Georgia chain gang, and that this denied him due process, Johnson first tried to get a writ of habeas corpus in the state courts. The trial court denied the writ, and this holding was affirmed by the intermediate

144. See Note, "Beyond the Ken of the Courts: A Critique of Judicial Refusal to Review Complaints of Convicts," *Yale Law Journal,* 72 (January 1963): 506-58.

145. Sutton v. Settle, 302 F.2d 286, 288 (8th Cir. 1962). Compare the remarks of Justice Murphy in Price v. Johnston, 334 U.S. 266, 285 (1948): "Lawful incarceration brings about the necessary withdrawal or limitation of many privileges and rights, a retraction justified by the considerations underlying our penal system."

146. See Note, "Prisoner's Remedies for Mistreatment," *Yale Law Journal,* 59 (March 1950): 800-808.

147. This story is summarized by Arthur E. Sutherland, Jr., "Due Process and Cruel Punishment," *Harvard Law Review,* 64 (December 1950): 271-79. See also Note, "The Case of the Fugitive from the Chain Gang," *Stanford Law Review,* 2 (December 1949): 174-83, and Note, *Minnesota Law Review,* 34 (January 1950): 134-37.

appellate court.[148] Without taking an appeal to the Pennsylvania Supreme Court, Johnson then tried the federal district court, which also denied his petition for a writ of habeas corpus,[149] but the Court of Appeals reversed, holding that the evidence established that Georgia authorities treated chain gang prisoners with "persistent and deliberate cruelty."[150] Without saying that the Fourteenth Amendment applies the Eighth Amendment to the states, the Court of Appeals held that it had no doubt of the fact that the Fourteenth Amendment prohibits the infliction of cruel and unusual punishment by a state, and that freedom from such punishment is a "basic" and "fundamental" right. The Supreme Court, however, promptly reversed the Court of Appeals on the ground, stated summarily, that Johnson had not exhausted his state remedies before going to the federal courts for relief.[151]

But this decision left an area of confusion, since it was not clear whether the state convict must exhaust the remedies available in the demanding or in the asylum state. Finally, in *Sweeney* v. *Woodall,*[152] decided soon thereafter, the Court held that the fugitive must exhaust the remedies of the demanding state. Woodall, a fugitive from an Alabama prison, was arrested in Ohio. Alleging brutal mistreatment in Alabama, to which he would again be subjected if returned, he litigated a petition for habeas corpus all through the Ohio courts, including a petition for certiorari in the U.S. Supreme Court. Then he started over again in a federal district court. The Supreme Court held that Woodall made no showing that relief was unavailable to him in the courts of Alabama. By resorting to self-help, he had changed his status from a prisoner of Alabama to that of a fugitive from Alabama. "But this," said the Court, "should not affect the authority of the Alabama courts to determine the validity of his imprisonment in Alabama." Both the rendition clause of the Constitution and the federal rendition statute, the Court noted, contemplate prompt return of a fugitive from justice as soon as the demanding state asks for him. "Considerations fundamental to our federal system," including considerations of convenience, require the prisoner to test the claim of unconstitutional treatment by Alabama in the courts of that state.[153] In a concurring opinion Justice Frankfurter argued that it ought to be assumed

148. Com. *ex rel.* Johnson v. Dye, 159 Pa. Super, 542, 49 A.2d 195 (1946).
149. Johnson v. Dye, 71 F. Supp. 262 (W.D. Pa. 1947).
150. Johnson v. Dye, 175 F.2d 250, 253 (3rd Cir. 1949). See also Harper v. Wall, 85 F. Supp. 783 (D.N.J. 1949), which held that the conditions of imprisonment in a county work camp in Alabama were so bad as to entitle an escaped prisoner to a writ of habeas corpus.
151. Dye v. Johnson, 338 U.S. 864 (1949).
152. 344 U.S. 86 (1952).
153. The Court's decision in Sweeney v. Woodall was foreshadowed by several similar holdings in Courts of Appeals: Johnson v. Matthews, 182 F.2d 677 (D.C. Cir. 1950), cert. denied, 340 U.S. 828 (1950); Ross v. Middlebrooks, 188 F.2d 308 (9th Cir. 1951); Davis v. O'Connell, 185 F.2d 513 (8th Cir. 1950).

that Alabama's prison officials would not prevent Woodall from invoking the aid of the local courts. Justice Douglas, who dissented alone, thought that this assumption was wholly unrealistic.

These cases involving fugitives from particularly gruesome prison conditions foreshadowed a change in attitude on the part of the courts, particularly the federal courts.[154] The Supreme Court encouraged this change with a ruling in 1967 that due process applies to the revocation of probation,[155] and a 1969 holding which affirmed the right of a prisoner to have the aid of "jail-house lawyers" for the preparation of legal papers.[156] Actually, at a somewhat earlier date a federal court of appeals ruled that the government has a duty to protect a prisoner against assault and injury, and that habeas corpus will lie even though freedom from incarceration cannot result.[157] It is important to note that the federal habeas statute no longer limits the successful petitioner's remedy to release from prison; the habeas corpus court is authorized to "dispose of the matter as law and justice require."[158]

Increasingly, federal courts take the position that while they are reluctant to interfere with the administration of prisons,[159] and especially state prisons,[160] they will inquire into "exceptional circumstances," such as compelling a prisoner to work at something which would be deleterious to his physical condition,[161] or denying him reasonable medical care.[162] Many federal courts have, during the past few years, discovered prison

154. For an exhaustive survey, see Ronald L. Goldfarb and Linda R. Singer, "Redressing Prisoners' Grievances," *George Washington Law Review,* 39 (December 1970): 175-320. For an earlier state case see State v. Carpenter, 231 N.C. 229, 56 S.E. 2d 713 (1949), where it was held that handcuffing a prisoner to the bars of the cell was not lawful, because it was unreasonable, excessive, and repugnant to natural justice. In 1962, the Supreme Court of California took jurisdiction, on writ of habeas corpus, to review allegations of prison mistreatment, though it put the burden of proof on the prisoner and reached the conclusion that there was no mistreatment as alleged. *In re* Jones, 22 Cal. 2d 478, 372 P.2d 310 (1962); *In re* Riddle, 22 Cal. 2d 472, 372 P.2d 304 (1962).

155. Mempa v. Rhay, 389 U.S. 128 (1967).

156. Johnson v. Avery, 393 U.S. 483 (1969).

157. Coffin v. Reichard, 143 F.2d 443 (6th Cir. 1944), cert. denied, 325 U.S. 887 (1945).

158. 28 U.S.C. §2243 (1964).

159. See, e.g., Lee v. Tahash, 352 F.2d 970 (8th Cir. 1965) (postal censorship upheld); Austin v. Harris, 226 F. Supp. 304 (W.D. Mo. 1964) (sane prisoner may be confined in a U.S. medical center).

160. See, e.g., U.S. *ex rel.* Knight v. Ragen, 337 F.2d 425, 426 (7th Cir. 1964): "Except under exceptional circumstances, internal matters in state penitentiaries are the sole concern of the states and federal courts will not inquire concerning them."

161. Black v. Ciccone, 324 F. Supp. 129 (W.D. Mo. 1970).

162. Talley v. Stephens, 247 F. Supp. 683 (E.D. Ark. 1965). Cf. Pisacano v. State, 8 App. Div. 2d 335, 340, 188 N.Y.S. 2d 35, 40 (1959): "Prison physicians owe no less duty to prisoners who must accept their care, than do private physicians to their patients who are free to choose." See also: Newman v. Alabama, 349 F. Supp. 278 (M.D. Ala. 1972).

conditions to be so intolerably bad as to amount to cruel and unusual punishment.[163]

One remedy for state prisoners is the writ of habeas corpus,[164] but this is available only after all available state remedies have been exhausted. The other important remedy in the federal courts is a suit of some sort, whether for damages, an injunction, or a declaratory judgment, under §1983 of Title 42 of the U.S. Code, which was originally a section of the Civil Rights Act of 1871.[165] This statute reads as follows: "Every person who, under color of any statute, ordinance, regulation, custom, or usage, of any State or Territory, subjects, or causes to be subjected, any citizen of the United States or other person within the jurisdiction thereof to the deprivation of any rights, privileges, or immunities secured by the Constitution and laws, shall be liable to the party injured in an action at law, suit in equity, or other proper proceeding for redress." The Supreme Court has ruled that one may sue the police for damages arising from unconstitutional police practices, under this statute, without first exhausting state remedies,[166] and that a prisoner may sue under §1983 for discriminatory denial of permission to purchase religious publications.[167]

Many lower federal courts have taken jurisdiction and have given remedies to prisoners under this statute. It has been held, for example, that intentional deprivation of essential medical care states a cause of action within the scope of this statute.[168] Above all, federal courts will give remedies to state prisoners under §1983 in extreme situations where

---

163. See Hamilton v. Schiro, 338 F. Supp. 1016 (E.D. La. 1970) (conditions so bad as to "shock the conscience as a matter of elemental decency"); Hamilton v. Love, 328 F. Supp. 1182 (E.D. Ark. 1971) (Pulaski County Jail wholly unfit); Brenneman v. Madigan, 343 F. Supp. 128 (N.D. Calif. 1972) ("shocking, debasing and subhuman conditions"); Gates v. Collier, 349 F. Supp. 881 (N.D. Miss. 1972) (Mississippi State Prison System condemned); Johnson v. Lark, 365 F. Supp. 289 (E.D. Mo. 1973) (conditions in the St. Louis City jail "unquestionably deplorable"). Cf. Com. *ex rel.* Bryant v. Hendrick, 444 Pa. 83, 280 A.2d 110 (1971) (conditions in a Philadelphia prison "cruel and callous," "disgusting and degrading"). For a general summary, see W. S. McAninch, "Penal Incarceration and Cruel and Unusual Punishment," *South Carolina Law Review,* 25 (November 1973): 579–603.

164. For a leading state case, see Com. *ex rel.* Bryant v. Hendrick, 280 A.2d 110 (Pa. 1971), where habeas corpus, in the form of transfer to another institution, was granted where the petitioner was in a county jail which the court found to be "a cruel, degrading and disgusting place."

165. This was §1 of the Ku Klux Klan Act of April 20, 1871, 17 Stat. 13. See Note, "Penal Institutions and the Eighth Amendment—A Broadened Conception of Cruel and Unusual Punishment," *Louisiana Law Review,* 31, no. 2 (1970–71): 395–404.

166. Monroe v. Pape, 365 U.S. 167 (1961). See also Lewis v. Kugler, 446 F.2d 1343 (3rd Cir. 1971) (prior resort to state courts not required to have standing to sue to enjoin arbitrary stops and searches on the public highways of New Jersey).

167. Cooper v. Pate, 378 U.S. 546 (1964).

168. Redding v. State, 220 F. Supp. 124 (N.D. Ill. 1963).

conditions are intolerably bad,[169] and where such conditions are alleged, a claim is entitled to be heard.[170] On the ground that the Eighth Amendment forbids "certain hard core inhuman treatment," that "we deal with human beings, not dumb, driven cattle," a federal Court of Appeals recently ruled that an action under §1983 may be brought by persons who have merely been arrested and are held in confinement pending trial.[171]

In 1970, the federal District Court for the Eastern District of Arkansas was, for the first time ever, confronted with a class action brought by a group of convicts who attacked a whole prison system on Eighth Amendment grounds.[172] The judge concluded that the testimony established that the system was "substandard and outmoded when measured by accepted penological standards." There is cruel and unusual punishment in the constitutional sense, he declared, "where the confinement is characterized by conditions and practices so bad as to be shocking to the conscience of reasonably civilized people." He characterized the Arkansas Petintentiary system as "a dark and evil world completely alien to the free world," and as "inherently dangerous." The "degrading and disgusting conditions"[173] included grueling manual labor, use of armed prisoners as guards, insufficient guards, frequent stabbings and sexual assaults, widespread use of liquor and drugs, inadequate medical facilities, overcrowding, poor food, and total absence of rehabilitative efforts. The Court ordered "a prompt and reasonable start toward eliminating the conditions," and required the submission of interim reports of compliance.

As the country moved into the 1970s, it became increasingly clear that the courts had abandoned the traditional "hands-off" attitude, and were increasingly willing to look into the acceptability of prison treatment. Even so, it remained true that judges are quick to observe that prison discipline is not under the supervisory direction of the courts, and that they will not intervene except where highly exceptional circumstances are

169. See, e.g., Jones v. Wittenberg, 323 F. Supp. 93, 95 (N.D. Ohio 1971) ("Most jails are bad, but this one is unusually bad"); Pierce v. La Vallee, 293 F.2d 233 (2nd Cir. 1961); Jackson v. Bishop, 404 F.2d 571 (8th Cir. 1968). In Rhem v. McGrath, 326 F. Supp. 681 (S.D. N.Y. 1971), the Court took jurisdiction under §1983, but concluded that while the situation in the jail was bad, it was not bad enough, and was getting better. The test, said the Court, is whether conditions "sink into the dismal area of man's inhumanity to man." 326 F. Supp. 689. See Note, "Conditions in Prison Render Confinement Unconstitutional," *Tulane Law Review,* 45 (February 1971): 403-7.

170. So the Supreme Court ruled squarely, for the first time, in Haines v. Kerner, 408 U.S. 238 (1972). For earlier rulings to this effect, see Beard v. Lee, 396 F.2d 749 (5th Cir. 1968); Sewell v. Pegelow, 291 F.2d 196 (4th Cir. 1961).

171. Anderson v. Nosser, 438 F.2d 183, 191, 193 (5th Cir. 1971).

172. Holt v. Sarver, 309 F. Supp. 362 (E.D. Ark. 1970), aff'd. 442 F.2d 304 (8th Cir. 1971), noted in *Harvard Law Review,* 84 (December 1970): 456-63.

173. 309 F. Supp. 369, 372-73, 381.

found to exist. To cite one problem which is frequently litigated, courts have in recent years repeatedly ruled that solitary confinement is not unconstitutional *per se,*[174] and does not in and of itself create a cause of action under the federal Civil Rights Act (§1983).[175] Nevertheless, there have been cases of solitary confinement where conditions were found to be so "inexcusable and shocking"[176] that courts were willing to conclude that the prisoner's right to be free from cruel and unusual punishment was violated.[177]

Whether conditions in a prison are so very bad that they amount to the infliction of cruel and unusual punishment within the meaning of the Constitution is but a part of a larger interest which American courts are now taking in the whole subject of the rights of prisoners.[178] Thus, the Supreme Court recently ruled that a prisoner has a right to a hearing on a complaint filed under §1983 of Title 42 of the U.S. Code alleging a violation of the free exercise of religion.[179] While it was asserted that federal courts do not sit to supervise prisons, they do protect the constitutional rights of all "persons," including prisoners, and prisoners have the same right that all other people have to petition the government for a redress of grievances. Similarly, a prisoner has a right under §1983 to sue for damages on account of injuries asserted to have arisen from alleged

---

174. U.S. *ex rel.* Verde v. Case, 326 F. Supp. 701 (E.D. Penna. 1971); Ford v. Board of Managers of N.J. State Prison, 407 F.2d 937 (3rd Cir. 1969); Roberts v. Pepersack, 256 F. Supp. 415 (D. Md. 1966); U.S. *ex rel.* Knight v. Ragen, 337 F.2d 425 (7th Cir. 1964); Conway v. State, 483 P.2d 350 (Okla. Cr. App. 1971).

175. U.S. *ex rel.* Pope v. Hendricks, 326 F. Supp. 699 (E.D. Penna. 1971); Roberts v. Barbosa, 227 F. Supp. 20 (S.D. Calif. 1964).

176. Mahaffey v. State, 392 P.2d 279, 281 (Ida. 1964).

177. In Sostre v. Rockefeller, 312 F. Supp. 863 (S.D. N.Y. 1970), the prisoner was put in solitary for a year, with less food, confinement in the cell twenty-four hours a day, one shower a week, no reading matter, no work, and total isolation. The man's offense was preparation of a legal motion for another prisoner. The Court felt that this treatment was "physically harsh, destructive of morale, dehumanizing in the sense that it is needlessly degrading, and dangerous to the maintenance of sanity . . . ,"and, wholly disproportionate to the offense for which it was imposed. 312 F. Supp. 868. The Court of Appeals reversed, Sostre v. McGinnis, 442 F.2d 178 (2nd Cir. 1971), on a finding that the conditions were not as inhumane as the District Judge thought they were. See Comment, *Washington University Law Quarterly,* 1972 (Spring 1972): 347–53. See also Wright v. McMann, 321 F. Supp. 127 (N.D. N.Y. 1970); U.S. *ex rel.* Cleggett v. Pate, 229 F. Supp. 818 (N.D. Ill. 1964); Jordan v. Fitzharris, 257 F. Supp. 674, 682 (N.D. Calif. 1966) (one in solitary confinement "is entitled to receive the essentials for survival"). For an early case on mistreatment of prisoners, see *In re* Birdsong, 39 Fed. 599 (S.D. Ga. 1889).

178. See Righard Singer, "Bringing the Constitution to Prison: Substantive Due Process and the Eighth Amendment," *University of Cincinnati Law Review,* 39 (Fall 1970): 650–84.

179. Cruz v. Beto, 405 U.S. 319 (1972).

mistreatment as a result of solitary confinement.[180] Furthermore, a claim under this statute may be prosecuted in a federal court by way of habeas corpus without first exhausting state remedies, where there is no showing that other relief was actually available.[181] In addition, in a 1974 decision the Supreme Court laid down certain minimum due process requirements in prison disciplinary cases, such as written notice of charges before a hearing, a written statement of reasons by the factfinders as to the evidence relied upon for the disciplinary action, and some right on the part of the prisoner to call witnesses and present documentary evidence; but neither confrontation (cross-examination) nor counsel was regarded as constitutionally required.[182] On the other hand, the Court upheld in 1974 state and federal prison rules limiting the access of journalists to prisoners as being reasonable limitations designed to further such significant governmental interests as security.[183] The right of prison officials to censor mail addressed to prisoners, however, has been subjected by the Court to some minimum procedural safeguards.[184]

The mistreatment of juvenile offenders is also a matter of current concern on the part of the courts. One federal district court, in an action under §1983, recently found a violation of the Eighth Amendment in the incarceration of juveniles in a county jail because of poor conditions and the absence of any attempt at rehabilitation.[185] Other federal district courts have given relief to juveniles where the finding was that the detention facilities were "so severe as to degrade human dignity,"[186] or "insidiously destructive of the humanity" of the inmates.[187]

Finally, a problem quite analogous to that of the treatment of prisoners which has been the subject of recent litigation is that of the confinement of persons in mental institutions.[188] Many courts have ruled that continued confinement in a mental institution without providing treatment is a cruel

---

180. Haines v. Kerner, 404 U.S. 519 (1972).

181. Wilwording v. Swenson, 404 U.S. 249 (1971).

182. Wolff v. McDonnell, 418 U.S. 538 (1974). Three dissenting Justices would have extended to the prisoner both the right of confrontation and the right to counsel.

183. Pell v. Procunier, 417 U.S. 817 (1974); Saxbe v. Washington Post Co., 417 U.S. 843 (1974). The vote in both cases was 5-4.

184. Procunier v. Martinez, 416 U.S. 396 (1974).

185. Baker v. Hamilton, 345 F. Supp. 345 (W.D. Ky. 1972).

186. Morales v. Turman, 364 F. Supp. 166, 173 (E.D. Tex. 1973).

187. Inmates of Boys' Training School v. Affleck, 346 F. Supp. 1354, 1365 (D. R.I. 1972).

188. See "Developments in the Law: Civil Commitment of the Mentally Ill," *Harvard Law Review,* 87 (April 1974): 1190-406; Note, "The Rights of the Mentally Ill during Incarceration: The Developing Law," *University of Florida Law Review,* 25 (Spring 1973): 494-519.

and unusual punishment contrary to the Eighth Amendment.[189] Similarly courts have come to the aid of patients in correctional institutions where conditions were found to be grossly inadequate,[190] or where aversion therapy (which induces vomiting) is employed without the inmate's consent.[191]

Reduction of Sentences

Apart from the constitutional question of cruel and unusual punishments, some American courts have the authority to reduce sentences, within the statutory limits, on the nonconstitutional ground that the sentence is excessive. As a general rule, appellate courts will not reduce a sentence as excessive, if within the limits prescribed by the legislature, without express statutory authority.[192] Federal appeals courts have no such power.[193] But a minority of fifteen states have given their appellate courts statutory power to reduce sentences they regard as excessive, though most of them will not permit the reviewing court to increase the sentence. New York enacted such a statute in 1882.[194] Some courts, even without statutory authorization, will reverse the judgments and grant new trials on the ground that the sentence is excessive.[195] An interesting recent

---

189. See United States v. Pardue, 354 F. Supp. 1377 (D. Conn. 1973); Martarella v. Kelley, 349 F. Supp. 575 (S.D. N.Y. 1972); United States v. Walker, 335 F. Supp. 705 (N.D. Cal. 1971); United States v. Jackson, 306 F. Supp. 4, 6 (N.D. Cal. 1969) (U.S. may not confine an unconvicted person in an institution similar to a prison without giving him "true medical treatment"); Horacek v. Exon, 357 F. Supp. 71 (D. Nebr. 1973); Ronse v. Cameron, 373 F.2d 451 (D.C. Cir. 1966); *In re* Ballay, 482 F.2d 648 (D.C. Cir. 1973).

190. Rozecki v. Gaughan, 459 F.2d 6 (1st Cir. 1972); Vann v. Scott, 467 F.2d 1235 (7th Cir. 1972).

191. Knecht v. Gillman, 488 F.2d 1136 (8th Cir. 1973). See also Nelson v. Heyne, 355 F. Supp. 451 (N.D. Ind. 1972), where the court expressed disapproval of the administration of tranquilizers without the specific authorization of a physician.

192. See, e.g., State v. Wright, 261 N.C. 356, 134 S.E. 2d 624 (1964); Mason v. State, 375 S.W. 2d 916 (Tex. Cr. App. 1964); Michell v. State, 154 So. 2d 701 (Fla. App. 1963). See also Lester B. Orfield, *Criminal Appeals in America* (Boston: Little, Brown & Co., 1939), chap. V; Livingston Hall, "Reduction of Criminal Sentences on Appeal," *Columbia Law Review,* 37 (April, May 1937): 521-56, 762-83.

193. See, e.g., United States v. Martell, 335 F.2d 764, 767-68 (4th Cir. 1964).

194. See N.Y. Code of Crim. Proc., §450.30. For other state statutes which permit appellate review of the sentence, see Ariz. Rev. Stat. Ann. §13-1717 (1956); Conn. Gen. Stat. §51-196 (1968); Ida. Code Ann. § 19-2821 (1948); Iowa Code Ann. §793.18 (1950); Mass. Ann. Laws, c. 278, §28B (1968); Neb. Rev. Stat. §29-2308 (1964); Pa. Stat. Tit. 17, §41 (1962).

195. See, e.g., Bailey v. State, 381 S.W. 2d 467, 474 (Ark. 1964); State v. Tuttle, 21 Wis. 2d 147, 124 N.W. 2d 9 (1963); Com. v. Green, 396 Pa. 137, 151 A.2d 241 (1959); State v. Laws, 51 N.J. 494, 242 A.2d 333 (1968), where the New Jersey Supreme Court held that it had the inherent judicial power to change a sentence for murder from death to a life term; People v. Smith, 14 Ill. 2d 95, 150 N.E. 2d 815 (1958); People v. Sinclair, 387 Mich. 91, 194 N.W. 2d 878 (1972). The Michigan Court declared that its repeated assertions that

example of a reduction of sentence by an appellate court was an Ohio case in which the defendant was convicted of two violations of law by using a false name and address in an application for a certificate of title to an automobile.[196] For this offense he was given a sentence of six months to ten years in the penitentiary. The maximum penalty under the statute was five years, but the trial judge sentenced the defendant to consecutive terms of five years each. The Ohio Supreme Court was unanimously of the opinion that the trial court had "abused its discretion" in ordering the sentence on each count to be served consecutively and not concurrently. And it was remarked, "The record discloses that the trial court probably did this because he was advised that defendant was a Communist. However, a Communist is entitled to even-handed justice in our courts."

It is a sign of the times that the trial judge took such strong exception to the holding that he had abused his discretion that he petitioned the state Supreme Court to expunge from its opinion the two sentences just quoted. The judges of the Ohio Supreme Court disqualified themselves, and appellate court judges were substituted, who proceeded to rule that a trial judge has no right to file an application to expunge all or any part of an opinion rendered by the Supreme Court.[197] When the case has been appealed, the trial judge's responsibility is completely at an end, "and when a case reaches the Supreme Court, the decision and the word structure of the opinion are within the sole and complete discretion of the members of that court."

Judicial review of sentences would provide our legal system with a useful tool for softening excessively harsh sentences without invoking a constitutional principle which courts are understandably reluctant to apply. Great Britain[198] and the civil law countries of Western Europe all give the defendant the option of appealing the sentence to a higher court.[199] Chief Judge Sobeloff of the Court of Appeals for the Fourth Circuit has explained that

---

an appellate court is without power to review a sentence has no basis in law or logic, and that it is ludicrous to suppose that the constitution vests an unbridled power in sentencing judges.

196. Ohio v. Hashmall, 160 O.S. 565, 117 N.E. 2d 606 (1954), cert. denied, 348 U.S. 842 (1954).

197. Ohio v. Hashmall, 164 O.S. 170, 128 N.E. 2d 1 (1955).

198. 7 Edw. 7, c. 23 §3(c) (1907). For a thorough review of the English experience, see Daniel J. Meador, "The Review of Criminal Sentences in England," in American Bar Association Project on Standards of Criminal Justice, *Appellate Review of Sentences* (March 1968), Appendix C, pp. 94–157.

199. See Gerhard O. W. Mueller and Fre Le Poole, "Appellate Review of Legal but Excessive Sentences: A Comparative Study," *Vanderbilt Law Review,* 21 (May 1968): 411–32; G. O. W. Mueller, "Penology on Appeal: Appellate Review of Legal but Excessive Sentences," *Vanderbilt Law Review,* 15 (June 1962): 671–97.

"excessive and disproportionate penalties are a primary reason today why our courts are swamped by criminal appeals."[200] He wrote as follows: "Why appellate judges should be bound and gagged with respect to the sentence poses something of a mystery. They can examine the indictment to see whether a comma is misplaced; they can review any order; any ruling on the evidence. But the really important question is shielded against review. There is scarcely a court of appeals . . . whose calendars are not already congested with thinly veiled entreaties imploring it to find a loophole in the law so that a Draconian sentence may be upset. Many appeals are docketed today only because of the severity of the sentence pronounced in the district court and since the appellate tribunal cannot tackle the real issue in a forthright manner, it may, and often does, in its endeavor to strike down a harsh penalty, give the law a strained construction liable to work havoc in a future case." It is beyond much question that appellate review of sentences would be a very useful device to add to the Eighth Amendment guaranty as protection against punishments which are cruel and unusual because they are excessive.[201]

While the constitutional principle which forbids cruel and unusual punishments has been invoked by many defendants, few indeed have succeeded in the appellate courts, though in recent years the Eighth Amendment has been given an expanded meaning. Appeals judges are understandably reluctant to set aside the view of the legislature on what is essentially a policy question in the resolution of which a wide latitude of judgment is inescapable, and to second-guess the trial judges who are normally in the best position to assess the measure of punishment, since they are closest to the facts. Nevertheless, the principle stands as a constant admonition that in extreme cases shocking to the sense of justice, appellate courts can interfere. A decision made in a moment of great feeling, or in response to a popular wave of fear or indignation, can be set aside. The sober second thought of reason may prevail.

200. 32 F.R.D. 264, 272 (1962). See the remarks of Judge Clark in United States v. Hoffman, 137 F.2d 416, 422 (2nd Cir. 1943): "Yet in weighing whether error is prejudicial we have allowed an unusually harsh sentence to turn the balance."

201. Alan H. Kirshen, "Appellate Court Implementation of the Standards for the Administration of Criminal Justice," *American Criminal Law Quarterly*, 8 (Winter 1970): 105-17, 111; Note, "Appellate Review of Primary Sentencing Decisions; A Connecticut Case Study," *Yale Law Review*, 69 (July 1960):1453-78. For a thorough review of the whole problem, together with specific recommendations, see A.B.A. Project, *Appellate Review of Sentences*, 198, above.

Addendum on Capital Punishment

Following the 5-4 decision of the Supreme Court in *Furman* v. *Georgia,* 408 U.S. 238 (1972), thirty-five states promptly readopted statutes providing for capital punishment, tailored to meet the objections perceived to have been expressed by a bare majority of the Court. Twenty states responded by reducing the number of offenses punishable by the death penalty, but making the death penalty mandatory on conviction, thus denying the trial judge and jury any discretion at all. The other fifteen states adopted statutes which sought to provide guidance for convicting juries in capital cases in terms of aggravating and mitigating factors. In addition, in 1974 Congress adopted a statute adding to the existing list of federal offenses punishable by death the crime of air piracy. It is also worth noting that the decision of the Supreme Court of California in *California* v. *Anderson,* 493 P.2d 880 (1972), was quickly set aside by a constitutional amendment adopted by the people of California, and that the voters of Massachusetts and Illinois rejected the abolition of capital punishment in referenda by a margin of almost 2 to 1. Popular attitudes towards capital punishment were also reflected in the fact that by the end of March 1976 juries had sentenced 460 persons to death; presumably juries reflect public opinion. It has been argued that these juries convicted defendants because they knew the sentences would not be carried out, but this is only an unproved assumption.

In three cases decided on July 2, 1976, dividing 7-2, the Supreme Court upheld the capital punishment laws of three states where the juries were given guidance by legislative enactments, *Gregg* v. *Georgia,* 44 U.S.L.W. 5230, *Proffitt* v. *Florida,* 44 U.S.L.W. 5256, and *Jurek* v. *Texas,* 44 U.S. L.W. 5262. All three cases involved convictions for first-degree murder. The Court majority ruled that the punishment of death is not cruel and unusual in violation of the Eighth and Fourteenth Amendments. The Justices argued that a punishment selected by a democratically elected legislature is presumed to be valid, that the legislature is not obliged to select the least severe penalty possible so long as the penalty is not cruelly inhuman or disproportionate to the crime involved, that a heavy burden of proof rests upon those who attack the judgment of the people's representatives, and that the question of punishments is peculiarly one of legislative policy. According to the Court majority, the death penalty serves two acceptable purposes, retribution and deterrence. "In part," said Justice Stewart, "capital punishment is an expression of society's moral outrage at particularly offensive conduct. This function may be unappealing to many, but it is essential in an ordered society that asks its citizens to rely on legal processes rather than self-help to vindicate their wrongs." The

Court majority recognized that there is a considerable debate as to whether the death penalty is a deterrent to crime, but after reviewing various studies of the subject, the Justices concluded that the results are inconclusive since there is no convincing empirical evidence either way, but also that the death penalty may be a deterrent for some, and that in the present state of our knowledge it is for the legislature to make a decision.

Justices Brennan and Marshall, who had argued in *Furman* that the death penalty is unconstitutional *per se,* restated their objections, maintaining that the death penalty cannot be squared with evolving standards of decency, and insisting that it has no deterrent value.

In two additional cases decided on the same day, by 5–4 votes, *Woodson* v. *North Carolina,* 44 U.S.L.W. 5267, and *Roberts* v. *Louisiana,* 44 U.S.L.W. 5281, the Court held unconstitutional state statutes which made the death sentence mandatory with respect to certain specified crimes. The majority Justices argued that legislation requiring mandatory death sentences is regressive, and that it simply papers over the problem of unguided and unchecked jury discretion. Since a mandatory death penalty statute provides no standards to guide the jury, they declared that the problem is made worse by allowing the jury to make an arbitrary decision. In addition, they objected that such a statute does not allow for the particularized consideration of relevant aspects of the character and record of each convicted defendant, and excludes the consideration of mitigating factors. "It treats all persons of a designated offense not as uniquely individual human beings, but as members of a faceless, undifferentiated mass to be subjected to the blind infliction of the penalty of death." Enlightened policy and justice, they maintained, requires that all circumstances relating both to the offender and the offense be taken into consideration. The fourth dissenting Justices argued that individualized consideration of offenders is not constitutionally required.

It remains to be noted that the 1976 cases upholding capital punishment over Eighth and Fourteenth Amendment objections all dealt with first-degree murder. That is all that was decided. Whether capital punishment is cruel and unusual in the constitutional sense for other offenses—such as armed robbery and rape—remains to be settled in future litigation.

Table of Cases

(The full citations are in the footnotes)

Abbate v. United States, 367
Abel v. United States, 275
Ableman v. Booth, 146
Abraham v. State, 227
Achtien v. Dowd, 225
Adams v. Illinois, 222
Adams v. Maryland, 324
Adams v. New York, 292
Adams v. U.S. *ex rel.* McCann, 140, 182, 226, 236
Adams v. Williams, 282
Adamson v. California, 18, 321
Adkins v. E. I. Dupont de Nemours, 242
Adler v. Board of Education, 314
Affonso Bros. v. Brock, 88
Agnello v. United States, 270, 300
Aguilar v. Texas, 267
Air Pollution Variance Board of Colorado v. Western Alfalfa Corp., 270
Akins v. Texas, 195
Albertson v. Subversive Activities Control Board, 310
Albrecht v. United States, 375
Alcorta v. Texas, 20, 124
Alderman v. United States, 299
Aldridge v. United States, 192
Alegata v. Com. of Massachusetts, 80, 81
Alexander v. Louisiana, 196
Alford v. United States, 94
Allen v. United States, 119, 188
Almeida-Sanchez v. United States, 282-83
American Publ. Co. v. Fisher, 169
American Tobacco Co. v. United States, 376
Amos v. United States, 293, 300
Anaya v. Baker, 242
Anders v. California, 224
Anderson v. Nelson, 322
Anderson v. Nosser, 413
Anderson v. United States, 340
Anderson National Bank v. Luckett, 74
Andres v. United States, 169

Anonymous, 198
Anonymous v. Baker, 253
Anon. Case, 160
Apodaca v. Oregon, 171
Argersinger v. Hamlin, 18, 85, 216-17, 231
Armstrong v. Manzo, 74
Armstrong v. State, 268
Arnold v. State, 221
Ashby v. White, 134
Ashcraft v. Tennessee, 20, 41, 344, 346
Ashdown v. Utah, 345
Ashe v. Swenson, 377
Ashton v. Kentucky, 80
Atlantic Coast Line R. Co. v. Ford, 108
Austin v. Harris, 411
Austin v. State, 234
Avery v. Alabama, 213
Avery v. Georgia, 196

B, *In re,* 250
Babington v. Yellow Taxi Corp., 29
Badders v. United States, 398
Bailey v. Richardson, 100
Bailey v. State, 416
Baker v. Hamilton, 415
Baldwin v. Hale, 75
Baldwin v. New York, 163
Ballard v. United States, 185
Ballay, *In re,* 416
Bancroft v. Board of Governors of Registered Dentists, 252
Bankers Trust Co., v. Blodgett, 100
Bar Assoc. of City of Boston v. Sleeper, 74
Barber v. Page, 97
Bard v. Chilton, 120
Bargesser v. State, 382
Barker v. Hardway, 253
Barker v. Wingo, 114
Barnes v. Com., 209
Barnes v. United States, 108

421

Table of Cases

Barr v. Columbia, 20, 106
Barrett v. United States, 59, 201
Barron v. Baltimore, 16
Bart v. United States, 311
Bartholomey v. State, 388, 393
Bartkus v. Illinois, 366
Barton v. Barbour, 161
Bassing v. Cady, 364
Baumgartner v. United States, 252
Beacon Theatres, Inc. v. Westover, 161
Beard v. Lee, 413
Beard v. United States, 308
Beavers v. Haubert, 113
Beazell v. Ohio, 101
Beck v. Ohio, 31
Beck v. Washington, 43, 123
Beecher v. Alabama, 345
Begalke v. United States, 246
Beilan v. Board of Education of Philadelphia, 316
Bell v. Alabama, 229
Bellis v. United States, 308
Ben Gold v. United States, 175
Benanti v. United States, 287
Bennett v. Com., 364
Bennett v. United States, 57
Benton v. Maryland, 19, 355
Berger v. California, 97
Berger v. New York, 288
Berger v. United States, 127, 174
Berkowitz v. United States, 362
Berry v. City of Cincinnati, 217
Besser Manufacturing Co. v. United States, 92
Betts v. Brady, 213–14, 215, 356
Billie Sol Estes v. Texas, 123
Binion v. United States, 54
Birdsong, *In re,* 414
Bivens v. Six Unknown Federal Narcotics Agents, 297, 298
Black v. Ciccone, 411
Black v. United States, 289
Blackburn v. Alabama, 344
Blackledge v. Perry, 358–59
Blackmer v. United States, 325
Blair v. United States, 325
Blair v. White, 371
Blockburger v. United States, 375
Bloom v. Illinois, 179
Blue v. United States, 45
Blumberg v. United States, 308
Blunt v. United States, 65
Board of Commissioners v. Pollard, 249
Boles v. Stevenson, 350
Bolkovac v. State, 217
Bollman, *Ex parte,* 146, 157
Bonham's Case, 116
Bornee, *Ex parte,* 355
Boruski v. S.E.C., 252
Boudreau v. The King, 341
Bowen v. Johnston, 131, 143
Bowen v. United States, 283
Boyce Motor Lines, Inc. v. United States, 77
Boyd v. Dutton, 224
Boyd v. United States, 257, 261–62
Boykin v. Alabama, 86
Bozza v. United States, 357
Bradford v. Territory *ex rel.* Woods, 169
Bradshaw v. Ball, 239
Brady v. Maryland, 10, 20, 125
Brady v. United States, 164, 231
Branzburg v. Hayes, 334-35
Bratcher v. United States, 188
Breed v. Jones, 362
Breithaupt v. Abram, 347
Brenneman v. Madigan, 412
Bridges v. United States, 71
Brinegar v. United States, 255, 281, 292
Brock v. North Carolina, 352, 374
Brookhart v. Janis, 96
Brooks v. Florida, 343
Brooks v. Tennessee, 316
Brown v. Air Pollution Control Board, 251
Brown v. Allen, 41, 145, 148, 149, 341
Brown v. Illinois, 340
Brown v. Louisiana, 106
Brown v. Mississippi, 41, 342, 346
Brown v. State, 400
Brown v. United States, 128, 299, 318
Brown v. Walker, 314, 327, 330
Browne v. State, 403
Brubaker v. Dickson, 228
Bruno v. State of Louisiana, 403
Bruno v. United States, 320
Bruton v. United States, 97
Bryan v. United States, 233
Bryant v. United States, 370
Buchalter v. New York, 86, 118
Buchanan v. O'Brien, 215
Bumper v. North Carolina, 193, 300

Burdeau v. McDowell, 259
Burgett v. Texas, 217
Burkett v. McCarty, 87
Burns v. Wilson, 155, 246
Burrell v. State, 268
Burton v. United States, 375, 377
Bushell's Case, 133, 160
Bute v. Illinois, 214
Butler v. United States, 248
Byars v. United States, 260, 267

Cain, *In re,* 157
Calder v. Bull, 99
Calhoun v. State, 389
California v. Anderson, 419
California v. Byers, 317
California v. Green, 23, 97
California Bankers Assoc. v. Shultz, 276
Callan v. Wilson, 176
Camara v. Municipal Court of San Francisco, 273
Cammer v. United States, 128
Campbell Painting Corp. v. Reid, 308
Cancemi v. People, 181
Candido, *In re,* 396
Canizio v. New York, 214
Cantwell v. Connecticut, 17
Capital Traction Co. v. Hof, 161
Capler v. State, 393
Carafas v. LaVallee, 135, 139
Carbo v. United States, 54, 132
Cardwell v. Lewis, 282
Care v. United States, 270
Carlson v. Landon, 50, 57
Carnley v. Cochran, 236
Carroll v. United States, 281
Carter v. Illinois, 214, 226
Carter v. Jury Commission of Greene County, 194, 195
Carter v. McClaughry, 376
Case of Davis, 58
Casey v. United States, 107
Cash v. Culver, 215
Cassell v. Texas, 196, 197
Chaffin v. Stynchcombe, 359
Chambers v. Florida, 20, 343
Chambers v. Maroney, 281
Chambers v. Mississippi, 96
Chandler v. Fretag, 218

Chapman, *In re,* 375
Chapman v. California, 322
Chapman v. United States, 301
Chase Securities Corp. v. Donaldson, 112
Cheff v. Schnackenberg, 129, 178–79
Chessman v. Teets, 125, 145
Chewning v. Cunningham, 223
Chicago & A. R. Co. v. Tranbarger, 102
Chimel v. California, 278–79
Cicenia v. LaGay, 343
Cipolla v. State, 397
City of Miami v. Aronovitz, 284
City of Monroe v. Ducas, 36
Ciucci v. Illinois, 379
Civil Rights Cases, 17
Clawans v. Rives, 363, 372
Cleaver v. Wilcox, 249
Clewis v. Texas, 345
Cline v. Frink Dairy Co., 76
Coates v. Cincinnati, 81, 398
Cochran v. Kansas, 72, 125
Codispoti v. Pennsylvania, 179
Cody v. Dombrowski, 282
Coffin v. Reichard, 411
Coffman v. Bomar, 228
Cohen v. Beneficial Industrial Loan Corp., 86
Cohen v. Hurley, 315
Cole v. Arkansas, 74
Colegrove v. Battin, 168
Coleman v. Alabama, 46, 197, 222
Coleman v. State, 71
Coleman v. Tennessee, 368
Coles v. Peyton, 228
Collins v. Johnston, 402, 408
Collins v. Kentucky, 76
Collins v. Loisel, 364
Collins v. United States, 114
Colonnade Catering Corp. v. United States, 276
Colten v. Kentucky, 81, 82
Com. v. Agoston, 219
Com. v. Beam, 37
Com. v. Bryant, 219
Com. v. Evans, 380
Com. v. Gorman, 31
Com. v. Green, 416
Com. v. Lopes, 221
Com. v. McCormick, 371
Com. v. Mitchell, 284

Com. v. Olds, 353
Com. v. Pierce, 124
Com. v. Ramunno, 380
Com. v. Rice, 364
Com. v. Slome, 75
Com. v. Turner, 341
Com. v. Wyatt, 396
Com. v. Wyman, 101
Com. *ex rel.* Bryant v. Hendrick, 412
Com. *ex rel.* Johnson v. Dye, 410
Com. of Pa. v. Ellis (Smith), 127
Com. of Pa. *ex rel.* Herman v. Claudy, 236
Connally v. General Construction Co., 76
Connley v. United States, 57
Conway v. State, 414
Cooke v. United States, 128, 200
Cool v. United States, 104
Cooley v. Strickland Transportation Co., 168
Coolidge v. New Hampshire, 24, 263
Cooper v. California, 281
Cooper v. Pate, 412
Coplon v. United States, 219
Cornero v. United States, 363, 372
Costello v. United States, 48, 70
Cottrell v. Com., 209
Couch v. United States, 307
Counselman v. Hitchcock, 306-7, 326
Countess of Shrewsbury's Case, 325
County of Dane v. Smith, 238
Covey v. Town of Somers, 74
Craig v. Harney, 20
Crawford v. United States, 190
Crocker v. Justices of the Superior Court, 121
Cruikshank v. United States, 77
Cruz v. Beto, 414
Culombe v. Connecticut, 345
Cummings v. Missouri, 86, 87
Cupp v. Murphy, 271
Cupp v. Naughten, 104
Curcio v. United States, 308
Curry v. State, 388
Curtis v. Loether, 161

Daeche v. United States, 337
Dairy Queen, Inc. v. Wood, 161
Dancy v. United States, 222
Danforth v. State Department of Health and Welfare, 250

Daniel v. Louisiana, 186
Daniman v. Board of Education of New York, 313
Darr v. Burford, 149, 246
Dartmouth College v. Woodward, 84
Davidson v. Dill, 35
Davis v. Alaska, 97
Davis v. Berry, 397
Davis v. Mississippi, 271
Davis v. North Carolina, 344
Davis v. O'Connell, 410
Davis v. United States, 103, 110, 301
Day-Bright Lighting, Inc., v. Missouri, 189
Dean v. Gadsen Times Publishing Corp., 189
Dear Wing Jung v. United States, 407
De Bord v. People, 369
Debs, *In re,* 179
Decker v. State, 217
Delli Paoli v. United States, 97
De Maris v. United States, 249
DeMeerleer v. Michigan, 214
Dennis v. United States, 56, 191
Dent v. West Virginia, 100
De Stefano v. Woods, 162
Diaz v. United States, 91, 380
Dickey v. Florida, 114
Dickinson v. United States, 156
Dier v. Banton, 270
Diggs v. Welch, 226
Dimes v. Grand Junction Canal Co., 116
District of Columbia v. Clawans, 89, 94, 176
District of Columbia v. Colts, 176
District of Columbia v. Little, 272
Dolan v. United States, 238
Donaldson v. Sack, 393
Donnelly v. DeChristoforo, 126
Dorsey v. Gill, 150, 225
Douglas v. Alabama, 96
Douglas v. California, 224
Dowd v. Cook, 149
Downum v. United States, 372
Drake v. State, 364
Dranow v. United States, 182
Draper v. United States, 267
Dreyer v. Illinois, 370
Dreyer v. People, 370
Driver v. Hinnant, 403
Drury v. Hurley, 313, 333
Dugan v. Ohio, 117

Table of Cases / 425

Duke v. United States, 69
Dukes v. Warden, 231
Dumbra v. United States, 30, 266
Duncan v. Kahanamoku, 159
Duncan v. Louisiana, 19, 162, 165, 170, 179, 186
Duncan v. Missouri, 101
Dunn v. Lyons, 120
Dutton v. Evans, 98
Dutton v. Smart, 401
Dutton v. State, 109
Dye v. Johnson, 410
Dyke v. Taylor Implement Mfg. Co., 179
Dynes v. Hoover, 152, 175

Earle, *Ex parte,* 371
Earnest v. Willingham, 224
Easter v. District of Columbia, 403
Eddy v. Moore, 35
Edgemon v. State, 237
Edwards v. State, 219
Edwards v. United States, 228
Elkins v. United States, 23, 260
Ellis v. Buchkoe, 235
Emspak v. United States, 311
Endo, *Ex parte,* 156
Entick v. Carrington, 257
Entsminger v. Iowa, 224
Escobedo v. Illinois, 23, 220-21
Essgee Co. v. United States, 270
Estep v. United States, 156
Evans v. Rives, 211, 236
Everson v. State, 407
E. W. Scripps Co. v. Fulton, 111

Fahy v. Connecticut, 296
Fair, *In re,* 368
Falsone v. United States, 308
Faretta v. California, 226, 235
Faulkner v. State, 406
Faxon v. School Committee of Boston, 313
Fay v. New York, 198-200
Fay v. Noia, 149, 246
F.C.C. v. Schreiber, 253
Feldman v. United States, 22, 323, 324
Fenster v. Leary, 81
Ferguson v. Georgia, 223
Fernicola v. Keenan, 33
Field v. United States, 56
Fikes v. Alabama, 344

Finnegan v. United States, 188
Fisher v. Baker, 158
Fiske v. Kansas, 20, 86
Fitzpatrick v. Williams, 55
Five Knights' Case, 133
Fong Foo v. United States, 360
Fontaine v. California, 322
Foote v. Maryland, 396
Ford v. Board of Managers of N.J. State Prison, 414
Forman v. United States, 357, 360
Foster v. California, 221
Foster v. Illinois, 215
Fox v. State of Washington, 77
Frank v. Mangum, 17, 120, 121, 143, 145
Frank v. Maryland, 272
Frank v. United States, 179
Frankel v. Woodrough, 113
Franklin v. Brown, 385
Frazier v. Cupp, 97
Frazier v. United States, 190-91
Freeman v. United States, 371
Freidus v. Leary, 407
Frisbie v. Collins, 109
Fry v. State, 341
Fucini, *In re,* 176
Fuentes v. Shevin, 75
Fuller v. Oregon, 242
Furman v. Georgia, 390-92, 419
Fusco v. Moses, 251

Gaines v. Washington, 68
Gagnon v. Scarpelli, 225
Gallegos v. Colorado, 345
Gallegos v. Nebraska, 41, 341
Galvan v. Press, 100
Gambino v. United States, 260
Garcia v. Territory, 396
Gardner v. Broderick, 315
Garland, *Ex parte,* 87, 100
Garland v. Torre, 334
Garner v. Board of Public Works of Los Angeles, 88, 100, 314
Garner v. Lousiana, 20, 106
Garrity v. New Jersey, 315
Gasquet v. Lapeyre, 157
Gates v. Collier, 412
Gault, *In re,* 89-90, 253
Gavieres v. United States, 375
Gelhard v. United States, 289

426 / Table of Cases

Gerstein v. Pugh, 32, 43
Giaccio v. Pennsylvania, 79
Gibbs v. Burke, 145, 214, 215
Gibson v. Hutchinson, 363
Gibson v. Mississippi, 101
Gideon v. Wainwright, 18, 85, 215–16, 217, 356
Giglio v. United States, 125
Gilbert v. California, 221
Gilbert v. State, 365
Giles v. Maryland, 20, 124
Giordenello v. United States, 48
Gitlow v. New York, 17
Glasgow v. Moyer, 140
Glasser v. United States, 183, 218, 229
Glenn, *Ex parte*, 372
Go-Bart Importing Co. v. United States, 267, 278
Goldberg v. Kelly, 252
Golden v. State, 371
Goldman v. United States, 284
Goldstein v. United States, 287
Gompers v. United States, 179
Goodson v. Peyton, 229
Goodwin v. Swenson, 228
Gordon v. Justice Court, 86
Gordon v. State, 388
Gore v. United States, 375
Gosa v. Mayden, 164
Goss v. Lopez, 253
Goto v. Lane, 147
Gouled v. United States, 264, 300
Grafton v. United States, 368
Graham v. West Virginia, 397
Grau v. United States, 267
Grayned v. City of Rockford, 81
Great Lakes Screw Corp. v. N.L.R.B., 251
Green, *Re*, 180
Green v. State, 363
Green v. United States, 129, 178, 354, 356, 381
Greenwald v. Wisconsin, 343
Gregg v. Georgia, 419
Gregory, *In re*, 140
Griffin v. California, 321
Griffin v. Illinois, 125, 224
Grimley, *Re*, 154
Grisham v. Hagan, 165
Groban, *In re*, 253
Groppi v. Leslie, 84

Groppi v. Wisconsin, 123
Grosso v. United States, 309, 310
Grunewald v. United States, 316
Gryger v. Burke, 101, 215
Gunsolus v. Gagnon, 224
Gusik v. Schilder, 153
Gustafson v. Florida, 283

Hagar v. Reclamation District, 84
Hagner v. United States, 72
Haines v. Kerner, 413, 415
Hairston v. United States, 59
Hale v. Henkel, 270
Hale v. Kentucky, 196
Haley v. Ohio, 345
Hall v. Johnson, 198
Halloran v. State, 369
Halprin v. United States, 402
Ham v. South Carolina, 192
Hamilton v. Alabama, 222
Hamilton v. Love, 412
Hamilton v. Schiro, 412
Hanson v. State, 405
Harisiades v. Shaughnessy, 100
Harlan v. McGourin, 142
Harlan v. State, 370
Harper v. Wall, 410
Harrington v. California, 97
Harris v. Nelson, 145–46
Harris v. New York, 340
Harris v. South Carolina, 344
Harris v. State, 379
Harris v. United States, 128, 269, 277, 278, 281
Harris v. Washington, 379
Harrison v. United States, 350
Hart v. State, 388
Haverstick v. State, 269
Hawk, *Ex parte*, 124, 148
Hawker v. New York, 101
Haynes v. United States, 310
Haynes v. Washington, 344
Helvering v. Mitchell, 376
Hemans v. United States, 400
Hendrickson v. Overlade, 229
Henry v. United States, 31
Hensley v. Municipal Court, 140
Hepner v. United States, 180
Herb v. Pitcairn, 16
Herbert v. Louisiana, 365

Hernandez v. State, 386
Hernandez v. Texas, 197-98
Herschel v. Dyra, 33
Herzog v. United States, 57
Hess v. Pawloski, 109
Hester v. United States, 270
Hiatt v. Brown, 154, 246
Hibben v. Smith, 118
Hibbs, *Ex parte,* 397
Hill v. California, 279
Hill v. Texas, 196
Himmelfarb v. United States, 371
Hirota v. MacArthur, 152
H. L. Doherty & Co. v. Goodman, 109
Ho Ah Kow v. Nunan, 407
Hoag v. New Jersey, 377
Hobbs v. State, 405
Hodges v. Com., 393
Hoffa v. United States, 285
Hoffman v. United States, 311
Holden v. Minnesota, 101
Holiday v. Johnston, 151, 235
Hollins v. Oklahoma, 196
Holt v. Sarver, 385, 413
Holt v. United States, 70
Holt v. Virginia, 180
Honaker v. Cox, 236
Hopkin Hugget's Case, 36
Hopt v. Utah, 101
Horacek v. Exon, 416
Howard v. Fleming, 398
Howland v. State, 401
Hoyt v. Florida, 186
Hudson v. North Carolina, 218
Hudson v. Parker, 51
Hughes v. Rizzo, 35
Hulett v. Julian, 118
Hull, *Ex parte,* 125, 138
Hunter v. Wade, 156
Hurtado v. California, 18, 68, 85
Husty v. United States, 281
Hysler v. Florida, 125

Ianneli v. United States, 376
Illinois v. Allen, 92
Illnois v. Birnbaum, 37
Illinois v. Somerville, 372
Ingraham v. Wright, 396
Inmates of Boys' Training School v. Affleck, 415

International Harvester Co. v. Kentucky, 76
Irvin v. Dowd, 122, 148
Irvine v. California, 40, 294
Ivan v. City of New York, 90, 104

Jaben v. United States, 48
Jack v. Kansas, 323
Jackson, *Ex parte,* 270
Jackson v. Bishop, 397, 413
Jackson v. Com., 181
Jackson v. Denno, 349
Jackson v. Dickson, 388
Jackson v. Indiana, 94
James v. Headley, 211
James v. Louisiana, 279
James v. Strange, 243
Jarl v. United States, 362
Jencks v. United States, 95-96
Jenkins v. Delaware, 339
Jenkins v. United States, 173
Jennings v. Illinois, 148
Johannessen v. United States, 100
John Bad Elk v. United States, 36
John Doe v. Commander, Wheaton Police Department, 34
Johnsen v. United States, 364
Johnson, *In re,* 217
Johnson v. Avery, 138, 411
Johnson v. Dye, 410
Johnson v. Eisentrager, 153
Johnson v. Florida, 20, 106
Johnson v. Hoy, 136
Johnson v. Lark, 412
Johnson v. Louisiana, 171
Johnson v. Matthews, 410
Johnson v. Mississippi, 129
Johnson v. State, 268
Johnson v. United States, 227, 263, 266, 277
Johnson v. Whiteside County, 238
Johnson v. Zerbst, 144, 150, 235, 244
Johnston v. United States, 200
Joint Anti-Fascist Committee v. McGrath, 7, 13
Jones, *In re,* 411
Jones v. Board of Registrars, 88
Jones v. Cunningham, 138
Jones v. Huff, 227
Jones v. Kentucky, 213
Jones v. United States, 200, 267, 299
Jones v. Wittenberg, 413

Jordan v. Com., 55
Jordan v. Fitzharris, 414
Jordan v. State, 37
Jurek v. State, 394
Jurek v. Texas, 419

Kastigar v. United States, 327
Katz v. United States, 288
Kaufman v. United States, 148
Kearney, *Ex parte,* 142
Keeler, *Ex parte,* 405
Kemmler, *In re,* 386, 387
Kennedy v. Commandant, 248
Kenney v. United States, 268
Kent v. United States, 90
Kepner v. United States, 368
Ker v. California, 31, 268, 296
Ker v. Illinois, 109
King v. Voisin, 341
Kinsella v. Krueger, 154
Kinsella v. Singleton, 165
Kirby v. Illinois, 221
Kirby v. United States, 94
Kitchens v. Smith, 217
Klapprott v. United States, 252
Klopfer v. North Carolina, 19, 112, 114
Knapp v. Schweitzer, 323, 324
Knauer v. United States, 252
Knecht v. Gillman, 416
Knox County Council v. State *ex rel.* McCormick, 238
Kolb v. O'Connor, 33
Kotteakos v. United States, 12
Kowall v. United States, 34
Kremen v. United States, 267
Krench v. United States, 380
Kring v. Missouri, 101

Labat v. Bennett, 185
Lambert v. California, 82
Lamont v. Solano County, 238
Lancaster, *Ex parte,* 71
Lange, *Ex parte,* 143, 357
Lanza v. New York, 270
Lanzetta v. New Jersey, 76, 398
LaVallee v. Rose, 343
Lawn v. United States, 70
Leary v. United States, 310
LeBallister v. Warden, 248
Lee v. Florida, 287

Lee v. Mississippi, 345
Lee v. Tahash, 411
Lefkowitz v. Newsome, 148
Lefkowitz v. Turley, 315
Lego v. Twomey, 350
Leigh v. United States, 54
Leland v. Oregon, 4, 103, 388
Lem Woon v. Oregon, 43
Lerner v. Casey, 316
Levine v. Hudspeth, 236
Levine v. United States, 109
Lewis v. Kugler, 412
Lewis v. United States, 300, 309
Leyra v. Denno, 145, 345
Liddell v. State, 388
Lindsey v. Washington, 101
Linkins v. State, 219
Lisenba v. California, 343, 346
Little, *In re,* 130
Little v. Com., 365
Loftus v. Illinois, 246
Logan v. United States, 370
Long v. District Court, 138
Longoria, *Ex parte,* 370
Loper v. Beto, 237
Lopez v. United States, 285, 291
Louisiana *ex rel.* Willie Francis v. Resweber, 354, 387, 408
Lovato v. New Mexico, 372
Ludecke v. Watkins, 153
Luria v. United States, 161, 252
Lustig v. United States, 260
Lynch, *In re,* 401
Lynum v. Illinois, 344
Lyons v. Oklahoma, 345

McAllister v. State, 119
McCardle, *Ex parte,* 146
McCarthy v. Arndstein, 307, 319
McConnell, *In re,* 180
McCray v. Illinois, 267
McDonald v. Com., 398
McDonald v. Johnston, 218
McDonald v. Massachusetts, 101
McDonald v. United States, 279, 302
McDougle v. Maxwell, 405
McElrath v. United States, 161
McElroy v. Guagliardo, 165
McElvaine v. Brush, 386
McGautha v. California, 389

McGuire v. State, 101
McKane v. Durston, 60
McKeiver v. Pennsylvania, 90, 176
Mackey v. United States, 309
McLaughlin v. Royster, 228
McMann v. Richardson, 16, 231
McNabb v. United States, 41, 45, 47, 340
McNally v. Hill, 136
McNeal v. Culver, 215
McNeil v. Director, Patuxent Institution, 94
Macomber v. Hudspeth, 235
McWilliams v. United States, 402
Madsen v. Kinsella, 154
Maffie v. United States, 332
Mahaffey v. State, 414
Mahler v. Eby, 100
Malinski v. New York, 7, 343
Mallon v. State, 400
Mallory v. United States, 41, 47, 341
Malloy v. Hogan, 19, 322, 324, 356
Malloy v. South Carolina, 101
Mancusi v. DeForte, 299
Mancusi v. Stubbs, 96
Maness v. Meyers, 307
Manley v. Georgia, 106
Mapp v. Ohio, 19, 40, 287, 294-95
Marchetti v. United States, 309
Marino v. Ragen, 246
Marron v. United States, 277
Martarella v. Kelley, 416
Martin v. State, 371
Mason v. State, 416
Massiah v. United States, 219
Mastrian v. Hedman, 50
Mathis v. United States, 339
Mattox v. Sacks, 148
Mattox v. United States, 96
Matysek v. United States, 136
Maxwell v. Dow, 18, 162, 165
Maxwell v. Stephens, 388
May v. Anderson, 250
Mayberry v. Pennsylvania, 92, 129
Mayor and Council of Hoboken v. Bauer, 406
Medley, *In re,* 101
Melanson v. O'Brien, 110
Meltzer v. United States, 59
Mempa v. Rhay, 224, 411
Menard v. Mitchell, 34
Menard v. Saxbe, 34

Merryman, *Ex parte,* 158
Mesarosh v. United States, 20, 124
Meyer v. Nebraska, 250
Michaelson v. Beemer, 181
Michaelson v. United States, 177
Michell v. State, 416
Michener v. Johnston, 236
Michigan v. Payne, 358
Michigan v. Tucker, 340
Mickle v. Henrichs, 397
Milam v. United States, 269
Milburn, *Ex parte,* 55
Miller v. Com., 55
Miller v. Pate, 20, 124
Miller v. State, 401
Miller v. United States, 255
Milligan, *Ex parte,* 14, 158
Mincy v. District of Columbia, 284
Minn. & St. Louis R.R. Co. v. Bombolis, 170
Minor v. United States, 310
Miranda v. Arizona, 220-21, 236, 338-39
Missouri *ex rel.* Hurwitz v. North, 73
Mitchell v. Illinois, 228, 230
Mobile, J. & K.C. R.R. v. Turnipseed, 106
Monroe v. Pape, 41, 412
Monroe v. Tielsch, 34
Mooney v. Holohan, 20, 124, 145
Moore v. Aderhold, 59
Moore v. Arizona, 115
Moore v. Dempsey, 17, 85, 119-20, 145
Moore v. Illinois, 126, 365
Moore v. Michigan, 236
Moore v. Missouri, 397
Moore v. New York, 198, 200
Moore v. State, 119
Moore v. United States, 228
Morales v. Turman, 415
Morey v. Com., 377
Morford v. United States, 192
Morgan v. Devine, 375
Morrison v. California, 107
Morrison v. Flowers, 108
Morrissey v. Brewer, 84
Mulkey v. Purdy, 33
Mullane v. Central Hanover Bank & Trust Co., 75
Mullaney v. Wilbur, 104
Muniz v. Hoffman, 179
Munn v. Illinois, 7

430 / Table of Cases

Murch v. Mottram, 148
Murchison, *In re,* 118
Murphy v. Florida, 123
Murphy v. Waterfront Commission of New York, 306, 324
Murphy and Glover Test Oath Case, 87
Murray's Lessee v. Hoboken Land & Improvement Co., 88
Musser v. Utah, 76
Myers v. United States, 179
Mylock v. Saladine, 187

Nabb v. United States, 238
Napue v. Illinois, 124
Nardone v. United States, 286, 287
Nash v. United States, 77
Nathanson v. United States, 267
N.L.R.B. v. Jones & Laughlin Steel Corp., 161
Neal v. Delaware, 194
Near v. Minnesota, 17
Nees v. S.E.C., 252
Neil v. Biggers, 142
Nelson v. Heyne, 416
Nelson v. O'Neil, 98
Newman v. Alabama, 411
Nickerson v. United States, 253
Nielson, *Ex parte,* 380
Nielson, Hans, *Re,* 144
Norris v. Alabama, 20, 194–95
North American Cold Storage Co. v. Chicago, 88
North Carolina v. Alford, 232
North Carolina v. Pearce, 357
North Carolina v. Rice, 358
Nowling v. State, 405
Noyd v. Bond, 153
Nye v. United States, 178

Oakley v. United States, 248
O'Brien v. United States, 289
O'Callahan v. Parker, 164
Oceanic Navigation Co. v. Stranahan, 180
Offutt v. United States, 128
Ohio v. Hashmall, 417
Ohio *ex rel.* Eaton v. Price, 273
Oliver, *In re,* 19, 84, 109, 110, 119
Oliver v. Postel, 111
Olmstead v. United States, 22, 255, 285–86
Omaechevarria v. Idaho, 78

Omaha v. Olmstead, 118
On Lee v. United States, 284
One Lot Emerald Cut Stones v. United States, 377
One 1958 Plymouth Sedan v. Pennsylvania, 296
O'Neil v. Vermont, 402, 408
Opinion of the Justices, *In re,* 319, 397
Oregon v. Hass, 340
Orloff v. Willoughby, 156
Ormento v. United States, 402
Orozco v. Texas, 339
Osborn v. United States, 288
Otton v. Zaborac, 251

Palko v. Connecticut, 19, 162, 354
Palmer v. Euclid, 81, 398
Pannell v. United States, 59, 62
Papachristou v. City of Jacksonville, 81
Paper v. United States, 269
Pappas, *In re,* 334
Parisi v. Davidson, 153
Parker v. Ellis, 139
Parker v. Gladden, 97
Parker v. Levy, 78–79
Parker v. North Carolina, 164, 231
Pate v. Robinson, 94
Paterno v. Lyons, 74
Patricia Blau v. United States, 311
Patton v. Mississippi, 196
Patton v. United States, 165, 181, 196
Pavesich v. New England Life Insurance Co., 254
Payne v. Arkansas, 344
Pell v. Procunier, 415
People v. Agnew, 217
People v. Alfinito, 268
People v. Anderson, 390
People v. Baum, 406
People v. Blevins, 228
People v. Borrero, 403
People v. Bradley, 270
People v. Carpenter, 192
People v. Carroll, 183
People v. Chiagles, 277
People v. Coaley, 226
People v. Coli, 119
People v. Conway, 277
People v. Cox, 229
People v. Curtis, 37

Table of Cases / 431

People v. Davis, 371, 403
People v. Defore, 293
People v. Den Uyl, 323
People v. Dillon, 364
People v. Eggers, 242
People v. Elmore, 341
People v. Garcia, 363
People v. Gilmore, 380
People v. Gitlow, 11
People v. Gnatz, 37
People v. Harter, 269
People v. Ibarra, 228
People v. Jackson, 405
People v. Jelke, 110
People v. Jenkins, 407
People v. Koehn, 382
People v. Letterio, 217
People v. Lewis, 89
People v. Lo Cicero, 367
People v. Lohman, 55
People v. Lorentzen, 403
People v. McDaniels, 379
People v. McIntyre, 227
People v. Marsh, 283
People v. Martin, 280
People v. Mason, 302
People v. Mire, 400
People v. Modesto, 321
People v. Morris, 228, 385
People v. Moten, 268
People v. Mummiani, 337
People v. Neal, 119
People v. Nitti, 228
People v. Odom, 229
People v. Peters, 280
People v. Quider, 72
People v. Rivera, 280
People v. Robinson, 218
People v. Rodgers, 400
People v. Rose, 218
People v. Saffore, 407
People v. Sharp, 226
People v. Simon, 284
People v. Sinclair, 401, 403, 416
People v. Smith, 416
People v. Sovetsky, 268
People v. Spegal, 182
People v. Tweed, 58
People v. Ventura, 229
People v. Walcher, 387

People v. West, 234
People v. White, 401
People v. Winfrey, 113
People ex rel. Garling v. Van Allen, 247
People ex rel. Hodson v. Miner, 355
People ex rel. Kemmler v. Durston, 386
People ex rel. Liss v. Superintendent, 367
People ex rel. Lobell v. McDonnell, 59
People ex rel. Menechino v. Warden, 224
People ex rel. Ransom v. Niagara County, 238
People ex rel. Rao v. Adams, 59
People ex rel. Rubinstein v. Warden of City Prison, 57
People ex rel. Sabatino v. Jennings, 137
People ex rel. Sammons v. Snow, 59
People ex rel. Taylor v. Forbes, 319
People ex rel. Whitman v. Wilson, 124
Pereira v. United States, 376
Perkins v. North Carolina, 401
Pernell v. Southall Realty, 161
Perry v. Williard, 224
Peters v. Hobby, 363
Peters v. Kiff, 186
Petite v. United States, 379
Peyton v. Coles, 226
Peyton v. Rowe, 136, 137
Picard v. Connor, 148
Pierce v. LaVallee, 413
Pierre v. Louisiana, 196
Pierson v. Ray, 41
Pietch v. United States, 114
Pilkinton v. Circuit Court of Howell County, Mo., 50
Pines v. District Court of Woodbury County, 114
Pinkerton v. United States, 376
Pinto v. Pierce, 350
Pisacano v. State, 411
Pointer v. Texas, 19, 96
Posey v. Mobile County, 238
Powell v. Alabama, 18, 210, 211, 212, 225
Powell v. California, 85
Powell v. Texas, 403
Preiser v. Rodriguez, 149
Preston v. United States, 260, 282
Price v. Georgia, 381
Price v. Johnston, 150, 151, 409
Procunier v. Atchley, 350
Procunier v. Martinez, 415

432 / Table of Cases

Proffitt v. Florida, 419
Provoo, Petition of, 113–14
Pyle v. Kansas, 124, 145

Queen v. Tooley, 36
Quercia v. United States, 173
Quicksall v. Michigan, 214
Quinn v. United States, 311
Quirin, *Ex parte*, 154

R. v. McKenna, 160
R. v. Schama, 3
Rabe v. Washington, 80
Rabinowitz v. United States, 256
Ralph v. Pepersack, 388
Ralph v. Warden, Maryland Penitentiary, 389
Rambo v. State, 365
Rathbun v. United States, 286
Rawlins v. Georgia, 189
Rea v. United States, 260
Reck v. Pate, 345
Rector v. State, 364
Redding v. State, 412
Reed, *Ex parte*, 154, 246
Reed v. Anderson, 222
Reeves v. State, 59
Regina v. Garbett, 318
Reid v. Covert, 154, 165
Reina v. United States, 324
Relford v. Commandant, 165
Remmer v. United States, 94, 174–75
Resolute Insurance Co. v. Seventh Judicial District Court of Oklahoma County, 56
Rex v. Edmonds, 198
Rex Trailer Co. v. United States, 376
Reynolds v. Cochran, 218
Reynolds v. United States, 95, 121, 226
Rhem v. McGrath, 413
Rhinelander, *Ex parte*, 375
Rice v. Olson, 215
Richards v. State, 293
Ricks v. District of Columbia, 81
Riddle, *In re*, 411
Rideau v. Louisiana, 123
Riggins v. Rhay, 224
Rios v. United States, 260
Roberts v. Barbosa, 414
Roberts v. Louisiana, 420
Roberts v. People, 108

Roberts v. Pepersack, 414
Robinson, *Ex parte*, 127
Robinson v. California, 19, 402, 408
Robinson v. Hanrahan, 75
Robinson v. Neil, 367
Rochin v. California, 346
Rogers, *Ex parte*, 403
Rogers v. Richmond, 345
Rogers v. United States, 174, 307, 318
Ronse v. Cameron, 416
Roseman v. United States, 72, 183
Ross, *In re*, 175
Ross v. Bernhard, 162
Ross v. Middlebrooks, 410
Ross v. Moffitt, 224
Ross v. Oregon, 100
Rosser v. Com., 363, 372
Roviaro v. United States, 267
Royall, *Ex parte*, 148
Rozecki v. Gaughan, 416
Rudolph v. Alabama, 388
Ruffalo, *In re*, 74
Ruthenberg v. United States, 184–85, 201

Sacher v. United States, 177, 179
Salinger v. Loisel, 141
Salistean v. State, 371
Samuels v. McCurdy, 102
Sanders v. State, 369
Sanders v. United States, 148
Sandoval v. Rattikin, 249
Sanford v. Robbins, 368
Santobello v. New York, 232–33
Sapir v. United States, 360
Sarah, The, 161
Saxbe v. Washington Post Co., 415
Scalf v. Com., 364, 380
Schechtman v. Foster, 24
Schenck v. United States, 271
Scher v. United States, 281
Schick v. United States, 176, 181
Schilb v. Kuebel, 63
Schita v. King, 156, 219
Schmerber v. California, 265, 348
Schmittler v. State, 226
Schneckloth v. Bustamonte, 151, 300
Schneiderman v. United States, 252
Schuble v. Youngblood, 218
Schwartz v. Texas, 287
Scott, *In re*, 57

Table of Cases / 433

Scott v. United States, 228
Screws v. United States, 40, 77
Sealfon v. United States, 375
Seattle v. Drew, 81
See v. City of Seattle, 273
Segurola v. United States, 300
Serfass v. United States, 364
Seven Cases v. United States, 77
Sewell v. Pegelow, 413
Sgro v. United States, 302
Shadwick v. City of Tampa, 263
Shapiro v. United States, 308, 326
Shaughnessy v. United States *ex rel.* Mezei, 7, 8
Shepherd v. People, 101
Sheppard v. Maxwell, 123
Sherwin v. People, 75
Shields v. United States, 91
Shillitani v. United States, 180
Shipley v. California, 279
Shuttlesworth v. Birmingham, 20, 106
Sibron v. New York, 35, 280
Siebold, *Ex parte,* 144
Silverman v. United States, 284
Silverthorne Lumber Co. v. United States, 270, 292
Simmons v. United States, 300, 371, 372
Simon, *Ex parte,* 147
Simpson v. Florida, 379
Sims v. Balkcom, 388
Sims v. Georgia, 350
Singer v. United States, 182
Six Members' Case, 133
Skinner v. Oklahoma, 250
Slaughter-House Cases, 17
Slochower v. Board of Higher Education of New York City, 313
Smayda v. United States, 285
Smith, *In re,* 228
Smith v. Bennett, 138
Smith v. Hooey, 114
Smith v. Illinois, 97
Smith v. O'Grady, 145, 215
Smith v. Texas, 195, 196, 198
Smith v. United States, 68, 319, 327, 337, 401
Smith v. Warden, 224
Smith v. Wisconsin, 32
Smith v. Yeager, 142
Smotherman v. Beto, 228

Snow, *Ex parte,* 237
Snyder v. Massachusetts, 8, 9, 91, 162, 342
Solesbee v. Balkcom, 93
Sostre v. McGinnis, 414
Sostre v. Rockefeller, 414
Southern Express Co. v. Com. *ex rel.* Walker, 407
Spano v. New York, 345
Sparf v. United States, 172
Specht v. Patterson, 86
Spector v. United States, 57
Spencer v. State, 405
Spencer v. Texas, 16, 93
Spevack v. Klein, 315
Spinelli v. United States, 268
Spock v. District of Columbia, 33
Stack v. Boyle, 50, 51, 58, 60
Staley, *In re,* 248
Stanford v. Texas, 267
Stanley v. Illinois, 250
State v. Anderson, 401
State v. Atkinson, 388, 401
State v. Austin, 369
State v. Baker, 406
State v. Bates, 364
State v. Becker, 400, 405
State v. Bell, 369
State v. Bey, 150
State v. Borst, 217
State v. Bouse, 227
State v. Brannon, 379
State v. Bridges, 403
State v. Browning, 341
State v. Brownridge, 401
State v. Buchanan, 334
State v. Burris, 385
State v. Butchek, 385
State v. Caldwell, 369
State v. Cannon, 396
State v. Carpenter, 411
State v. Cerny, 388
State v. Colcord, 400
State v. Coleman, 388
State v. Cooper, 353
State v. Cripps, 388
State v. Crook, 388
State v. Diamond, 76
State v. Dickerson, 393
State v. Di Paglia, 405
State v. Dixon, 394

State v. Dreher, 229
State v. Driver, 406
State v. Emery, 370
State v. Evjue, 355
State v. Farmer, 355
State v. Farne, 370
State v. Feilen, 397
State v. Felch, 355
State v. Ferguson, 321
State v. Fletcher, 367
State v. Folkes, 341
State v. Forcella, 387
State v. Gardner, 341
State v. Gee, 386
State v. Gillis, 380
State v. Givens, 81
State v. Goetz, 364
State v. Griffin, 385
State v. Gutterman, 174
State v. Harper, 229
State v. Height, 306
State v. Helm, 371-72
State v. Hoa, 377
State v. Hoag, 357
State v. Holton, 364
State v. Howland, 45
State v. James, 402
State v. Jewett, 365
State v. Johnson, 226
State v. Jones, 353, 364
State v. Kasherman, 363
State v. Keefe, 114
State v. Kimbrough, 405
State v. Kisik, 321
State v. Klapprott, 76
State v. Knops, 334
State v. Konigsberg, 54
State v. Koonce, 37
State v. Kremens, 388
State v. Krozel, 218
State v. Kuhnhausen, 113
State v. Laws, 416
State v. Lee, 355, 367
State v. Longley, 202
State v. Menillo, 54
State v. Merchant, 228
State v. Mikesell, 379
State v. Milano, 71
State v. Nance, 405
State v. Nipper, 396

State v. O'Brien, 383
State v. Pace, 202
State v. Parsons, 382
State v. Popolos, 72
State v. Quintana, 400
State v. Rankin, 368
State v. Reynolds, 81, 353
State v. Ross, 406
State v. Rush, 239
State v. Schabert, 47
State v. Schmit, 111
State v. Simpson, 369
State v. Sinclair, 393
State v. Smith, 369, 401
State v. Snyder, 363
State v. Sommers, 363
State v. Sparks, 157
State v. Spiller, 108
State v. Switzer, 380
State v. Talken, 181
State v. Tatman, 371
State v. Taylor, 400
State v. Tomasi, 386
State v. Tune, 219
State v. Tuttle, 416
State v. Vallejos, 242
State v. Waddell, 393
State v. Ward, 234
State v. Wertheimer, 59
State v. White, 369
State v. Witte, 355
State v. Wolfe, 319
State v. Wolski, 233
State v. Wright, 416
State v. Yokum, 363
State v. Zdanowicz, 306
State v. Zukauskas, 341
State ex rel. Argersinger v. Hamlin, 216
State ex rel. Baker v. Utecht, 209
State ex rel. Blouin v. Walker, 403
State ex rel. Drexel v. Alvis, 397
State ex rel. Garvey v. Whitaker, 406
State ex rel. Hunt v. Warden, 361
State ex rel. May v. Boles, 217
State ex rel. Mitchell v. Kelly, 323
State ex rel. Nelson v. Smith, 405
Steele v. United States, 266
Steigler v. State, 388
Stein v. New York, 348
Stephens v. State, 406

Table of Cases / 435

Sterling v. City of Oakland, 33
Stevens v. Marks, 315
Stewart v. State, 228
Stewart v. United States, 316
Stilson v. United States, 187
Stirone v. United States, 74
Stone v. Powell, 159
Stoner v. California, 301
Storti, *In re,* 386
Stoutenburgh v. Frazier, 398
Strauder v. West Virginia, 194
Strobhar v. State, 367
Stroble v. California, 41, 344
Stroud v. United States, 270, 360, 380
Strunk v. United States, 115
Stubbs, *In re,* 368
Sullivan v. Murphy, 34
Sullivan v. State, 393
Sutton v. Settle, 409
Swain v. Alabama, 197
Sweeney v. Woodall, 148, 410
Swenson v. Bosler, 224

Tacoma v. Heater, 218
Takahashi v. United States, 269
Talley v. Stephens, 411
Tanksley v. United States, 110
Tarble's Case, 146, 152
Taylor v. Alabama, 344
Taylor v. Hayes, 179
Taylor v. Louisiana, 20, 106, 186
Taylor v. Taintor, 55
Taylor v. United States, 91, 364
Territory v. Ketchum, 385
Terry, *Ex parte,* 128
Terry v. Ohio, 29, 35, 280
Test Oath Cases, 87
Test v. United States, 197
Testa v. Katt, 16
Tezeno v. State, 392
Thiel v. Southern Pacific Co., 184
Thies v. State, 45
Thomas v. Arizona, 345
Thompson v. Louisville, 20, 105
Thompson v. Missouri, 101
Thompson v. United States, 371
Thompson v. Utah, 101
Tollett v. Henderson, 148, 231
Tomkins v. Missouri, 214
Tot v. United States, 106-7

Toth v. Quarles, 165
Toussie v. United States, 112
Townsend v. Burke, 215, 223
Townsend v. Sain, 345
Travelers Health Assoc. v. Virginia, 109
Tremble v. Stone, 50
Tritico v. United States, 380
Trono v. United States, 380
Trop v. Dulles, 385, 387, 399
Trupiano v. United States, 30, 279
Tucker v. Howard, 213
Tumey v. Ohio, 117
Turner v. Arkansas, 379
Turner v. Fouche, 194, 195
Turner v. Louisiana, 175
Turner v. Pennsylvania, 344
Turner v. United States, 107
Twining v. New Jersey, 18, 320, 356

Ullman, *In re,* 330
Ullmann v. United States, 330
United Press Associations v. Valente, 111
United States v. Adams, 375
United States v. Ash, 222
United States v. Ball, 356, 364, 369
United States v. Bandy, 51
United States v. Barnett, 178
United States v. Bayer, 345, 376
United States v. Behrens, 91
United States v. Berkeness, 267
United States v. Berrigan, 206
United States v. Billy Joe Wade, 221
United States v. Biswell, 276
United States v. Brown, 270
United States v. Brunett, 268
United States v. Bryan, 325
United States v. Buntin, 40
United States v. Burr, 121, 187, 306
United States v. Calandra, 297
United States v. Candelaria, 357, 365
United States v. Capson, 253
United States v. Cardiff, 76
United States v. Carignan, 348
United States v. Charles, 269
United States v. Clark, 368
United States v. Cohen Grocery Co., 75, 79
United States v. Collins, 400
United States v. Coplon, 95
United States v. Culp, 248
United States v. Davis, 229

436 / Table of Cases

United States v. Dawson, 200, 400
United States v. Debrow, 71
United States v. Dewinsky, 103
United States v. Dionisio, 271, 317
United States v. DiRe, 36, 38, 282
United States v. Douglas, 94
United States v. Edwards, 279
United States v. Evans, 368
United States v. Ewell, 112
United States v. Field, 56
United States v. Figueroa, 60
United States v. Fischer, 252
United States v. Fitzgerald, 45
United States v. Fox, 309
United States v. Freed, 310
United States v. Furlong, 367
United States v. Gainey, 107
United States v. Giles, 371
United States v. Gilligan, 233
United States v. Gutterman, 218
United States v. Hale, 340
United States v. Hall, 100
United States v. Hammonds, 228
United States v. Harris, 267
United States v. Hartenfeld, 219
United States v. Hayman, 148
United States v. Helwig, 219
United States v. Hill, 114
United States v. Hoffman, 418
United States v. Holman, 402
United States v. Hood, 77
United States v. Huff, 248
United States v. Hunter, 248
United States v. Jackson, 163, 252, 416
United States v. Jeffers, 299
United States v. Jenkins, 362
United States v. Johnson, 200
United States v. Jones, 369, 397
United States v. Jorn, 354, 373
United States v. Kahn, 289
United States v. Kahriger, 309
United States v. Kalish, 35
United States v. Kellerman, 401
United States v. Kobli, 109
United States v. Krulewitch, 95
United States v. La Franca, 362
United States v. Lanza, 365
United States v. Lattimore, 72–73
United States v. Lee, 281
United States v. Lefkowitz, 277

United States v. Lovett, 87, 88
United States v. McCunn, 371
United States v. McFarlane, 248–49
United States v. McLeod, 35
United States v. McMahan, 248
United States v. McWilliams, 113
United States v. Mara, 271
United States v. Marion, 29, 115
United States v. Martell, 416
United States v. Michener, 375
United States v. Mitchell, 341
United States v. Monia, 327
United States v. Montgomery, 372
United States v. Moreland, 69
United States v. Mule, 57
United States v. Murdock, 323, 324
United States v. National Assoc. of Real Estate Boards, 377
United States v. National Dairy Products Corp., 79
United States v. Nelson, 319
United States v. Nimerick, 103
United States v. Nugent, 15
United States v. Oppenheimer, 378
United States v. Pardue, 416
United States v. Parker, 248
United States v. Peltier, 283
United States v. Perez, 370
United States v. Petrillo, 77
United States v. Plattner, 226
United States v. Potash, 371
United States v. Provoo, 113
United States v. Rabinowitz, 278, 279
United States v. Raudenbush, 377
United States v. Regan, 180
United States v. Robinson, 283
United States v. Rogoff, 372
United States v. Romano, 107
United States v. Rosenberg, 387
United States v. Sanges, 368
United States v. Seltzer, 269
United States v. Sing Tuck, 147
United States v. Smith, 173, 253
United States v. Spector, 77
United States v. Stone, 40
United States v. Stromberg, 252
United States v. Sullivan, 309
United States v. Tempia, 249
United States v. Trans-Missouri Freight Association, 102

Table of Cases / 437

United States v. Ullmann, 330
United States v. U.S. Coin and Currency, 309
United States v. U.S. District Court, 289
United States v. VanLeeuwen, 270
United States v. Ventresca, 266
United States v. Vuitch, 79
United States v. Walker, 416
United States v. Weissman, 405
United States v. Weller, 253
United States v. Wezel, 252
United States v. White, 271, 288, 308
United States v. Williams, 376
United States v. Willis, 253
United States v. Wilson, 54, 129, 292, 361
United States v. Wood, 190
United States v. Wurzbach, 77
United States v. Young, 181
United States v. Zucker, 181
U.S. *ex rel.* Bongiorno v. Ragen, 400
U.S. *ex rel.* Bruno v. Herold, 110
U.S. *ex rel.* Caminito v. Murphy, 344
U.S. *ex rel.* Clark v. Zelker, 400
U.S. *ex rel.* Cleggett v. Pate, 414
U.S. *ex rel.* Darcy v. Handy, 120, 123
U.S. *ex rel.* Feeley v. Ragen, 225
U.S. *ex rel.* Gardner v. Madden, 249
U.S. *ex rel.* Hirschberg v. Cooke, 154
U.S. *ex rel.* Innes v. Hiatt, 156
U.S. *ex rel.* Knight v. Ragen, 411, 414
U.S. *ex rel.* Maldonado v. Denno, 226
U.S. *ex rel.* Marcus v. Hess, 353, 376
U.S. *ex rel.* Milwaukee Social Democratic Publishing Co. v. Burleson, 407
U.S. *ex rel.* Mitchell v. Thompson, 226
U.S. *ex rel.* Nortner v. Hiatt, 236
U.S. *ex rel.* Pope v. Henricks, 414
U.S. *ex rel.* Rubenstein v. Mulcahy, 60
U.S. *ex rel.* Rutz v. Levy, 364
U.S. *ex rel.* Swanson v. Reincke, 403
U.S. *ex rel.* Toth v. Quarles, 154
U.S. *ex rel.* Turner v. Williams, 181
U.S. *ex rel.* Verde v. Case, 414
U.S. *ex rel.* Williams v. Brierley, 228
Upshaw v. United States, 47, 341
Urbasek, *In re,* 90
Uveges v. Pennsylvania, 215

Vale v. Louisiana, 279
Vallandingham, *Ex parte,* 152, 246
Vann v. Scott, 416
Various Items of Personal Property v. United States, 362
Viereck v. United States, 126, 174
Virginia, *Ex parte,* 193
Vlandis v. Kline, 107
Voll, *Ex parte,* 55
Von Cleef v. New Jersey, 278
Von Moltke v. Gillies, 236

Wade v. Hunter, 373
Wade v. Mayo, 145, 148, 215, 246
Wagers v. Sizemore, 118
Wainwright v. New Orleans, 36
Wainwright v. Stone, 79
Wales v. Whitney, 135
Waley v. Johnston, 144
Walker v. Johnston, 144, 151, 235
Walker v. Sauvinet, 166
Walker v. State, 209, 401
Walker v. Wainright, 136
Walleck v. Hudspeth, 219
Waller v. Florida, 367
Walmer v. Tittenmore, 136
Walter v. State, 185
Walton v. Arkansas, 222
Ward v. Texas, 343
Ward v. Village of Monroeville, 117-18
Warden v. Hayden, 264-65
Wardius v. Oregon, 126
Ware v. Estes, 396
Warszower v. United States, 337
Washington v. Rodriguez, 401
Washington v. Texas, 19, 98, 325
Waters-Pierce Oil Co. v. Texas, 407, 408
Watkins, *Ex parte,* 142, 398
Watson v. United States, 403
Watts v. Indiana, 344, 346
Webb v. Texas, 98
Weber v. Com., 400, 404
Weeks v. United States, 40, 292
Weems v. United States, 398
Weisberg v. Village, 33
Weiss v. United States, 287
Weller v. Dickson, 249
West Coast Hotel Co. v. Parrish, 8
Western & Atlantic R. Co. v. Henderson, 106
Wheeler v. Goodman, 12, 81
Wheeler v. United States, 402

Whelchel v. McDonald, 155
White v. Maryland, 222
White v. Ragen, 124, 125
White v. Texas, 343
White v. United States, 57
Whiteley v. Warden of Wyoming Penitentiary, 30
Whitley v. Cunningham, 209
Whitus v. Georgia, 196
Wieman v. Updegraff, 314
Wilkerson v. Utah, 386
Williams v. Beto, 227, 228, 229
Williams v. Com., 388
Williams v. Florida, 166-67, 317
Williams v. Huff, 236
Williams v. Illinois, 407
Williams v. Kaiser, 214
Williams v. New York, 92-93
Williams v. Oklahoma, 360
Williams v. United States, 279
Williamson v. Lee Optical Co., 7
Williamson v. United States, 57
Wilson, *Ex parte,* 68
Wilson v. Rose, 229
Wilson v. Schnettler, 261
Wilson v. State, 183
Wilson v. United States, 308, 320, 332
Wilwording v. Swenson, 415
Wingo v. Wedding, 152, 235
Winship, *In re,* 90-91, 103-4

Winters v. New York, 76, 77
Wisconsin v. Constantineau, 84
Wise v. Mills, 292
Witherspoon v. Illinois, 192
Witmer v. United States, 156
Wolf v. Colorado, 260, 294, 298
Wolff v. McDonnell, 415
Wong Doo v. United States, 141
Wong Sun v. United States, 31
Wong Wing v. United States, 69
Wood v. United States, 222
Woods v. Nierstheimer, 245
Woodson v. North Carolina, 420
Woolmington v. D.P.P., 3, 102
Workman v. Com. of Kentucky, 406
Worthington v. United States, 255
Wright v. Georgia, 80
Wright v. McMann, 414
Wyman v. James, 274-75

Yamashita, *In re,* 154
Yates v. United States, 363
Yerger, *Ex parte,* 131
Yick Wo v. Hopkins, 144
Young v. Ragen, 149, 246

Zakonaite v. Wolf, 181
Zap v. United States, 269, 301, 302
Zasada v. State, 219
Zimmerman, *Ex parte,* 159

Index

Accusation, 67–71; seriousness of, 5; by grand juries, 67; by information, 68; right to a specific accusation, 71–75
Ad deliberandum et recipiendum, writ of, 132
Administrative searches, 272–77
Ad prosequendum, writ of, 132
Ad respondendum, writ of, 132
Ad subjiciendum et recipiendum, writ of, 132
Ad testificandum, writ of, 132
Anti-Narcotics Act of 1914, 107
Appeal by the state, 368
Arnold, Thurman: on significance of a criminal trial, 10
Arrests, 25–42; nature of, 28–30; by private persons, 29; by peace officers, 29; warrant of, 30; without warrant, 30; for felonies, 30; for misdemeanors, 30–31; and probable cause, 31–32; reform of law of, 32–33; expungement of records of, 33–35; right to resist, 36–39; remedies for illegal arrests, 39–42; search incidental to arrest, 277–81; stop-and-frisk, 280–81

Bail, 49–65; historical origins of, 49–50; reasons for, 50–52; present rules of, 52–55; forfeiture of, 55–56; and the judge's discretion, 56–60; excessive bail, 58–60; remedies, 60–64; bail bond racket, 60–61; and preventive detention, 64–65
Bail Reform Act of 1966, 52–54
Bank Secrecy Act of 1970, 276
Bazelon, David L., Judge: on effective assistance of counsel, 225, 230
Bennett, James V.: on public defenders, 241
Bill of Rights of 1689: and bail, 49; and punishments, 383, 408
Bills of attainder, 86–87

Black, Hugo L., Justice: on construction of Bill of Rights, 18; on grand jury procedure, 70; on notice of specific charges, 74; on statutory vagueness, 77; on bills of attainder, 87; on exclusion of defendant from courtroom for disruptive behavior, 92; on use of out-of-court sources, 93; on statutes of limitations, 111–12; on the right to an unbiased judge, 119; on indigent defendants, 125; on habeas corpus, 144; on jury trial, 163; on jury trial in contempt cases, 178; on jury impartiality, 191; on right to counsel in noncapital cases, 215–16; on the meaning of incrimination, 312, 317, 318, 319, 321, 331; on coerced confessions, 343, 347; on double jeopardy, 353, 357, 358, 366, 373, 381; on the death penalty, 389; on cruel and unusual punishments, 404
Blackmun, Harry A., Justice: on professional bail bondsmen, 63; on justice for juveniles, 90–91; on welfare searches, 274; on corporal punishment, 397
Blackstone, Sir William: on bail, 49; on habeas corpus, 131; on double jeopardy, 353; on punishments, 384
Blatchford, Samuel, Justice: on the privilege against self-incrimination, 307
"Blue-ribbon" juries, 198–200
Bok, Curtis, Judge: on due process, 6
Bradley, Joseph P., Justice: on searches and seizures, 261
Brandeis, Louis D., Justice: on procedure, 8; on governmental lawlessness, 22; on the right to privacy, 254; on search and seizure by private parties, 259; on wiretapping, 286; on double jeopardy, 375
Brennan, William J., Jr., Justice: on value of the preliminary hearing, 46; on justice for

439

Brennan, William J., Jr. (*cont.*)
  juveniles, 90; on exclusion of disorderly defendants from courtroom, 92; on the right of accused to inspect government documents, 96; on the right to an unbiased judge, 118; on habeas corpus, 140, 149; on right to counsel at pretrial lineup, 221; on the right of privacy, 255; on the "mere evidence" rule, 264–65; on the exclusionary rule, 297; on remedies for unreasonable searches and seizures, 298; on the privilege against self-incrimination, 310, 322; on double jeopardy, 366; on the death penalty, 389, 391
Bridges, Harry: proceedings against, 71
Burden of proof: views of Justice Frankfurter, 3–4; in juvenile proceedings, 90–91, 103; general principles of, 102–5
Burger, Warren E., Chief Justice: on justice as a state function, 21; on diversity in law enforcement, 23; on the exclusionary rule, 24, 296–97; on the contempt power, 129; on jury trial, 163; on plea bargaining, 232–33; on self-incrimination, 317; on the *Miranda* rules, 340; on double jeopardy, 364; on the death penalty, 391–92

Camden, Lord: on general search warrants, 257–58
Campbell, William J., Judge: on abolition of grand juries, 70
Cardozo, Benjamin N., Justice: on citizen assistance in arrests, 29; on right to be present at the trial, 91; on search incidental to arrest, 277; on double jeopardy, 354
Casper, Jonathan D.: on treatment of the guilty, 10
Chafee, Zechariah, Jr.: on habeas corpus, 131
Challenges for jury service, peremptory and for cause, 187–88
Chase, Salmon P., Chief Justice: on habeas corpus, 131
Chase, Samuel, Justice: on the *ex post facto* clauses, 99–100
Chatham, Lord: on the privacy of the home, 256
Civil Rights Act of 1866, 40
Civil Rights Act of 1871, 412
Civil Rights Act of 1957, 178
Civil Rights Act of 1964, 178
Civil Rights Congress Bail Fund, 56
Clark, Charles E., Judge: on self-incrimination, 330
Clark, Tom C., Justice: on vague statutes, 77; on pretrial publicity, 122; on the exclusionary rule, 294–95; on the meaning of incrimination, 314–15; on the corroboration rule for confessions, 337; on confessions and coercion, 347; on double jeopardy, 360
Clayton Act, 177
Coke, Lord: on the right to an unbiased judge, 116
Comment: and self-incrimination, 319–22
Common law, principles regarding criminal justice, 3
Competence to stand trial, 73–74
Compulsory process to secure witnesses, 98
Confessions: how different from self-incrimination, 336; problem of, 336–51; and the *Miranda* rules, 338–40; and unlawful detention, 340–42; and the issue of coercion, 342–51
Confessions and torture, 12
Confrontation: right of, 94–98; waiver of right of, 96–97
Contempt of court procedure, 127–30
Counsel: right to, 208–53; growth of the right, 208–10; scope of the right, 210–18; effective representation by, 218–25; competence of, 225–31; and plea bargaining, 231–35; waiver of right to, 235–38; question of compensation of, 238–43; and representation of unpopular defendants, 243; remedies for denial of right to, 243–46; right to, in military justice, 246–49; right to, in noncriminal cases, 249–53
Crime, definition of, 4
Crime Control Act of 1968, 342
Criminal contempt and right to trial by jury, 177–80
Criminal Justice Act of 1964, 240
Cruel and unusual punishments, 383–420; the constitutional rule, 383–84; scope of the guaranty, 384–85; the death penalty, 385–95, 419–20; other forms of punishment, 395–98; the issue of severity, 398–

Cruel and unusual punishments (*cont.*) 407; fines and penalties, 407; treatment of prisoners, 409-16; reduction of sentences, 416-18

Davis, David, Justice: on the suspension of constitutional rights, 14
Davis, Jefferson: and bail, 58
Davis, Kenneth Culp: on police discretion, 26
Day, William R., Justice: on the exclusionary rules, 292
Death penalty, 385-95, 419-20
De Homine Replegiando, writ of, 132
De Manucaptione, writ of, 132
De Otio et Atia, writ of, 132
De Tocqueville, Alexis: on the advantages of trial by jury, 205
District of Columbia Court Reform and Criminal Procedure Act, 64
Double jeopardy, 352-82; nature of the right, 352-54; nationalization of the concept, 354-57; scope of the right, 357-63; when does jeopardy attach?, 363-64; offenses against two sovereigns, 365-68; right of the government to appeal, 368; some exceptions to the general rule of double jeopardy, 369-70; termination of proceedings, 370-75; closely related offenses, 375-79; included offenses, 379-82
Douglas, William O., Justice: on procedural rights, 6-7; on due process, 7; on construction of Bill of Rights, 18; on arrest warrants, 31; on prosecution of lawless police, 40; on bail, 56-57; on vague statutes, 76, 80; on suppression of evidence by the prosecution, 125; on jury trial, 163; on jury representativeness, 185; on right to counsel, 214; on right to counsel in misdemeanor cases, 216-17; on plea bargaining, 231; on use of unlawful evidence, 260-61; on the "mere evidence" rule, 265; on administrative searches, 272-73, 276; on welfare searches, 275; on stop-and-frisk, 280; on wiretapping, 289; on the Fourth Amendment, 302; on the privilege against compulsory self-incrimination, 306, 307, 308, 315, 317, 321, 328, 331; on the newsman's privilege, 335; on the voluntariness of confessions, 347; on double jeopardy, 358, 376; on the death penalty, 389, 391; on interstate rendition of prisoners, 411
Dudley, Joseph, Judge: on refusal of writ of habeas corpus, 134
Due process: centrality of, 6-9; as a flexible concept, 13; expansion of, 18-21

Eisenhower, Dwight D.: on justice and fair play, 15; on taking the privilege against self-incrimination, 333
Electronic surveillance, 284-92
Emergency Price Control Act, 29
Enforcement Act of 1970, 40
Entick, John: and general warrants, 257
Equal justice, right to, 10-15
Exclusionary rule, 292-97; views of Chief Justice Burger, 24
Ex post facto rule, 99-102
Expungement of arrest records, 33-35

Fair hearing, right to, 84-129; in the federal context, 84-86; right to a trial, 86-89; juvenile delinquency proceedings, 89-91; right to be present at the trial, 91-92; the necessity to present evidence in court, 92-94; right of confrontation, 94-98; compulsory process to secure witnesses, 98; the *ex post facto* rules, 99-102; the burden of proof, 102-5; the no-evidence rules, 105-6; statutory presumptions of guilt, 106-8; jurisdiction, 108-9; right to a public trial, 109-11; right to a speedy trial, 111-16; right to an unbiased judge, 116-19; freedom from mob domination, 119-20; pretrial publicity, 121-24; knowing use of perjured testimony by the prosecution, 124-27; prosecution and the boundaries of propriety, 126-27; contempt procedure, 127-30
Fair Labor Standards Act, 256, 334
Federal Communications Act, 286, 287, 290
Federal Criminal Justice Act of 1964, 230
Federal Firearms Act of 1938, 106
Federalism: and the problems of criminal justice, 15-21; and the right to a fair hearing, 80-84; and self-incrimination, 322-24; and double jeopardy, 354-57, 365-68; and cruel and unusual punishments, 408-9

Federal Kidnaping Act, 163
Federal Magistrates Act, 47
Federal Rules of Criminal Procedure: Rule 5 (initial appearance before the magistrate), 47–48, 337; Rule 7 (the indictment and the information), 68, 71; Rule 11 (pleas), 233; Rule 23 (trial by jury or by the court), 166, 182; Rule 24 (trial jurors), 187; Rule 26 (evidence), 94; Rule 31 (verdict), 168–69; Rule 41 (search and seizure), 262, 264, 266, 298; Rule 42 (criminal contempt), 127–29, 177; Rule 43 (presence of the defendant), 91; Rule 44 (right to and assignment of counsel), 211, 235; Rule 46 (release from custody), 52–54; Rule 48 (dismissal), 71, 112, 168
Field, Stephen J., Justice: on the due process right to notice and a hearing, 84; on taking the privilege against self-incrimination, 332
Fines and penalties, 407
Fleming, Macklin: on perfectionism in criminal law, 24
Fortas, Abe, Justice: on justice for juveniles, 89–90; on the writ of habeas corpus, 135–36, 139, 146; on the "mere evidence" rule, 265
Fourteenth Amendment, adoption of, 17
Fourth and Fifth Amendments, relations with each other, 261–62
Frank, Jerome, Judge: on immunity from self-incrimination, 330; on the death penalty, 387–88
Frankfurter, Felix, Justice: on the American criminal justice system, 3; on due process, 13; on fair procedures and security, 15; on the Bill of Rights, 22; on vague statutes, 77; on the presumption of innocence, 103; on pretrial publicity, 122; on the contempt power, 128; on waiver of jury trial, 182–83; on the "silver platter" doctrine, 260; on the limits of the right of search, 269; on administrative searches, 272; on the exclusionary rule, 293; on standing to challenge illegal searches, 299; on the privilege against self-incrimination, 308, 330; on the voluntariness of confession, 344, 346, 347; on double jeopardy, 353, 366, 374; on interstate rendition of prisoners, 410

Fuller, Melville W., Chief Justice: on the death penalty, 386, 387

Gambler's Occupational Tax Act of 1951, 309
Goldberg, Arthur J., Justice: on the American bail system, 61–62; on assistance of counsel, 220; on probable cause for search warrants, 267; on scope of the privilege against self-incrimination, 324; on the death penalty, 386, 388
Goldfarb, Ronald: on the bail system, 62
Goodman, Louis E., Judge: on habeas corpus, 150
Grand juries, use of, 67–71
Gray, Horace, Justice: on bail, 50–51
Griswold, Erwin N.: on the privilege against self-incrimination, 306
Guilt by association, 4
Gun Control Act of 1968, 276

Habeas corpus, writ of, 131–59; significance of, 131; English origins of, 131–34; American origins, 134–35; uses of, 135–40; and appeal, 140–42; expansion of, 142–46; some limiting factors, 146–52; and military detention, 152–56; suspension of, 156–59
Habeas Corpus Act of 1679, 133–34, 142
Hall, Jerome: on police lawlessness, 42
Hand, Learned, Judge: on right to resist arrest, 37; on disclosure of evidence to the accused, 95
Harlan, John M., Justice, 1877–1911: on the Fourteenth Amendment, 18; on the contempt power, 128; on judge's supervisory responsibility, 172
Harlan, John Marshall, Justice, 1955–71: on federal control of state rules of criminal procedure, 16; on jury trial, 162; on jury size, 167; on jury trial in civil cases, 181; on the exclusionary rule, 295; on use of testimony on standing, 300; on the privilege against self-incrimination, 310, 322; on double jeopardy, 358, 377; on the death penalty, 389; on cruel and unusual punishments, 404
Harrison Narcotics Act, 190
Hobbs Act, 74
Holdsworth, William S.: on magistrates and

Holdsworth, William S. (*cont.*)
  police, 43; on habeas corpus, 131; on the merits of trial by jury, 205
Holmes, Oliver Wendell, Justice: on governmental lawlessness, 22; on presumptions in the law, 107; on freedom from mob domination, 120; on pretrial publicity, 121; on habeas corpus, 147; on search and seizure by private parties, 259; on wiretapping, 285-86; on the exclusionary rule, 293
Hoover, J. Edgar: on protecting the individual, 15
Hughes, Charles E., Chief Justice: on federal review of state courts, 20; on habeas corpus, 131, 143; on the role of the judge in relation to the jury, 173; on jury impartiality, 190; on exclusion of Negroes from jury service, 194-96; on search warrant law, 302; on the citizen's duty to testify, 324-25; on coerced confessions, 342-43

Immunity Act of 1954, 330
Immunity and self-incrimination, 324-31
Incrimination, meaning of, 311-17
Internal Security Act of 1950, 83
Interstate Commission on Crime, 32
Irvin, Sam, Jr.: on preventive detention, 64

Jackson, Robert H., Justice: on importance of procedure, 7, 8; on right to resist arrest, 36; on submission to arrest, 38; on right to bail, 51; on federal review of state legislation, 86; on military habeas corpus, 156; on jury selection, 190-91; on "blue-ribbon" juries, 198; on searches and seizures, 255; on the underlying rationale of the Fourth Amendment, 263; on the exclusionary rule, 292; on the voluntariness of confessions, 344
Jefferson, Thomas: on suspension of habeas corpus, 157
Jenkes, Francis: and habeas corpus, 133
Johnson, Lyndon B.: on crime as a local matter, 21; on bail reform, 54
Johnson, Samuel: on habeas corpus, 131
Judiciary Act of 1789, 135, 178, 201, 210
Judiciary Act of 1867, 143
Jurisdiction, requirement of, 108-9

Jury Selection Act of 1968, 183
Jury service for women, 185-86; general eligibility rules, 188; eligibility of government employees, 189-91
Jury trial, 160-207; constitutional origins, 160-65; right as binding on the states, 162-63; requirement of twelve members, 165-68; requirement of unanimity, 168-72; judge's supervisory responsibility, 172-75; scope of right to, in federal courts, 175-81; waiver of right to, 181-83; jury representativeness, 183-86; jury impartiality, 187-93; exclusion of Negroes from jury service, 193-98; the "blue-ribbon" jury, 198-200; trial by a local jury, 200-202; merits of trial by jury, 202-7
Juvenile delinquency proceedings, 89-91

Ku Klux Klan Act of 1871, 158

Lattimore, Owen: and the right to specific charges, 73
Lilburne, "Freeborn John": and self-incrimination, 305
Lincoln, Abraham: on suspension of habeas corpus, 157

McAllister, Thomas F., Judge: on the right of privacy, 255
McKenna, Joseph, Justice: on cruel and unusual punishments, 398
Magna Carta, 112, 131, 304, 382
Magruder, Calvert, Judge: on taking the privilege against self-incrimination, 332
Maitland, Frederic W.: on bail, 49
Manhattan Bail Project, 62
Mansfield, Lord: on jury impartiality, 187
Marijuana Tax Act, 310
Marshall, John, Chief Justice: on impartial jurors, 121; on habeas corpus, 142; on jury impartiality, 187
Marshall, Thurgood, Justice: on jury size, 167; on the privilege against self-incrimination, 328; on double jeopardy, 356, 358, 360, 361; on the death penalty, 389, 391; on cruel and unusual punishments, 404
"Mere evidence" rule on searches and seizures, 264

Merriam, Charles E., 3
Military detention: problem of, 152–56; and right to habeas corpus, 153
Military justice: right to counsel, 246–49
Minton, Sherman, Justice: on jury tampering, 174; on unreasonable searches, 256
Miranda rules, 220–21, 236–37, 300, 338–40, 350–51
Mob domination, freedom from, 119–20
Model Penal Code, 36, 37
Models of the criminal process, 21–24
Moley, Raymond: on merits of prosecution by information, 69
Moody, William H., Justice: on the privilege against compulsory self-incrimination, 320–21
Murphy, Frank, Justice: on arrest procedure, 30; on jury representativeness, 183; on "blue-ribbon" juries, 199–200; on search incidental to arrest, 278; on suits for damages for illegal searches, 298
Murphy, Michael: on the imbalance in law enforcement, 23

National Advisory Commission on Civil Disorders, 27
National Commission on Law Observance and Enforcement (Wickersham), 203
National Commission on Reform of Federal Criminal Laws, 389
National Labor Relations Act, 334
National Prohibition Act, 362, 365
National Stolen Property Act, 278
Negroes and jury service, 193–98
No-evidence rule, 105–6
Norris–La Guardia Act of 1932, 177
Northwest Ordinance, 135
Notice, right to, 66–83; and the accusation, 67–71; right to a specific accusation, 71–75; in noncriminal cases, 74–75; and the void-for-vagueness rule, 75–82; notice of what?, 82–83

Oaks, D. H.: on the exclusionary rule, 296
O'Meara, Joseph: on equality of rights, 11
Omnibus Crime Control and Safe Streets Act of 1968, 21, 289
Organized Crime Control Act of 1970, 327

Packer, Herbert L.: on crime control models, 21–22

Perjured testimony, knowing use of by the prosecution, 124–27
Petition of Right of 1627, 133, 304
Petty offenses and the right to trial by jury, 176–77
Pitney, Mahlon, Justice: on federal review of state courts, 120
Plea bargaining, 231–35
Police: number of, 25; problems of, 25–26; discretion of, 26; lawlessness of, 27–28; limited powers of, 35; right to resist, 36–39; and use of force, 38–39
Police power, abuses of, 9–10
Pollock, Frederick: on bail, 49
Pound, Cuthbert, Judge: on equality of rights, 11
Powell, Lewis F., Jr., Justice: on pretrial confinement, 43–44; on habeas corpus, 151; on jury unanimity, 171; on the exclusionary rule, 297; on the privilege against self-incrimination, 307, 327–28; on double jeopardy, 359, 360; on the death penalty, 392
Preliminary hearing, 42–49; legal basis for, 42–44; purpose of, 44–45; value of, 45–46; waiver of, 46; required procedure for, 47–49; right to counsel at, 222
President's Commission on Law Enforcement and Administration of Justice: on lawlessness, 12, 234, 386; on size of police forces, 25
President's Committee on Civil Rights, 28, 42
Presumption of innocence, 102–5
Pretrial publicity and a fair trial, 121–24
Preventive detention, 64–65
Price Control Act, 308
Prisoners, treatment of, 409–16
Privacy, rights of, 12, 254–56
Privileged communications, 331–36; newsman's privilege, 334–36
Probation, right to counsel, 224
Procedure, importance of, 3–24
Prosecution and the boundaries of propriety, 126–27
Public defenders, 240–42
Public trial, right to, 109–11

Radin, Max: on the right to a public trial, 110

Recoupment of costs of appointed counsel, 242–43
Reed, Stanley F., Justice: on double jeopardy, 354–55; on the death penalty, 387; on cruel and unusual punishments, 408
Rehnquist, William H., Justice: on standards in military justice, 79; on right to counsel for discretionary appeals, 224; on search of automobiles, 283; on double jeopardy, 372; on the death penalty, 392
Remington, William W.: proceedings against, 71
Roberts, Owen J., Justice: on unreasonable presumptions, 107; on the right to counsel in state courts, 213
Robinson-Patman Act, 79
Rutledge, Wiley B., Justice: on importance of historic rights, 11; on jury selection, 190; on postconviction remedies, 245–46; on search of automobiles, 282

Santarelli, Donald E.: on the exclusionary rule, 295–96
Schaefer, Walter V., Illinois Justice: on importance of the right to counsel, 208
Schweitzer, Louis: on bail reform, 62
Searches and seizures, 254–303; rights of privacy, 254–56; historical origins, 256–59; search and seizure by private parties, 259–61; relation of Fourth to Fifth Amendments, 261–62; the search warrant, 262–69; scope of the guaranty, 269–72; administrative searches, 272–77; search without warrants incident to arrest, 277–81; search of automobiles without warrant, 281–84; electronic surveillance, 284–92; exclusionary rule, 292–97; remedies, 298–300; waiver, 300–302; conclusions, 302–3
Self-incrimination, 304–51; historical roots, 304–6; scope of the privilege, 306–11; how the privilege is pleaded, 311; what is incrimination?, 311–17; waiver, 317–19; the issue of comment, 319–22; self-incrimination and federalism, 322–24; the problem of immunity, 324–31; the problem of motive, 331–33; other privileged communications, 331–36; the problem of confessions, 336–51
Sentences, reduction of, 416–18

Sherman Anti-Trust Act, 77, 334, 376
"Silver platter" doctrine on searches and seizures, 260
Smith Act, 310, 312, 332
Soboleff, Simon E., Judge: on appeals from sentence, 417–18
Speedy trial, right to, 111–16
Speedy Trial Act of 1974, 112
Spencer, Herbert: on the merits of trial by jury, 203
Star Chamber, 3, 133, 256, 304
State appellate court decisions, federal review of, 17–18
State prisoners and the right to federal habeas corpus, 148–52
Statutes of limitations, 111
Statutory presumptions of guilt, 106–8
Stephen, Sir James Fitzjames: on early ritualistic proofs of guilt, 66–67; on self-incrimination, 333
Stewart, Potter, Justice: on judicial integrity, 23; on vague statutes, 81; on jury trial, 162, 163; on jury selection, 193; on searches and seizures, 260; on electronic eavesdropping, 288; on waiver of Fourth Amendment rights, 301; on self-incrimination, 321; on the newsman's privilege, 335; on double jeopardy, 378; on the death penalty, 391
Stone, Harlan F., Chief Justice: on the specificity of criminal charges, 73; on probable cause for search warrants, 266
Stop-and-frisk, 280–81
Story, Joseph, Justice: on double jeopardy, 370
Strafford, Earl of, attaint of, 87
Subversive Activities Control Act, 310
Sutherland, George, Justice: on the sufficiency of the indictment, 72; on meaning of trial by jury, 165; on the function of the prosecutor, 174; on the right to counsel, 210, 225

Taft, William H., Chief Justice: on the right to an unbiased judge, 117; on search of automobiles, 281; on wiretapping, 285; on double jeopardy, 365
Taney, Roger B., Chief Justice: on suspension of habeas corpus, 158
Trial, right to, 86–89; in civil cases, 88; in

Trial, right to (*cont.*)
petty criminal cases, 88–89; right to a public trial, 109–11; right to a speedy trial, 111–16
Truman, Harry S.: on the distinction between opinions and crimes, 83; on duty to represent unpopular defendants, 243
Tweed, William M., "Boss": and bail, 58

Unbiased judge, right to, 116–19
Uniform Arrest Act, 32–33, 35, 36, 37
Uniform Code of Military Justice, 78–79, 152–53, 155, 164, 247
Universal Declaration of Human Rights, 384

Vanderbilt, Arthur T., Judge: on right to a fair trial, 5
Vera Foundation, 51, 62
Vicinage and jury trial, 200–202
Vinson, Fred M., Chief Justice: on right to bail, 50; on excessive bail, 58; on military habeas corpus, 155; on the privilege against compulsory self-incrimination, 318; on double jeopardy, 374
Void-for-vagueness rule, 75–82
Voir dire examination, 187

Waite, J. O., Judge: on prosecutorial propriety, 127
Waite, Morrison R., Chief Justice: on pretrial publicity, 121; on jury impartiality, 188
Warrants: of arrest, 30; general warrants, 256–59; requirements for search warrants, 262–69
Warren, Earl, Chief Justice: on right to resist arrest, 36; on informing juries of prior convictions, 93; on habeas corpus, 136; on right to trial by jury, 182; on discrimination in selecting jurors, 198; on the *Miranda* rules, 236–37; on military justice, 247; on the "mere evidence" rule, 265; on stop-and-frisk, 280–81; on pleading the privilege against self-incrimination, 311; on cruel and unusual punishments, 385, 399; on the death penalty, 387
Warren, Samuel D.: on the right to privacy, 254
Washington, Bushrod, Justice: on the *ex post facto* rule, 100
Webster, Daniel: on the law of the land, 84
Welfare visits as searches, 274–75
White, Byron R., Justice: on the crippling of law enforcement, 23; on the nature of an arrest, 28–29; on the vagueness doctrine, 81–82; on the right to a speedy trial, 112; on jury trial, 162; on jury size, 166–67; on makeup of juries, 197; on administrative searches, 273; on self-incrimination, 321; on the newsman's privilege, 334–35; on confessions, 349; on double jeopardy, 358; on the death penalty, 391
White, Edward D., Chief Justice: on vague statutes, 76
Wigmore, John H.: on the laws of evidence, 5; on the right of cross-examination, 6; on the presumption of innocence, 102–3; on the merits of trial by jury, 204; on the exclusionary rule, 293; on the meaning of incrimination, 312, 320, 325
Wilkes, John: and general search warrants, 257
Wiretapping, 285–92
Wright, Donald R., California Chief Justice: on the death penalty, 390
Wright, J. Skelly, Judge: on professional bail bondsmen, 62

Youngdahl, Luther W., Judge: on specificity of charges, 72–73

DESIGNED BY TED SMITH/GRAPHICS
COMPOSED BY FOX VALLEY TYPESETTING, MENASHA, WISCONSIN
MANUFACTURED BY CUSHING MALLOY, INC., ANN ARBOR, MICHIGAN
TEXT IS SET IN TIMES ROMAN, DISPLAY LINES IN BODONI

Library of Congress Cataloging in Publication Data
Fellman, David, 1907-
The defendant's rights today.
Includes bibliographical references and index.
1. Criminal procedure—United States. I. Title.
KF9625.F44   1976   345'.73'056   76-41869
ISBN 0-299-07200-2